Brihat Parasara Hora Sastra

of

Maharshi Parasara

महर्षि पराशर कृत

बृहत्पाराशर होरा शास्त्र

VOL. I

English translation, commentary, annotation and editing

by

R. Santhanam

RANJAN PUBLICATIONS

16, Ansari Road, Darya Ganj, New Delhi-110002 (*INDIA*)

Published by :

Ranjan Publications

16, Ansari Road, Darya Ganj

New Delhi - 110002 (INDIA)

Ph. : 91-11-2327 88 35, 2328 29 98.

email:ranjanpublications@rediffmail.com

ISBN : 81-88230-60-X (Set)

Edition : **2016**

Price : Rs. 400.00
U$ 30.00

Printed at : Goyal Enterprises, Delhi-110032 Ph. : 22385770

CONTENTS

Preface

Presented herewith with pleasure is the first-ever English translation of the full text of the available version of Maharshi Parasara's Brihat Parasara Hora Sastra. But for the blessings of Lord Ganesa this would have been as uphill task for me.

Sri Maha Vishnu is the god f gods. So is ParasaraHora—the book of books in the field of astrology.

The work is in the form of a carritch between sage Parasara and his disciple Maitreya who later himself became a worthy sage. Parasara belonging to Vasishta's lineage was Veda Vyasa's father. As could be seen in the course of progressing thorugh the text, sage Saunaka was the preceptor of Parasara in the matter of astrology. Saunaka was one of the earliest sages and was Garga's disciple.

The date of Parasara could be attributed to be roughly the era of Dharma Raja of Maha Bharata. This can be understood when the sage states "in the present Yuga, Dharma Raja is born with the combination of..." He further states that Salivahana 'will be born with the same combination...' Further, the reader could find statements relating to the horoscopic yogas of Maha Vishnu, Prajapati, Swayambhu Manu etc. which statement could possibly be made by no ordinary mortal.

Varaha Mihira in Brihat Samhita, Kalyana Varma in Saravali and many such other illustrious authors gave references of Parasara's astrological statements.

Parasara Hora finds its translation in Bengali, Malayalam etc. which translations however have not been seen by me. I have with me the following versions.

1. Sri Venkateswata Press, Bombay, partly rendered in Hindi. For a majority of slokas, one can find Sanskrit commentary only.

2. Hindi translation by Sitaram Jha. (Master Khelari Lal, Varanasi edition)

3. Hindi translation by Devachandra Jha (Chaukambha edition)

4. Hindi translation by Ganesa Datta Pathak (Thakur Prasad edition)

After scrutinizing critically the four manuscripts, I have for reasons of more credibility chosen the Sanskrit version rendered by Sitararm Jha. The Chaukambha version is almost the same as that of Khelari Lal's.

Other versions that I have come across are :

1. Tamil translation by C. G. Rajan—for only 36 chapters, without Sanskrit verses.

2. English translation by N. N. K. Rao for only 25 chapters, without Sanskrit slokas.

Thus, I have felt a need to make the original version available in English to the fullest possible extent. Our version has 97 chapters containing English translation and exhaustive annotations and examples.

To handle the publication easily, we have divided the work in two volumes. The present Volume—first volume—contains 45 chapters while the remaining 52 chapters have been put in the second volume.

Chapter 1 and chapter 2 give some preliminary extra-astrological information. From chapter 3, the astrological information begins. In this chapter, planetary descriptions, benefics and malefics, planetary deities, complexions, sex, primordial compounds, seasons, relationships, dignities etc. are given. Methods of calculating the 5 Upagrahas like Dhooma and Muhurta Velas like Gulika are given. These are totally ten and have their own say on a nativity, as the other nine main Grahas have. So to say, these Upagrahas and Muhurta velas can alter in suitable proportions the effects due to Nava Grahas.

In the matter of calculation of Gulika, a different concept comes to light from this oldest work. The later authors have given an altogether variable in knowing Gulika's position whereas Parasara advised that it should be cast for the **beginning** of Saturn's Muhurta. Whereas some suggest that it should be for the ending Muhurta of Saturn.

In chapter 4, each Rasi is described from various angles. Slokas 25-30 are the climax of this chapter. An unerring method to find out the Nisheka Lagna (or the moment of intercourse causing conception) from the time of birth is outlined. Though the process of calculation is as simple as a school student's mathematical quiz, it has great truth in it which even modern science could not discover. To prove the truth of the statement in the sage's instruction, a practical example has been given by me. An assumed example cannot better solve the problem. A practical case where the time of coitus is astrologically chosen is taken in hand; time of birth has also been got accurately noted. From the time of birth, the time of Nisheka (or of coitus) is traced which is not in variation, even to the slightest extent, with the originally noted Nisheka time. Again from the time of Nisheka, the birth time is traced in a forward manner using only traditional rules of astrology. This exercise proves three important points, viz.

1. The point of M.C. is to be found out in the natal horoscope and houses intersected accordingly. This is popularly called Sripati Paddhati. Originally Parasara advocated this system.

2. Gulika's position should be found out for the beginning of Saturn's Muhurta only.

3. Lahiri's Ayanamsa is the first best. The reader will find that we have used Moon's **exact** longitude in the above process. Simple angular distance by any Ayanamsa will not alter the solution, but a slight change in Moon's position will take us far away from the truth. With Lahiri's Ayanamsa, we can safely work out even Nadiamsas, which change fast.

The method given by me in working out the future birth time from the time of coition can very well help the astrologers to foretell the exact moment of birth from the time of query. Reseaches reveal that time of query has a perfect alignment with the time of Nisheka.

Chapter 5 touches various special Lagnas, like Ghatika Lagna, Hora Lagna and Bhava Lagna. The importance of these ascendanss cannot be underestimated. A final Bhava chart can emerge after merging the different bhava charts caused by these various special ascendants. This final bhava chart can only reveal the extent of planetary effects when considered housewise whereas the bhava chart exclusively prepared on natal ascendant alone can sometimes mislead. This is what the sage emphasises in sloka 9.

Come to chapter 6. The zodiac is divided in to sixteen Vargas or divisions. These are called Shodasa Vargas. How to find out such Vargas and their use are fully explained. These are from Rasi down to Shashtiamsa. In the classification, the vargas are made in four groups, i.e. 6 vargas, 7 Vargas, 10 Vargas and 16 Vargas and special technical names have been given for the total number of desirable vargas a planet attained for easy identification. For example if a planet is said to be in Golokamsa, it indicates that out of 16 Vargas, it is in 15 good Vargas. These technical names appear in the gradation of Raja Yogas.

Each Varga finds a certain specific use in preference to a planet's Rasi position. For example, without considering the Dvadasamsa chart no tangible resuits due to the native's parents can be known. In deciding one's career, the Dasamsa positions of the planets are of supreme importance. These are highlighted in chapter 7. In this very chapter the sage enunciates what is called Vimsopaka strength of a planet. He assigns a maximum of 20 points taking again differently the four Varga classifications, viz. Shadvarga, Sapta Varga, Dasa Varga and Shodasa Varga. The consideration here is whether a planet is placed in own sign, friendly sign, enemy's sign and the like in the concerncd Varga scheme. Then an evaluaton is done to get Vimsopaka strength. This strength enables us decide the extent of auspicious effects a planet will be capable of revealing in a dasa.

Chapter 8 deals with what is called Jaimini aspects on Rasi basis. Maharshi Jaimini was the sage who expanded these Parasari principles very extensively in Sutra form for easy memorization and successful applicability. The original concept is however from the pen of Parasara.

Childhood evils are discussed in chapter 9 whiie chapter 10 prescribes planetary combinations to combat such possible evils.

Basic information about the 12 houses could be found in chapter 11 while specific attention may be given to slokas 14-16. Thesc 3 slokas serve an important key in knowing how a Bhava is going to give effects under various circumstances.

Chapters 12-23 give a variety of information and instructions in analysing the 12 houses of a horoscope in a systematic manner. A close study of these rules will tame one's mind to scientifically approach the horoscope for fruitful resuts.

Chapter 24 is again one of the most important chapters. Here, the various effects of a Bhava lord being in a specific house are given. All the 12 lords are fully covered. How to sort out a situation in case of contrary indications is given in slokas 145-148.

The bhava effects of Dhooma, Vyatipata, Gulika etc. are narrated fully in chapter 25. Pranapada Lagna's position vis-a-vis natal ascendant also reveals certain special effects as could be seen in this very chapter.

Shadbala calculations, Ishta and Kashta phalas and other related mathematical aspects are elaborately laid down in the 3 chapters, viz. 26, 27 and 28.

It is not in order if planets are studied with reference to mere natal chart. Padas for various houses will further alter the planetary effects. This is what is taught in chapter 29. Raja Yogas, inter alia are best analysed through Arudha chart or Pada chart. The sage suggests Graha Padas as well, but unfortunately he leaves it at that without adding much information.

For still deeper research, Upapada will be more effective. This area will give more clues particularly about marriage, financc and diseases. See chapter 30.

Chapter 31 entitled 'Argaladhyaya' though brief has worthy information on planetary interventions, obstructions and effects thereof.

Significance of planets is treated in chapter 32.

Karakamsa is the Navamsa Rasi occupied by Atma Karaka. Plenets forming a certain relationship with Karakamsa and their effects are narrated in chapter 33 extending to 99 slokas.

Chapter 34 is again one of the most instructive. Planets assume a certain tendency by virtue of owning a certain house. The sage elaborately touches such roles for various planets for all the 12 ascendants. He decides on such principles the Yoga Karakas, Yoga Bhanga, Karakas and Marakas for each ascendant. This will enable us understand whether planet will give beneficial results or adverse effects. Death dealing planets or Mrakas allow us to guess the period of one's death,

As the name implies, chapter 35 lists Nabhasa Yogas which are available in most standard texts. Many new Raja Yogas could be found in chapter 36, like Khadga, Mridanga, Chamara, Kahala etc.

Chapters 37 and 38 deal with Lunar and Solar yogas which are popularly known. Raja yogas in chapter 39, Yogas for royal association in chapter 40, and financial combinations in chapter 41 deserve special mention, containing a variety of authoritative information.

Maraka or death dealing planets have a say on the finances of the native apart from causing his end. These are tersely enlightened in the 42nd chapter.

The chapter on longevity, bearing No. 43, is among the most important ones. Pindayu, Naisargayu, Amsayu and the like, and computations based on ascendant/planetary pairs linking with movable, fixed and common signs contain instructive information. In the notes, I have taken Pindayu calculations and worked out a fullfledged example touching all aspects of computation. I have adopted a scientific method for deductions for planetary contributions arising by placement in bhavas 12 to 7. I have simply not considered bhava positions in these deductions but degree-wise positions of the various planets. I have given one common formula covering the six bhavas and the reader can work out the exact loss of longevity. This can be usefully extened to any loss of years as far as bhavas 12 to 7 is concerned in other systems as well. Other longevity calculations have been suitably annotated by me.

The reader will also do well to study chapter 44 concerning Marakas before he takes a decision on longevity. Rahu/Ketu have also been assigned Marakatwa roles.

The concluding chapter of Vol 1 is the 45th dealing with a number of kinds of Avasthas of the planets. Out of these, the 12 Avasthas, known as Sayanadi Avasthas are of supreme importance. If one tries to interpret these Avasthas in proper spirit, he will be able to detect the diseases the native will suffer. I have supported my views with the help of information from Adbhuta Sagara of Ballala Sena and Hora Ratna of Balabhadra. For example, if Mars is in Agamanavastha, one will suffer from deep ear pains. In the normal parlance, we consider only Jupiter in the context of ear defects. Diseases of hand and foot are assigned to Venus in Agamanavastha. If one conducts a scientific research in the matter of diseases with the help of planetary Avasthas, viz. Sayanadi Avasthas, one is bound to reach many brilliant clues.

The present work offers a vast scope for success in predictive astrology. One can build up his own applied astrology instead of theoretical astrology if he works on the lines suggested by Maharshi Parasara.

A word of caution is necessary for the benefit of the reader, In order to understand the hidden aspects of the various rules given herein, what is required is a thorough understanding of these principles. Skipping over fast to an ensuing chapter may not convey the real idea of a 'present' chapter. To make the reader's Job easier, I have explained every difficult aspect as clearly as I understand based on my own experience and study of other authoritative texts,

In the end, I would like to mention that my attempt to translate this great work and annotate may not have been wholly successful. I surely would have left some shortcomings unnoticed and unrectified. From the readers, I can only expect the affection of forgiving me for any innocent lapses.

New Delhi R. Santhanam
Vijaya Dasami 1984

श्रीगणेशाय नमः

अथ बृहत्पाराशरहोराशास्त्रम्

BRIHAT PARASARA HORA SASTRA

[गजाननं भूतगणादिसेवितं कपित्थजम्बूफलसारभक्षणम् ।
उमासुतं शोकविनाशकारणं नमामि विघ्नेश्वरपादपंकजम् ॥

I prostrate before the lotus-feet of Lord Vighneswara, the offspring of Uma, the cause of destruction of sorrow, who is served by Bhuta ganas (the five great elements of the universe) etc; who has the face of a tusker and who consumes the essence of *Kapiththa* and *Jambu* fruits.]

सृष्टिक्रमकथनाध्यायः ॥१॥

Chapter 1

The Creation

अथैकदा मुनिश्रेष्ठं त्रिकालज्ञं पराशरम् ।
पप्रच्छोपेत्य मैत्रेयः प्रणिपत्य कृताञ्जलिः ॥१॥

भगवन् ! परमं पुण्यं गुह्यं वेदाङ्गमुत्तमम् ।
त्रिस्कन्धं ज्यौतिषं-होरा गणितं संहितेति च ॥२॥

एतेष्वपि त्रिषु श्रेष्ठा होरेति श्रूयते मुने ! ।
त्वत्तस्तां श्रोतुमिच्छामि कृपया वद मे प्रभो ! ॥३॥

कथं सृष्टिरियं जाता जगतश्च लयः कथम् ? ।
खस्थानां भूस्थितानां च सम्बन्धं वद विस्तरात् ? ॥४॥

1-4. Offering his obeisance to all-knowing sage **Parasara** and with folded hands, **Maitreya** said, "O Venerable, Astrology, the supreme limb of the Vedas, has three divisions, viz. Hora,

Ganita and Samhita. Among the said three divisions, Hora or genethliac part of astrology is still more excellent. I desire to know of its glorious aspects from you. Be pleased to tell me, "How this Universe is created ? How does it end ? What is the relationship of the animals born on this earth with the heavenly bodies ? Please speak elaborately".

Notes : Maitreya was Parasara's ardent disciple. Sage Parasara was the illustrious father of Bhagawan Veda Vyasa. **Parasara Smriti, Parasara Samhita** and the present work **Parasara Hora** are some of the immortal contributions made by our sage.

Parasara's preceptor was sage Saunaka, the reputed author of **Rigveda Pratisakhya** and other vedic compositions, from whom he took instructions in astrology. Saunaka was taught by Narada, son of Lord Brahma Pitamaha in the matter of astrology and others. Narada got direct instructions from Pitamaha. These details are stated by sage Parasara in the concluding chapter of the present work.

The sage predicts in the course of his treatise that Salivahana *will* be born in a yoga caused by relationship between an angular lord and a trinal lor as both are in Simhasanamsa, *vide* ch. 41 sloka 32. While the technicalities of the astrological part of this statement will be understood by the reader as he progresses with the study of this work, it will be evident that Parasara was much before Salivahana. The era of Salivahana commenced in AD 72. Since Veda Vyasa is reverentially referred as *Parasaratmaja*, meaning the offspring of Parasara, Sage Parasara lived during Maha Bharata era.

Sage Maitreya's name appears in Veda Vyasa's *Srimad Bhagavata Purana*. Maitreya was sage Kusaru's offspring. Sage Maitreya achieved a great deal of knowledge in spiritual and other topics. Vidura abandoned his kith and kin and met sage Maitreya to achieve religious merits.

As can be seen, our text is in the form of a carritch between sage Parasara and Maitreya, the Master and the Disciple respectively.

Astrology has three divisions, *viz.* Hora, Ganita and Samhita. Hora deals with genethliac part while mathematical aspects like planetary movements, strengths *etc.* are taught by the Ganita branch. Samhita means a collection or compendium of law, code and digest of any branch of learning. These are like *Rig Veda Samhita. Charaka Samhita, Vasishta Samhita etc.* Thus *Samhita* is not an original work.

साधु पृष्टं त्वया विप्र ! लोकानुग्रहकारिणा ।
अथाहं परमं ब्रह्म तच्छक्तिं भारतीं पुनः ॥५॥

सूर्यं नत्वा ग्रहपतिं जगदुत्पत्तिकारणम् ।
वक्ष्यामि वेदनयनं यथा ब्रह्ममुखाच्छ्रुतम् ॥६॥

शान्ताय गुरुभक्ताय सर्वदा सत्यवादिने ।
आस्तिकाय प्रदातव्यं ततः श्रेयो ह्यवाप्स्यति ॥७॥

न देयं परशिष्याय नास्तिकाय शठाय वा ।
दत्ते प्रतिदिनं दुःखं जायते नात्र संशयः ॥८॥

5-8. Parasara answered, 'O Brahmin, your query (so to say, the desire to know of the intricacies of astrology) has an auspicious purpose in it for the welfare of the Universe. Praying Lord Brahma and Sri Saraswati, His power (and consort), and the Sun God, the leader of the planets and the cause of Creation, I shall proceed to narrate to you the science of astrology as heard through Lord Brahma. Only good will follow the teaching of this science to the students who are peacefully disposed, who honour the preceptors (and elders) who speak only truth and who are God-fearing. Woeful for ever doubtlessly will it be to impart knowledge of this science to an unwilling student, to a heterodox and to a crafty person.

एकोऽव्यक्तात्मको विष्णुरनादिः प्रभुरीश्वरः ।
शुद्धसत्वो जगत्स्वामी निर्गुणस्त्रिगुणान्वितः ॥९॥

संसारकारकः श्रीमान्निमित्तात्मा प्रतापवान् ।
एकांशेन जगत्सर्वं सृजत्यवति लीलया ॥१०॥

त्रिपादं तस्य देवस्य ह्यमृतं तत्त्वदर्शिनः ।
विदन्ति तत्प्रमाणं च सप्रधानं तथैकपात् ॥११॥

व्यक्ताव्यक्तात्मको विष्णुर्वासुदेवस्तु गीयते ।
यदव्यक्तात्मको विष्णुः शक्तिद्वयसमन्वितः ॥१२॥

9-12. Sri Vishnu who is the lord (of all matters), who has undefiled spirit, who is endowed with the three *Gunas* although he transcends the grip of *Gunas* (i.e. *Gunatita*), who is the Author of this Universe, who is glorious, who is the Cause and who is endowed with valour has no beginning. He authored the Universe and administers it with a quarter of his power. The other three quarters of Him, filled with nectar, are knowable to (only) the philosophers (of maturity). The Principal Evolver who is both perceptible and imperceptible is Vasu Deva. The Imperceptible part of the Lord is endowed with dual powers while the Perceptible with triple powers.

व्यक्तात्मकस्त्रिभिर्युक्तः कथ्यतेऽनन्तशक्तिमान् ।
सत्त्वप्रधाना श्रीशक्ति—र्भूशक्तिश्च रजोगुणा ॥१३॥

शक्तिस्तृतीया या प्राक्ता नीलाख्या ध्वान्तरूपिणी ।
वासुदेवश्चतुर्थोऽभूच्छ्रीशक्त्या प्रेरितो यदा ॥१४॥

संकर्षणश्च प्रद्युम्नोऽनिरुद्ध इति मूर्तिधृक् ।
तमःशक्त्याऽन्विता विष्णुर्देवः संकर्षणाभिधः ॥१५॥

13-15. The three powers are : *Sri Sakti* (Mother Lakshmi) with *Sattwa Guna, Bhoo Sakti* (Mother Earth) with *Rajoguna* and *Neela Sakti* with *Tamoguna.* Apart from the three, the fourth kind of Vishnu, influenced by *Sri Sakti* and *Bhoo Sakti,* assumes the form of *Sankarshana* with *Tamo Guna,* of *Pradyumna* with *Rajoguna* and of *Anirudha* with *Satwa Guna.*

प्रद्युम्नो रजसा शक्त्याऽनिरुद्धः सत्त्वया युतः ।
महान् संकर्षणाज्जातः प्रद्युम्नाद्यदहंकृतिः ॥१६॥

अनिरुद्धात् स्वयं जातो ब्रह्माहंकारमूर्तिधृक् ।
सर्वेषु सर्वशक्तिश्च स्वशक्त्याऽधिकया युतः ॥१७॥

16-17. *Mahattatwa, Ahamkara* and *Ahamkara Murthi, Brahma,* are born from *Samkarshana, Pradyumna* and *Anirudha* respectively. All these three forms are endowed with all the three gunas, with predominance of the *Guna* due to their origin.

अहंकारस्त्रिधा भूत्वा सर्वमेतदविस्तरात् ।
सात्त्विको राजसश्चैव तामसश्चेदहंकृतिः ॥१८॥

देवा वैकारिकाज्जातास्तैजसादिन्द्रियाणि च ।
तामसाच्चैवभू तानि खादीनि स्वस्वशक्तिभिः ॥१९॥

18-19. *Ahamkara* is of three classes, *i.e.* with *Satwik*, *Rajasik* and *Tamasik* dispositions. Divine class, sensory organs and the five primordial compounds (air, earth etc.) are respectively from the said three *Ahamkaras*.

श्रीशक्त्या सहितो विष्णुः सदा पाति जगत्त्रयम् ।
भूशक्त्या सृजते ब्रह्मा नीलशक्त्या शिवोऽत्ति हि ॥२०॥

20. Lord Vishnu coupled with *Sri Sakti* rules over the three worlds. Coupled with *Bhoo Sakti*, He is Brahma causing the Universe. Coupled wtth *Neela Sakti*, He is Siva, destroying the Universe.

सर्वेषु चैव जीवेषु परमात्मा विराजते ।
सर्वं हि तदिदं ब्रह्मन् ! स्थितं हि परमात्मनि ॥२१॥

सर्वेषु चैव जीवेषु स्थितंह्यंशद्वयं क्वचित् ।
जीवांशो ह्यधिकस्तद्वत् परमात्मांशकः किल ॥२२॥

सूर्यादयो ग्रहाः सर्वे ब्रह्मकामद्विषादयः ।
एते चान्ये च बहवः परमात्मांशकाधिकाः ॥२३॥

शक्तयश्च तथैतेषामधिकांशाः श्रियादयः ।
स्वस्वशक्तिषु चान्यासु ज्ञेया जीवांशकाधिकाः ॥२४॥

21-24. The Lord is in all beings and the entire Universe is in Him. All beings contain both *Jeevatma* and *Paramatma Amsas*. Some have predominance of the former while yet some have the latter in predominance. *Paramatmamsa* is predominant in the *Grahas* viz. Sun *etc.* and Brahma, Siva and others. Their powers or consorts too have predominance of *Paramatmamsa*. Others have more of *Jeevatmamsa*.

अथावतारकथनाध्यायः ॥२॥

Chapter 2

Great Incarnations (Of The Lord)

रामकृष्णादयो ये ये ह्यवतारा रमापतेः।
तेऽपि जीवांशसंयुक्ताः किंवा ब्रूहि मुनिश्वर ! ॥१॥

1. Maitreya : "O sage, are the incarnations of Vishnu, *viz.* Sri Rama, Sri Krishna *etc.* endowed with *Jeevamsa ?*

रामः कृष्णश्च भो विप्र ! नृसिंहः सूकरस्तथा।
एते पूर्णावताराश्च ह्यन्ये जीवांशकान्विताः ॥२॥

2. Parasara : "O Brahmin, the four incarnations, *viz.* Rama, Krishna, Narasimha and Varaha are wholly with *Paramatmamsa.* The other incarnations (than these, out of the ten) have in them *Jeevamsa* too.

अवताराण्यनेकानि ह्यजस्य परमात्मनः।
जीवानां कर्मफलदो ग्रहरूपी जनार्दनः ॥३॥

दैत्यानां बलनाशाय देवानां बलवृद्धये।
धर्मसंस्थापनार्थाय ग्रहाज्जाताः शुभाः क्रमात् ॥४॥

3-4. The Unborn lord has many incarnations. He has incarnated as the planets (*Nava Grahas*) to bestow on the living beings the results due to their Karmas. He is Janardana. He assumed the auspicious form of *Grahas* to destroy the demons (evil forces) and sustain the divine beings.

रामोऽवतारः सूर्यस्य चन्द्रस्य यदुनायकः।
नृसिंहो भूमिपुत्रस्य बुद्धः सोमसुतस्य च ॥५॥

वामनो विबुधेज्यस्य भार्गवो भार्गवस्य च।
कूर्मो भास्करपुत्रस्य सैंहिकेयस्य सूकरः ॥६॥

केतोर्मीनावतारश्च ये चान्ये तेऽपि खेटजाः।
परात्मांशोऽधिको येषु ते सर्वे खेचराभिधाः ॥७॥

5-7 From the Sun God the incarnation of Rama, from the Moon that of Krishna. from Mars that of Narasimha, from Mercury that of Budhdha, from Jupiter that of Vamana, from Venus that of Parasu Rama, from Saturn that of Koorma (Tortoise), from Rahu that of Varaha (Pig) and from Ketu that of Meena (Fish) occurred. All other incarantaions than these also are through the *Grahas*. The beings with more *Paramatmamsa* are called divine beings.

जीवांशोह्यधिको येषु जीवास्ते वै प्रकीर्तिताः।
सूर्यादिभ्यो ग्रहेभ्यश्च परमात्मांशनिःसृताः ॥८॥

रामकृष्णादयः सर्वे ह्यवतारा भवन्ति वै।
तत्रैव ते विलीयन्ते पुनः कार्योत्तर सदा ॥९॥

जीवांशनिःसृतास्तेषां तेभ्यो जाता नरादयः।
तेऽपि तत्रैव लीयन्ते तेऽव्यक्ते समयन्ति हि ॥१०॥

इदं ते कथितं विप्र! सर्वं यस्मिन् भवेदिति।
भूतान्यपि भविष्यन्ति तत्तज्जानन्ति तद्विदः ॥११॥

विना तज्ज्यौतिषं नान्यो ज्ञातुं शक्नोति कर्हिचित्।
तस्मादवश्यमध्येयं ब्राह्मणेश्च विशेषतः ॥१२॥

यो नरः शास्त्रमज्ञात्वा ज्यौतिषं खलु निन्दति।
रौरवं नरकं भुक्त्वा चान्धत्वं चान्यजन्मनि ॥१३॥

8-13. The beings with more *Jeevatmamsa* are (mortal) beings. The high degree of *Paramatmamsa* from the *Grahas*, viz. Sun *etc.* did incarnate as Rama, Krishna *etc.* After completing the mission, the *Paramatmamsas* (of the respective) *Grahas* again merge (in the respective) *Grahas*. The Jeevatma portions from the *Grahas* take births as human beings and live their lives according to their Karmas and again merge in the *Grahas*. And at the time of Great Destruction, the *Grahas* as well merge in the Lord Vishnu. One who knows of all these, will become versed in the knowledge of the past, present and future. Without a knowledge of astrology these cannot be known. Hence everyone should have a knowledge of Astrology particularly the Brahmin. One who, devoid of astrological knowledge, blames this science will go to the hell called 'Raurava', and will be reborn blind.

अथ ग्रहगुणस्वरूपाध्यायः ॥३॥

Chapter 3

Planetary Characters And Description

कथितं भवता प्रेम्णा ग्रहावतरणं मुने ! ।
तेषां गुणस्वरूपाद्यं कृपया कथ्यतां पुनः ॥१॥

1. Maitreya : "O Sage, you have affectionately explained about the planetary incarnations. Now kindly detail their characters and dispositions."

शृणु विप्र ! प्रवक्ष्यामि भग्रहाणां परिस्थितिम् ।
आकाशे यानि दृश्यन्ते ज्योतिर्बिम्बान्यनेकशः ॥२॥

तेषु नक्षत्रसंज्ञानि ग्रहसंज्ञानि कानिचित् ।
तानि नक्षत्रनामानि स्थिरस्थानानि यानि वै ॥३॥

2-3. Parasara : "O Brahmin, listen to the account of placement of the heavenly bodies. Out of the many luminous bodies sighted in the skies, some are stars; yet some are planets (i.e. *Grahas*). Those that have no movements are the Nakshatras (or asterisms).

Notes : Placed in the firmaments are many stars among which we have, for astrological purposes, 27 stars and 7 planets. Rahu and Ketu though recognised as planets for astrological delineations are shadowy. These two are nodes of the Moons

and are exactly apart 180 degrees mutually. Their positions are formed when the Moon crosses the ecliptic from northern latitude to southern one and *vice versa.*

गच्छन्तो भानि गृह्णन्ति सततं ये तु ते ग्रहाः ।
भचक्रस्य नगाश्व्यंशा अश्विन्यादि-समाह्वयाः ॥४॥

तद्द्वादशविभागास्तु तुल्या मेषादिसंज्ञकाः ।
प्रसिद्धा राशयः सन्ति ग्रहास्त्वर्कादिसंज्ञकाः ॥५॥

राशीनामुदयो लग्नं तद्वशादेव जन्मिनाम् ।
ग्रहयोग-वियोगाभ्यां फलं चिन्त्यं शुभाशुभम् ॥६॥

4-6. Those are called planets (or *Grahas*) that move through the Nakshatras (or asterisms) in the zodiac. The said zodiac comprises of 27 asterisms commencing from Aswini. The same area is divided in 12 parts equal to 12 Rasis (or signs) commencing from Aries. The names of the planets commence from the Sun. The sign rising is known as Lagna (or the ascendant). Based on the ascendant and the planets joining and departing from each other, the native's good and bad effects are deduced.

Notes : Planets move in the zodiac through stellar mansions or Nakshatras. The names of the 27 Nakshatras are :

1. Aswini	2. Bharani	3. Krittika
4. Rohini	5. Mrigasira	6. Arudra
7. Punarvasu	8. Pushyami	9. Aslesha
10. Makha	11. Poorva Phalguni	12. Uttara Phalguni
13. Hastha	14. Chitta	15. Swati
16. Visakha	17. Anuradha	18. Jyeshta
19. Moola	20. Poorvashadha	21. Uttarashadha
22. Sravana	23. Dhanishta	24. Sathabhishak
25. Poorvabhadra	26. Uttarabhadra	27. Revati

The names of the planets are given in sloka 10 of this chapter.

The ascendant is a very importat point in the horoscope. It is the sign that rises in the east, on the latitude of birth. The apparent rising of a sign is due to the rotation of the earth on its own axis at a rate of motion causing every degree of the zodiac seems to ascend on the eastern horizon. Approximately, two hours are required for a sign to pass *via* the horizon, thereby every degree taking four minutes to ascend. This duration, however, is actually dependent on the concerned latitude.

Actually the Sun has no motion. His is an apparent one as viewed from the rotating earth. Other planets including the nodes have varied rates of motion. The average daily motions of the planets, which are not, however standard, are as follows :

The Sun	:	1°
The Moon	:	13—15°
Mars	:	30—45′
Mercury	:	65—100′
Venus	:	62—82′
Jnpiter	:	5—15′
Saturn	:	2′
Node	:	3′

With such different motions, a planet forms various aspects with others. These aspects through longitudinal distances have a great deal of utility in astrology. This is what the sage suggests to be considered.

संज्ञा नक्षत्रवृन्दानां ज्ञेयाः सामान्यशास्त्रतः।
एतच्छास्त्रानुसारेण राशि-खेटफलं ब्रुवे ॥७॥

7. Details (of astronomical nature) of stars be understood by general rules while I narrate to you about the effects of planets and signs.

Notes : Planetary movements can be fully understood from astronomical literature and *Samhitas. Narada Samhita, Garga Samhita, Vasishta Samhita etc.* are hinted at by Parasara, by "general rules" or सामान्य शास्त्र. This may well mean other ordinary literature devoted to stellar movements.

यस्मिन् काले यतः खेटा यान्ति दृग्गणितैकताम् ।
तत एव स्फुटाः कार्याः दिक्कालौ च स्फुटौ विदा ॥८॥

स्वस्वदेशोद्भवैः साध्यं लग्नं राश्युदयैः स्फुटम् ।
अथादौ वच्मि खेटानां जातिरूपगुणानहम् ॥६॥

8-9. The positions of the planets for a given time be taken as per **Drikganita.** And with the help of Rasi durations applicable to the respective places, the ascendant at birth should be known. Now I tell you about the castes, descriptions and dispositions of the planets.

अथ खेटा रविश्चन्द्रो मङ्गलश्च बुधस्तथा ।
गुरुः शुक्रः शनी राहुः केतुश्चैते यथाक्रमम् ॥१०॥

10. *NAMES OF PLANETS :* The names of the nine planets respectively are : the Sun, the Moon, Mars, Mercury, Jupiter, Venus, Saturn, Rahu and Ketu.

Notes : In the Sanskrit literature on astrology, the planets are denoted by different names. Please see. ch. 2 of my English translation of **Horasara,** for additional information in this regard.

तत्रार्क-शनि-भूपुत्राः क्षीणेन्दु-राहु-केतवः ।
क्रूराः, शेषग्रहा सौम्याः, क्रूरः क्रूर-युतो बुधः ॥११॥

11. *BENEFICS AMD MALEFICS :* Among these, the Sun, Saturn, Mars, decreasing Moon, Rahu and Ketu (the ascending and the descending nodes of the Moon) are malefics while the rest are benefics. Mercury, however, is a malefic if he joins a malefic.

Notes : That decreasing Moon and increasing Moon are respectively a malefic and a benefic is the view conveyed by the sage. Yet some exponents and commentators hold the following view :

When the Moon is ahead of the Sun but within 120°, she has medium strength. Between 120° to 240° she is very auspicious, see अतिशुभप्रदो. From 240° to 0° she is bereft of strength. This is Yavanas' view, *vide* P. 70 of my English Translation of **Saravali.** This view is, however, related to the Moon's strength or otherwise, while waning Moon (Krishna Paksha or dark half Moon) is a malefic and waxing Moon (Sukla Paksha or bright half Moon) is a benefic.

Should the Moon be conjunct a benefic or aspected by a benefic, she turns a benefic, even if in a waning state.

As regards Mercury, we have clear instructions from Parasara, that he becomes a malefic if he joins a malefic. If waning Moon and Mercury are together, both are benefics.

सर्वात्मा च दिवानाथो मनः कुमुदबान्धवः ।
सत्त्वं कुजो बुधैः प्रोक्तो बुधो वाणीप्रदायकः ॥१२॥

देवेज्यो ज्ञानसुखदो भृगुर्वीर्यप्रदायकः ।
ऋषिभिः प्राक्तनैः प्रोक्तश्छायासूनुश्च दुःखदः ॥१३॥

12-13. *PLANETARY GOVERNANCES :* The Sun is the soul of all. The Moon is the mind. Mars is one's strength. Mercury is speech-giver while Jupiter confers Knowledge and happiness. Venus governs semen (potency) while Saturn denotes grief.

Notes : The degree of benefic effects of the indications mentioned above will be commensurate with the strength of the concerned planet. If the Sun is strong, one will have a matured soul and will make abundant spiritual progress. Knowledge and general happiness will be well acquired if Jupiter is well-disposed. Grief will not be there, if Saturn is bereft of strength.

रविचन्द्रौ तु राजानौ नेता[1] ज्ञेयो धरात्मजः ।
बुधो राजकुमारश्च सचिवौ गुरुभार्गवौ ॥१४॥

प्रेष्यको रविपुत्रश्च सेना स्वर्भानुपुच्छकौ ।
एवं क्रमेण वै विप्र ! सूर्यादीन् प्रविचिन्तयेत् ॥१५॥

14-15. *PLANETARY CABINET :* Of royal status are the Sun and the Moon while Mars is the army chief. Prince-apparent is Mercury. The ministerial planets are Jupiter and Venus. Saturn is a servant. Rahu and Ketu form the planetary army.

रक्तश्यामो दिवाधीशो गौरगात्रो निशाकरः ।
नात्युच्चाङ्गः कुजो रक्तो दूर्वाश्यामो बुधस्तथा ॥१६॥

गौरगात्रो गुरुर्ज्ञेयः शुक्रः श्यावस्तथैव च ।
कृष्णदेहो रवेः पुत्रो ज्ञायते द्विजसत्तम ! ॥१७॥

1. नेतृ—Leader of elephants, animals etc.

16-17. *PLANETARY COMPLEXIONS* : The Sun is blood-red. The Moon is tawny. Mars who is not very tall is blood-red while Mercury's hue is akin to that of green grass. Tawny, variegated and dark are Jupiter, Venus and Saturn in their order.

वह्न्यम्बुशिखिजा विष्णुविडौजः शचिका द्विज !।
सूर्यादीनां खगानां च देवा ज्ञेयाः क्रमेण च ॥१८॥

18. *PLANETARY DEITIES* : Fire (Agni), Water (Varuna), Subrahmanya (Lord Siva's son following Ganesa). Maha Vishnu, Indra, Sachi Devi (the consort of Lord Indra) and Brahma are the presiding deities of the 7 planets in their order.

Notes : The deities or Adhidevatas of the planets as given above may be invoked to get the respective planets' afflictions cured. For example, evils indicated by Mercury can be brought under control by offering prayers to Sri Vishnu Bhagawan.

The names of the planetary deities are additionally employed by Varaha Mihira in selecting a name for the child. The consonants and vowels are attributed to the seven planets as under.

Sun	: The Vowels (12 in number from अ to औ)
Moon	: Semi Vowels **viz.** य, र, ल and व
	: Sibilants **viz.** श, ष and स
	: Aspirate **viz.** ह
Mars	: Guttural **viz.** क, ख, ग, घ and ङ
Venus	: Palatals **viz** च, छ, ज, झ and ञ
Mercury	: Cerebrals **viz.** ट, ठ, ड, ढ and ण
Jupiter	: Dentals **viz.** त, थ, द, ध and न
Saturn	: Labials **viz.** प, फ, ब, भ and म

The name of the child can be selected with an initial letter as above based on the stronger of the two, **viz.** natal ascendant lord and Navamsa ascendant lord. For example, if Mars is stronger, the name can have a guttural in the beginning appropriate to the presiding deity. In this case, Subrahmanya is the deity and the name can be Kumara (कुमार) or Guha (गुह). Similar deductions can be suitably made in other cases. **If the**

initial letter belongs to a planet without dignity, it will bring bad luck.

Likewise, the Nakshatras too have presiding deities. Any affliction caused to natal star by way of malefic occupation or by eclipses at birth or in a future date, can be warded off by suitable propitiation to the deity concerned. The 27 deities are denoted below :

Aswini	—	Aswini Kumara
Bharani	—	Yama
Krittika	—	Agni
Rohini	—	Brahma
Mrigasira	—	Moon
Arudra	—	Siva
Punarvasu	—	Aditi
Pushyami	—	Jupiter
Aslesha	—	Rahu
Makha	—	Sun
Poorva Phalguni	—	Aryama
Uttara Phalguni	—	Sun
Hastha	—	Viswa Karma
Chitta	—	Vayu
Swati	—	Indra
Visakha	—	Mitra
Anuradha	—	Indra
Jyeshta	—	Niruti
Moola	—	Varuna
Poorvashadha	—	Viswadeva
Uttarashadha	—	Brahma
Sravana	—	Vishnu
Dhanishta	—	Vasu (वसु)
Sathabishak	—	Varuna
Poorvabhadra	—	Ajacharana
Uttarabhadra	—	Ahirbudhanya
Revati	—	Poosha

A malefic planet in a particular star will yield its evil effects in the Dasa related to that star. For example, if Ketu is in Krittika in the 9th house, the evil effects due to father will be given by Ketu in Sun's dasa (related to Krittika). Hence propitiation of Fire god will counter the possible evil.

Alternatively, Lord Ganesa representing Ketu may also be pleased suitably.

क्लीबौ द्वौ सौम्यसौरी च युवतीन्दुभृगू द्विज ! ।
नराः शेषाश्च विज्ञेया भानुर्भौमो गुरुस्तथा ॥१९॥

19. *SEX OF THE PLANETS* : Mercury and Saturn are neuters. The Moon and Venus are females while the Sun, Mars and Jupiter are males.

अग्निभूमिनभस्तोयवायवः क्रमतो द्विज ! ।
भौमादीनां ग्रहाणां च तत्त्वानीति यथाक्रमम् ॥२०॥

20. *PRIMORDIAL COMPOUNDS* : The **Pancha Bhootas,** *viz.* fire, earth. ether, water and air are respectively governed by Mars, Mercury, Jupiter, Venus and Saturn.

गुरुशुक्रौ विप्रवर्णौ कुजार्कौ क्षत्रियौ द्विज ! ।
शशिसौम्यौ वैश्यवर्णौ शनिः शूद्रो द्विजोत्तम ! ॥२१॥

21. *PLANETARY CASTES* : Jupiter and Venus are Brahmins. The Sun is a royal planet while the Moon and Mercury belong to commercial community. Saturn rules the Sudras (4th caste).

जीवसूर्येन्द्रवः सत्त्वं बुध-शुक्रौ रजस्तथा ।
सूर्यपुत्र-धरापुत्रौ तमः-प्रकृतिकौ द्विज ! ॥२२॥

22. Satwik planets are the luminaries and Jupiter, Venus and Mercury are Rajasik while Mars and Saturn are Tamasik planets.

Notes : The Satwa, Rajas and Tamasik natures of planets will have a say on the disposition of the native. For further information, see my notes, *vide* P. 51 of **Saravali.**

मधुपिङ्गलदृक्सूर्यश्चतुरस्रः शुचिर्द्विज ! ।
पित्तप्रकृतिको धीमान् पुमानल्पकचो द्विज ! ॥२३॥

23. *DESCRIPTION OF THE SUN* : The Sun's eyes are honey-coloured. He has a square body. He is of clean habits, bilious, intelligent and has limited hair (on his head).

Notes : Much additional details could be gathered from my notes in ch. 4 of **Saravali** and ch. 2 of **Horasara.** The native will be influenced in appearance, disposition etc. by the strongest planet or the ascendant lord or the Navamsa ascendant lord.

बहुवातकफः 'प्राज्ञश्चन्द्रो वृत्ततनुर्द्विज! ।
शुभदृङ्मधुवाक्यश्च चञ्चलो मदनातुरः ॥२४॥

24. *DESCRIPTION OF THE MOON* : The Moon is very windy and phlegmatic. She is learned and has a round body. She has auspicious looks and sweet speech, is fickleminded and very lustful.

क्रूरो रक्तेक्षणो भौमश्चपलोदारमूर्तिकः ।
पित्तप्रकृतिकः क्रोधी कृशमध्यतनुर्द्विज! ॥२५॥

25. *DESCRIPTION OF MARS* : Mars has blood-red eyes, is fickle-minded, liberal, bilious, given to anger and has thin waist and thin physique.

वपुःश्रेष्ठः श्लिष्टवाक्च ह्यतिहास्यरुचिर्बुधः ।
पित्तवान् कफवान् विप्र! मारुतप्रकृतिस्तथा ॥२६॥

26. *DESCRIPTION OF MERCURY* : Mercury is endowed with an attractive physique and the capacity to use words with many meanings. He is fond of jokes. He has a mix of all the three humours.

बृहद्गात्रो गुरुश्चैव पिङ्गलो मूर्द्धजेक्षणे ।
कफप्रकृतिको धीमान् सर्वशास्त्रविशारदः ॥२७॥

27. *DESCRIPTION OF JUPITER* : Jupiter has a big body, tawny hair and tawny eyes, is phlegmatic, intelligent and learned in all sastras.

सुखी कान्तवपु श्रेष्ठः सुलोचनो भृगोः सुतः ।
काव्यकर्ता कफाधिक्योऽनिलात्मा वक्रमूर्धजः ॥२८॥

28. *DESCRIPTION OF VENUS* : Venus is charming, has a splendorous physique, is excellent or great in disposition, has charming eyes, is a poet, is phlegmatic and windy and has curly hair.

Notes : The word सुखी in the text has many purports like happy, virtuous, charming etc. Since Venus is a charming planet, the said meaning 'charming' has been used. However, I do not imply that Venus is not a virtuous planet *etc.*

कृशदीर्घतनुः शौरिः पिङ्गदृष्टयनिलात्मकः ।
स्थूलदन्तोऽलसः पंगुः खररोमकचो द्विज ! ॥२९॥

29. *DESCRIPTION OF SATURN :* Saturn has an emaciated and long physique, has tawny eyes, is windy in temperament, has big teeth, is indolent and lame and has coarse hair.

धूम्राकारो नीलतनुर्वनस्थोऽपि भयंकरः ।
वातप्रकृतिको धीमान् स्वर्भानुस्तत्समः शिखी ॥३०॥

30. *DESCRIPTION OF RAHU AND KETU :* Rahu has smoky appearance with a blue-mix physique. He resides in forests and is horrible. He is windy in temperament and is intelligent. Ketu is akin to Rahu.

अस्थि रक्तस्तथा मज्जा त्वग् वसा वीर्यमेव च ।
स्नायुरेषामधीशाश्च क्रमात् सूर्यादयो द्विज ! ॥३१॥

31. *PRIMARY INGREDIENTS (OR SAPTA DHATUS) :* Bones, blood, marrow, skin, fat, semen and muscles are respectively denoted by the planets from the Sun etc.

Notes : The Sun and others upto Saturn rule the Sapta Dhatus or primary ingredients of the body, as denoted above. Their strength or weakness indicate safety or otherwise to the Dhatu concerned. For example, if the Sun is afflicted at birth, the native is liable to suffer disorders of bones, breakage of bones, and the like. The native will incur disorders of blood if the Moon is primarily ill-disposed. Similarly other aspects of the Dhatus may be considered.

देवालयजलं वह्निक्रीडादीनां तथैव च ।
कोशशय्योत्कराणान्तु नाथाः सूर्यादयः क्रमात् ॥३२॥

32. *PLANETARY ABODES :* Temple, watery place, place of fire, sport-ground, treasure-house, bed-room and filthy ground : these are respectively the abodes for the seven planets from the Sun onward.

Notes : The abodes denoted have varied uses, particularly in horary astrology. If, for example, Mercury is related to the recovery of a lost article, it will be near a sport-ground. If it is Venus, it is in the bed-room, and so on and so forth.

अयनक्षणवारर्तुमासपक्षसमा द्विज !।
सूर्यादीनां क्रमाज्ज्ञेया निर्विशंकं द्विजोत्तम ! ॥३३॥

33. *PLANETARY PERIODS :* Ayana, Muhurtha, a day (consisting day and night), Ritu, month, fortnight and year : These are the periods allotted to the planets from the Sun to Saturn.

Notes : The durations cited can be related to the maturity of an event, particularly in horary astrology and in Dasa bhukti judgements. Should the Sun, for example, be related to the fruition of an event, it will be in about six months.

Ayana is the time taken by the Sun to complete one course—northern or southern in the zodiac. This is about six months. The Moon indicates Muhurtha, which is equal to 48 minutes. Ritu is approximately two months or the time required for ths Sun's transit of two Rasis.

The period indicated by Rahu is 8 months and Ketu 3 months (vide sloka 46 of this ch.). Also see sloka 18, ch. 4 of **Saravali** which states further use of these indications.

कटु-क्षार-तिक्त-मिश्र-मधुराम्ल-कषायकाः ।
क्रमेण सर्वे विज्ञेयाः सूर्यादीनां रसा इति ॥३४॥

34. *PLANETARY TASTES :* Pungent, saline, bitter, mixed, sweet, aciduous and astringent are respectively tastes lorded by the Sun *etc.*

Notes : The strongest planet will give the native a penchant for the particular taste ruled by it. Alternatively, one may like the taste denoted by the 2nd lord or the planet conjunct the 2nd lord. The planet in the 2nd too has a say in the matter. If many are thus related, the strongest one prevails.

बुधेज्यौ बलिनौ पूर्वे रवि-भौमौ च दक्षिणे ।
पश्चिमे सूर्यपुत्रश्च सित-चन्द्रौ तथोत्तरे ॥३५॥

निशायां बलिनश्चन्द्र-कुज-सौरा भवन्ति हि।
सर्वदा ज्ञो बली ज्ञेयो दिने शेषा द्विजोत्तम! ॥३६॥
कृष्णे च बलिनः क्रूराः सौम्या वीर्ययुताः सिते।
सौम्यायने सौम्यखेटो बली याम्यायनेऽपरः ॥३७॥
वर्षमासाहहोराणां पतयो बलिनस्तथा।
शमंबुगुशुचंराद्या वृद्धितो वीर्यवत्तराः ॥३८॥

35-38. *PLANETARY STRENGTHS :* Strong in the east are Mercury and Jupiter. The Sun and Mars are so in the south while Saturn is the only planet that derives strength in the west. The Moon and Venus are endowed with vigour when in the north. Again, strong during night are the Moon, Mars and Saturn while Mercury is strong during day and night. The rest (i.e. Jupiter, the Sun and Venus) are strong only in day time. During the dark half malefics are strong. Benefics acquire strength in the bright half of the month. Malefics and benefics are respectively strong in Dakshinayana and Uttarayana. The lords of the year, month, day and Hora (planetary hour) are stronger than the other in ascending order. Again stronger than the other in the ascending are : Saturn, Mars, Mercury, Jupiter, Venus, the Moon and the Sun.

Notes : Indicated in the first instance are directional strengths or digbala. The following are the directions related to a horoscope.

East	: ascendant
North	: 4th house or the Nadir
West	: 7th house or the descendant
South	: 10th house or the meridian

These are to be reckoned only from the ascendant and not from the Moon.

Jupiter and Mercury have Digbala in the ascendant. The Sun and Mars acquire this strength in the 10th house; Saturn does so in the 7th. The 4th gives directional strength to the Moon and Venus. The planet gets no Digbala if it is in the opposite sign with reference to its Digbala house. For example, Saturn has no Digbala if he rises.

The use of Digbala is : The planet with Digbala will direct the native fruitfully in its Dasa periods to the respective direction lorded by it. If Jupiter is in the ascendant, the periods of Jupiter will give success in north-east, the direction ruled by it. The directions of the planets may be understood as under :

The Sun	— east
Saturn	— west
Venus	— south-east
The Moon	— north-west
Mars	— south
Mercury	— north
Jupiter	— north-east
Rahu	— south-west

Conversely, if one undertakes living in or journeying to the direction denoted by a planet without directional strength, there will be obstructions and losses.

To understand other strengths, the reader is referred to **Saravali, Part I**, my English translation and notes thereof in this context.

सूर्यो जनयति स्थूलान् दुर्भगान् सूर्यपुत्रकः ।
क्षीरोपेतांस्तथा चन्द्रः कटुकाद्यान् धरासुतः ॥३९॥
पुष्पवृक्षं भृगोः पुत्रो गुरु-ज्ञौ सफलाफलौ ।
नीरसान् सूर्यपुत्रश्च एवं ज्ञेयाः खगा द्विज ! ॥४०॥

39-40. *RELATED TO TREES* : The Sun rules strong trees (i.e. trees with stout trunks). Saturn useless trees, the Moon milky trees (like rubber yielding plants), Mars bitter ones (like lemon plants), Venus floral plants, Jupiter fruitful ones and Mercury fruitless ones.

Note : Much information can be seen in **Brihat Jataka** and **Saravali** in regard to birth of trees.

राहुश्चाण्डालजातिश्च केतुर्जात्यन्तरस्तथा ।
शिखिस्वर्भानुमन्दानां वल्मीकं स्थानमुच्यते ॥४१॥
चित्रकन्था फणीन्द्रस्य केतोश्छिद्रयुतो द्विज ! ।
सीसं राहोर्नीलमणिः केतोर्ज्ञेयो द्विजोत्तम ! ॥४२॥

गुरोः पीताम्बरं विप्र ! भृगोः क्षौमं तथैव च।
रक्तक्षौमं भास्करस्य इन्दोः क्षौमं सितं द्विज ! ॥४३॥
बुधस्य कृष्णक्षौमं तु रक्तवस्त्रं कुजस्य च।
वस्त्रं चित्रं शनेर्विप्र ! पट्टवस्त्रं तथैव च ॥४४॥

41-44. *OTHER MATTERS* : Rahu rules the outcaste while Ketu governs mixed caste. Saturn and the nodes indicate anthills. Rahu denotes multi-coloured clothes and Ketu rags. Lead and blue gem belong to Rahu and Ketu. Jupiter, Venus, the Sun, the Moon, Mercury, Mars and Saturn in their order govern saffron, silken, red silken, white silken, black silken, red and multi-coloured robes.

Notes : "*Chandala*" is translated as outcaste, though it additionally means one cruel in deeds (like a butcher, for instance). It further means a person illegally born to a *Sudra* (4th caste in Hindu tradition of ancient days) father and Brahmana mother. Ketu denotes a person born through an intercaste marriage.

Some authorities hold the following view about planetary robes :

The Sun—coarse, the Moon—new, Mars—burnt, Mercury —water soaked, Jupiter—of recent origin but not new, Venus—durable, Saturn—torn, Rahu—multi-coloured and Ketu—much torn.

भृगोर्ऋतुर्वसन्तश्च कुजभान्वोश्च ग्रीष्मकः।
चन्द्रस्य वर्षा विज्ञेया शरच्चैव तथा विदः ॥४५॥
हेमन्तोऽपि गुरोर्ज्ञेयः शनेस्तु शिशिरो द्विज !।
अष्टौ मासाश्च स्वर्भानोः केतोर्मासत्रयं द्विज ! ॥४६॥

45-46. *PLANETARY SEASONS* : Vasanta, Greeshma, Varsha, Sarad, Hemanta and Sisira are the six Ritus respectively governed by Venus, Mars, Moon, Mercury, Jupiter and Saturn. Rahu and Ketu denote 8 months and 3 months respectively.

Notes : Since the Sun is the cause of the seasons, he is not specifically allotted any season. However, the Sun is a co-ruler of Greeshma Ritu apart from Mars.

The durations of Ritus or seasons are as follows :

Vasanta	— 20th March to 19th May
Greeshma	— 20th May to 19th July
Varsha	— 20th July to 19th September
Sarat	— 20th September to 19th November
Hemanta	— 20th November to 19th January
Sisira	— 20th January to 19th March

But in the matter of lost horoscopy, a different nomenclature is followed by many to ascertain natal Sun's placement by Ritu. For details, please see page 12 of my English rendering of **Nashta Jataka.**

राह्वारपंगुचन्द्राश्च विज्ञेया धातुखेचराः ।
मूलग्रहौ सूर्यशुक्रौ अपरा जीवसंज्ञकाः ॥४७॥

47. *DHATU, MOOLA AND JEEVA DIVISIONS :* Dhatu planets are Rahu, Mars, Saturn and the Moon while the Sun and Venus are Moola planets. Mercury, Jupiter and Ketu rule Jeevas.

Notes : The divisions of Dhatu (metals), Moola (roots, vegetables etc.) and Jeeva (living beings) have a great use in horary astrology, particularly to know the unexpressed query. If, for example, Rahu is in the ascendant or is a significant planet in a horary chart, then the query relates to a metal. For a fuller appreciation, see **Bhuvana Deepaka** of Padma Prabhu Soori.

ग्रहेषु मन्दो वृद्धोऽस्ति आयुर्वृद्धिप्रदायकः ।
नैसर्गिके बहुसमान् ददाति द्विजसत्तम ! ॥४८॥

48. *SATURN :* Out of all the planets Saturn is the eldest (i.e. with the highest age). He bestows maximum number of years in Naisargika Dasa.

मेषो वृषो मृगः कन्या कर्को मीनस्तथा तुला ।
सूर्यादीनां क्रमादेते कथिता उच्चराशयः ॥४९॥
भागा दश त्रयोऽष्टाश्व्यस्तिश्योऽक्षा भमिता नखाः ।
उच्चात् सप्तमभं नीचं तैरेवांशैः प्रकीर्तितम् ॥५०॥

49-50. *EXALTATION AND DEBILITATION :* For the seven planets from the Sun on, the signs of exaltation are respectively Aries, Taurus, Capricorn, Virgo, Cancer, Pisces and Libra.

The deepest exaltation degrees are respectively 10,3, 28, 15, 5, 27 and 20 in those signs. And in the seventh sign from the said exaltation sign each planet has its own debilitation. The same degrees of deep exaltation apply to deep fall.

Notes : Each planet assumes significance in a certain sign. In the opposite sign therefrom, it is debilitated. Even in the exaltation sign or the debilitation sign, it is very highly favourable or highly detrimental as the case may be, in a certain degree. For example, the Sun is exalted in Aries and is the most powerful on the 10th degree therein. In Libra he gets debilitated and if be in 10th degree of Libra, he is worst affected. Similarly suitable deductions be made for other planets.

As for the exaltations and debilitation of the nodes, there are different views. Please see page 20 of my English translation of **Horasara** for necessary information.

रवेः सिंहे नखांशाश्च त्रिकोणमपरे स्वभम् ।
उच्चमिन्दोर्वृषे त्र्यंशास्त्रिकोणमपरेंऽशकाः ॥५१॥
मेषेऽर्कांशास्तु भौमस्य त्रिकोणमपरे स्वभम् ।
उच्चं बुधस्य कन्यायामुक्तं पञ्चदशांशकाः ॥५२॥
ततः पञ्चांशकाः प्रोक्तं त्रिकोणमपरे स्वभम् ।
चापे दंशांशा जीवस्य त्रिकोणमपरे स्वभम् ॥५३॥
तुले शुक्रस्य तिथ्यंशास्त्रिकोणमपरे स्वभम् ।
शनेः कुम्भे नखांशाश्च त्रिकोणमपरे स्वभम् ॥५४॥

51-54. *ADDITIONAL DIGNITIES :* In Leo the first 20 degrees are the Sun's Moolatrikona while the rest is his own house. After the first 3 degrees of exaltation portion in Taurus, for the Moon the rest is her Moolatrikona. Mars has the first 12 degrees in Aries as Moolatrikona with the rest therein becoming simply his own house. For Mercury, in Virgo the first 15 degrees are exaltation zone, the next 5 degrees Moolatrikona and the last 10 degrees are own house. The first one third of Sagittarius is the Moolatrikona of Jupiter while, the remaining part thereof is his own house. Venus divides Libra into two halves keeping the first as Moolatrikona and the second as own house. Saturn's arrangements are same in Aquarius as the Sun has in Leo.

त्रिकोणात् स्वात्-सुख-स्वाऽन्त्यधीधर्मायुःस्वतुङ्गपाः।
सुहृदो रिपवश्वान्ये समाश्चोभयलक्षणाः ॥५५॥

55. *NATURAL RELATIONSHIPS :* Note the signs which are the 4th, 2nd, 12th, 5th, 9th and the 8th from the Moolatrikona of a planet. The planets ruling such signs are its friends, apart from the lord of its exaltation sign. Lords other than these are its enemies. If a planet becomes its friend as well as its enemy (on account of the said two computations) then it is neutral or equal.

Notes : A simple formula is given in this sloka to compute planetary relationships. From the Moolatrikona sign of a planet, the 2nd, 4th, 5th, 8th, 9th and 12th lords are its friends. The rest *viz.* 3rd, 6th, 7th, 10th and 11th lords from Moolatrikona are its enemies. The exaltation sign's lord is always friendly even if he owns the 3rd, 6th, 7th, 10th or the 11th from Moolatrikona. If, however, friendship and enmity occur simultaneously none prevails but equality or neutrality.

Take for example the case of Mars. The Moolatrikona for him is Aries. The 11th lord from there is Saturn and hence he is inimical. But he is as well a friend, as he is the lord of exaltation sign of Mars. Since we get enmity on one count and friendship on the other, Saturn becomes equal to Mars. Take again the relationship of Venus. He owns the 2nd and 7th from the Moolatrikona of Mars, thus becoming friend and enemy respectively. Hence he is neutral to Mars.

See table below for an easy grasp of relationship :

Planet	Friends	Enemies	Equals
Sun	Moon, Mars, Jupiter	Venus, Sat	Mercury
Moon	Sun, Mercury	—	Mars, Jup, Venus, Saturn
Mars	Sun, Moon, Jupiter	Mercury	Venus, Saturn
Mercury	Sun, Venus	Moon	Mars,J upiter Saturn
Jupiter	Sun, Moon, Mars,	Mercury, Venus	Saturn
Venus	Mercury, Saturn	Moon, Sun	Mars, Jupiter
Saturn	Mercury, Venus	Sun, Moon, Mars	Jupiter

The Moon does not consider anyone as her enemy as per the following statement of Parasara (Benares edition by Chaukamba "चन्द्रस्य नारी रविचन्द्रपुत्रोमित्रे समा: शेषनभश्चरा: meanning meaning further that the Sun and Mercury are Moon's friends while others are her neutrals. **Saravali** also has an identical view.

As for Rahu and Ketu, the following may be of additional interest.

Rahu : The Sun, Moon and Mars are his enemies. Jupiter, Venus and Saturn are his friends. Mercury is his neutral.

Ketu : The luminaries are his enemies. Mars, Venus and Saturn are his friends, while Mercury and Jupiter are his neutrals.

दशबन्ध्वाय-सहज-स्वान्त्यस्थास्ते परस्परम् ।
तत्काले मित्रतां यान्ति रिपवोऽन्यत्र संस्थिता: ।।५६।।

56. *TEMPORARY (HOROSCOPIC) RELATIONSHIPS :* The planet posited in the 10th, 4th, 11th, 3rd, 2nd or the 12th from another becomes mutual friend. There is enmity otherwise. (This applies to a given horoscope).

Notes : The hints given in sloka 55 are to understand the constant relationship among planets. In the present sloka we are advised of planets having a certain relationship based on their positions, i.e. for given moment. If two are mutually in 4th and 10th, or in 3rd and 11th or in 2nd and 12th, they become temporarily cordial to each other. Should they be otherwise, there prevails mutual temporary enmity. This rule is very simple and needs no explanation.

तत्काले च निसर्गे च मित्रं चेदधिमित्रकम् ।
मित्रं मित्रसमत्वे तु शत्रु: शत्रुसमत्वके ।।५७।।
समो मित्ररिपुत्वे तु शत्रुत्वे त्वधिशत्रुता ।
एवं विविच्य दैवज्ञो जातकस्य फलं वदेत् ।।५८।।

57-58. *COMPOUND RELATIONSHIP :* Should two planets be naturally and temporarily friendly, they become extremely friendly. Friendship on one count and neutrality on another count make them friendly. Enmity on one count combined with affinity on the other turns into equality. Enmity and neutralship cause only enmity. Should there be enmity in both manners, extreme enmity is obtained. The astrologer should consider these and declare horoscopic effect accordingly.

Notes : The final relationship, as a result of natural and temporary dispositions is called 5-fold relationship, or पंचधा संबंध. The same is shown below in an easy form :

Speculum of Compound Relationships

One relationship		Another relationship	Net relationship
Friendship	+	Friendship	Extreme triendship
Neutrality	+	Friendship	Friendship
Enmity	+	Enmity	Extreme enmity
Neutrality	+	Enmity	Enmity
Enmity	+	Friendship	Neutral

It is understood that if there is friendship with enmity, then also neutrality will prevail.

स्वोच्चे शुभं फलं पूर्णं त्रिकोणे पादवर्जितम् ।
स्वर्क्षेऽर्धं मित्रगेहे तु पादमात्रं प्रकीर्तितम् ॥५९॥
पादार्धं समभे प्रोक्तं शून्यं नीचास्तशत्रुभे ।
तद्वद्दुष्टफलं ब्रूयाद् व्यत्ययेन विचक्षणः ॥६०॥

59-60. *RATIO OF EFFECTS* : A planet in exaltation gives fully good effects while in Moolatrikona it is bereft of its auspicious effects by one fourth. It is half beneficial in its own house. Its beneficence is in one fourth in a friendly sign. In an equal's sign one eighth of auspicious disposition is useful. The good effects are nil in debilitation or enemy's camp. Inauspicious effects are quite reverse with reference to what is stated.

त्र्यंशाढ्यविश्वभागैश्च चतुर्भैः सहितो रविः ।
धूमो नाम महादोषः सर्वकर्मविनाशकः ॥६१॥

धूमो मण्डलतः शुद्धो व्यतीपातोऽत्र दोषदः ।
सषड्भोऽत्र व्यतीपातः परिवेषोऽतिदोषकृत् ॥६२॥
परिवेषश्च्युतश्चक्रादिन्द्रचापस्तु दोषदः ।
विव्यंशात्यष्टिभागाढ्यश्चापः केतुखगोऽशुभः ॥६३॥
एकराशियुतः केतुः सूर्यतुल्यः प्रजायते ।
अप्रकाशग्रहाश्चैते पापा दोषप्रदाः स्मृताः ॥६४॥

61-64. *NON-LUMINOUS UPAGRAHAS (SUB-PLANETS) :* Add 4 signs 13 degrees and 20 minutes of arc to the Sun's longitude at a given moment to get the exact position of the all-inauspicious Dhooma. Reduce Dhooma from 12 signs to arrive at Vyatipata. Vyatipata is also inauspicious. Add six signs to Vyatipata to know the position of Parivesha. He is extremely inauspicious. Deduct Parivesha from 12 signs to arrive at the position of Chapa (Indra Dhanus) who is also inauspicious. Add 16 degrees 40 minutes to Chapa which will give Ketu (Upaketu) who is a malefic. By adding a sign to Upaketu, you get the original longitude of the Sun. These are planets devoid of splendour which are malefics by nature and cause affliction.

Notes : The *Aprakasa Grahas* or upagrahas are to be calculated as under based on the above four verses :

1. Sun	+	133°20′	=	Dhooma
2. Dhooma	+	53°20′	=	Vyatipata
3. Vyatipata	+	180°	=	Parivesha
4. Parivesha	—	53°20′	=	Indra Cahpa (Indra Dhanus)
5. Chapa	+	16°40′	=	Upaketu (Sikhi)

Upaketu, if increased by 30 degrees, will reach the Sun's exact position at a given moment.

Let us assume that the Sun is in Taurus 10 degrees and Calculate the 5 Upagrahas, as under :

Sun	(40°)+133°20′	=	Dhooma	=	173°20′
Dhooma	(173°20′)+ 53°20′	=	Vyatipata	=	226°40′
Vyatipata	(226°40′)+180°	=	Parivesha	=	406°40′ (or 46°40′)
Parivesha	(46°40′)— 53°20′	=	Chapa	=	353°20′
Chapa	(353°20′)+ 16°40′	=	Upaketu	=	10°
Upaketu	(10°)+ 30°	=	Sun	=	40°

It may be seen that by adding 30^0 to Upaketu, the last calculated Upagraha, we reached the Sun's original point which is the basis for Upagraha calculations.

सूर्येन्दुलग्नगेष्वेषु वंशायुर्ज्ञाननाशनम् ।
इति धूमादिदोषाणां स्थितिः पद्मासनोदिता ॥६५॥

65. *EFFECTS OF SUB-PLANETS :* If one of these afflicts the Sun, the native's dynasty will decline while the Moon and the ascendant respectively associated with one of these will destroy the longevity and wisdom. So declared Lord Brahma, the lotus-born.

Notes : If the Sun is afflicted by one of these Upagrahas. the native's dynasty will not spread, so to say there will be loss of all sons or lack of sons. If the ascendant is afflicted short life will come to pass. The Moon in the grip of an Upagraha will cause mental afflictions. Though the text denotes 'conjunction' of an Upagraha with the Sun. we better treat it as 'affliction' for the Suh can never be conjunct any of the five Upagrahas, except Vyatipata as can be seen from the example calculation.

रविवारादिशन्यन्तं गुलिकादि निरूप्यते ।
दिवसानष्टधा भक्त्वा वारेशाद् गणयेत् क्रमात् ॥६६॥
अष्टमोंऽशो निरीशः स्याच्छन्यंशो गुलिकःस्मृतः ।
रात्रिमप्यष्टधा कृत्वा वारेशात् पञ्चमादितः ॥६७॥
गणयेदष्टमः खण्डो निष्पतिः परिकीर्तितः ।
शन्यंशो गुलिकः प्रोक्तो रव्यंशः कालसंज्ञकः ॥६८॥
भौमांशो मृत्युरादिष्टो गुर्वंशो यमघण्टकः ।
सोम्यांशोऽर्धप्रहरकः स्वस्वदेशोद्भवः स्फुटः ॥ ६९॥

66-69. *CALCULATIONS OF GULIKA ETC :* The portions of the Sun etc. upto Saturn denote the periods of Gulika and others. Divide the day duration (of any week day) into eight equal parts. The eighth portion is lordless. The seven portions are distributed to the seven planets commencing from the lord of the week day. Whichever portion is ruled by Saturn will be the portion of Gulika. Similarly make the night duration into eight equal parts and distribute these commencing from the 5th weeklord. Here again the eighth portion is lordless while Saturn's portion is Gulika. The Sun's portion is Kala (काल), Mars' portion is Mrityu, Jupiter's portion is Yamaghantaka and Mercury's portion is Ardha Prahara. These (durations) differently apply to different places (commensurate with variable day and night durations).

Notes : Ardha Prahara, Yamaghantaka, Mrityu, Kala and Gulika are the 5 Kala Velas, suggested by the sage. The day duration according to latitude is divided into eight equal parts. The eighth portion is unlorded. The first portion is allotted to the week day lord. Other portions follow in the order of week day lords. We consider 5 planetary portions ignoring that of the Moon and Venus. The portions of the Sun, Mars, Mercury, Jupiter and Saturn are respectively called Kala, Mrityu, Ardhaprahara, Yamaghantaka and Gulika.

In the case of night, the durations or 1/8th parts are allotted in a different order. The first portion goes to the planet ruling the 5th weekday lord counted from the day in question. The others follow in the usual order. Here again, the 8th part is lordless. The planetary portions from Kala to Gulika are the same in nomenclature, in the night also.

Guliks and Mandi are one and the same and not different. This is borne by the statement of Parasara (vide **Brihat Parasara Hora Sastra,** ch. 4, sloka 15, Benares Hindi edition of Chaukhambha Sanskrita Sansthana), viz. "**Namantaram tu tasyaiva Mandirityabhidheeyate**". This quarter is not available in our version. In this connection, please refer to **Prasna Marga** and **Jataka Parijatha.**

Keeranuru Nataraja of **Jatakalankaram** (Tamil version) gives signs of dignities for these Upagrahas and Gulika *etc.* The same is as under :

Upagraha & Gulika etc.	**Exaltation**	**Debilitation**	**Swakshetra (own sign)**
Dhooma	Leo	Aquarius	Capricorn
Vyatipata	Scorpio	Taurus	Gemini
Parivesha	Gemini	Sagittarius	Sagittarius (?)

Indrachapa	Sagittarius	Gemini	Cancer
Upaketu	Aquarius	Leo	Cancer
Gulika	...	...	Aquarius
Yamaghantaka	...	...	Sagittarius
Ardhaprahara	...	...	Gemini
Kala	...	...	Capricorn
Mrityu	...	...	Scorpio

From the Sun to Saturn, no one is exalted in the above-mentioned exaltation signs, nor debilitated in the above mentioned debilitation signs.

Out of the 5 Kalavelas, viz. Gulika etc. four except Kala (related to the Sun) have own sign system in the respective signs ruled by their fathers. Gulika, son of Saturn, has Aquarius as own house. Jupiter's son, Yamaghantaka, has it in Sagittarius. Ardhaprahara, Mercury's son, is in own sign if in Gemini. Mrityu, son of Mars has Scorpio as own house. It is not known why Kala, a son of the Sun shifted to Capricorn, a sign of his brother (Saturn) leaving his father's Leo. Obviously, Saturn has given his Moolatrikona to his son Gulika while he gave Capricorn (a secondary sign) to his 'brother' Kala.

गुलिकेष्टवशाल्लग्नं स्फुटं यत् स्वस्वदेशजम् ।
गुलिकं प्रोच्यते तस्माज्जातकस्य फलं वदेत् ॥७०॥

70. *GULIKA'S POSITION* : **The degree ascending at the time of start of Gulika's portion (as above) will be the longitude of Gulika at a given place. Based on this longitude only, Gnlika's effects for a particular nativity be estimated.**

Notes : The day duration or night duration as the case may be for calculation the five Kalavelas, viz. Gulika etc. be considered for the latitude of birth. Some authorities suggest to use the end of the period for ascertaining longitudes of these. Sage Parasara's view is correct in this respect, as exemplified in the notes for slokas 25-30, ch. 4 *infra.* "Mandi" and "Gulika" are interchanged in our own text to mean one and the same.

भांशपादसमैः प्राणैश्चराद्यर्कत्रिकोणभात् ।
उदयादिष्टकालान्तं यद्भं प्राणपदं हि तत् ॥७१॥

स्वेष्टकालं पलीकृत्य तिथ्याप्तं भादिकं च यत् ।
चरागद्विभसंस्थेऽर्के भानौ युङ् नवमे सुते ॥७२॥
स्फुटं प्राणपदाख्यं तल्लग्नं ज्ञेयं द्विजोत्तम ! ।
लग्नाद् द्विकोणे तुर्ये च राज्ये प्राणपदं तदा ॥७३॥
शुभं जन्म विजानीयात्तथैवैकादशेऽपि च ।
अन्यस्थाने स्थितं चेत् स्यात् तदा जन्माशुभं वदेत् ॥७४॥

71-74. *CALCULATION OF PRANAPADA* : Convert the given time into vighatikas and divide the same by 15. The resultant Rasi, degrees etc. be added to the Sun if he is in a movable sign which will yield Paranapada. If the Sun is in a fixed sign, add 240 degrees additionally and if in dual sign add 120 degrees in furtherance to get Pranapada. The birth will be auspicious if Pranapada falls in the 2nd, 5th, 9th, 4th, 10th or 11th from the natal ascendant. In other houses, Pranapada indicates an inauspicious birth.

Notes : The calculation of Pranapada Lagna is exemplified below, as per the above slokas :

Assume birth is at 16gh 25vi. When this is converted into vighatikas, we get 985. Divided by 15, this yields 65.66. Rasi which means 65 signs and 20 degrees. Expunging the multiples of 12, we have 5s 20^0 or 170^0.

The next step is to add this straightaway to the Sun's longitude if he is in a movable sign. Suppose the Sun is in Aries 15 degrees, we get $170+15=185$ or Libra 5 degrees as Pranapada ascendant.

In the same example if the Sun is in a fixed sign, say Taurus 15 degrees, we have to add another 240 degrees, So to say, 45 (the Sun)$+240+170=455$ or 95 degrees (Cancer 5 degrees) as Pranapada asceadant.

Again, alternatively if the Sun is in a dual sign, say Gemini 15^0, we have to add only 120 degrees in place of 240 degrees. That is 75 (Sun's longitude)$+120+170=365=5^0$ Aries is Pranapada Lagna.

अथ राशिस्वरूपाध्यायः ॥४॥

Chapter 4

Zodiacal signs Described

अहोरात्रस्य पूर्वान्त्यलोपाद् होराऽवशिष्यते।
तस्य विज्ञानमात्रेण जातकर्मफलं वदेत् ॥१॥
यदव्यक्तात्मको विष्णुः कालरूपो जनार्दनः।
तस्याङ्गानि निबोध त्वं क्रमान्मेषादिराशयः ॥२॥

1-2. *IMPORTANCE OF HORA :* The word Hora (होरा) is derived from Ahoratra (अहोरात्र) after dropping the first and last syllables. Thus Hora (ascendants) remains in between Ahoratra (i.e. day and night) and after knowing Hora, the good and bad effects of a native be known. Sri Vishnu, the Invisible, is Time personified. His limbs are the 12 Rasis commencing from Aries.

मेषो वृषश्च मिथुनः कर्क-सिंह-कुमारिकाः।
तुलालिऽश्च धनुर्नक्रे कुम्भो मीनस्ततः परम् ॥३॥

3. *NAMES OF SIGNS :* The 12 signs of the zodiac in order are : Aries, Taurus, Gemini, Cancer, Leo, Virgo, Libra, Scorpio, Sagittarius, Capricorn, Aquarius and Pisces.

शीर्षाननै तथा बाहू हृत्क्रोडकटिबस्तयः।
गुह्योरुयुगले जानुयुग्मे वै जङ्घके तथा ॥४॥
चरणौ द्वौ तथा मेषात् ज्ञेयाः शीर्षादयः क्रमात्।

4-4½. *LIMBS OF KALAPURUSHA :* The time personified has his limbs as under with reference to the 12 signs respectively : Head, face, arms, heart, stomach, hip, space below navel, privities, thighs, knees, ankles and feet.

Notes : The limbs of Kalapurusha or Time Personified are divided treating Aries as ascendant. For an individual, the ascending sign will denote head, 2nd sign face and so on and so forth. See the diagram given below in the case of a Scorpio native, for an easy grasp.

(5) Stomach	(6) Hip	(7) Below navel	(8) Privities
(4) Heart			(9) Thighs
(3) Arms			(10) Knees
(2) Face	Ascdt head	(12) Feet	(11) Ankles

The use of the above is to know of the planetary influences on the concerned limb. In the above case, if Rahu is in Scorpio ascendant, there will be a scar etc. on the head. Or when his Dasa starts, if he is afflicted at birth, he will cause danger to head. The limbs related to malefics will suffer defects and adversities while the ones related to benefics will be beautiful, strong and immune to danger. These are *sthoola* (broad) scheme. For *Sookshma* (minute) scheme of limbs, the 36 decanates are resorted to.

चरस्थिरद्विस्वभावाः क्रूराक्रूरौ नरस्त्रियौ ॥५॥
पित्तानिलत्रिधात्वैक्यश्लेष्मिकाश्च क्रियादयः ।

5-5½ :-*CLASSIFICATION OF SIGNS* : Movable, Fixed and Dual are the names given to the 12 signs in order. These are again known as malefic and benefic, successively. Similarly these are male and female. Aries, Leo and Sagittarius are bilious. Taurus, Virgo and Capricorn are windy. Gemini, Libra and Aquarius are mixed while the rest are phlegmatic.

Notes : The 12 signs are divided into movable, fixed and dual. Movable are Aries, Cancer, Libra and Capricorn. The signs Taurus, Leo, Scorpio and Aquarius are fixed or immovable. Gemini, Virgo, Sagittarius and Pisces are dual or common.

Aries, Gemini, Leo, Libra, Sagittarius and Aquarius are male signs. These are also known as malefic or cruel signs. Taurus, Cancer, Virgo, Scorpio, Capricorn and Pisces are female signs. These are beneficial or soft signs.

Aries and its trines are bilious. Taurus and its trines are windy. Gemini and its trincs have a mix of all the three temperaments, viz. bile, wind and phlegm. Cancer and its trines are phlegmatic.

The temperaments of the signs have a specific use in medical astrology. If, for example, a phlegmatic sign happens to be the 6th house and is occupied by an afflicted planet with phlegmatic temperament, tuberculosis, severe cough and other pulmonary disorders will crop up. If a windy sign is afflicted by a windy planet, rheumatism, colics, paralysis etc. will trouble the native. When a bilious planet affects a bilious sign, one will be liable to premature grey hair, yellowish body, secretion of bile, jaundice etc. If a mixed sign gets affected by Mercury, the native will be predisposed to suffer many imbalances. The planets have been described as windy, phlegmatic and bilious as could be seen in ch. 3 **supra**.

रक्तवर्णो बृहद्गात्रश्चतुष्पाद्रात्रिविक्रमी ॥६॥
पूर्ववासी नृपज्ञातिः शैलचारी रजोगुणी ।
पृष्ठोदयी पावकी च मेषराशिः कुजाधिपः ॥७॥

6-7. *ARIES DESCRIBED :* The sign Aries is blood-red in complexion. It has a prominent (big) physique. It is a quadruped sign and strong during night. It denotes courage. It resides in the east and is related to kings. It wanders in hills and predominates in Rajoguna (रजस् is the second of the three constituent qualities and is the cause of great activity in living beings). It rises with its back (a Prishtodaya sign) and is fiery. Its ruler is Mars.

श्वेतः शुक्राधिपो दीर्घश्चतुष्पाच्छर्वरीबली ।
याम्येट् ग्राम्यो वणिग्भूमिरजः पृष्ठोदयो वृषः ॥८॥

8. *TAURUS DESCRIBED :* Its complexion is white, and is lorded by Venus. It is long and is a quadruped sign. It has strength in night and resides in the south. It represents villages and businessmen. An earthy sign, Taurus rises with its back.

शीर्षोदयी नृमिथुनं सगदं च सवीणकम् ।
प्रत्यग् वायुर्द्विपाद्रात्रिबली ग्रामव्रजोऽनिली ॥९॥
समगात्रो हरिद्वर्णो मिथुनाख्यो बुधाधिपः ।

9-9½. *GEMINI DESCRIBED :* The sign Gemini rises with its head and represents a male and a female holding a mace and lute. It lives in the west and is an airy sign. It is a biped sign as well and is strong in nights. It lives in villages and is windy in temperament. It has an even body with greengrass hue. Its ruler is Mercury.

पाटलो वनचारी च ब्राह्मणो निशि वीर्यवान् ॥१०॥
बहुपादचरः स्थौल्यतनुः सत्त्वगुणी जली ।
पृष्ठोदयी कर्कराशिर्मृगांकाऽधिपतिः स्मृतः ॥११॥

10-11. *CANCER DESCRIBED :* The sign Cancer is pale-red. It resorts to forests and represents Brahmins. It is strong in nights. It has many feet (i.e. it is a centipede sign) and has a bulky body. It is Satwic in disposition (seen in gods) and is a watery sign. It rises with its back and is ruled by the Moon.

सिंहः सूर्याधिपः सत्त्वी चतुष्पात् क्षत्रियो वनी ।
शीर्षोदयी बृहद्गात्रःपाण्डुः पूर्वेड् द्युवीर्यवान् ॥१२॥

12. *LEO DESCRIBED :* Leo is ruled by the Sun and is Satwic. It is a quadruped sign and a royal sign. It resorts to forests and rises with its head. It has a large, white body. It resides in the east and is day-strong.

पार्वतीयाथ कन्याख्या राशिर्दिनबलान्विता ।
शीर्षोदया च मध्यांगा द्विपाद्याम्यचरा च सा ॥१३॥
सा सस्यदहना वैश्या चित्रवर्णा प्रभञ्जिनी ।
कुमारी तमसा युक्ता बालभावा बुधाधिपा ॥१४॥

13-14. *VIRGO DESCRIBED :* This sign is a hill-resorter, and is strong in day-time. It rises with its head and has a medium build. It is a biped sign and resides in the south. It has grains and fire in its hands. It belongs to business community and is variegated. It relates to hurricanes (प्रभञ्जिनी). It is a Virgin and is Tamasa (a disposition of demons). Its ruler is Mercury.

शीर्षोदयी द्युवीर्याढ्यस्तुलः कृष्णो रजोगुणी ।
पश्चिमो भूचरो घाती शूद्रो मध्यतनुर्द्विपात् ॥१५॥
शुक्राऽधिपोऽथ स्वल्पांगो बहुपाद्ब्राह्मणो बिली ।
सौम्यस्थो दिनवीर्याढ्यः पिशंगो जलभूवहः ॥१६॥
रोमस्वाढ्योऽतितीक्ष्णाग्रो वृश्चिकश्च कुजाधिपः ।

15-16½. *LIBRA AND SCORPIO DESCRIBED :* Libra is a Seershodaya sign rising with its head and is strong in day time. It is black in complexion and is predominant with **Rajoguna**. It relates to the western direction and resorts to land. It is destructive or mischievous (घातिन्). It represents Sudras or the 4th Varna and has a medium build and is a biped sign. Its lord is Venus. Scorpio has a slender physique and is a centipede sign. It denotes Brahmins and resides in holes. Its direction is north and is strong in day time. It is reddish-brown and resorts to water and land. It has a hairy physique and is very sharp (or passionate). Mars is its ruler.

पृष्ठोदयी त्वथ धनुर्गुरुस्वामी च सात्त्विकः ॥१७॥
पिंगलो निशिवीर्याढ्यः पावकः क्षत्रियो द्विपात् ।
आदावन्ते चतुष्पादः समगात्रो धनुर्धरः ॥१८॥
पूर्वस्थो वसुधाचारी तेजस्वी ब्रह्मणा कृतः ।

17-18½. *SAGITTARIUS DESCRIBED :* The sign Sagittarius rises with its head and is lorded by Jupiter. It is a **Satwic** sign and is tawny in hue. It has strength in night and is fiery. A royal sign, Sagittarius is biped in first half. Its second half is quadruped. It has an even build and adores an arch. It resides in the east, resorts to land and is splendorous.

मन्दाधिपस्तमी भौमी याम्येट् च निशि वीर्यवान् ॥१९॥
पृष्ठोदयी बृहद्गात्रः कर्बुरो वनभूचरः ।
आदौ चतुष्पदोन्ते तु विपदो जलगो मतः ॥२०॥

19-20. *CAPRICORN DESCRIBED :* Capricorn is lorded by Saturn and has predominance of Tamoguna (a disposition seen in demons). It is an earthy sign and represents the southern direction. It is strong in nights, and rises with back. It has a large body. Its complexion is variegated and it resorts to both forests and lands. Its first half is quadruped and second half footless moving in water.

कुम्भः कुम्भी नरो बभ्रुवर्णो मध्यतनुर्द्विपात्।
द्युवीर्यो जलमध्यस्थो वातशीर्षोदयी तमः ॥२१॥
शूद्रः पश्चिमदेशस्य स्वामी दैवाकरिः स्मृतः।

21-21½. *AQUARIUS DESCRIBED :* The sign Aquarius represents a man holdig a pot. Its complexion is deep-borwn. It has a medium build and a biped sign. It is very strong in day time. It resorts to deep water and is airy. It rises with its head and is **Tamasic.** It rules Sudras, the 4th Varna and the west. Its lord is Saturn, the Sun's offspring.

मीनौ पुच्छास्यसंलग्नौ मीनराशिर्दिवाबली ॥२२॥
जली सत्वगुणाढ्यश्च स्वस्थो जलचरो द्विजः।
अपदो मध्यदेही च सौम्यस्थो ह्युभयोदयी ॥२३॥
सुराचार्याधिपश्चेति राशीनां गदिता गुणाः।
त्रिंशद्भागात्मकानां च स्थूलसूक्ष्मफलाय च ॥२४॥

22-24. *PISCES DESCRIBED :* Pisces resembles a pair of fish, one tailed with the head of the other. This sign is night-strong. It is a watery sign and is predominant with **Satwa guna.** It denotes resoluteness and is a water-resorter. It is footless and has a medium build. It rules the north and rises with both head and back. It is ruled by Jupiter. This is how the 12 Rasis each of 30 degree extent are described to evaluate gross and specific effects.

अथातः सम्प्रवक्ष्यामि शृणुष्व मुनिपुंगव !
जन्मलग्नं च संशोध्य निषेकं परिशोधयेत् ॥२५॥
तदहं संप्रवक्ष्यामि मैत्रेय ! त्वं विधारय।
जन्मलग्नात् परिज्ञानं निषेकं सर्वजन्तु यत् ॥२६॥
यस्मिन् भावे स्थितो मन्दस्तस्य मान्देर्यदन्तरम्।
लग्नभाग्यान्तरं योज्यं यच्च राश्यादि जायते ॥२७॥

मासादि तन्मितं ज्ञेयं जन्मतः प्राक् निषेकजम् ।
यद्यदृश्यदलेऽङ्गेशस्तदेन्दोर्भुक्तभागयुक् ॥२८॥
तत्काले साधयेल्लग्नं शोधयेत् पूर्ववत्तनुम् ।
तस्माच्छुभाशुभं वाच्यं गर्भस्थस्य विशेषतः ॥२९॥
शुभाशुभं वदेत् पित्रोर्जीवनं मरणं तथा ।
एवं निषेकलग्नेन सम्यग् ज्ञेयं स्वकल्पनात् ॥३०॥

25-30. *NISHEKA LAGNA* **: O excellent of the sages, explained now is a step to arrive at the Nisheka Lagna when the natal ascendant is known. Note the angular distance between Saturn and Mandi (Gulika). Add this to the difference between the ascendant Lagna bhava (Madhya or cusp) and the 9th bhava (cusp). The resultant product in Rasis, degrees etc. will represent the months, days etc. that elapsed between Nisheka and birth. At birth if the ascendant lord is in the invisible half (i.e. from ascendental cusp to descendental cusp) add the degrees etc. the Moon moved in the particular Rasi occupied by her to the above-mentioned product. Then the ascendant at Nisheka can be worked out and the good and bad experienced by the native in the womb can be guessed. One can also guess, with the help of Nisheka Lagna, effects like longevity, death etc. of the parents.**

Notes : If birth time is accurately noted, we can trace out the correct time and date of coitus that caused the conception in question. Adhana Lagna or Nisheka Lagna means the ascendant that prevailed at the time of coitus and not the one at conception. The Sanskrit word 'Adhana' or 'Nisheka' means a sexual cohabitation. (Some texts call the first union between a couple as 'Adhaana' and the later ones in the usual course as 'Nisheka'.)

As per our present verses, we consider the birth chart of a male child born on Friday, the 17th February 1984 at 22h 35m IST at New Delhi. The birth time has been correctly noted with a special request to the attending doctor. The time of coitus was astrologically chosen and promptly noted down in the records. And hence this case will serve as a foolpro of example. The natus as per Lahiri Ayanamsa (i.e. 23^0 37′ 51″) is given below :

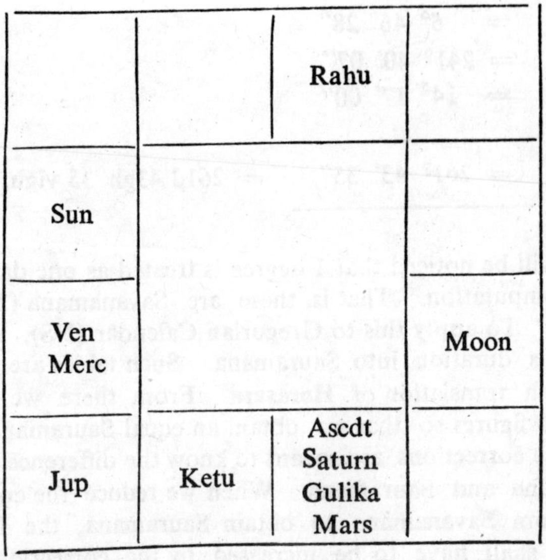

The longitudes of required planets and important cusps are as given below :

Ascendant Cusp : 182° 23′ 06″ 9th cusp : 64° 03′ 13″

10th cusp or M.C. : 94° 36′ 06″ Gulika : 208° 32′ 06″

Saturn : 202° 45′ 38″ Moon : 134° 17′ 00″

Sidereal Time at birth : 8h 1m 21s

The longitude of Gulika is cast for the beginning of Saturn's Muhurta, as suggested by the sage in ch. 3 *supra.*

With the above data, we should be able to trace back the Adhana date and time. The formula is :

Adhana Lagna=Date of birth and time minus "x"

where "X" is obtained thus= A+B+C

Now A, B and C are explained. "A" is the angular distance between Saturn and Gulika at birth. "B" is the distance between the cusp of the ascendant and that of the 9th house counted in a direct order (i.e. *via* 4th and 7th cusps). "C" is required if the ascendant lord is in the invisible half (i.e. ascendant and descendant intersected by the *nadir*). Otherwise, "C" is not required. In the example case, these are :

A	=	5° 46′ 28″
B	=	241° 40′ 07″
C	=	14° 17′ 00″
X	=	261° 43′ 35″ = 261d 43gh 35 vigh.

It will be noticed that 1 degree is treated as one day in the above computation. That is, these are Savanamana (360 days per year). To apply this to Gregorian Calendar (NS), we must reduce this duration into Sauramana. Such tables are given in my English translation of **Horasara**. From there we take the correction figures so that we obtain an equal Sauramana duration. Those corrections are meant to know the difference between Savanamana and Sauramana. When we reduce the correction factor from Savanamana to obtain Sauramana, the figure so obtained shall have to be increased by the correction factors excessively considered in the first mentioned correction factors. A reader even with average intelligence will appreciate this exercise. From the tables referred we obtain correction factors for 261d 43gh 35vigh as under :

	d	gh	vigh	Lip	Vilipta
200 days :	2	55	16	56	40
60 days :	0	52	35	05	00
1 day :	0	00	52	35	05
43.58 gh :	0	00	38	00	00
Correction :	3	49	22	36	45

We can take the above figure to be 3d 49gh 23 vigh as a round figure for convenience sake. When this correction factor is deducted from 261d 43gh 35vigh, we get 257d 54gh 12vigh. This needs a slight increase due to excessive correction contained by the above correction factor, 3d 49gh 23vigh. From the same table, we get a factor of 3gh 22 vigh which should be added to 257d 54gh 12vigh. Thus we get 257d 57gh 34vigh. That is, the Adhana ought to have been so many days behind the birth date while the birth is on 17th Feb 1984 at 22-35 hrs. The time of

Adhana as noted is : 4th June 1983 at 10.40 PM, IST, at New Delhi. (The last menses period, or LMP date, as recorded is 31-5-1983.) The duration between the two is shown below month by month.

Month	Days	Hrs	Min
June 1983	26	01	20
July 1983	31	00	00
August 1983	31	00	00
September 1983	30	00	00
October 1983	31	00	00
November 1983	30	00	00
December 1983	31	00	00
January 1984	31	00	00
February 1984	16	22	35
Total gap	257	23	55
=	257d	59gh.	47.5 Vigh

The above duration in June 1983 devoid of 3d 22h 40m as Adhana took place on 4th at the said hour. Similarly, in February 84, the duration is considered only upto the moment of birth. For calculation of ghatis, 12 midnight is treated as the starting point as English dates begin at 12 midnight.

The reader will note that we got the actual duration between birth and coitus counted backwards as 257 59gh 47 5Vigh whereas with the help of the rules, we could get 257d 57gh 34 vigh, having a difference of less than 2.5 ghatis. This difference is not inexplicable. We have considered the longitudinal difference of 1 degree equalling a day (of 60 ghatis). This means one minute of longitude is one ghati. Since the birth time and coitus time have been perfectly noted, the difference could be attributed to not considering the fraction of second of arc in the various longitudes. Thus 2.5 gh difference means 2.5 minutes of arc. Please note that we have totally used the longitudes of five positions, viz. ascendant, 9th house, Gulika, Saturn and Moon. A small fraction of seconds of difference at everv stage can well cause some difference.

Albeit the time of coitus (or Adhana) has been recorded properly and albeit we got the same by reverse process with the help of birth time as per Maharshi's principle, one may be yet wondering whether it is a coincidence. To allay such a misconception, we make again an exercise to arrive at the birth date and time in a forward manner with the help of coitus time indicated above. In such a process, we consider only classical rules as per standard books on Hindu Astrology, ignoring any suggestion from any ambiguous quarter.

Stage 1 : Firstly we find out whether the delivery should be before 273 days or after 273 days from Adhana. The relevant principle is from my translation of **Nashta Jatakam** which principle owes its acknowledgment to **Manushya Jatakm** and **Jataka Sagaram.** 273 days is the basis as the Moon takes 273.2 days to complete ten zodiacal revolutions The Adhana chart is as per the time 22 40 hours IST for June 4, 1983 at New Delhi. See the zodiac as under as per Lahiri Ayanamsa.

	Merc	Sun Mars	Rahu
Moon 29°15'36"			Ven
Ascdt 10°20'37"			
Ketu	Jup (R)	Sat (R)	

The Adhana Moon is waning in state and is in the invisible half of the zodiac. Should the Adhana Moon be waning and be in the invisible half, or with increasing rays in the visible half, then the birth takes place before 273 days from Adhana. So to say, the transit Moon will not complete ten revolutions. Adhana

Moon with increasing rays in the invisible half or Adhana Moon with decreasing rays in the visible half will cause the birth only after 273 days. To wit, she will in transit exceed ten revolutions of the firmaments. In the Adhana chart before us, the Moon is decreasing (i.e. approaching the Sun) and is in the 2nd house (i.e. invisible half). Hence it suggests a possibility of delivery before 273 days. The answer is known to the reader in the affirmative.

Stage 2 : It is not enough if we state that the delivery will be before 273 days. We must narrow down the period still briefly. The Sun's position at Adhana will tell us the possible month of delivery. One of the rules in this context is from **Suka Jataka** (vide p. 49 of my English translation of **Hora Sara** stating that deilvery will be in the 9th, 10th or 11th month according to the Adhana ascendant being in a movable sign, fixed sign or common sign. In the case cited by me, Capricorn, a movable sign, is on the east suggesting delivery in the 9th month (i.e. between 240-270 days).

Stage 3 : After the above step, our job is to dig out the possible Moon sign at birth. According to Kalyana Varma's **Saravali** (ch.8, Verses 46-47), the natal Moon will be either in the 7th or in the 10th from her Adhana position. In the Adhana chart before us, the Moon is in Aquarius and hence the natal Moon should be Leo or in Scorpio. The reader will observe the natal Moon in Leo.

Stage 4 : Leo, as any other sign, is 30 degrees in length. Then where should the Moon exactly be ? Is her birth position justified vis a vis Adhana position ? This is known by the ascendant at birth.

The signs Aries, Taurus, Gemini, Cancer, Sagittarius and Capricorn are nocturnal signs as these are strong during night time. The other six, viz. Leo, Virgo, Libra, Scorpio, Aquarius and Pisces are called diurnal signs being strong during day time.

If the Adhana Lagna is a nocturnal sign, birth will be in a day sign. If birth occurs in a night sign, then the ascending sign at Adhana should have been a day sign. (In the Adhana chart given, the ascendant is Capricorn—a nocturnal sign and hence birth in Libra—a diurnal sign, is justified.)

Stage 5 : Nocturnal sign can ascend in day time as well. Similarly diurnal sign can ascend in night time also. If the

Adhana Lagna is a night sign, birth will be in day time and in a diurnal sign. If the said Lagna is a day sign, birth will occur in night time in a nocturnal ascendant. The fraction of sign natally ascending will correspond to the fraction past in the Adhana Lagna.

In the Adhana chart given, the ascendant is Capricorn and portion past is 10° 20′37″. We convert this longitude into seconds of arc to have accuracy. The longitude thus is 37237″. Similarly, 30 degrees make 1,08,000 seconds of arc. The night duration at birth in our example is 12h 50m 48s as the Sunrise on 17.2 1984 is at 6h 59m 58s and Sunset 18h 9m 10s, for New Delhi. Now see the process as under :

108000 seconds (30 deg.) = 46248 seconds of time (or 12h 50m 48s)
37237″ (or 10° 20′37″) = ?
= (46248 × 37237)/108000
= 15945.711 seconds of time
= 4.4293641 hours
= 4h 26m (4h 25m 45.71 sec)

So to say, 4h 2′m have past from the Sunset, i.e. from 18h 9m 10s. This denotes 22h 34m 55s which should be the birth time. And we have the birth time recorded as 22h 35m. This cannot be a coincidence or manipulation for a serious student of astrology like me, but a meaningful and scientific astrological process.

When the Adhana Moon's Dwadasamsa is known correctly, the natal Moon can be well checked. She, at birth, should be in the same Dwadasamsa as she was at Adhana. Please note this agreeability—Adhana Moon as well as natal Moon being in Capricorn Dwadasamsa similarly. Hence our natal Moon is just the correct one.

Another verification factor, which however need not exist if the Moon's Dwadasama coincides, is : Whatever the angular distance is between Adhana Moon and Adhana Lagna will prevail between the natal Moon and natal ascendant. In our example, the difference between Adhana Moon and Adhana Lagna is 48°44′ whereas natal Moon and natal ascendant are 49°6′ apart.

The curious reader may note one thing. There are many rules to note the birth month, natal Moon, natal ascendant etc. with the help of Adhana (or prasna). And the correct ones bringing the various possibilities to a coincidental manner should be correctly judged without rushing to conclusions simply theoretically.

Thus the reader will be convinced of the fact that Adhana time noted is correct as we got back to the birth details from Adhana and *vice versa* accurately without any ambiguity whatsoever.

From the said two processes based on accurately maintained records for purposes of scientific research, I, rather we, firmly can conclude the following without a shadow of doubt :

1. Gulika's longitude will correspond to the beginning of Saturn's Muhurta only, as suggested by the sage, irrespective of any other authority stating that it should be for the end of Muhurta ruled by Saturn. In fact, I have not come across any sage's work stating contrarily to what Parasara stated in this regard. Suppose we have calculated Gulika for the given birth chart for the end of Saturn's muhurta, the longitude of Gulika would have advanced by 24 degrees. That would put the Adhana still 24 days behind the noted date. Please note that we have exactly reached the Adhana date as per the record maintained without any variation. This proves that Gulika should be at the beginning of Saturn's Muhurta.

2. Accurate Ayanamsa is only that of Lahiri and that accurate it is as to the seoond of arc. This contention is proved by the fact that we have made use of the Moon's longitude. Other 4 longitudes used by us in the process of getting back to Adhana are simply angular distances which will not be affected by any Ayanamsa. But the Moon's longitude will vary plus or minus according to the Ayanamsa, and Adhana time will be minus or plus according to the variation. Whereas with Lahiri's position of the Moon, we did not experience any anamoly in the Adhana computation. Similarly in progressing towards the birth date from the Adhana date, Moon's longitude played a significant role. If for example with another Ayanamsa, the Moon goes to Pisces in the Adhana, her natal position, will yet be in Leo but inconsistent with Adhana position. Hence Lahiri Ayanamsa has all the perfection required for calculation of even the Nadiamsas.

अथ विशेषलग्नाध्याय: ॥५॥

Chapter 5

Special Ascendants

अथाहं सम्प्रवक्ष्यामि तवाग्रे द्विजसत्तम !।
भाव-होरा-घटी-संज्ञलग्नानीति पृथक् पृथक् ॥१॥

1. Oh excellent of the Brahmins, I explain below again some special ascendants, viz. Bhava Lagna, Hora Lagna and Ghatika Lagna.

सूर्योदयं समारभ्य घटिकानां तु पंचकम् ।
प्रयाति जन्मपर्यन्तं भावलग्नं तदेव हि ॥२॥

इष्टं घटचादिकं भक्त्वा पंचभिर्भादिजं फलम् ।
योज्यमौदयिके सूर्ये भावलग्नं स्फुटं च तत् ॥३॥

2-3. *BHAVA LAGNA* : From Sunrise to the time of birth every 5 ghatis (or 120 minutes) constitute one Bhava Lagna. Divide the time of birth (in ghatis, vighatis etc.) from Sun-rise by 5 and add the quotient etc. to the Sun's longitude as at Sun rise. This is called Bhava Lagna.

Notes : To work out the various ascendants, assume that the birth is at 12gh 30vi and the Sun's longitude as prevalent at the time of Sun rise is 4s 12°. Find out the Bhava Lagna in the first instance, as under ;

When birth time is divided by 5 we get 2.5 signs or 75°. This is to be added to the Sun's longitude as given which is 132°. We get 207° or Libra 27° as Bhava Lagna.

तथा सार्धद्विघटिकामितादर्कोदयाद् द्विज !।
प्रयाति लग्नं तन्नाम होरालग्नं प्रचक्षते ॥४॥

इष्टघटचादिकं द्विघ्नं पञ्चाप्तं भादिकं च यत् ।
योज्यमौदयिके भानौ होरालग्नं स्फुटं हि तत् ॥५॥

4-5. *HORA LAGNA :* Again from Sun-rise till the time of birth, Hora Lagna repeats itself every 2½ ghatis (i. e. 60 minutes). Divide the time past upto birth from the Sunrise by 2½ and add the quotient etc. in signs, degrees and so on to the longitude of the Sun as at the Sunrise. This will yield Hora Lagna in Rasi, degrees etc.

Notes : Let us find out the Hora Lagna for the same example.

Birth time is to be divided by 2.5. When done so, we get 5 signs or 150 degrees. Add this to the Sun's longitude as at sunrise (i.e. 132 plus 150=282°). We thus get Hora Lagna as Capricorn 12°.

कथयामि घटीलग्नं शृणु त्वं द्विजसत्तम ।
सूर्योदयात् समारभ्य जन्मकालावधि क्रमात् ॥६॥

एकैकघटिकामानात् लग्नं यद्याति भादिकम् ।
तदेव घटिकालग्नं कथितं नारदादिभिः ॥७॥

राशयस्तु घटीतुल्याः पलार्धप्रमितांशकाः ।
योज्यमौदयिके भानौ घटीलग्नं स्फुटं हि तत् ॥८॥

6-8. *GHATI LAGNA* (*GHATIKA LAGNA*) *:* Now listen to the method of working out Ghatika Lagna. This Lagna changes along with every Ghatika (24 minutes) from the Sunrise. Note the birth time in Ghati and vighatis. Consider the number of ghatis past as number of Rasis or Ghatika Lagnas. The Vighatis be divided by 2 to arrive at degrees and minutes of arc past in the said Ghatika Lagna. The product so arrived in Rasis, degrees and minutes be added to the Sun's longitude as at Sunrise to get the exact location of Ghatika Lagna. So say sages like Narada.

Notes : Let us find out the Ghatika Lagna in the above example case.

Birth time is 12 ghatis which gives 12 Rasis. Vighatis left are 30 which are to be divided by 2 and treated as degrees. 30 divided by 2 yields 15, i.e. 15°. Thus, we note 12 signs

15 degrees to be away from the Sun (as at rise of the day). When 12s 15° or 375° are added to the Sun (132°), we get 507° which after expunging 360° results in 147° or Leo 27° as Ghatika Lagna.

क्रमादेषां च लग्नानां भावकोष्ठं पृथक् लिखेत् ।
ये ग्रहा यत्र भे तत्र ते स्थाप्या राशिलग्नवत् ॥६॥

9. *USE OF SPECIAL ASCENDANTS :* Keeping the planets at birth as it is, prepare various Bhava charts with respect to each special ascendant and analyse as done for the natal ascendant.

Notes : This is a very important clue given by the sage. We get the longitudes of the three special ascendants, viz. Bhava Lagna, Hora Lagna and Ghatika Lagna. Apart from the natal ascendant, the planets will remain in different bhavas according to the special ascendant being considered. Thus we get four different Bhava charts. If a planet remains in the same bhava in all the four bhava charts, it will specially reveal the bhava effects due to it. Otherwise, its effects are proprt-ionately altered in respect of that bhava.

The Benares edition (Chaukambha series) has the following special hints in this chapter respecting planets and bhavas, thus : The planet on the cusp of a house will give full effects due to the bhava concerned. The one in Bhava Sandhi (end of house) gives no results due to **that** bhava. (This does not mean that the planet is wholly ineffective. It is, suffice to say, ineffective as far as that bhava is concerned.) If a planet is ahead of the Bhava sphuta (longitude) of the various Lagnas (i.e. Natal, Bhava, Hora and Ghatika Lagnas) but within 15°, its effects due to the Bhava concerned start diminishing. Conversely if it is prior to the cusp but not beyond 15°, the effects proportionately increase. Needless to mention that on the 'cusp', the effects are more revealed. This gives us a clue that longitude arrived in the case of Bhava Lagna, Hora Lagnaetc and Ghatika Lagna are the center points of those Lagnas, just as for the natal ascendant.

वर्णदाख्यदशां भानां कथयाम्यथ तेऽग्रतः ।
यस्य विज्ञानमात्रेण वदेदायुर्भवं फलम् ॥१०॥

ओजलग्नप्रसूतानां मेषादेर्गणयेत् क्रमात् ।
समलग्नप्रसूतानां मीनादेरपसव्यतः ॥११॥
मेषमीनादितो जन्मलग्नान्तं गणयेत् सुधीः ।
तथैव होरालग्नान्तं गणयित्वा ततः परम् ॥१२॥
ओजत्वेन समत्वेन सजातीये उभे यदि ।
तर्हि संख्ये योजयीत वैजात्ये तु वियोजयेत् ॥१३॥
मेषमीनादितः पश्चाद्यो राशिः स तु वर्णदः ।

10-13½. *VARNADA DASA :* I now detail Varnada Dasa just by knowing which, one can deal with the longevity of a native. If the natal ascendant is an odd sign count dirctly from Aries to natal ascendant. If the natal ascendant is an even sign, count from Pisces to the natal ascendant, in the reverse order. Similarly, if the Hora Lagna is an odd one, count from Aries to Hora Lagna in direct order. If the Hora Lagna is an even one, count from Pisces to Hora Lagna in the reverse order. If both the products are odd signs or even signs, then add both the figures. If one is odd and the other is even, then know the difference between the two products. If the latest product, in this process, is an odd one, count so many signs from Aries in a direct manner; if an even one, count so many signs from Pisces in reverse order. The sign so known will be the Varnada for the ascendant.

Notes : Take the case of a native who has Libra (an odd sign) as natal ascendant and Scorpio (an even sign) as Hora Lagna. When we count from Aries to Libra (odd sign—hence direct), we get 7. Again from Pisces to Scorpio (Hora Lagna, an even sign—hence reverse) we have 5 signs. We have to add these two figures, as they are of the same class, i.e. odd. We get 12. This product is an even one. Hence we have to count 12 signs from Pisces in a reverse manner to get Varanada for the Lagna. Thus we get Aries. This is the Varnada Rasi for natal ascendant.

There is a suggestion from one quarter that longitudes of natal ascendant and Hora Lagna be also taken into consideration. In that case, the counting when done from Aries, is to be done from zero degree. And from Pisces, it is from the last degree of Pisces, i.e. the 30th degree of Pisces is the starting point.

एतत्प्रयोजनं वक्ष्ये श्रुणु त्वं द्विजपुंगव: !।
होरालग्नभयोर्नेया सबलाद्वर्णदा दशा ।।१४।।
यत्संख्यो वर्णदो लग्नात् तत्तत्संख्याक्रमेण तु ।
क्रमव्युत्क्रमभेदेन दशा स्यादोज-युग्मयो ।।१५।।

14-15. *EFFECTS OF VARANADA :* Now listen to the use of the above. Out of the two, viz. natal ascendant and Hora Lagna, whichever is stronger, from there Varnada starts. If the natal ascendant is an old sign, the counting of Dasas is clockwise. Otherwise anti-clockwise. The Lagna dasa years will equal the number of signs intervening between the natal ascendant and Varnada. Similarly for other houses.

पापदृष्टि: पापयोगो वर्णदस्य त्रिकोणके।
यदि स्यात् तर्हि तद्राशिपर्यन्तं तस्य जीवनं ।।१६।।
रुद्रशूले यथैवायुर्मरणादि निरूप्यते ।
तथैव वर्णदस्यापि त्रिकोणे पापसंगमे ।।१७।।
वर्णदादपि भो विप्र ! लग्नवच्चिन्तयेत् फलम् ।
वर्णदात् सप्तमाद् भावात् कलत्रायुर्विचिन्तयेत् ।।१८।।
एकादशादग्रजस्य तृतीयात्तु यवीयस: ।
सुतस्य पंचमे विद्यान्मातुश्चतुर्थभावत: ।।१९।।
पितुश्च नवमाद् भावादायुरेवं विचिन्तयेत् ।
शूलराशिदशायां वै प्रबलायामरिष्टकम् ।।२०।।

16-20. Should a trine from the ascendant's Varnada be occupied or aspected by a malefic, the native will live only upto the Dasa of the said Rasi. Just as the Rudra planet in Soola Dasa is capable of causing evils, the above mentioned planets related to Varnada's trine be treated. The Varnada Lagna be considered as natal ascendant while the 7th from Varnada will denote the longevity of the spouse, the 11th longevity of elder brothers and sisters, the 3rd longevity of younger brothers and sisters, the 5th the longevity of sons, the 4th longevity of mother and the 9th longevity of father. The dasa of the Soola Rasi will inflict greater evils.

Notes : Rudra planet is the one which has more strength when the lords of 2nd and 8th are considered. The planet with

Rudra designation normally features in Soola Dasa to know the possible time of death. The Dasas of the Rasis are calculated in direct or reverse order according to the natal ascendant being odd or even.

Soola Dasa calculations are akin to that of Sthira Dasa. But in the case of Sthira Dasa, Rudra's counterpart is Brahma Graha. The two Dasas are discussed in ch. 46 of the 2nd part of our treatise, among various Dasas.

एवं तन्वादिभावानां कर्तव्या वर्णदा दशा ।
पूर्ववच्च फलं ज्ञेयं देहिनां च शुभाशुभम् ॥२१॥
ग्रहाणां वर्णदा नैव राशीनां वर्णदा दशा ।
कृत्वार्कंधा राशिदशां क्रमादन्तर्दशां वदेत् ॥२२॥
एवमन्तर्दशादिं च कृत्वा तेन फलं वदेत् ।
क्रमव्युत्क्रमभेदेन लिखेदन्तर्दशामपि ॥२३॥
स्वस्वदेशोद्‌भवं लग्नं जन्मलग्नमिहोच्यते ।
भावहोरादिलग्नानां सर्वत्रैव समक्रिया ॥२४॥

21-24. Similar assessments be made with reference to the Varnada of each Bhava commencing the first and the evils and goods due to a nativity be known. These Varnada Dasas are only for Bhavas (Rasis) and not their occupants. The sub period of each Dasa will be one twelfth of the Dasa and the order will also be clockwise or anti-clockwise as explained earlier. The natal ascendant is to be calculated according to birth place while Bhava Lagna, Hora Lagna etc. are common to all places.

अथ षोडशवर्गाध्यायः ॥६॥

Chapter 6

The Sixteen Divisions Of A Sign

श्रुता ग्रहगुणास्त्वत्तस्तथा राशिगुण मुने ।
श्रोतमिच्छामि भावानां भेदांस्तान् कृपया वद ॥१॥

1. O sage, I have known from you about the planets, signs and their descriptions. I desire to know the details of various divisions of a sign, which please narrate.

वर्गान् षोडश यानाह ब्रह्मा लोकपितामहः।
तानहं सम्प्रवक्ष्यामि मैत्रेय ! श्रूयतामिति ॥२॥
क्षेत्रं होरा च द्रेष्काणस्तुर्यांशः सप्तमांशकः।
नवांशो दशमांशश्च सूर्यांशः षोडशांशकः ॥३॥
विंशांशो वेदबाह्वंशो भांशस्त्रिंशांशकस्ततः।
खवेदांशोऽक्षवेदांशः षष्ठ्यंशश्च ततः परम् ॥४॥

2-4. *NAMES OE THE 16 VARGAS :* Lord Brahma has described 16 kinds of Vargas (Divisions) for each sign. Listen to those. The same are : Rasi, Hora, Drekkana, Chathurthamsa, Sapthamamsa, Navamsa, Dasamamsa, Dvadasamsa, Shodasamsa, Vimsamsa, Chaturvimsamsa, Sapthavimsamsa, Trimsamsa, Khavedamsa, Akshavedamsa and Shashtiamsa.

तत्क्षेत्रं तस्य खेटस्य राशेर्यो यस्य नायकः।
सूर्येन्द्वोर्विषमे राशौ समे तद्विपरीतकम् ॥५॥
पितरश्चन्द्रहोरेशा देवाः सूर्यस्य कीर्तिताः।
राशेरर्द्धं भवेद्धोरा ताश्चतुर्विंशतिः स्मृता ॥
मेषादि तासां होराणां परिवृत्तिद्वयं भवेत् ॥६॥

5-6. *RASI AND HORA :* The Rasi owned by a planet is called its Kshetra (one sign). The first half of an old sign is the Hora ruled by the Sun while the second half is the Hora of the Moon. The reverse is true in the case of an even sign. Half of Rasi is called Hora. These are totally 24 counted from Aries and repeat twice (at the rate of 12) in the whole of the zodiac.

Notes : The names of planets lording over the 12 signs have been given earlier. The following table throws light on lordships of Horas (15° each) of the 12 signs.

Speculum Of Horas

Sign	Hora lord (0—15°)	Hora lord (15—30°)
Aries	Sun	Moon
Taurus	Moon	Sun
Gemini	Sun	Moon
Cancer	Moon	Sun
Leo	Sun	Moon
Virgo	Moon	Sun
Libra	Sun	Moon
Scorpio	Moon	Sun
Sagittarius	Sun	Moon
Capricorn	Moon	Sun
Aquarius	Sun	Moon
Pisces	Moon	Sun

राशित्रिभागा द्रेष्काणास्ते च षट्त्रिंशदीरिताः ।
परिवृत्तित्रयं तेषां मेषादेः क्रमशो भवेत् ॥७॥
स्वपंचनवमानां च राशीनां क्रमशश्च ते ।
नारदा-ऽगस्ति-दुर्वासा द्रेष्काणेशाश्चरादिषु ॥८॥

7-8. *DECANATE :* One third of a Rasi is called Drekkana (decanate). These are totally 36, counted from Aries (to Pisces), repeating thrice at the rate of 12 per round. The 1st, 5th and the 9th Rasis from a sign are its three decanates, and are respectively lorded by Narada, Agasthya and Doorvasa.

Notes : Each Rasi has three decanates or Drekkanas. The first one is ruled by the lord of the very sign. The second one belongs to the planet that rules the 5th from the sign in question. The lord of the 9th from the sign in question is the lord of the 3rd decanate. Each decanate is 10 degrees in length. The 3 decanates along with the signs in which they fall are as per table given belaw :

Speculum Of Decanates

(**Note** : The signs in this and other tables are indicated by numericals, e.g. 1 is Aries, 2 is Taurus & *C*.)

Sign	1st decanate	2nd decanate	3rd decanate
Aries	1	5	9
Taurus	2	6	10
Gemini	3	7	11
Cancer	4	8	12
Leo	5	9	1
Virgo	6	10	2
Libra	7	11	3
Scorpio	8	12	4
Sagittarius	9	1	5
Capricorn	10	2	6
Aquarius	11	3	7
Pisces	12	4	8

स्वर्क्षादिकेन्द्रपतयस्तुर्यांशेशाः क्रियादिषु ।
सनकश्च सनन्दश्च कुमारश्च सनातनः ॥९॥

9. *CHATURTHAMSA* : The lords of the 4 angles from a sign are the rulers of respective Chaturthamsa of a Rasi commencing from Aries. Each Chathurthamsa is one fourth of a Rasi. The deities respectively are Sanaka, Sananda, Kumara and Sanatana.

Notes : Each Chaturthamsa is one fourth of a sign or 7° 30′. The 1st, 2nd, 3rd and 4th Chaturthamsas are ruled respectively by the same sign, the 4th, 7th and 10th signs therefrom. See the table given below :

Speculum Of Chaturthamsas

Signs	1	2	3	4	5	6	7	8	9	10	11	12
7° 30′	1	2	3	4	5	6	7	8	9	10	11	12
15°	4	5	6	7	8	9	10	11	12	1	2	3
22° 30′	7	8	9	10	11	12	1	2	3	4	5	6
30°	10	11	12	1	2	3	4	5	6	7	8	9

Example : The four Chaturthamsas of Aries are respectively ruled by Aries, Cancer, Libra and Capricorn.

सप्तांशपास्त्वोजगृहे गणनीया निजेशतः ।
युग्मराशौ तु विज्ञेयाः सप्तमर्क्षादिनायकात् ॥१०॥
क्षार-क्षीरौ च दध्याज्यौ तथेक्षुरससम्भवः ।
मद्यशुद्धजलावोजे समे शुद्धजलादिकाः ॥११॥

10-11. *SAPTHAMAMSA* : The Sapthamamsa (one seventh of a Rasi) counting commences from the same sign in the case of an odd sign. It is from the seventh sign thereof while an even sign is considered. The names of the seven divisions in odd sings are : Kshaara, Ksheera, Dadhi, Ghritha, Ikshu Rasa, Madhya and Suddha Jala. These designations are reversed for an even sign.

Notes : Each sign is made in 7 equal parts of 4° 17′ 8.57″ which is called Saptamamsa. As far as odd signs are concerned, the Saptamamsas fall in the successive signs commencing from the odd sign in question. The counting in the same manner is from the 7th sign thereof for an even sign. Example : For Aries, these divisions are Aries, Taurus Gemini etc., while for Taurus these are Scorpio, Sagittarius, Capricorn etc. See the table given below :

Speculum Of Sapthamamsas

	Signs	1	2	3	4	5	6	7	8	9	10	11	12
D													
I	1st Dvn	1	8	3	10	5	12	7	2	9	4	11	6
V	2nd Dvn	2	9	4	11	6	1	8	3	10	5	12	7
I	3rd Dvn	3	10	5	12	7	2	9	4	11	6	1	8
S	4th Dvn	4	11	6	1	8	3	10	5	12	7	2	9
I	5th Dvn	5	12	7	2	9	4	11	6	1	8	3	10
O	6th Dvn	6	1	8	3	10	5	12	7	2	9	4	11
N	7th Dvn	7	2	9	4	11	6	1	8	3	10	5	12
S													

नवांशेशाश्चरे तस्मात्स्थिरे तन्नवमादितः ।
उभये तत्पंचमादेरिति चिन्त्यं विचक्षणैः ।।
देवा नृराक्षसाश्चैव चरादिषु गृहेषु च ।।१२।।

12. *NAVAMSA :* The Navamsa calculation are for a movable sign from there itself, for a fixed sign from the 9th thereof and for a dual sign from the 5th thereof. They go by designations Deva (divine), Manushya (human) and Rakshasa (devilish) in a successive and repetitive order for a movable sign. (Manushya, Rakshasa and Deva are the order for a fixed sign while Rakshasa Manushya and Deva are a dual sign's order.)

Notes : Navamsa is 1/9th part of a sign or 3° 20′. The 9 Navamsas in order commence from the same sign for a movable sign, from the 9th for a fixed sign and from 5th for a dual sign. For example : the Navamsas of Aries are counted from Aries itself; from Capricorn for Taurus and from Libra for Gemini. These are fully shown in the table below :

Speculum Of Navamsas

	Signs	1	2	3	4	5	6	7	8	9	10	11	12
D	1st	1	10	7	4	1	10	7	4	1	10	7	4
I	2nd	2	11	8	5	2	11	8	5	2	11	8	5
V	3rd	3	12	9	6	3	12	9	6	3	12	9	6
I	4th	4	1	10	7	4	1	10	7	4	1	10	7
S	5th	5	2	11	8	5	2	11	8	5	2	11	8
I	6th	6	3	12	9	6	3	12	9	6	3	12	9
O	7th	7	4	1	10	7	4	1	10	7	4	1	10
N	8th	8	5	2	11	8	5	2	11	8	5	2	11
S	9th	9	6	3	12	9	6	3	12	9	6	3	12

दशमांशाः स्वतश्चौजे युग्मे तन्नवमात् स्मृताः ।
दश पूर्वादिदिक्पाला इन्द्रा-ऽग्नि-यम-राक्षसाः ।।१३।।
वरुणो मारुतश्चैव कुबेरेशान-पद्मजाः ।
अनन्तश्च क्रमादोजे समे वा व्युत्क्रमेण तु ।।१४।।

13-14. *DASAMSA* : Starting from the same sign for an odd sign and from the 9th with reference to an even sign, the 10 Dasamsas each of 3° are reckoned. These are presided over by the ten rulers of the cardinal directons *viz.* Indra, Agni, Yama, Rakshasa, Varuna, Vayu, Kubera, Isana, Brahma and Anantha in case of an odd sign. It is in the reverse order that these presiding deities ore reckoned when an even sign is given.

Notes : In the case of an odd sign, the Dasamamsas (3° each) are successively counted from the same sign. The counting is from the 9th in case of an even sign. See the table below :

Speculun Of Dasamsa

	Signs	1	2	3	4	5	6	7	8	9	10	11	12
	1st	1	10	3	12	5	2	7	4	9	6	11	8
D	2nd	2	11	4	1	6	3	8	5	10	7	12	9
I	3rd	3	12	5	2	7	4	9	6	11	8	1	10
V	4th	4	1	6	3	8	5	10	7	12	9	2	11
I	5th	5	2	7	4	9	6	11	8	1	10	3	12
S	6th	6	3	8	5	10	7	12	9	2	11	4	1
I	7th	7	4	9	6	11	8	1	10	3	12	5	2
O	8th	8	5	10	7	12	9	2	11	4	1	6	3
N	9th	9	6	11	8	1	10	3	12	5	2	7	4
S	10th	10	7	12	9	2	11	4	1	6	3	8	5

Example : For odd sings, the Dasamsas are the 10 signs counted successively therefrom. For even signs, these fall in 10 successive signs counted from the 9th thereof.

द्वादशांशस्य गणना तत्तत्क्षेत्राद्विनिर्दिशेत् ।
तेषामधीशाः क्रमशो गणेशाऽश्वि-यमाऽहयाः ॥१५॥

15. *DVADASAMSA* : The reckoning of the Dvadasamsa (one twelfth of a sign or 2½ degrees each) commences from the same sign. In each sign the presidentship repeats thrice in the order of Ganesa, Aswini Kumara, Yama and Sarpa for the 12 Dvadasamsas.

Notes : Each Dvadaṣamsa is 2° 30′ and the 12 divisions fall successively in the successive 12 signs from the sign in question. The following table will show the details.

Speculum Of Dvadasamsa

	Signs	1	2	3	4	5	6	7	8	9	10	11	12
	Ist	1	2	3	4	5	6	7	8	9	10	11	12
	2nd	2	3	4	5	6	7	8	9	10	11	12	1
D	3rd	3	4	5	6	7	8	9	10	11	12	1	2
I	4th	4	5	6	7	8	9	10	11	12	1	2	3
V	5th	5	6	7	8	9	10	11	12	1	2	3	4
I	6th	6	7	8	9	10	11	12	1	2	3	4	5
S	7th	7	8	9	10	11	12	1	2	3	4	5	6
I	8th	8	9	10	11	12	1	2	3	4	5	6	7
O	9th	9	10	11	12	1	2	3	4	5	6	7	8
N	10th	10	11	12	1	2	3	4	5	6	7	8	9
S	11th	11	12	1	2	3	4	5	6	7	8	9	10
	12th	12	1	2	3	4	5	6	7	8	9	10	11

Example : The Dvadasamsas in Aries in order are : Aries, Taurus, Gemini, Cancer, Leo, Virgo, Libra, Scorpio, Sagittarius, Capricorn, Aquarius and Pisces. Similarly, for other signs these be known from the Table.

अज-सिंहाऽश्वितो ज्ञेया षोडशांशाश्चरादिषु ।
अज-विष्णू हरः सूर्यो ह्योजे युग्मे प्रतीपकम् ॥१६॥

16. *SHODASAMSA* : Starting from Aries for a movable sign, from Leo for a fixed sign and from Sagittarius for a dual sign, the 16 Shodasamsas (16th part of a sign i.e. of 1°52′ 30″) are regularly distributed. The presiding deities of these repeat in the order Brahma, Vishnu, Siva and Sun four times in the case of an odd sign. It is reverse in the case of an even sign that these ruling deities are understood.

Notes : Each sign is made into 16 equal parts of Shodasamsas of 1° 52′ 30″. The 16 divisions for any movable sign commence from Aries and are distributed successively. Similarly from Leo for all fixed signs and from Sagittarius for all dual signs. See the table given below :

Speculum of Shodasamsas (or Kalamsas)

	Signs	Aries, Cancer Libra & Capri	Taurus, Leo Scorp & Aquarius	Gemini, Virgo, Sagi & Pisces
	Ist/13th	Aries	Leo	Sagittarius
	2nd/14th	Taurus	Virgo	Capri
	3rd/15th	Gemini	Libra	Aqua
DIVISIONS	4th/16th	Cancer	Scorp	Pisces
	5th	Leo	Sagi	Aries
	6th	Virgo	Capri	Taurus
	7th	Libra	Aqua	Gemini
	8th	Scorp	Pisces	Cancer
	9th	Sagi	Aries	Leo
	10th	Capri	Taurus	Virgo
	11th	Aqua	Gemini	Libra
	12th	Pisces	Cancer	Scorpio

Example : The 16 Shodasamsas for Aries or Cancer, or Libra or Capricorn (movable signs) are distributed to the 16 signs (12+4) commencing from Aries. Similarly for fixed signs fron Leo and for dual signs from Sagittarius as shown in the above Speculum.

अथ विंशतिभागानामधिपा ब्रह्मणोदिताः ।
क्रियाच्चरे स्थिरे चापान् मृगेन्द्राद् द्विस्वभावके ॥१७॥

काली गौरी जया लक्ष्मीविजया विमला सती ।
तारा ज्वालामुखी श्वेता ललिता बगलामुखी ॥१८॥
प्रत्यङ्गिरा शची रौद्री भवानी वरदा जया ।
त्रिपुरा सुमुखी चेति विषमे परिचिन्तयेत् ॥१९॥
समराशौ दया मेधा छिन्नशीर्षा पिशाचिनी ।
धूमावती च मातङ्गी बाला भद्र-ऽरुणानला ॥२०॥
पिङ्गला छुच्छुका घोरा वाराही वैष्णवी सिता ।
भुवनेशी भैरवी च मङ्गला ह्यपराजिता ॥२१॥

17-21. *VIMSAMSA* : From Aries for a movable sign, from Sagittarius for a fixed sign and from Leo for a common sign—this is how the calculations of Vimsamsa (1/20th of a sign or 1°30′ each) are to commence. The presiding deities of the 20 Vimsamsas in an odd sign are respectively : Kaali (काली), Gauri, Jaya (जया), Lakshmi, Vijaya, Vimala, Sati, Tara, Jvala-Mukhi, Sveta, Lalita, Bagala-mukhi, Pratyangira, Sachi, Raudri, Bhavani, Varada, Jaya (जया), Tripura and Sumukhi. In an even sign these 20 deities respectively are : Daya, Megha, Chinnasi, Pisachini, Dhoomavathi, Matangi, Bala, Bhadra, Aruna, Anala, Pingala, Chuchchuka, Ghora, Vaarahi, Vaishnavi, Sita (सिता), Bhuvanesvari, Bhairavi, Mangala and Aparajita.

Notes : There are 20 Vimsam sas at the rate of 1°30′ degrees in the whole of a sign. See the speculum of Vimsamsas given below :

Speculum of Vimsamsas

	Signs	Aries, Cancer, Libra & Capri	Taurus, Leo Scorp & Aqua	Gemini, Virgo, Sagi & Pisces
DIVISIONS	Ist/13th	Aries	Sagi	Leo
	2nd/14th	Taurus	Capri	Virgo
	3rd/15th	Gemini	Aqua	Libra
	4th/16th	Cancer	Pisces	Scorp
	5th/17th	Leo	Aries	Sagi

6th/18th	Virgo	Taurus	Capri
7th/19th	Libra	Gemini	Aqua
8th/20th	Scorp	Cancer	Pisces
9th	Sagi	Leo	Aries
10th	Capri	Virgo	Taurus
11th	Aqua	Libra	Gemini
12th	Pisces	Scorp	Cancer

EXAMPLE : For Aries and other movable signs, the 20 divisions are in order distributed from Aries; for fixed signs from Sagittarius and for dual signs from Leo as could be seen from the Table.

सिद्धांशकानामधिपाः सिंहादोजभगे ग्रहे।
कर्काद्युग्मभगे खेटे स्कन्दः पर्शुधरोऽनलः ॥२२॥
विश्वकर्मा भगो मित्रो मयोऽन्तकवृषध्वजाः।
गोविन्दो मदनो भीमः सिंहादौ विषमे क्रमात् ॥
कर्कादौ समभे भीमाद्विलोमेन विचिन्तयेत् ॥२३॥

22-23. *SIDDHAMSA :* The Siddhamsa (1/24th part of a sign or 1°15′ each) distribution commences from Leo and Cancer respectively for an odd sign and an even sign. In the case of an odd sign the ruling deities repeat twice in the order of Skanda, Parsudhara, Anala, Viswakarma, Bhaga, Mitra, Maya, Antaka, Vrisha-dhwaja, Govinda, Madana and Bhima. Reverse these from Bhishma (to Skanda) twice to know the deities for the Siddhamsa in an even aign.

Notes : Siddhamsa is also called Chaturvimsamsa, each being of a length of 1°15′, (24 in number in the whole of a sign). The successively distributed Siddhamsas commence from Leo for any odd sign and from Cancer for any even sign, as per the Table :

Speculum of Siddhamsa

	Signs	Odd	Even
DIVISIONS	1st/13th	Leo	Cancer
	2nd/14th	Virgo	Leo
	3rd/15th	Libra	Virgo
	4th/16th	Scorp	Libra
	5th/17th	Sagi	Scorp
	6th/18th	Capri	Sagi
	7th/19th	Aqua	Capri
	8th/20th	Pisces	Aqua
	9th/21st	Aries	Pisces
	10th/22nd	Taurus	Aries
	11th/23rd	Gemini	Taurus
	12th/24th	Cancer	Gemini

भांशाधिपाः क्रमाद्दस्रयमवह्निपितामहाः ।
चन्द्रेशादितिजीवाहिपितरो भगसंज्ञिताः ॥२४॥
अर्यमार्कत्वष्ट्टमरुच्छक्राग्निमित्रवासवाः ।
निऋत्युदकविश्वेऽजगोविन्दो वसवोऽम्बुपः ॥२५॥
ततोऽजपादहिर्बुध्न्यः पूषा चैव प्रकीर्तिताः ।
नक्षत्रेशास्तु भांशेशा मेषादिचरभक्रमात् ॥२६॥

24-26. *BHAMSA* (*NAKSHATRAMSA OR SAPTAVIMSAMSA*) *:* The Bhamsa lords are respectively the presiding deities of the 27 Nakshatras as under : Dasra (Aswini Kumara), Yama,

Agni, Brahma, Chandra, Isa, Aditi, Jıva, Ahi, Pitara, Bhaga, Aryama, Surya, Tvashta, Marut, Sakragni, Mitra, Vasava, Rakshasa, Varuna, Visvadeva, Govinda, Vasu, Varuna, Ajapa, Ahirbudhanya and Pusha. These are for an odd sign. Count these deities in a reverse order for an even sign. The Bhamsa distribution commences from Aries and other movable signs for all the 12 signs.

Notes : One Bhamsa is of 1° 6′ 40″ of arc and there are 27 such divisions in a sign. See the speculum given below :

Speculum Of Bhamsa

	Signs	1	2	3	4	5	6	7	8	9	10	11	12
	1st/13th/25th	1	4	7	10	1	4	7	10	1	4	7	10
D	2nd/14th/26th	2	5	8	11	2	5	8	11	2	5	8	11
I	3rd/15th/27th	3	6	9	12	3	6	9	12	3	6	9	12
V	4th/16th	4	7	10	1	4	7	10	1	4	7	10	1
I	5th/17th	5	8	11	2	5	8	11	2	5	8	11	2
S	6th/18th	6	9	12	3	6	9	12	3	6	9	12	3
I	7th/19th	7	10	1	4	7	10	1	4	7	10	1	4
O	8th/20th	8	11	2	5	8	11	2	5	8	11	2	5
N	9th/21st	9	12	3	6	9	12	3	6	9	12	3	6
S	10th/22nd	10	1	4	7	10	1	4	7	10	1	4	7
	11th/23rd	11	2	3	8	11	2	5	8	11	2	5	8
	12th/24th	12	3	6	9	12	3	6	9	12	3	6	9

The Bhamsas (or Nakshatramsas or Sapthavimsamsas) are distributed from Aries for fiery signs, from Cancer for earthy signs, from Libra for airy signs and Capricorn for watery signs. I have on P. 31 of my English translation of SARAVALI given different calculation for Nakshatramsa. That source obviously is defective and I would prefer Parasara's version as given in our present text.

त्रिशांशेशाश्च विषमे कुजार्कीज्यज्ञभार्गवा: ।
पंचपंचाष्टसप्ताक्षभागानां व्यत्ययात् समे ।।२७।।

वह्निः समीरशक्रौ च धनदो जलदस्तथा।
विषमेषु क्रमाज्ज्ञेयाः समराशौ विपर्ययात् ॥२८॥

27-28. *TRIMSAMSA :* The Trimsamsa lords for an odd sign are Mars, Saturn, Jupiter, Mercury and Venus. Each of them in order rules 5,5,8,7 and 5 degrees, The deities ruling over the Trimsamsas are respectively, Agni, Vayu, Indra, Kubera, and Varuna. In the case of an even sign, the quantum of Trimsamsa, planetary lordship and deities get reversed.

Notes : For Trimsamsa divisions, see the table given below :

Speculum of Trimsamsas

	Signs	1,3,5,7,9 and 11	Signs	2,4,6,8,10 and 12
D I	First 5°	Aries	First 5°	Taurus
V I	Next 5°	Aquarius	Next 7°	Virgo
S I	Next 8°	Sagittarius	Next 8°	Pisces
O N	Next 7°	Gemini	Next 5°	Capricorn
S	Next 5°	Libra	Next 5°	Scorpio

चत्वारिंशद्विभागानामधिपा विषमे क्रियात्।
समभे तुलतो ज्ञेयाः स्वस्वाधिपसमन्विताः ॥२९॥
विष्णुश्चन्द्रो मरीचिश्च त्वष्टा धाता शिवो रविः।
यमो यक्षश्च गन्धर्वः कालो वरुण एव च ॥३०॥

29-30. *CHATVARIMSAMSA (1/40th part of a sign) :* For odd signs count from Aries and for an even sign from Libra in respect of Chatvarimsamsas (each of 45′ of arc). Vishnu, Chandra, Marichi, Tvashta, Dhata, Siva, Ravi, Yama, Yaksha, Gandharva, Kala and Varuna repeat successively as presiding deities in the same order for all sings.

Notes : Chatvarimsamsa or Khavedamsa is a fortieth part of a sign or 45′ of arc. These are successively distributed in the various signs from Aries in case of any odd sign, and from Libra in case of any even sign. See the table noted below :

Speculum of Chatvarimsamsa

	Signs	1	2	3	4	5	6	7	8	9	10	11	12
	1st, 13th, 25th, 37th	1	7	1	7	1	7	1	7	1	7	1	7
D	2nd, 14th, 26th, 38th	2	8	2	8	2	8	2	8	2	8	2	8
I	3rd, 15th, 27th, 39th	3	9	3	9	3	9	3	9	3	9	3	9
V	4th, 16th, 28th, 40th	4	10	4	10	4	10	4	10	4	10	4	10
I	5th, 17th, 29th	5	11	5	11	5	11	5	11	5	11	5	11
S	6th, 18th, 30th	6	12	6	12	6	12	6	12	6	12	6	12
I	7th, 19th, 31st	7	1	7	1	7	1	7	1	7	1	7	1
O	8th, 20th, 32nd	8	2	8	2	8	2	8	2	8	2	8	2
N	9th, 21st, 33rd	9	3	9	3	9	3	9	3	9	3	9	3
S	10th, 22nd, 34th	10	4	10	4	10	4	10	4	10	4	10	4
	11th, 23rd, 35th	11	5	11	5	11	5	11	5	11	5	11	5
	12th, 24th, 36th	12	6	12	6	12	6	12	6	12	6	12	6

As regards ruling deities Vishnu to Varuna repeat 3 times while in the 4th round the rulership is only upto Tvashta.

तथाक्षवेदभागानामधिपाश्चरभे क्रियात्।
स्थिरे सिंहाद् द्विभेचापात् विधीशविष्णवश्चरे ॥३१॥
ईशाच्युतसुरज्येष्ठा विष्णुकेशाः स्थिरे द्विभे।
देवाः पंचदशावृत्त्या विज्ञेया द्विजसत्तम ! ॥३२॥

31-32. *AKSHA VEDAMSA* (*1/45th part of a sign*) *:* Aries, Leo and Sagittarius are the signs from which the distributions respectively commence for movable, immovable and common signs. In movable signs, Brahma, Siva and Vishnu; in immovable sings Siva, Vishnu and Brahma and in common sings Vishnu, Brahma and Siva repeat 15 times the presidentship over these Akshavedamsas.

Notes : Each Akshavedamsa is of 40′ arc as a sign is divided into 45 equal parts. Aries is the starting point for all movable signs, Leo for all fixed signs and Sagittarius for all dual signs. The distribution is through in successive signs in each case. See the Table given on the next page :

Speculum of Akshavedamsa

	Signs	1	2	3	4	5	6	7	8	9	10	11	12
	1st, 13th, 25th, 37th	1	5	9	1	5	9	1	5	9	1	5	9
	2nd, 14th, 26th, 38th	2	6	10	2	6	10	2	6	10	2	6	10
D	3rd, 15th, 27th, 39th	3	7	11	3	7	11	3	7	11	3	7	11
I	4th, 16th, 28th, 40th	4	8	12	4	8	12	4	8	12	4	8	12
V	5th, 17th, 29th, 41st	5	9	1	5	9	1	5	9	1	5	9	1
I	6th, 18th, 30th, 42nd	6	10	2	6	10	2	6	10	2	6	10	2
S	7th, 19th, 31st, 43rd	7	11	3	7	11	3	7	11	3	7	11	3
I	8th, 20th, 32nd, 44th	8	12	4	8	12	4	8	12	4	8	12	4
O	9th, 21st, 33rd, 45th	9	1	5	9	1	5	9	1	5	9	1	5
N	10th, 22nd, 34th	10	2	6	10	2	6	10	2	6	10	2	6
S	11th, 23rd, 35th	11	3	7	11	3	7	11	3	7	11	3	7
	12th, 24th, 36th	12	4	8	12	4	8	12	4	8	12	4	8

राशीन् विहाय खेटस्य द्विघ्नमंशाद्यमर्कहृत् ।
शेषं सैकं च तद्राशेर्भपाः षष्ट्यंशपाः स्मृताः ॥३३॥
घोरश्च राक्षसो देवः कुबेरो यक्ष-किन्नरौ ।
भ्रष्टः कुलघ्नो गरलो वह्निर्माया पुरीषकः ॥३४॥
अपाम्पतिर्मरुत्वांश्च कालः सर्पामृतेन्दुकाः ।
मृदुः कोमल-हेरम्ब-ब्रह्म-विष्णु-महेश्वराः ॥३५॥
देवार्द्रौ कलिनाशश्च क्षितीश-कमलाकरौ ।
गुलिको मत्युकालश्च दावाग्निर्घोरसंज्ञकः ॥३६॥
यमश्च कण्टकसुधाऽमृतौ पूर्णनिशाकरः ।
विषदग्धकुलान्तश्च मुख्यो वंशक्षयस्तथा ॥३७॥
उत्पातकालसौम्याख्याः कोमलः शीतलाभिधः ।
करालदंष्ट्रचन्द्रास्यौ प्रवीणः कालपावकः ॥३८॥
दण्डभृन्निर्मलः सौम्यः क्रूरोऽतिशीतलोऽमृतः ।
पयोधिभ्रमणाख्यौ च चन्द्ररेखा त्वयुग्मपाः ॥३९॥
समे भे व्यत्ययाज्ज्ञेयाः षष्ट्यंशेशाः प्रकीर्तिताः ।
षष्ट्यंशस्वामिनस्त्वोजे तदीशाद्व्यत्ययः समे ॥४०॥

शुभषष्टयंशसंयुक्ता ग्रहाः शुभफलप्रदाः ।
क्रूरषष्टयंशसंयुक्ता नाशयन्ति खचारिणः ॥४१॥

33-41. *SHASHTIAMSA (1/60th part a of sign or half-a-degree each) :* To calculate the Shashtiamsa lord, ignore the sign position of a planet and take the degrees etc. it traversed in that sign. Multiply that figure by 2 and divide the degrees by 12. Add 1 to the remainder which will indicate the sign in which the Shashtiamsa falls. The lord of that sign is the planet ruling the said Shashtiamsa. In odd signs, the names of Shashtiamsas are : 1. Ghora, 2. Rakshasa, 3. Deva, 4. Kubera, 5. Yaksha, 6. Kinnara, 7. Bhrashta, 8. Kulaghna, 9. Garala, 10. Vahni, 11. Maya, 12. Purishaka, 13. Apampathi, 14. Marutwan, 15. Kala, 16. Sarpa, 17. Amrita 18. Indu, 19. Mridu, 20. Komala, 21. Heramba, 22. Brahma, 23. Vishnu, 24. Maheswara, 25. Deva, 26. Ardra, 27. Kalinasa, 28. Kshiteesa, 29. Kamalakara, 30. Gulika, 31. Mrithyu, 32. Kaala, 33. Davagni, 34. Ghora, 35. Yama, 36 Kantaka, 37. Sudha, 38. Amrita, 39. Poornachandra, 40. Vishadagdha, 41, Kulanasa, 42. Vamsakshaya, 43. Utpata, 44. Kaala, 45. Saumya, 46. Komala, 47. Seetala, 48. Karala Damshtra 49. Chandramukhi, 50. Praveena, 51. Kalapavaka, 52. Dandayudha, 53. Nirmala. 54. Saumya, 55. Kroora, 56. Atiseetala, 57. Amrita 58. Payodhi, 59. Bhràmana, 60. Chandrarekha (Indurekha). The reverse is the order for even signs insomuch as these names are concerned. Planets in benefic Shashtiamsas produce auspicious results while the opposite is true in case of planets in malefic Shashtiamsas.

Notes : The method of calculating the ruling planet for each Shashtiamsa (or 1/60th pat of a sign or 30′ of arc) is advised in sloka 33 above. Assume that Venus is placed in Capricorn 13° 25′. To find out the Shashtiamsa lord, ignore the sign position and multiply the degrees and minutes by 2. Hence $13° 25' \times 2 = 26° 50'$. The degrees i.e. 26 (ignoring minutes) be divided by 12. The remainder is 2 which should be increased by 1. Thus we get 3. Count 3 signs from Capricorn. The resulting Shashtiamsa position is Pisces whose lord is Jupiter. These positions can also be marked in a zodiacal diagram for the planets and ascendant for an easy grasp.

The order of Shashtiamsas along with the meanings of

their designations are denoted below. These will be very helpful in delineation and to know whether a particular Shashtiamsa is benefic or malefic in nature, (as marked against each Shashtiamsa).

Odd sign		Even sign
0°-0° 30′	1. **Ghora** (M)—aweful, violent.	29° 30′-30°
0°30′-1°	2. **Rakshasa** (M)—demoniacal.	29°-29°30′
1°-1°30′	3. **Deva** (B)—divine, spiritual side.	28°30′-29°
1°30′-2°	4. **Kubera** (B)—celestial treasurer.	28°-28°30′
2°-2°30′	5. **Yaksha** (B)—celestial singer.	27°30′-28°
2°30′-3°	6. **Kinnara** (B)—a mythical being with a human head in the form of a horse, a bad or deformed man.	27°-27° 30′
3°-3°30′	7. **Bhrashta** (M)—fallen, vicious.	26°30-27°
3°30′-4°	8. **Kulaghna** (M)—ruining a family.	26°-26°30′
4°-4°30′	9. **Garala** (M)—poison or venom.	25°30′-26°
4°30′-5°	10. **Vahni** (M)—fire, gastric fluid, digestive faculty, appetite.	25°-25°30′
5°-5°30′	11. **Maya** (M)—deceit, jugglery.	24°30′-25°
5°30′-6°	12. **Purishaka** (M)—dirt.	24°-24°30′
6°-6°30′	13. **Apampathi** (B)—the ocean, Varuna, (the rain god).	23°30′-24°
6°30′-7°	14. **Marut** (B)—the wind god.	23°23°30′
7°-7°30′	15. **Kaala** (M)—dark blue colour, weather, Time considered as one of the nine dravyas by the Vaiseshikas, a person who distils and sells liquor, Saturn, Siva, a personification of the destructive principle.	22°30′-23°
7°30′-8°	16. **Sarpa** (M)—snake.	22°-22°30′
8°-8°30′	17. **Amrita** (B)—immortal, nectar.	21°30′-22°
8°30′-9°	18. **Indu** (B)—Moon, the number 1, camphor.	21°-21°30′
9°-9°30′	19. **Mridu**(B)—moderate, soft.	20°30′-21°

9°30′-10°	20. **Komala** (B)—tender, agreeable.	20°-20°30′
10°-10°30′	21. **Heramba** (B)—Ganesa, (the elephant faced god), a boastful hero, buffalo.	19°30′-20°
10°30′-11°	22. **Brahma** (B)—the Universal Father, a missile, sacred knowledge.	19°-19°30′
11°-11°30′	23. **Vishnu** (B)—the second deity of the sacred Triad, name of Agni, name of a lawgiver (author of Vishnusmriti), a pious man.	18°30′-19°
11°30′-12°	24. **Maheswara** (B)—the third deity of the Triad entrusted wlth the task of Great Destruction, also name of Vishnu, a great lord (sovereign).	18°-18°30′
12°-12°30′	25. **Deva** (B)—same as S. No. 3	17°30′-18°
12°30′-13°	26. **Ardra** (B)—moist	17°-17°30′
13°-13°30′	27. **Kalinasa** (B)—destruction of strife (according to some, this is a malefic Shashtiamsa)	16°30′-17°
13°30′-14°	28. **Kshiteesa** (B)—ruler of the earth	16°-16°30′
14°-14°30′	29. **Kamalakara** (B)—a lake full of lotuses, an assemblage of lotuses.	15°30′-16°
14°30′-15°	30. **Gulika** (M)—Saturn's son.	15°-15°30′
15°-15°30′	31. **Mrithyu** (M)—son of Mars, death.	14°30′-15°
15°30′-16°	32. **Kaala** (M)—same as S.No. 15	14°-14°30′
16°-16°30′	33. **Davagani** (M)—a forest conflagration.	13°30′-14°
16°30′-17°	34. **Ghora** (M)—same as S.No. 1	13°-13°30′
17°-17°30′	35. **Yama** (M)—death personified	12°30′-13°
17°30′-18°	36. **Kantaka** (M)—thorn, any troublesome fellow to the state and enemy of order and government.	12°-12°30′
18°-18°30′	37. **Sudha** (B)—nectar, ambrosia, name of the Ganges.	11°30′-12°
18°30′-19°	38. **Amrita** (B)—same as S.No. 17	11°-11°30′
19°-19°30′	39. **Poornachandra** (B)—Full Moon.	10°30′-11°

19°30′-20°	40. **Vishadagdha** (M)—destroyed by venom, consumed by grief.	10°-10°30′
20°-20°30′	41. **Kulanasa** (M)—same as 8.	9°30′-10°
20°30′-21°	42. **Vamsakshaya** (M)—descent not growing further.	9°-9°30′
21°-21°30′	43. **Utpata** (M)—a portentous or unusual phenomenon boding calamity, any public calamity like an eclipse, earthquake & *C.*	8°30′-9°
21°30′-22°	44 **Kaala** (M)—same as No. 15	8°-8°30′
22°-22°30′	45. **Saumya** (B)—relating or sacred to the Moon, handsome, auspicious.	7°30′-8°
22°30′-23°	46. **Komala** (B)—same as 20	7°-7°30′
23°-23°30′	47. **Seetala** (B)—cold, Moon, camphor, turpentine, sandal.	6°30′-7°
23°30′-24°	48. **Karaladamshtra** (M)—frightful teethed	6°-6°30′
24°′-24°30′	49. **Chandramukhi** (B)—having the beauty of the Moon.	5°30′-6°
24°30′-25°	50. **Praveena** (B)—clever, versed in.	5°-5°30′
25°-25°30′	51. **Kala Pavaka** (M)—the destructive fire at the end of the world.	4°30′-5°
25°30′-26°	52. **Dandayudha** (M)—the staff held by an ascetic (or by a Brahmin).	4°-4°30′
26°-26°30′	53. **Nirmala** (B)—resplendent, sinless. stainless, virtuous.	3°30′-4°
26°30′-27°	54. **Saumya** (B)—same as S.No. 45	3°-3°30′
27°-27°30′	55. **Kroora** (M)—pitiless, mischievous, bloody, disagreeable, terrible.	2°30′-3°
27°30′-28°	56. **Atiseetala** (B)—very cold.	2°-2°30′
28°-28°30′	57. **Amrita** (B)—same as S.No. 17	1°30′-2°
28°30′-29°	58. Payodhi (B)—Ocean.	1°-1°30′
29°-29°30′	59. **Bhramana** (M)—wandering.	0°30′-1°
29°30′-30°	60. **Chandra Rekha** (B)—the digit or streak of the Moon.	0°-0°30′

With the above interpretation of the names of the Shashtiamsas, we will be wellguided in the matter of predictions. For example, if a benefic planet is in the 3rd house identical with a benefic's Rasi in 'Yaksha' shashtiamsa, the native will have high musical achievements. If Jupiter or the 2nd lord be in 'Kubera' Shashtiamsa, one will be very affluent. If a planet in the 8th is in 'Payodhi' shashtiamsa, fear from water may be expected. If the 10th lord occupies 'Bhrashta' shashtiamsa, the native will be wretched in profession. In this manner, many incidents can be clearly estimated which may not be 'visible' to ordinary eye from the horoscope.

Now, we have before us the details of all the 16 divisions as dealt with by sage Parasara. One more minute division, the minutest in Hindu Astrology, is Nadi Amsa or 150th part of a sign which will complete the system of Divisionalisation. For details, please see my works **"Doctrines of Suka Nadi — Retold"** and **"An Epitome of Nadi Granthas"**.

वर्गभेदानहं वक्ष्ये मैत्रेय ! त्वं विधारय।
षड्वर्गाः सप्तवर्गाश्च दिग्वर्गा नृपवर्गकाः ॥४२॥
भवन्ति वर्गसंयोगे षडवर्गे किंशुकादयः।
द्वाभ्यां किंशुकनामा च त्रिभिर्व्यंञ्जनमुच्यते ॥४३॥
चतुर्भिश्चामराख्यं च छत्रं पञ्चभिरेव च।
षड्भिः कुण्डलयोगः स्यान्मुकुटाख्यं च सप्तभिः ॥४४॥
सप्तवर्गेऽथ दिग्वर्गे पारिजातादिसंज्ञकाः।
पारिजातं भवेद्द्वाभ्यामुत्तमं त्रिभिरुच्यते ॥४५॥
चतुर्भिर्गोपुराख्यं स्याच्छरैः सिंहासनं तथा।
पारावतं भवेत् षड्भिर्देवलोकं च सप्तभिः ॥४६॥
वसुभिर्ब्रह्मलोकाख्यं नवभिः शक्रवाहनम्।
दिग्भिः श्रीधामयोगः स्यादथ षोडशवर्गके ॥४७॥
भेदकं च भवेद्द्वाभ्यां त्रिभिः स्यात् कुसुमाख्यकम्।
चतुर्भिर्नागपुष्पं स्यात् पंचभिः कन्दुकाह्वयम् ॥४८॥
केरलाख्यं भवेत् षड्भिः सप्तभिः कल्पवृक्षकम्।
अष्टभिश्चन्दनवनं नवभिः पूर्णचन्द्रकम् ॥४९॥

दिग्भिरुच्चैःश्रवा नाम रुद्रैर्धन्वन्तरिर्भवेत् ।
सूर्यकान्तं भवेद् सूर्यैर्विश्वैः स्याद्विद्रुमाख्यकम् ॥५०॥
शक्रसिंहासनं शक्रैर्गोलोकं तिथिभिर्भवेत् ।
भूपैः श्रीवल्लभाख्यं स्याद्वर्गा भेदैरुदाहृताः ॥५१॥
स्वोच्चमूलत्रिकोणस्वभवनाधिपतेः शुभाः ।
स्वारूढात् केन्द्रनाथानां वर्गा ग्राह्याः सुधीमता ॥५२॥
अस्तंगता ग्रहजिता नीचगा दुर्बलाश्च ये ।
शयनादिगतास्तेभ्य उत्पन्ना योगनाशकाः ॥५३॥

42-53. *VARGA CLASSIFICATION* : Maitreya, explained now are the sum effects of classifications of different divisions (or Vargas so far narrated). These are four kinds, viz. Shad Varga (6 divisions considered), Saptha Varga (7 divisions considered), Dasa Varga (10 divisions considered) and Shodasa Varga (all the 16 divisions considered). In the Shadvarga classification, the Varga designations arc Kimsuka, Vyanjana, Chaamara, Chatra and Kundala according to a planet being in 2 to 6 combinations of good Vargas. Next is the Sapt avarga in which these classifications continue in the same manner upto six combinations of good Vargas, the 7th additional Varga getting classified as Mukuta. In the Dasa Varga scheme, the designations commence from Parijata etc. such as 2 good Vargas—Parijatha. 3. Uttama, 4. Gopura, 5. Simhasana, 6. Paaravata, 7. Devaloka, 8. Brahmaloka, 9. Sakravahana and 10. Vargas—Sridhama. In the Shodasa Varga scheme the combinations of Vargas go with designations thus : two good Vargas—Bhedaka, 3. Kusuma, 4. Nagapushpa, 5. Kanduka, 6. Kerala, 7. Kalpavriksha, 8. Chandana Vana, 9. Poornachandra, 10. Uchchaisrava, 11. Dhanvantari, 12. Suryakanta, 13. Vidruma, 14. Sakrasimhasana, 15. Goloka and 16. Vargas—Sri Vallabha. In these divisions, the divisions falling in the planet's exaltation sign, Moolatrikona sign, own sign, and the signs owned by the lord of an angle from the Arudha ascendant are all to be considered (as good Vargas). The divisions of a combust planet, defeated planet, weak planet and a planet in bad Avasthas like Sayana be all ignored to be auspicious, for these destroy the good yogas.

Notes : Four kinds of summary of the Vargas or divisions are suggested thus :

(a) Shadvarga (considering six Vargas) *viz.* Rasi, Hora, Decanate, Navamsa Dvadasamsa and Trimsamsa.

(b) Sapta Varga (seven Vargas) adding Saptamamsa to the Shad Varga.

(c) Dasa Varga (ten Vargas) adding Shodasamsa, Dasamamsa and Shashtiamsa divisions to the Sapta Varga.

(d) Shodasa Varga (all the 16 Vargas so far narrated by the sage).

The groups as above are as per slokas 17-20 of ch. 7 *infra*.

The Vargas to be considered (as good) are :

1. Exaltation divisions.
2. Moolatrikona divisions.
3. Own divisions.
4. The divisions of the owners of the four angles counted from the Arudha Pada or Pada Lagna.

The first three are clear. The fourth one needs a clarification. In sloka 52 above, the word "स्वारुढात्" (*Swarudhath*) has been used which means from the Arudha Pada or Pada Lagna. Hence the last quarter of sloka 52 hints at the "divisions of the lords of angles from the Arudha Pada". (Similarly "Swamsa" or स्वांश means the Navamsa occupied by Atma Karaka i.e. Karakamsa ascendant, *vide* ch. 33, *infra*.)

The sage suggests that the signs owned by the lords of Arudha Lagna and of its angles are considered good for Varga Division. This will bring many signs—sometimes as many as 8—in the purview of this rule. It has been felt necessary to bring this liberal approach contained in the sloka to the attention of the reader. In my opinion, the truer strength of a planet lies in its Moolatrikona, exaltation and own sign positions.

For the sake of brevity, the good Vargas in number in the context of Shadvarga through Shodasa Varga are given special designations as detailed below :

If Shadvarga scheme is considered two or more such good Vargas are known thus :

2. Kimsuka 3. Vyanjana 4. Chamara 5. Chatra 6. Kundala.

If Sapta Varga scheme is used the same names upto six good Vargas apply while seven good Vargas go under the name Mukuta.

If Dasa Varga scheme is resorted to, the good Vargas in number are called thus :

2. Parijata 3. Uttama 4. Gopura 5. Simhasana 6. Paravata 7. Devaloka 8. Brahmaloka 9. Sakravahana 10. Sridhama.

The author of **Sarvartha Chintamani** designates 8, 9 and 10 respectively as Amara, Iravata and Vaiseshikamsas. In fact, these three are popularly known with these names *viz.* Amara etc. rather than with the ones given by Maharshi.

When Shodasa Varga scheme is wholly considered, the number of good divisions are known as :

2. Bhedaka 3. Kusuma 4. Nagapushpa 5. Kanduka 6. Kerala 7. Kalpavriksha 8. Chandanavana 9. Poornachandra 10. Uchchaisrava 11. Dhanvantari 12 Suryakanta 13. Vidruma 14. Sakrasimhasana 15. Goloka 16. Sri Vallabha.

It may be noted that most of even the hoary authors have not gone beyond Dasa Varga scheme. The sage has fully explained all the 16 Vargas involved so that a planet's actual disposition is properly known.

As far as Hora or half of a sign is concerned "good Vargas" should be flexibly used as except the Sun and Moon, none has rulership of Hora. Jupiter is in exaltation Varga if in Moon's Hora. Then, for Jupiter in Sun's Hora, and for other four in any Hora, how do we classify the Varga? In my opinion, we have to follow the hint given in sloka 13 of the next chapter that Jupiter, Sun and Mars give effects if in Sun's Hora (as far as Hora is concerned) and the rest of the planets except Mercury in Moon's Hora. Mercury is good in both the Horas. So to say, these are good Horas for the concerned planets. It follows that Jupiter and Mercury are good in any Hora for Varga classification. (There are further hints about Hora, vide ch.7, sloka 13 onwards.)

Nextly, a brief clarification is required about the Sun and Moon not having own Trimsamsas. The Sun can occupy Aries in Trimsamsas and the Moon can be in Taurus in Venusian Trimsamsa. They cannot be in Leo or Cancer in Trimsamsa charts. Hence only exaltation will apply to them in Trimsamsa.

Now, coming back to the Varga names, we will take up some for clarifications. The word "Suryakantamsa" denotes that the planet or the ascendant, as the case may be, has obtained 12 good Vargas in the Shodasa Varga or 16 divisions. Similarly "पारावतांश" or Paravatamsa indicates six good Vargas in Dasa Varga scheme. One can understand these terms on these lines.

अथ वर्गविवेकाध्यायः ॥७॥

Chapter 7

Divisional Consideration

अथ षोडशवर्गेषु विवेकं च वदाम्यहम् ।
लग्ने देहस्य विज्ञानं होरायां सम्पदादिकम् ॥१॥
द्रेष्काणे भ्रातृजं सौख्यं तुर्यांशे भाग्यचिन्तनम् ।
पुत्रपौत्रादिकानां वै चिन्तनं सप्तमांशके ॥२॥
नवमांशे कलत्राणां दशमांशे महत्फलम् ।
द्वादशांशे तथा पित्रोश्चिन्तनं षोडशांशके ॥३॥
सुखाऽसुखस्य विज्ञानं वाहनानां तथैव च ।
उपासनाया विज्ञानं साध्यं विंशतिभागके ॥४॥
विद्याया वेदबाह्वंशे भांशे चैव बलाऽबलम् ।
त्रिंशांशके रिष्टफलं खवेदांशे शुभाऽशुभम् ॥५॥
अक्षवेदांशके चैव षष्ट्यंशेऽखिलमीक्षयेत् ।
यत्र कुत्रापि सम्प्राप्तः क्रूरषष्ट्यंशकाधिपः ॥६॥
तत्र नाशो न सन्देहो गर्गादीनां वचो यथा ।
यत्र कुत्रापि सम्प्राप्तः कलांशाधिपतिः शुभः ॥७॥
तत्र वृद्धिश्च पुष्टिश्च गर्गादीनां वचो यथा ।
इति षोडशवर्गाणां भेदास्ते प्रतिपादिताः ॥८॥

1-8. *USE OF THE 16 DIVISIONS :* I now explain the use of these sixteen divisions. The physique from the ascendant, wealth from Hora, happiness through coborn from decanate, fortunes from Chaturthamsa, sons and grandsons from sapthamsa, spouse from Navamsa, power (and position) from Dasamsa, parents from Dvadasamsa, benefits and adversities through conveyances from Shodasamsa, worship from Vimsamsa, learning from Chathur Vimsamsa. strength and weakness from Bhamsa,evil effects from Trimsamsa, auspicious and inauspicious effects from Khavedamsa, and all indications from both Akshavedamsa and Shashtiamsa : these are the considerations to be made through the respective Vargas or divisions. The bhava whose lord is in a malefic Shashtiamsa will diminish, so say Garga and others. The bhava whose lord is in a benefic Shodasamsa (or Kalamsa) flourish. This is how the 16 Vargas are to be evaluated.

Notes : The Shodasavargas, apart from giving clues as to the dignity of a planet, can be used to delineate various Bhava effects. The proper instruments are :

1. Ascendant for the wellbeing or otherwise of the physique.
2. Hora for wealth.
3. Decanate for happiness through coborn.
4. Chaturthamsa for fortunes.
5. Saptamamsa for dynasty (i.e. progeny etc.)
6. Navamsa for spouse.
7. Dasamamsa for power and position (i.e. livelihood etc.)
8. Dvadasamas for parents.
9. Shodasamsa for conveyances and related happiness.
10. Vimsamsa for worship, spiritual progress, religious activities etc.
11. Chaturvimsamsa for academic achievements.
12. Bhamsa for strength and weakness.
13. Trimsamsa for evils.
14. Khavedamsa for auspicious and inauspicious effects.
15. Akshavedamsa for all general indications.
16. Shashtiamsa for all general indications.

When, for example, considering the academic achievements of a native, take the 2nd and 4th lords. If these occupy favourable Chaturvimsamsas, the subject will progress with education unhindered. Or if the Dasa lord related to education is dignified in Chaturvimsamsa, he will confer wide learning. Similarly the other events be delineated accordingly.

Slokas 6-8 need a clearer approach. Take a bhava owned by a planet. If the said planet is in a malefic Shashtiamsa, then the bhava in question suffers a defect. Good and bad Shashtiamsas have been specified earlier.

Another clarification is about the lord of Shodasamsa being benefic. If a planet is in the Shodasamsa (Kalamsa) of a benefic, then the house owned by the first-mentioned flourishes. The word "शुभ" means "benefic" without reference to "good Vargas" vide sloka 52 of the previous chapter. Why the sage chose these exceptions is inexplicable.

उदयादिषु भावेषु खेटस्य भवनेषु वा ।
वर्गविंशोपकं वीक्ष्य ज्ञेयं तेषां शुभाऽशुभम् ॥९॥
अथातः सम्प्रवक्ष्यामि वर्गविंशोपकं बलम् ।
यस्य विज्ञानमात्रेण विपाकं दृष्टिगोचरम् ॥१०॥
गृहविंशोपकं वीक्ष्यं सूर्यादीनां खचारिणाम् ।
स्वगृहोच्चे बलं पूर्णं शून्यं तत्सप्तमस्थिते ॥११॥

9-12. After assessing the 20 point strength of the ascending degree, other houses and the planets, the good and bad effects be declared. I explain below the method of knowing the Vimsopaka strength (20 point strength) just by knowing which an idea of the results of actions of this birth and of former birth will clearly emerge. The planets from the Sun on get full strength when in exaltation or in own sign and are bereft of strength when in the 7th (from exaltation). In between, the strength be known by rule of three process. In the case of a planet owning two signs, distinction of placement in odd/even sign identical with own sign be made.

Notes : The method of calculating Vimsopaka strength is given in slokas 17-27 of the present chapter. The sage instructs that this strength will be highly suggestive.

Other sources of strength are suggested in slokas 11-16. These are related to assess a planet's proper disposition.

A planet in exaltation is fully powerful while in debilitation it is devoid of Vigour. If it is descending, i.e. leaving the exaltation and transitting towards debilitation, degree by degree, its strength diminishes and the planet becomes fully void in the debilitation sign. Again when it climbs from fall to exaltation, gradually it gains and becomes fully potential in exaltation.

It is also stated that planets in own signs get full strength. Here a distinction is to be noted. Male planets in male signs and female planets in female sings get full strength. Mars and others each have two signs. Mars, a male planet, in own sign if in Aries is better than Mars in Scorpio, a female sign. Venus in Taurus is better placed than in Libra. Such inference may be wisely made. These details are elaborately discussed in the relevant chapters in the matter of calculation of Shadbala etc.

ग्रहस्थितिवशाज्ज्ञेयं द्विराश्यधिपतिस्तथा ।
मध्येऽनुपाततो ज्ञेयं ओजयुग्मर्क्षभेदतः ॥१२॥
सूर्यहोराफलं दद्युर्जीवार्कवसुधात्मजाः ।
चन्द्रास्फूजिदर्कपुत्राश्चन्द्रहोराफलप्रदाः ॥१३॥
फलद्वयं बुधो दद्यात् समे चान्द्रं तदन्यके ।
रवेः फलं स्वहोरादौ फलहीनं विरामके ॥१४॥
मध्येऽनुपातात् सर्वत्र द्रेष्काणेऽपि विचिन्तयेत् ।
गृहवत् तुर्यभागेपि नवांशादावपि स्वयम् ॥१५॥
सूर्यः कुजफलं धत्ते भार्गवस्य निशापतिः ।
त्रिंशांशके विचिन्त्यैवमत्रापि गृहवत् स्मृतम् ॥१६॥

13-16. *HORA, DECANATE AND TRIMSAMSA EFFECTS :* Jupiter, the Sun and Mars give (pronounced) effects in the hora of the Sun. The Moon, Venus and Saturn do so when in Moon's hora. Mercury is effective in both the Horas. In the case of an even Rasi the hora of the Moon will be powerful in effects while the Sun's hora in an odd sign will be so. Full, medium and nil will be the effects respectively in the beginning, middle and the end of a hora. Similar applications be made for a decanate, Turyamsa, Navamsa etc. As for Trimsamsa effects the Sun is akin to Mars and the Moon is akin to Venus. The effects applicable to Rasi will apply to Trimsamsa.

Notes : The three male planets in Sun's Hora will be revealing while Venus, Moon and Saturn are good in Moon's Hora.

Here again, Sun's Hora of odd signs and Moon's Hora in even signs are given preference. Now from this, it emerges that Sun, Mars and Jupiter are highly powerful in the first half of an odd sign and Moon, Venus and saturn are very revealing in the second half of an even sign. Mercury is powerful in any Hora whether an odd sign or otherwise.

The effects due to a Hora will be derived fully if the planet is in the first one-third part of the Hora. The effects will be medium or nil according to the placements being in the second or third part of the Hora.

लग्नहोराद्रृकाणांकभागसूर्यंका इति ।
त्रिंशांशकश्च षड्वर्गा अत्र विंशोपकाः क्रमात् ॥१७॥
रसनेत्राब्धिपंचाश्विभूमयः सप्तवर्गके ।
ससप्तमांशके तत्र विश्वकाः पंच लोचनम् ॥१८॥
त्रयः सार्द्धं द्वयं सार्द्धवेदा द्वौ रात्रिनायकः ।
स्थूलं फलं च संस्थाप्य तत्सूक्ष्मं च ततस्ततः ॥१९॥

17-19. *VIMSOPAKA STRENGTH :* The Shadvargas (six divisions) consist of Rasi, Hora, decanate, Navamsa, Dvadasamsa and Trimsamsa. The full strength, for each of the divisions respectively are 6, 2, 4, 5, 2 and 1. This is the Vimsopaka strength relating to Shadvarga division. Adding the Sapthamamsa to the Shad Vargas, we get Sapta Varga, the Vimsopaka strength for which is : 5, 2, 3, 2½, 4½, 2 and 1. These are gross strengths while subtle ones should be understood by exact positions.

Notes : Vimsopaka strength is the 20 point strength obtained by a planet in continuously occupying own Vargas etc. in the various schemes like Shad Varga to Shodasa Varga. For fuller appreciation, see the notes given under slokas 26-27 of the current chapter.

दशवर्गे दिगंशाढ्याः कलांशाः षष्टिभागकाः ।
त्रयं क्षेत्रस्य विज्ञेयाः पंचषष्ट्यंशकस्य च ॥२०॥

20. Add Dasamsa, Shodasamsa and Shastiamsa to the said Saptha Varga Divisions, to get the scheme of Dasa Varga (10

divisions) The Vimsopaka strength in this context is 3 for Rasi, 5 for Shashtiamsa and for the other 8 divisions, 1½ each.

साद्धैंकभागाः शेषाणां विश्वकाः परिकीर्तिता।
अथ वक्ष्ये विशेषेण बलं विंशोपकाह्वयम् ॥२१॥
क्रमात् षोडशवर्गाणां क्षेत्रादीनां पृथक् पृथक्।
होरात्रिंशांशदृक्काणे कुचन्द्रशशिनः क्रमात् ॥२२॥
कलांशस्य द्वयं ज्ञेयं त्रयं नन्दांशकस्य च।
क्षेत्रे सार्द्धं च त्रितयं वेदाः षष्ट्यंशकस्य हि ॥२३॥
अर्द्धमर्धं तु शेषाणां ह्येतत् स्वीयमुदाहृतम्।
पूर्णं विंशोपकं विंशो धृतिः स्यादधिमित्रके ॥२४॥
मित्रे पंचदश प्रोक्तं समे दश प्रकीर्तितम्।
शत्रौ सप्ताधिशत्रौ च पंचविंशोपकं भवेत् ॥२५॥

21-25. When the 16 divisions (Shodasa Varga Scheme) are considered together, the Vimsopaka score goes thus : Hora 1 Trimsamsa 1, decanate 1, Shodasamsa 2, Navamsa 3, Rasi 3½, Shashtiamsa 4, and the rest of the nine divisions each a half. The Vimsopaka strength remains as 20 (in the above computations) only when the planet is in own house Vargas. Otherwise the total strength from 20 declines to 18 in extreme friend's Vargas, to 15 in friendly Vargas, to 10 in equal's divisions, to 7 in enemy's Vargas and to 5 in sworn enemy's Vargas. (These figures are called Varga Viswa.)

वर्गविश्वाः स्वविश्वघ्नाः पुनर्विंशतिभाजिताः।
विश्वाफलोपयोग्यं तत्पञ्चोनं फलदो न हि ॥२६॥
तदूर्ध्वं स्वल्पफलदं दशोर्ध्वं मध्यमं स्मृतम्।
तिथ्यूर्ध्वं पूर्णफलदं बोध्यं सर्वं खचारिणाम् ॥२७॥

26-27. *VIMSOPAKA PROPORTIONAL EVALUATION :* Multiply the figure due to full strength for the division by the Varga Viswa and divide by 20 to get the exact strength of the planet. If the such total is below 5 the planet will not be capable of giving auspicious results. If it is above 5 but below 10, the planet will yield some good effects. Later on upto 15 it is indicative of mediocre effect. A planet with above 15 will yield wholly favourable effects.

Notes : Vimsopaka or 20 point strength is calculated for Shad Varga, Saptha Varga, Dasa Varga or Shodasa Varga, whichever is being considered by the astrologer. These Vargas are detailed in the earlier slokas. By being in own Vargas a planet gets full points of strength allotted to it in the concerned scheme. These are tabulated below for easy grasp :

Varga	Shad Varga	Saptha Varga	Dasa Varga	Shodasa Varga
Rasi	6	5.0	3.0	3.5
Hora	2	2.0	1.5	1.0
Drekkana	4	3.0	1.5	1.0
Navamsa	5	2.5	1.5	3.0
Dvadasamsa	2	4.5	1.5	0.5
Trimsamsa	1	2.0	1.5	1.0
Saptamsa	—	1.0	1.5	0.5
Dasamsa	—	–	1.5	0.5
Kalamsa	—	—	1.5	2.0
Shastiamsa	—	—	5.0	4.0
Vimsamsa	—	—	—	0.5
Chatur Vimsamsa	—	—	—	0.5
Bhamsa	—	—	—	0.5
Turyamsa	—	—	—	0.5
Khavedamsa	—	—	—	0.5
Akshavedamsa	—	—	—	0.5
Total	20	20.0	20.0	20.0

The figure against each individual division is called "Swaviswa". For example, in Rasi Division under Shodasa Varga, you find 3.5 which is the Swaviswa.

Varga Viswa is the total strength as shown in sloka 25 for the various dignities like placement in own house, extreme friend's house *etc.*

If a planet is continuously in own Vargas in the whole of Shad Varga scheme or any other, it gets all the 20 points or full of Vimsopaka strength. This is always not possible. By virtue of a placement in other than own house, the points diminish. In this context, Panchadha Sambandha or compound relationship is to be considered, as learnt by us from slokas 57-58 of ch. 3, **supra**.

To arrive at the net Vimsopaka, note the following formula :

$$\frac{\text{Swaviswa} \times \text{Varga Viswa}}{20}$$

Now see the following horoscope of a native born on 17-2-1984 at 2235 hrs. IST at New Delhi.

		Rahu	
Sun			
Venus Mercury			Moon
Jup	Ketu	Lag Sat Mars	

Let us consider the Vimsopaka strength for the ascendant lord Venus. His Varga dignities and his relationship with each of the Varga Lords is noted simultaneously along with Vimsopaka. The longitude of Venus is 9s 4° 32′ 30″.

Division	**occupation**	**Lord**	**Relationship**	**SV**	**VV**	**VS**
Rasi	Capricorn	Sat.	Adhimitra	6	18	5.4
Hora	Cancer	Moon	Adhisatru	2	5	0.5
Drekkana	Capricorn	Sat.	Adhimitra	4	18	3.6
Navamsa	Aquarius	Sat.	Adhimitra	5	18	4.5
Dvadasamsa	Aquarius	Sat.	Adhimitra	2	18	1.8
Trimsamsa	Taurus	Ven.	Own	1	20	1.0

In the above table, SV=Swavisva, VV=Varga Viswa and VS=Vimsopaka strength.

The rest of the points will be clear to the reader from the above calculations. And the Vimsopaka strengths be estimated accordingly.

Maharshi Parasara fixes broad guidelines to know the use of this strength as under :

5 points	:	Inauspicious results (or neutralisation of good effects)
5-10 points	:	Some good effects
10-15 points	:	Mediocre effects
15-20 points	:	Wholly favourable effects.

In our example, Venus gets 16.8 points and hence he should confer wholly favourable effects when Shad Varga scheme is considered. I would, however, prefer use of all the 16 Vargas for a truer picture.

Minute evaluations of Vimsopaka are given on p. 101 for a better understanding.

अथाऽन्यदपि वक्ष्येऽहं मैत्रेय ! त्वं विधारय ।
खेटाः पूर्णफलं दद्युः सूर्यात् सप्तमके स्थिताः ॥२८॥
फलाभावं विजानीयात् समे सूर्यनभश्चरे ।
मध्येऽनुपातात् सर्वत्र ह्युदयास्तविशोपकाः ॥२९॥

28-29. *OTHER SOURCES OF STRENGTH :* Maitreya, there are other kinds of sources as I explain below. Planets in the 7th from the Sun will be fully effective. One with an identical longitude in comparison to the Sun's will destroy the good effects. Rule of three process be applied to the planet in between these positions.

Notes : A planet away from the Sun is immune to loss of rays, and can express itself fully. This need not be literally misinterpreted that the one not being in the 7th from the Sun will be ineffective. For example, we have Ubhayachari and other yogas in which case, a planet other than the Moon is related to the Sun by close positions. This does not mean that these yogas will not fructify. If a planet is eclipsed in the Sun, it proves impotent. This applies to Venus and Saturn as well, against the common belief that these two do not lose rays even if combust and hence are free from Astangata dosha. This suggestion is only for Ayurdaya calculations and rectifications of planetary rays (or Graha Kiranas). Please see the following table for degrees of combustion.

Planet	Combustion in direct motion	Combustion in (R) motion
Moon	12°	—
Mars	17°	8°
Mercury	14°	12°
Jupiter	11°	11°
Venus	10°	8°
Saturn	16°	16°

Rahu and Ketu should not be treated as combust although they may be longitudinally close to the Sun. For they are only mathematical points. On the contrary, they eclipse or obstruct the Sun. A basic phenomenon in combustion is the planet combust does not heliacally rise during the period of combustion but is set.

वर्गविशोपकं ज्ञेयं फलमस्य द्विजर्षभ ! ।
यच्च यत्र फलं बुद्ध्वा तत्फलं परिकीर्तितम् ॥३०॥
वर्गविशोपकं चादावुदयास्तमतः परम् ।
पूर्णं पूर्णेतिपूर्णंस्यात् सर्वदैवं विचिन्तयेत् ॥३१॥
हीनं हीनेतिहीनं स्यात् स्वल्पेल्पात्यल्पकं स्मृतम् ।
मध्यं मध्येतिमध्यं स्याद्यावत्तस्य दशास्थितिः ॥३२॥

30-32. *DASA EFFECTS WITH VIMSOPAKA STRENGTH* : Maitreya, after assessing the Vimsopaka strength through the various divisions, the rising and setting of the planets be considered. The Vimsopaka strength is classified as under: Poorna, Atipoorna, Madhya, Atimadhya, Heena. Atiheena, Swalpa and Atiswalpa. Thus should be classified the Vimsopaka strength and the Dasa period results declared accordingly.

Notes : The sage uses 8 distinct terms to classify the effects of Vimsopaka strength. I have used the same original terms for the sake of identity while the table given below with percentages of effects due to the various grades will enlighten the student as to what these terms imply.

Grade	Vimsopaka points	Beneficial effects due
Atipoorna	17.5 to 20.0	87.5—100%
Poorna	15.0 to 17.5	75.0—87.5%
Atimadhya	12.5 to 15.0	62.5—75.0%
Madhya	10.0 to 12.5	50.0—62.5%
Swalpa	7.5 to 10.0	37.5—50.0%
Atiswalpa	5.0 to 7.5	25.0—37.5%
Heena	2.5 to 5.0	12.5—25.0%
Atiheena	0 to 2.5	0—12.5%

The percentages given by me are numerical assignments for a comparative study so that an idea is gained of the gradations originally suggested.

अथाऽन्यदपि वक्ष्यामि मैत्रेय ! श्रृणु सुव्रत ! ।
लग्नतुर्यास्तवियतां केन्द्रसंज्ञा विशेषतः ॥३३॥
द्विपंचरन्ध्रलाभानां ज्ञेयं पणफराभिधम् ।
त्रिषष्ठभाग्यरिष्फानामापोक्लिममिति द्विज ! ॥३४॥
लग्नात् पंचमभाग्यस्य कोणसंज्ञा विधीयते ।
षष्ठाष्टव्ययभावानां दुःसंज्ञास्त्रिकसंज्ञकाः ॥३५॥
चतुरस्त्रं तुर्यरन्ध्रं कथयन्ति द्विजोत्तम ! ।
स्वस्थादुपचयर्क्षाणि त्रिषडायाम्बराणि हि ॥३६॥

33-36. *ANGLES, TRINES ETC. DEFINED* : O Maitreya, listen to other matters which I am explaining. The Kendras (angles) are specially known as ascendant, the 4th house the descendant and the mid-heaven (the 10th house). The 2nd, 5th, 8th and the llth are Panapharas or succedents while the 3rd, 6th, 9th and the 12th are called Apokliinas or cadents. The 5th and 9th from the ascendant are known by the name Kona or trine. Evil houses or Trika houses are the 6th, 8th and the 12th. Chatuıasras are the 4th and 8th. The 3rd, 6th, 10th and 11th houses are Upachaya.

Notes : The 12 houses including the ascendant are classified into various groups which are as under :

Kendras or angles	: Ascendant 4th, 7th and 10th
Panapharas or Succedents	: 2nd, 5th, 8th and 11th
Apoklimas or Cadents	: 3rd, 6th, 9th and 12th
Konas or Trines	: 5th and 9th
Trikas or evil houses	: 6th, 8th and 12th
Chaturasras	: 4th and 8th
Upachayas	: 3rd, 6th, 10th and 11th.

तनुर्धनं च सहजो बन्धुपुत्रारयस्तथा ।
युवतीरन्ध्रधर्माख्यकर्मलाभव्ययाः क्रमात् ॥३७॥
संक्षेपेणैतदुदितमन्यद् बुद्ध्यनुसारतः ।
किञ्चिद्विशेषं वक्ष्यामि यथा ब्रह्ममुखाच्छ्रुतम् ॥३८॥

37-38. *NAMES OF BHAVAS* : The 12 houses are : Thanu, Dhana, Sahaja, Bandhu, Putra, Ari (अरि), Yuvati, Randhra, Dharma, Karma, Laabha and Vyaya are in order the names of houses. I explained these briefly and leave it to you to grasp more according to your intelligece. As delivered by Lord Brahma, some further information is added thus (i.e. in the following verses).

Notes : Each house is given a special name for easy identity. The indications are known thus :

Thanu	: physique
Dhana	: wealth
Sahaja	: younger brother/sister

Bandhu	: relatives
Putra	: progeny
Ari	: enemies
Yuvati	: wife
Randhra	: longevity
Dharma	: religion
Karma	: acts (or livelihood)
Laabha	: gains
Vyaya	: expenditure

"Randhra" actually means a vulnerable or assailable point. A planet in the 8th becomes vulnerably placed. The various houses in a nativity are related to various spheres of life. Ch. 11 deals with the houses in this context.

नवमेऽपि पितुर्ज्ञानं सूर्याच्च नवमेऽथवा ।
यत्किञ्चिद्दशमे लाभे तत्सूर्याद्दशमे भवे ॥३९॥
तुर्ये तनौ धने लाभे भाग्ये यच्चिन्तनं च तत् ।
चन्द्रात्तुर्ये तनौ लाभे भाग्ये तच्चिन्तयेद् ध्रुवम् ॥४०॥
लग्नाद् दुश्चिक्यभवने यत्कुजाद्विक्रमेऽखिलम् ।
विचार्यं षष्ठभावस्य बुधात् षष्ठे विलोकयेत् ॥४१॥
पुत्रस्य च गुरोः पुत्रे, जायायाः सप्तमे भृगोः ।
अष्टमस्य व्ययस्यापि मन्दान्मृत्यौ व्यये तथा ॥४२॥
यद्भावाद्यत्फलं चिन्त्यं तदीशात्तत्फलं विदुः ।
ज्ञेयं तस्य फलं तद्धि तत्र चिन्त्यं शुभाऽशुभम् ॥४३॥

39-43. *INDICATIONS FROM HOUSES :* The 9th from the ascendant and the 9th from the Sun deal with one's father. Whatever effects are to be known from the 10th and 11th counted from ascendant be also known from similar houses counted from the Sun. Whatever results are to be known from the 4th, 1st, 2nd, 11th and the 9th should also be known from the 4th of the Moon, from the Moon sign itself and 2nd, 11th and 9th from the Moon respectively. Whatever has to be known through the 3rd from the ascendant be also analysed through the 3rd from Mars. The 6th from Mercury be also considered in regard to indications derivable from the 6th counted from the ascendant. The 5th from Jupiter, the 7th from Venus and both the 8th and 12th from Saturn stand for consideration respectively in respect of offspring, spouse and death. The lord of the Bhava is equally important when estimating the indications of a particular Bhava (house).

Notes : We get important clues from the above five verses.

It is not enough if the house concerned as counted from the ascendant is strong and well disposed for the prosperity of the house. Such a house from the signifying planet should also be strong. For example, one will enjoy paternal happiness if the 9th from the ascendant and the 9th from the Sun are both well disposed. The 9th from the Sun if occupied by a debilitated planet or if the 9th lord from the Sun is weak, then the good indications through Pitru Bhava are neutralized. Now see a gist of the slokas :

(a) Father to be considered from the 9th both from the Sun and Lagna.

(b) 10th from Lagna to be correlated with the 10th from the Sun—for patrimony, paternal rites etc.

(c) 11th from Lagna to be correlated with the 11th from the Sun for gains (and for father's longevity—as the 11th is the 3rd from the 9th.)

(d) The 4th from the Lagna and from the Moon are related to mother.

(e) The ascendant and the Moon sign relate the physical felicity of the native, and general strength of the radix.

(f) The 2nd from the ascendant and from the Moon be investigated about one's sight, speech, learning, wealth etc.

(g) The 11th from ascendant and from Moon for gains, elder brothers, friends etc.

(h) The 9th from ascendant and from the Moon for general fortunes, religion, meritorious activities etc.

(i) The 3rd from Mars and from the ascendant be seen for coborn, courage etc.

(j) The 6th from ascendant and from Mercury for diseases, debts, enemies, cousins and the like.

(k) The 5th from the ascendant and from Jupiter for obtainment of progeny, their well being, their prosperity etc.

(For a female the 9th from Lagna and from Jupiter in connection with children are to be scrutinized.)

(l) The 7th from Lagna and from Venus for marriage, its nature, consequences, duration etc.

(m) Both the 8th and 12th from both the Lagna and Saturn for death.

From this it will be seen that each of the 12 houses is related to some specific planet apart from the ascendant. These rules are very highly suggestive.

अथ राशिदृष्टिकथनाध्याय: ॥८॥

Chapter 8

Aspects Of The Signs

अथ मेषादिराशीनां चरादीनां पृथक् पृथक् ।
दृष्टिभेदं प्रवक्ष्यामि शृणु त्वं द्विजसत्तम ! ॥१॥
राशयोऽभिमुखं विप्र ! तथा पश्यन्ति पार्श्वभे ।
यथा चर: स्थिरानेवं स्थिर: पश्यति वै चरान् ॥२॥
द्विस्वभावो विनाऽऽत्मानं द्विस्वभावान् प्रपश्यति ।
समीपस्थं परित्यज्य खेटास्तत्र गतास्तथा ॥३॥

1-3. *SIGN ASPECTS :* O Maitreya, now detailed are the aspects emanating from the signs Aries etc. Every movable sign aspects the 3 fixed signs leaving the fixed sign adjacent to it. Every fixed sign lends aspect to the 3 movable signs barring the adjacent movable sign. And a common sign aspects the other three common signs. The planet in a sign lends the same aspect as the sign (in which the planet is) does.

Notes : Apart from usual aspects of planets, Maharshi Parasara deals with Rasi aspects or sign aspects. These are also used by sage Jaimini (a disciple of Vedavyasa and author of Poorva Meemamsa etc.) and this system came to be known as Jaimini system though the original propounder is Parasara.

Jaimini Maharshi is also an equally worshipped authority on astrology. He mainly uses Rasi aspects, Rasi Dasas apart from many other Dasas, Arudha Pada, Atma Karaka etc. by longitudes, Karakamsa etc.

The current 3 slokas throw light on the sign aspects. Each movable Rasi aspects 3 fixed signs, leaving the nearest fixed sign. For example, Aries—movable sign—does not aspect Taurus but Leo, Scorpio and Aquarius. Taurus—a fixed sign aspects 3 movable signs, viz. Cancer, Libra and Capricorn but does not aspect Aries, the nearest movable sign. Gemini's aspects are on Virgo, Sagittarius and Pisces. The planet in a sign aspects similar signs as above and also the occupant thereof. Hence, in these aspects, longitudes of the aspector and the aspected are ignorable.

The following table will represent the aspects detailed above :

Sign/occupant aspecting	Sign/occupant aspected
Aries	Leo, Scorpio and Aquarius
Taurus	Cancer, Libra and Capricorn
Gemini	Virgo, Sagittarius and Pisces
Cancer	Scorpio, Aquarius and Taurus
Leo	Libra, Capricorn and Aries
Virgo	Sagittarius, Pisces and Gemini
Libra	Aquarius, Taurus and Leo
Scorpio	Capricorn, Aries and Cancer
Sagittarius	Pisces, Gemini and Virgo
Capricorn	Taurus, Leo and Scorpio
Aquarius	Aries, Cancer aud Libra
Pisces	Gemini, Virgo and Sagittarius

चरेषु संस्थिताः खेटाः पश्यन्ति स्थिरसङ्गतान् ।
स्थिरेषु संस्थिता एवं पश्यन्ति चरसंस्थितान् ॥४॥
उभयस्थास्तु सूर्याद्या पश्यन्त्युभयसंस्थितान् ।
निकटस्थं विना खेटाः पश्यन्तीत्ययमागमः ॥५॥

4-5. *PLANETARY ASPECTS* : A planet in a movable sign aspects the other 3 fixed signs leaving the fixed sign next to it. A planet in a fixed sign does not aspect the next movable sign but the remaining 3 movable signs. The one in a common sign throws aspect over the remaining 3 common signs. Simultaneously a planet in the aspected sign is also subjected to the aspect concerned.

Notes : The idea conveyed in the two verses can be well conceived from the notes given for the first three slokas above. With the help of these five slokas, one can deduce the following from the horoscope given as example below :

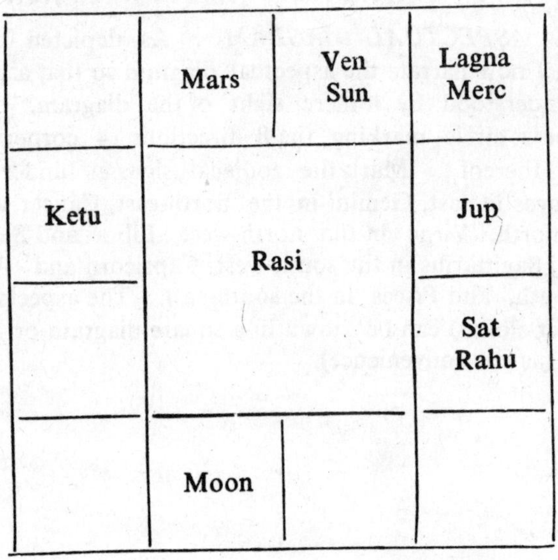

(a) Mars aspects Saturn, Moon and the nodes.

(b) Venus, the Sun and Mercury aspect none.

(c) Jupiter aspects the Moon, Ketu, Sun and Venus.

(d) Saturn and Rahu aspect Mars.

(e) Moon aspects Mars and Jupiter.

(f) Ketu aspects Mars and Jupiter.

In the above, we considered only planet to planet aspect so that we know the difference between this system of aspects and the usual one.

दृष्टिचक्रमहं वक्ष्ये यथावद् ब्रह्मणोदितम्।
यस्य विन्यासमात्रेण दृष्टिभेदः प्रकाश्यते ॥६॥
प्राचि मेषवृषौ लेख्यौ कर्कसिंहौ तथोत्तरे।
तुलाऽली पश्चिमे विप्र! मृगकुम्भौ च दक्षिणे ॥७॥
ईश—कोणे तु मिथुनं वायव्ये कन्यकां तथा।
नैर्ऋत्यां चापमालिख्य वह्निकोणे झषं लिखेत् ॥८॥
एवं चतुर्भुजाकारं वृत्ताकारमथापि वा।
दृष्टिचक्रं प्रविन्यस्यैवं ततो दृष्टि विचारयेत् ॥९॥

6-9. *ASPECTUAL DIAGRAM* : As depicted by Lord Brahma, I now narrate the aspectual diagram so that aspects are easily understood by a mere sight of the diagram. Draw a square or a circle marking the 8 directions (4 corners and 4 quarters thereof). Mark the zodiacal signs as under : Aries and Taurus in east, Gemini in the north-east, Cancer and Leo in the north, Virgo in the north-west, Libra and Scorpio in the west, Sagittarius in the south-west, Capricorn and Aquarius in the south, and Pisces in the south-east. The aspects (as per the earlier slokas) can be shown in a square diagram or circular diagram (as per convenience).

अथारिष्टाध्याय: ॥९॥

Chapter 9

Evils At Birth

आदौ जन्माङ्गतो विप्र ! रिष्टाऽरिष्टं विचारयेत् ।
ततस्तन्वादिभावानां जातकस्य फलं वदेत् ॥१॥

1. O Brahmin, first of all, estimate the evils and checking factors thereof through the ascendant and then declare the effects of the 12 bhavas.

Notes : The ascendant is the most important in the matter of causing evils or counteracting evils till a native is 32. Hence, the sage refers to the ascendant specifically in the matter of Balarishta or infant mortality and cautions (in the next sloka) that upto the age of 24, no definite assurances about longevity be made.

The Moon becomes important in the matter of evils and checking factors for longevity from the age of 32 upto 64th year. And the Sun is the centre in this respect from the age of 64. This does not mean that the evils from the Moon do not operate till the 32nd year of age, and so on and so forth.

चतुर्विशतिवर्षाणि यावद् गच्छन्ति जन्मत: ।
जन्मारिष्टं तु तावत् स्यादायुर्दायं न चिन्तयेत् ॥२॥

2. Evils causing premature end exist upto the 24th year of one's age. As such, no definite calculation of life span should be made till such year of age.

Notes : While the sage declares that upto the 24th year, it will not be possible to declare definitely in the matter of longevity. Other works like **Horasara, Jyotisharnava Navaneethamu** (Telugu version), **Sarvartha Chintamani, Jathaka Parijatha, Phala Deepika** *etc.* say that longevity calculations will be futile till the 12th year of age.

षष्ठाष्टरिष्फगश्चन्द्रः क्रूरैः खेटैश्च वीक्षितः।
जातस्य मृत्युदः सद्यस्त्वष्टवर्षैः शुभेक्षितः ॥३॥
शशिवन्मृत्युदाः सौम्याश्चेद्वक्राः क्रूरवीक्षिताः।
शिशोर्जातस्य मासेन लग्ने सौम्यविवर्जिते ॥४॥
यस्य जन्मनि धीस्थाः स्युः सूर्यार्कीन्दुकुजाभधाः।
तस्य त्वाशु जनित्री च भ्राता च निधनं व्रजेत् ॥५॥
पापेक्षितो युतो भौमो लग्नगो न शुभेक्षितः।
मृत्युदस्त्वष्टमस्थोऽपि सौरेणार्केण वा युतः ॥६॥

3-6. *SHORT-LIFE COMBINATIONS (upto sloka 23) :* Should the Moon be in the 6th, 8th, or the 12th from the ascendant and be in aspect to a malefic, the child will die soon. If in the process there be a benefic's aspect, it may live upto 8. If a benefic is retrograde in the 6th, 8th or the 12th being in aspect to a malefic, death will occur within a month of birth. This is true only when the ascendant is unoccupied by a benefic. Should the 5th be occupied by Saturn, Mars and the Sun jointly, (early) death of mother and brother will come to pass. Mars placed in the ascendant or in the 8th and be conjunct Saturn or Sun or be in aspect to a malefic, being bereft of benefic aspect will prove a source of (immediate) death.

Notes : Here a pertinent query may emerge as to why the sage mentions combinations for premature death while longevity cannot be decidedly declared upto the 24th year of age as per his own statement. These yogas will guide us to detect the immediate defects for longevity and resort to remedial measures like fire sacrifice, prayers, donations, medicine etc. and save the from Akala Mrityu or premature death, vide ch. 5 of **Horasara**.

The Moon in an evil house at birth and in aspect to a malefic will cause early death. Even a benefic's aspect on the Moon, in the said Yoga, will cause the end at the age of 8, suggests the sage. If she is increasing, this need not be feared.

चन्द्रसूर्यग्रहे राहुश्चन्द्रसूर्ययुतो यदि।
सौरिभौमेक्षितं लग्नं पक्षमेकं स जीवति ॥७॥
कर्मस्थाने स्थितः सौरिः शत्रुस्थाने कलानिधिः।
क्षितिजः सप्तमस्थाने सह मात्रा विपद्यते ॥८॥

लग्ने भास्करपुत्रश्च निधने चन्द्रमा यदि।
तृतीयस्थो यदा जीवः स याति यममन्दिरम् ॥९॥
होरायां नवमे सूर्यः सप्तमस्थः शनैश्चरः।
एकादशे गुरुः शुक्रो मासमेकं स जीवति ॥१०॥
व्यये सर्वे ग्रहा नेष्टाः सूर्यशुक्रेन्दुराहवः।
विशेषान्नाशकर्तारो दृष्ट्या वा भङ्गकारिणः ॥११॥

7-11. If Saturn and Mars aspect the ascendant as the luminaries join Rahu (elsewhere), the child will live only for a fortnight. Immediate death of the child along with its mother will occur if Saturn is in the 10th, the Moon in the 6th and Mars in the 7th. One will immediately go to the abode of Yama (the Hindu god of death) if Saturn is in the ascendant while the Moon and Jupiter are in their order in the 8th and the 3rd. Only a month will be the span of one's life who has the Sun in the 9th, Mars in the 7tha nd Jupiter and Venus in the 11th. All planets (i.e. any planet) in the 12th will be source of short life, specifically the luminaries, Venus and Rahu. But the aspect of one of these four planets (on the 12th) will counteract such evils.

Notes : One of the 4 planets among the Sun, Moon, Rahu and Venus in the 12th will contribute to premature end. If there is aspect of one of these on the 12th, the evils for premature death are checked. (This goes to prove that Rahu has aspects.) The Sun, however, in the 12th for Libra ascendant will confer a life span of 100 years, *vide* sloka 16, ch. 10, *infra*

पापान्वितः शशी धर्मे द्यूनलग्नगतो यदि।
शुभैरवेक्षितयुतस्तदा मृत्युप्रदः शिशोः ॥१२॥

12. The Moon is capable of causing early end if she is with a malefic in the 8th, 7th or the ascendant and unrelated to a benefic.

सन्ध्यायां चन्द्रहोरायां गण्डान्ते निधनाय वै।
प्रत्येकं चन्द्रपापैश्च केन्द्रगैः स्याद्विनाशनम् ॥१३॥

13. Early death will come to pass if there be a birth in the morning or evening junctions or in a hora ruled by the Moon

or in Gandanta while the Moon and malefics occupy angles from the ascendant.

Notes : There are three yogas denoted for premature death :

(a) Birth in **Sandhya** (as defined in the next sloka).

(b) Birth (i.e. asendant) in a Hora ruled by the Moon. (For Hora, see slokas 5-6, ch. 6.)

(c) Birth in Gandanta.

In each of the three yogas, it is a prerequisite that the angles from the ascendant be captured by the Moon and malefics.

Gandanta : The last Navamsas of Cancer, of Scorpio and of Pisces are called as Gandanta. According to a host of authors, mere Gandanta Lagna or the Moon in Gandanta will cause premature death.

रवेस्तु मण्डलार्द्धस्तात् सायं संध्या त्रिनाडिका ।
तथैवार्द्धोदयात् पूर्वं प्रातः संध्या त्रिनाडिका ।।१४।।

14. *DEFINITION OF SANDHYA* : 3 Ghatikas before the sight of the semi disc (half) of the rising Sun and a similar duration following the Sun set are called as morning twilight and evening twilight, respectively.

Notes : Morning twilight (or **Pratah Sandhya**) lasts for 72 minutes in the morning before the sight of the Sun's disc (locally) and evening twilight for a similar duration after the Sun set. This definition of Sandhya by the sage is for deciding evils to longevity in childhood.

In the context of Kala Dasa, Sandhya is defined differently by the sage, obviously with a purpose, *vide* ch. 46 of Vol. II.

चक्रपूर्वापरार्द्धेषु क्रूरसौम्येषु कीटभे ।
लग्नगे निधनं याति नाऽत्र कार्या विचारणा ।।१५।।

15. *EARLY DEATH :* Should all the malefics be in the oriental half while benefics are in the occidental half, early death of one born in Scorpio will follow. In this case there is no need of any rethinking.

Notes : The area of the horoscope from the 4th cusp to the 10th cusp via the 7th house is known as occidental (or western) half while the rest half is oriental (or eastern) half.

One born in Scorpio ascendant with malefics in the oriental half and bhenfics in the occidental half will face immediate death. This yoga is called as Vajra Mushti yoga by Yavanacharyas, as quoted by Kalyana Varma. The Moon should be in the occidental half if she is a benefic or be in the oriental half if she is a malefic. If Mercury remains unafflicted, by a malefic, this yoga will not come to pass.

व्ययशत्रुगतैः क्रूरैर्मृत्युव्रव्यगतैरपि ।
पापमध्यगते लग्ने सत्यमेव मृतिं वदेत् ॥१६॥

16. Malefics in the 12th and the 6th, *or* in the 8th and the 2nd while the ascendant is hemmed between other malefics will bring early death.

लग्नसप्तमगौ पापौ चन्द्रोऽपि क्रूरसंयुतः ।
यदा नावेक्षितः सौम्यैः शीघ्रान्मृत्युर्भवेत्तदा ॥१७॥

17. Malefics occupying the ascendant and the 7th while the Moon is conjunct a malefic with no relief from a benefic will also cause premature death.

क्षीणे शशिनि लग्नस्थे पापैः केन्द्राष्टसंस्थितैः ।
यो जातो मृत्युमाप्नोति स विप्रेश ! न संशयः ॥१८॥

18. Early death will be inflicted on the native if decreasing Moon is in the ascendant while malefics capture the 8th and an angle. There is no doubt about that.

पापयोर्मध्यगश्चन्द्रो लग्नाष्टान्तिमसप्तमः ।
अचिरान्मृत्युमाप्नोति यो जातः स शिशुस्तदा ॥१९॥

19. The Moon in the ascendant, 8th, 12th or the 7th and hemmed between malefics will confer premature death.

पापद्वयमध्यगते चन्द्रे लग्नसमाश्रिते :
सप्ताष्टमेन पापेन मात्रा सह मृतः शिशुः ॥२०॥

20. Should the Moon be in the ascendant hemmed between two malefics while the 7th or the 8th has a malefic in it, the child will face immediate death along with its mother.

शनैश्चरार्कभौमेषु रिष्फधर्माष्टमेषु च ।
शुभैरवीक्ष्यमाणेषु यो जातो निधनंगतः ॥२१॥

21. Should Saturn, the Sun and Mars be in the 12th, 9th and 8th without benefic's aspect, the child will face instant death.

यद्द्रेष्काणे च यामित्रे यस्य स्याद्दारुणो ग्रहः ।
क्षीणचन्द्रो विलग्नस्थः सद्यो हरति जीवितम् ॥२२॥

22. With a malefic in the 7th house or in the rising decanate while decreasing Moon is in the ascendant, death will be experienced early.

आपोक्लिमस्थिताः सर्वे ग्रहा बलविवर्जिताः ।
षण्मासं वा द्विमासं वा तस्यायुः समुदाहृतम् ॥२३॥

23. The life span of the child will be either 2 months or 6 months only, if all planets devoid of strength are relegated to Apoklima houses (i.e. 3rd, 6th, 9th and 12th.)

त्रिभिः पापग्रहैः सूतौ चन्द्रमा यदि दृश्यते ।
मातृनाशो भवेत्तस्य शुभदृष्टे शुभं वदेत् ॥२४॥

24. *EVILS TO MOTHER* (*upto sloka 33*) : The mother of the native will incur evils (will die soon) if the Moon at birth is aspected by three malefics. Benefics aspecting the Moon will bring good to the mother.

धने राहुर्बुधः शुक्रः सौरिः सूर्यो यदा स्थितः ।
तस्य मातुर्भवेन्मृत्युर्मृते पितरि जायते ॥२५॥

25. Should the 2nd be occupied by Rahu, Mercury, Venus, Sun and Saturn the child's birth has been after its father's death while even the mother will face early death.

पापात्सप्तमरन्ध्रस्थे चन्द्रे पापसमन्विते ।
बलिभिः पापकैर्दृष्टे जातो भवति मातृहा ॥२६॥

26. If the Moon is in the 7th/8th from a malefic, be herself with a malefic, and be aspected by a strong malefic, predict mother's end to be early.

उच्चस्थो वाऽथ नीचस्थः सप्तमस्थो यदारविः।
पानहीनो भवेद्बाल अजाक्षीरेण जीवति ॥२७॥

27. The child will not live on mother's milk but on that of a she-goat if the Sun is exalted or debilitated in the 7th.

Notes : For an Aries native, if the Sun is in the 7th in debilitation, or in the 7th in exaltation for a Libra native, it deprives one of mother's milk. The 7th rules the 4th from the 4th and hence the 7th is referred to.

Saturn in the 4th house will also deprive one of mother's milk.

Atmakaraka in Scorpio Navamsa will produce similar effects. For a definition of Atmakaraka, see ch. 32, *infra.*

चन्द्राच्चतुर्थगः पापो रिपुक्षेत्रे यदा भवेत्।
तदा मातृवधं कुर्यात् केन्द्रे यदि शुभो न चेत् ॥२८॥

28. Should a malefic be in the 4th, identical with an inimical sign, counted from the Moon while there is no benefic in an angle, the child will lose its mother in a premature manner.

द्वादशे रिपुभावे च यदा पापग्रहो भवेत्।
तदा मातुर्भयं विद्याच्चतुर्थे दशमे पितुः ॥२९॥

29. Malefics in the 6th *and* 12th will bring evils to mother. The child's father will receive similar effects if the 4th *and* 10th are captured by malefics.

लग्ने क्रूरो व्यये क्रूरो धने सौम्यस्तथैव च।
सप्तमे भवने क्रूरः परिवारक्षयंकरः ॥३०॥

30. Mercury in the 2nd while malefics occupy the ascendant, 7th and 12th : this yoga will destroy the entire family.

लग्नस्थे च गुरौ सौरौ धने राहौ तृतीयगे।
इति चेज्जन्मकाले स्यान्माता तस्य न जीवति ॥३१॥

31. Jupiter, Saturn and Rahu respectively posited in the ascendant, 2nd and 3rd will cause mother's death early.

क्षीणचन्द्रात्त्रिकोणस्थैः पापैः सौम्यविवर्जितैः।
माता परित्यजेद्बालं षण्मासाच्च न संशयः ॥३२॥

32. Doubtlessly the mother will give up the child if it has malefics in trines counted from the decreasing Moon. No benefic shall be in conjunction with the said malefics.

एकांशकस्थौ मन्दारौ यत्र कुत्रस्थितौ यदा।
शशिकेन्द्रगतौ तौ वा द्विमातृभ्यां न जीवति ॥३३॥

33. If Mars and Saturn are together in an angle with reference to the Moon and occupy one and the same Navamsa, the child will have two mothers. Yet it will be short-lived.

लग्ने सन्दो मदे भौमः षष्ठस्थाने च चन्द्रमाः।
इति चेज्जन्मकाले स्यात् पिता तस्य न जीवति ॥३४॥

34. *EVILS TO FATHER* (*upto sloka 42*) *:* One's father will incur early death if Saturn, Mars and the Moon in their order are in the ascendant, the 7th and the 6th.

लग्ने जीवो धने मन्दरविभौमबुधास्तथा।
विवाहसमये तस्य बालस्य म्रियते पिता ॥३५॥

35. The native will at the time of his marriage lose his father if Jupiter is in the ascendant while Saturn, Sun, Mars and Mercury are together in the 2nd.

सूर्यः पापेन संयुक्तो ह्यथवा पापमध्यगः।
सूर्यात् सप्तमगः पापस्तदा पितृवधो भवेत् ॥३६॥

36. Early loss of father will take place if the Sun is with a malefic or is hemmed between malefics as there is another malefic in the 7th from the Sun.

सप्तमे भवने सूर्यः कर्मस्थो भूमिनन्दनः।
राहुर्व्यये च यस्यैव पिता कष्टेन जीवति ॥३७॥

37. Remote will be the possibility of one's father sustaining if the Sun is in the 7th while Mars is in the 10th and Rahu is in the 12th.

दशमस्थो यदा भौमः शत्रुक्षेत्रसमाश्रितः ।
म्रियते तस्य जातस्य पिता शीघ्रं न संशयः ॥३८॥

38. Early and doubtless will be one's father's death if Mars is in the 10th identical with his enemy's sign.

Notes : Mercury is the sole enemy of Mars, vide ch. 3, verse 55. Mercury's camps are Gemini and Virgo. Hence, for a Sagittarius native or for a Virgo native, Mars in the 10th (alone) will cause early death of father.

रिपुस्थाने यदा चन्द्रो लग्नस्थाने शनैश्चरः ।
कुजश्च सप्तमे स्थाने पिता तस्य न जीवति ॥३९॥

39. The Moon in the 6th, Saturn in the ascendant and Mars in the 7th : this array of heavenly bodies at birth will not ensure a long span of life for the father.

भौमांशकस्थिते भानौ शनिना च निरीक्षिते ।
प्राग्जन्मनो निवृत्तिः स्यान्मृत्युर्वाऽपि शिशोः पितुः ॥४०॥

40. If the Sun is aspected by Saturn and be in Aries/Scorpio Navamsa, the father would have given up the family before the birth of the child or would have passed away.

चतुर्थे दशमे पापौ द्वादशे च यदा स्थितौ ।
पितरं मातरं हत्वा देशाद्देशान्तरं व्रजेत् ॥४१॥

41. If the 4th, 10th and 12th are all occupied by malefics, both the parents will leave the child to its own fate and wander from place to place.

Notes : Also see sloka 8, ch. 10 *infra*.

राहु-जीवौ रिपुक्षेत्रे लग्ने वाऽथ चतुर्थके ।
त्रयोविंशतिमे वर्षे पुत्रस्तातं न पश्यति ॥४२॥

42. The father will not see the native till his (the native's) 23rd year if Rahu and Jupiter are together in an inimical sign identical with the ascendant or the 4th.

Notes : The inimical signs for Jupiter are that of Mercury and Venus. Rahu is inimically placed in Cancer, Leo, Aries and Scorpio. Jupiter is friendly in these signs. It is hence implied that these two should join in one of these signs as 4th or the 10th so that the father cannot see the native till the latter is 23.

However, the rule needs a cautious approach in view of the clash between inimical places for the two planets. Mercury is Rahu's neutral. Hence if Mercury is temporarily inimical for Rahu, then Rahu's placement (along with Jupiter) in Gemini or Virgo as the 4th or the ascendant will cause the event. In other cases, this will have to be wisely interpreted.

भानुः पिता च जन्तूनां चन्द्रो माता तथैव च।
पापदृष्टियुतो भानुः पापमध्यगतोऽपि वा ॥४३॥
पित्ररिष्टं विजानीयाच्छिशोर्जातस्य निश्चितम्।
भानोः षष्ठाष्टमर्क्षस्थैः पापैः सौम्यविवर्जितैः।
सुखभावगतैर्वाऽपि पित्ररिष्टं विनिर्दिशेत् ॥४४॥
एवं चन्द्रात् स्थितैः पापैर्मातु कष्टं विचारयेत्।
बलाऽबलविवेकेन कष्टं वा मृत्युमादिशेत् ॥४५॥

43-45. *PARENTS* : The Sun is the indicator of father for all beings while the mother is indicated by the Moon. Should the Sun be aspected by malefics or be hemmed between them will cause evils to father. Similarly the Moon be considered in respect of mother. Malefics in the 6th, 8th or 4th from the Sun will bring inauspicious results about the father. Malefics in such places from the Moon will be adverse for the mother. The strength or otherwise of the occupants concerned be suitably estimated.

अथाऽरिष्टभंगाध्यायः ॥१०॥

Chapter 10
Antidotes For Evils

इत्यरिष्टं मया प्रोक्तं तद्भङ्गश्चापि कथ्यते।
यत् समालोक्यं जातानां रिष्टाऽरिष्टं वदेद्बुधः ॥१॥

1. Those are the evils (due to a native). I now narrate the antidotes for such evils as well, which will be helpful to assess the extent of inauspiciousness.

Notes : The antidotes mentioned here are in the context of short life. While some may carry with them the concept of fortunate yogas, every principle does not.

एकोऽपि ज्ञार्यशुक्राणां लग्नात् केन्द्रगतो यदि ।
अरिष्टं निखिलं हन्ति तिमिरं भास्करो यथा ॥२॥

2. Should one among Mercury, Jupiter and Venus be in an angle from the ascendant, all evils are destroyed as the Sun eliminates darkness.

एक एव बली जीवो लग्नस्थो रिष्टसंचयम् ।
हन्ति पापक्षयं भक्त्या प्रणाम इव शूलिनः ॥३॥

3. Just as a single reverential obeisance before Lord Siva, the Trident holder, frees one from all sins, a single but strong Jupiter in the ascendant will ward off all the evils.

Notes : In the case of Capricorn ascendant, Jupiter therein should be exceedingly strong by other virtues, as otherwise he can lead to short-life. For, sage Bhrigu specifically hints at Madhyayu or medium span of life with Jupiter in the ascendant identical with debilitation or inimical sign or malefic's sign.

एक एव विलग्नेशः केन्द्रसंस्थो बलान्वितः ।
अरिष्टं निखिलं हन्ति पिनाकी त्रिपुरं यथा ॥४॥

4. The ascendant lord is singly capable of counteracting all evils if he is strongly placed in an angle just as Lord Siva, the holder of Bow, destroyed the three cities (built of gold, silver and iron by Maya for the demons).

शुक्लपक्षे क्षपाजन्म लग्ने सौम्यनिरीक्षिते ।
विपरीतं कृष्णपक्षे तथारिष्टविनाशनं ॥५॥

5. All evils are destroyed if a benefic aspects the ascendant of one born during night in the bright half. Similarly, a malefic's aspect on the ascendant of one born during day time in the dark half.

Notes : The second statement does not imply evils to longevity if a benefic aspects the ascendant for a day-birth in Krishna Paksha (or dark-half). That is however not enough, if exists, but a malefic's aspect is required.

व्ययस्थाने यदा सूर्यस्तुलालग्ने तु जायते।
जीवेत् स शतवर्षाणि दीर्घायुर्बालको भवेत् ॥६॥

6. The Sun in the 12th will confer a hundred-year life span on one born in Libra ascendant.

गुरु-भौमौ यदा युवतौ गुरुदृष्टोऽथवा कुजः।
हत्वाऽरिष्टमशेषं च जनन्याः शुभकृद्भवेत् ॥७॥

7. It will prove auspicious for the mother as well as the native if Mars joins or is aspected by Jupiter.

चतुर्थदशमे पापः सौम्यमध्ये यदा भवेत्।
पितुः सौख्यकरो योगः शुभैः केन्द्रत्रिकोणगैः ॥८॥

8. Though malefics in the 4th/10th are a source of evil for the father, they turn auspicious if hemmed by benefics or if benefics are in trines or in angles.

सौम्यान्तरगतैः पापैः शुभैः केन्द्रत्रिकोणगैः।
सद्यो नाशयतेऽरिष्टं तद्भावोत्थफलं न तत् ॥९॥

9. If malefics are surrounded by benefics while angles/ trines are themselves benefic-occupied evils disappear soon. Not only this, evils will not follow from the bhavas concerned.

अथ भावविवेकाध्यायः ॥११॥

Chapter 11

Judgement of Houses

अरिष्टं तत्प्रभङ्गं च श्रुतं त्वत्तो मया मुने!।
कस्माद् भावात् फलं किं किं विचार्यमिति ? मे वद ॥१॥

1. O sage, I have come to know of the evils and antidotes thereof as well from you. Please tell me, what is to be deduced from each house.

देहं रूपं च ज्ञानं च वर्णं चैव बलाबलम् ।
सुखं दुःखं स्वभावञ्च लग्नभावान्निरीक्षयेत् ॥२॥

2. *INDICATIONS OF THE FIRST HOUSE :* (The sage replies) : physique, appearance, intellect (or the organ of intelligence, *i.e.* brain), complexion of the body, vigour, weakness, happiness, grief and innate nature are all to be guessed through the ascending sign.

Notes : We ar tersely told here of the prime indications to be deduced from each house. There are many matters related to each house which I have listed rather exhaustively in my English translation of **Horasara**. See pp 183-187 **ibid.**

धनधान्यं कुटुम्बांश्च मृत्युजालममित्रकम् ।
धातुरत्नादिकं सर्वं धनस्थानान्निरीक्षयेत् ॥३॥

3. *SECOND HOUSE :* Wealth, grains (food etc.), family, death, enemies, metals, precious stones etc. are to be understood through the 2nd house.

विक्रमं भृत्यभ्रात्रादि चोपदेशप्रयाणकम् ।
पित्रोर्वै मरणं विज्ञो दुश्चिक्याच्च निरीक्षयेत् ॥४॥

4. *THIRD HOUSE :* From the 3rd house, know of the following : tilour, servants (attendants etc.), brothers, sisters etc. initiatory instrucitons (उपदेश), journey, and parent's death.

वाहनान्यथ बन्धूंश्च मातृसौख्यादिकान्यपि ।
निधि क्षेत्रं गृहं चापि चतुर्थात् परिचिन्तयेत् ॥५॥

5. *FOURTH HOUSE :* Conveyances, relatives, mother, happiness, treasure, lands and houses are to be consulted through the 4th house.

यन्त्र-मन्त्रौ तथा विद्यां बुद्धेश्चैव प्रबन्धकम् ।
पुत्रराज्यापभ्रंशादीन् पश्येत् पुत्रालयाद् बुधः ॥६॥

6. *FIFTH HOUSE :* The learned should deduce from the 5th house amulets, sacred spells, learning, knowledge, sons, royalty (or authority), fall of position etc.

मातुलान्तकशंकानां शत्रूंश्चैव व्रणादिकान्।
सपत्नीमातरं चापि षष्ठभावान्निरीक्षयेत् ॥७॥

7. *SIXTH HOUSE :* Maternal uncle, doubts about death, enemies, ulcers, step mother etc. are to be estimated from the 6th house.

जायामध्वप्रयाणं च वाणिज्यं नष्टवीक्षणम्।
मरणं च स्वदेहस्य जायाभावान्निरीक्षयेत् ॥८॥

8. *SEVENTH HOUSE :* Wife, travel, trade, loss of sight, death etc. be known from the 7th house .

आयु रणं रिपुं चापि दुर्गं मृतधनं तथा।
गत्यनुकादिकं सर्वं पश्येद्रन्ध्राद्विचक्षणः ॥९॥

9. *EIGHTH HOUSE :* The 8th house indicates longevity, battle, enemies, forts, wealth of the dead, and things that have happened and are to happen (in the past and future births).

भाग्यं श्यालं च धर्मं च भ्रातृपत्न्यादिकांस्तथा।
तीर्थयात्रादिकं सर्वं धर्मस्थानान्निरीक्षयेत् ॥१०॥

10. *NINTH HOUSE :* Fortunes, wife's brother, religion, brother's wife, visits to shrines etc. be known from the 9th house.

राज्यं चाकाशंवृत्ति च मानं चैव पितुस्तथा।
प्रवासस्य ऋणस्यापि व्योमस्थानान्निरीक्षणम् ॥११॥

11. *TENTH HOUSE :* Royalty (authority), place, profession (livelihood), honour, father, living in foreign lands and debts are to be understood from the 10th house.

Notes : "Father" is to be studied through the 10 house, as per the above sloka. The sage obviously refers to the 10th in this context as the 10th is the 7th from the 4th. Western astrologers too follow this view.

Here we need some elaboration. The status of the father, his family (i.e. consisting of the native's mother etc.), and the final rites the native will perform to his father will all have to be known through the 10th house. The father as an individual and his well being etc. be examined from the 9th house. The sage also discusses the father with reference to the 9th house in one of the ensuing chapters.

Thus it follows that both the 9th and 10th are primary houses related to father.

नानावस्तुभवस्यापि पुत्रजायादिकस्य च ।
आयं वृद्धिं पशूनां च भवस्थानान्निरीक्षणम् ॥१२॥

12. *ELEVENTH HOUSE :* All articles, son's wife, income, prosperity, quadrupeds etc. are to be understood from the 11th house.

व्ययं च वैरिवृत्तान्त-रिःफमन्त्यादिकं तथा ।
व्ययाच्चैव हि ज्ञातव्यमिति सर्वत्र धीमता ॥१३॥

13. *TWELFTH HOUSE :* From the 12th house, one can know about expenses, history of enemies, one's own death etc.

यो यो शुभैर्युतो दृष्टो भावो वा पतिदृष्टयुक् ।
युवा प्रवृद्धो राज्यस्थः कुमारो वाऽपि यत्पतिः ॥१४॥
तदीक्षणवशात् तत्तद्भावसौख्यं वदेद् बुधः ।
यद्यद् भावपतिर्नष्टस्त्रिकेशाद्यैश्च संयुतः ॥१५॥
भावं न वीक्षते सम्यक् सुप्तो वृद्धोमृतोऽथवा ।
पीडितो वाऽस्य भावस्य फलं नष्टं वदेद् ध्रुवम् ॥१६॥

14-16. *PROSPERITY OR ANNIHILATION OF A HOUSE :* Predict prosperity of the house which is conjunct or is aspected by a benefic. Also when its lord is in Yuvavastha or in Prabuddhavastha or in Kaumaravastha or in the 10th house, the bhava's wellbeing is indicated. The bhava which is not aspected by its lord or whose lord is with a malefic planet or with one of the lords of evil and such other houses (i.e. 3rd, 6th, 8th, llth and 12th) or is defeated in a planetary war or is in one of the three Avasthas, viz, Vriddhavastha, Mritavastha and Suptavastha.

Notes : The prosperity or wellbeing of a house is assured under the following conditions :

(a) The house that contains a benefic.

(b) The house that is aspected by a benefic.

(c) The house whose lord is in Yuvavastha or in Kumaravastha. These two Avasthas are among the 5 Avasthas, viz. Baala, Kumara, Yavana, Vriddha and Mrita by being in 6° portions respectively. This is for an odd sign placement. It is reverse in the case of an even sign. Aslo see ch. 45 infra.

So to say if the lord of a house is in 6° to 18° of an odd sign, he will be in one of the two Avasthas required. Alternatively, it should be between 12° and 24° of an even sign. (If a planet is debilitated or is combust, the goods cited are void).

(d) Prabuddhavastha is another name for Jagradavastha, meaning a state of awakenness. This applies to a planet in own sign or in exaltation sign. The bhava owned by an exalted planet or placed in own sign flourishes. Except the luminaries, the other five own each two houses. It is true that a planet owning two houses if placed in own house, it predominantly acts on behalf of that house occupied by it. Simultaneously, its another house also gets strengthened by virtue of such a placement. For example, Saturn owns the 3rd and 4th for Scorpio ascendant and if he is in the 4th, he will mainly give good effects of the 4th (his Moola-trikona house). This does not mean that the 3rd house is left uncared by him.

(e) The house owned by a planet placed in the 10th from the ascendant will produce good results. I would prefer it to be closely related to the 10th cusp (or meridian) for it is the most effective point of the natus. For details, see notes for rule 1, ch. 2 of my work, **"Doctrines of Suka Nadi—Retold."**

Next we are told of the conditions under which a house suffers annihilations which are :

(a) The bhava unaspected by its lord does not flourish. Each bhava cannot be under the aspect of its lord. Then this does not mean that the bhava suffers annihilation. It may be construed that in tne absence of such an aspect, the bhava can look upto alternative sources as mentioned earlier. If a malefic relation is there for a bhava, its lord's aspect on it is an antidote.

(b) The lord of a bhava joining a malefic is a disadvantage for the bhava. If the said malefic is a friendly planet to the bhava lord or if they join in favourable houses, then the evil is minimized. Even if it is an exalted malefic, then also good effects may be expected.

(c) The lord of a house in conjunction with the lord of 6th/8th/12th cannot be productive of good. If he himself is an evil lord, then some relief can be expected. This is mainly from a yoga point and not in all respects.

(d) If a planet is defeated in planetary war, its bhava's potence is void.

Normally, we are taught that when two planets are on the same degree there occurs a war and the one with lesser longitude is declared winner. The luminaries do not enter into war.

In this connection, please refer to ch. 79 (Vol. II of our present work).

The late C. G. Rajan has a detailed and elaborate account of planetary war. According to him if two planets have identical longitudes to the **minute** of arc there is a planetary war, (This does not involve luminaries). He adds that they should be on the same latitude, i. e. both northern or both southern. The one with higher latitude is declared winner. He gives an example involving Saturn and Mars as under, for 0347 hrs on 15th December 1925 :

	Longitude	Latitude
Mars	209° 24′	0 N 21
Saturn	209° 24′	2 N 25

He declares Saturn as the winner as he has advanced latitude.

We need not rush to the conclusion that Mr. Rajan's version is contrary to Parasara's. We should appreciate the pains taken by Mr. Rajan in throwing **more** light on the subject. He gives more advanced and sound arguments which are not being reproduced here for the sake of achieving brevity.

For practical purposes, we are well guided by the elaboration of Mr. Rajan.

(e) The house whose lord is in Vriddhavastha (i.e. of an advanced age) becomes ineffective from the view point of good results. A planet in the area of 18°-24° of an odd sign or between 6° and 12° of an even sign is said to be in such an Avastha.

(f) If a planet is in Mritavastha (*in extremis*) its bhava will be destroyed. This state occurs to a planet in the first 6° of an even sign or in the last 6° of an odd sign.

(g) Lastly, a planet in Suptavastha neutralises the effect of the bhava owned by it. This Avastha is due to a debilitated planet or the one in an inimical camp.

The reader will thus see the significance of the present two slokas.

Hemaprabha Suri, a Jain astrologer of eminence, enumerates a principle in his work **"Trailokya Prakasa"** (edited by Ram Sarup Sharma, Lahore) that the bhava occupied or aspected by the Moon undergoes good or bad effects. That is, if the Moon is increasing, good effects will increase; otherwise effects will diminish.

अथ तनुभावफलाध्यायः ॥१२॥

Chapter 12

Effects Of First House

सपापो देहपोऽष्टारिव्ययगो देहसौख्यहृत् ।
केन्द्रे कोणे स्थितोऽङ्गेशः सदा देहसुखं दिशेत् ॥१॥
लग्नपोऽस्तङ्गतो नीचे शत्रुभे रोगकृद् भवेत् ।
शुभाः केन्द्रत्रिकोणस्था सर्वरोगहराः स्मृताः ॥२॥

1-2. *PHYSICAL COMFORTS :* Should the ascendant lord be conjunct a malefic or be in the 8th, 6th or 12th, physical felicity will diminish. If he is in an angle/trine there will be at all times comforts of the body. If the ascendant lord is in debilitation, combustion or enemy's sign, there will be diseases. With a benefic in an angle or trine, all diseases will disappear.

Notes : The ascendant lord going to an evil house together with a malefic is a dire defect in the matter of not only health but also luck and progress. If the ascendant lord in the process is a benefic or is exalted, then some relief in the course of time can be hoped.

The ascendant's angles (i.e. 4th, 7th or the 10th) or its trine (5th/9th) containing a benefic is a powerful remedy for all ills related to health.

लग्ने चन्द्रेऽथवा क्रूरग्रहैर्दृष्टेऽथवा युते ।
शुभदृष्टिविहीने च जन्तोर्देहसुखं न हि ॥३॥

3. There will not be bodily health if the ascendant or the Moon be aspected by or conjunct a malefic, being devoid of a benefic's aspect.

लग्ने सौम्ये सुरूपः स्यात् क्रूरे रूपविवर्जितः ।
सौम्यखेटैर्युते दृष्टे लग्ने देहसुखान्वितः ॥४॥

4. *BODILY BEAUTY :* A benefic in the ascendant will give a pleasing appearance, while a malefic will make one bereft of good appearance, Felicity of the body will be enjoyed if the ascendant is aspected by or conjunct a benefic.

लग्नेशो ज्ञो गुरुर्वाऽपि शुक्रो वा केन्द्रकोणगः ।
दीर्घायुर्धनवान् जातो बुद्धिमान् राजवल्लभः ॥५॥
लग्नेशे चरराशिस्थे शुभग्रहनिरीक्षिते ।
कीर्तिश्रीमान् महाभोगी देहसौख्यसमन्वितः ॥६॥
बुधो जीवोऽथवा शुक्रो लग्ने चन्द्रसमन्वितः ।
लग्नात् केन्द्रगतो वाऽपि राजलक्षणसंयुतः ॥७॥

5-7. *OTHER BENEFITS :* If the ascendant lord, Mercury, Jupiter or Venus be in an angle or in a trine, the native will be longlived, wealthy, intelligent and liked by the king. Fame, wealth, abundant pleasures and comforts of the body will be acquired if the ascendant lord is in a movable sign and be aspected by a benefic planet. One will be endowed with royal marks (of fortune) if Mercury, Jupiter or Venus be in the ascendant along with the Moon, or be in angle from the ascendant.

Notes : **"Rajalakshana"** means mark of fortune. There are 32 Lakshanas of major category in Samudrika Sastra or physiognomy. Some of these could be found in ch. 81 of our present work (vol II).

If Mercury, Jupiter or Venus be in 4th, 7th or 10th from the ascendant, or be in the company of the Moon in the ascendant, the native will enjoy royal fortunes.

ससौरे सकुजे वापि लग्ने मेषे वृषे हरौ ।
राश्यंशसदृशै गात्रे स जातो नालवेष्टितः ॥८॥

8. *COILED BIRTH :* If there be a birth in one of Aries, Taurus and Leo ascendants containing either Saturn or Mars, the birth of the child is with a coil around. The corresponding limb will be in accordance with the Rasi or Navamsa rising.

Notes : This rule applies to only three ascendants, viz. Aries, Taurus and Leo. Mars or Saturn should be in the ascendant. The limbs indicated by the Rasis are shown in sloka 4-4½ of ch. 4 **supra**. These apply to the Navamsas as well. The limbs denoted in slokas 12-15 of the present chapter have a different use and should not be mixed for the purpose of coiled birth, which will be simply obvious to the reader.

चतुष्पदगतो भानुः परे वीर्यसमन्विताः ।
द्विस्वभावगता जातौ यमलाविति निर्दिशेत् ॥९॥

9. *BIRTH OF TWINS :* The native, who has the Sun in a quadruped sign while others are in dual signs with strength, is born as one of the twins.

Notes : Quadruped signs are : Aries, Taurus, Leo, first half of Capricorn and second part of Sagittarius. If the Sun is in a quadruped sign while all others are in dual signs—Gemini and its angles—the native will be one of the twins. The other six planets be endowed with strength.

रवीन्दू एकभावस्थावेकांशकसमन्वितौ ।
त्रिमात्रा च त्रिभिर्मासैः पित्रा भ्रात्रा च पोषितः ॥१०॥

10. *TO BE NURTURED BY 3 MOTHERS :* If the Sun and the Moon join in one and the same bhava (house) and fall in one Navamsa, the native will be nurtured by 3 different mothers for the fiirst 3 months from its birth and will later on be brought up by its father and brother.

Notes : In my opinion, the Vargothama position of the luminaries in conjunction seems to be excepted. They should be in the same quarter of a constellation and will naturally be in one Navamsa. This combination obviously implies loss of mother within the first three months.

भ्रातृ apart from meaning a brother calls for interpretation as a near relative in general.

एवमेव फलं वाच्यं चन्द्रादपि सदा बुधैः ।
अथ जातनरस्याङ्गे व्रणचिह्नादिकं ब्रुवे ॥११॥

11. *IMPORTANT :* The learned in astrology should base the effects on the Moon also as are applicable to the ascendant. Now explained are clues to know of ulcers, identity marks etc. on one's person.

Notes : This wellknown rule is a speciality in Hindu Astrology and has the sage's sanction. The Moon is given a significant status equal to the ascendant for she rules one's mind and the mind in turn functions according to one's *Karma,* see *Buddhih Karmanusarini.*

शिरो नेत्रे तथा कर्णौ नासिके च कपोलकौ ।
हनूर्मुखं च लग्नाद्या तनावाद्यदृकाणके ॥१२॥
मध्यद्रेष्काणगे लग्ने कण्ठोंऽसौ च भुजौ तथा ।
पार्श्वे च हृदये क्रोडे नाभिश्चेति यथाक्रमम् ॥१३॥
बस्तिर्लिङ्गगुदे मुष्कावूरू जानू च जंघके ।
पादश्चेत्युदितैर्वाममङ्गं ज्ञेयं तृतीयके ॥१४॥

12-14. *DECANATES AND BODILY LIMBS :* Head, eyes, ears, nose, temple, chin and face is the order of limbs denoted (by the various houses) when the first decanate of a sign ascends. In the case of the second decanate ascending, the order is : neck, shoulder, arm, side, heart, stomach and navel. The order for the third decanate ascending is : pelvis, anus/penis, testicles, thigh, knee, calf and foot. The portion already risen indicates left side of the body (while the one yet to rise—i e. invisible half—denotes right side of the body).

Notes : The portion that has already risen is known as visible half of the horoscope. From the cusp of the ascendant to the cusp of the descendant counted backwards (i e. via the 10th cusp) is visible half. The rest is invisible half. Visible half represents the left side of the body while invisible half right side of the body.

The limbs suggested by the 2 slokas in three different orders are shown in the three diagrams for an easy grasp. The assumption is that the first decanate, second decanate and the third decanate of Aries rise in the respective cases :

Left eye	Left side of head	Right side of head	Right eye	Right ear
Left ear		Aries ascendant first decanate		Right nostril
Left nostril				Right side temple
Left side temple	Chin (left side)	Face (left side)	Face (right side)	Chin (right side)

Shoulder (left)	Neck (left)	Neck (right)	Shoulder (right)	Arm (right)
Arm (left)		Aries ascendant second decanate		Right side of trunk
Left side of trunk				Right side of heart
Left side of heart	Left side of stom-ach	Left side of navel	Right side of navel	Right side of stomach

Anus/ penis (left)	Left side of pelvis	Right side of pelvis	Anus/ penis (right)	Right testicle
Left testicle		Aries ascendant third decanate		Right thigh
Left thigh				Right knee
Left knee	Left calf	Left foot	Right foot	Right calf

The above three diagrams are made for the three decanates of Aries ascendant. The reader can change the sign positions according to the ascendant and its decanate as prevailing at birth. The two halves in the ascendant and 7th may please be noted attentively.

The corresponding part for female is ovary as against male's testicle. Similarly female's privity prevails in exchange of male organ. Pelvis is made into two parts, viz. **false pelvis** and **true pelvis**. The true pelvis is denoted by the portion of the zodiac yet to rise while false pelvis by the half of zodiac already rose.

यस्मिन्नङ्गे स्थितः पापो व्रणं तत्र समादिशेत् ।
नियतं सबुधैः क्रूरैः सौम्यैर्लक्ष्म वदेद् बुधः ॥१५॥

15. *LIMBS AFFECTED :* The limb related to a malefic by occupation will have ulcers or scars while the one by benefic will have a mark (like moles etc). So say the learned (in astrology).

Notes : Also see sloka 6, ch. 4 of **Saravali**, which states that a malefic or a benefic if be in own Rasi or Navamsa, the effects will be right from birth. In other cases, it will be in the course of one's life that these effects will come to pass.

अथ धनभावफलाध्यायः ॥१३॥

Chapter 13

Effects of Second House

धनभावफलं वच्मि श्रृणु त्वं द्विजसत्तम ! ।
धनेशो धनभावस्थः केन्द्रकोणगतोऽपि वा ॥१॥
धनवृद्धिकरो ज्ञेयस्त्रिकस्थो धनहानिकृत् ।
धनदश्च धने सौम्यः पापो धनविनाशकृत् ॥२॥

1-2. *COMBINATIONS FOR WEALTH* : O excellent of the Brahmanas, listen to me speaking on the effects of the 2nd house. If the lord of the 2nd is in the 2nd or is in an angle or in a trine, he will promote one's wealth(or monetary state). Should he be in the 6th/8th/12th, financial conditions will decline. A benefic in the 2nd will give wealth while a malefic instead will destroy the same.

Notes : Venus or Mercury in the 2nd will be favourable for wealth while Jupiter will not be wholly auspicious. If however, Jupiter is in the 2nd ruling the 2nd, then financial aspects will be smooth. That is why the sage specifically mentions this fact in the next sloka. It does not mean that Jupiter, otherwise in the 2nd will be wholly harmful. This denotes a problematic situation in money matters. Various authors have given different views in their works for a summary of which the reader may switch over to p. 491 of my English translation of **Saravali.**

धनाधिपो गुरुर्यस्य धनभावगतो भवेत् ।
भौमेन सहितो वाऽपि धनवान् स नरो भवेत् ॥३॥

3. One will be wealthy if Jupiter is in the 2nd as the lord of the 2nd or is with Mars.

Notes : There are two independent conditions in this verse denoting wealth. Jupiter, if in the 2nd, should be the ruler of 2nd for the native becoming wealthy. This applies to Scorpio ascendant and Aquarius ascendant. In that case, his lonely position itself in the 2nd will confer wealth rather abundant wealth. Whether or not Jupiter owns the 2nd, if be conjunct Mars, wealth will be acquired by the native; the **house** occupied by them not standing for consideration.

धनेशे लाभभावस्थे लाभेशे वा धनं गते ।
तावुभौ केन्द्रकोणस्थौ धनवान् स नरो भवेत् ॥४॥

4. If the 2nd lord is in the 11th while the lord of the 11th is in the 2nd, wealth will be acquired by the native. Alternatively these two lords may join in an angle or in a trine.

Notes : The 11th lord has a say in financial matters apart from the 2nd lord. One's gains are indicated by the 11th lord. If he is in exchange with the 2nd lord, the native will be wealthy, These two planets joining in the ascendant, 4th, 7th, 10th, 5th or 9th will also lead to financial gains.

धनेशे केन्द्रराशिस्थे लाभेशे तत्त्रिकोणगे।
गुरुशुक्रयुते दृष्टे धनलाभमुदीरयेत् ॥५॥

5. If the lord of the 2nd is in an angle while the 11th lord is in a trine thereof or is aspected by or conjunct by Jupiter and Venus, the supject will be wealthy.

Notes : The lord of the 2nd should be in the ascendant, or 4th/7th/10th house. The 11th lord should be in the 5th/9th counted from the house occupied by the 2nd lord. Alternatively the 2nd lord should be related to Jupiter (and) or Venus by conjunction or by aspect. Both the combinations are for gaining wealth.

धनेशो रिपुभावस्थो लाभेशस्तद्गतो यदि।
धनायौ पापयुक्तौ वा दृष्टौ निर्धन एव सः ॥६॥
धनलाभाधिपावस्तौ पापग्रहसमन्वितौ।
जन्मप्रभृतिदारिद्र्यं भिक्षान्नं लभते नरः ॥७॥

6-7. *YOGAS FOR POVERTY* : One will be penniless if the lord of the 2nd is in an evil house while the 11th lord is also so placed and the 2nd is occupied by a malefic. There will be penury right from birth and the native will have to beg even for his food if the lords of the 2nd and the 11th are both combust or be with malefics.

Notes : The lords of the 2nd and 11th can be jointly in the 6th/8th/12th or individually disposed in any two of the said three houses. Simultaneously the 2nd house needs a malefic in it. Thus there are afflictions from three directions which will make the native extremely poor. Even food is denied to one having combust 2nd lord and combust 11th lord. Alternatively the 2nd lord may be with a severe malefic while the 11th lord is also similarly placed. The conjunction of the 2nd lord with a Yogakarka, although a malefic, will not be adverse in the matter of finace. On the contrary it will prove very auspicious. For example, Mercury, the 2nd lord, joining Saturn in the case of a Taurus native, will make financial prospects superior.

षष्ठेऽष्टमे व्यये वाऽपि धनलाभाधिपौ यदि।
लाभे कुजो धने राहू राजदण्डाद् धनक्षयः ॥८॥

8. *LOSS OF WEALTH THROUGH THE KING :* Should the lords of the 2nd and 11th be relegated to the 6th/8th/12th (jointly or separately) while Mars is in the 11th and Rahu is in the 2nd, the native will lose his wealth on account of royal punishments.

Notes : This combination will cause financial losses through penalties, fines etc. imposed by the government, in the modern context. Monetary deficiencies will as well persist throughout.

लाभे जीवे धने शुक्रे धनेशे शुभसंयुते ।
व्यये च शुभसंयुक्ते धर्मकार्ये धनव्ययः ॥९॥

9. *EXPENSES ON GOOD ACCOUNTS :* Jupiter in the 11th, Venus in the 2nd, and a benefic in the 12th while the 2nd lord is conjunct a benefic there will be expenses on religious or charitable grounds.

स्वभोच्चवस्थे धनाधीशे जातको जनपोषकः ।
परोपकारी ख्यातश्च विज्ञेयो द्विजसत्तम ! ॥१०॥

10. *FAME ETC. :* If the 2nd lord is in own sign or is exalted the native will look after his people, will help others and will become famous.

Notes : Our text requires the 2nd lord to be in exaltation or in own sign so that the native will look after his people & C.

It has been practically seen that the 2nd lord's dignity is essential for one to be helpful to others and be dutiful towards his family members. Chaukhamba edition has almost a different condition in this place : It states that the 2nd lord should be in deep exaltation or in own sign and be in aspect to Jupiter. The net result given therein is "fame and liked bypall". The condition of 'deep' exaltation seems to me to be somewhat in excess of the requirement while a simple own sign position is given as an alternative. As such, I feel mere exaltation of the 2nd lord is enough for obtaining the said results.

स्थिते पारावतांशादौ धनेशे शुभसंयुते ।
तद्गृहे सर्वसम्पत्तिर्विनाऽऽस्यासेन जायते ॥११॥

11. *EFFORTLESS ACQUISITION :* If the 2nd lord is conjunct a benefic and be in a good division like Paravatamsa, there will be all kinds of wealth in his family effortlessly.

Notes : "Paravatamsa" denotes six good Vargas out of Dasavarga scheme (*vide* ch. 6, *supra*). "Paravatamsadau" of the text denotes Paravata or such other higher Vargas. To wit, the 2nd lord should be in Paravatamsa or in Devalokamsa, Brahmalokamsa, Sakravahanamsa or Sridhamamsa in the Dasavarga scheme. The eorresponding superior Amsas whem the entire Shodasavarga scheme is used should be above Poornachandramsa. In the Dasavarga scheme, why the sage fixes the minimum Varga as Paravatha is obvious. This varga denotes 6 good divisions in Dasavarga scheme i.e. above 50% of good divisions.

The 2nd lord being endowed with such a Varga dignity and conjunct another benefic brings in effortless wealth and wealth of all kinds. It follows that the 2nd lord's disposition (or the disposition of Jupiter) will decide the financial status of a native.

नेत्रेशे बलसंयुक्ते शोभनाक्षो भवेन्नरः ।
षष्ठाष्टमव्ययस्थे च नेत्रवैकल्यवान् भवेत् ॥१२॥

12. *EYES :* If the 2nd lord is endowed with strength, the native will possess beautiful eyes. Should the said planet be in the 6th, 8th or 12th, there will be disease or deformity of eyes.

Notes : "Netresa" denotes the lord of the 2nd, i.e. significator of eyes. This does not mean that the 12th lord has nothing to do with eyes. Precisely, 2nd lord and 12th lord respectively lord over right eye and left eye respectively. This is from the health point of view of eye. However, when the beauty of the eyes is to be known, it is from the 2nd house only. Jupiter well placed in the 2nd, or the 2nd lord in exaltation, or with a benefic will give one beautiful eyes. While Venus in the 2nd or Full Moon in the 2nd will not deprive one of beautiful eyes, defects of sight at an early stage will result from the said position. Mercury in the 2nd will have a say on the speech rather than on the sight. Hence Jupter's position in the 2nd is a safe bet for strong sight and beauty of the eyes, if the planet is not with evils of fall and the like.

धनेशे पापसंयुक्ते धने पापसमन्विते ।
पिशुनोऽसत्यवादी च वातव्याधिसमन्वितः ॥१३॥

13. *UNTRUTHFUL PERSON :* If the 2nd house and its lord are conjunct malefics, the native will be a tale-bearer, will speak untruth and will be afflicted by windy diseases.

Notes : The 2nd house and its lord are referred in the matter of windy diseases. Gastric troubles, rheumatism and the like are classified under windy disorders. If the 2nd house or its lord is associated with Saturn or Mercury it will cause rheumatism and such other disorders. If Jupiter in affliction is so related, gastric troubles will come to pass.

अथ सहजभावफलाध्यायः ॥१४॥

Chapter 14

Effects Of The Third House

अथ विक्रमभावस्य फलं वक्ष्यामि भो द्विज ! ।
सहजे सौम्ययुग्दृष्टे भ्रातृमान् विक्रमी नरः ॥१॥

1. O Brahmin, I now tell you about the 3rd house. Should the 3rd house be conjunct or aspected by a benefic, the native will be endowed with co-born and be courageous.

Notes : 'Bhratru' in Sanskrit simply means a brother. Proper adjective is to be added, viz. **Jyeshta** for elder and **Kanishta** for younger, to the word **Bhratru**. The 3rd house specifically deals with the after-born while the 11th house deals with preborn. This can be seen from sloka 32, Ch. 32 **infra**. In the said chapter the sage instructs us to consider Mars for the 3rd bhava and Jupiter for 11th bhava.

Younger sister is denoted by the 3rd house and Mars while elder sister by the 11th house and Jupiter.

स-भौमो भ्रातृभावेशो भ्रातृभावं प्रपश्यति ।
भ्रातृक्षेत्रगतो वाऽपि भ्रातृभावं विनिर्दिशेत् ॥२॥

2. If the 3rd lord along with Mars aspects the 3rd house the native will enjoy good results due to the 3rd house. Alternatively these two planets may be in the 3rd itself.

Notes : Mars alone in the 3rd, except in Capricorn or in Scorpio or in Aries, is not conductive to brothers. The form of our sloka is different in that the 3rd house be jointly aspected or occupied by Mars and the 3rd lord for the prosperity of coborn.

पापयोगेन तौ पापक्षेत्रयोगेन वा पुनः ।
उत्पाट्य सहजान् सद्यो निहन्तारौ न संशयः ॥३॥

3. Destruction at once of coborn will come to pass if the said 2 planets are together with a malefic or in a sign owned by a malefic.

Notes : "The coborn will not live long" is the hint given by the phrase "*Sadyo nihantarau*". Mars and the 3rd lord joining in a malefic's sign or joining a malefic is said to be adverse for the longevity of coborn. Similarly Jupiter and the 11th lord in such a state is adverse for elder brothers and elder sisters; Venus and the 7th lord so placed for the spouse, Jupiter and the 5th lord so placed for progeny; Sun and the 9th lord so placed for father, the Moon and the 4th lord so placed for mother, and so on and so forth. So to say the significator and the lord of the concerned house together in a malefic's sign or with a malefic (or in an evil house) will bring harm to the said relative.

स्त्रीग्रहो भ्रातृभावेशः स्त्रीग्रहो भ्रातृभावगः ।
भगिनी स्यात् तथा भ्राता पुंगृहे पुंग्रहो यदि ॥४॥
मिश्रे मिश्रफलं वाच्यं बलाबलविनिर्णयात् ।

4-4½. *FEMALE AND MALE COBORN :* If the 3rd lord is a female planet or if the 3rd house be occupied by female planets, one will have sisters born after him. Similarly male planets and male signs denote younger brothers. Should it be of mixed nature, coborn of both sexes will be obtained. These effects be declared after assessing the strength and weakness of the concerned.

Notes : Saturn and Mercury are termed as neutral planets. Rahu and Ketu are shadowy ones. In the matter of deciding the sex of coborn or progeny, Saturn and Rahu be treated as males while Mercury and Ketu are females.

(**Trailokyaprakasika** vide sloka 12 treats Ketu as a female and Rahu as a eunuch. **Daivagnabharana** vide ch. I, s. 14-15 considers the reverse of this at one place and imediately quotes a different school of thought, thus : Rahu is a male planet and Ketu a eunuch.)

All odd signs are male signs and all even signs are female signs. Male signs exclusively occupied by male planets will cause birth of brothers. Converse is the case with female signs occupied by female planets. This should be known from the 3rd house being male or female sign & C. If the 3rd house is occupied by a male planet as well as a female planet, there will be brothers and sisters as well. The contribution will come to pass if the contributor is strong. For example, Jupiter in the 3rd in a male sign if strong will cause the birth of a brother. If he is weak, acquisition of brother through Jupiter will not be fruitful. Then one has to look upto alternative sources whether the native will have a brother or not.

मृतौ कुजतृतीयेशौ सहोदरविनाशकौ ॥५॥
केन्द्रत्रिकोणगे वाऽपि स्वोच्चमित्रस्ववर्गगे ।
कारके सहजेशे या भ्रातृसौख्यं विनिर्दिशेत् ॥६॥

5-6. Should the 3rd lord and Mars be together in the 8th, destruction of coborn will result. Happiness in this respect will come to pass if Mars or the 3rd lord is in an angle or in a trine or in exaltation/friendly divisions.

Notes : The suggestions given in the notes for sloka 3 about spouse, elder brother, mother etc. may be suitably extended in this respect with the help of the present verse. For example, if Venus and 7th lord are together in the 8th, the native's married life will be short (and in bad taste.)

Similarly, their conjunction in an angle or in a trine will confer longlasting benefic effects.

Further hint that can be taken from the verse in question is : If a significator and house lord join together in a sign which is identical with debilitation/inimical sign for one of them, the significance of the planet is lost. If they join in a sign which is exaltation/friendly sign for one of them, then the significance of the planet gains prosperity.

भ्रातृभे बुधसंयुक्ते तदीशे चन्द्रसंयुते ।
कारके मन्दसंयुक्ते भगिन्येकाग्रतो भवेत् ॥७॥
पश्चात् सहोदरोऽप्येकस्तृतीयस्तु मृतो भवेत् ।
कारके राहुसंयुक्ते सहजेशे तु नीचगे ॥८॥
पश्चात् सहोदराभावं पूर्वं तु तत्त्रयं वदेत् ।
भ्रातृस्थानाधिपे केन्द्रे कारके तत्त्रिकोणगे ॥९॥
जीवेन सहिते चोच्चे ज्ञेया द्वादश सोदराः ।
तत्र ज्येष्ठद्वयं तद्वज्जातकाच्च तृतीयकम् ॥१०॥
सप्तमं नवमं चैव द्वादशं च मृतं वदेत् ।
शेषाः सहोदराः षड् वै भवेयुर्दीर्घजीवनाः ॥११॥

7-11. *NUMBER OF BROTHERS AND SISTERS* : If Mercury is in the 3rd while the 3rd lord and Moon are together as the indicator (Mars) joins Saturn, the effects are : there occurred the birth of an **elder sister** and there will be younger brothers. Further the third brother will die. Should Mars and Rahu be conjunct while the 3rd lord is in his sign of debilitation, there will be loss of younger brothers/sisters while 3 elder brothers/sisters were attained by the native. If the 3rd lord is in an angle while the significator is exalted in a trine and be in the company of Jupiter, 12 will be the number of total coborn. Out of these 2 elders and the 3rd, 7th, 9th and 12th of younger coborn will be shortlived while six of the said twelve will be longlived.

Notes : The word 'Karaka' or significator in sloka 7 etc. should be wisely noted as Mars only and not as Jupiter, which is borne by sloka 11.

In the context of indication of one's having 12 coborn, this may be taken in the present age to be a number of coborn, if not literally 12. Mars exalted and being in the company of Jupiter is denoted which means Jupiter will be in fall. Some of the coborn will die obviously because of Jupiter's debilitation taking away some potence of exalted Mars.

व्ययेशेन युतो भौमो गुरुणा सहितोऽपि वा।
भ्रातृभावे स्थिते चन्द्रे सप्तसंख्यास्तु सोदराः ॥१२॥
भ्रातृस्थाने शशियुते केवलं पुङ् ग्रहेक्षिते।
सहजा भ्रातरो ज्ञेयाः शुक्रयुक्तेक्षितेऽन्यथा ॥१३॥

12-13. There will be 7 coborn if the 12th lord (some texts read as the 11th lord) joins Mars and Jupiter while the 3rd is occupied by the Moon. If the Moon is lonely placed in the 3rd in aspect to male planets, there will be younger brothers while the aspect of Venus denotes younger sisters.

अग्रे जातं रविर्हन्ति पृष्ठे जातं शनैश्चरः।
अग्रजं पृष्ठजं हन्ति सहजस्थो धरासुतः ॥१४॥

14. *ADVERSE PLANETS* : The Sun in the 3rd will destroy the preborn. The afterborn will be destroyed if Saturn is found in the 3rd. In the same situation Mars will destroy both the preborn and later born.

Notes : Sage Bhrigu also opines that the Sun in the 3rd house will not allow the native to retain his elder brothers. This position will affect one's relationship with brothers and sisters. Regarding Mars in the 3rd, Garga Maharshi states that the native will obtain two brothers and two sisters all the 4 of whom will pass away early. The placement of Mars in the 3rd has also adverse say on the native's character. For further details, see my detailed notes in the chapter "Effects of Planets in Bhavas", of Saravali.

एतेषां विप्र! योगानां बलाबलविनिर्णयात्।
भ्रातृणां भगिनीनां वा जातकस्य फलं वदेत् ॥१५॥

15. After estimating the strength and weakness of such yogas, the effects related to brothers and sisters be announced.

अथ सुखभावफलाध्याय: ॥१५॥

Chapter 15

Effects Of The Fourth House

उक्तं तृतीयभावस्य फलं संक्षेपतो मया।
सुखभावफलं चाऽथ कथयामि द्विजोत्तम ! ॥१॥

1. O excellent of the Brahmins, thus have been briefly told about the effects of the 3rd house. Now listen to the results related to the 4th house.

सुखेशे सुखभावस्थे लग्नेशे तद्गतेऽपि वा।
शुभदृष्टे च जातस्य पूर्णं गृहसुखं वदेत् ॥२॥

2. *HOUSING COMFORTS :* One will have residential comforts in full degree if the 4th is occupied by its lord or by the ascendant lord and be aspected by a benefic.

स्वगेहे स्वांशके स्वोच्चे सुखस्थानाधिपो यदि।
भूमि-यान-गृहादीनां सुखं वाद्यभवं तथा ॥३॥

3. *MISCELLANEOUS :* Should the 5th lord be in his own house, or in own Navamsa or in exaltation, the native will be endowed with comforts related to lands, conveyances, houses etc. and musical instruments.

कर्माधिपेन संयुक्ते केन्द्रे कोणे गृहाधिपे।
विचित्रसौधप्राकारैर्मण्डितं तद्गृहं वदेत् ॥४॥

4. *HOUSING COMFORTS :* If the 10th lord joins the 4th lord in an angle or in a trine, the native will acquire beautiful mansions.

बन्धुस्थानेश्वरे सौम्ये शुभग्रहयुतेक्षिते।
शशिजे लग्नसंयुक्ते बन्धुपूज्यो भवेन्नरः ॥५॥

5. *RELATIVES :* Should Mercury be in the ascendant while the 4th lord being a benefic is aspected by another benefic, the native will be honoured by his relatives.

मातुःस्थाने शुभयुते तदीशे स्वोच्चराशिगे।
कारके बलसंयुक्ते मातुर्दीर्घायुरादिशेत् ॥६॥

6. *LONG-LIVING MOTHER* : If the 4th house is occupied by a benefic while its lord is in his exaltation sign as the indicator of mother is endowed with strength, the native will have a long-living mother.

Notes : The stronger among the Moon and Mars is denoted as the significator of mother, vide slokas 18-19 ch. 32, *infra*. There are still many more views about the karakatwas for parents given by various authors.

सुखेशे केन्द्रभावस्थे तथा केन्द्रस्थितो भृगुः।
शशिजे स्वोच्चराशिस्थे मातुः पूर्णं सुखं वदेत् ॥७॥

7. *HAPPINESS TO MOTHER :* The native's mother will be happy if the 4th lord is in an angle while Venus is also in an angle as Mercury is exalted.

सुखे रवियुते मन्दे चन्द्रे भाग्यगते सति।
लाभस्थानगतो भौमो गो-महिष्यादिलाभकृत् ॥८॥

8. *QUADRUPEDS :* The Sun in the 4th, Moon and Saturn in the 9th and Mars in the 11th—this yoga will confer cows and buffaloes on the native.

चरगेहसमायुक्ते सुखे तद्राशिनायके।
षष्ठे व्यये स्थिते भौमे नरः प्राप्नोति मूकताम् ॥९॥

9. *DUMBNESS :* Should the 4th house be a movable one while its lord and Mars are together in the 6th or the 8th house, the native will be dumb.

लग्नस्थानाधिपे सौम्ये सुखेशे नीचराशिगे।
कारके व्ययभावस्थे सुखेशे लाभसङ्गते ॥१०॥
द्वादशे वत्सरे प्राप्ते वाहनस्य सुखं वदेत्।
वाहने सूर्यसंयुक्ते स्वोच्चे तद्भावनायके ॥११॥
शुक्रेण संयुते वर्षे द्वात्रिंशे वाहनं भवेत्।
कर्मेशेन युते बन्धुनाथे तुङ्गांशसंयुते ॥१२॥

द्विचत्वारिंशके वर्षे नरो वाहनभाग् भवेत्।
लाभेशे सुखराशिस्थे सुखेशे लाभसंयुते ॥१३॥
द्वादशे वत्सरे प्राप्ते जातो वाहनभाग् भवेत्।
शुभं शुभत्वे भावस्य पापत्वे फलमन्यथा ॥१४॥

10-14. *CONVEYANCES :* If the ascendant lord is a benefic while the 4th lord is in fall or in the 11th and the significatoı (Venus) is in the 12th, the native will obtain conveyances in his 12th year. Should the Sun be in the 4th house, as the 4th lord is exalted and be with Venus, one will acquire conveyanees in his 32nd year. It will be in the 42nd year that one will be endowed with conveyances if the 4th lord joins the 10th lord in his (4th lord's) exaltation Navamsa. An exchange between the 11th and the 4th lords will confer conveyances in the 12th year. A benefic related to the 4th house (and to its lord) will bring with him auspicious effects while a malefic will produce only malefic effects (in respect of conveyances).

Notes : It is not known why the 4th lord should be in fall for early obtainment of conveyances. This condition seems to be the result of defective text as the next line adds that the 4th lord may be in the 11th. To me it occurs that the correct version should read as : If the ascendant lord is a benefic while the 11th is tenanted by Venus and the 4th lord, early obtainment of conveyance (around the 12th year) will come to pass. Another rule given by the sage to get similar effect is an exchange between the lord of 4th and 11th.

Should a benefic be in the 4th, aspect the 4th, or is conjunct with or aspect the lord of the 4th house, then the native will be happy with conveyances and be free from accidents and dangers. A malefic replacing the said benefic will cause losses concerning vehicles and reduce one to severe accidents.

अथ पञ्चमभावफलाध्यायः ॥१६॥

Chapter 16

Effects Of The Fifth House

अथ पञ्चमभावस्य कथयामि फलं द्विज ! ।
लग्नपे सुतभावस्थे सुतपे च सुते स्थिते ॥१॥
केन्द्रत्रिकोणसंस्थे वा पूर्णं पुत्रसुखं वदेत् ।
षष्ठाष्टमव्ययस्थे तु सुताधीशे त्वपुत्रता ॥२॥
सुतेशेऽस्तंगते वाऽपि पापाक्रान्ते च निर्बले ।
तदा न जायते पुत्रो जातो वा म्रियते ध्रुवम् ॥३॥

1-3. O Brahmin, now I tell you the effects related to the 5th house. If the lords of the ascendant and the 5th are in their own signs or in an angle or in a trine, one will enjoy thorough happiness through his children. Should the 5th lord be in the 6th, 8th or 12th, there will be no offspring. Should the lord of the 5th be combust or be with malefics and be weak, there will be no children; even if per chance issues are obtained they will only quit the world soon.

Notes : "Suta" in Sanskrit used in compound word or as an adjective does not exclude a female issue for it means "begotten". There are however specific occasions where the expression "son" is exclusively denoted by this term. A logical approach according to circumstances is needed in interpreting such expressions.

The conjunction of the 5th lord with the ascendant lord in a good house will ensure early obtainment of children apart from happiness through them. If they join in an evil house, they will prove a defect in this respect.

षष्ठस्थाने सुताधीशे लग्नेशे कुजसंयुते ।
म्रियते प्रथमापत्यं काकबन्ध्या च गेहिनी ॥४॥

4. If the 5th lord is in the 6th as the ascendant lord is conjunct Mars, the native will lose his very first child whereafter his female will not be fertile to yield an offspring.

सुताधीशो हि नीचस्थो व्ययषष्ठाष्टमस्थितः ।
काकबन्ध्या भवेन्नारी सुते केतुबुधौ यदि ॥५॥

5. Should the 5th lord be in fall in the 6th, 8th or the 12th while Mercury and Ketu are in the 5th, the native's wife will give birth to one child only.

सुतेशो नीचगो यत्र सुतस्थानं न पश्यति ।
तत्र सौरिबुधौ स्यातां काकबन्ध्यात्वमाप्नुयात् ॥६॥

6. If the 5th lord is in fall and be not in aspect to the 5th while Saturn and Mercury are in the 5th, the native's wife will give birth to one child only.

भाग्येशो मूर्तिवर्ती चेत् सुतेशो नीचगो यदि ।
सुते केतु-बुधौ स्यातां सुतं कष्टाद् विनिर्दिशेत् ॥७॥

7. Should the 9th lord be in the ascendant while the 5th lord is in fall and Ketu is in the 5th along with Mercury, obtainment of progeny will be after a great deal of ordalium.

Notes : The very presence of Mercury, or Ketu, or Saturn in the 5th will present a doubtful picture of progeny. If two of them join in the 5th, then there will be *Kakavandhya Dosha* (obtaining only a single issue) for the wife of the native, or even childlessness.

षष्ठाष्टमव्ययस्थो वा नीचो वा शत्रुराशिगः ।
सुतेशश्च सुते तस्य कष्टात् पुत्रं विनिर्दिशेत् ॥८॥

8. If the 5th lord is in the 6th, 8th or the 12th or be in an inimical sign or be in fall or in the 5th itself, the native will beget issues with difficulty.

पुत्रभावे बुधक्षेत्रे मन्दक्षेत्रेऽथवा पुनः ।
मन्दे मान्दियुते दृष्टे तदा दत्तादयः सुताः ॥९॥

9. Should the 5th house be owned by Saturn or Mercury and be occupied or aspected by Saturn and Mandi, one will have adopted issues.

Notes : "Mandi" is the word used in the text which means Gulika. This identicality has been narrated in a previous Chapter.

Aspect of Mandi is suggested by the sage. Though there is no authentic information on aspect of Mandi (and other Upagrahas), it may be said that it aspects the 7th house.

The rule as per the sloka applies to Aquarius, Taurus, Virgo and Libra. In the case of the latter two Lagnas, Saturn though rules the 5th is helpless obviously because of affliction by Gulika. Otherwise Saturn related to the 5th house as its owner will not deprive one of progeny, making him go in for an adoption.

रवि-चन्द्रौ यदैकस्थावेकांशकसमन्वितौ ।
त्रिमातृभिरसौ याद्वा द्विपित्राऽपि च पोषितः ॥१०॥

10. Should the Sun and the Moon be together in a Rasi and in the same Navamsa, the native will be brought up by 3 mothers or 2 **fathers.**

Notes : The luminaries should be in the same Rasi and same Navamsa. As a result of this yoga, the child will be brought up by 3 females equal to mother or two men as father (i.e. paternal reatives etc.). This obviously hints at the possible loss of mother or father soon after birth.

पञ्चमे षड्ग्रहैर्युक्ते तदीशे व्ययराशिगे ।
लग्नेशेन्दू बलाढयौ चेत् तदा दत्तसुतोद्भवः ॥११॥

11. Adopted issue is indicated if the 5th is tenanted by six planets while its lord is in the 12th, and the Moon and ascendant are endowed with strength.

सुते ज्ञजीवशुक्रैश्च सबलैरवलोकिते[1] ।
भवन्ति बहवः पुत्राः सुतेशे हि बलान्विते ॥१२॥

12. There will be many children if the 5th lord is strong while the 5th is aspected by strong Mercury, Jupiter and Venus.

---

1. संयुतेक्षिते is another reading which includes placement in the 5th.

सुतेशे चन्द्रसंयुक्ते तद्द्रेष्काणगतेऽपि वा।
तदा हि कन्यकोत्पत्तिः प्रवदेद् दैवचिन्तकः ॥१३॥

13. If the 5th lord is with the Moon or be in her decanate, the native will beget daughters, so say astrologers.

Notes : The 5th lord's joining the Moon will confer daughters (rather more daughters) than sons. The Moon is a planet of multiplicity and hence there will be a number of daughters.

An alternative suggested by the sage is that the 5th lord should be in a decanate owned by the Moon. The Moon's decanates are : the first ten degrees of Cancer, the second ten degrees of Pisces and the third ten degrees of Scorpio. If the 5th lord occupies a degree as above, he will fall in the Moon's decanate. Then the native will obtain daughters.

सुतेशे चरराशिस्थे राहुणा सहिते विधौ।
पुत्रस्थानं गते मन्दे परजातं वदेच्छिशुम् ॥१४॥

14. If the 5th lord is in a movable sign while Saturn is in the 5th, as Rahu is with the Moon the child (so born) is of questionable birth.

Notes : There are 3 conditions denoted so that the owner of the horoscope is an illegal product. These are : (a) The 5th lord should be in a movable sign. (b) The 5th house should be occupied by Saturn, and (c) The Moon should be with Rahu (anywhere).

The combinations indicating illegal birth get nullified under certain conditions. For details see p. 55 of my English translation of **Horasara** also.

लग्नादष्टमगे चन्द्रे चन्द्रादष्टमगे गुरौ।
पापग्रहैर्युते दृष्टे परजातो न संशयः ॥१५॥

15. Undoubtedly the native is born of other's loins if the Moon is in the 8th from the ascendant while Jupiter is in the 8th from the Moon. Malefic's aspect/association is essential in this Yoga.

पुत्रस्थानाधिपे स्वोच्चे लग्नाद्वा द्वित्रिकोणगे।
गुरुणा संयुते दृष्टे पुत्रभाग्यमुपैति सः ॥१६॥

16. If the 5th lord is exalted or be in the 2nd, 5th or 9th from the ascendant or be conjunct or aspected by Jupiter, obtainment of children will be there.

Notes : Anyone of the following 3 states of the 5th lord will ensure birth of children :

1. The 5th lord in exaltation.
2. The 5th lord in the 2nd/5th/9th house.
3. The 5th lord related to Jupiter by aspect or conjunction.

Even though Jupiter may be the ruler of the 6th or 8th or 12th, his association with the 5th lord will ensure obtainment of children.

त्रिचतुःपापसंयुक्ते सुते सौम्याविवर्जिते ।
सुतेशे नीचराशिस्थे नीचसंस्थो भवेच्छिशुः ॥१७॥

17. One will obtain children that will indulge in mean deeds if the 5th is occupied by 3 or 4 malefics while the 5th lord is in fall. A benefic (including Mercury) in the 5th is excluded in the said combination.

पुत्रस्थानं गते जीवे तदीशे भृगुसंयुते ।
द्वात्रिंशे च त्र्यस्त्रिंशे वत्सरे पुत्रसंभवः ॥१८॥

18. If the 5th is occupied by Jupiter while its lord is with Venus, one will obtain an offspring in his 32nd/33rd year.

सुतेशे केन्द्रभावस्थे कारकेण समन्विते ।
षट्त्रिंशे त्रिंशदब्दे च पुत्रोत्पत्तिं विनिर्दिशेत् ॥१९॥

19. Should the 5th lord be in an angle along with Jupiter, the Karaka, one will beget a child at the age of 30 or 36.

लग्नाद् भाग्यगते जीवे जीवाद् भाग्यगते भृगौ ।
लग्नेशे भृगुयुक्ते वा चत्वारिंशे सुतं वदेत् ॥२०॥

20. If Jupiter is in the 9th from the ascendant while Venus is in the 9th from Jupiter along with the ascendant lord, one will beget a child at the age of 40.

पुत्रस्थानं गते राहौ तदीशे पापसंयुते ।
नीचराशिगतो जीवो द्वात्रिंशे पुत्रमृत्युदः ॥२१॥

21. The native will at the age of 32 lose his child if Rahu is in the 5th, the 5th lord is conjunct a malefic and Jupiter is in debilitation.

जीवात् पञ्चमगे पापे लग्नात् पञ्चमगेऽपि च ।
षट्त्रिंशे च त्रयस्त्रिंशे चत्वारिंशे सुतक्षयः ॥२२॥

22. There will be loss of children at 33 and 36 if a malefic is in the 5th from Jupiter while another is in the 5th from the ascendant.

लग्ने मान्दितमायुक्ते लग्नेशे नीचराशिगे ।
षट्पञ्चाशत्तमेऽब्दे च पुत्रशोकसमाकुलः ॥२३॥

23. Should Mandi be in the ascendant while the ascendant lord is in fall, grief on account of loss of child at the age of 56 will come to pass.

Notes : Mandi and Gulika are one and the same as described *supra.* The placement of Gulika in the ascendant while its lord is in debilitation will cause death of an offspring at the native's age of 56. Similarly, the debilitation of Gulika's dispositor will cause harm to the bhava concerned, i.e. the bhava occupied by Gulika.

चतुर्थे पापसंयुक्ते षष्ठभावे तथैव हि ।
सुतेशे परमोच्चस्थे लग्नेशेन समन्विते ॥२४॥
कारके शुभसंयुक्ते दशसंख्यास्तु सूनवः ।
परमोच्चगते जीवे धनेशे राहुसंयुते ॥२५॥
भाग्येशे भाग्यसंयुक्ते संख्याता नव सूनवः ।
पुत्रभाग्यगते जीवे सुतेशे बलसंयुते ॥२६॥
धनेशे कर्मभावस्थे वसुसंख्यास्तु सूनवः ।
पञ्चमात् पञ्चमे मन्दे सुतस्थे च तदीश्वरे ॥२७॥
सूनवः सप्तसंख्यश्च द्विगर्भे यमलौ वदेत् ।
वित्तेशे पञ्चमस्थाने सतस्थे च सुताधिपे ॥२८॥

जायन्ते षट् सुतास्तस्य तेषां च त्रिप्रजामृतिः।
मन्दात् पञ्चमगे जीवे जीवात् पञ्चमगे शनौ ।।२९।।
सुतभे पापसंयुवते पुत्रमेकं विनिर्दिशेत्।
पञ्चमे पापयुवते वा जीवात् पञ्चमगे शनौ ।।३०।।
पत्न्यन्तरे पुत्रलाभं कलत्रत्रयभाग् भवेत्।
पञ्चमे पापसंयुवते जीवात् पञ्चमगे शनौ ।।३१।।
लग्नेशे धनभावस्थे सुतेशो भौमसंयुतः।
जातं जातं शिशुंहन्ति दीर्घायुश्च स्वयं भवेत् ।।३२।।

24-32. *NUMBER OF CHILDREN* : There will be 10 sons if the 4th and the 6th are occupied by malefics while the 5th lord is in deep exaltation joining the ascendant lord as Jupiter is with another benefic. Nine will be the number of sons that one will beget if Jupiter is in deep exaltation as Rahu is with the 2nd lord and the 9th is occupied by its own lord. There will be eight sons if Jupiter is in the 5th/9th while the 5th lord is endowed with strength and the 2nd lord is in the 10th. Saturn in the 9th from the ascendant while the 5th lord is in the 5th itself, will give 7 sons out of which twins will be born twice. If the 5th lord in the 5th in conjunction with the 2nd lord, there will be birth of 7 sons out of which 3 will pass away. Only one son is denoted if there be a malefic in the 5th from the ascendant while Jupiter is in the 5th from Saturn or *vice versa.* If the 5th house has a malefic in it or if Saturn is in the 5th from Jupiter, the native will beget offspring only through his 2nd or 3rd wife. Should the 5th be occupied by a malefic while Jupiter has Saturn in the 5th as the ascendant lord is in the 2nd, and the 5th lord is with Mars, one will live long but lose his children one after the other as they are born.

अथ षष्ठभावफलाध्यायः ॥१७॥

Chapter 17

Effects Of The Sixth House

अथ विप्र ! फलं वक्ष्ये षष्ठभावसमुद्भवम् ।
देहे रोगव्रणाद्यं तत् श्रूयतामेकचेतसा ॥१॥

1. O Brahmin, following are the effects produced by the 6th house, relating to diseases, ulcers etc. Listen to the same attentively.

षष्ठाधिपः स्वगेहे वा देहे वाऽप्यष्टमे स्थितः ।
तदा व्रणो भवेद्देहे षष्ठराशिसमाश्रिते ॥२॥

2. *ULCERS/BRUISES :* Should the 6th lord be in the 6th itself or in the ascendant/8th, there will be ulcers or bruises on the body. The sign becoming the 6th house will lead to the knowledge of the concerned limb.

एवं पित्रादिभावेशास्तत्तत्कारकसंयुताः ।
व्रणाधिपयुताश्चापि षष्ठाष्टमयुता यदि ॥३॥
तेषामपि व्रणं वाच्यमादित्येन शिरोव्रणम् ।
इन्दुना च मुखे कण्ठे भौमेन ज्ञेन नाभिषु ॥४॥
गुरुणा नासिकायां च भृगुणा नयने पदे ।
शनिना राहुणा कुक्षौ केतुना च तथा भवेत् ॥५॥

3-5. *RELATIVES AFFECTED :* The Karaka of a relative or the lord of such a house joining the 6th lord or being in the 6th/8th house indicates ulcers/bruises to such a relative like father. The Sun with such lordship and in such a house denotes such affectation of head, the Moon face, Mars neck, Mercury navel, Jupiter nose, Venus eyes, Saturn feet and the nodes abdomen.

Notes : In these three slokas, we are instructed to know of the possible afflictions to the natlve's relatives and to the native himself — both from the horoscope of the native.

Firstly a certain significator or a certain bhava lord should join the 6th lord or be in the 6th/8th house so that the relative signified by the said Karaka incurs ulcers, bruises etc. For example, in a Sagittarius Lagna horoscope, the 6th lord is Venus. The 6th is Taurus and the 8th is Cancer. Suppose the 4th lord Jupiter or the Matrukaraka Moon (signifying mother) joins Venus or is in Taurus. (Cancer though the 8th house, the Moon therein should not be deemed harmful in this regard and Jupiter in Cancer will not also afflict the mother as he is exalted there and protects the 4th by aspect.) As a result, the mother will incur ulcer, bruises etc.

The relatives signified by planets and Bhavas are denoted in ch. 32, *infra.*

The second clue is to know the possible affliction, to the native, of a particular area in the body. If the Sun is the lord of the 6th house or is with the 6th lord or is in the 6th/8th, the native will be apt to incur affliction of head, and so on and forth. As regards, Rahu and Ketu, they do not own any house in the normal context. Hence their position in the 6th/8th or goining the 6th lord need only be considered. Rahu or Ketu in the 6th/8th will cause stomachial disorders.

लग्नाधिपः कुजक्षेत्रे बुधभे यदि संस्थितः ।
यत्र कुत्र स्थितो ज्ञेन वीक्षितो मुखरुक्प्रदः ॥६॥

6. *FACIAL DISEASES :* Should the lord of the ascendant be in a sign of Mars or of Mercury and be aspected Merury, there will be diseases of the face.

Notes : The lord of the ascendant should be in Aries, Scorpio, Gemini or Virgo and be aspected by Mercury. Even if Mars, ruling the ascendant, is in Gemini or in Virgo and is aspected by Mercury, the native will suffer facial diseases. The occupation can be in any bhava.

As regards Aries Lagna and Scorpio Lagna a different look be given to the placement of Mars in own sign. For Aries Lagna, Mars in Scorpio or for Scorpio Lagna, Mars in Aries and aspected by Mercury will not produce the said adversity, unless Mars is seriously afflicted otherwise.

लग्नाधिपौ कुजबुधौ चन्द्रेण यदि संयुतौ।
राहुणा शनिना सार्द्धं कुष्ठं तत्र विनिर्दिशेत् ॥७॥
लग्नाधिपं विना लग्ने स्थितश्चेत्तमसा शशी।
श्वेतकुष्ठं तदा कृष्णकुष्ठं च शनिना सह ॥८॥
कुजेन रक्तकुष्ठं स्यात्तत्तदेवं विचारयेत् ॥८½॥

7-8½. *LEPROSY :* Mars or Mercury having ownership of the ascending sign and joining the Moon, Rahu and Saturn, will cause leprosy. If the Moon is in the ascendant which is not however Cancer and be with Rahu, there will occur white leprosy. Saturn in place of Rahu will cause black leprosy while Mars similarly will afflict one with blood-leprosy.

लग्ने षष्ठाष्टमाधीशौ रविणा यदि संयुतौ ॥९॥
ज्वरगण्डः कुजे ग्रन्थिः शस्त्रव्रणमथापि वा।
बुधेन पित्तं गुरुणा रोगाभावं विनिर्दिशेत् ॥१०॥
स्त्रीभिः शुक्रेण, शशिना वायुना संयुतो यदि।
गण्डश्चाण्डालतो नाभौ तमःकेतुयुते भयम् ॥११॥
चन्द्रेण गण्डः सलिलैः कफश्लेष्मादिना भवेत्।
एवं पित्रादिभानां तत्तत्कारकयोगतः ॥१२॥
गण्डं तेषां वदेदेवमूह्यमत्र मनीषिभिः ॥१२½॥

9-12½. *DISEASES IN GENERAL :* If the ascendant is occupied by the lords of the 6th and 8th along with the Sun, the native will be afflicted by fever and tumours. Mars replacing the Sun will cause swelling and hardening of the blood vessels and wounds and hits by weapons. Mercury so featuring will bring in billious diseases while Jupiter in similar case will destroy any disease. Similarly Venus will cause diseases through females, Saturn windy diseases, Rahu danger through low-castemen and Ketu navel diseases, The Moon in such a conjunction will inflict dangers through water and phlegmatic disorders. Similar estimates be made from the respective significators and Bhavas for relatives like father.

Notes : The hints given above can be summed up as under :

Lords of the 6th and 8th in the ascendant being

with the Sun	: Tumours, fever etc.
,, Mars	: Diseases of blood vessels, hits, wounds etc.
,, Mercury	: Bilious disease (like : jaundice).
,, Jupiter	: Freedom from diseases.
,, Venus	: Diseases caused by sexual union.
,, Saturn	: Windy diseases like rheumatism, artheritis, paralysis etc.
,, Rahu	: Danger from the so called low-caste men.
,, Ketu	: Diseases of the navel.
,, the Moon	: Drowning, cough, tuberculosis, asthma and other lung disorders.

Replacing the ascendant with a certain bhava, these afflictions to the concerned relatives be predicted. For example, if the 6th and 8th lords join the Moon in the 3rd bhava, danger to coborn by drowning, lung disorders etc. be known. Should Venus join the 6th and 8th lords in the 11th house, an elder brother of the native will incur venereal diseases.

Thus the clues given by the sage should be extensively and effectively applied in regard to diseases for the native and his relatives.

The afflictions to be caused by the planets, signs etc. have been rather exhaustively given in the notes in ch. 47 of my English translation of **Saravali.** Though it was in the context of death, the same may be carefully used in knowing diseases as well. The reader may accordingly consult the said Notes.

Dr. H. L. Cornell, M. D., in his **'Encyclopaedia of Medical Astrology'** enlists some important diseases under different planetary captions. By way of adding useful information for the benefit of the inquisitive reader, I quote some as below :

The Sun : diseases of the nerves of the brain, cellular excitation, blood affliction, weak constitution, dryness, apoplexy, diseases of arteries, bowel disorders, pimples, skin and throat affliction, chronic inflamation, conjuctivities, diphtheria, dizziness, dropsy (Hindu astrology relates dropsy to Jupiter), fever, fistula, giddiness, glaucoma, violent pains and headaches, organic heart troubles, palpitation disorders, hyperanaemia, afflictions to excretory and generative systems, measles, obstruction in the stomach, quinsy, scrofula, scurvy, sharpness of urine, smallpox, disorders of spine, strangury, sunstrokes, swellings in neck or feet, tremblings, tumours, venereal distempers *etc.*

The Moon : gaseous distention of abdomen, abscesses, diseases of alimentary canal, disorders of bladder, blindness, disorders of bowels, disorders of the brain substance, bronchial disorders, cancer, carditis, catarrh, cellular zymosis, worms in children, colds, conjuctivitis, rotten coughs, delirium (Rahu is the main planet for delirium according to Hindu astrology), diarrhoea, irregular menses, menstrual disorders, dyspepsia, effusions, epilepsy, eruptions, disorders of eyes, gout in feet, osmosis, leucorrhoea, diseases of genetals, defects in haemoglobin, hysteria, mental ill health, stone in Kidneys (also Venus indicates this disorder), scrofula, disorders of larynx, disorders of breasts, diseases of mucous and serous membranes, miscarriage. obstruction of bowels and lungs, phthisis, premature births, profluvial effusions, thin blood, disorders of uterus, vomitting *etc.* She will also cause liver defects for women (while Jupiter afflicts the male's liver).

Mars : death by abortions, disorders of vessels, bleeding, excessive menses, boils, affections and pains in breasts, burns, bruises, carbuncles, chickenpox, cholera, congestion of blood, consumption, contagious fevers, cutaneous eruptions, fatty degeneration of the heart, dysentery, epidemics, fractures and falls, disorders of geneto-urinary system, gonorrhoea, haemoptysis, hernia, hysteria, itches, loss of blood, hemorrhage of lungs, malaria (also under Rahu), ulceration of penis, perityphlitis, piles, semitertial fevers, syphilis, extreme heat in throat, tonsils, vascular excitement, abscess of vulva, yellow jaundice *etc.*

Mercury : nervous complaints, asthma, apoplexy, impure blood, disorders caused to brain by overwork, rapid breathing, shortness of breathing, colic in the bowels, cramps in the arms, shoulders, legs and feet, dumbness, falling fits, flatulent colic, gastro—abdominal troubles, hyperasthesia, insomnia, neuralgia in and obstruction of kidneys, paralysis of the nervous system, pulmonary diseases, quivering, griplings in stomach, suppression of urine, heart tremours, lowering or exhausting of the vital fluids of the nerves, worms in bowels *etc.*

Jupiter : Jupiter will not cause any disease by himself but when afflicted in the figure by adverse heavenly bodies. Such are : Adiposis (excessive formation of adipose tissue), disorders of adrenals, diseases from corrupt air, alterations in the red blood particles, disorders of arterial blood, disorders in the back and of backbone, stone in bladder, cancer of the breast, cerebral congestion, digestive disorders, dropsy, affections of the ear, eczema, tumour of kidneys, disturbances of milk glands, fatty degeneration of muscles, plethoric and sthenic distentions, potato like cancer, thoracic diathesis, pains in vertebrae, diseases of viscera, liver and spleen.

Venus : comedo, disorders of bowels (like distempers, flux and mucus in bowels), breathing disorders (caused by tight lacing and indiscretions in dress), Bright's Disease, poor circulation of venous blood, clogging of the system, disorders caused by wrong use of cosmetics, diabetes, diphtheria, enlarged tonsils, humorous discharge from eyes, skin eruptions and diseases in feet, bilious flatulency, hysteria, diseases of kidneys, King's Evil, diseases of matrix, Night Losses (discharge in sleep), venereal disorders, disorders of thorax, Typhus Fever, urine infection, *etc.*

Saturn : antiperistalsis, arthritis, articular rheumatism, black jaundice, fractures of and pains in bones, chronic bronchitis, impotence, club feet, colds, deafness, dyspnoea, typhoid, disorders of foetus and troubles during conception, narrowing of passages heart affected by poison, depression in skull, lumpy and hard stools, ablation of tonsils, dental diseases *etc.*

How to apply these diseases is entirely a different matter. The reader will have to make judgements of his based on his own experience, and from various angles.

रोगस्थानगते पापे तदीशे पापसंयुते ॥१३॥
राहुणा संयुते मन्दे सर्वदा रोगसंयुतः ।
रोगस्थानगते भौमे तदीशे रंध्रसंयुते ॥१४॥

षड्वर्षे द्वादशे वर्षे ज्वररोगी भवेन्नरः।
षष्ठस्थानगते जीवे तद्गृहे चन्द्रसंयुते ॥१५॥
द्वाविंशैकोनविंशेऽब्दे कुष्ठरोगं विनिर्दिशेत्।
रोगस्थानं गतो राहुः केन्द्रे मान्दिसमन्विते ॥१६॥
लग्नेशे नाशराशिस्थे षड्विंशे क्षयरोगता।
व्ययेशे रोगराशिस्थे तदीशे व्ययराशिगे ॥१७॥
त्रिंशद्वर्षैकोनवर्षे गुल्मरोगं विनिर्दिशेत्।
रिपुस्थनगते चन्द्रे शशिना संयुते सति ॥१८॥
पञ्चपञ्चाशदब्देषु रक्तकुष्ठं विनिर्दिशेत्।
लग्नेशे लग्नराशिस्थे मन्दे शत्रुसमन्विते ॥१९॥
एकोनषष्टिवर्षे तु वातरोगादितो भवेत् ॥१९½॥

13-19½. *TIMING OF ILLNESS :* The native will be afflicted by illness throughout life if Saturn is with Rahu while the 6th lord and 6th house are conjunct malefics. One will suffer from (severe) fever at the age of 6 and at the age of 12 if Mars is in the 6th while the 6th lord is in the 8th. If the Moon is in Sagittarius/Pisces while Jupiter is in the 6th from the ascendant, one will suffer from leprosy at the age of 19 and 22. If Rahu is in the 6th, ascendant lord is in the 8th and Mandi is in an angle, consumption will trouble the native at the age of 26. Spleenary disorders will be experienced at the age of 29 and 30 if the lords of 6th and 12th are in exchange of their signs. Saturn and the Moon together in the 6th will inflict blood—leprosy at the age of 45. If Saturn is with an inimical planet while the ascendant lord is in the ascendant itself windy disorders (like rheumatism) will trouble the native at the age of 59.

रंध्रेशे रिपुराशिस्थे व्ययेशे लग्नसंस्थिते ॥२०॥
चन्द्रे षष्ठेशसंयुक्ते वसुवर्षे मृगाद्भयम्।
षष्ठाष्टमगतो राहुस्तस्मादष्टगते शनौ ॥२१॥
जातस्य जन्मतो विप्र! प्रथमे च द्वितीयके।
वत्सरेऽग्निभयं तस्य त्रिवर्षे पक्षिदोषभाक् ॥२२॥

20-22. *UNFORTUNATE YEARS :* Should the Moon be conjunct the 6th lord while the 8th lord is in the 6th and the

12th lord is in the ascendant, the native will be troubled by animals at the age of eight. O Brahmin, if Rahu is in the 6th while Saturn is in the 8th from the said Rahu, the child will have danger through fire at the age 1 and 2 while in the 3rd year birds will bring some evils.

षष्ठाष्टमगते सूर्ये तद्व्यये चन्द्रसंयुत।
पंचमे नवमेऽब्दे तु जलभीतिं विनिर्दिशेत् ॥२३॥
अष्टमे मन्दसंयुक्ते तस्माद्वा द्वादशे कुजः।
त्रिंशाब्दे दशमेऽब्दे तु स्फोटकादि विनिर्दिशेत् ॥२४॥
रंध्रेशे राहुसंयुक्ते तदंशे रंध्रकोणगे।
द्वाविंशेऽष्टादशे वर्षे ग्रन्थिमेहादिपीडनम् ॥२५॥

23-25. *UNFORTUNATE YEARS (continued) :* Danger through water will have to be feared during the 5th and the 9th years if the Sun is in the 6th or 8th while the Moon is in the 12th from the said Sun. Saturn in the 8th as Mars is in the 7th will cause small-pox, in the 10th year and 30th year of age. If 8th lord joins Rahu in an angle/trine from the 8th house and be in the 8th in Navamsa, the subject will be troubled by swelling of blood vessels, urinary disorders etc. during the 18th year and the 22nd year.

Notes : The evils narrated above relating to the 18th/22nd year of age need some clarification. The 8th lord should be conjunct Rahu in the 2nd, 4th, 5th, 11th or 12th from the ascendant. The said 8th lord should simultaneously be in the 8th place from the Navamsa ascendant (i.e. in the 8th in Navamsa chart). As a result, the native will incur urinary and blood vessel disorders in 18th/22nd year of age.

लाभेशे रिपुभावस्थे रोगेशे लाभराशिगे।
एकत्रिंशत्समे वर्षे शत्रुमूलाद्धनव्ययः ॥२६॥

26. *LOSS THROUGH ENEMIES :* Loss of wealth will come to pass during the 31st year if the 11th and 6th lords exchange their Rasis.

सुतेशे रिपुभावस्थे षष्ठेशे गुरुसंयुते।
व्ययेशे लग्नभावस्थे तस्य पुत्रो रिपुर्भवेत् ॥२७॥

27. *INIMICAL SONS :* One's own sons will be his enemies if the 5th lord is in the 6th while the 6th lord is with Jupiter. Simultaneously the 12th lord should be in the ascendant.

लग्नेशे षष्ठराशिस्थे तदीशे षष्ठराशिगे।
दशमैकोनविंशेऽब्दे शुनकाद्भीतिरुच्यते ॥२८॥

28. *FEAR FROM DOGS :* There will be fear from dogs during the 10th and 19th year if the ascendant lord and the 6th lord are in exchange.

अथ जायाभावफलाध्याय: ॥१८॥

Chapter 18

Effects Of The Seventh House

जायाभावफलं वक्ष्ये श्रृणु त्वं द्विजसत्तम!।
जायाधिपे स्वभे स्वोच्चे स्त्रीसुखं पूर्णमादिशेत् ॥१॥

1. O excellent of the Brahmins, listen to me detailing the effects of the 7th house. If the 7th lord is in his own sign or in exaltation, one will derive full happiness through his wife (and marriage),

कलत्रपो विना स्वर्क्षं व्ययषष्ठाष्टमस्थित:।
रोगिणीं कुरुते नारीं तथा तुङ्गादिकं विना ॥२॥

2. *SICK WIFE :* Should the 7th lord be in the 6th, 8th or the 12th, the wife will be sickly. This, however, does not apply to own house or exaltation placement as above.

Notes : The placement of the 7th lord in the 6th/8th/12th will cause a sickly wife. (Similarly Venus in an evil house). If the said house happens to be exaltation or own sign, then this need not be feared. For example, Saturn in Capricorn for a Leo native or Venus in Pisces for an Aries native.

सप्तमे तु स्थिते शुक्रेऽतीवकामी भवेन्नरः।
यत्र-कुत्र-स्थिते पापयुते स्त्रीमरणं भवेत् ॥३॥

3. *EXCESSIVE LIBIDINOUSNESS/DEATH OF WIFE :* If Venus is in the 7th, the native will be exceedingly libidinous. Venus joining a malefic in any house will cause loss of wife.

जायाधीशः शुभैर्युक्तो दृष्टो वा बलसंयुतः।
तदा जातो धनी मानी सुखसौभाग्यसंयुतः ॥४॥
नीचे शत्रुगृहेऽस्ते वा निर्बले च कलत्रपे।
तस्यापि रोगिणी भार्या बहुभार्यो नरो भवेत् ॥५॥

4-5. *THE 7TH LORD :* Should the 7th lord be endowed with strength and be conjunct or be aspected by a benefic, the native will be wealthy, honourable, happy and fortunate. Conversely, if the 7th lord is in fall or is combust or is in an enemy's sign, one will acquire sick wives and many wives.

Notes : Plurality of wives and sickness to them will come to pass with the 7th lord's occupying his sign of debilitation or having got combust or inimical placement. There is more to the 7th lord for plurality of wives than what it stated, as it will be evident from practical experience. However, this affliction to the 7th lord will cause delays and disappointments in respect of marriage apart from sickness to spouse. If the 7th lord is in an enemy's sign, the native's wife will scarcely honour him.

मन्दभे शुक्रगेहे वा जायाधीशे शुभेक्षिते।
स्वोच्चगे तु विशेषेण बहुभार्यो नरो भवेत् ॥६॥

6. *PLURALITY OF WIVES :* If the 7th lord is in a sign of Saturn or of Venus and be aspected by a benefic, there will be many wives. Should the 7th lord be particularly in exaltation, the same effects will come to pass.

वन्ध्यासङ्गो भवे भानौ चन्द्रे राशिसमस्त्रियः।
कुजे रजस्वलासङ्गो वन्ध्यासङ्गश्च कीर्तितः ॥७॥

बुधे वेश्या च हीना च वणिक् स्त्री वा प्रकीर्तिता ।
गुरौ ब्राह्मणभार्या स्याद्गर्भिणीसङ्ग एव च ॥८॥
हीना च पुष्पिणी वाच्या मन्दराहुफणीश्वरैः ।

7-8½. *MISCELLANEOUS MATTERS :* The native will befriend barren females (for sexual union) if the Sun is in the 7th. The Moon therein will cause association with such females as corresponding to the sign becoming the 7th. Mars placed in the 7th will denote association with marriageable girls (or those with menses) or with barren females. Mercury indicates harlots, mean females and females belonging to traders' community. Wife of a Brahmin or a pregnant female will be in the native's association if Jupiter is in the 7th. Base females and females having attained their courses are denoted by Saturn/Rahu/Ketu in the 7th.

Notes : Any planet in the 7th (including the 7th lord, vide ch. 24, sloka 79) is normally indicative of absence of sterlingness in character in the mattet of sexual union.

If the Sun is in the 7th in a horoscope promising lose character, the native will seek pleasures from females who are barren. As regards the Moon, the kind of females to sexually intercourse with, will correspond to the sign becoming the 7th house. For example, when Virgo becomes the 7th house the female is a virgin; Libra prostitutes, Gemini a house wife and so on and so forth. Mars in the 7th denotes a female that has come of marriageable age or one who is in her monthly course or one devoid of conceiving ability. Similarly, in other cases. Jnpiter in the 7th is also no exception.

The above results should be declared, only after ensuring that the native is primarily disposed to go out of the way for sexual union, with the support of other horoscopic indications.

कुजेऽथ सुस्तनी मन्दे व्याधिदौर्बल्यसंयुता ॥९॥
कठिनोर्ध्वकुचार्ये च शुक्रे स्थूलोत्तमस्तनी ।

9-9½. Mars denotes a female with attractive breasts. Saturn indicates sick and weak spouse. Jupiter will bring a spouse with hard and prominent breasts while Venus will bring one with bulky and excellent breasts.

Notes : Though there is no specific word in the above lines to mean "spouse", these planets (related to 7th house by occupation, aspect or ownership) will cause obtainment of such wives. These can also indicate the kind of females that one sexually unites with.

पापे द्वादशकामस्थे क्षीणचन्द्रस्तु पञ्चमे ॥१०॥
जातश्च भार्यावश्यः स्यादिति जातिविरोधकृत् ।
जामित्रे मन्दभौमे च तदीशे मन्दभूमिजे ॥११॥
वेश्या वा जारिणी वाऽपि तस्य भार्या न संशयः ।
भौमांशकगते शुक्रे भौमक्षेत्रगतेऽथवा ॥१२॥
भौमयुक्ते च दृष्टे वा भगचुम्बनभाग् भवेत् ।
मन्दांशकगते शुक्रे मन्दक्षेत्रगतेऽपि च ॥१३॥
मन्दयुक्ते च दृष्टे च शिश्नचुम्बनतत्परः ।

10-13½. Malefics in the 12th and 7th while decreasing Moon is in the 5th denote that the native will be controlled by his spouse who will be inimical to the race (or family). If the 7th house is occupied or owned by Saturn/Mars, the native will beget a harlot as his spouse or she will be attached to other men illegally. Should Venus be in a Navamsa of Mars or in a Rasi of Mars or be in aspect to or conjunct Mars, the native will "kiss" the private parts of the female. If Venus is so related to Saturn, the native will "kiss" the private parts of the male.

Notes : There are four hints given in the above verses, as under :

1. The Moon with decreasing rays in the 5th house while the 12th and the 7th are occupied by malefic planets the spouse will be high-handed and will be at loggerheads with the family members of the native.

2. Saturn or Mars in the 7th house, or owning the 7th house : the spouse will be of questionable character. While the placement of Saturn (and) or Mars in the 7th house is bad for the character of the spouse, Mars or Saturn ruling the 7th house should not simply lead to the fruition of the said effect. Cancer, Leo, Taurus and Libra or such ascendants have the 7th lordship of Saturn or Mars. So to say, in the case of

these four ascendants, there must be severe affliction to the 7th from other sources so that the spouse is not chaste in character.

3. The native will indulge in kissing the privities of the female if Venus is in a Rasi or Navamsa of Mars, or is aspected by or in conjunction with Mars. That is, he will have unusual habits in the matter of sexual gratification from the female.

4. Venus, if related to Saturn and his divisions instead of to Mars and his divisions as stated in point 3 above, the native will have ugly relations with another male, for subduing his mad lust.

दारेशे स्वोच्चराशिस्थे मदे शुभसमन्विते ॥१४॥
लग्नेशो बलसंयुक्तः कलत्रस्थानसंयुतः ।
तद्भार्या सद्गुणोपेता पुत्रपौत्रप्रवर्धिनी ॥१५॥

14-15. *WORTHY SPOUSE :* The native will beget a spouse endowed with (the seven principal) virtues who will expand his dynasty by sons and grandsons if the 7th lord is exalted while the 7th is occupied by strong ascendant lord and a benefic.

Notes : The above verses hint at the possibility of the native obtaining children (and grandchildren) if the ascendant lord with strength is in the 7th with a benefic as the 7th lord is disposed in exaltation sign. The combination in question is meant for the native begetting a virtuous wife as well. The mere exaltation of the 7th lord is capable of bestowing a virtuous wife, if not progeny.

कलत्रे तत्पतौ वापि पापग्रहसमन्विते ।
भार्याहानिं वदेत् तस्य निर्बले च विशेषतः ॥१६॥

16. *EVILS TO SPOUSE :* If the 7th house or its lord is conjunct a malefic the native's wife will incur evils, especially if the 7th house or its lord is bereft of strength.

षष्ठाष्टमव्ययस्थाने मदेशो दुर्बलो यदि ।
नीचराशिगतो वापि दारनाशं विनिर्दिशेत् ॥१७॥

17. *LOSS OF SPOUSE :* If the 7th lord is devoid of strength and is relegated to the 6th, 8th or the 12th, or if the 7th

lord is in fall, the native's wife will be destroyed (i.e. she will die early).

कलत्रस्थानगे चन्द्रे तदीशे व्ययराशिगे।
कारको बलहीनश्च दारसौख्यं न विद्यते ॥१८॥

18. *LACK OF CONJUGAL FELICITY* : If the Moon is in the 7th as the 7th lord is in the 12th and the Karaka (indicator Venus) is bereft of strength, the native will not be endowed with marital happiness.

Notes : The Moon referred to here should obviously be decreasing. The Moon increasing, while although the other part of the planetary conditions as stated in the sloka is fulfilled, will stall the adversity and improve the situation.

सप्तमेशे स्वनीचस्थे पापर्क्षे पापसंयुते।
सप्तमे क्लीबराश्यंशे द्विभार्यो जातको भवेत् ॥१९॥
कलत्रस्थानगे भौमे शुक्रे जामित्रगे शनौ।
लग्नेशे रन्ध्रराशिस्थे कलत्रत्रयवान् भवेत् ॥२०॥
द्विस्वभावगते शुक्रे स्वोच्चे तद्राशिनायके।
दारेशे बलसंयुक्ते बहुदारसमन्वितः ॥२१॥

19-21. *PLURALITY OF WIVES* : One will have two wives if the 7th lord is in fall, or in a malefic's sign along with a malefic while the 7th house or the 7th Navamsa belongs to a eunuch planet. If Mars and Venus are in the 7th or if Saturn is in the 7th while the lord of the ascendant is in the 8th, the native will have 3 wives. There will be many wives if Venus is in a dual sign while its lord is in exaltation as the 7th lord is endowed with strength.

Notes : For a dual marriage, the 7th from the natal ascendant or the 7th from Navamsa ascendant should be owned by a eunuch planet. So to say, Gemini, Virgo, Capricorn or Aquarius should be the 7th as above. While this is fulfilled, the 7th lord (from natal ascendant) should be in his sign of debilitation or in a malefic's sign along with a malefic.

The other two yogas are simple and need no elaboration.

दारेशे शुभराशिस्थे स्वोच्चस्वर्क्षगतो भृगुः ।
पञ्चमे नवमेऽब्दे तु विवाहः प्रायशो भवेत् ॥२२॥

22. *TIME OF MARRIAGE (upto sloka 34) :* If the 7th lord is in a benefic's house (or in the 9th as subha Rasi so means) while Venus is exalted or is in own sign, the native will marry at the age of 5 or 9.

Notes : The age of marriage indicated in the text will not be practical in all cases in the modern social conditions. These will be simply helpful in knowing of early and belated marriages. For example, the present sloka should tell us of the possibility of early marriage, if not literally at the age of 5 or 9.

दारस्थानं गते सूर्ये तदीशे भृगुसंयुते ।
सप्तमैकादशे वर्षे विवाहः प्रायशो भवेत् ॥२३॥

23. If the Sun is in the 7th while his dispositor is conjunct Venus, there will be marriage at 7th or 11th year of age.

कुटुम्बस्थानगे शुक्रे दारेशे लाभराशिगे ।
दशमे षोडशाऽब्दे च विवाहः प्रायशो भवेत् ॥२४॥

24. Venus in the 2nd while the 7th lord is in the 11th will give marriage at the age of 10 or 16.

लग्नकेन्द्रगते शुक्रे लग्नेशे मन्दराशिगे ।
वत्सरैकादशे प्राप्ते विवाहं लभते नरः ॥२५॥

25. Marriage will take place during the 11th year if Venus is in an angle from the ascendant while the ascendant lord is in Capricorn/Aquarius.

लग्नात् केन्द्रगते शुक्रे तस्मात् कामगते शनौ ।
द्वादशैकोनविंशे च विवाहः प्रायशो भवेत् ॥२६॥

26. The native will marry at 12 or 19 if Venus is in an angle from the ascendant while Saturn is in the 7th counted from Venus.

चन्द्राज्जामित्रगे शुक्रे शुक्राज्जामित्रगे शनौ ।
वत्सरेऽष्टादशे प्राप्ते विवाहं लभते नरः ॥२७॥

27. Should Venus be in the 7th from Moon while Saturn is in the 7th from Venus, marriage will be in the 18th year.

धनेशे लाभराशिस्थे लग्नेशे कर्मराशिगे।
अब्दे पञ्चदशे प्राप्ते विवाहं लभते नरः ॥२८॥

28. Marriage will be in the 15th year if the 2nd lord is in the 11th while the ascendant lord is in the 10th.

धनेशे लाभराशिस्थे लाभेशे धनराशिगे।
अब्दे त्रयोदशे प्राप्ते विवाहं लभते नरः ॥२९॥

29. An exchange between the lords of the 2nd and the 11th will bring marriage 13 years after birth.

रन्ध्राज्जामित्रगे शुक्रे तदीशे भौमसंयुते।
द्वाविंशे सप्तविंशेऽब्दे विवाहं लभते नरः ॥३०॥

30. One's 22nd/27th year will confer marriage if Venus is in the 7th from the 8th house (i.e. the 2nd from ascendant), while his dispositor is conjunct Mars.

Notes : The Yogas given from this sloka through sloka 34 will delay one's marriage as could be easily understood.

दारांशकगते लग्न-नाथे दारेश्वरे व्यये।
त्रयोविंशे च षड्विंशे विवाहं लभते नरः ॥३१॥

31. Should the 7th lord be in the 12th while the natal ascendant lord is in the 7th in Navamsa, marriage will be in 23rd/26th year of age.

Notes : The ascendant lord (in Rasi chart) should be in the 7th sign in Navamsa chart while the 7th lord in Rasi is in the years 12th in Rasi to give marriage at 23/26 of age.

रन्ध्रेशे दारराशिस्थे लग्नांशे भृगुसंयुते।
पञ्चविंशे त्रयस्त्रिंशे विवाहं लभते नरः ॥३२॥

32. Either the 25th year or the 33rd year will bring marriage if the 8th lord is in the 7th as Venus is in Navamsa ascendant.

भाग्याद्भाग्यगते शुक्रे तद्द्वये राहुसंयुते।
एकत्रिंशात्त्रयस्त्रिंशे दारलाभं विनिर्दिशेत् ॥३३॥

33. Should Venus be in the 9th from the 9th (i.e. in the

5th house), while Rahu is in one of the said houses (i.e. in the 5th/9th), marriage will take place during 31st or 33rd year.

भाग्याज्जामित्रगे शुक्रे तद्द्यूने दारनायके।
त्रिंशे वा सप्तविंशाब्दे विवाहं लभते नरः ॥३४॥

34. The native will marry at 30 or 27 if Venus is in the ascendant while the 7th lord is in the 7th itself.

दारेशे नीचराशिस्थे शुक्रे रन्ध्रारिसंयुते।
अष्टादशे त्रयस्त्रिंशे वत्सरे दारनाशनम् ॥३५॥
मदेशे नाशराशिस्थे व्ययेशे मदराशिगे।
तस्य चैकोनविंशाब्दे दारनाशं विनिर्दिशेत् ॥३६॥
कुटुम्बस्थानगो राहुः कलत्रे भौमसंयुते।
पाणिग्रहे च त्रिदिने सर्पदष्टे वधूमृतिः ॥३७॥
रन्ध्रस्थानगते शुक्रे तदीशे सौरिराशिगे।
द्वादशैकोनविंशाब्दे दारनाशं विनिर्दिशेत् ॥३८॥
लग्नेशे नीचराशिस्थे धनेशे निधनं गते।
त्रयोदशे तु सम्प्राप्ते कलत्रस्य मृतिर्भवेत् ॥३९॥

35-39. *TIMING OF WIFE'S DEATH :* Loss of wife will occur in the 18th year or 33rd year of age of the native if the 7th lord is in fall while Venus is in the 8th. One will lose his spouse in his 19th year if the 7th lord is in the 8th while the 12th lord is in the 7th. The native's wife will die within three days of marriage due to snake bite if the native has Rahu in the 2nd and Mars in the 7th. If Venus is in the 8th while his dispositor is in a sign of Saturn, death of wife will take place during the native's 12th or 21st year of age. Should the ascendant lord be in his sign of debilitation as the 2nd lord is in the 8th, loss of wife will occur in the 13th year of age.

शुक्राज्जामित्रगे चन्द्रे चन्द्राज्जामित्रगे बुधे।
रन्ध्रेशे सुतभावस्थे प्रथमं दशमाब्दिकम् ॥४०॥
द्वाविंशे च द्वितीयं च त्रयस्त्रिंशे तृतीयकम्।
विवाहं लभते मर्त्यो नाऽत्र कार्या विचारणा ॥४१॥

40-41. *THREE MARRIAGES :* Should the Moon be in the 7th from Venus while Mercury is in the 7th from the Moon and the 8th lord is in the 5th (from the ascendant), there will be marriage in the 10th year followed by another in the 22nd year and yet another in the 33rd year.

षष्ठे च भवने भौमः सप्तमे राहुसंस्थितिः ।
अष्टमे च यदा सौरिस्तस्य भार्या न जीवति ॥४२॥

42. *DEATH OF WIFE :* If the 6th, 7th and 8th are in their order occupied by Mars, Rahu and Saturn, the native's wife will not live (long).

अथ आयुर्भावफलाध्याय: ॥१९॥

Chapter 19

Effects Of The Eighth House

आयुर्भावफलं चाऽथ कथयामि द्विजोत्तम ! ।
आयुःस्थानाधिपः केन्द्रे दीर्घमायुः प्रयच्छति ॥१॥

1. *LONG LIFE :* O excellent of the Brahmins, listen to me speaking on the effects of the 8th house. If the 8th lord is in an angle, long life is indicated.

आयुस्थानाधिपः पापैः सह तत्रैव संस्थितः ।
करोत्यल्पायुषं जातं लग्नेशोऽप्यत्र संस्थितः ॥२॥

2. *SHORT LIFE :* Should the 8th lord join the ascendant lord or a malefic and be in the 8th itself, the native will be short-lived.

एवं हि शनिना चिन्ता कार्या तर्कैर्विचक्षणैः ।
कर्माधिपेन च तथा चिन्तनं कार्यमायुषः ॥३॥

3. *SATURN AND TENTH LORD ABOUT LONGEVITY :* Similarly consider Saturn and **10th lord** in the matter of longevity.

Notes : To get the actual import of this verse, we should read it in the context of the previous verse. So to say, short life will come to pass if :

1. The 8th lord is in the 8th along with a malefic or along with the ascendant lord or

2. Saturn joins a malefic/ascendant lord in the 8th house or

3. The 10th lord is in the 8th along with a malefic planet/ ascendant lord.

षष्ठे व्ययेऽपि षष्ठेशो व्ययाधीशो रिपौ व्यये ।
लग्नेऽष्टमे स्थितो वाऽपि दीर्घमायुः प्रयच्छति ॥४॥
स्वस्थाने स्वांशके वाऽपि मित्रेशे मित्रमन्दिरे ।
दीर्घायुषं करोत्येव लग्नेशोऽष्टमपः पुनः ॥५॥
लग्नाष्टमपकर्मेशमन्दाः केन्द्रत्रिकोणयोः ।
लाभे वा संस्थितास्तद्वद् दिशेयुर्दीर्घमायुषम् ॥६॥
एवं बहुविधा विद्वन्नायुर्योगाः प्रकीर्तिताः ।
एषु यो बलवांस्तस्याऽनुसारादायुरादिशेत् ॥७॥

4-7. *LONG LIFE :* There will be long life if the 6th lord is in the 12th or if the 6th lord is in the 6th as the 12th lord is in the 12th or if the 6th lord and 12th lord are in the ascendant and the 8th. If the lords of the 5th, 8th and ascendant are in own navamsas, own Rasis or in friendly signs, the native will enjoy a long span of life. Should the lords of the ascendant, 8th and 10th and Saturn are all disposed severally in an angle, in a trine or in the 11th, the subject will live long. Like these, there are many other yogas dealing with the issue of longevity. The strength and weakness of the planets concerned be estimated in deciding longevity.

Notes : In sloka 4, we have three yogas for long life. These are :

1. The 6th lord in the 12th.

2. The 6th and 12th lords simultaneously in the 6th and the 12th.

3. The 6th lord in the ascendant while the 12th lord is in the 8th.

The combinations given in the other two verses are quite clear.

अष्टमाधिपतौ केन्द्रे लग्नेशे बलवर्जिते ।
विंशद्वर्षाण्यसौ जीवेद् द्वात्रिंशत्परमायुषम् ॥८॥
रन्ध्रेशे नीचराशिस्थे रन्ध्रे पापग्रहैर्युते ।
लग्नेशे दुर्बले जन्तुरल्पायुर्भवति ध्रुवम् ॥९॥
रन्ध्रेशे पापसंयुक्ते रन्ध्रे पापग्रहैर्युते ।
व्यये क्रूरग्रहाक्रान्ते जातमात्रं मृतिर्भवेत् ॥१०॥
केन्द्रत्रिकोणगाः पापाः शुभाः षष्ठाष्टगा यदि ।
लग्ने नीचस्थ-रन्ध्रेशो जातः सद्यो मृतो भवेत् ॥११॥
पञ्चमे पापसंयुक्ते रन्ध्रेशे पापसंयुते ।
रन्ध्रे पापग्रहैर्युक्ते स्वल्पमायुः प्रजायते ॥१२॥
रन्ध्रेशे रन्ध्रराशिस्थे चन्द्रे पापसमन्विते ।
शुभदृष्टिविहीने च मासान्ते च मृतिर्भवेत् ॥१३॥

8-13. *SHORT LIFE :* One's span of life will be between 20 and 32 years if the ascendant lord is weak while the 8th lord is in an angle. The native will only be short-lived if the 8th lord is in fall while the 8th has a malefic in it and the ascendant lord is bereft of strength. Death will be instant at birth if the 8th house, 8th lord and the 12th house are all conjunct malefics. Malefic in angles/trines and benefics in 6th/8th while the ascendant has in it the 8th lord in fall : this yoga will cause immediate end. If the 5th house, 8th house and the 8th lord are all conjunct malefics, the life span will be very brief. Within a month of birth, death will befall the child if the 8th lord is in the 8th itself while the Moon is with malefics and be bereft of beneficial aspect.

Notes : If the 8th lord is in an angle, the native will be long-lived, according to sloka 1 of the present chapter. The ascendant lord bereft of strength, in such a case, will reduce the life span as per verse 8 above. Hence it follows that the 8th lord's good disposition is alone not enough, but the power of ascendant lord is a simultaneous need, for a long life.

In sloka 12, it is stated that 8th lord should be in fall in the ascendant. For no ascendant, the 8th lord is debilitated in the ascending sign. This is possible when only the 8th bhava falls in the 7th or 9th sign. For example, in certain latitudes, suppose the last portion of Virgo rises. Then there is a possibility of the 8th cusp falling in Taurus. In that case, its ruler, Venus, can be debilitated in Virgo, the ascending sign. Otherwise, by signs it is not possible.

Should the 8th lord be in the 8th,, long life to the native is denoted. But when simultaneously the Moon is captured by a malefic and be without any help from a benefic, then early evils to life span will have to be predicted, vide sloka 13 above.

लग्नेशे स्वोच्चराशिस्थे चन्द्रे लाभसमन्विते।
रन्ध्रस्थानगते जीवे दीर्घमायुर्न संशयः ॥१४॥
लग्नेशोऽतिबली दृष्टः केन्द्रसंस्थैः शुभग्रहैः।
धनैः सर्वगुणैः सार्धं दीर्घमायुः प्रयच्छति ॥१५॥

14-15. *LONG LIFE (again)* : One will be longlived if the ascendant lord is in exaltation while the Moon and Jupiter are respectively in the 11th and 8th from the ascendant. If the ascendant lord is exceedingly strong and be aspected by a benefic from an angle, the person concerned will be wealthy, virtuous and longlived.

Notes : Even if Jupiter is lonely well-placed in the 8th house, it leads to a long span of life. If he is further helped by the Moon being in the 11th house and by the ascendant lord's exaltation, doubtlessly the life will be exceedingly lengthy.

अथ भाग्यभावफलाध्याय: ॥२०॥

Chapter 20

Effects Of The Ninth House

अथ भाग्यभावं विप्र ! फलं वक्ष्ये तवाऽग्रतः ।
सबलो भाग्यपे भाग्ये जातो भाग्ययुतो भवेत् ॥१॥
भाग्यस्थानगते जीवे यदीशे केन्द्रसंस्थिते ।
लग्नेशे बलसंयुक्ते बहुभाग्ययुतो भवेत् ॥२॥

1-2. *COMBINATIONS FOR FORTUNES :* O Brahmin, now listen to effects of the 9th house. One will be fortunate (or affluent) if the 9th lord is in the 9th with strength. Should Jupiter be in the 9th house while 9th lord is in an angle and the ascendant lord is endowed with strength, one will be extremely fortunate.

Notes : "Bhagyasthana" is a name given to the 9th house. "Bhagya" denotes fortunes, affluence etc. Hence from the 9th house, one's capacity to retain the wealth earned should be studied.

भाग्येशे बलसंयुक्ते भाग्ये भृगुसमन्विते ।
लग्नात् केन्द्रगते जीवे पिता भाग्यसमन्वितः ॥३॥

3. *FORTUNATE (AFFLUENT) FATHER :* If the 9th lord is with strength as Venus is in the 9th while Jupiter is in an angle from the ascendant, the native's father is fortunate.

भाग्यस्थानाद् द्वितीये वा सुखे भौमसमन्विते ।
भाग्येशे नीचराशिस्थे पिता निर्धन एव हि ॥४॥

4. *INDIGENT FATHER :* If the 9th lord is debiltated while the 2nd/4th from the 9th is occupied by Mars, the native's father is poor.

Notes : It is stated that Mars in the 10th or 12th from the ascendant (i.e. the 2nd or the 4th from the 9th) while the

9th lord is in debilitation denotes poverty of wealth for the father. Even if there be some wealth of the father, Mars in the 10th/12th (not being in own house or in exaltation) will make the native disinherit patrimony or enter into litigations. So to say, such patrimony will not come to the hands of the native, that too easily.

भाग्येशे परमोच्चस्थे भाग्यांशे जीवसंयुते ।
लग्नाच्चतुष्टये शुक्रे तत्पिता दीर्घजीवनः ॥५॥

5. *LONG LIVING FATHER :* Should the 9th lord be in deep exaltation while Venus is in angle from the ascendant and Jupiter is in the 9th from Navamsa Ascendant, the father of the native will enjoy a long-span of life.

भाग्येशे केन्द्रभावस्थे गुरुणा च निरीक्षिते ।
तत्पिता वाहनैर्युक्तो राजा वा तत्समो भवेत् ॥६॥

6. *ROYAL STATUS FOR FATHER :* If the 9th lord is an angle in aspect to Jupiter, the native's father will be a king endowed with conveyances or be equal to a king.

भाग्येशे कर्मभावस्थे कर्मेशे भाग्यराशिगे ।
शुभदृष्टे धनाढ्यश्च कीर्तिमांस्तत्पिता भवेत् ॥७॥

7. *WEALTHY AND FAMOUS FATHER :* Should the lord of the 9th be in the 10th while the 10th lord being aspected by a benefic the native's father will be very rich and famous.

परमोच्चांशगे सूर्ये भाग्येशे लाभसंस्थिते ।
धर्मिष्ठो नृपवात्सल्यः पितृभक्तो भवेन्नरः ॥८॥
लग्नात्त्रिकोणगे सूर्ये भाग्येशे सप्तमस्थिते ।
गुरुणा सहिते दृष्टे पितृभक्तिसमन्वितः ॥९॥

8-9. *VIRTUOUS AND DEVOTED TO FATHER :* Should the Sun be in deep exaltation as the 9th lord is in the 11th, the native will be virtuous, dear to king and devoted to father. If the Sun is in a trine from the ascendant while the 9th lord is in the 7th in conjnction with or in aspect to Jupiter, the native will be devoted to his father.

भाग्येशे धनभावस्थे धनेशे भाग्यराशिगे।
द्वात्रिंशात्परतो भाग्यं वाहनं कीर्तिसम्भवः ॥१०॥

10. *FORTUNES ETC. :* Aquisition of fortunes, conveyances and fame will follow the 32nd year of age if the 9th lord is in the 2nd while the 2nd lord is in the 9th.

लग्नेशे भाग्यराशिस्थे षष्ठेशेन समन्विते।
अन्योन्यवैरं ब्रुवते जनकः कुत्सितो भवेत् ॥११॥

11. *INIMICAL TO FATHER :* There will be mutual enmity between the father and the native if the ascendant lord is in the 9th but with the lord of the 6th. Further, the native's father will be of contemptible disposition.

कर्माधिपेन सहितो विक्रमेशोऽपि निर्बलः।
भाग्यपो नीचमूढस्थो योगो भिक्षाशनप्रदः ॥१२॥

12. *BEGGED FOOD :* If the 10th lord and 3rd lord are both bereft of strength while the 9th lord is in fall or in combustion, the native will go abegging for his food.

षष्ठाष्टमव्यये भानू रन्ध्रेशे भाग्यसंयुते।
व्ययेशे लग्नराशिस्थे षष्ठेशे पञ्चमे स्थिते ॥१३॥
जातस्य जननात्पूर्वं जनकस्य मृतिर्भवेत्।
रन्ध्रस्थानगते सूर्ये रन्ध्रेशे भाग्यभावगे ॥१४॥
जातस्य प्रथमाब्दे तु पितुर्मरणमादिशेत्।
व्ययेशे भाग्यराशिस्थे नीचांशे भाग्यनायके ॥१५॥
तृतीये षोडशे वर्षे जनकस्य मृतिर्भवेत्।
लग्नेशे नाशराशिस्थे रन्ध्रेशे भानुसंयुते ॥१६॥
द्वितीये द्वादशे वर्षे पितुर्मरणमादिशेत्।
भाग्याद्रन्ध्रगते राहौ भाग्याद्भाग्यगते रवौ ॥१७॥
षोडशेऽष्टादशे वर्षे जनकस्य मृतिर्भवेत्।
राहुणा सहिते सूर्ये चन्द्राद्भाग्यगते शनौ ॥१८॥
सप्तमैकोनविंशाब्दे तातस्य मरणं ध्रुवम्।
भाग्येशे व्ययराशिस्थे व्ययेशे भाग्यराशिगे ॥१९॥

वदाब्धिमितवर्षाच्च पितुर्मरणमादिशत् ।
रव्यंशे च स्थिते चन्द्रे लग्नेशे रन्ध्रसंयुते ॥२०॥
पञ्चत्रिंशैकचत्वारिंशद्वर्षे मरणं पितुः ।
पितृस्थानाधिपे सूर्ये मन्दभौमसमन्विते ॥२१॥
पञ्चाशद्वत्सरे प्राप्ते जनकस्य मृतिर्भवेत् ।
भाग्यात् सप्तमगे सूर्ये भ्रातृसप्तमगस्तमः ॥२२॥
षष्ठेऽब्दे पञ्चविंशाब्दे पितुर्मरणमादिशेत् ।
रन्ध्रजामित्रगे मन्दे मन्दाज्जामित्रगे रवौ ॥२३॥
त्रिंशैकविंशे षड्विंशे जनकस्य मृतिर्भवेत् ।
भाग्येशे नीचराशिस्थे तदीशे भाग्यराशिगे ॥२४॥
षड्विंशेऽब्दे त्र्यस्त्रिंशे पितुर्मरणमादिशेत् ।
एवं जातस्य दैवज्ञो फलं ज्ञात्वा विनिर्दिशेत् ॥२५॥

13-25. *COMBINATIONS FOR FATHER'S DEATH* : The father of the native would have passed away prior to the native's birth if the Sun is in the 6th/8th/12th as the 8th lord is in the 9th, the 12th lord is in the ascendant, and the 6th lord is in the 5th house. Should the Sun be in the 8th while the 8th lord is in the 9th, the native's father will pass away within a year of his birth. If the lord of the 12th is in the 9th while the 9th lord is in debilitation Navamsa, the native's father will face his end during the 3rd/16th year of the native. Death of father will occur in the 2nd or 12th year if the ascendant lord is in the 8th as the 8th lord is with the Sun. Should Rahu be in the 8th from the 9th (i.e. 4th from the ascendant) as the Sun is in the 9th from the 9th (i.e. 5th from the ascendant), death of father will take place in the 16th/18th year of the native. If Saturn is in the 9th from the Moon as the Sun is with Rahu, the native's father will die in the 7th or the 19th year of the native. The native in his 44th year will lose his father if the 9th lord is in the 12th as the 12th lord is in the 9th. If the ascendant lord is in the 8th as the Moon is in the Sun's Navamas, the native in his 35th/41st year will lose his father. One will lose his father in the 50th year if the Sun, being the lord of the 9th, is conjunct Mars and Saturn. If the Sun is in the 7th from the 9th (i. e. 3rd from the ascendant) as Rahu is in the 7th from the 3rd (i.e. 9th from the ascendant), the 6th/25th year of the native will be fatal for father. If Saturn is in the 7th from the 8th (i. e. 2nd from the ascendant) as the Sun is in the 7th from Saturn (i.e. 8th from the ascendant), the ages of 30, 21 or 26 will be fatal for the father. If the 9th lord is in debilitation while his dispositor is in the 9th, the native will lose his father at 26 or 30. Thus the astrologers may know the effects (of the 9th house).

परमोच्चांशगे शुक्रे भाग्येशेन समन्विते।
भ्रातृस्थाने शनियुते बहुभाग्याधिपो भवेत् ॥२६॥

26. *FORTUNES :* One will enjoy abundant fortunes if Venus is in deep exaltation and be in the company of the 9th lord as Saturn is in the 3rd.

गुरुणा संयुते भाग्ये तदीशे केन्द्रराशिगे।
विंशद्वर्षात् परं चैव बहुभाग्यं विनिर्दिशेत् ॥२७॥
परमोच्चांशगे सौम्ये भाग्येशे भाग्यराशिगे।
षट्त्रिंशाच्च परं चैव बहुभाग्यं विनिर्दिशेत् ॥२८॥

27-28. *FORTUNATE PERIODS :* Abundant fortunes will be acquired after the 20th year if the 9th has Jupiter in it as its lord is in an angle from the ascendant. Should Mercury be in his deep exaltation as the 9th lord is in the 9th itself, abundant fortunes will be earned after the 36th year.

लग्नेशे भाग्यराशिस्थे भाग्येशे लग्नसंयुते।
गुरुणा संयुते द्यूने धनवाहनलाभकृत् ॥२९॥

29. Should the ascendant lord be in the 9th as the 9th lord is in the ascendant, and Jupiter is in the 7th, there will be gains of wealth and conveyances.

भाग्याद्भाग्यवतो राहुस्तदीशे निधनं गते।
भाग्येशे नीचराशिस्थे भाग्यहीनो भवेन्नरः ॥३०॥

30. *LACK OF FORTUNES :* If Rahu is in the 9th from the 9th (i. e. 5th from the ascendant), as his dispositor is in the 8th from the ascendant and the 9th lord is in fall, the native will be devoid of fortunes.

भाग्यस्थानगते मन्दे शशिना च समन्विते।
लग्नेशे नीचराशिस्थे भिक्षाशी च नरो भवेत् ॥३१॥

31. *FOOD BY BEGGING :* Should Saturn be in the 9th along with the Moon as the ascendant lord is in fall, the native will acquire food by begging.

एवं भाग्यफलं विप्र! संक्षेपात् कथितं मया।
लग्नेशभाग्यभावेशस्थित्याऽन्यदपि निर्दिशेत् ॥३२॥

32. O Brahmin, these are the effects related to the 9th house. I have explained (these) briefly. These may be (further) estimated with the help of the state of the lords of the ascendant and 9th and in other manners as well.

अथ कर्मभावफलाध्याय: ॥२१॥

Chapter 21

Effects of The Tenth House

कर्मभावफलं चाऽथ कथयामि तवाग्रतः।
शृणु मैत्रेय! तत्त्वेन ब्रह्म-गर्गादिभाषितम् ॥१॥

1. I now explain the effects of the 10th house. Listen to these, O Maitreya, in the words of Brahma, Garga and others.

Notes : Statements like **"Brahma Gargadi Bhashitam"** go to prove that sage Parasara, had access to such expositions of Lord Brahma which would not be possible to an ordinary mortal. The history of Parasara has been explained in the notes for the initial slokas of ch. 1 **supra** and ch. 41 **infra.**

सबले कर्मभावेशे स्वोच्चे स्वांशे स्वराशिगे।
जातस्तातसुखेनाढ्यो यशस्वी शुभकर्मकृत् ॥२॥

2. *PATERNAL HAPPINESS :* If the 10th lord is strong and be in exaltation or in own Rasi/Navamsa, the native will

derive extreme paternal happiness, will enjoy fame and will perform good deeds.

Notes : Though the word "Karma" means deed, it actually in the context of astrology denotes one's profession, job, livelihood etc. The 10th house rules one's patrimony, paternal happiness, last offices to father and such other matter while the 9th house, as explained earlier deals with one's father as an individual.

कर्माधिपो बलोनश्चेत् कर्मवैकल्यमादिशेत् ।
सैंहिः केन्द्रत्रिकोणस्थो ज्योतिष्टोमादियागकृत् ॥३॥

3. If the 10th lord is devoid of strength, the native will face obstructions in his work. If Rahu is in an angle or in a trine, he will perform religious sacrifices like *Jyotishtoma.*

Notes : Should Rahu be strongly disposed in an angle or in a trine, the native will perform *"Jyotishtoma."* This is Soma sacrifice deemed as a whole class of sacrificial ceremonies consisting of sixteen vedic rites. To wit, the native will be extremely religious and meritorious.

कर्मेशे शुभसंयुक्ते शुभस्थानगते तथा ।
राजद्वारे च वाणिज्ये सदा लाभोऽन्यथान्यथा ॥४॥

4. If the 10th lord is with a benefic or be in an auspicious house, one will always gain through royal patronage and in business. In a contrary situation, only opposite results will come to pass.

Notes : Should the 10th lord be with a benefic or in a benefic's Rasi, the native will ever gain in his undertakings with the king (*i.e.* in his calling). "अन्यथान्यथा" means that if the 10th lord is with a malefic or in a malefic's Rasi, the native will be a loser in his calling and will not serve the king (or a worthy person). The short and the long of the verse is to convey the idea that the 10th lord should be related to a benefic's sign for a happy and prosperous calling. Connections with a malefic will cause grief.

दशमे पापसंयुक्ते लाभे पापसमन्विते ।
दुष्कृतिं लभते मर्त्यः स्वजनानां विदूषकः ॥५॥

5. Should the 10th and 11th be both occupied by malefics the native will indulge only in bad deeds and will defile his own men.

कर्मेशे नाशराशिस्थे राहुणा संयुते तथा ।
जनद्वेषी महामूर्खो दुष्कृतिं लभते नरः ॥६॥

6. If the lord of the 10th is relegated to the 8th along with Rahu, the native will hate others, be a great fool and will do bad deeds.

Notes : The 8th house occupied by Rahu in the company of the 10th lord will spoil professional happiness of the native apart from making him perform questionable and foolish deeds as well as incurring misconceptions with one and all

कर्मेशे द्यूनराशिस्थे मन्दभौमसमन्विते ।
द्यूनेशे पापसंयुते शिश्नोदरपरायणः ॥७॥

7. If Saturn, Mars and the 10th lord are in the 7th as the 7th lord is with a malefic, the native will be fond of carnal pleasures and of filling his belly.

Notes : The effects for the combination as above are described by the words *"Sisnodara Parayana"* (शिश्नोदरपरायणः) and as far as I understand, the meaning is as above. (Sisna= male organ, Udara=belly.)

तुङ्गराशिं समाश्रित्य कर्मेशे गुरुसंयुते ।
भाग्येशे कर्मराशिस्थे मानैश्वर्यप्रतापवान् ॥८॥
लाभेशे कर्मराशिस्थे कर्मेशे लग्नसंयुते ।
तावुभौ केन्द्रगौ वापि सुखजीवनभाग् भवेत् ॥९॥
कर्मेशे बलसंयुक्ते मीने गुरुसमन्विते ।
वस्त्राभरणसौख्यादि लभते नात्र संशयः ॥१०॥

8-10. Should the 10th lord be in exaltation and be in the company of Jupiter as the 9th lord is in the 10th the native will be endowed with honour, wealth, and valour. One will lead a happy life if the 11th lord is in the 10th and the 10th lord is in the ascendant or if the lords of the 10th and 11th are conjunct in an angle. Should the 10th lord in strength be in Pisces along with Jupiter, the native will doubtless obtain robes, ornaments and happiness.

लाभस्थानगते सूर्ये राहुभौमसमन्विते ।
रविपुत्रेण संयुक्ते कर्मच्छेत्ता भवेन्नरः ॥११॥

11. Should Rahu, Sun, Saturn and Mars be in the 11th, the native will incur cessation of his duties.

Notes : The 4 planets, *viz.* the Sun, Mars, Rahu and Saturn joining in the 11th house will ensure that the native will not be successful in his performance. As a consequence, he will not have a happy calling or profession worth the name, and will gain nothing.

मीने जीवे भृगुयुते लग्नेशे बलसंयुते ।
स्वोच्चराशिगते चन्द्रे सम्यग्ज्ञानार्थवान् भवेत् ॥१२॥

12. One will be learned and wealthy if Jupiter is in Pisces along with Venus while the ascendant lord is strong and the Moon is in exaltation.

Notes : ज्ञान means learning in the normal context. Apart, this denotes sacred knowledge derived from meditation on the higher truths of religion and philosophy which instructs the seeker how to understand his own nature within him and to reunite with the Almighty avoiding reincarnation. This is taught by ज्ञानयोग (Gnana yoga). Jupiter and Venus joining in Pisces (the terminal house, denoting final emancipation) will endow the native with such supreme knowledge. The lord of the ascendant simultaneously joining the exalted Moon renders the mind fertile enough to produce knowledge of one's own self. For one cannot attain the Lord without first knowing what he himself is. Material wealth will also come to the native as a by-product of the planetary configuration in question. So to say one will be spiritually and materially wealthy.

कर्मेशे लाभराशिस्थे लाभेशे लग्नसंस्थिते ।
कर्मराशिस्थिते शुक्रे रत्नवान् स नरो भवेत् ॥१३॥

13. Should the 10th lord be in the 11th while the 11th lord is in the ascendant and Venus is in the 10th, the native will be endowed with precious stones.

Notes : To wit the planets so disposed as mentioned in the sloka will confer a huge influx of material wealth on the native.

केन्द्रत्रिकोणगे कर्मनाथे स्वोच्चसमाश्रिते ।
गुरुणा सहिते दृष्टे स कर्मसहितो भवेत् ॥१४॥

14. If the lord of the 10th is exalted in an angle or a trine and be in the company of or in aspect to Jupiter, one will be endowed with (worthy) deeds.

कर्मेशे लग्नभावस्थे लग्नेशेन समन्विते ।
केन्द्रत्रिकोणगे चन्द्रे सत्कर्मनिरतो भवेत् ॥१५॥

15. Should the 10th lord be in the ascendant along with the ascendant lord as the Moon is in an angle or in a trine, the native will be interested in good deeds.

कर्मस्थानगते मन्दे नीचखेचरसंयुते ।
कर्मांशे पापसंयुक्ते कर्महीनो भवेन्नरः ॥१६॥

16. If Saturn is in the 10th along with a debilitated planet while the 10th from Navamsa ascendant is occupied by a malefic, the native will be bereft of (virtuous) acts.

कर्मेशे नाशराशिस्थे रन्ध्रेशे कर्मसंस्थिते ।
पापग्रहेण संयुक्ते दुष्कर्म निरतो भवेत् ॥१७॥

17. One will indulge in bad acts if the 10th lord is in the 8th while the 8th lord is in the 10th with a malefic.

कर्मेशे नीचराशिस्थे कर्मस्थे पापखेचरे ।
कर्मभात्कर्मगे पापे कर्मवैकल्यमादिशेत् ॥१८॥

18. Obstructions to the native's acts will crop up if the 10th lord is in fall, as both the 10th house from the ascendant and the 10th from the 10th (*i.e.* 7th from the ascendant) have malefic occupations.

कर्मस्थानगते चन्द्रे तदीशे तत्त्रिकोणगे।
लग्नेशे केन्द्रभावस्थे सत्कीर्तिसहितो भवेत् ॥१९॥
लाभेशे कर्मभावस्थे कर्मेशे बलसंयुक्ते।
देवेन्द्रगुरुणा दृष्टे सत्कीर्तिसहितो भवेत् ॥२०॥
कर्मस्थानाधिपे भाग्ये लग्नेशे कर्मसंयुते।
लग्नात् पञ्चमगे चन्द्रे ख्याततनामा नरो भवेत् ॥२१॥

19-21. *COMBINATIONS FOR FAME :* One will be endowed with fame if the Moon is in the 10th while the 10th lord is in a trine from the 10th and the ascendant lord is in ascendant's angle. Similar effects will come to pass if the 11th lord is in the 10th while the 10th lord is strong and be in aspect to Jupiter. Fame will come to the native if the 10th lord is in the 9th as the ascendant lord is in the 10th and the Moon is in the 5th from the ascendant.

इति कर्मफलं प्रोक्तं संक्षेपेण द्विजोत्तम!।
लग्नकर्मेशसम्बन्धादूह्यमन्यदपि स्वयम् ॥२२॥

22. O excellent of the Brahmins, thus have been told about the effects of the 10th house in a brief manner. Other related effects be guessed by you based on the relationship of the lords of the ascendant and of the 10th.

अथ लाभभावफलाध्याय: ॥२२॥

Chapter 22

Effects Of The Eleventh House

लाभभावफलञ्चाथ कथयामि द्विजोत्तम!।
श्रूयतां जातको लोके यच्छुभत्वे सदा सुखी ॥१॥

1. O excellent of the Brahmins, I now explain effects relating to the 11th house, the auspiciousness of which bhava will make one happy at all times.

लाभाधिपो यदा लाभे तिष्ठेत् केन्द्रत्रिकोणयोः ।
बहुलाभं तदा कुर्यादुच्चे सूर्यांशगोऽपि वा ।।२।।

2. Should the 11th lord be in the 11th itself or be in an angle or in a trine from the ascendant, there will be many gains. Similarly if the 11th lord is exalted, though in combustion, there will be many gains.

Notes : The second line of the above verse deserves a proper approach. सूर्यांशगोऽपि means "although in combustion or having lost rays in the Sun". The word "अपि" meaning "although" in this context deters the otherwise possible interpretation as "Sun's Navamsa or Sun's Rasi" which of course will be an extreme rendering. To wit, the correct import is that even though the 11th lord is combust but be in exaltation the native will gain abundantly.

लाभेशे धनराशिस्थे धनेशे केन्द्रसंस्थिते ।
गुरुणा सहिते भावे गुरुलाभं विनिर्दिशत् ।।३।।

3. If the 11th lord is in the 2nd while the 2nd lord is in angle (from the ascendant) along with Jupiter, the gains will be great.

लाभेशे विक्रमे भावे शुभग्रहसमन्विते ।
षट्त्रिंशे वत्सरे प्राप्ते सहस्रद्वयनिष्कभाक् ।।४।।

4. If the 11th lord is in the 3rd while the 11th is occupied by a benefic, the native will gain 2000 Nishkas in his 36th year.

Notes : "भावे" means in the Bhava or house in question, i.e. the 11th bhava and not the 3rd bhava. Since विक्रमे already preceeds, भावे to mean "in the 3rd house" will be redundant.

निष्क (Nishka) though meaning a gold coin was generally taken to indicate one Karsha or Suvarna of 16 Mashas. This also denotes a certain weight of gold in the hoary days. The sage thus obviously hints at the opulence of the native in varied measures by quantifying the resultant Nishkas according to the merits of the planetary formations at birth.

केन्द्रत्रिकोणगे लाभनाथे शुभसमन्विते ।
चत्वारिंशे तु सम्प्राप्ते सहस्रार्धसुनिष्कभाक् ।।५।।

5. If the 11th lord is conjujct a benefic in an angle or in a trine (from the ascendant), the native will acquire 500 Nishkas in his 40th year.

लाभस्थाने गुरुयुते धने चन्द्रसमन्विते।
भाग्यस्थानगते शुक्रे षट्सहस्राधिपो भवेत्॥६॥

6. The native will own 6000 Nishkas if the 11th is occupied by Jupiter while the 2nd and 9th are respectively taken over by the Moon and Venus by position.

लाभाच्च लाभगे जीवे बुधचन्द्रसमन्विते।
धनधान्याधिपः श्रीमान्रत्नाद्याभरणैर्युतः॥७॥

7. Should Jupiter, Mercury and the Moon be in the 11th from the 11th (i.e. 9th from the ascendant) the native will be endowed with wealth, grains, fortunes, diamonds, ornaments *etc*.

लाभेशे लग्नभावस्थे लग्नेशे लाभसंयुते।
त्रयस्त्रिंशे तु सम्प्राप्ते सहस्रनिष्कभाग् भवेत्॥८॥

8. One will gain 1000 Nishkas in his 33rd year if the 11th lord is in the ascendant and the ascendant lord is in the 11th.

धनेशे लाभराशिस्थे लाभेशे धनराशिगे।
विवाहात्परतश्चैव बहुभाग्यं समादिशेत्॥९॥

9. If the 11th lord is in the 2nd as the 2nd lord is in the 11th, one will amass abundant fortunes after marriage.

भ्रातृपे लाभराशिस्थे लाभेशे भ्रातृसंस्थिते।
भ्रातृभावाद्धनप्राप्तिदिव्याभरणसंयुतः॥१०॥

10. If the 11th lord is in the 3rd as the 3rd lord is in the 11th, one will gain wealth through co-born and be endowed with excellent ornaments.

लाभेशे नीचभेऽस्ते वा त्रिके पापसमन्विते।
कृते भूरिप्रयत्नेऽपि नैव लाभः कदाचन॥११॥

11. There will be no gains in spite of numerous efforts if the 11th lord is in fall, in combustion or be in the 6th/8th/12th with a malefic.

अथ व्ययभावफलाध्यायः ॥२३॥

Chapter 23

Effects Of The Twelfth House

अथाह व्ययभावस्य कथयामि फलं द्विज!।
व्ययेशे शुभसंयुक्ते स्वभे स्वोच्चगतेऽपि वा ॥१॥
व्यये च शुभसंयुक्ते शुभकार्ये व्ययस्तदा।
चन्द्रो व्ययाधिपो धर्मलाभमन्त्रेषु संस्थितः ॥२॥
स्वोच्चे स्वर्क्षे निजांशे वा लाभधर्मात्मजांशके।
दिव्यागारादिपर्यंको दिव्यगन्धैकभोगवान् ॥३॥
पराध्यर्यरमणो दिव्यवस्त्रमाल्यादिभूषणः।
पराध्यर्यवित्तसंयुतो विज्ञो दिनानि नयति प्रभुः ॥४॥

1-4. O Brahmin, now I tell you about the effects of the 12th house. There will be expenses on good accounts if the 12th lord is with a benefic, or be in own house or be exalted or if a benefic occupies the 12th. One will own beautiful houses and beds and be endowed with superior scented articles and pleasures if the Moon happens to be the 12th lord and be exalted or be in own sign/Navamsa or in the 11th/9th/5th in Rasi/Navamsa. The said native will live with rich clothes, and ornaments, be learned and lordly.

एवं स्वशत्रुनीचांशेऽष्टमांशे वाऽष्टमे रिपौ।
संस्थितः कुरुते जातं कान्तासुखविवर्जितम् ॥५॥
व्ययाधिक्यपरिक्लान्तं दिव्यभोगनिराकृतम्।
स हि केन्द्रत्रिकोणस्थः स्वस्त्रियाऽलंकृतः स्वयम् ॥६॥

5-6. And if the 12th lord is in the 6th/8th or be in enemy's Navamsa, debilitation Navamsa or in 8th in Navamsa, one will be devoid of happiness from wife, be troubled by expenses and deprived of general happiness. If he be in an angle/trine, the native will beget a spouse.

यथा लग्नात् फलं चैतदात्मनः परिकीर्तितम् ।
एवं भ्रात्रादिभावेषु तत्तत्सर्वं विचारयेत् ॥७॥

7. Just as these effects are derived from the ascendant in regard to the native, similar deductions be made about co-born etc. from the 3rd and other houses.

Notes : Hints are given here to know from the native's horoscope the effects related to his co-born, uncles etc. For example, brother's finances from the 4th house (2nd from the 3rd), brother's marriage from the 9th house (7th from the 3rd), father's health from the 2nd house (6th from the 9th), mother's health from the 9th (6th from the 4th), wife's spending nature from the 6th house (i.e. 12th from the 7th) and so on and so forth. Proceeding on these lines, we can see the possibility of predicting many important events for other relatives from the native's horoscope itself.

दृश्यचक्रार्धगाः खेटाः प्रत्यक्षफलदायकाः ।
अदृश्यार्धगताः खेटाः परोक्षे फलदाः स्मृताः ॥८॥

8. Planets placed in the visible half of the zodiac will give explicit results while the ones in the invisible half will confer secret results.

Notes : Visible half is the half of the zodiac within a range of 180 degrees from the ascendant's cusp seen backwards. The other half is invisible.

A planet in the visible half of the zodiac will be more potential in effects while in the invisible half it is less potential and unmanifest.

व्ययस्थानगतोः राहुर्भौमार्किरविसंयुतः ।
तदीशेऽप्यर्कसंयुक्ते नरके पतनं भवेत् ॥९॥

9. If Rahu is in the 12th along with Mars, Saturn and the Sun, the native will go to hell. Similar effect will occur if the 12th lord is with the Sun.

Notes : The 12th house relates to one's fate after death. Whether he will reincarnate, or attain infernal region or the Lotus Feet of the Lord will have to be studied from the 12th house. In this connection, refer to ch. 26 of **Horasara** also.

व्ययस्थानगते सौम्ये तदीशे स्वोच्चराशिगे।
शुभयुक्ते शुभैर्दृष्टे मोक्षः स्यान्नात्र संशयः ॥१०॥

10. If there is a benefic in the 12th while its lord is exalted or is conjunct or aspected by a benefic, one will attain final emancipation.

व्ययेशे पापसंयुक्ते व्यये पापसमन्विते।
पापग्रहेण संदृष्टे देशाद्देशान्तरं गतः ॥११॥

11. One will wander from country to country if the 12th lord and 12th house are with malefics and be in aspect to malefics.

व्ययेशे शुभराशिस्थे व्ययर्क्षे शुभसंयुते।
शुभग्रहेण संदृष्टे स्वदेशात् सञ्चरो भवेत् ॥१२॥

12. One will move in his own country if the 12th lord and 12th house are with benefics and be in aspect to benefics.

Notes : In the previous sloka and the present one, clues are given to know as to whether one will be in his own place or outside the native place. If the 12th house and its lord are connected with benefics, one will progress in his own place while he will wander hither and thither (without progress) if 12th lord and 12th house are spoilt by malefics.

व्यये मन्दादिसंयुक्ते भूमिजेन समन्विते।
शुभदृष्टेर्न सम्प्राप्तिः पापमूलाद्धनार्जनम् ॥१३॥

13. Earnings will be through sinful measures if the 12th is occupied by Saturn or Mars etc. and be not aspected by a benefic.

लग्नेशे व्ययराशिस्थे व्ययेशे लग्नसंयुते।
भृगुपुत्रेण संयुक्ते धर्ममूलाद्धनव्ययः ॥१४॥

14. If the ascendant lord is in the 12th while the 12th lord is in the ascendant with Venus, expenses will be on religious grounds.

अथ भावेशफलाध्याय: ॥२४॥

Chapter 24

Effects Of The Bhava Lords

लग्नेशे लग्नगे देहसुखभाग् भुजविक्रमी ।
मनस्वी चञ्चलश्चैव द्विभार्यो परगोऽपि वा ॥१॥

1. *EFFECTS OF ASCENDANT LORD IN VARIOUS HOUSES (upto sloka 12)* : Should the ascendant lord be in the asecndant itself, the native will be endowed with physical happiness (i.e. good health) and prowess. He will be intelligent, fickle-minded, will have two wives and will unite with other females.

Notes : The position of the ascendant lord in the ascendant itself will make the native fearless and longlived.

लग्नेशे धनगे बालो लाभवान् पण्डितः सुखी ।
सुशीलो धर्मविन्मानी बहुदारगुणैर्युतः ॥२॥

2. If the lord of the ascendant is in the 2nd, he will be gainful, scholarly, happy, endowed with good qualities, be religious, honourable and will have many wives.

Notes : The native having the ascendant lord in the 2nd house will face obstacles in obtaining progeny and thus he will be left with a longing for issues. He will further become wealthy through his own efforts.

लग्नेशे सहजे जातः सिंहतुल्य-पराक्रमी ।
सर्वसम्पद्युतो मानी द्विभार्यो मतिमान् सुखी ॥३॥

3. If the lord of the ascendant is in the 3rd, the native will equal a lion in valour, be endowed with all kinds of wealth, be honourable, will have two wives, be intelligent and happy.

Notes : Should the 3rd house contain the ascendant lord, one will be equal to a king, respected by others and will indulge in unnatural methods of sexual gratification.

लग्नेशे सुखगे बालः पितृमातृसुखान्वितः ।
बहुभ्रातृयुतः कामी गुणरूपसमन्वितः ॥४॥

4. If the ascendant lord is in the 4th, the native will be endowed with paternal and maternal happiness, will have many brothers, be lustful virtuous and charming.

Notes : With the ascendant lord in the 4th house, the native is of a noble descent. He will prosper by his own efforts. He will be ambitious and beautiful. Prosperity will come to him easily. He will ever enjoy physical felicity.

लग्नेशे सुतगे जन्तोः सुतसौख्यं च मध्यमम् ।
प्रथमापत्यनाशः स्यान्मानी क्रोधी नृपप्रियः ॥५॥

5. If the ascendant lord is in the 5th, the native will have mediocre progenic happiness, will lose his first child, be honourable, given to anger and be dear to king.

लग्नेशे षष्ठगे जातो देहसौख्यविवर्जितः ।
पापाढ्ये शत्रुतः पीडा सौम्यदृष्टिविवर्जिते ॥६॥

6. If the ascendant lord is in the 6th and related to a malefic the native will be devoid of physical happiness, and will be troubled by enemies if there is no benefic aspect.

Notes : The ascendant lord going to the 6th house will mar the prospects of health. However, for Scorpio and Taurus ascendant, it will be a felicitous augury for freedom from diseases.

The 6th house position of Lagna Lord in general will give abundant wealth and respect apart from royal status. There is, however, a possibility of more than one marriage or losing the spouse early.

लग्नेशे सप्तमे पापे भार्या तस्य न जीवति ।
शुभेऽटनो दरिद्रो वा विरक्तो वा नृपोऽपि वा ॥७॥

7. If the ascendant lord is a malefic and be in the 7th, the native's wife will not live (long). If the planet in question be a benefic, one will wander aimlessly, face penury and be dejected. He will alternatively become a king (if the said planet is strong).

लग्नेशेऽष्टमगे जातः सिद्धविद्याविशारदः।
रोगी चौरो महाक्रोधी द्यूती च परदारगः॥८॥

8. If the ascendant lord is in the 8th, the native will be an accomplished scholar, be sickly, thievish, be given to much anger, be a gambler and will join others' wives.

Notes : The only good effect of the ascendant lord being in the 8th house is one's academic accomplishment. This position will cause **Balarishta** or child mortality. The native's health will be poor. He will be a repository of misfortunes. He will see many deaths in the family to his grief. His married life will be a hell. He will be a profligate and will incur ill-fame and disrepute. Penury will ever be after him.

In case of Aries and Libra ascendant, this approach for evil results should be avoided and results declared after further scanning the radix.

लग्नेशे भाग्यगे जातो भाग्यवाञ्जनवल्लभः।
विष्णुभक्तः पटुर्वाग्मी दारपुत्रधनैर्युतः॥९॥

9. If the ascendant lord is in the 9th, the native will be fortunate, dear to people, be a devotee of Sri Vishnu, be skilful, eloquent in speech and be endowed with wife, sons and wealth.

Notes : One will gain abundantly from his father. Every undertaking of his will be fruitful. He will be well-disposed to his co-born, These are additional results of the ascendant lord occupying the 9th house.

लग्नेशे दशमे जातः पितृसौख्यसमन्वितः।
नृपमान्यो जने ख्यातः स्वार्जितस्वो न संशयः॥१०॥

10. If the ascendant lord is in the 10th, the native will be endowed with paternal happiness, royal honour (or patronage), fame among men and will doubtlessly have self-earned wealth.

Notes : The 10th house occupied by the ascendant lord denotes obtainment of co-born. The native will possess ambitions and will prosper in his pursuits.

लग्नेशे लाभगे जातः सदा लाभसमन्वितः।
सुशीलः ख्यातकीर्तिश्च बहूदारगुणैर्युतः॥११॥

11. If the ascendant lord is in the 11th, the native will always be endowed with gains, good qualities, fame and many wives.

लग्नेशे व्ययभावस्थे देहसौख्यविवर्जितः।
व्यर्थव्ययी महाक्रोधी शुभदृग्योगवर्जिते॥१२॥

12. If the ascendant lord is in the 12th and be devoid of benefic aspect/conjunction, the native will be bereft of physical happiness, will spend unfruitfully and be given to much anger.

Notes : If the ascendant lord is in the 12th, the native's life will not be prosperous. He will be addicted to gambling, thieving, debauchery and other vices. He will expend wastefully.

धनेशे लग्नगे जातः पुत्रवान् धनसंयुतः।
कुटुम्बकण्टकः कामी निष्ठुरः परकार्यकृत्॥१३॥

13. *EFFECTS OF 2ND LORD IN VARIOUS HOUSES* (upto sloka 24) : If the 2nd lord is in the ascendant, the native will be endowed with sons and wealth, be inimical to his family, lustful, hard-hearted and will do others' jobs.

Notes : One will be fraudulent and will face financial upheavals with the lord of the 2nd occupying the ascendant. These evil effects will not wholly apply to Capricorn ascendant, but with some modifications.

धनेशे धनगे जातो धनवान् गर्वसंयुतः।
द्विभार्यो बहुभार्यो वा सुतहीनः प्रजायते॥१४॥

14. If the 2nd lord is in the 2nd, the native will be wealthy, proud, will have two or more wives and be bereft of progeny.

धनेशे सहजे जातो विक्रमी मतिमान् गुणी।
कामी लोभी शुभाढ्ये च पापाढ्ये देवनिन्दकः ॥१५॥

15. If the 2nd lord is in the 3rd, the native will be valorous, wise, virtuous, lustful and miserly—all these when related to a benefic. If related to a malefic, the native will be a heterodox.

Notes : Should the 2nd lord be in the 3rd house, the native will be ill-related to females and will earn through prostitutes. If a malefic is related to the 2nd lord in the 3rd, the person concerned will not be God-fearing and will have dirty conduct.

धनेशे सुखभावस्थे सर्वसम्पतसमन्वितः।
गुरुणा संयुते स्वोच्चे राजतुल्यो नरो भवेत् ॥१६॥

16. If the 2nd lord is in the 4th, the native will acquire all kinds of wealth. If the 2nd lord is exalted and be conjunct Jupiter, one will be equal to a king.

Notes : The placement of the 2nd lord in the 4th will also produce a heterodox and one of questionable character.

The exaltation of the 2nd lord in the 4th applies only to Libra ascendant. Obviously the sage suggests that the exaltation of Mars in the company af Jupiter (in debilitation) in the 4th house will prove extremely favourable for a Libra native conferring near-regalhood. It is also not unmeaningful to conclude that the 2nd lord exalted and joining Jupiter becoming a good omen for any ascendant.

धनेशे सुतभावस्थे जातो धनसमन्वितः।
धनोपार्जनशीलाश्च जायन्ते तत्सुता अपि ॥१७॥

17. If the 2nd lord is in the 5th the native will be wealthy. Not only the native, but also his sons, will be intent on earning wealth.

Notes : The 2nd lord going to the 5th house will make one resort to trickery. His family life will not be happy. He will not be kind to others. He will be very lustful and will be prone to lose a child prematurely.

धनेशे रिपुभावस्थे सशुभे शत्रुतो धनम् ।
सपापे शत्रुतो हानिर्जंघावैकल्यवान् भवेत् ॥१८॥

18. If the 2nd lord is in the 6th along with a benefic the native will gain wealth through his enemies; if be with a malefic, there will be loss through enemies apart from mutilation of shanks.

Notes : There will be severe loss of wealth through thefts and servants. He will have defects of privities. These are further effects of the 2nd lord occupying the 6th house.

धनेशे सप्तमे जातः परदाररतो भिषक् ।
पापेक्षितयुते तस्य भार्या च व्यभिचारिणी ॥१९॥

19. If the 2nd lord is in the 7th, the native will be addicted to others' wives and be a doctor. If a malefic is related to the said placement by conjunction or by aspect, the native's wife will (also) be of questionable character.

Notes : The 2nd lord in the 7th house and related to a dire malefic will render the mother of the native being of questionable character according to some hoary authors. However, the 4th house and its lord deserve a special attention in the context of mother's disposition.

धनेशेऽष्टमगे जातो भूरिभूमिधनैर्युतः ।
पत्नीसुखं भवेत् स्वल्पं ज्येष्ठभ्रातृसुखं न हि ॥२०॥

20. If the 2nd lord is in the 8th, the native will be endowed with abundant land and wealth. But he will have limited marital felicity and be bereft of happiness from his elder brother.

धनेशे धर्मभावस्थे धनवानुद्यमी पटुः ।
बाल्ये रोगी सुखी पश्चात् तीर्थधर्मव्रतादिकृत् ॥२१॥

21. If the 2nd lord is in the 9th, the native will be wealthy, diligent, skilful, sick during childhood and will later on be happy (i. e. healthy) and will visit shrines, observing religious code *etc.*

धनेशे कर्मगे जातः कामी मानी च पण्डितः ।
बहुदारधनैर्युक्तः किञ्च पुत्रसुखोज्झितः ॥२२॥

22. If the 2nd lord is in the 10th, the native will be libidinous, honourable, learned, will have many wives and much wealth but be bereft of filial happiness.

धनेशे लाभभावस्थे सर्वलाभसमन्वितः ।
सदोद्योगयुतो मानी कीर्तिमान् जायते नरः ॥२३॥

23. If the 2nd lord is in the 11th, the native will have all kinds of wealth, be ever diligent, honourable and famous.

Notes : The native will undergo miseries due to ill-health during childhood and with the march of time he will be endowed with health throughout, if the 2nd lord is in the 11th house.

धनेशे व्ययभावस्थे साहसी धनवर्जितः ।
परभाग्यरतस्तस्य ज्येष्ठापत्यसुखं नहि ॥२४॥

24. If the 2nd lord is in the 12th, the native will be adventurous, be devoid of wealth, and be interested in other's wealth while his eldest child will not keep him happy.

Notes : According to the saying "वित्तेशे व्ययगेवापि ग्रहद्वय-समन्विते अधिकैश्वर्यं संपन्न त्रयादिग्रहसंयुते वा

Meaning that if the 2nd lord is in the 12th house with two or more (favourable) planets, the native will be extremely wealthy. This is found to be a sound clue in actual cases. However, the 2nd lord lonely in the 12th is bad for riches, except in the case of Aries ascendant with Venus in the 12th in high dignity.

लग्नगे सहजाधीशे स्वभुजार्जितवित्तवान् ।
सेवाज्ञः साहसी जातो विद्याहीनोऽपि बुद्धिमान् ॥२५॥

25. *EFFECTS OF 3RD LORD IN VARIOUS HOUSES (upto sloka 36)* : If the 3rd lord is in the ascendant, the native will have self-made wealth, be disposed to worship, be valorous and be intelligent although devoid of learning.

Notes : One will have a lean body with the ascendant having the 3rd lord in it. He will have such sexual lust that cannot be subdued. He will be short-tempered and ill-disposed to others.

द्वितीये सहजाधीशे स्थूलो विक्रमवर्जितः।
स्वल्पारम्भी सुखी न स्यात् परस्त्रीधनकामुकः ॥२६॥

26. If the 3rd lord is in the 2nd, the native will be corpulent, devoid of valour, will not make much efforts, be not happy and will have an eye on others' wives and others' wealth.

Notes : Should the 3rd lord be in the 2nd house, one will resort to unnatural sexual means of gratification. He will not show enthusiasm in his undertakings.

सहजे सहजाधीशे सहोदरसुखान्वितः।
धनपुत्रयुतो हृष्टो भुनक्ति सुखमद्भुतम् ॥२७॥

27. If the 3rd lord is in the 3rd, the native will be endowed with happiness through co-born and will have wealth and sons, be cheerful and extremely happy.

सुखस्थे सहजाधीशे सुखी च धनसंयुतः।
मतिमान् जायते बालो दुष्टभार्यापतिश्च सः ॥२८॥

28. If the 3rd lord is in the 4th, the native will be happy, wealthy and intelligent but will acquire a wicked spouse.

सुतस्थे सहजाधीशे पुत्रवान् गुणसंयुतः।
भार्या तस्य भवेत् क्रूरा क्रूरग्रहयुतेक्षिते ॥२९॥

29. If the 3rd lord is in the 5th, the native will have sons, and be virtuous. If in the process the 3rd lord be conjunct or aspected by a malefic, the native will have a formidable wife.

षष्ठभावे तृतीयेशे भ्रातृशत्रुर्महाधनी।
मातुलैश्च समं वैरं मातुलानीप्रियो नरः ॥३०॥

30. If the 3rd lord is in the 6th, the native will be inimical to his co-born, be affluent, will not be well-disposed to his maternal uncle and be dear to his maternal aunt.

Notes : The student's attention is drawn to the statement of the text, *viz.* मातुलानी प्रियो नरः which has been without any misconception, rendered to denote the native's being "dear to his maternal aunt". At the same time, **Sanketa Nidhi** while commenting on the 3rd lord's placement in the 6th house gives an overt clue to the native being fond of physicallp matiny with his maternal aunt. One wonders whether sage Parasara covertly points out to one and the same thing. Possibly so, for the Sanskrit expression is so flexible.

सप्तमे सहजाधीशे राजसेवापरो नरः।
बाल्ये दुःखी सुखी चान्ते जायते नाऽत्र संशयः ॥३१॥

31. If the 3rd lord is in the 7th, the native will be interested in serving the king and be not happy during boyhood but at the end of his life.

Notes : It is not a favourable indication to have an independent profession or business when the 3rd lord is in the 7th house. The 7th denotes one's public relationship, business prospects etc. and an evil lord is not welcome there. As a result, the native will be destined to be in the employ of others.

Further, this position will give a tendency to steal. The native will incur a legal award like death.

अष्टमे सहजाधीशे जातश्चौरो नरो भवेत्।
दासवृत्त्योपजीवी च राजद्वारे मृतिर्भवेत् ॥३२॥

32. If the 3rd lord is in the 8th, the native will be a thief, will derive his livelihood serving others and will die at the gate of royal palace.

नवमे सहजाधीशे पितुः सुखविवर्जितः।
स्त्रीभिर्भाग्योदयस्तस्य पुत्रादिसुखसंयुतः ॥३३॥

33. If the 3rd lord is in the 9th, the native will lack paternal bliss, will make fortunes through wife and will enjoy progenic and other pleasures.

Notes : Although one may have fortunes and progenic happiness, one will unendingly feel miserable if the 3rd lord occupies the 9th house. His father will be a contemptible person.

दशमे सहजाधीशे जातः सर्वसुखान्वितः।
स्वभुजार्जितवित्तश्च दुष्टस्त्रीभरणे रतः ॥३४॥

34. If the 3rd lord is in the 10th, the native will have all kinds of happiness and self-made wealth and be interested in nurturing wicked females.

लाभगे सहजाधीशे व्यापारे लाभवान् सदा।
विद्याहीनोऽपि मेधावी साहसी परसेवकः ॥३५॥

35. If the 3rd lord is in the 11th, the native will always gain in trading, be intelligent although not literate, be adventurous and will serve others.

Notes : One will have an emaciated body with the 3rd lord's position in the 11th house. He will incur misunderstandings with others and will not be a worthy friend.

व्ययस्थे सहजाधीशे कुकार्ये व्ययकृज्जनः।
पिता तस्य भवेत् क्रूरः स्त्रीभिर्भाग्योदयस्तथा ॥३६॥

36. If the 3rd lord is in the 12th, the native will spend on evil deeds, will have a wicked father and will be fortunate through a female (or wife).

Notes : The 3rd lord going to the 12th will bestow every happiness in life. Yet the native will feel highly miserable. This view is held by Ramadayalu.

This placement will further spoil the prospects of co-born. If Mars also joins the said 3rd lord, sustenance of co-born will be doubtful.

सुखेशे धग्नगे जातो विद्यागुणविभूषितः।
भूमि-वाहनसंयुक्तो मातुः सुखसमन्वितः ॥३७॥

37. *EFFECTS OF THE 4TH LORD IN VARIOUS HOUSES (upto sloka 48) :* If the 4th lord is in the ascendant, the native will be endowed with learning, virtues, ornaments, lands, conveyances and maternal happiness.

Notes : As a result of the 4th lord coming to occupy the ascendant, the subject will acquire incomparable learning in various branches. However, there is an element of risk of being deprived of one's ancestral properties. After leading married life for some time, the native will give up worldly life and may turn into an ascetic.

सुखेशे धनगे जातो भोगी सर्वधनान्वितः।
कुटुम्बसहितो मानी साहसी कुहकान्वितः ॥३८॥

38. If the 4th lord is in the 2nd, the native will enjoy pleasures, all kinds of wealth, family life and honour and be adventurous. He will be cunning in disposition.

Notes : The 2nd house tenanted by the 4th lord will bring abundant gains from mother and maternal relatives. The mother of the native will be able to receive great help from her brothers and sisters. The subject will join evil company and face some risks. He will build up self-earned wealth and his lust for lucre will never be subdued.

सुखेशे सहजे जातो विक्रमी भृत्यसंयुतः।
उदारोऽरुग् गुणी दाता स्वभुजार्जितवित्तवान् ॥३९॥

39. If the 4th lord is in the 3rd, the native will be valorous. He will have servants, be liberal, virtuous and charitable and will possess self-earned wealth. He will be free from diseases.

सुखेशे सुखभावस्थे मन्त्री सर्वधनान्वितः।
चतुरः शीलवान् मानी ज्ञानवान् स्त्रीप्रियः सुखी ॥४०॥

40. If the 4th lord is in the 4th, the native will be a minister and will possess all kinds of wealth. He will be skilful, virtuous, honourable, learned, happy and be welldisposed to his spouse.

सुखेशे पुत्रभावस्थे सुखी सर्वजनप्रियः।
विष्णुभक्तो गुणी मानी स्वभुजार्जितवित्तवान् ॥४१॥

41. If the 4th lord is in the 5th, the native will be happy and be liked by all. He will be devoted to Sri Vishnu, be virtuous, honourable and will have self-earned wealth.

सुखेशे रिपुभावस्थे मातुः सुखविवर्जितः।
क्रोधी चोरोऽभिचारी च स्वेच्छाचारश्च दुर्मनाः ॥४२॥

42. If the 4th lord is in the 6th, the native will be devoid of maternal happiness, be given to anger, be a thief and a conjurer (or magician), be independent in action and be ill-disposed.

Notes : The native will be brought up by another female in the place of his mother. He will be careless about his own matters. He will have litigations on account of properties. His mother will be sickly in constitution and be a source of worry to the family members. He will not be welldisposed toward his mother. These are additional effects for the 6th house placement of the 4th lord in a nativity.

सुखेशे सप्तमे जातो बहुविद्यासमन्वितः।
पित्रार्जितधनत्यागी सभायां मूकवद् भवेत् ॥४३॥

43. If the 4th lord is in the 7th, the native will be endowed with a high degree of education, will sacrifice his patrimony and be akin to the dumb in an assembly.

Notes : When the 4th lord occupies the 7th house, the person concerned will not enjoy paternal properties. He may either lose or sacrifice the same. He will not be a householder for a long time and will give up his family burdens sooner or later as a husband and as a father. Though he will achieve a great degree of education, he will be unable to express himself before a group of men.

सुखेशे रन्ध्रभावस्थे गृहादिसुखवर्जितः।
पित्रोः सुखं भवेदल्पं जातः क्लीबसमो भवेत् ॥४४॥

44. If the 4th lord is in the 8th the native will be devoid of domestic and other comforts, will not enjoy much parental happiness and be equal to a neuter.

Notes : The 4th lord's relegation to the 8th house will affect the progenic ability of the native and he will not be able to carnally satisfy his spouse. His happiness in household life will not be appreciable; some problem or the other will accost him. His education will face many an obstacle. His childhood will be with many difficulties.

सुखेशे भाग्यभावस्थे जातः सर्वजनप्रियः।
देवभक्तो गुणी मानी भवेत् सर्वसुखान्वितः ॥४५॥

45. If the 4th lord is in the 9th, the native will be dear to one and all, be devoted to God, be virtuous, honourable and endowed with every kind of happiness.

सुखेशे कर्मभावस्थे राजमान्यो नरो भवेत्।
रसायनी महाहृष्टो सुखभोगी जितेन्द्रियः ॥४६॥

46. If the 4th lord is in the 10th, the native will enjoy royal honours, be an alchemist, be extremely pleased, will enjoy pleasures and will conquer his five senses.

Notes : One will be professionally happy and prosperous with the 4th lord in the 10th house. He will have abundant self-made properties. He will, however, lack maternal happiness if the 4th lord in the said house is not happily placed.

सुखेशे लाभगे जातो गुप्तरोगभयान्वितः।
उदारो गुणवान् दाता परोपकरणे रतः ॥४७॥

47. If the 4th lord is in the 11th, the native will have fear of secret disease, be liberal, virtuous, charitable and helpful to others.

Notes : Some say that the 11th house having the 4th lord will ensure freedom from diseases while our sage attributes secret diseases (like venereal affliction or any other diseases caused by physical union). Apparently the sage does not prefer the 4th lord (lord of happiness) getting relegated to the 11th (the 8th from the 4th).

सुखेशे व्ययभावस्थे गृहादिसुखवर्जितः।
जातो दुर्व्यसनी मूढः सदाऽऽलस्यसमन्वितः ॥४८॥

48. If the 4th lord is in the 12th the native will be devoid of domestic and other comforts, will have vices and be foolish and indolent.

Notes : Complete absense of happiness, particularly paternal, will come to pass. One will be bereft of masculine vigour. His mother is of doubtful character. These are additional effects for the 4th lord being in the 12th house, according to classical works.

सुतेशे लग्नगे जातो विद्वान् पुत्रसुखान्वितः।
कदर्यो वक्रचित्तश्च परद्रव्यापहारकः ॥४९॥

49. *EFFECTS OF THE 5th LORD IN VARIOUS HOUSES (upto sloka 60)* : If the 5th lord is in the ascendant, the native will be scholarly, be endowed with progenic happiness, be a miser, be crooked, and will steal others' wealth.

Notes : The native having the 5th lord in the ascendant will be of unsteady disposition. Though progenic happiness is denoted by our text, there are other exponents warning of an unpleasant situation in respect of one of the native's sons.

सुतेशे धनगे जातो बहुपुत्रो धनान्वितः।
कुटुम्बपोषको मानी स्त्रीप्रियः सुयशा भुवि ॥५०॥

50. If the 5th lord is in the 2nd, the native will have many sons and wealth, be a *pater familias,* be honourable, be attached to his spouse and be famous in the world.

Notes : Maharshi Parasara praises very highly the placement of the 5th lord in the 2nd house and attributes worldwilde fame for the native. It is actually true in the case of Smt. Indira Gandhi, Prime Minister of India, whose map of birth is furnished below : born on 19th November 1917 (Monday) at 2317 hrs IST at Allahabad, 81E54 25N28.

		Jup (R) 15-0	Ketu 10-34
	Rasi		Asc 28-05 Sat 21-48
Moon 5-35			Mars 16-23
Ven 20-57 Rahu 10-34	Merc 13-11 Sun4-04		

Note the lord of the 5th Mars occupying the 2nd house in Leo. The nativity has a number of splendid planetary influences apart from this. As indicated by sage Parasara, the 2nd house position of the 5th lord gave her a world-wide position and honour for a very long number of years.

One can notice that the native will have ample opportunities of shining brilliantly, whether or not on a world level, with the 2nd house placement of the 5th lord in strength and dignity. Should there further be sufficient Raja Yogas etc. as in the case of the example chart given, the native will be sure to hit the headlines of the world press.

The position of the 5th lord in the 2nd will further cuase asthma and catarrh and the native will have infected lungs. He will become proud owing to his possessions.

सुतेशे सहजे भावे जायते सोदरप्रियः।
पिशुनश्च कदर्यश्च स्वकार्यनिरतः सदा ॥५१॥

51. If the 5th lord is in the 3rd, the native will be attachced to his co-born, be a talebearer and a miser, and be always interested in his own work.

Notes : The native will further be an imposter. He will not be helpful to anybody in any manner.

सुतेशे सखभावस्थे सुखी मातृसुखान्वितः।
लक्ष्मीयुक्तः सुबुद्धिश्च राज्ञोऽमात्योऽथवा गुरुः ॥५२॥

52. If the 5th lord is in the 4th, the native will be happy, endowed with maternal happiness, wealth and intelligence, and be a king or a minister or a preceptor.

Notes : A very long life will come to the native's mother. The native will start acquiring prosperity, right from his youth. He will also own a posh or beautiful house. These are additional effects that will come to pass with the 4th house having the 5th lord in it.

सुतेशे सुतभावस्थे शुभाढ्ये पुत्रवान् नरः।
पापाढ्येऽपत्यहीनोऽसौ गुणवान् मित्रवत्सलः ॥५३॥

53. If the 5th lord is in the 5th, the native will hava progeny if related to a benefic; there will be no issues if malefic

is related to the said 5th lord placed in 5th. The 5th lord in 5th will, however, make one virtuous and dear to friends.

सुतेशे रिपुभावस्थे पुत्रः शत्रुसमो भवेत्।
मृतापत्योऽथवा जातो दत्तक्रीतसुतोऽथवा ॥५४॥

54. If the 5th lord is in the 6th, the native will obtain such sons who will be equal to his enemies or will lose them, or will acquire an adopted or purchased son.

Notes : Maharshi Parasara enunciates four different possibilities if the 5th lord is in the 6th house.

1. Obtaining sons that will be inimical to the native : The 6th house denotes one's enemies. The planet occupying the 6th will signify the class of enemy. 5th lord indicates sons, 9th lord indicates father, 4th lord indicates mother and so on and so forth. Such relative will be inimical to the native corresponding to the rulership of the occupant of the 6th house.

2. Loss of children : The 6th is the maraka sthana for children as it is the 2nd from the 5th. Hence loss of progeny is denoted.

3. Obtaining an adopted issue : Normally this occurs when one is unable to have progeny of his own loins, or fails to have living children. Point 2 above answers the circumstances.

4. Purchase of a child : This is also like adoption. Hence it follows that the situation of the 5th lord in the 6th house is not very desirable, of course excepting Saturn for Virgo ascendant.

It is also not advisable for a female to have her 9th lord in the 10th house from the point of view of filial happiness.

सुतेशे सप्तमे मानी सर्वधर्मसमन्वितः।
पुत्रादिसुखयुक्तश्च परोपकरणे रतः ॥५५॥

55. If the 5th lord is in the 7th, the native will be honourable, very religious, endowed with progenic happiness and be helpful to others.

Notes : With the 5th lord going to the 7th house, the native will be tall in stature and will speak only truth. He will honestly serve his employer, and his dealings will be honest. He will be firm in disposition.

सुतेशे रन्ध्रभावस्थे स्वल्पपुत्रसुखान्वितः ।
कासश्वाससमायुक्तः क्रोधी च सुखवर्जितः ॥५६॥

56. If the 5th lord is in the 8th, the native will not have much progenic happiness, be troubled by cough and pulmonary disorders, be given to anger and be devoid of happiness.

सुतेशे भाग्यगे पुत्रो भपो वा तत्समो भवेत् ।
स्वयं वा ग्रन्थकर्ता च विख्यातः कुलदीपकः ॥५७॥

57. If the 5th lord is in the 9th, the native will be a prince or equal to him, will author treatises, be famous and will shine in his race.

Notes : The placement of the 5th lord in the 9th house is a good augury for writership, authorship, editorship and the like. See the following horoscope of the most venerable Jagadguru Adi Sankaracharya.

Mars	Sun Merc Ven	Rahu	Moon
Jup	Rasi		Asc
Sat	Ketu		

Please note that the 5th lord is in the 9th in a house of Jupiter. Mars is a favourable planet for Cancer ascendant and his dispositor himself is in a mystique house (Aquarius) in aspect to Saturn in exchange. This great person's philosophical expositions in an endeavour to re-stand Hinduism on firm grounds are of perennial importance and his horoscope should serve a perfect example of our above rule.

I have given another horoscope dealing with authorship on page 88 of **"Doctrines of Suka Nadi—Retold"** which is as under :

Born on 21.5.1944 at 1902 hrs War time, 13N40, 79E20.

	Merc Ven Moon	Sun	Sat
	Rasi		Rahu Mars Jup
Ketu			
	Asc		

The native has authored a number of books on a subject dear to his heart. Mark the 5th lord Jupiter in exaltation in the 9th.

Apart from the 5th lord being in the 9th for fame *via* authorship, the 7th house having the 5th lord will equally contribute to such achievements. See the horoscope of late Sri C. G. Rajan on the next page.

The birth data are : born 5th July 1894 AD as taken from his preface given to 'Cancer Ascendant Volume' of Saptarshi Nadi series of Madras Govt. Publications. Sri C. G. Rajan did a great service to the lovers of astrology by bringing out dozens of volumes on astrology in Tamil and English. He had

Mars Rahu		Jup Ven	Sun
			Moon Merc
	Rasi		
	Asc		Sat Ketu

also edited a couple of volumes in Tamil of **Saptarshi Nadis** on behalf of the Oriental Manuscripts Library, University of Madras. He had as well produced a couple of astronomical treatises like **Siddhanta Raja Siromani (Graha Karanam)** containing planetary tables from 3200 BC to 3100 AD. Note the 5th lord in the 7th in his natus along with Venus.

सुतेशे राज्यभावस्थे राजयोगो हि जायते ।
अनेकसुखभोगी च ख्यातकीर्तिर्नरो भवेत् ॥५८॥

58. If the 5th lord is in the 10th, the native will enjoy a Rajayoga and various pleasures, and be very famous.

Notes : For enjoying a superior degree of material benefits like wealth, position, fame *etc.* the 5th lord is the best placed in the 10th house than elsewhere. This one position with sterling qualities will equal many Rajayogas. It is a prerequisite of course that in such a placement the 5th lord is very close to the meridian, if not exactly on the meridian, preferably with exaltation or such other dignities. If he is placed in an enemy's house or such other afflictions tormenting him, he will prove rather adverse than a Rajayoga maker.

सुतेशे लाभगे जातो विद्यावान् जनवल्लभः ।
ग्रन्थकर्ता महादक्षो बहुपुत्रधनान्वितः ॥५९॥

59. If the 5th lord is in the 11th, the native will be learned, dear to people, be an author of treatises, be very skilful and be endowed with many sons and wealth.

Notes : The 5th lord's station in the 11th house will keep one free from misfortunes and unhappiness. He will be of helping nature. His academic achievements will be abundant. He will be happy in respect of his children, but the said 11th house should be a friendly sign for the 5th lord (*vide* rule 48, p. 96 of **Doctrines of Suka Nadi—Retold**). If the 5th lord is inimically placed in the 11th house, for example the Sun in Aquarius in the 11th in the case of Aries ascendant, the progeny will be inimical to the native. However, obtainment of progeny will not be obstructed in that case even.

सुतेशे व्ययभावस्थे जातः पुत्रसुखोज्झितः ।
दत्तपुत्रयुतो वाऽसौ क्रीतपुत्रान्वितोऽथवा ॥६०॥

60. If the 5th lord is in the 12th, the native will be bereft of happiness from his own sons, will have an adopted or purchased son.

Notes : The placement of the 5th lord in the 12th in terminal house will cause various kinds of miseries in the matter of children. One may not obtain a child at all, or may incur inimical relations with his own child. Adoption will surely come to pass if Saturn or Mercury ruling the 5th is in the 12th. In other cases, the disposition of Saturn/Mercury/Jupiter will have to be seen while the 5th lord is in the 12th. Further grave defects with the 5th lord in the 12th are difficulties in digestion and abdominal disorders.

षष्ठेशे लग्नगे जातो रोगवान् कीर्तिसंयुतः ।
आत्मशत्रुर्धनी मानी साहसी गुणवान् नरः ॥६१॥

61. *EFFECTS OF THE 6TH LORD IN VARIOUS HOUSES (upto sloka 72) :* If the 6th lord is in the ascendant, the native will be sickly, famous, inimical to his own men, rich, honourable, adventurous and virtuous.

Notes : The 6th lord in the ascending sign will bring various diseases to the native. He will incur adverse effects in the matter of acquisition of progeny.

Venus in Taurus ascendant will particularly give benefic results in full measure as stated. He will also not stall obtainment of children. There will, however, be more daughters than sons, while the first child will be a male.

षष्ठेशे धनभावस्थे साहसी कुलविश्रुतः।
परदेशी सुखी वक्ता स्वकर्मनिरतः सदा ॥६२॥

62. If the 6th lord is in the 2nd, the native will be adventurous, famous among his racemen, will live in alien countries (or places), be happy, be a skilful speaker and be always interested in his own work.

Notes : The native will further be skilful in dealing with hoary lore. His financial position will be somewhat shaky. He will enjoy good health.

षष्ठेशे सहजः जातः क्रोधी विक्रमवर्जितः।
भ्राता शत्रुसमस्तस्य भृत्यश्चोत्तरदायकः॥६३॥

63. If the 6th lord is in the 3rd, the native will be given to anger, be bereft of courage, inimical to all of his co-born and will have disobedient servants.

Notes : The 3rd house containing the 6th lord will not serve the native with intelligence at all times. To wit, he will be partly deprived of benefits due to his intelligence. He will also not be steady in disposition.

षष्ठेशे सुखभावस्थे मातुः सुखविवर्जितः।
मनस्वी पिशुना द्वेषी चलचित्तोऽतिवित्तवान् ॥६४॥

64. If the 6th lord is in the 4th, the native will be devoid of maternal happiness, be intelligent, be a talebearer, be jealous, fickle-minded and very rich.

षष्ठेशः सुतगो यस्य चलं तस्य धनादिकम्।
शत्रुता पुत्रमित्रैश्च सुखी स्वार्थी दयान्वितः॥६५॥

65. If the 6th lord is in the 5th, the native will have fluctuating finances. He will incur enmity with his sons and friends. He will be happy, selfish and kind.

षष्ठेशे रिपुभावस्थे वैरं स्वज्ञातिमण्डलात् ।
अन्यैः सह भवेन् मैत्री सुखं मध्यं धनादिजम् ॥६६॥

66. If the 6th lord is in the 6th, the native will have enmity with the group of his kinsmen but be friendly to others and will enjoy mediocre happiness in matters like wealth.

Notes : The native will enjoy happiness of conveyances and be free from diseases. His life span will also be considerably lengthy. These are additional effects for the 6th lord in the 6th itself.

षष्ठेशे दारभावस्थे जातो दारसुखोज्झितः ।
कीर्तिमान् गुणवान् मानी साहसी धनसंयुतः ॥६७॥

67. If the 6th lord is in the 7th, the native will be deprived of happiness through wedlock. He will be famous, virtuous, honourable, adventurous and wealthy.

Notes : Apart from denying marital happiness, the 6th lord's occupancy of the 7th house will dissatisfy the native in the matter of progeny. His own spouse will be his sworn enemy.

षष्ठेशेऽष्टमगे जातो रोगी शत्रुर्मनीषिणाम् ।
परद्रव्याभिलाषी च परदाररतोऽशुचिः ॥६८॥

68. If the 6th lord is in the 8th, the native will be sickly, inimical, will desire others' wealth, be interested in others' wives and be impure (or degraded).

Notes : It is not good for one's purity of character if the 8th house is occupied by the 6th lord. The native will be ever incurring enmity with others and be not happy. He will have a green eye on others' learning and an eye on others' wealth.

षष्ठेशे भाग्यगे जातः काष्ठपाषाणविक्रयी ।
व्यवहारे क्वचिद्धानिः क्वचिद्वृद्धिश्च जायते ॥६९॥

69. If the 6th lord is in the 9th, the native will trade in wood and stones (पाषाण also means poison), and will have fluctuating professional fortunes.

Notes : The Maharshi seems to suggest that one will deal in building construction material by saying that one will sell wood and stones with the 6th lord in the 9th. It will further cause ups and downs in one's livelihood.

षष्ठेशे दशमे भावे मानवः कुलविश्रुतः।
अभक्तश्च पितुर्वक्ता विदेशे च सुखी भवेत् ॥७०॥

70. If the 6th lord is in the 10th, the native will be well-known among his men, will not be respectfully disposed to his father and will be happy in foreign countries. He will be a gifted speaker.

Notes : One will be greatly valorous and learned in Sastras (or ancient lore). There will be litigations on account of ancestral properties. Dutifulness and living in foreign place will also come to pass. These are in furtherance to the sage's views for the placement of the 6th lord in the 10th house.

षष्ठेशे लाभगे जातः शत्रुतो धनमाप्नुयात्।
गुणवान् साहसी मानी किन्तु पुत्रसुखोज्झितः ॥७१॥

71. If the 6th lord is in the 11th, the native will gain wealth through his enemies, be virtuous, adventurous and will be somewhat bereft of progenic happiness.

Notes : One will, to some extent, be happy and to yet some extent be unhappy if the 6th lord occupies the 11th house. This is in regard to progeny. There is also a view that this position can wholly deny acquisition of a child.

षष्ठेशे व्ययभावस्थे व्यसने व्ययकृत् सदा।
विद्वद्द्वेषी भवेज्जातो जीवहिंसासु तत्परः ॥७२॥

72. If the 6th lord is in the 12th the native will always spend on vices, be hostile to learned people and will torture living beings.

Notes : The native will be of questionable morality and will ever be intent on deriving sexual pleasures from other females as well.

दारेशे लग्नगे जातः परदारेषु लम्पटः।
दुष्टो विचक्षणोऽधीरो जनो वातरुजान्वितः ॥७३॥

73. *EFFECTS OF THE 7TH LORD IN VARIOUS HOUSES (upto sloka 84)* : If the 7th lord is in the ascendant, the native will go to others' wives, be wicked, skilful, devoid of courage and afflicted by windy diseases.

Notes : The native will not be firm in his words and actions. He will impart courage in others although he himself will be bereft of courage. So say learned astrologers in the context of the ascendant being occupied by the 7th lord.

दारेशे धनगे जातो बहुस्त्रीभिः समन्वितः।
दारयोगाद्धनाप्तिश्च दीर्घसूत्री च मानवः ॥७४॥

74. If the 7th lord is in the 2nd, the native will have many wives, will gain wealth through his wife and be procrastinating in nature.

Notes : This position will further give corrupt character making one addicted to many women. He will lose his wife early. His prosperity will ascend with his marriage.

दारेशे सहजे जातो मृतापत्यो हि मानवः।
कदाचिज्जायते पुत्री यत्नात् पुत्रोऽपि जीवति ॥७५॥

75. If the 7th lord is in the 3rd, the native will face loss of children and sometimes with great difficulty there will exist a living son. There is also the possibility of birth of a daughter (who will sustain).

Notes : Three salient features in regard to progeny are denoted by sage Parasara for the 3rd house placement of the 7th lord. Firstly, loss of children in general. Secondly, possibility of (rarely) acquiring a daughter. Lastly, no possibility of having a living son. In fine, probably a female child will live long to keep the native happy, while male children will pass away as they are born.

दारेशे सुखभावस्थे जाया नास्य वशे सदा।
स्वयं सत्यप्रियो धीमान् धर्मात्मा दन्तरोगयुक् ॥७६॥

76. If the 7th lord is in the 4th, the wife of the native will not be under his control. He will be fond of truth, be intelligent and religious. He will suffer from dental diseases.

Notes : A disobedient wife follows the 4th house position of the 7th lord. This is Maharshi's instruction. However, Ramadayalu states in this context thus, पातिव्रत्योद्भासिता तस्यभार्या meaning that the native's wife will brilliantly shine with chastity or devotion to husband. Lord Rama's sacred horoscope is a classic example having Cancer ascendant with Saturn, the 7th lord, in the 4th—of course in exaltation. I do not possess even the slightest competence to say that the Maharshi's view is untenable.

In this context, however, I quote a horoscope from **"Saptarshi Nadi"** (Volume for Taurus ascendant). The whole Nadi was a product of intercourse between four groups of sages, each group having seven great sages, in the benign presence of Parvati, a consort of Lord Siva. In the seminar on Taurus ascendant, Parasara was also a participant. The horoscope in particular (bearing No. 25 in the original volume) was analysed by Parasara himself as one of the seven Rishis in dialogue. See the nativity :

Jup	Saturn	Ascdt	Ketu
	RASI		Merc Sun Ven
			Mars
Rahu	Moon		

Dealing with the above horoscope, Parasara describes the native's spouse thus : "she will be somewhat short-tempered. She will deliver auspicious words. She will be dear to her husband. She will live begetting fame from all the four directions. She will be fortunate. She will be free from any blemish (or Dosha). She will be dark in complexion. She will feed the needy. In beauty, she will be akin to *Rathi* (the extremely charming spouse of the extremely charming Cupid, the Hindu God of beauty and son of Maha Vishnu). She will possess many ornaments and be intelligent. She will be modest and will not have any desire for other men (than her spouse, i.e. the native in question)." This is how sage Parasara describes the wife of the native in question in verses 27-29 *ibid.* Though no direct reason has been attributed for the chastity of the spouse, we cannot ignore the disposition of the 7th lord, particularly with debilitated Moon in the 7th. The 7th lord is in the 4th giving the native a spouse who would be extremely devout proving an asset to the husband. As such the view of our present sloka in regard to the spouse is at the outset defective. Thus the wife cannot be out of the control of the native. The Chaukambha edition also clearly states that the native's wife will not be chaste, see जायानैवपतिव्रता and hence the version of our sloka is also rightly interpreted.

दारेशे पञ्चमे जातो मानी सर्वगुणान्वितः ।
सर्वदा हर्षयुक्तश्च तथा सर्वधनाधिपः ॥७७॥

77. If the 7th lord is in the 5th, native will be honourable, endowed with all (i.e. seven principal) virtues, always delighted and endowed with all kinds of wealth.

Notes : I have observed two salient features in the 7th lord's getting into the 5th house. These are : (1) Delay and disappointments in married life. The conjugal life seldom proves happy. (2) Severe affliction to progenic indications. Either there will be unhappiness on account of children or loss of children.

The effects mentioned by the sage, *viz.* virtues, wealth, honour and (general) happiness will also come to pass. The happiness about marriage and progeny will visibly be absent.

This will further give rise to the native's association with great people. He will be endowed with boosted spirits.

दारेशे रिपुभावस्थे भार्या तस्य रुजान्विता।
स्त्रिया सहाऽथ वा वैरं स्वयं क्रोधी सुखोज्झितः ॥७८॥

78. If the 7th lord is in the 6th, the native will beget a sickly wife, be inimical to her, given to anger and devoid of happiness.

Notes : The 7th lord in the 6th will reduce the general happiness of the native apart from severely inflicting his conjugal bliss. His own health will be poor while his wife will be weak in constitution. She will equally have adverse health conditions The native will coaleasce with harlots.

दारेशे सप्तमे भावे जातो दारसुखान्वितः।
धीरो विचक्षणो धीमान् केवलं वातरोगवान् ॥७९॥

79. If the 7th lord is in the 7th, the native will be endowed with happiness through wife, be courageous, skilful and intelligent but only afflicted by windy diseases.

Notes : By using the word "केवलं" in the text meaning "only", the sage hints that the only possible defect in the 7th lord's placement in the 7th itself will be troubles from windy diseases (like rheumatism, artheritis *etc.*).

One undesirable quality will, however, be found in the native, contrary to no adverse indication in the text, and that is his addiction to other females. This is an exception to Venus occupying the 7th house identical with Taurus or Libra.

दारेशे मृत्युभावस्थे जातो दारसुखोज्झितः।
भार्याऽपि रोगयुक्ताऽस्य दुःशीलाऽपि न चानुगा ॥८०॥

80. If the 7th lord is in the 8th, the native will be deprived of marital happiness. His wife will be troubled by diseases, be devoid of good disposition and will not obey the native.

Notes : As the 7th lord goes to the 8th house, the native's spouse will be liable to incur afflictions to her longevity. However, marriage may bring some pecuniary gains for the native.

दारेशे धर्मभावस्थे नानास्त्रीभिः समागमः ।
जायाहृतमना जातो बह्वारम्भकरो नरः ॥८१॥

81. If the 7th lord is in the 9th, the native will have union with many women, be well-disposed to his own wife and will have many undertakings (or assignments).

दारेशे कर्मभावस्थे नास्य जाया वशानुगा ।
स्वयं धर्मरतो जातो धनपुत्रादिसंयुतः ॥८२॥

82. If the 7th lord is in the 10th, the native will beget a disobedient wife, will be religious and endowed with wealth, sons etc.

दारेशे लाभभावस्थे दारैरर्थसमागमः ।
पुत्रादिसुखमल्पं च जनः कन्याप्रजो भवेत् ॥८३॥

83. If the th lord is in the 11th, the native will gain wealth through his wife, be endowed with less happiness from sons etc. and will have daughters.

Notes : If the 7th lord is in the 11th house, there is a possibility of the native losing his children to his grief. He will obtain (more) daughters. His own sons will be hostile to him and will cause him no happiness. Living son also seems to be very remote a probability.

दारेशे व्ययगे जातो दरिद्रः कृपणोऽपि वा ।
भार्याऽपि व्ययशीलाऽस्य वस्त्राजीवी नरो भवेत् ॥८४॥

84. If the 7th lord is in [the 12th, the native will incur penury, be a miser and his livelihood will be related to clothes. His wife will be a spendthrift.

अष्टमेशे तनौ जातस्तनुसौख्यविवर्जितः ।
देवानां ब्राह्मणानां च निन्दको व्रणसंयुतः ॥८५॥

85. *EFFECTS OF THE 8TH LORD IN VARIOUS HOUSES (upto sloka 96)* : If the 8th lord is in the ascendant, the native will be devoid of physical felicity and will suffer from wounds. He will be hostile to gods and brahmins (or religious people).

अष्टमेशे धने बाहुबलहीनः प्रजायते।
धनं तस्य भवेत् स्वल्पं नष्ट वित्तं न लभ्यते ॥८६॥

86. If the 8th lord is in the 2nd, the native will be devoid of bodily vigour, will enjoy a little wealth and will not regain lost wealth.

रन्ध्रेशे सहजे भावे भ्रातृसौख्यं न जायते।
सालस्यो भृत्यहीनश्च जायते बलवर्जितः ॥८७॥

87. If the 8th lord is in the 3rd, the native will be devoid of fraternal happiness, be indolent and devoid of servants and strength.

रन्ध्रेशे सुखभावस्थे मातृहीनो भवेच्छिशुः।
गृहभूमिसुखैर्हीनो मित्रद्रोही न संशयः ॥८८॥

88. If the 8th lord is in the 4th, the child will be deprived of its mother. He will be devoid of a house, lands and happiness and will doubtlessly betray his friends.

Notes : Maharshi Parasara uses the word "शिशु" meaning child. Hence it is apparent that the native will lose his mother in the very childhood if the 8th lord is in the 4th house.

रन्ध्रेशे सुतभावस्थे जडबुद्धिः प्रजायते।
स्वल्पप्रज्ञो भवेज्जातो दीर्घायुश्च धनान्वितः ॥८९॥

89. If the 8th lord is in the 5th, the native will be dull-witted, will have limited number of of children, be longlived and wealthy.

Notes : One's financial acquisitions, though abundant, will not be steady and be subjected to fluctuations. Though his intentions and actions will be *bona fide,* they will go unrecognized. He will not be steady in disposition and will off and on change his line of thinking. He will not enjoy filial bliss. These are additional hints for the 8th lord's stationing in the 5th house at birth.

रन्ध्रेशे रिपुभावस्थे शत्रुजेता भवेज्जनः।
रोगयुक्तशरीरश्च बाल्ये सर्पजलाद् भयम् ॥९०॥

90. If the 8th lord is in the 6th, the native will win over his enemies, be afflicted by diseases and during childhood will incur danger through snakes and water.

Notes : The position of the 8th lord in the 6th house is a sureshot of success over enemies and in litigations. The native will be reduced to danger through snakes, scorpions etc. during childhood. Afterwards he will be free from such calamities. However, this position is not very favourable for one's health. This also indicates a long span of life.

रन्ध्रेशे दारभावस्थे तस्य भार्याद्वयं भवेत् ।
व्यापारे च भवेद्हानिस्तस्मिन् पापयुते ध्रुवम् ॥९१॥

91. If the 8th lord is in the 7th, the native will have two wives. If the 8th lord is conjunct a malefic in the 7th there will surely be downfull in his business (or livelihood).

Notes : The 7th house being occupied by the 8th lord is a forerunner of difficulties in married life. There will be want of understanding between the native and his spouse. The constitution of the spouse will be quite weak and she will always be subjected to uncertainties or dangers.

Outwardly the native may pose to be God-fearing. But he will not be sincerely devoted to the Almighty. He will be an expert in stealing others' things.

रन्ध्रेशे मृत्युभावस्थे जाता दीर्घायुषा युतः ।
निर्बले मध्यमायुः स्याच्चौरो निन्द्योऽन्यनिन्दकः ॥९२॥

92. If the 8th lord is in the 8th the native will be long-lived. If the said planet be weak being in the 8th, the longevity will be medium, while the native will be a thief, be blameworthy and will blame others well.

Notes : In remaining in the 8th itself, the 8th lord should be quite strong in Shadbala, so the native will be long-lived. If he is bereft of strength, the native will not enjoy full span of life.

The 8th house in occupation by its own lord will give a spouse with questionable character. However she will be a source of financial help to the native by her own earnings or properties. The native will inherit ancestral properties as well. The evil effects cited above will not come to pass for an Aquarius native having Mercury in exaltation in the 8th in Virgo. He should be within the first half of Virgo to stall the said evils. In the later portion of Virgo his potence considerably decreases.

अष्टमेश तपःस्थाने धर्मद्रोही च नास्तिकः।
दुष्टभार्यापतिश्चैव परद्रव्यापहारकः ॥९३॥

93. If the 8th lord is in the 9th, the native will betray his relig on, be a heterodox, will beget a wicked wife and will steal others' wealth.

Notes : The native will suffer frequent misfortunes and downfalls. His prosperity will not be unobstructed and he will find it difficult to cope up with professional adversities. His father will suffer a cut in longevity. His understanding with his father will be deficient. Progenic happiness will not come to him in full measure. His wife will be of "questionable birth". She will go to other men and beget progeny. The native himself will be addicted to others' housewives. These are additional effects of the 8th lord occupying the 9th house in a nativity. In the case of a Gemini native, Saturn occupying the 9th house (his Moolatrikona) will not produce these malefic effects. But his benefic tendencies will be quite meagre.

रन्ध्रेशे कर्मभावस्थे पितृसौख्यविवर्जितः।
पिशुनः कर्महीनश्च यदि नैव शुभेक्षिते ॥९४॥

94. If the 8th lord is in the 10th the native will be devoid of paternal bliss, be a tale-bearer and be bereft of livelihood. If there is an aspect in the process from a benefic, then these evils will not mature.

Notes : There is a school of thought to say that the 8th lord occupying the 9th house will cause the deaths of parents right in the native's boyhood. Apparently one will not enjoy parental happiness for a long duration.

This placement of the 8th lord will produce all kinds of miseries in livelihood, fortunes, fame, properties and the like.

According to Maharshi Parasara, if the 8th lord in the 10th house is (well) related to a benefic, no evils will come to pass.

रन्ध्रेशे लाभभावस्थे सपापे धनवर्जितः ।
बाल्ये दुःखी सुखी पश्चात् दीर्घायुश्च शुभान्विते ॥९५॥

95. If the 8th lord along with a malefic is in the 11th, the native will be devoid of wealth and will be miserable in boyhood but happy later on. Should the 8th lord be in conjunction with a benefic and be in the 11th, the native will be long-lived.

Notes : The 8th lord in the 11th house, unless related to a malefic, particularly by conjunction, will not deprive the native of financial benefits. If he is alone in the 11th, he will not prove that bad in this respect. Moreover, for Taurus ascendant, Jupiter in the 11th house is not baneful. And for Scorpio ascendant, Mercury in the 11th will prove a highly favourable bargain in the matter of wealth, fame, knowledge etc.

रन्ध्रेशे व्ययभावस्थे कुकार्ये व्ययकृत् सदा ।
अल्पायुश्च भवेज्जातः सपापे च विशेषतः ॥९६॥

96. If the 8th lord is in the 12th, the native will spend on evil deeds and will incur a short life. More so, if there be additionally a malefic in the said house.

भाग्येशे लग्नगे जातो भाग्यवान् भूपवन्दितः ।
सुशीलश्च सुरूपश्च विद्यावान् जनपूजितः ॥९७॥

97. *EFFECTS OF THE 9TH LORD IN VARIOUS HOUSES (up to sloka 108) :* If the 9th lord is in the ascendant, the native will be fortunate (or prosperous), will be honoured by the king, be virtuous, charming, learned and honoured by the public.

Notes : If the 9th lord is in the rising sign, the native will hold a very high position which will bring him wealth and fame. He will be free from enemies. A female having the said position will prove a worthy housewife and be rid of afflictions from other planetary sources. [(These effects will not be enjoyed by a Scorpio native.)

भाग्येशे धनभावस्थे पण्डितो जनवल्लभः ।
जायते धनवान् कामी स्त्रीपुत्रादिसुखान्वितः ॥९८॥

98. If the 9th lord is in the 2nd, the native will be a scholar, be dear to all, wealthy, sensuous and endowed with happiness from wife, sons etc.

भाग्येशे भ्रातृभावस्थे जातो भ्रातृसुखान्वितः ।
धनवान् गुणवांश्चापि रूपशीलसमन्वितः ॥९९॥

99. If the 9th lord is in the 3rd, the native will be endowed with fraternal blies, be wealthy, virtuous and charming.

भाग्येशे तुर्यभावस्थे गृहयानसुखान्वितः ।
सर्वसम्पत्तियुक्तश्च मातृभक्तो भवेन्नरः ॥१००॥

100. If the 9th lord is in the 4th, the native will enjoy houses, conveyances and happiness, will have all kinds of wealth and be devoted to his mother.

भाग्येशे सुतभावस्थे सुतभाग्यसमन्वितः ।
गुरुभक्तिरतो धीरो धर्मात्मा पण्डितो नरः ॥१०१॥

101. If the 9th lord is in the 5th the native will be endowed with sons and prosperity, devoted to elders, bold, charitable and learned.

भाग्येशे रिपुभावस्थे स्वल्पभाग्यो भवेन्नरः ।
मातुलादिसुखैर्हीनः शत्रुभिः पीडितः सदा ॥१०२॥

102. If the 9th lord is in the 6th, the native will enjoy meagre prosperity, be devoid of happiness from maternal relatives and be always troubled by enemies.

भाग्येशे दारभावस्थे दारयोगात् सुखोदयः ।
गुणवान् कीर्तिमांश्चापि जायते द्विजसत्तमः ॥१०३॥

103. O Brahmin, If the 9th lord is in the 7th, the native will beget happiness after marriage, be virtuous, and famous.

Notes : One will further be able to achieve success in all his undertakings. His prosperity will pick up after marriage. The native will be not well disposed to his father. These are additional effects due to the 7th house placement of the 9th lord.

भाग्येशे मृत्युभावस्थे भाग्यहीनो नरो भवेत् ।
ज्येष्ठभ्रातृसुखं नैव तस्य जातस्य जायते ॥१०४॥

104. If the 9th lord is in the 8th, the native will not be prosperous and will not enjoy happiness from his elder brother.

Notes : Having got the 9th lord relegated to the 8th house, one will be devoid of fortunes. He will face failures in all his undertakings. He will not achieve professional and financial stability. His father will primarily incur a cut in longevity. The native will be a source of miseries to his elder brothers/sisters.

A blessing in disguise with this position is a probable inheritence of patrimony by the native.

भाग्येशे भाग्यभावस्थे बहुभाग्यसमन्वितः ।
गुणसौन्दर्यसम्पन्नो सहजेभ्यः सुखं बहु ॥१०५॥

105. If the 9th lord is in the 9th, the native will be endowed with abundant fortunes, virtues and beauty and will enjoy much happiness from co-born.

Notes : Should the 9th lord be in the 9th itself, one will obtain fraternal bliss. His co-bron will amass fortune. The native himself will own properties in a large scale. He will achieve easy success in each and every undertaking. His father will play a significant role in his (i.e. the native's) progress. The native's mother will be free from diseases. The native will be nurtured by his maternal grand parents.

भाग्येशे कर्मभावस्थे जातो राजाऽथ तत्समः ।
मन्त्री सेनापतिर्वाऽपि गुणवान् जनपूजितः ॥१०६॥

106. If the 9th lord is in the 10th, the native will be a king or equal to him or be a minister or an army chief, be virtuous and dear to all.

Notes : The sage suggests that with the 9th lord going to the 10th the native will be either a king or a minister or an army chief. Apparently, if the 9th lord is prepotent, one will enjoy royal status. The strength proportionately falling down will make the native enjoy comparatively lesser positions.

भाग्येशे लाभभावस्थे धनलाभो दिने दिने।
भवतो गुरुजनानां च गुणवान् पुण्यवानपि ॥१०७॥

107. If the 9th lord is in the 11th, the native will enjoy financial gains day by day, be devoted to elders, virtuous and meritorious in acts.

Notes : The native who has the 9th lord in the 11th house will see increasing phases of fortunes and prosperity. The 9th lord indicates one's prosperity and the 11th house gains. Hence the said position is extremely favourable for material upliftment. This will, however, not apply to Gemini ascendant having Saturn, the 9th lord, in the 11th house. On the contrary it will prove highly detrimental for the prosperity of the native.

Additional effects due to the 9th lord's placement in the 11th house (excepting of course Gemini ascending), high honours, spiritual success, metaphysical achievements and gains through father.

भाग्येशो व्ययभावस्थो भाग्यहानिकरो नृणाम्।
शुभकार्ये व्ययो नित्यं निर्धनोऽतिथिसङ्गमात् ॥१०८॥

108. If the 9th lord is in the 12th, the native will incur loss of fortunes, will always spend on auspicious acts and will become poor on account of entertaining guests.

Notes : The 9th lord in the 12th is said to cause loss of wealth on account of entertaining guests. In the modern context lavish parties will take this role. The native will land in financial difficulties on account of throwing parties and the like.

This position is not also auspicious for the happiness of elder brothers and sisters.

कर्मेशे लग्नगे जातो विद्वान् ख्यातो धनी कविः।
बाल्ये रोगी सुखी पश्चाद् धनवृद्धिर्दिने दिने ॥१०९॥

109. *EFFECTS OF THE 10TH LORD IN VARIOUS HOUSES (upto sloka 120)* : If the 10th lord is in the ascendant, the native will be scholarly, famous, be a poet, will incur diseases in boyhood and be happy later on. His wealth will increase day by day.

Notes : The 10th lord occupying the ascendant is very favourable for riches giving a royal status to the native. The following figure belongs to Sarabhoji Maharaja of Tanjore.

			Rahu Moon Sat
	RASI		Jup Ven
Ketu	Mars		Ascdt Sun Merc

In the above chart, the lord of the 10th is Mercury who is in the ascendant in own sign. The 2nd lord Venus is in the company of exalted Jupiter. The native amassed a vast kingdom and wealth. He established the Tanjore Saraswati Mahal Library which is a treasure-house of literature of ancient lore.

The ascendant having the 10th lord in it will contribute to the native's becoming well educated and learned. It will also make one widely famous.

If there are no Balarishta combinations and if the 6th lord is sufficiently favourable, then the position of the 10th lord in the ascendant will not cause diseases in boyhood.

राज्येशे धनभावस्थे धनवान् गुणसंयुत: ।
राजमान्यो वदान्यश्च पित्रादिसुखसंयुत: ॥११०॥

110 If the 10th lord is in the 2nd, the native will be wealthy, virtuous, honoured by the king, charitable and will enjoy happiness from father and others.

Notes : The placement of the 10th lord in the 2nd will give immeasurable financial success through one's own profession or calling, apart from a large scale patrimony. (This will be more effective for Gemini ascendant having the 10th lord Jupiter in the 2nd in exaltation). His fame will spread in all corners, according to other classical exponents.

The horoscope of Mr. Morarji Desai, an erstwhile Prime Minister of India, as given below, is a perfect example to depict professional fame etc.

Born on 29.2.1896 at1258 hrs (LMT) in Bulsar (Gujrat).

			Asc
Sun Rahu	RASI		Jup
Mars Merc Venus			Moon Ketu
		Saturn	

The 10th lord is in the 2nd house speaking for the wide political famė he earned through a number of years. He also occupied the coveted position of Prime Minister. He has been a successful person both financially and professionally. The exaltation of Saturn in a trine, and of Jupiter in the 2nd have been key factors in the native's success. The 11th house receives its own lord's aspect from exaltation sign giving gains in a better manner.

Also refer to the birth chart of Mrs Indira Gandhi, where Mars ruling the 10th house is in the 2nd house. Except for a brief period, she continues to be the Prime Minister from 1966 onwards. Her fame has spread in all corners and she is considered to be one of the most skilful administrators.

कर्मेशे सहजे जातो भ्रातृभृत्यसुखान्वितः।
विक्रमी गुणसम्पन्नः वाग्मी सत्यरतो नरः ॥१११॥

111. If the 10th lord is in the 3rd, the native will enjoy happiness from brothers and servants, be valorous, virtuous, eloquent and truthful.

कर्मेशे सुखभावस्थे सुखी मातृहिते रतः।
यान-भूमि-गृहाधीशो गुणवान् धनवानपि ॥११२॥

112. If the 10th lord is in the 4th, the native will be happy, be always interested in his mother's welfare, will lord over conveyances, lands and houses, be virtuous and wealthy.

कर्मेशे सुतभावस्थे सर्वविद्यासमन्वितः।
सर्वदा हर्षसंयुक्तो धनवान् पुत्रवानपि ॥११३॥

113. If the 10th lord is in the 5th, the native will be endowed with all kinds of learning, be always delighted and be wealthy and endowed with sons.

Notes : The lord of the 10th house occupying the 5th house will prove a great asset for the native bestowing abundant wealth which will never leave him. He will have a number of children. There will seldom be filial grief for him. He will always move among wealthy people. In the matter of learning and education, sky is the limit in his case. He will be very truthfully disposed and command all material comforts of life. Dr. Rabindranath Tagore's natus is given below which will describe his radiant intelligence, brilliant learning and unparalleled poetic abilities. Birth data : born May 7, 1861 at 3.15 AM IST at 22N35 88E30.

Note the 10th lord Jupiter in exaltation in the 5th obtaining a potential status over other planets in the horoscope. Jupiter's

Moon Ascdt	Sun Merc Venus		Mars Ketu
	RASI		Jup
			Sat
Rahu			

powerful aspect on his dispositor, the Moon, lent that tremendous mental impetus to the native that he was a preeminent poet with a matchless learning. Mercury ruling the 4th house is unaffected by the Sun, being 16° apart.

कर्मेशे रिपुभावस्थे पितृसौख्यविवर्जितः।
चतुरोऽपि धनैर्हीनः शत्रुभिः परिपीडितः॥११४॥

114. If the 10th lord is in the 6th, the native will be bereft of paternal bliss. Although he may be skilful he will be bereft of wealth and be troubled by enemies.

Notes : The 10th lord going to the 6th house is a dire blemish for professional and monetary stability. One will undergo frequent changes in his calling and will suffer losses therein. His financial growth will be severely paralyzed. He will have a number of enemies contributing to his decline. He will incur lasting diseases. An advantage, however, will come to him in the form of extreme intelligence.

राज्येशे दारभावस्थे जातो दारसुखान्वितः।
मनस्वी गुणवान् वाग्मी सत्यधर्मरतः सदा॥११५॥

115. If the 10th lord is in the 7th, the native will be

endowed with happiness through wife, be intelligent, virtuous, eloquent, truthful and religious.

कर्मेशे रन्ध्रभावस्थे कर्महीनो भवेन्नरः।
दीर्घायुरप्यसौ जातः परनिन्दापरायणः॥११६॥

116. If the 10th lord is in the 8th, the native will be devoid of (good) acts, longlived and intent on blaming others.

Notes : The 10th lord's placement in the 8th house denotes potence of longevity. The 10th lord is the indicator of one's Karmic credit and his strength or his position in the 8th house will contribute to great longevity. That the 10th lord should be considered akin to Saturn in the matter of life span is a fact taught to us by Maharshi Parasra, vide sloka 3 in ch. 19. The rule as per the present verse will, however, not apply to Gemini ascendant horoscope having Jupiter in the 8th (in fall) which will in fact adversely affect longevity. And a Leo native will be a significant beneficiary with Venus in the 8th in exaltation and will enjoy a considerably long span of life.

राज्येशे भाग्यभे जातो राजा राजकुलोद्भवः।
तत्समोऽन्यकुलोत्पन्नो धनपुत्रादिसंयुतः॥११७॥

117. If the 10th lord is in the 9th, one born of royal scion will become a king whereas an ordinary native will be equal to a king. This placement will confer wealth and progenic happiness etc.

कर्मेशे राज्यभावस्थे सर्वकर्मपटुः सुखी।
विक्रमी सत्यवक्ता च गुरुभक्तिरतो नरः॥११८॥

118. If the 10th lord is in the 10th, the native will be skilful in all jobs, be valorous, truthful and devoted to elders.

राज्येशे लाभभावस्थे जातो धनसुतान्वितः।
हर्षवान् गुणवांश्चापि सत्यवक्ता सदा सुखी॥११९॥

119. If the 10th lord is in the 11th, the native will be endowed with wealth, happiness and sons. He will be virtuous, truthful and always delighted.

राज्येशे व्ययभावस्थे तस्य राजगृहे व्ययः ।
शत्रुतोऽपि भयं नित्यं चतुरश्चापि चिन्तितः ॥१२०॥

120. If the 10th lord is in the 12th, the native will spend through royal abodes (*i e.* kings), will have fear from enemies and will be worried in spite of being skilful.

Notes : Expenditure through royal abodes possibly indicates that the native will lose on taxes, fines etc. to the government as the 12th house is involved. Otherwise, this can mean luxurious political expenses. This placement will cause troubles in financial matters through the Government.

लाभेशे लग्नगे जातः सात्त्विको धनवान् सुखी ।
समदृष्टिः कविर्वाग्मी सदा लाभ-समन्वितः ॥१२१॥

121. *EFFECTS OF THE 11TH LORD IN VARIOUS HOUSES (upto sloka 132)* : If the 11th lord is in the ascendant, the native will be genuine in disposition, be rich, happy, even-sighted, be a poet, be eloquent in speech and be always endowed with gains.

Notes : When the 11th lord is in the ascendant, the native will always befriend the virtuous and reject evil associations. He will be extremely prosperous after marriage.

लाभेशे धनभावस्थे जातः सर्वधनान्वितः ।
सर्वसिद्धियुतो दाता धार्मिकश्च सुखी सदा ॥१२२॥

122. If the 11th lord is in the 2nd, the native will be endowed with all kinds of wealth and all kinds of accomplishments, be charitable, religious and always happy.

लाभेशे सहजे जातः कुशलः सर्वकर्मसु ।
धनी भ्रातृसुखोपेतः शूलरोगभयं क्वचित् ॥१२३॥

123. If the 11th lord is in the 3rd, the native will be skilful in all jobs, wealthy, endowed with fraternal bliss and may sometimes incur gout pains.

लाभेशे सुखभावस्थे लाभो मातृकुलाद् भवेत् ।
तीर्थयात्राकरो जातो गृहभूमिसुखान्वितः ॥१२४॥

124. If the 11th lord is in the 4th, the native will gain

from maternal relatives, will undertake visits to shrines and will possess happiness of house and lands.

लाभेशे सुतभावस्थे भवन्ति सुखिनः सुताः।
विद्यावन्तोऽपि सच्छीलाः स्वयं धर्मरतः सुखी ॥१२५॥

125. If the 11th lord is in the 5th, the native's children will be happy, educated and virtuous. He will be himself religious and happy.

लाभेशे रोगभावस्थे जातो रोगसमन्वितः।
क्रूरबुद्धिः प्रवासी च शत्रुभि परिपीडितः ॥१२६॥

126. If the 11th lord is in the 6th. the native will be afflicted by diseases, be cruel, living in foreign places and troubled by enemies.

Notes : The placement of the 11th lord in the 6th house will augment the chances of 'acquisition' of diseases. The native will incur defects of hearing organ. (In Aquarius, the 11th lord will particularly afflict a Virgo native with dire deafness.) The native will be so selfish that for his own happiness he will leave his family members and live away from his home or hometown. Servitude will befit him rather than an independent profession. He will often undergo financial reversals.

लाभेशे दारभावस्थे लाभो दारकुलात् सदा।
उदारश्च गुणी कामी जनो भार्यावशानुगः ॥१२७॥

127. If the 11th lord is in the 7th, the native will always gain through his wife's relatives, be liberal, virtuous, sensuous and will remain at the command of his spouse.

Notes : Should the 7th house be occupied by the 11th lord, the native will always look upto and receive help from his wife's relatives. He will be quite affluent as well. He will lack in wisdom. Judgement will lack in him in the matter of expenses and he cannot make out where to spend and where not

A strong urge to seek union with others' females will always be prevalent in him but none will bother for him. Even his own spouse will boss over him.

लाभेशे रन्ध्रभावस्थे हानिः कार्येषु जायते।
तस्यायुश्च भवेद्दीर्घं प्रथमं मरणं स्त्रियः ॥१२८॥

128. If the 11th lord is in the 8th, the native will incur reversals in his undertakings and will live long while his wife will predecease him.

Notes : The 11th lord in the 8th house increases the native's longevity. The geniture given earlier of Sri Morarji Desai having Mars in the 8th being the 11th lord bears an ample testimony to this effect. However, this rule should not be applied to Leo ascendant having Mercury, the 11th lord, in the 8th house in debilitation.

लाभेशे भाग्यभावस्थे भाग्यवान् जायते नरः।
चतुरः सत्यवादी च राजपूज्यो धनाधिपः ॥१२९॥

129. If the 11th lord is in the 9th the native will be fortunate, skilful, truthful, honoured by the king and be affluent.

लाभेशे कर्मभावस्थे भूपवन्द्यो गुणान्वितः।
निजधर्मरतो धीमान् सत्यवादी जितेन्द्रियः ॥१३०॥

130. If the 11th lord is in the 10th, the native will be honoured by the king, be virtuous, attached to his religion, intelligent, truthful and will subdue his senses.

Notes : with the 11th lord occupying the 10th house, one will be primarily intent on public welfare and redemption. He will delve deep into the core of his religion and bring out myriad truths to educate the public. He will create an epoch of his own which will go into the pages of history. The sacred horoscope of Sri Bhakti Vedanta Swamiji is a fitting example as given below. He was born on September Ist, 1896 AD, at 1530 hrs at Calcutta.

In this chart, the 11th lord Venus is in the 10th in debilitation and in the company of the 10th lord Mercury in exaltation. The Neechabhanga occurring to Venus enhanced his merits and took him to matchless heights. Swamiji had many other brilliant features in his horoscope, *viz.* Saturn in peak in the 11th house, the 3 important planets—the Sun, Ketu and Jupiter — all effectively joining in the 9th house (and being in one and same Navamsa) and so on and so forth. He founded Hare

		Moon Mars	
Rahu			
			Sun Jup Ketu
Lagna		Sat	Merc Venus

Krishna movement spreading the sacred name of Lord Krishna to the West. He brought out in print his commentaries on Vedas, Gita etc. in uncountable volumes. Above all, he is a magic word on the lips of millions.

It is my experience that a planet with cancelled debilitation would give such splendid results keeping other planets behind and make the world conscious of such a native. It is of course a prerequisite that the ascendant lord should primarily be strong enough. In the case of Swamiji, the soul stands well-fortified and robed with identity with the praise-worthy Lord. Mark the prepotent 9th house containing ascendant lord along with the Sun and Ketu.

The reader can always note that if the 11th lord is well disposed in the 10th house, the native concerned will dedicate his life for others and be devoid of desires to meeting personal ends. That is the moral we learn from the Swamiji's radix.

लाभेशे लाभभावस्थे लाभः सर्वेषु कर्मसु ।
पाण्डित्यं च सुखं तस्य वर्द्धते च दिने दिने ॥१३१॥

131. If the 11th lord is in the 11th, the native will gain in all his undertakings while his learning and happiness will be on the increase day by day.

लाभेशे व्ययभावस्थे सत्कार्येषु व्ययः सदा।
कामुको बहुपत्नीको म्लेच्छसंसर्गकारकः ॥१३२॥

132. If the 11th lord is in the 12th, the native will always expend on good deeds, be sensuous, will have many wives and will befriend barbarians (or foreigners in general).

व्ययेशे लग्नगे जातो व्ययशीलो जनो भवेत्।
दुर्बलः कफरोगी च धनविद्याविवर्जितः ॥१३३॥

133. *EFFECTS OF THE 12TH LORD IN VARIOUS HOUSES (upto sloka 144) :* If the 12th lord is in the ascendant, the native will be a spendthrift, be weak in constitution, will suffer from phlegmatic disorders, and be devoid of wealth and learning.

Notes : Phlegmatic disorders relate to breathing troubles, lung disorders, tuberculosis etc. With the 12th lord going to the rising sign, the native will always suffer from one disease or the other. He will ever be in the grip of fear of death. He will acquire many vices. His undertakings will not yield success.

व्ययेशे धनभावस्थे शुभकार्ये व्ययः सदा।
धार्मिकः प्रियवादी च गुणसौख्यसमन्वितः ॥१३४॥

134. If the 12th lord is in the 2nd, the native will always spend on auspicious deeds, be religious, will speak sweetly and be endowed with virtues and happiness.

व्ययेशे सहजे जातो भ्रातृसौख्यविवर्जितः।
भवेदन्यजनद्वेषी स्वशरीरस्य पोषकः ॥१३५॥

135. If the 12th lord is in the 3rd, the native will be devoid of fraternal bliss, will hate others and will promote self-nourishment (*i.e.* be quite selfish).

व्ययेशे सुखभावस्थे मातुः सुखविवर्जितः।
भूमियानगृहादीनां हानिस्तस्य दिने-दिने ॥१३६॥

136. If the 12th lord is in the 4th the native will be devoid of maternal happiness and will day by day accrue losses in respect of lands, conveyances and houses.

व्ययेशे सुतभावस्थे सुतविद्याविवर्जितः ।
पुत्रार्थे च व्ययस्तस्य तीर्थाटनपरो नरः ॥१३७॥

137. If the 12th lord is in the 5th, the native will be bereft of sons and learning. He will spend as well as visit shrines in order to beget a son.

व्ययेशे रिपुभावस्थे जातः स्वजनवैरकृत् ।
क्रोधी पापी च दुःखी च परजायारतो नरः ॥१३८॥

138. If the 12th lord is in the 6th, the native will incur enmity with his own men, be given to anger, be sinful, miserable and will go to others' wives.

व्ययेशे दारभावस्थे व्ययो दारकृतः सदा ।
तस्य भार्यासुखं नैव बल-विद्याविवर्जितः ॥१३९॥

139. If the 12th lord is in the 7th, the native will incur expenditure on account of his wife, will not enjoy conjugal bliss and will be bereft of learning and strength.

व्ययेशे मृत्युभावस्थे जातो लाभान्वितः सदा ।
प्रियवाङ् मध्यमायुश्च सम्पूर्णगुणसंयुतः ॥१४०॥

140. If the 12th lord is in the 8th, the native will always gain, will speak affably, will enjoy a medium span of life and be endowed with all good qualities.

Notes : By 'medium life' it is meant to denote a span of life of 60 years. So to say the 12th lord in the 8th will not be in a position to contribute to higher bracket of longevity.

व्ययेशे भाग्यभावस्थे गुरुद्वेषी भवेन्नरः ।
मित्रैरपि भवेद्वैरं स्वार्थसाधनतत्परः ॥१४१॥

141. If the 12th lord is in the 9th, the native will dishonour his elders, be inimical even to his friends and be always intent on achieving his own ends.

व्ययेशे राज्यभावस्थे व्ययो राजकुलाद्भवेत् ।
पितृतोऽपि सुखं तस्य स्वल्पमेव हि जायते ॥१४२॥

142. If the 12th lord is in the 10th, the native will incur expenditure through royal persons and will enjoy only moderate paternal bliss.

व्ययेशे लाभभावस्थे लाभे हानिः प्रजायते।
परेण रक्षितं द्रव्यं कदाचिल्लभते नरः ॥१४३॥

143. If the 12th lord is in the 11th, the native will incur losses, be brought up by others and will sometimes gain through others.

Notes : One will face obstacles in begetting a child if the 12th lord occupies the 11th house. He will at last adopt a child.

व्ययेशे व्ययभावस्थे व्ययाधिक्यं हि जायते।
न शरीरसुखं तस्य क्रोधी द्वेषपरो नृणाम् ॥१४४॥

144. If the 12th lord is in the 12th, the native will only face heavy expenditure, will not have physical felicity, be iritable and spiteful.

इति ते कथितं विप्र! भावेशानां च यत् फलम्।
बलाबलविवेकेन सर्वेषां तत्समादिशेत् ॥१४५॥
द्विराशीशस्य खेटस्य विदित्वोभयथा फलम्।
विरोधे तुल्यफलयोर्द्वयोर्नाशः प्रजायते ॥१४६॥
विभिन्नयोस्तु फलयोर्द्वयोः प्राप्तिर्भवेद्ध्रुवम्।
ग्रहे पूर्णबले पूर्णमर्धमर्धबले फलम् ॥१४७॥
पादं हीनबले खेटे ज्ञेयमित्थं बुधैरिति।
उक्तं भावस्थितानां ते भावेशानां फलं मया ॥१४८॥

145-148. *MISCELLANEOUS* : O Brahmin, those are the effects of house lords which are to be deduced considering their strengths and weaknesses. In the case of a planet owning two bhavas, the results are to be deducted based on its two lordships (for the same placement). If contrary results are thus indicated, the results will be nullified, while results of varied nature will come to pass. The planet will yield full, half or a quarter of the effects according to its strength being full, medium and negligible respectively. Thus I have told you about the effects due to bhava lords in various bhavas.

Notes : We get important and key clue to analyse the effects of a bhava lord placed in a certain bhava. Except the Sun and the Moon, the other 5 planets own two bhavas each. In the case of the Sun and the Moon, the results cited will come to pass. (Here also one should give due consideration to various other relative factors. Simply applying the effects without checking other sources will lead to pitfalls.)

When a planet owns two signs, its placement in a certain bhava is affected by its two lordships. For example, take the case of Saturn in the 5th house for a Pisces native. His position in the 5th as the 11th lord will give children and happiness through them. And as the 12th lord, he will deny progeny so that the native resorts to visiting shrines *etc.* in a bid to obtain a progeny. In such a contrary situation the different results mentioned for Saturn's position in the 5th should not be straightaway declared but alternative sources like Jupiter (the significator of progery) and the Moon (the owner of the 5th house) should be looked upto.

Next we are clearly instructed in regard to results of mutually different spheres. For example again take the same case of Pisces ascendant having Saturn in the 5th house. Other results mentioned for the 11th lord being in the 5th house are : native being religious and happy. As the 12th lord in the 5th, the result mentioned is that the native will be devoid of education. After sorting out the controversy about progeny, it should be declared that Saturn in the 5th will deprive the native born in Pisces ascendant of learning (as due to 12th lordship) and will make the native religious and happy (as the 11th lord).

अथाऽप्रकाशग्रहफलाध्याय: ॥२५॥

Chapter 25

Effects Of Non-Luminous Planets

रव्यादिसप्तखेटानां प्रोक्तं भावफलं मया ।
अप्रकाशग्रहाणां च फलानि कथयाम्यहम् ॥१॥

1. Thus I have explained the effects of the seven planets *viz.* the Sun *etc.* Now I tell you about the effects of non-luminous planets.

शूरो विमलनेत्रांशः सुस्तब्धो निर्घृणः खलः।
मूर्तिस्थे धूमसंज्ञे च गाढरोषो नरः सदा ॥२॥

2. *EFFECTS OF DHUMA IN VARIOUS BHAVAS (upto sloka 13) :* If Dhuma is in the ascendant, the native will be valiant, endowed with beautiful eyes, stupefied in disposition, unkind, wicked and highly short-tempered.

Notes : Before declaring results due to placements of non-luminous planets (**i.e.** Dhuma etc.), the student will do well to refer to the sage's instruction in the concluding verses of the present chapter.

I have given in my notes for slokas 66-69 in ch.3 details of ownership, exaltation and debilitation signs for the 10 Upagrahas and Muhurta planets as culled out from Keeranuru Nataraja's **Jatakalankaram.** These will benefit the reader to consider lordships (or secondary lordships) of these also for each sign. For example, Gulika is 'lord' of Aquarius. Hence in the case of a Cancer native, he is the '8th lord' apart from Saturn's candidacy for 8th lordship. Of course primary importance be given to Saturn and he should not be underrated in that case.

The results due to Dhuma, Gulika etc. will mature in the Dasa periods of their dispositors. For example, if Gulika is placed in Virgo, the effects due to Gulika will come to pass in the major and sub periods of Mercury.

In giving effects Gulika is compared to Saturn, Kala to Rahu, Ardha Prahara to Mercury and Yamaghantaka to Jupiter. The first two are malefic in nature while the latter two are benefics. Of all, Gulika is the most powerful in adverse results while Yamaghantaka (son of Jupiter) is the mighty benefic.

रोगी धनी तु हीनाङ्गो राज्यापहृतमानसः।
धूमे द्वितीये संप्राप्ते मन्दप्रज्ञो नपुंसकः ॥३॥

3. If Dhuma is in the 2nd, the native will be sickly, wealthy, devoid of a limb, will incur humiliation at royal level, be dullwitted and be a eunuch.

मतिमान् शौर्यसम्पन्न इष्टचितः प्रियंवदः।
धूमे सहजभावस्थे जनाढ्यो धनवान् भवेत्॥४॥

4. If Dhuma is in the 3rd, the native will be intelligent, very bold, delighted, eloquent, and be endowed with men and wealth.

कलत्राङ्गपरित्यक्तो नित्यं मनसि दुःखितः।
धूमे चतुर्थे सम्प्राप्ते सर्वशास्त्रार्थचिन्तकः॥५॥

5. If Dhuma is in the 4th, the native will be grieved on account of being given up by his female but will be learned in all sastras.

स्वल्पापत्यो धनैर्हीनो धूमे पञ्चमसंस्थिते।
गुरुता सर्वभक्षं च सुहृन्मन्त्रविवर्जितः॥६॥

6. If Dhuma is in the 5th, the native will have limited progeny, be deviod of wealth, be great, will eat anything and be bereft of friends and Mantras.

बलवाञ्छत्रुवधको धूमे च रिपुभावगे।
बहुतेजोयुतः ख्यातः सदा रोगविवर्जितः॥७॥

7. If Dhuma is in the 6th, the native will be strong, will conquer his enemies, be very brilliant, famous and free from diseases.

निर्धनः सततं कामी परदारेषु कोविदः।
धूमे सप्तमगे जातो निस्तेजाः सर्वदा भवेत्॥८॥

8. If Dhuma is in the 7th, the native will be penniless, be ever sensuous, skilful in goining to others' females and be always devoid of brilliance.

विक्रमेण परित्यक्तः सोत्साहो सत्यसङ्गरः।
अप्रियो निष्ठुरः स्वार्थी धूमे मृत्युगते सति॥९॥

9. If Dhuma is in the 8th, the native will be bereft of courage but be enthusiastic, be truthful, disagreeable, hard-hearted and selfish.

सुतसौभाग्यसम्पन्नो धनी मानी दयान्वितः।
धर्मस्थाने स्थिते धूमे धर्मवान् बन्धुवत्सलः॥१०॥

10. If Dhuma is in the 9th, the native will be endowed with sons and fortunes, be rich, honourablo, kind, religious and well disposed to his relatives.

सुतसौभाग्यसंयुक्तः सन्तोषी मतिमान् सुखी।
कर्मस्थे मानवो नित्यं धूमे सत्यपदस्थितः॥११॥

11. If Dhuma is in the 10th, the native will be endowed with sons and fortunes, be delighted, intelligent, happy and truthful.

धनधान्यहिरण्याढ्यो रूपवांश्च कलान्वितः।
धूमे लाभगते चैव विनीतो गीतकोविदः॥१२॥

12. If Dhuma is in the 11th, the native will be endowed with wealth, grains and gold, be beautiful, will have knowledge of arts, be modest and be skilful in singing.

पतितः पापकर्मा च धूमे द्वादशसङ्गते।
परदारेषु संसक्तो व्यसनी निर्घृणः शठः॥१३॥

13. If Dhuma is in the 12th, the native will be morally fallen, will indulge in sinful acts, be interested in others' wives, addicted to vives, unkind and crafty.

लग्ने पाते च सम्प्राप्ते जातको दुःखीपीड़ितः।
क्रूरो घातकरो मूर्खो द्वेषी बन्धुजनस्य च॥१४॥

14. *EFFECTS OF VYATIPATA IN VARIOUS HOUSES* (*upto sloka 25*) : If Vyatipata (also known in short as Pata) is in the ascendant, the native will be troubled by miseries, be cruel, will indulge in destructive acts, be foolish and will be ill-disposed to his relatives.

जिह्मोऽतिपित्तवान् भोगी धनस्थे पातसंज्ञके।
निर्घृणश्चाऽकृतज्ञश्च दुष्टात्मा पापकृत्तथा॥१५॥

15. If Vyatipata is in the 2nd, the native will be morally crooked, be bilious, will enjoy pleasures, be unkind but grateful, be wicked and sinful.

स्थिरप्रज्ञो रणी दाता धनाढ्यो राजवल्लभः।
सम्प्राप्ते सहजे पाते सेनाधीशो भवेन्नरः ॥१६॥

16. If Vyatipata is in the 3rd, the native will be firm in disposition, be a warrior, be liberal, very rich, dear to king, and be head of an army.

बन्धव्याधिसमायुक्तः सुतसौभाग्यवर्जितः।
चतुर्थगो यदा पातस्तदा स्यान्मनुजश्च सः ॥१७॥

17. If Vyatipata is in the 4th, the native will be endowed with relatives etc. but not sons and fortunes.

दरिद्रो रूपसंयुक्तः पाते पञ्चमगे सति।
कफपित्तानिलैर्युक्तो निष्ठुरो निरपत्रपः ॥१८॥

18. If Vyatipata is in the 5th, the native will be poor, be charming in appearance, will have imbalances of phlegm, bile and wind, be hard-hearted and shameless.

शत्रुहन्ता सुपुष्टश्च सर्वास्त्राणां च चालकः।
कलासु निपुणः शान्तः पाते शत्रुगते सति ॥१९॥

19. If Vyatipata is in the 6th, the native will destroy his enemies, be physically mighty, skilful in use of all kinds of weapons and in arts, and be peaceful in disposition.

धनदारसुतैस्त्यक्तः स्त्रीजितो दुःखसंयुतः।
पाते कलत्रगे कामी निर्लज्जः परसौहृदः ॥२०॥

20. If Vyatipata is in the 7th, the natiue will be bereft of wealth, wife and sons, will subdue to females, be miserable, sensuous, shameless and friendly to others.

विकलाक्षो विरूपश्च दुर्भगो द्विजनिन्दकः।
मृत्युस्थाने स्थिते पाते रक्तपीडापरिप्लुतः ॥२१॥

21. If Vyatipata is in the 8th, the native will have deformity of eyes, be ugly, unfortunate, spiteful to Brahmins and be troubled by disorders of blood.

बहुव्यापारको नित्यं बहुमित्रो बहुश्रुतः ।
धर्मभे पातखेटे च स्त्रीप्रियश्च प्रियंवदः ।।२२।।

22. If Vyatipata is in the 9th, the native will have many kinds of business and many friends, be very learned, well-disposed to his wife and be eloquent.

स-श्रीको धर्मकृच्छान्तो धर्मकार्येषु कोविदः ।
कर्मस्थे पातसंज्ञे हि महाप्राज्ञो विचक्षणः ।।२३।।

23. If Vyatipata is in the 10th, the native will be rich, religious, peaceful, skilful in religious acts, very learned and farsighted.

प्रभूतधनवान् मानी सत्यवादी दृढव्रतः ।
अश्वढ्यो गीतसंसक्तः पाते लाभगते सति ।।२४।।

24. If Vyatipata is in the 11th, the native will be extremely opulent, be honourable, truthful, firm in policy, endowed with many horses and be interested in singing.

कोपी च बहुकर्माढ्यो व्यंगो धर्मस्य दूषकः ।
व्ययस्थाने गते पाते विद्वेषी निजबन्धुषु ।।२५।।

25. If Vyatipata is in the 12th, the native will be given to anger, associated with many activities, disabled, irreligious and will hate his own relatives.

विद्वान् सत्यरतः शान्तो धनवान् पुत्रवाञ्छुचिः ।
परिधौ तनुगे दाता जायते गुरुवत्सलः ।।२६।।

26. *EFFECTS OF PARIDHI (OR PARIVESHA) IN VARIOUS HOUSES (upto sloka 37) :* If Paridhi is in the ascendant, the native will be learned, truthful, peaceful, rich, endowed with sons, pure, charitable and dear to elders.

ईश्वरो रूपवान् भोगी सुखी धर्मपरायणः ।
धनस्थे परिधौ जातः प्रभुर्भवति मानवः ।।२७।।

27. If Paridhi is in the 2nd, the native will be wealthy, charming, will enjoy pleasures, be happy, very religious and be a lord.

स्त्रीवल्लभः सुरूपांगो देवस्वजनसंगतः ।
तृतीये परिधौ भृत्यो गुरुभक्तिसमन्वितः ॥२८॥

28. If Paridhi is in the 3rd, the native will be fond of his wife, be very charming, pious, well disposed to his men, be a servant and be respectful of his elders.

परिधौ सुखभावस्थे विस्मितं त्वरिमंगलम् ।
अक्रूरं त्वथ सम्पूर्णं कुरुते गीतकोविदम् ॥२९॥

29. If Paridhi is in the 4th, the native will be wonder-struck, helpful to enemies as well, kind, endowed with everything and be skilful in singing.

लक्ष्मीवान् शीलवान् कान्तःप्रियवान् धर्मवत्सलः ।
पञ्चमे परिधौ जातः स्त्रीणां भवति वल्लभः ॥३०॥

30. If Paridhi is in the 5th, the native will be affluent, virtuous, splendorous, affectionate, religious and dear to his wife.

व्यक्तोऽर्थपुत्रवान् भोगी सर्वसत्त्वहिते रतः ।
परिधौ रिपुभावस्थे शत्रुहा जायते नरः ॥३१॥

31. If Paridhi is in the 6th, the native will be famous and wealthy, be endowed with sons and pleasures, be helpful to all and will conquer his enemies.

स्वल्पापत्यः सुखैर्हीनो मन्दप्रज्ञः सुनिष्ठुरः ।
परिधौ द्यूनभावस्थे स्त्रीणां व्याधिश्च जायते ॥३२॥

32. If Paridhi is in the 7th, the native will have limited number of children, be devoid of happiness, be of mediocre intelligence, very hard-hearted, and will have a sickly wife.

अध्यात्मचिन्तकः शान्तो दृढकायो दृढव्रतः ।
धर्मवांश्च ससत्त्वश्च परिधौ रन्ध्रसंस्थिते ॥३३॥

33. If Paridhi is in the 8th, the native will be spiritually disposed, peaceful, strong-bodied, firm in decision, religious and gentle.

पुत्रान्वितः सुखी कान्तो धनाढयो लौल्यवर्जितः ।
परिधौ धर्मगे मानी स्वल्पसन्तुष्टमानसः ॥३४॥

34. If Paridhi is in the 9th, the native will be endowed with sons, be happy, brilliant, very affluent, be devoid of excessive passion, be honourable and be happy with even an iota.

कलाभिज्ञस्तथा भोगी दृढकायो ह्यमत्सरः ।
परिधौ दशमे प्राप्ते सर्वशास्त्रार्थपारगः ॥३५॥

35. If Paridhi is in the 10th, the native will be versed in arts, will enjoy pleasures, be strong-bodied, and be learned in all sastras.

स्त्रीभोगी गुणवांश्चैव मतिमान् स्वजनप्रियः ।
लाभगे परिधौ जातो मन्दाग्निरूपपद्यते ॥३६॥

36. If Paridhi is in the 11th, the native will enjoy pleasures through women, be virtuous, intelligent, dear to his people and will suffer disorders of digestive fire.

व्ययस्थे परिधौ जातो व्ययकृत् मानवः सदा ।
दुःखभाग् दुष्टवुद्धिश्च गुरुनिन्दापरायणः ॥३७॥

37. If Paridhi is in the 12th, the native will always be a spendthrift, be miserable, firm and will dishonour elders.

धनधान्यहिरण्याढयः कृतज्ञः सम्मतः सताम् ।
सर्वदोषपरित्यक्तश्चापे तनुगते नरः ॥३८॥

38. *EFFECTS OF CHAPA (INDRA DHANUS OR KODANDA) IN VARIOUS HOUSES (upto sloka 49) :* If Chapa is in the ascendant, the native will be endowed with wealth, grains and gold, be grateful, agreeable and devoid of all afflictions.

प्रियंवदः प्रगल्भाढयो विनीतो विद्ययाऽन्वितः ।
धनस्थे चापखेटे च रूपवान् धर्मतत्परः ॥३९॥

39. If Chapa is in the 2nd, the native will speak affably, be very rich, modest, learned, charming and religious.

कृपणोऽतिकलाभिज्ञश्चौर्यकर्मरतः सदा ।
सहजे धनुषि प्राप्ते हीनाङ्गो गतसौहृदः ॥४०॥

40. If Cbapa is in the 3rd, the native will be a miser, be versed in many arts, will indulge in thieving, be devoid of some limb and be unfriendly.

सुखी गोधनधान्याद्यैं राजसन्मानपूजितः ।
कार्मुके सुखसंस्थे तु नीरोगो तनु जायते ॥४१॥

41. If Chapa is in the 4th, the native will be happy, endowed with quadrupeds, wealth, grains *etc* , be honoured by the king and be devoid of sickness.

रुचिमान् दीर्घदर्शी च देवभक्तः प्रियंवदः ।
चापे पञ्चमगे जातो विवृद्धः सर्वकर्मसु ॥४२॥

42. If Chapa is in the 5th, the native will be splendorous, far-sighted, pious, affable and will acquire prosperity in all his undertakings.

शत्रुहन्ताऽतिधर्तश्च सुखी प्रीतिरुचिः शुचिः ।
षष्ठस्थानगते चापे सर्वकर्मसमृद्धिभाक् ॥४३॥

43. If Chapa is in the 6th, the native will destroy his enemies, be happy, affectionate, pure and will achieve plentifulness in all his undertakings.

ईश्वरो गुणसम्पूर्णः शास्त्रविद्धार्मिकः प्रियः ।
चापे सप्तमभावस्थे भवतेति न संशयः ॥४४॥

44. If Chapa is in the 7th, the native will be wealthy, endowed with all virtues, learned in sastras, religious, and agreeable.

परकर्मरतः क्रूरः परदारपरायणः ।
अष्टमस्थानगे चापे जायते विकलांगकः ॥४५॥

45. If Chapa is in the 8th, the native will be interested in other's jobs, be cruel, interested in other's wives and be defective limbed.

तपस्वी व्रतचर्यासु निरतो विद्ययाऽधिकः ।
धर्मस्थे जायते चापे मानवो लोकविश्रुतः ॥४६॥

46. If Chapa is in the 9th, the native will perform, penance, will take to religious observations, be highly learned, and be famous among men.

बहुपुत्रधनैश्वर्यो गोमहिष्यादिमान् भवेत् ।
कर्मभे चापसंयुक्ते जायते लोकविश्रुतः ॥४७॥

47. If Chapa is in the 10th, the native will be endowed with many sons, abundant wealth, cows, buffaloes etc. and will be famous among men.

लाभगे चापखेटे च लाभयुक्तो भवेन्नरः ।
निरोगो दृढकोपाग्निर्मन्त्रस्त्रीपरमास्त्रवित् ॥४८॥

48. If Chapa is in the 11th, the native will be gainful, free from diseases, very fiery in disposition, affectionate to his wife and will have knowledge of mantras and weapons (or missiles).

खलोऽतिमानी दुर्बुद्धिर्निर्लज्जो व्ययसंस्थिते ।
चापे परस्त्रीसंयुक्तो जायते निर्धनः सदा ॥४९॥

49. If Chapa is in the 12th the native will be wicked, very honourable, evil in disposition, shameless, will go to other's females and be ever poor.

कुशलः सर्वविद्यासु सुखी वाङ्निपुणः प्रियः ।
तनौ शिखिनि सञ्जातः सर्वकामान्वितो भवेत् ॥५०॥

50. *EFFECTS OF DHWAJA* (*i e. SIKHI OR UPAKETU) IN VARIOUS HOUSES (upto sloka 61) :* If Dhwaja is in the ascendant, the native will be skilful in all branches of learning, be happy, efficient in speech, agreeable and be very affectionate.

वक्ता प्रियंवदः कान्तो धनस्थानगते ध्वजे ।
काव्यकृत् पण्डितो मानी विनीतो वाहनान्वितः ॥५१॥

51. If Dhwaja is in the 2nd, the native will be a good and affable speaker, be splendorous, will write poetry, be scholarly, honourable, modest and endowed with conveyances.

कदर्यः क्रूरकर्ता च कृशाङ्गो धनवर्जितः ।
सहजस्थे तु शिखिनि तीव्ररोगी प्रजायते ॥५२॥

52. If Dhwaja is in the 3rd, the native will be miserly, cruel in acts, thin-bodied, poor and will incur severe diseases.

रूपवान् गुणसम्पन्नः सात्त्विकोऽपि श्रुतिप्रियः ।
सुखसंस्थे तु शिखिनि सदा भवति सौख्यभाक् ॥५३॥

53. If Dhwaja is in the 4th, the native will be charming, very virtuous, gentle, interested in Vedas and be always happy.

सुखी भोगी कलाविच्च पञ्चमस्थानगे ध्वजे ।
युक्तिज्ञो मतिमान् वाग्मी गुरुभक्तिसमन्वितः ॥५४॥

54. If Dhwaja is in the 5th, the native will be happy, will enjoy pleasures, be versed in arts, skilled in expedients, intelligent, eloquent and will respect elders.

मातृपक्षक्षयकरः शत्रुहा बहुबान्धवः ।
रिपुस्थाने ध्वजे प्राप्ते शूरः कान्तो विचक्षणः ॥५५॥

55. If Dhwaja is in the 6th, the native will be ominous for maternal relatives, will win over his enemies, be endowed with many relatives, valiant, splendorous and skilful.

द्यूतक्रीडाव्यभिरतः कामी भोगसमन्वितः ।
ध्वजे तु सप्तमस्थाने वेश्यासु कृतसौहृदः ॥५६॥

56. If Dhwaja is in the 7th, the native will be interested in gambling, be sensuous, will enjoy pleasures and will befriend prostitutes.

नीचकर्मरतः पापो निर्लज्जो निन्दकः सदा ।
मृत्युस्थाने ध्वजे प्राप्ते गतस्त्र्यपरपक्षकः ॥५७॥

57. If Dhwaja is in the 8th, the native will be interested in base acts, be sinful, shameless, will blame others' will lack in marital happiness and will take others' side.

लिङ्गधारी प्रसन्नात्मा सर्वभूतहिते रतः।
धर्मभे शिखिनि प्राप्ते धर्मकार्येषु कोविदः॥५८॥

58. If Dhwaja is in the 9th, the native will wear (religious) badges, be delighted, helpfully disposed to all and be skilled in religious deeds.

सुखसौभाग्यसम्पन्नः कामिनीनां च वल्लभः।
दाता द्विजैः समायुक्तः कर्मस्थे शिखिनि द्विज! ॥५९॥

59. O Brahmin, if Dhwaja is in the 10th, the native will be endowed with happiness and fortunes, be fond of females, be charitable and will befriend Brahmins.

नित्यलाभः सुधर्मो च लाभे शिखिनि पूजितः।
धनाढ्यः सुभगः शूरः सुयज्ञश्चाति कोविदः॥६०॥

60. If Dhwaja is in the 11th, the native will ever acquire gains, be very religious, honourable, affluent, fortunate, valiant and skilled in sacrificial rites.

पापकर्मरतः शूरः श्रद्धाहीनोऽघृणो नरः।
परदाररतो रौद्रः शिखिनि व्ययगे सति॥६१॥

61. If Dhwaja is in the 12th, the native will be interested in sinful acts, be valiant, untrustworthy, unkind, interested in others' females and be short-tempered.

रोगार्त्तः सततं कामी पापात्माधिगतः शठः।
तनुस्थे गुलिके जातः खलभावोऽतिदुःखितः॥६२॥

62. *EFFECTS OF GULIKA IN VARIOUS HOUSES (upto sloka 73)* : If Gulika is in the ascendant, the native will be afflicted by diseases, be lustful, sinful, crafty, wicked and very miserable.

Notes : Out of all the non-luminous planets, Gulika deserves a special consideration in natal horoscopy as well as horary astrology. This is also a very important factor in birth rectification, and such other important calculations.

If Gulika is in the ascendant, the native will incur severe defects of eyes. He will take to bad acts like thieving. He will disregard religion, be deprived of progeny and be dullheaded. His longevity will incur a severe cut.

As already stated, in the case of each Upagraha and Muhurta Vela, the dispositor should invariably be considered before coming to a conclusion.

विकृतो दुःखितः क्षुद्रो व्यसनी च गतत्रपः।
धनस्थे गुलिके जातो निःस्वो भवति मानवः ॥६३॥

63. If Gulika is in the 2nd, the native will be unsightly in appearance, miserable, mean, given to vices, shameless and penniless.

Notes : Should Gulika be in the 2nd house, the native will further be unfortunate. His learning will be obstructed off and on. He will have speech defects, be harsh in speech, will live away from his people, will not have family happiness, be untruthful, will involve in a scandal, be unfit to move among others and will in the Dasa periods of the 2nd lord face troubles equal to death.

चार्वङ्गो ग्रामपः पुण्यसंयुक्तः सज्जनप्रियः।
सहजे गुलिके जातो मान्यो राजपूजितः ॥६४॥

64. If Gulika is in the 3rd, the native will be charming in appearance, will head a village, be fond of virtuous men, and be honoured by the king.

Notes : With Gulika in the 3rd house, one will face destruction of co-born. Though fairly rich, he will feel distressed.

रोगी सुखपरित्यक्तः सदा भवति पापकृत्।
गुलिके सुखभावस्थे वातपित्ताधिको भवेत् ॥६५॥

65. If Gulika is in the 4th, the native will be sickly, devoid of happiness, sinful and afflicted due to windy and bilious excesses.

Notes : The native will not befriend anybody but be inimical to others inclusive of his relatives. He will be devoid of conveyances or will face risks through conveyances. He will not have a good house to live in. His last days will be miserable and death will be painful after a long confinement.

विस्तुतिर्विधनोऽल्पायुर्द्वेषी क्षुद्रो नपुंसकः।
गुलिके सुतभावस्थे स्त्रीजितो नास्तिको भवेत् ॥६६॥

66. If Gulika is in the 5th, the native will not be praise-worthy, be poor, short-lived, spiteful, mean, be a eunuch, be subdued by his wife and be a heterodox.

Notes : The native's virility or progenic ability will be significantly affected by Gulika's occupying the house of progeny. He will not be in a position to obtain issues unless Jupiter and the 5th lord are favourable. Gulika in this house will make one devoid of God-fearing tendency and be at the disposal of his wife. His personal disposition will not be agreeable.

वीतशत्रुः सुपुष्टाङ्गो रिपुस्थाने यमात्मजे।
सुदीप्तः सम्मतः स्त्रीणां सोत्साहः सुदृढो हितः ॥६७॥

67. If Gulika is in the 6th, the native will be devoid of enemies, be strong-bodied, splenorous, liked by his wife, enthu-siastic, very friendly and helpful in disposition.

Notes : When Gulika is in the 6th house, the native will be interested in controlling evil spirits and make a livelihood from such achievements. He will obtain children. He will be very courageous. There will be freedom from diseases if the 6th house containing Gulika is a benefic sign.

स्त्रीजितः पापकृज्जारः कृशाङ्गो गतसौहृदः।
जीवितः स्त्रीधनेनैव गुलिके सप्तमस्थिते ॥६८॥

68. If Gulika is in the 7th, the native will subdue to his spouse, be sinful, will go to others' females, be emaciated, devoid of friendship and will live on wife's (or a female's) wealth.

Notes : Gulika occupying the 7th house, will make the native thrive on a female's wealth or through the contributions of his own spouse. His conjugal life will not cause him any happiness. He will possibly have more than one marriage.

His knowledge will not be quite much. In relation to public dealings, he will incur misunderstandings and enmity.

क्षुधालुर्दुःखित क्रूरस्तीक्ष्णरोषोऽतिनिर्घृणः ।
रन्ध्रगे गुलिके निःस्वो जायते गुणवर्जितः ॥६९॥

69. If Gulika is in the 8th, the native will be troubled by hunger, be miserable, cruel, very much short-tempered, very unkind, poor and bereft of good qualities.

Notes : The native will find it difficult to get even a square meal. His face will be ugly. His eyes will be diseased. His teeth will be yellowish. He will be quite short in stature. These are additional effects as due to the 8th house position of Gulika, son of Saturn.

बहुक्लेशः कृशतनुर्दुष्टकर्मातिनिर्घृणः ।
गुलिके धर्मगे मन्दः पिशुनो बहिराकृतिः ॥७०॥

70. If Gulika is in the 9th, the native will undergo many ordeals, be emaciated, will perform evil acts, be very unkind, sluggish and be a tale-bearer.

Notes : If Gulika is in the 9th house one will be devoid of paternal bliss and good fortunes His father will pass away in the native's childhood itself. None of the native's undertakings will bear fruits.

पुत्रान्वितः सुखी भोक्ता देवाग्न्यर्चनवत्सलः ।
दशमे गुलिके जातो योगधर्माश्रितः सुखी ॥७१॥

71. If Gulika is in the 10th, the native will be endowed with sons, be happy, will enjoy many things, be fond of worshipping gods and fire and will practise meditation and religion.

Notes : The placement of Gulika in the 10th house, will prove favourable for Yoga, Meditation and such other achievements. The native, at one stage, will turn into a heterodox and discard his religious code.

सुस्त्रीभोगी प्रजाध्यक्षो बन्धूनां च हिते रतः ।
लाभस्थे गुलिके जातो नीचाङ्गः सार्वभौमकः ॥७२॥

72. If Gulika is in the 11th, the native will enjoy women of class, be a leader of men, be helpful to his relatives, be short in stature and be an emperor.

Notes : If Gulika is in the 11th house, the subject will be in the company of many females. He will be devoid of good character. He will enjoy progenic happiness, wealth status *etc.* and be charming in appearance.

नीचकर्माश्रितः पापो हीनाङ्गो दुर्भगोऽलसः ।
व्ययगे गुलिके जातो नीचेषु कुरुते रतिम् ॥७३॥

73. If Gulika is in the 12th, the native will indulge in base deeds, be sinful, defective-limbed, unfortunate, indolent, and will join mean people.

Notes : Gulika's tenancy in the 12th house at birth will bring innumerable misfortunes and cause loss of wealth on evil missions. One will, however, enjoy progenic happiness.

लग्ने प्राणपदे क्षणो रोगी भवति मानवः ।
मूकोन्मत्तो जडाङ्गस्तु हीनाङ्गो दुखितः कृशः ॥७४॥

74. *EFFECTS OF PRANAPADA'S POSITION WITH REFERENCE TO THE ASCENDANT (upto sloka 85) :* If Pranapada is in the ascendant, the native will be weak, sickly, dumb, lunatic, dullwitted, defective-limbed, miserable and emaciated.

Notes : Pranapada is a special ascendant. How to calculate this special sensitive point could be found on p. 47 *supra.*

Pranapada will fall in a certain degree and its relation with referance to natal ascendant will portend many an event as tersely shown in the present 12 verses.

बहुधान्यो बहुधनो बहुभृत्यो बहुप्रजः ।
धनस्थानस्थिते प्राणे सुभगो जायते नरः ॥७५॥

75. If Pranapada is in the 2nd, the native will be endowed with abundant grains (rice, wheat etc.), abundant wealth, abundant attendants, abundant children and be fortunate.

हिंस्रो गर्वसमायुक्तो निष्ठुरोऽतिमलिम्लुचः।
तृतीयगे प्राणपदे गुरुभक्तिविवर्जितः ॥७६॥

76. If Pranapada is in the 3rd, the native will be injurious, (or mischievous), proud, hard-hearted, very dirty and be devoid of respect for elders.

सुखस्थे तु सुखी कान्तः सुहृद्रमासु वल्लभः।
गुरौ परायणः शीतः प्राणे वै सत्यतत्परः ॥७७॥

77. If Pranapada is in the 4th, the native will be happy, friendly, attached to females and elders, soft and truthful.

सुखभाक् सुक्रियोपेतस्त्वपचारदयान्वितः।
पञ्चमस्थे प्राणपदे सर्वकामसमन्वितः ॥७८॥

78. If Pranapada is in the 5th, the native will be happy, will do good acts, be kind, and very affectionate.

बन्धुशत्रुवशस्तीक्ष्णो मन्दाग्निर्निर्दयः खलः।
षष्ठे प्राणपदे रोगी वित्तपोऽल्पायुरेव च ॥७९॥

79. If Pranapada is in the 6th, the native will be subdued by his relatives and enemies, be sharp, will have defective digestive fire, be wicked, sickly, affluent and shortlived.

ईर्ष्यालु सततं कामी तीव्ररौद्रवपुर्नरः।
सप्तमस्थे प्राणपदे दुराराध्यः कुबुद्धिमान् ॥८०॥

80. If Pranapada is in the 7th, the native will be green-eyed, ever libidinous, fierce in appearance, be not worth respect and be ill-disposed.

रोगसन्तापिताङ्गश्च प्राणपादेऽष्टमे सति।
पीडितः पार्थिवैर्दुःखैर्भृत्यबन्धुसुतोद्भवैः ॥८१॥

81. If Pranapada is in the 8th, the native will be afflicted by diseases, be troubled and will incur misery on account of the king, relatives, servants and sons.

पुत्रवान् धनसम्पन्नः सुभगः प्रियदर्शनः।
प्राणे धर्मस्थिते भृत्यः सदाऽदुष्टो विचक्षणः ॥८२॥

82. If Pranapada is in the 9th, the native will be endowed with sons, be very rich, fortunate, charming, will serve others and be not wicked but be skilful.

वीर्यवान् मतिमान् दक्षो नृपकार्येषु कोविदः।
दशमे वै प्राणपदे देवार्चनपरायणः ॥८३॥

83. If Pranapada is in the 10th, the native will be heroic, intelligent, skilful, be an expert in carrying out royal orders, and will worship gods.

विख्यातो गुणवान् प्राज्ञो भोगीध नसमन्वितः।
लाभस्थानस्थिते प्राणे गौराङ्गो मातृवत्सलः ॥८४॥

84. If Pranapada is in the 11th, the native will be famous, virtuous, learned, wealthy, fair-complexioned and attached to mother.

क्षुद्रो दुष्टस्तु हीनाङ्गो विद्वेषी द्विजबन्धुषु।
व्यये प्राणे नेत्ररोगी काणो वा जायते नरः ॥८५॥

85. If Pranapada is in the 12th, the native will be mean, wicked, defective-limbed, will hate Brahmins and relatives and will suffer from eye diseases or be one-eyed.

इत्यप्रकाशखेटानां फलान्युक्तानि भूसुर!।
तथा यानि प्रकाशानां सूर्यादीनां खचारिणाम् ॥८६॥
तानि स्थितिवशात्तेषां स्फुटदृष्टिवशात् तथा।
बलाऽबलविवेकेन वक्तव्यानि शरीरिणाम् ॥८७॥

86-87. O Brahmin, these are the effects for Dhooma etc. (and Pranapada ascendant). Before declaring these results, the effects of the Sun and other planets should be wisely conceived by their positions, relations and aspects apart from their strength or weakness.

Notes : We are advised to look upto the Sun and others while declaring the effects due to Dhooma, Gulika etc. So to say the dispositors of Dhooma etc. Should be scrutinized to know the extent of effects. For example if Gulika is due to give bad effects, but his dispositor is well-aspected, well-placed or well-related, the evils are minimised. Conversely if favourable effects are due to Gulika etc. the weakness or adverse placement of the respective dispositor will not allow maturity of such good effects.

Another hint we take from these two verses is : We should balance the results due to Dhooma, Gulika etc. with the results due to the planets from Sun to Saturn (and of course the nodes). For example, Gulika is in the 11th and good effects are due. If a planet posited in the same 11th denotes contrary results, then the strength of the two will lead to correct estimation of the situation.

अथ ग्रहस्फुटदृष्टिकथनाध्यायः ॥२६॥

Chapter 26

Evaluation of Planetary Aspects

भगवन् ! कतिधा दृष्टिर्बलं कतिविधं तथा ।
इति मे संशयो जातस्तं भवान् छेत्तुमर्हति ॥१॥

1. O Glorious, it is said that aspects (of planets) and strengths are to be known in deciding the effects. How many kinds are these ? Please clarify my doubts.

एका राशिवशाद् दृष्टिः पूर्वमुक्ता च या द्विज ।
अन्या खेटस्वभावोत्था स्फुटा तां कथयाम्यहम् ॥२॥
त्रिदशे च त्रिकोणे च चतुरस्रे च सप्तमे ।
पादवृद्धया प्रपश्यन्ति प्रयच्छन्ति फलं तथा ॥३॥
पूर्णं च सप्तमं सर्वे, शनि-जीव-कुजाः पुनः ।
विशेषतश्च त्रिदश-त्रिकोण-चतुरष्टमान् ॥४॥
इति सामान्यतः पूर्वैराचार्यैः प्रतिपादिता ।
स्फुटान्तरवशाद्या च दृष्टिः साऽतिस्फुटा यथा ॥५॥

2-5. *PLANETARY ASPECTS :* O Brahmin, I have earlier stated aspects based on signs. The other kind is between planets which I detail below. 3rd and 10th, 5th and 9th, 4th and 8th and lastly 7th—on these places the aspects increase gradually in slabs of quarters i.e 1/4, 1/2, 3/4th and full. The effects (due to such aspects) will also be proportionate. All planets aspect the 7th fully. Saturn, Jupiter and Mars have special aspects respectively on 3rd and 10th, 5th and 9th, and 4th and 8th. The ancient preceptors have explained these which are ordinary (arising by mere sign positions). By subtle mathematical calculations, these aspects will have to be clearly understood as under.

दृश्याद् विशोध्य द्रष्टारं षड्राशिभ्योऽधिकान्तरम् ।
दिगभ्यः संशोध्य तद् भागा द्विभक्ता दृक् स्फुटा भवेत् ।।६।।
पञ्चाधिके विना राशिं भागाद्विघ्नाश्च दृक् स्फुटा ।
वेदाधिके त्यजेद् भूताद् भागा दृष्टिः, त्रिभाधिके ।।७।।
विशोध्यार्णवतो द्वाभ्यां लब्धं त्रिंशद्युतं च दृक् ।
द्व्यधिके तु विना राशिं भागास्तिथियुतास्तथा ।।८।।

6-8. *ASPECTUAL EVALUATIONS :* Deduct the longitude of the aspected planet (or house) from that of the aspecting planet. If the sum exceeds six signs (or 180 deg) deduct the sum again from 10 signs (or 300 deg). Convert the latest sum into degrees and divide by two. The resultant product is Drishti Kona or aspectual angle. If the difference (between aspector and aspected) is in excess of 5 signs, ignore. signs and multiply the degrees etc. by 2 which is the aspectual value. If the difference is in excess of 4 signs deduct it from 5 signs (or 150 deg) and the resultant degree etc. beeome Drishti value. If the difference is in excess of 3 signs deduct it from 4 signs (or 120 degress) and halve the product to be increased by 30 to get Drishti value. If the difference is above 2 signs ignore signs and add 15 to the degrees etc. to get Drishti value. If it is in excess of one sign, ignore Rasis and divide the degrees etc. by 2 to get Drishti value.

रूपाधिके विना राशिं भागा द्वयाप्ताश्च दृग् भवेत् ।
एवं राश्यादिके शेषे शनौ द्रष्टरि भो द्विज ! ।।९।।

एकभे नवभे भागा भुक्ता भोग्या द्विसंगुणाः।
द्विभेंऽशार्धोनिताः षष्टिरष्टभे खाग्नियुग् लवाः ॥१०॥

9-10. *SPECIAL CONSIDERATION FOR SATURN'S ASPECTS :* O Brahmin, if Saturn is the aspecting planet find out the difference between him and the aspected planet; if the sum is above 1 sign, multiply the degrees etc. (ignoring sign) by 2 to get Drishti value. If the sum is above nine sings, the degrees to elapse be doubled to get aspectual value. If the sum is above 2 signs, the degrees etc. (in excess of 2 signs) be halved and deducted from 60. If the sum exceeds 8 signs, add to the degrees etc, a figure of 30 to get Drishti value. In other cases, the sums be processed as explained earlier.

त्रिसप्तभे तु भौमस्य षष्टिरत्र लवोनिता।
सार्धांशास्तिथिसंयुक्ता द्विभे, रूपं सदाऽङ्गभे ॥११॥

11. *SPECIAL CONSIDERATION FOR MARS' ASPECTS :* Deduct the longitude of Mars from that of the planet aspected (by Mars). If the sum is 3 Rasis & *c* or 7 Rasis & *c,* the degrees etc. (after ignoring Rasis) be reduced from 60. If it is above 2 Rasis, the degrees etc. be increased by half of it (i.e. add 50%) and superadd 15. If the sum is 6 signs, one Rupa is the value.

त्रिसप्तभे तु जीवस्य भागार्धं शर-वेद-युक्।
द्विगुणैस्तु लवैश्चोनाः खरसाश्चतुरष्टभे ॥१२॥
एवं रव्यादिखेटानां स्फुटा दृष्टिः प्रजायते।
तद्वशादेव भावानां जातकस्य फलं वदेत् ॥१३॥

12. *SPECIAL CONSIDERATION FOR JUPITER'S ASPECTS :* Deduct the longitude of Jupiter from that of the planet aspected by him. If the resultant sum is 3 Rasis & *c* or 7 Rasis & *c,* halve the degrees etc. (ignoring Rasis) and increase it by 45. If the sum is 4 Rasis & *c* or 8 Rasis & *c,* the degrees etc. (ignoring Rasis) be subtracted from 60. This will be the aspectual value. The sum being in conformity with others than these be treated as stated earlier.

Notes : Throughout this chapter and others related to calculation of strengths of planets and houses, the term 'Virupa' has been used which denotes 'Shashtiamsas' or 'Kalas'. 60 such units make one Rupa.

The planet that aspects is Drishti Graha or the aspector. The planet that is aspected is known as Drisya Graha or the aspected. The longitude of 'the aspected' is to be deducted from that of the aspector. If the longitude of the aspected is lesser than that of the aspector, increase the longitude of 'the aspected' by 360 to facilitate deduction, which will yield the aspectual or Drishti angle.

After finding out the Drishti angles, the various quantities will have to be processed as under with the relevant principles :

Rule 1. When aspectual angle is between 30 and 60 degrees, reduce 30 degrees from the resultant aspectual angle and divide by 2 to get aspectual value.

Rule 2. If the aspectual angle is above 60 but below 90 degrees, reduce 60 from the aspectual angle and add 15 to get aspectual value.

Rule 3. In case the aspectual angle is above 90 but less than 120 degrees the aspectual angle be reduced from 120, then halved and then increased by 30, to get aspectual value.

Rule 4. If the aspectual angle is between 120 and 150 degrees, reduce the angle of aspect from 150 to get aspectual va lue,

Rule 5. If the aspectual angle is between 150 and 180 degrees reduce 150 from aspectual angle and double the resultant sum to get aspectual value.

Rule 6. When the aspectual angle is above 180 but below 300 degrees deduct the aspectual angle from 300 and halve the resultant sum, to get aspectual value.

Needless to mention there is no aspectual value if the angle is between 300 and 30 degrees.

For house in aspect, consider the cusp of the house, akin to a planetary degree.

In the case of aspects from Saturn, Mars and Jupiter, the following additions may be noted as a simple formula.

A) Mars : When the aspect angle is 90-120 degrees or 210-240 degrees, add 15 Virupas to the value obtained from the speculum.

B) Jupiter : When the aspect angle is 120-150 degrees or 240-270 degrees increase the speculum value by 30 Virupas.

C) Saturn : When the aspect angle is 60-90 degrees or 270-300 degrees and 45 Virupas to the value obtained from the speculum.

Without undergoing these ordeals, the student can easily find out the Drishti values on the above lines from the Speculum of Aspectual Values given below :

Speculum of Aspetual Values (Computerized)

Deg:Mn	Virupa	Deg:Mn	Virupa	Deg:Mn	Virupa
30: 0	.00	41:30	5.75	53: 0	11.50
30:30	.25	42: 0	6.00	53:30	11.75
31: 0	.50	42:30	6.25	54: 0	12.00
31:30	.75	43: 0	6.50	54:30	12.25
32: 0	1.00	43:30	6.75	55: 0	12.50
32:30	1.25	44: 0	7.00	55:30	12.75
33: 0	1.50	44:30	7.25	56: 0	13.00
33:30	1.75	45: 0	7.50	56:30	13.25
34: 0	2.00	45:30	7.75	57: 0	13.50
34:30	2.25	46: 0	8.00	57:30	13.75
35: 0	2.50	46:30	8.25	58: 0	14.00
35:30	2.75	47: 0	8.50	58:30	14.25
36: 0	3.00	47:30	8.75	59: 0	14.50
36:30	3.25	48: 0	9.00	59:30	14.75
37: 0	3.50	48:30	9.25	60: 0	15.00
37:30	3.75	49: 0	9.50	60:30	15.50
38: 0	4.00	49:30	9.75	61: 0	16.00
38:30	4.25	50: 0	10.00	61:30	16.50
39: 0	4.50	50:30	10.25	62: 0	17.00
39:30	4.75	51: 0	10.50	62:30	17.50
40: 0	5.00	51:30	10.75	63: 0	18.00
40:30	5.25	52: 0	11.00	63:30	18.50
41: 0	5.50	52:30	11.25	64: 0	19.00

Deh:Mn	Virupa	Deg:Mn	Virupa	Deg:Mn	Virupa
64:30	19.50	82: 0	37.00	99:30	40.25
65: 0	20.00	82:30	37.50	100: 0	40.00
65:30	20.50	83: 0	38.00	100:30	39.75
66: 0	21.00	83:30	38.50	101: 0	39.50
66:30	21.50	84: 0	39.00	101:30	39.25
67: 0	22 00	84:30	39.50	102: 0	39.00
67:30	22.50	85: 0	40.00	102:30	38.75
68: 0	23.00	85:30	40.50	103: 0	38.50
68:30	23.50	86: 0	41.00	103:30	38.25
69: 0	24.00	86:30	41.50	104: 0	38.00
69:30	24.50	87: 0	42.00	104:30	37.75
70: 0	25.00	87:30	42.50	105: 0	37.50
70:30	25.50	88: 0	43.00	105:30	37.25
71: 0	26.00	88:30	43.50	106: 0	37.00
71:30	26.50	89: 0	44.00	106:30	36.75
72: 0	27.00	89:30	44.50	107: 0	36.50
72:30	27.50	90: 0	45.00	107:30	36.25
73: 0	28.00	90:30	44.75	108: 0	36.00
73:30	28.50	91: 0	44.50	108:30	35.75
74: 0	29.00	91:30	44.25	109: 0	35.50
74:30	29 50	92: 0	44.00	109:30	35.25
75: 0	30.00	92:30	43.75	110: 0	35.00
75:30	30.50	93: 0	43.50	110:30	34.75
76: 0	31.00	93:30	43.25	111: 0	34.50
76:30	31.50	94: 0	43.00	111:30	34.25
77: 0	32.00	94:30	42.75	112: 0	34.00
77:30	32.50	95: 0	42.50	112:30	33.75
78: 0	33.00	95:30	42.25	113: 0	33.50
78:30	33 50	96: 0	42.00	113:30	33.25
79: 0	34.00	96:30	41.75	114: 0	33.00
79:30	34.50	97: 0	41.50	114:30	32.75
80: 0	35.00	97·30	41.25	115: 0	32.50
80:30	35.50	98: 0	41.00	115:30	32.25
81: 0	36.00	98:30	40.75	116: 0	32.00
81:30	36.50	99: 0	40.50	116:30	31.75

Deg:Mn	Virupa	Deg:Mn	Virupa	Deg:Mn	Virupa
117: 0	31.50	134:30	15.50	152: 0	4.00
117:30	31.25	135: 0	15.00	152:30	5.00
118: 0	31.00	135:30	14.50	153: 0	6.00
118:30	30.75	136: 0	14.00	153:30	7.00
119: 0	30.50	136:30	13.50	154: 0	8.00
119:30	30.25	137: 0	13.00	154:30	9.00
120: 0	30.00	137:30	12.50	155: 0	10.00
120:30	29.50	138: 0	12.00	155:30	11.00
121: 0	29.00	138:30	11.50	156: 0	12.00
121:30	28.50	139: 0	11.00	156:30	13.00
122: 0	28.00	139:30	10.50	157: 0	14.00
122:30	27.50	140: 0	10.00	157:30	15.00
123: 0	27.00	140:30	9.50	158: 0	16.00
123:30	26.50	141: 0	9.00	158:30	17.00
124: 0	26.00	141:30	8.50	159: 0	18.00
124:30	25.50	142: 0	8.00	159:30	19.00
125: 0	25.00	142:30	7.50	160: 0	20.00
125:30	24.50	143: 0	7.00	160:30	21.00
126: 0	24.00	143:30	6.50	161: 0	22.00
126:30	23.50	144: 0	6.00	161:30	23.00
127: 0	23.00	144:30	5.50	162: 0	24.00
127:30	22.50	145: 0	5.00	162:30	25.00
128: 0	22.00	145:30	4.50	163: 0	26.00
128:30	21.50	146: 0	4.00	163:30	27.00
129: 0	21.00	146:30	3.50	164: 0	28.00
129:30	20.50	147: 0	3.00	164:30	29.00
130: 0	20.00	147:30	2.50	165: 0	30.00
130:30	19.50	148: 0	2.00	165:30	31.00
131: 0	19.00	148:30	1.50	166: 0	32.00
131:30	18.50	149: 0	1.00	166:30	33.00
132: 0	18.00	149:30	.50	167: 0	34.00
132:30	17.50	150: 0	.00	167:30	35.00
133: 0	17.00	150:30	1.00	168: 0	36.00
133:30	16.50	151: 0	2.00	168:30	37.00
134: 0	16.00	151:30	3.00	169: 0	38.00

Deg:Mn	Virupa	Deg:Mn	Virupa	Deg:Mn	Virupa
169:30	39.00	187: 0	56.50	204:30	47.75
170: 0	40.00	187:30	56.25	205: 0	47.50
170:30	41.00	188: 0	56.00	205:30	47.25
171: 0	42.00	188:30	55.75	206: 0	47.00
171:30	43.00	189: 0	55.50	206:30	46.75
172: 0	44.00	189:30	55.25	207: 0	46.50
172:30	45.00	190: 0	55.00	207:30	46.25
173: 0	46.00	190:30	54.75	208: 0	46 00
173:30	47.00	191: 0	54.50	208:30	45.75
174: 0	48.00	191:30	54.25	209: 0	45 50
174:30	49.00	192: 0	54.00	209:30	45.25
175: 0	50.00	192:30	53.75	210: 0	45.00
175:30	51.00	193: 0	53.50	210:30	44.75
176: 0	52.00	193:30	53.25	211: 0	44.50
176:30	53.00	194: 0	53.00	211:30	44.25
177: 0	54.00	194:30	52.75	212: 0	44.00
177:30	55.00	195: 0	52.50	212:30	43.75
178: 0	56.00	195:30	52.25	213: 0	43.50
178:30	57.00	196: 0	52.00	213:30	43.25
179: 0	58.00	196:30	51.75	214: 0	43.00
179:30	59.00	197: 0	51.50	214:30	42.75
180: 0	60.00	197:30	51.25	215: 0	42.50
180:30	59.75	198: 0	51.00	215:30	42.25
181: 0	59.50	198:30	50.75	216: 0	42.00
181:30	59.25	199: 0	50.50	216:30	41.75
182: 0	59.00	199:30	50.25	217: 0	41.50
182:30	58.75	200: 0	50.00	217:30	41.25
183: 0	58.50	200:30	49.75	218: 0	41.00
183:30	58.25	201: 0	49.50	218:30	40.75
184: 0	58.00	201:30	49.25	219: 0	40.50
184:30	57.75	202: 0	49.00	219:30	40.25
185: 0	57.50	202:30	48.75	220: 0	40.00
185:30	57.25	203: 0	48.50	220:30	39.75
186: 0	57.00	203:30	48.25	221: 0	39.50
186:30	56.75	204: 0	48.00	221:30	39.25

Deg:Mn	Virupa	Deg:Mn	Virupa	Deg:Mn	Virupa
222: 0	39.00	239:30	30.25	257: 0	21.50
222:30	38.75	240: 0	30.00	257:30	21.25
223: 0	38.50	240:30	29.75	258: 0	21.00
223 30	38.25	241: 0	29.50	258:30	20.75
224: 0	38.00	241:30	29.25	259: 0	20.50
224:30	37.75	242: 0	29.00	259:30	20.25
225: 0	37.50	242:30	28.75	260: 0	20.00
225;30	37.25	243: 0	28.50	260:30	19.75
226: 0	37.00	243:30	28.25	261: 0	19.50
226:30	36.75	244: 0	28.00	261:30	19.25
227: 0	36.50	244:30	27.75	262: 0	19.00
227.30	36.25	245: 0	27.50	262:30	18.75
228: 0	36.00	245:30	27.25	263: 0	18.50
228:30	35.75	246: 0	27.00	263:30	18.25
229: 0	35.50	246:30	26.75	264: 0	18.00
229:30	35.25	247: 0	26.50	264:30	17.75
230: 0	35.00	247:30	26.25	265: 0	17.50
230:30	34.75	248: 0	26.00	265:30	17.25
231: 0	34.50	248:30	25.75	266: 0	17.00
231:30	34.25	249: 0	25.50	266:30	16.75
232: 0	34.00	249:30	25.25	267: 0	16.50
232:30	33:75	250: 0	25.00	267:30	16.25
233: 0	33,50	250:30	24.75	268: 0	16.00
233:30	33.25	251: 0	24.50	268:30	15.75
234: 0	33.00	251:30	24.25	269: 0	15.50
234:30	32.75	252: 0	24.00	269:30	15.25
235: 0	32.50	252:30	23.75	270: 0	15.00
235:30	32.25	253: 0	23.50	270:30	14.75
236: 0	32.00	253:30	23.25	271: 0	14.50
236:30	31.75	254: 0	23.00	271:30	14.25
237: 0	31.50	254:30	22.75	272: 0	14.00
237:30	31.25	255: 0	22.50	272:30	13.75
238: 0	31.00	255:30	22.25	273: 0	13.50
238:30	30.75	256: 0	22.00	273:30	13.25
239: 0	30.50	256:30	21.75	274: 0	13.00

Deg:Mn	Virupa	Deg:Mn	Virupa	Deg:Mn	Virupa
274:30	12.75	283: 0	8.50	291:30	4.25
275: 0	12.50	283:30	8.25	292: 0	4.00
275:30	12.25	284: 0	8.00	292:30	3.75
276: 0	12.00	284:30	7.75	293: 0	3.50
277:30	11.75	285: 0	7.50	293:30	3.25
276: 0	11.50	285:30	7.25	294: 0	3.00
277:30	11.25	286: 0	7.00	294:30	2.75
278: 0	11.00	286:30	6.75	295: 0	2.50
278;30	10.75	287: 0	6.50	295:30	2.25
279: 0	10.50	287:30	6.25	296: 0	2.00
279:30	10.25	288: 0	6.00	296:30	1.75
280: 0	10.00	288:30	5.75	297: 0	1.50
280;30	9.75	289: 0	5.50	297:30	1.25
281: 0	9.50	289:30	5.25	298: 0	1.00
281:30	9.25	290: 0	5.00	298:30	.75
282: 0	9.00	290:30	4.75	299: 0	.50
282;30	8.75	291; 0	4.50	299:30	.25

अथ स्पष्टबलाध्याय ॥२७॥

Chapter 27

Evaluation Of Strengths

अथ स्पष्टबलं वक्ष्ये स्थान-कालादिसम्भवम् ।
नीचोनं खचरं भार्धाधिक चक्राद् विशोधयेत् ॥१॥
भागीकृत्य त्रिभिर्भक्तं लब्धमुच्चबलं भवेत् ।

1-1½. *STHAANA BALA (upto sloka 6) FIRSTLY UCHCHABALA :* Now about the strengths by classes positional, temporal etc. (Firstly, Uchchabala forming part of positional strength or Sthaanabala). Deduct from the longitude of the planet its (deep) debilitation point. If the sum is less than 6 signs, consider it as it is; if it exceeds 6 signs, deduct the same from 12 signs. The sum so got be converted into degress etc. and divided by 3 which is the planet's Uchchabala or exaltation strength (in Virupas).

Notes : These strengths are called Shadbala. These consist of the following :

1. Sthaana Bala (or positional strength)
2. Dig Bala (or directional strength)
3. Kala Bala (Temporal Strength) inclusive of Ayana Bala (or equinoctial strength)
4. Cheshta Bala (or motional strength)
5. Naisargika Bala (or natural strength)
6. Drik Bala (or aspectual strength)

These strengths are computed for the seven planets from the Sun to Saturn. The nodes are not considered.

Firstly explained is Sthaana Bala due to a planet's position.

This strength comprises of the following considerations :

1. Uchcha Bala (or exaltation strength)
2. Saptavargaja Bala (or strength accruing out of positions in Rasi, Hora, Decanate, Saptamamsa, Navamsa, Dvadasamsa and Trimsamsa).
3. Ojhayugmarasiamsa Bala (strength acquired by placement in odd/even Rasi and in odd/even Navamsa).
4. Kendradi Bala (due to placement in angle, or succedent or cadent house).
5. Drekkana Bala (due to placement in first, second or third decanate of a sign).

In the present verses under comment the sage explains the method to know the Uchchabala of a planet. To find out this strength, we need two things. Firstly the planet's actual longitude. Secondly its debilitation point which is constant for all horoscopes. The deep debilitation points of the 7 planets are noted on pp 38-39 *supra*.

For example, assume the Sun's placement in a given case is Pisces 12° 15' (or 342° 15'). His deep debilitation point is Libra 10° (or 190°). Hence :

(Sun's position—Deep debilitation point) ÷ 3

$$= \frac{342°15' \text{ minus } 190°}{3}$$

$$= 152° \; 15' \div 3 = 50.75 \text{ Virupas}$$

If the sum before division by 3 is in excess of 180 degrees deduct it from 360 and then divide by 3 which will be the planet's uchcha bala in Virupas. Maximum Uchcha bala is always 60 shashtiamsas or 1 Rupa.

स्वत्रिकोण-स्वगेहाधिमित्रमित्र-समारिषु ॥२॥
अधिशत्रुगृहे चापि स्थितानां क्रमशो बलम् ।
भूताब्धयः खाग्नि-नखास्तिथ्यो दश युगाः कराः ॥३॥
एवं होरादृकाणाद्रि-भागांक-द्वादशांशजम् ।
त्रिंशांशजं तदैक्यञ्च सप्तवर्गसमुद्भवम् ॥४॥

2-4. *SAPTAVARGAJA BALA :* If a planet is in its Moolatrikona Rasi, it gets 45 Virupas, in own Rasi 30 Virupas, extreme friend's Rasi 20 Virupas, friend's Rasi 15 Virupas, neutral's Rasi 10 Virupas, enemy's Rasi 4 Virupas and in extreme enemy's Rasi 2 Virupas. Similarly these values occur for the other 6 divisional occupations, *viz.* Hora, Decanate, Saptamamsa. Navamsa, Dvadasamsa and Trimsamsa. When all these are added together the planet's Saptavargaja Bala emerges.

Notes : Next step is to find out the Saptavargaja bala of a planet. The tables of various Vargas as well as the compound relationships of the planets, are given in the previous pages. The compound relationships of two given planets, vide P. 42 *supra* (including Hora lordship etc.) be seen in the Rasi chart only and not in the concerned divisional chart. Then the strengths in Virupas for each of the Saptavargas be found out and added, which is then called saptavargaja bala of the planet.

शुक्रेन्दू समभांशेऽन्ये विषमेऽङ्घ्रिमितं बलम् ।

4½. *OJHAYUGMARASIAMSA BALA :* Each of Venus and the Moon in even Rasis and others in odd Rasis acquire a quarter of Rupa (i.e. 15 Virupas). These are applicable to such Navamsas also.

Notes : Each of Jupiter, the Sun, Mars, Mercury and Saturn get 15 Virupas if they are placed in odd Rasis. Venus and the Moon get similar strength for placement in an even sign. Similarly for placement in such odd or even Navamsas. The strengths acquired by Rasi and Navamsa positions be added together to know the Ojhayugmarasiamsa bala. (Male and neutral planets get this strength in male Rasi/Navamsa. Female planets get such strength in female Rasi/Navamsa.)

केन्द्रादिषुस्थिताः खेटाः पूर्णऽर्धऽङ्घ्रिमितं क्रमात् ॥५॥

5. *KENDRADI BALA :* A planet in an angle gets full strength while one in succedent house gets half and the one in cadent house gets a quarter (of Rupa) (as Kendradi bala),

Notes : Kendradi means angles etc. This denotes three groups of four Rasis each. These are angles, (i.e. 1st, 4th, 7th and 10th) succedents, (i.e. 2nd, 5th, 8th and 11th) and cadents, (i e. 3rd, 6th, 9th and 12th). The following are the Kendradi balas :

(1) Planet in angle=60 Virupas
(2) Planet in succedent=30 Virupas
(3) Planet in cadent=15 Virupas

आद्यमध्यावसानेषु द्रेष्काणेषु स्थिताः क्रमात् ।
पुंनपुंसकयोषाख्या दद्युरङ्घ्रिमितं बलम् ॥६॥

6. *DREKKANA BALA :* Male, female and hermaphrodite planets respectively get a quarter Rupa according to placements in the first, second and third decanates.

Notes : This strength is acquired by a planet with reference to its decanate position being in the 1st, 2nd or 3rd part of a sign. Male planets are : the Sun, Mars, and Jupiter. Female planets are Venus and the Moon. Saturn and Mercury are eunuch bodies. A Drekkana bala of 15 Virupas will be acquired by planets as under :

Male planet in 1st Drekkana.
Female planet in 2nd Drekkana.
Eunuch planet in 3rd Drekkana.

For calculations of Drekkana, see Speculum of Drekkanas, *supra.* Needless to mention that if the Drekkana position is other than what is required, then the strength on this count is nil. This strength is also called Linga Bala.

The Balas so far acquired, *viz*. (1) Uchcha bala, (2) Saptavargaja bala, (3) Ojhayugmarasiamsa bala, (4) Kendradi bala and (5) Drekkana bala be all added together to get net Sthaana bala or positional strength. These are in Virupas and hence be divided by 60 to know the strength in Rupas.

सूर्यात् कुजात् सुखं, जीवाज्ज्ञाच्चाऽस्तं लग्नमार्कितः ।
दशमं च भृगोश्चन्द्राद् हित्वा षड्भाधिके सति ॥७॥
चक्राद् विशोध्य तद्भागास्त्रिभिर्भक्ताश्च दिग्बलम् ।

7-7½. *DIGBALA OR DIRECTIONAL STRENGTH :*
Deduct the 4th house (i.e. Nadir) from the longitudes of Sun and Mars; the 7th house (i.e. descendant) from that of Jupiter and Mercury; the 10th house (i.e. meridian) from that of Venus and the Moon; and lastly the ascendant from that of Saturn. If the sum is above 180 degrees deduct the sum from 360. The sum arrived in either way be divided by 3 which will be the Digbala (or directional strength) of the planet.

Notes : As seen earlier, Jupiter and Mercury have Digbala in the ascendant. Venus and the Moon have this bala in the 4th house (i.e. Nadir), Saturn in the descendant and the Sun and Mars on the meridian. These strengths are full on the cusp of the respective house and nil on the cusp of the opposite house. Hence note down the longitude of the concerned planet and the cuspal degree on which it is bereft of directional strength. Deduct the latter from the former. If the product exceeds 180' deduct the same again from 360. The sum so arrived at be divided by 3, which will denote the Digbala of the planet in Virupas. The directional strength acquired by a planet when it is on its most powerful point is 1 Rupa or 60 Virupas. For example Saturn exactly on the 7th cusp gets 1 Rupa, and exactly on the ascending degree gets zero Virupa as directional strength.

इष्टाधटि निशीथात्तन्नतं त्रिशच्च्युतं नतम् ॥८॥
चन्द्रभौम-शनीनां च नतं द्विघ्नं कलादिकम् ।
षष्टिशुद्धं तदःयेषां सदा रूपं बुधस्य हि ॥९॥

8-9. *KAALA BALA OR TEMPORAL STRENGTH (upto sloka 17)* : Firstly NATHONNATHA BALA. Find out the difference between midnight and apparent birth time which is called Unnata. Deduct Unnata from 30 ghatis to obtain Nata (नत). Double the Nata in ghatis which will indicate identical Natha bala for the Moon, Mars and Saturn. Deduct the Natha from 60 to know the Unnatha bala of the Sun, Jupiter and Venus. Mercury, irrespective of day and night, gets full Nathonnatha Bala (i.e. of 1 Rupa or 60 Virupas).

Notes : Kaala Bala (or temporal strength) comprises of the following sub divisions :

1) Nathonnatha Bala (diurnal and nocturnal strengths).
2) Paksha Bala (Paksha=fortnight).
3) Tribhaga Bala (strength due to day/night being made in 3 parts).
4) Varsha-Masa-Dina-Hora Bala (Varsha=astrological year, Masa=month, Dina=week day and Hora=planetary hour).
5) Ayana Bala (equinoctial strength).
6) Yudhdha Bala (strength due to partaking in planetary war).

Though Naisargika bala discussed in between in sloka 14, this is an independent source of strength without reference to Kala bala.

Firstly Nathonnatabala, Moon, Mars and Saturn get this strength in the night. The Sun, Jupiter and Venus get diurnal strength or strength in day time. The same Virupas of strength will be identically held by all the planets of each group. That is whatever will be the Sun's Nathonnata strength will be identically held by Jupiter and Venus. Similarly the other group.

Formula : Natha ghatis (apparent) × 2=Natha bala for Moon group.

60 − Moon's Natha Bala=Bala for Sun group

Mercury always gets 1 Rupa as Nathonnatha bala irrespective of the birth being in day or night time.

Another simple method is as under :

$$\text{Natha Bala} = \frac{\text{Brith time in degrces}}{3}$$

$$\text{Unnatha Bala} = \frac{\text{180 Minus birth time in degrees}}{3}$$

For this purpose count from apparent midnight to birth time at the rate of one degree per minute of time, or 15° per hour. This will convert the birth time into degrees etc.

अथ पक्षबलं वक्ष्ये सूर्यं चन्द्राद् विशोध्य च।
षड्भाधिके विशोध्यार्काद् भागीकृत्य त्रिभिर्भजेत् ॥१०॥
पक्षजं बलमिन्दुज्ञशुक्रेज्यानां तु षष्टितः।
विशोध्य तब्दलं ज्ञेयं पापानां पक्षसंभवम् ॥११॥

10-11. *PAKSHA BALA :* Deduct from the Moon's longitude that of the Sun. If the sum exceeds 6 signs, deduct the same from 12. The product so obtained be converted into degrees etc. and divided by 3 which will indicate the Paksha bala of each of the benefic planets. The Paksha bala of benefic should be deducted from 60 which will go to each malefic as Paksha bala.

Notes : Paksha bala is decided on the following basis :

$$\text{Paksha bala for benefic} = \frac{\text{Moon minus Sun}}{3}$$

Paksha bala for malefic =60 minus benefic's Paksha bala,

Benefics form one group and each of them will get the same figure of Paksha bala. (Mercury is to be treated as a malefic if he is conjunct a malefic. The Moon in dark half is a malefic.) The bala of benefics should be deducted from 60 to get a malefic's Paksha bala. If Moon—Sun is above 180, deduct it from 360.

Whether the Moon is in a group of benefics or otherwise, her Paksha bala is always doubled just as the Sun's Ayana bala.

दिनत्र्यंशेषु सौम्यार्क-शनीनां, निट्त्रिभागके।
चन्द्रशुक्रकुजानां च बलं पूर्णं सदा गुरोः ॥१२॥

12. *TRIBHAGA BALA :* One Rupa is obtained by Mercury (if birth is) in the first one third part of day time, by the Sun in the second one third part of the day and by Saturn in the last third part of the day. Similarly, the Moon, Venus and Mars get full strength (of one Rupa) in the first, second and last one third parts of the night. Jupiter gets this strength at all times.

Notes : This strength goes to one planet only, as 1 rupa. Jupiter, however, gets 1 Rupa irrespective of birth time.

The day duration or night duration according to birth being in day or night must be divided by 3. With the following table, Tribhaga bala can be known, according to the birth being :

in 1st part of day=1 Rupa to Mercury
in 2nd part of day=1 Rupa to the Sun
in 3rd part of day=1 Rupa to Saturn
in 1st part of night=1 Rupa to the Moon
in 2nd part of night=1 Rupa to Venus
in 3rd part of night=1 Rupa to Mars
at any time=1 Rupa to Jupiter

Thus two planets will get 1 Rupa of Tribhaga bala. That is 1 Rupa to Jupiter and 1 Rupa to the respective planet in whose part the birth occurs. The other 5 planets do not get any Tribhaga bala.

वर्षमासदिनेशानां तिथ्यस्त्रिशच्छराणंवाः ।
होरेशस्य बलं षष्टिरुक्तं नैसर्गिकं पुरा ॥१३॥

13. *VARSHA-MAASA-DINA-HORA BALA :* 15, 30, 45 and 60 Virupas are in order given to Varsha lord, Maasa lord Dina lord and Hora lord. Naisargika bala (or natural,strength) has already been explained.

Notes : Under this heading, four different planets get certain Virupas. These strengths are :

Varsha (Abda) lord	=	15 Virupas
Masa (month) lord	=	30 Virupas
Dina (day) lord	=	45 Virupas
Hora (hour) lord	=	60 Virupas

How to decide the said lordships is explained as under.

Varsha lord : Astrological year is different from other measures. The day on which the astrological year begins can be found out from the Speculum of abbreviated Ahargana, vide p.272. To know the Varsha lord we should first ascertain the number of days past from the beginning of Creation. This is a very tedious process and hence we are concerned with the abbreviated Ahargana (or the number of days past from

Creation). According to late Rev. Ebenezer Burgess, who translated Surya Siddhanta in English, as on January 1, 1860, the number of days past from the beginning of Creation are 714, 404, 108, 573.

To know the day on which the astrological year in which birth took place began adopt the following formula. Divide the number of days past from the day of Creation till the day of birth by :60. Reject remainder and multiply the quotient by 3. Increase the post-multiplied product by 1 and divide by 7. The remainder will indicate the week day on which the astrological year giving birth to the native opened. Remainder 1 indicates Sunday, 2 Monday and so on and so forth.

Assume that birth took place on June 1, 1984. Locate from the Speculum of Abbreviated Ahargaņas for January O date 1984 as 65142. Add 153 being the number of days upto the day of birth (inclusive the birth date). Thus we get abbreviated days past from creation to birth as 65295. This product when divided by 360 yields a quotient of 181. Ramainder is tc be rejected. 181 multiplied by 3 indicates 543. Increased by 1, this gives 544. When 544 is divided by 7, the remainder is 5. That is, the astrological year of birth for one born on June 1, 1984 began on a Thursday. Hence this strength or Varsha bala goes to Jupiter, the ruler of Thursday.

Masa Lord : Divide the same Ahargana by 30 and the quotient (devoid of remainder) indicates months passed from Creation to birth. The completed months be multiplied by 2 and increased by 1. The latest sum should be divided by 7 and the remainder indicates on which the birth month began. Continuing with the same case, we divide 65295 by 30. Quotient is 2176. This sum multiplied by 2 and increased by 1 denotes 4353. Dividing 4353 by 7, we get a remainder of 6 denoting Friday. That is, the month of birth began on Friday and the Masa bala goes to Venus, the lord of Friday.

Dina lord : Though the week day of birth can be known from ephemeris or perpetual calendars, we better adopt the method prescribed which will confirm if the Ahargana followed is correct or is otherwise. The number of days as arrived above indicating Ahargana be divided by 7 and the remainder will indicate the week day of birth. In the example case 65295 divided by 7 leaves a remainder of 6. That is June 1,1984 is Friday. Hence the Ahargana followed by us is correct. While considering Dina bala, the birth should be treated from sunrise to sunrise.

Hence in this case, the Dina bala goes to Venus, ruler of Friday.

Hora Bala : Ho ra means planetary hour. Each day from sunrise to sunrise is divided into 24 equal parts of one hour or 2.5 ghatikas. These Horas are ruled by the 7 planets from the Sun to Saturn. The first Hora of the day is ruled by the lord of the week day. The 2nd one is ruled by the lord of the 6th week day counted from the first ruler. The 3rd Hora is ruled by the lord of the 6th week day counted from the 2nd Hora lord. Similarly it proceeds in the same manner till the first Hora of the next day is taken over by the lord of that day himself. Whichever planet rules the birth Hora gets the Hora Bala. Horas are to be calculated for mean local time and not standard time of birth.

For easy reference, consult the Speculum of Horas *Vide infra.*

Speculum of Abbreviated Ahargana for January 0

Yr.	Ahargana	Yr.	Ahargana	Yr.	Ahargana
1800	458	1813	2686	1826	7434
1801	823	1814	3051	1827	7799
1802	1188	1815	3416	1828*	8164
1803	1553	1816*	3781	1829	8530
1804*	1918	1817	4147	1830	8895
1805	2284	1818	4512	1831	9260
1806	2649	1819	4877	1832*	9625
1807	494	1820*	5242	1833	9991
1808*	859	1821	5608	1834	10356
1809	1225	1822	5963	1835	10721
1810	1590	1823	6338	1836*	11086
1811	1955	1824*	6703	1837	11452
1812*	2320	1825	7069	1838	11817

Yr.	Ahargana	Yr.	Ahargana	Yr.	Ahargana
1839	12182	1875	25334	1911	38479
1840*	12547	1876*	25696	1912*	38844
1841	12913	1877	26062	1913	39210
1842	13278	1878	26427	1914	39575
1843	13643	1879	26792	1915	39940
1844*	14008	1880*	27157	1916*	40305
1845	14374	1881	27523	1917	40671
1846	14739	1882	27888	1918	41036
1847	15104	1883	28253	1919	41401
1848*	15469	1884*	28618	1920*	41766
1849	15835	1885	28984	1921	42132
1850	16200	1886	29349	1922	42497
1851	16565	1887	29714	1923	42862
1852*	16930	1888*	30079	1924*	43227
1853	17296	1889	30445	1925	43593
1854	17661	1890	30810	1926	43958
1855	18026	1891	31175	1927	44323
1856*	18391	1892*	31540	1928*	44688
1857	18757	1893	31906	1929	45054
1858	19122	1894	32271	1930	45419
1859	19487	1895	32636	1931	45784
1860*	19852	1896*	33001	1932*	46149
1861	20218	1897	33367	1933	46515
1862	20583	1898	33732	1934	46880
1863	20948	1899	34097	1935	47245
1864*	21313	1900	34462	1936*	47610
1865	21679	1901	34827	1937	47976
1866	22044	1902	35192	1938	48341
1867	22409	1903	35557	1939	48706
1868*	22774	1904*	35922	1940*	49071
1869	23140	1905	36288	1941	49437
1870	23505	1906	36653	1942	49802
1871	23870	1907	37018	1943	50167
1872*	24235	1908*	37383	1944*	50532
1873	24601	1909	37749	1945	50898
1874	24966	1910	38114	1946	51263

Yr.	Ahargana	Yr.	Ahargana	Yr.	Ahargana
1947	51628	1965	58203	1983	64777
1948*	51993	1966	58568	1984*	65142
1949	52359	1967	58933	1985	65508
1950	52724	1968*	59298	1986	65873
1951	53089	1969	59664	1987	66238
1952*	53454	1970	60029	1988*	66603
1953	53820	1971	60394	1989	66969
1954	54185	1972*	60759	1990	67334
1955	54550	1973	61125	1991	67699
1956*	54915	1974	61490	1992*	68064
1957	55281	1975	61855	1993	68430
1958	55646	1976*	62220	1994	68795
1959	56011	1977	62586	1995	69160
1960*	56376	1978	62951	1996*	69525
1961	56742	1979	63316	1997	69891
1962	57107	1980*	63681	1998	70256
1963	57472	1981	64047	1999	70621
1964*	57837	1982	64412		

* **Leap years.**

Common Years—Days for Zero Dates of Months

Date	Days	Date	Days	Date	Days
Jan. 0	0	May 0	120	Sept. 0	243
Feb. 0	31	June 0	151	Oct. 0	273
Mar. 0	59	July 0	181	Nov. 0	304
April 0	90	Aug. 0	212	Dec. 0	334

Leap Years—Days for Zero Dates of Months

Date	Days	Date	Days	Date	Days
Jan. 0	0	May 0	121	Sept. 0	244
Feb. 0	31	June 0	152	Oct. 0	274
Mar. 0	60	July 0	182	Nov. 0	305
April 0	91	Aug. 0	213	Dec. 0	335

Speculum of Horas

Hora	Sun	Mon	Tue	Wed	Thu	Fri	Sat
1.	Sun	Moon	Mar	Merc	Jup	Ven	Sat
2.	Ven	Sat	Sun	Moon	Mar	Merc	Jup
3.	Merc	Jup	Ven	Sat	Sun	Moon	Mar
4.	Moon	Mar	Merc	Jup	Ven	Sat	Sun
5.	Sat	Sun	Moon	Mar	Merc	Jup	Ven
6.	Jup	Ven	Sat	Sun	Moon	Mars	Merc
7.	Mars	Merc	Jup	Ven	Sat	Sun	Moon
8.	Sun	Moon	Mars	Merc	Jup	Ven	Sat
9.	Ven	Sat	Sun	Moon	Mars	Merc	Jup
10.	Merc	Jup	Ven	Sat	Sun	Moon	Mars
11.	Moon	Mars	Merc	Jup	Ven	Sat	Sun
12.	Sat	Sun	Moon	Mars	Merc	Jup	Ven
13.	Jup	Ven	Sat	Sun	Moon	Mars	Merc
14.	Mars	Merc	Jup	Ven	Sat	Sun	Moon
15.	Sun	Moon	Mars	Merc	Jup	Ven	Sat
16.	Ven	Sat	Sun	Moon	Mars	Merc	Jup
17.	Merc	Jup	Ven	Sat	Sun	Moon	Mars
18.	Moon	Mars	Merc	Jup	Ven	Sat	Sun
19.	Sat	Sun	Moon	Mars	Merc	Jup	Ven
20.	Jup	Ven	Sat	Sun	Moon	Mars	Merc
21.	Mars	Merc	Jup	Ven	Sat	Sun	Moon
22.	Sun	Moon	Mars	Merc	Jup	Ven	Sat
23.	Ven	Sat	Sun	Moon	Mars	Merc	Jup
24.	Merc	Jup	Ven	Sat	Sun	Moon	Mars

तन्मानं सप्तहृत्षष्टिरेकाद्येकोत्तरैर्हता ।
शमंबुगुशुचंरादिखेटानां क्रमतो द्विज ! ॥१४॥

14. *NAISARGIKA BALA (NATURAL STRENGTH)* : Divide one Rupa (or 60 Virupas) by 7 and multiply the resultant product by 1 to 7 separately which will indicate the Natural Strength due to Saturn, Mars, Mercury, Jupiter, Venus, the Moon and the Sun, respectively.

Notes : As per the above rule, the Naisargika Bala in Rupas are indicated below so that the reader need not calculate himself.

Sun = 1.000 Rupa
Moon= 0.857 Rupa
Mars = 0.286 Rupa
Merc = 0.429 Rupa
Jup = 0.571 Rupa
Ven = 0.714 Rupa
Sat = 0.143 Rupa

This strength is acquired by a planet due to its luminosity. The brightest gets the highest Naisargika Bala while the least bright gets the least Naisargika Bala. The Sun is the brightest among the 7 planets while Saturn is the darkest. The brightness of the planets can be guessed from the above figures.

This is an independent strength and has nothing to do with Kala Bala, and is constant for all nativities and for ever. Hence no individual calculations need be done.

Naisargika Bala has a significant use in the Shadbala. If two planets are of equal Shadbala, then the one with higher Naisargika Bala prevails over the other.

पञ्चाब्धयः सुराः सूर्याः खण्डकांशाः क्रमादमी ।
सायनग्रहदोराशितुल्यखण्डयुतिश्च सा ॥१५॥

भागादिकहतादेष्यात् त्रिंशल्लब्धयुता लवाः ।
स्वमृणं तुलमेषाद्यौ शनीन्द्वोश्च त्रिराशिषु ॥१६॥

तथाऽऽरार्केज्यशुक्राणां व्यस्तं, ज्ञस्य सदा धनम् ।
तद्भागाश्च त्रिभिर्भक्ता ज्ञेयमायनजं बलम् ॥१७॥

15-17 *AYANA BALA* : 45, 33 and 12 are the Khandas for calculating Ayana Bala. Add Ayanamsa to the planet (for which Ayana Bala is required) and find out the Bhuja (distance from the nearest equinox). Add the figure corresponding to the Rasi (of the Bhuja) to the Bhuja. The degrees etc. of the Bhuja (devoid of Rasi) be multiplied by the figure corresponding to the higher of the left out Khandas and divided by 30. Add the resultant product to the sum obtained earlier. Convert this into Rasi etc. If the Moon and Saturn are in Libra or ahead add to this 3 Rasis, and if in Aries to Virgo reduce from 3 Rasis. Similarly it is reverse for the Sun, Mars, Venus and Jupiter, (i.e. addition or deduction is converse). For Mercury 3 Rasis are always additive. The resultant sum in Rasi, degrees and minutes be divided by 3 to get the Ayana Bala in Rupas.

Notes : Ayana Bala can be found out on the following simple formula.

$$\text{Ayana Bala} = \frac{23^\circ 27' \pm \text{Kranti}}{46^\circ 54'} \times 60$$

$$= (23^\circ 27' \text{ plus or minus Kranti}) \times 1.2793$$

The following points have to be remembered in respect of of Krantis. When the Moon or Saturn have Southern Kranti or when the Sun, Mars, Jupiter or Venus have Northern Kranti, take plus. In a contrary situation in respect of these 6 planets, take minus. As far as Mercury is concerned, it is always plus whether he has Southern Kranti or Northern Kranti. Krantis (or declinations) can be ascertained from standard modern ephemeris.

The Sun's Ayana Bala is again multiplied by 2 whereas for others the product arrived in Virupas is considered as it is.

The following speculum will help the reader to easily work out the Ayana Bala, when the Kranti of a planet is known.

Speculum of Ayana Bala

Kranti ± 23° 27′	Ayana Bala	Kranti ± 23° 27′	Ayana Bala	Kranti ± 23° 27′	Ayana Bala
° ′		° ′		° ′	
0 0	0.0	2 35	3.3	5 10	6.6
0 5	0.1	2 39	3.4	5 14	6.7
0 9	0.2	2 44	3.5	5 19	6.8
0 14	0 3	2 49	3.6	5 24	6.9
0 19	0.4	2 54	3.7	5 28	7.0
0 23	0.5	2 58	3.8	5 33	7.1
0 28	0.6	3 3	3.9	5 38	7.2
0 33	0.7	3 8	4.0	5 42	7.3
0 38	0.8	3 12	4.1	5 47	7.4
0 42	0.9	3 17	4.2	5 52	7.5
0 47	1.0	3 22	4.3	5 56	7.6
0 52	1.1	4 26	4.4	6 1	7.7
0 56	1.2	3 31	4.5	6 6	7.8
1 1	1.3	3 36	4.6	6 11	7.9
[illegible]	1.4	3 40	4.7	6 15	8.0
1 10	1.5	3 45	4.8	6 20	8.1
1 15	1.6	3 50	4.9	6 25	8.2
1 20	1.7	3 55	5.0	6 29	8.3
1 24	1.8	3 59	5.1	6 34	8.4
1 29	1.9	4 4	5.2	6 39	8.5
1 34	2.0	4 9	5.3	6 43	8.6
1 38	2.1	4 13	5.4	6 48	8.7
1 43	2.2	4 18	5.5	6 53	8.8
1 48	2.3	4 23	5.6	6 57	8.9
1 53	2.4	4 27	5.7	7 2	9.0
1 57	2.5	4 32	5.8	7 7	9.1
2 2	2.6	4 37	5.9	7 11	9.2
2 7	2.7	4 41	6.0	7 16	9.3
2 11	2.8	4 46	6.1	7 21	9.4
2 16	2.9	4 51	6.2	7 26	9.5
2 21	3.0	4 55	6.3	7 30	9.6
2 25	3.1	5 0	6.4	7 35	9.7
2 30	3.2	5 5	6.5	7 40	9.8

Kranti ± 23° 27′	Ayana Bala	Kranti ± 23° 27′	Ayana Bala	Kranti ± 23° 27′	Ayana Bala
° ′		° ′		° ′	
7 44	9.9	10 24	13.3	13 3	16.7
7 49	10.0	10 28	13.4	13 8	16.8
7 54	10.1	10 33	13.5	13 13	16.9
7 58	10.2	10 38	13.6	13 17	17.0
8 3	10.3	10 43	13.7	13 22	17.1
8 8	10.4	10 47	13.8	13 27	17.2
8 12	10.5	10 52	13.9	13 31	17.3
8 17	10.6	10 57	14.0	13 36	17.4
8 22	10.7	11 1	14.1	13 41	17.5
8 27	10.8	11 6	14.2	13 45	17.6
8 31	10.9	11 11	14.3	13 50	17.7
8 36	11.0	11 15	14.4	13 55	17.8
8 41	11.1	11 20	14.5	14 0	17.9
8 45	11.2	11 25	14.6	14 4	18.0
8 50	11.3	11 29	14.7	14 9	18.1
8 55	11.4	11 34	14.8	14 14	18.2
8 59	11.5	11 39	14.9	14 18	18.3
9 4	11.6	11 44	15.0	14 23	18.4
9 9	11.7	11 48	15.1	14 28	18.5
9 13	11.8	11 53	15 2	14 32	18.6
9 18	11.9	11 58	15.3	14 37	18.7
9 23	12.0	12 2	15.4	14 42	18.8
9 27	12.1	12 7	15.5	14 46	18.9
9 32	12.2	12 12	15.6	14 51	19.0
9 37	12.3	12 16	15.7	14 56	19.1
9 42	12.4	12 21	15.8	15 0	19.2
9 46	12.5	12 26	15.9	15 5	19.3
9 51	12.6	12 30	16.0	15 10	19.4
9 56	12.7	12 35	16.1	15 15	19.5
10 0	12.8	12 40	16.2	15 19	19.6
10 5	12.9	12 44	16.3	15 24	19.7
10 10	13.0	12 49	16.4	15 29	19.8
10 14	13.1	12 54	16.5	15 33	19.9
10 19	13.2	12 59	16.6	15 38	20.0

Kranti ± 23° 27′	Ayana Bala	Kranti ± 23° 27′	Ayana Bala	Kranti ± 23° 27′	Ayana Bala
° ′		° ′		° ′	
15 43	20.1	18 22	23.5	21 2	26.9
15 47	20.2	18 27	23.6	21 6	27.0
15 52	20.3	18 32	23.7	21 11	27.1
15 57	20.4	18 36	23.8	21 16	27 2
16 1	20.5	18 41	23.9	21 20	27.3
16 6	20.6	18 46	24.0	21 25	27.4
16 11	20,7	18 50	24.1	21 30	27.5
16 16	20.8	18 55	24.2	21 34	27.6
16 2C	20.9	19 0	24.3	21 39	27.7
16 25	21.0	19 4	24.4	21 44	27.8
16 30	21.1	19 9	24.5	21 49	27.9
16 34	21.2	19 14	24.6	21 53	28.0
16 39	21.3	19 18	24.7	21 58	28.1
16 44	21.4	19 23	24.8	22 3	28.2
16 48	21.5	19 28	24.9	22 7	28.3
16 53	21.6	19 33	25.0	22 12	28.4
16 58	21.7	19 37	25.1	22 17	28.5
17 2	21.8	19 42	25.2	22 21	28.6
17 7	21.9	19 47	25.3	22 26	28.7
17 12	22.0	19 51	25.4	22 31	28.8
17 16	22.1	19 56	25.5	22 35	28.9
17 21	22.2	20 1	25.6	22 40	29.0
17 26	22.3	20 5	25.7	22 45	29.1
17 31	22.4	20 10	25.8	22 49	29.2
17 35	22.5	20 15	25.9	22 54	29.3
17 40	22.6	20 19	26.0	22 59	29.4
17 45	22.7	20 24	26.1	23 4	29.5
17 49	22.8	20 29	26.2	23 8	29.6
17 54	22.9	20 33	26.3	23 13	29.7
17 59	23.0	20 38	26.4	23 18	29.8
18 3	23.1	20 43	26.5	23 22	29.9
18 8	23.2	20 48	26.6	23 27	30.0
18 13	23.3	20 52	26.7	23 32	30.1
18 17	23.4	20 57	26.8	23 36	30.2

Kranti ± 23° 27'	Ayana Bala	Kranti ± 23° 27'	Ayana Bala	Kranti ± 23° 27'	Ayana Bala
° '		° '		° '	
23 41	30.3	26 21	33.7	29 0	37.1
23 46	30.4	26 25	33.8	29 5	37.2
23 50	30.5	26 30	33.9	29 9	37.3
23 55	30.6	26 35	34.0	29 14	37.4
24 0	30.7	26 39	34.1	29 19	37.5
24 5	30.8	26 44	34.2	29 23	37.6
24 9	30.9	26 49	34.3	29 28	37.7
24 14	31.0	26 53	34.4	29 33	37.8
24 19	31.1	26 58	34.5	29 38	37.9
24 23	31.2	27 3	34.6	29 42	38.0
24 28	31.3	27 7	34.7	29 47	38.1
24 33	31.4	27 12	34.8	29 52	38.2
24 37	31.5	27 17	34.9	29 56	38.3
24 42	31.6	27 22	35.0	30 1	38.4
24 47	31.7	27 26	35.1	30 6	38.5
24 51	31.8	27 31	35.2	30 10	38.6
24 56	31.9	27 36	35.3	30 15	38.7
25 1	32 0	27 40	35.4	30 20	38.8
25 5	32.1	27 45	35.5	30 24	38.9
25 10	32.2	27 50	35.6	30 29	39.0
25 15	32.3	27 54	35.7	30 34	39.1
25 20	32.4	27 59	35.8	30 38	39.2
25 24	32.5	28 4	35.9	30 43	39.3
25 29	32 6	28 8	36.0	30 48	39.4
25 34	32.7	28 13	36.1	30 53	39.5
25 38	32.8	28 18	36.2	30 57	39.6
25 43	32.9	28 22	36.3	31 2	39.7
25 48	33.0	28 27	36.4	31 7	39.8
25 52	33.1	28 32	36.5	31 11	39.9
25 57	33.2	28 37	36.6	31 16	40.0
26 2	33.3	28 41	36.7	31 21	40.1
26 6	33.4	28 46	36.8	31 25	40.2
26 11	33.5	28 51	36.9	31 30	40.3
26 16	33.6	28 55	37.0	31 35	40.4

Kranti ± 23° 27′	Ayana Bala	Kranti ± 23° 27′	Ayana Bala	Kranti ± 23° 27′	Ayana Bala
° ′		° ′		° ′	
31 39	40.5	34 19	43.9	36 58	47.3
31 44	40.6	34 24	44.0	37 3	47.4
31 49	40.7	34 28	44.1	37 8	47.5
31 54	40.8	34 33	44.2	37 12	47.6
31 58	40.9	34 38	44.3	37 17	47.7
32 3	41.0	34 42	44.4	37 22	47.8
32 8	41.1	34 47	44.5	37 27	47.9
32 12	41.2	34 52	44.6	37 31	48.0
32 17	41.3	34 56	44.7	37 36	48.1
32 22	41.4	35 1	44.8	37 41	48.2
32 26	41.5	35 6	44.9	37 45	48.3
32 31	41.6	35 11	45.0	37 50	48.4
32 36	41.7	35 15	45.1	37 55	48.5
32 40	41.8	35 20	45.2	37 59	48.6
32 45	41.9	35 25	45.3	38 4	48.7
32 50	42.0	35 29	45.4	38 9	48.8
32 54	42.1	35 34	45.5	38 13	48.9
32 59	42.2	35 39	45.6	38 18	49.0
33 4	42.3	35 43	45.7	38 23	49.1
33 9	42.4	35 48	45.8	38 27	49.2
33 13	42.5	35 53	45.9	38 32	49.3
33 18	42.6	35 57	46.0	38 37	49.4
33 23	42.7	36 2	46.1	38 42	49.5
33 27	42.8	36 7	46.2	38 46	49.6
33 32	42.9	36 11	46.3	38 51	49.7
33 37	43.0	36 16	46.4	38 56	49.8
33 41	43.1	36 21	46.5	39 0	49.9
33 46	43.2	36 26	46.6	39 5	50.0
33 51	43.3	36 30	46.7	39 10	50.1
33 55	43.4	36 35	46.8	39 14	50.2
34 0	43.5	36 40	46.9	39 19	50.3
34 5	43.6	36 44	47.0	39 24	50.4
34 10	43.7	36 49	47.1	39 28	50.5
34 14	43.8	36 54	47.2	39 33	50.6

Kranti ± 23° 27′	Ayana Bala	Kranti ± 23° 27′	Ayana Bala	Kranti ± 23° 27′	Ayana Bala
° ′		° ′		° ′	
39 38	50.7	42 8	53.9	44 38	57.1
39 43	50.8	42 13	54.0	44 43	57.2
39 47	50 9	42 17	54.1	44 47	57.3
39 52	51.0	42 22	54.2	44 52	57.4
39 57	51.1	42 27	54.3	44 57	57.5
40 1	51.2	42 31	54.4	45 1	57.6
40 6	51.3	42 36	54.5	45 6	57.7
40 11	51.4	42 41	54.6	45 11	57.8
40 15	51.5	42 45	54.7	45 16	57.9
40 20	51.6	42 50	54.8	45 20	58.0
40 25	51.7	42 55	54.9	45 25	58.1
40 29	51.8	43 0	55.0	45 30	58.2
40 34	51.9	43 4	55.1	45 34	58.3
40 39	52.0	43 9	55.2	45 39	58.4
40 43	52.1	43 14	55.3	45 44	58.5
40 48	52·2	43 18	55.4	45 48	58.6
40 53	52.3	43 23	55.5	45 53	58.7
40 58	52.4	43 28	55.6	45 58	58.8
41 2	52.5	43 32	55.7	46 2	58.9
41 7	52.6	43 37	55.8	46 7	59.0
41 12	52.7	93 42	55.9	46 12	59.1
41 16	52.8	43 46	56.0	46 16	59.2
41 21	52.9	43 51	56.1	46 21	59.3
41 26	53.0	43 56	56.2	46 26	59.4
41 30	53.1	44 0	56.3	46 31	59.5
41 35	53.2	44 5	56.4	46 35	59.6
41 40	53.3	44 10	56.5	46 40	59.7
41 45	53.4	44 15	56.6	46 45	59.8
41 49	53.5	44 19	56.7	46 49	59.9
41 54	53.6	44 24	56.8	46 54	60.0
41 59	53.7	44 29	56.9		
42 3	53.8	44 33	57.0		

यद्रवेरायनं वीर्यं चेष्टाख्यं तावदेव हि।
विधोः पक्षबलं यावत् तावच्चेष्टाबलं स्मृतम् ॥१८॥

18. *MOTIONAL STRENGTH FOR SUN AND MOON :* The Sun's Cheshta Bala (or motional strength) will correspond to his Ayana Bala. The Moon's Paksha Bala will itself be her Cheshta Bala.

Notes : For the Sun and the Moon, there is no separate method of Cheshta Bala computation. The Sun's Ayana Bala will itself be his Cheshta Bala (or motional strength) while the Moon's Paksha Bala is her Cheshta Bala. For the other 5 planets, the method is described in slokas 24-25 infra.

पापदृक्पादहीनं तच्छुभदृक्पादयुक् तथा।
बलैक्यं ज्ञेज्यदृग्युक्तमेवं खेटबलं भवेत् ॥१९॥

19. *DRIG BALA (ASPECTUAL STRENGTH) :* Reduce one fourth of the Drishti Pinda if a planet has malefic aspects on it and add a fourth if it is aspected by a benefic. Super add the entire aspect of Mercury and Jupiter to get the net strength of a planet.

अथ तारग्रहाणां तु युद्धचतोश्च द्वयोर्मिथः।
बलान्तरं विजेतुः स्वं, निर्जितस्य बले त्वृणम् ॥२०॥

20. *PLANETARY WAR :* Should there be a war between the starry planets (i.e. between 2 planets from Mars to Saturn, in a given horoscope), the difference between the Shadbalas of the two should be added to the victor's shadbala and deducted from the Shadbala of the vanquished.

वक्रानुवक्रा विकला मन्दा मन्दतरा समा।
चरा चाऽतिचरा चेति ग्रहाणामष्टधा गतिः ॥२१॥
षष्टिर्वक्रगते वीर्यमनुवक्रगतेर्दलम्।
पादो विकलभुक्तेः स्यात् तथा मध्यगतेर्दलम् ॥२२॥
पादो मन्दगतेस्तस्य दलं मन्दतरस्य हि।
चरभुक्तेस्तु पादोनं, दलं स्यादतिचारिणः ॥२३॥

21-23 *PLANETARY MOTIONS (MARS TO SATURN) :* Eight kinds of motions are attributed to planets. These are Vakra (retrogression), Anuvakra (entering the previous sign in retrograde motion), Vikala (devoid of Motion or in stationary position), Manda (somewhat slower motion than usual), Mandatara (slower than the previous mentioned motion), Sama (somewhat increasing in motion as against Manda), Chara (faster than Sama) and Atichara (entering next sign in accelerated motion). The strengths allotted due to such 8 motions are : 60, 30, 15, 30, 15, 7.5, 45 and 30.

मध्यमस्फुटयोगार्धहीनं स्वस्वचलोच्चकम् ।
षड्भाधिकं च्युतं चक्राच्चेष्टाकेन्द्रं स्मृतं कुजात् ॥२४॥
भागीकृतं त्रिभिर्भक्तं लब्धं चेष्टाबलं त्विति ।
स्थानदिक्कालदृक्चेष्टानिसर्गोत्थं च षड्विधम् ॥२५॥

24-25 *MOTIONAL STRENGTH FOR MARS ETC.* : Add together the mean and true longitudes of a planet and divide the ame by two. Reduces this sum from the Seeghrocha (or apogee) of the planet. The resultant product will indicate the Cheshta Kendra (or Seeghra kendra) of the planet from 12 signs. The Rasi, degrees and minutes so arrived be converted into degrees, minutes etc. and divided by 3 which will denote the motional strength of the planet. Thus there are six sources of strength called Sthaana Bala Digbala, Kaalabala, Drigbala, Cheshta Bala and Naisargika Bala.

Notes : Take the average between a planet's mean longitude and true longitude (i. e. Mars to Saturn). Deduct this product from its Seeghrocha which will be its Cheshta Kendra. If this exceeds 180 degrees deduct again from 360 degrees. Divide the Cheshta Kendra by 3 which will be the motional strength of the planet.

एवं ग्रहबलं प्रोक्तमथ भावबलं श्रृणु ।
कन्यायुग्मतुलाकुम्भचापाद्याधश्च सप्तमम् ॥२६॥
गोऽजसिंहमृगाद्यार्ध-चापान्त्यार्धात् सुखं त्यजेत् ।
कर्कवृश्चिकतो लग्नं मृगान्त्यार्धज्झषाश्च खम् ॥२७॥
शोध्यमङ्गाधिकं चक्राच्च्युतं भागीकृतं त्रिहृत् ।
सद्दृष्टिपादयुक्-पापदृष्टिपादविवर्जितम् ॥२८॥

ज्ञेज्यदृष्टियुतं तच्च स्वस्वस्वामिबलान्वितम् ।
इति भावबलं स्पष्टं सामान्यं च पुरोदितम् ॥२६॥

26-29 *BHAVA BALAS :* Thus I explained about the planetary strengths. Deduct the 7th house (longitude of descendant) from the bhava if the bhava happens to be in Virgo, Gemini, Libra, Aquarius or the first half of Sagittarius. If Aries, Taurus, Leo or first half of Capricorn or the second half of Sagittarius happen to be the bhava, deduct the 4th house (Nadir) from it. Should the Bhava be in Cancer or in Scorpio deduct from it the ascendant. And deduct the 10th house (meridian) from the bhava happening to fall in Capricorn second half or Pisces. Convert the product so obtained (in the respective case) into degrees etc. and divide by 3 to get the strength of the bhava. If the balance in the process of deducting the Nadir, Meridian, ascendant or descendant exceeds 6 signs, deduct it again from 12 signs before converting into degrees and dividing by 3. The product after division should be increased by a fourth if the bhava in question has a benefic aspect on it. And a malefic's aspect will entail one fourth reduction. If Jupiter or Mercury aspect a bhava, add that planet's aspectual strength also. And then superadd the strength acquired by the lord of that Bhava. This will be the net strength of that Bhava.

बुधेज्ययुक्तभावस्य बलमेकेन संयुतम् ।
मन्दाररवियुक्तस्य बलमेकेन वर्जितम् ॥३०॥
दिने शीर्षोदयो भावः सन्ध्यायामुभयोदयः ।
निशि पृष्ठोदयाख्यश्च दद्यात् पादमितं बलम् ॥३१॥

30-31 *SPECIAL RULES :* The bhavas occupied by Jupiter and Mercury will each get an addition of 1 rupa while each of the bhava occupied by Saturn, Mars and the Sun suffer 1 rupa reduction. 15 virupas will have to be added to the bhavas falling in Seershodaya Rasis if birth happens to be in day time, to the bhavas falling in dual (or common) Rasis if birth happens to be in twilight and to the bhavas falling in Prishtodaya Rasis if birth be in night.

अंकाग्नयोऽङ्गरामाश्च खाग्नया करसिन्धवः ।
नवाग्नयः सुरास्त्रिशद् दशसंगुणिताः क्रमात् ॥३२॥

रव्यादीनां बलैक्यश्चेत् तदा सुबलिनो मताः ।
अधिकं पूर्णमेव स्याद् बलं चेद्बलिनो द्विज ! ॥३३॥

32-33. *SHADBALA REQUIREMENTS :* 390, 360, 300, 420, 390, 330 and 300 Virupas are the Shadbala Pindas needed for the Sun etc. (upto Saturn) to be considered strong. If the strength exceeds, the planet is deemed to be very strong.

Notes : The minimum Shadbala requirements of the planets are as under :

The Sun	=	6.5 Rupas
The Moon	=	6.0 Rupas
Mars	=	5.0 Rupas
Mercury	=	7.0 Rupas
Jupiter	=	6.5 Rupas
Venus	=	5.5 Rupas
Saturn	=	5.0 Rapas

If a planet has the required shadbala, it will prove favourable to the native by virtue of its strength. However, Saturn's exterme strength will give long life as well as miseries.

गुरुसौम्यरवीणां तु भूतषट्केन्दवो द्विज ! ।
पंचाग्नयः खभूतानि कर-भूमिसुधाकराः ॥३४॥
खाग्नयश्च क्रमात्स्थान-दिक्-चेष्टा-समयाऽयने ।
सितेन्द्वोस्त्र्यग्निचन्द्राश्च खेषवः खाग्नयः शतम् ॥३५॥
चत्वारिंशत् कला भौम-मन्दयोः षण्णव क्रमात् ।
त्रिंशत् खवेदाः सप्ताङ्गा नखांश्चेत्युदिता द्विज ! ॥३६॥

34-36. Jupiter, Mercury and the Sun are strong if each of their Sthaana Bala, Digbala, Kaalabala, Cheshta Bala and Ayana Bala are respectively 165, 35, 50, 112 and 30 Virupas. The same required for the Moon and Venus are 133, 50, 30, 100 and 40. For Mars and Saturn these are 96, 30, 40, 67 and 20.

Notes : Even if the Shadbala Pinda is short of the sums stipulated in the previous two slokas, certain minimum requirements of the constituent strengths will make the planet considerably favourable. For this purpose, Jupiter, Mercury and the Sun can be put in 'A' group. The Moon and Venus form 'B' group while Mars and Saturn 'C' group. The constituent Balas in Virupas that should be minimum are :

Type	Group 'A'	Group 'B'	Group 'C'
Sthaanabala	165	133	96
Digbala	35	50	30
Kaalabala	50	30	40
Cheshtabala	112	100	67
Ayanabala	30	40	20

Ayanabala has been separately shown above. It is normally a practice to include Ayana Bala in the Kaalabala itself. In that case, Ayanabala should be separately seen apart from seeing the rest of the Kaalabala, as per the requirements denoted above.

एवं कृत्वा बलैक्यंच ततश्चिन्त्यं फलं द्विज!।
भावस्थानग्रहैः प्रोक्तयोगे ये योगहेतवः ॥३७॥
तेषां मध्ये बली कर्ता स एवाऽस्य फलप्रदः।
योगेष्वाप्तेषु बहुषु नीतिरेवं प्रकीर्तिता ॥३८॥

37-38. *BHAVA EFFECTS :* O Brahmin, thus the various sources of strengths be gathered together and effects declared. Whatever yogas or effects have been stated with respect to a bhava will come to pass through the strongest planet.

गणितेषु प्रवीणो यः शब्दशास्त्रे कृतश्रमः।
न्यायविद् बुद्धिमान् देशदिक्कालज्ञो जितेन्द्रियः ॥३९॥
ऊहापोह-पटुर्होरास्कन्धश्रवणसम्मतः।
मैत्रेय ! सत्यतां याति तस्य वाक्यं न संशयः ॥४०॥

39-40. *ELIGIBILITY TO ISSUE FRUITFUL PREDICTIONS :* O Maitreya, the words of one who has achieved skill in mathematics, one who has put in industrious efforts in the branch of grammar, one who has knowledge of justice, one who is intelligent, one who has knowledge of geography, space and time, one who has conquered his senses, one who is skilfully logical (in estimation) and one who is favourable to astrology, will doubtless be truthful.

अथेष्टकष्टाध्यायः ॥२८॥

Chapter 28

Ishta And Kashta Balas

अथ चेष्टमनिष्टं च ग्रहाणां कथयाम्यहम्।
यद्वशाच्च प्रयच्छन्ति शुभाऽशुभदशाफलम् ॥१॥

1. Now I narrate the benefic and evil tendencies of the planets based on which the Dasa effects—good or bad—can be decided.

स्वनीचोनो ग्रह शोध्यः षड्भाधिवये भमण्डलात्।
सैको राशिभंवेदुच्च-रश्मिर्द्विघ्नांशसंयुतः ॥२॥

2. *EXALTATION RAYS :* Deduct the planet's debilitation point from its actual position. If the sum exceeds 6 sings, deduct from 12 signs. The said sum should then be increased by 1 Rasi. The degrees etc. be multiplied by 2 which when considered along with Rasis will indicate the Uchcha Rasmi of the planet.

चेष्टाकेन्द्राच्च तद्रश्मिं साधयेदुच्चरश्मिवत्।
चेष्टाकेन्द्रं कुजादीनां पूर्वमुक्तं मया द्विज! ॥३॥
सायनार्कस्त्रिभोऽर्कस्य व्यर्केन्दुश्च विधोस्तथा।
चेष्टाकेन्द्रं रसाल्पं तच्चक्राच्छोध्यं रसाधिके ॥४॥

3-4. *CHESHTA RASMI :* Cheshta Rasmis are to be calculated from Cheshta Kendra similar to Uchcha Rasmi computations. The Cheshta Kendras of planets from Mars to Saturn have already been explained. Add 3 Rasis to Sayana Sun (i.e. Sun with Ayanamsa), which will be the Cheshta Kendra for the Sun. The sidereal longitude of the Sun should be deducted from the Moon to get the Moon's Cheshta Kendra. If the Cheshta Kendra (for any planet) is in excess of 6 signs, deduct it from 12 signs. Add 1 sign and multiply the degrees etc. by 2 which will indicate the Cheshta Rasmi of the planet.

चेष्टोच्चरश्मियोगार्धं शुभरश्मिः प्रकीर्त्यते ।
अष्टभ्यश्च विशुद्धोऽसावशुभाख्यश्च कथ्यते ॥५॥

5. *BENEFICIAL AND MALEEIC RAYS :* Add the Uchcha Rasmis and Cheshta Rasmis together and divide by two. The result will be auspicious rays (Subha Rasmis). Deduct from 8 the Subha Rasmis to obtain inauspicious rays (or Asubha Rasmis).

उच्चचेष्टाकरान् व्येकान् दिग्भिर्हत्वा तु योजयेत् ।
तदर्धमिष्टसंज्ञं स्यात् कष्टं तत्षष्टितश्च्युतम् ॥६॥

6. *ISHTA AND KASHTA (BENEFIC AND MALEFIC TENDENCIES) :* Reduce 1 from each of Cheshta Rasmi and Uchcha Rasmi. Then multiply the products by 10 and add together. Half of the sum will represent the Ishta Phala (benefic tendency) of the planet. Reduce Ishta Phala from 60 to obtain the planet's Kashta Phala (or malefic tendency).

स्वोच्चे मूलत्रिकोणे च स्वभेऽधिसुहृदोष्टभे ।
समभे शत्रुभे चाधि-शत्रुभे नीचभे क्रमात् ॥७॥
षष्टिरिष्वब्धयस्त्रिंशदाकृतिस्तिथयो गजाः ।
चत्वारो द्वौ च शून्यं च शुभमेतत्फलं गृहे ॥८॥
षष्टितः पतितं चैतच्छेषं स्यादशुभं गृहे ।
तदर्धमन्यवर्गेषु ज्ञेयं विप्र ! शुभाऽशुभम् ॥९॥

7-9. *ISHTA KASHTA SAPTAVARGAJA PHALA :* 60, 45, 30, 22, 15, 8, 4, 2 and 0 are the Subhankas (or Subha Griha Pankthis or benefic points) due to a planet's placement respectively in exaltation, Moolatrikona, own sign, extreme friend's sign, friend's sign, equal's sign, enemy's sign, bitter enemy's sign and debilitation sign. If Subhanka is deducted from 60, Asubhanka (or Asubha Pankthi or inauspicious points) will emerge. O Brahmin, in other Vargas, these are halved.

पञ्चस्विष्टफलं चाद्यात् समं षष्ठे ततः परम् ।
अशुभं त्रिषु विज्ञेयमिति शास्त्रेषु निश्चितम् ॥१०॥

10. A planet is considered auspicious in the first five of the said places. In the sixth place it is equal, i.e. neither good nor bad. And in the other three places it is inauspicious.

दिग्बलं दिक्फलं तस्य तथा दिनफलं भवेत्।
तयोः फलं शुभं प्रोक्तमशुभं षष्टितश्च्युतम् ॥११॥
शुभेऽधिके शुभं ज्ञेयमशुभं त्वशुभेऽधिके।
दशाफलं नभोगस्य तथा भावफलं द्विज! ॥१२॥

11-12. *NATURE OF EFFECTS DUE TO DIGBALA ETC :* The directional strength of planet is itself representative of the effects due to the direction and Dinabala itself is indicative of effects due to day. Whatever quantum of Digbala etc. are obtained by a planet will be the extent of auspicious effects acquirable on account of that strength. Deducting those figures from 60, the extent of inauspiciousness is known. If auspiciousness is more in the case of planet's strength, the Dasa and Bhavas related to that planet will be auspicious. And these are converse if inauspiciousness is predominant.

बलैः षड्भिः समेधित्वा बलैक्येन भजेत् पृथक्।
तत्तद्बलफलानि स्युरशुभानि शुभानि च ॥१३॥
शुभपापफलाभ्यां च हन्याद् दृष्टि बलं तथा।
दृष्टी ते शुभपापाह्वये बले स्यातां तदाह्वये ॥१४॥

13-14. *SAPTAVARGAJA BALA AND ISHTA KASHTA (Continued) :* The various strengths (i.e. the other 6 vargas vide slokas 7-9 supra) be multiplied by the respective planet's shadbala pinda which will indicate the auspiciousness of the varga concerned. Auspicious or inauspicious aspect will be obtained by multiplying the Subha or Asubha Pankthi. Similarly auspicious or inauspicious effects will be known by multiplying the auspicious or inauspicious strength by the respective Pankthi.

भावानां च फले प्रोक्ते पतीनां च फले उभे।
राशौ शुभनभोगश्चेद् भावसाधनसंभवम् ॥१५॥
फलं तस्य शुभे युञ्ज्यादशुभे वर्जयेत् तथा।
पापश्चेदन्यथा चैवं बले दृष्टयां तथैव च ॥१६॥
युञ्ज्यादुच्चादिगे खेटे फलं नीचादिगे त्यजेत्।
एवं शुभाऽशुभं ज्ञात्वा जातकस्य फलं वदेत् ॥१७॥

अष्टवर्गफलं चैवं स्थाने च करणेऽन्यथा ।
राशिद्वयगते भावे तद्राश्यधिपतेः क्रिया ॥१८॥
स्थानाधिकेन भावेन भावलाभः प्रकीर्तितः ।
तत्समाने च तद्भावे तदानीं स्थानदान् ग्रहान् ॥१९॥
संयोज्य स्थानसंख्याया दलमेतत्समं फलम् ।
एवं सखेटभावानां फलं ज्ञेयं शुभाऽशुभम् ॥२०॥

15-20. *EFFECTS OF A BHAVA :* The strength of a Bhava and its lord have already been explained. The actual effects will be a combination of bhava strength and its lord's strength. If there is a benefic in the bhava add the same to the auspicious effects and deduct from inauspicious effects, which will denote the net auspicious or inauspicious effects. If a malefic is in the bhava, reverse the process, i.e. add inauspicious effects and deduct auspicious effects. Similarly aspects and strengths. If a planet is exalted or with such a dignity, add auspicious effects and reduce inauspicious effects. For debilitation etc. it is converse. In Ashtaka Varga, add Bindus (auspicious points) and deduct Karanas (inauspicious points). If a bhava extends to two Rasis, the rectification will be done as per both the lords. In that case whichever Rasi has more Bindus that Rasi will yield more favourable results concerning that Bhava. If both the Rasis have more auspicious Bindus take the average. Thus the auspicious and inauspicious effects of a bhava be understood.

अथ पदाध्यायः ॥२९॥

Chapter 29

Bhava Padas

कथयाम्यथ भावानां खेटानां च पदं द्विज ! ।
तद्विशेषफलं ज्ञातुं यथोक्तं प्राङ् महर्षिभिः ॥१॥
लग्नाद् यावतिथे राशौ तिष्ठेल्लग्नेश्वरः क्रमात् ।
ततस्तावतिथे राशौ लग्नस्य पदमुच्यते ॥२॥

सर्वेषामाप भावानां ज्ञेयमेवं पदं द्विज ।।
तनुभावपदं तत्र बुधा मुख्यपदं विदुः ।।३।।

1-3. *METHOD OF PADA* (पद) *CALCULATIONS* : O Brahmin, I shall now tell you about the Padas (or Arudhas) for bhavas and planets as well, as laid down by the earlier great sages. The Pada of the ascendant will correspond to the sign arrived at by counting so many signs from the ascendant lord as he is away from the ascendant. Similarly Padas for other houses be known through their lords. The word "Pada" exclusively denotes the Pada for ascendant (or Lagna Pada).

Notes : Maharshi Jaimini (author of Poorva Mimamsa) extensively dealt with this system of astrology as given in ch. 29-33 hereof. Though sage Parasara has originally sown seeds, later on Jaimini delved deep and located many pearls out of his great wisdom and intuition. Thus it has become to be known more by the name Jaimini astrology rather than Parasari.

To work out the Padas etc. enunciated in these chapters, we shall consider a nativity as indicated below calling it the standard nativity.

Date of birth : May 21, 1944 at 1902 hrs (War time) 79E 20 13 N40

	Merc Ven Moon	Sun	Sat
	Rasi		Mars Rahu Jup
	Ascdt O° 48′34″		

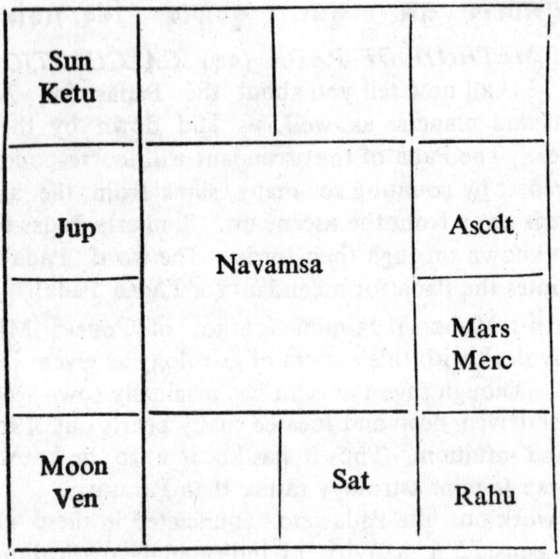

Longitudes

Planet	Deg	Min	Sec
The Sun	37	12	18
The Moon	27	35	46
Mars	96	18	46
Mercury	14	54	13
Jupiter	116	7	13
Venus	27	17	50
Saturn	63	9	41
Rahu	97	37	6
Ketu	277	37	6

In calculating the Arudhas for the various houses, we have to proceed as under. First of all we understand the 12 Arudhas thus :

1. Lagna Pada (or simply Pada) : Arudha of 1st house.
2. Dhana Pada : Arudha of 2nd house.
3. Vikrama (Bhratru) Pada : Arudha of 3rd house.
4. Matru (Sukha) Pada : Arudha of 4th house.
5. Mantra or Putra Pada : Arudha of 5th house.
6. Roga or Satru Pada : Arudha of 6th house.
7. Dara Pada (Kalatra Pada) : Arudha of 7th house.
8. Marana Pada : Arudha of 8th house.
9. Pitru Pada : Arudha of 9th house.
10. Karma Pada : Arudha of 10th house.
11. Labha Pada : Arudha of 11th house.
12. Vyaya Pada : Arudha of 12th house.

In calculating the Arudha Pada for a house, note the number of signs its lord moved away from that particular sign. Count so many signs from the lord in question. The sign so arrived will be the Arudha for the sign under consideration.

In the standard nativity, Scorpio is the ascendant and its lord Mars is 9 signs away from the ascendant and is in Cancer.

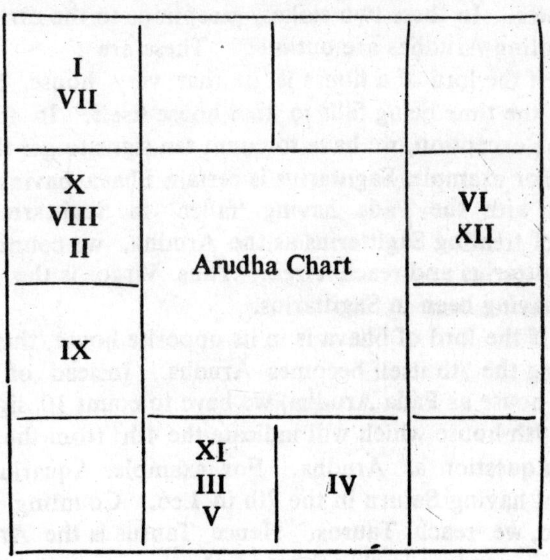

Hence we count 9 signs from Cancer and get Pisces. Pisces is thus the Arudha or Pada of the ascendant (i.e. Lagna Pada). Now see the Arudha chart for the said nativity on p. 295. (The figures marked in Roman numbers denote the Bhava for which it stands as Pada.)

In the said chart, for example, Scorpio has the Mantrarudha (5th), Vikramarudha (3rd) and Labharudha (11th). Sagittarius has none. Thus, one sign may contain more than one Arudha while another sign may not be an Arudha at all.

स्वस्थानं सप्तमं नैवं पदं भवितुमर्हति।
तस्मिन् पदत्वे विज्ञेयं मध्यं, तुर्यं क्रमात् पदम् ॥४॥
यथा तुर्यस्थिते नाथे तुर्यमेव पदं भवेत्।
सप्तमे च स्थिते नाथे विज्ञेयं दशमं पदम् ॥५॥

4-5. *SPECIAL EXCEPTIONS :* The same house or the 7th from it does not become its Pada. When the Pada falls in the same house, the 10th therefrom be treated as its Pada. Similarly when the 7th becomes the Pada of a house, the 4th from the original house in question be treated as its Pada. If the ruler of a bhava be in the 4th from the bhava, then the very house occupied be noted as the Pada.

Notes : In these two slokas, exceptions to the earlier rules in calculating Arudhas are outlined. These are :

1. If the lord of a house is in that very house, then the Pada for the time being falls in that house itself. In that case, as per the exception, we have to count ten signs to get the actual Pada. For example, Sagittarius is certain Bhava having Jupiter therein, with the Pada having 'fallen' in Sagittarius itself. Instead of treating Sagittarius as the Arudha, we count 10 signs from Sagittarius and reach Virgo. Thus Virgo is the Pada for Jupiter having been in Sagittarius.

2. If the lord of bhava is in its opposite house, then for the time being the 7th itself becomes Arudha. Instead of treating that 7th house as Pada Arudha, we have to count 10 signs from the said 7th house which will indicate the 4th from the original Bhava in question as Arudha. For example, Aquarius is the ascendant having Saturn in the 7th in Leo. Counting 10 signs from Leo, we reach Taurus. Hence Taurus is the Arudha for Aquarius ascendant having Saturn in Leo.

3. If the lord of a bhava is in the 4th from the bhava, no counting is required. The house occupied by the lord itself (i.e. 4th from the bhava) is the Arudha. For example, Leo ascendant having the Sun is the 4th sign in Scorpio gets Scorpio itself as Arudha Lagna.

यस्माद् यावतिथे राशौ खेटात् तद्भवनं द्विज ! ।
ततस्तावतिथं राशिं खेटारूढं प्रचक्षते ॥६॥
द्विनाथद्विभयोरेवं विज्ञेयं सबलावधि ।
विगणय्य पदं विप्र ! ततस्तस्य फलं वदेत् ॥७॥

6-7. *PADAS FOR PLANTES :* Note the position of a planet and see how many signs away is its own sign with reference to its position. Count so many sign from the said own sign and the resultant sign will become the Arudha of the planets. If a planet owns two Rasis or if a Rasi is owned by two planets, consider the stronger and declare effects accordingly.

Notes : Here we are taught of what can be called as Graharudha or planet's Arudha. From a perusal of the above verses, we can take it to mean that there are 9 planetary Arudhas. Since the sage uses "Rasi owned by two planets" he obviously hints at co-rulership of Rahu and Ketu. Rahu is a co-ruler of Aquarius while Ketu shares ownership of Scorpio (*Vide* sloka 157, ch. 46 *infra*).

Assume that the Sun is in Capricorn. Counting from Capricorn to Leo we get 8 signs. Again from Leo we count 8 signs and reach Pisces which is the Arudha for the Sun. The exceptions stated for Bhavarudhas do not apply to Graharudhas.

In case of other 5 planets (Mars to Saturn) each owns two signs. Then the counting of planet's Arudha in such a case is with reference to the stronger of the two signs. For deciding strengths of signs and planets one has to use his wise judgement apart from consulting hints given in ch. 46. However, we do not have any authentic information available as to how to use Graharudhas. Either we have to work on experience or keep silent on this issue. The literature available on Jaimini system being limited nothing more can be said about this.

अथाऽहं पदमाश्रित्य फलं किञ्चिद् ब्रुवे द्विज !
पदादेकादशे स्थाने ग्रहैर्युक्तेऽथवेक्षिते ॥८॥
धनवान् जायते बालस्तथा सुखसमन्वितः ।
शुभयोगात् सुमार्गेण धनाप्तिः पापतोऽन्तथा ॥९॥
मिश्रैर्मिश्रं फलं ज्ञेयं स्वोच्चमित्रादिगेहगैः ।
बहुधा जायते लाभो बहुधा च सुखागमः ॥१०॥
पदाल्लाभगृहं यस्य पश्यन्ति सकला ग्रहाः ।
राजा वा राजतुल्यो वा स जातो नात्र संशयः ॥११॥

8-11. *PADA AND FINANCE (upto sloks 15)* : O Brahmin, I now tell you of some effects of planets based on Pada. If the 11th from Lagna Pada is occupied or aspected by a planet, the native will be happy and rich; wealth will come through virtuous means if a benefic is related as above. A malefic will confer wealth through questionable means. If there be both a benefic and a malefic, it will be through both means. If the planet in question (i.e. the one so related to 11th from Lagna Pada) be in exaltation or in own sign etc., there will be plenty of gains and plenty of happiness.

पदाल्लाभगृहं पश्येद् व्ययं कश्चिन्न पश्यति ।
अविघ्नेन सदा लाभो जायते द्विजसत्तम ! ॥१२॥

12. O excellent of the Brahmins, if the 12th from Lagna Pada is unaspected as the 11th from Lagna Pada is being aspected by a planet, then the gains will be uninterrupted.

ग्रहदृग्योगबाहुल्ये पदादेकादशे द्विज ! ।
सार्गले चापि तत्रापि बह्वर्गलसमागमे ॥१३॥
शुभग्रहार्गले विप्र ! तत्राप्युच्चग्रहार्गले ।
शुभेन स्वामिना दृष्टे लग्नभाग्यादिगेन वा ॥१४॥
जातस्य भाग्यप्राबल्यं निर्दिशेदुत्तरोत्तरम् ।
उक्तयोगेषु चेत् खेटो द्वादशं नैव पश्यति ॥१५॥

13-15. O Brahmin, the quantum of gains will correspond to the number of planets in or aspecting the 11th from Lagna

Pada. If there is Argala for the said 11th there will be more gains while a benefic Argala will bring still more gains. If the said benefic causing Argala be in his exaltation, the gains will be still higher. If the said 11th is aspected by a benefic from the ascendant, the 9th etc. gains will increase in the ascending order. In all these cases, the 12th from Pada be simultaneously free from malefic association.

Notes : From the Arudha ascendant, the 11th house is important in deciding the financial gains to be enjoyed by the native. Simultaneously the 12th from Arudha Lagna should be free from malefic relationship. If the planet related to the 11th from Lagnarudha is stronger than the one related to 12th from Lagnarudha, even then there will be gains. If more are well related to the 11th gains will be still more.

For Argala, see ch. 31 *infra*

A benefic placed in the ascendant aspecting the 11th from Arudha Lagna will be still beneficial. If the aspect is from the 9th from Lagna, it will confer much more gains. The 11th Arudha aspected by a favourable planet will also confer abundant gains. In the standard nativity, Jupiter is in the 9th in exaltation and aspects the 11th house from Arudha Lagna and also the 11th Arudha (i e. Labharudha). Hence in Jupiter's Dasa, the native can hope for abundant financial and professional gains.

पदस्थानाद् व्यये विप्र ! शुभपापयुतेक्षिते ।
व्ययबाहुल्यमित्येवं विशेषोपार्जनात् सदा ॥१६॥
शुभग्रहे सुमार्गेण कुमार्गात् पापखेचरे ।
मिश्रे मिश्रफलं वाच्यमेवं लाभोऽपि लाभगे ॥१७॥

16-17. *PADA AND FINANCIAL LOSSES (upto sloka 21)* : If the 12th from Lagna Pada is aspected by conjunct both benefics and malefics, there will be abundant earnings but plenty of expenses, The benefic will cause through fair means, malefic through unfair means and mixed planets through both fair and unfair means.

Notes : In the standard nativity, the 12th house from Arudhapada is aspected by Mars (8th aspect). Hence the expenses are equally high.

पदारूढाद् व्यये शुक्रभानु-स्वर्भानुभिर्युते ।
राजमूलाद् व्ययो वाच्यश्चन्द्रदृष्ट्या विशेषतः ॥१८॥

18. If the 12th from Lagna Pada is conjunct the Sun, Venus and Rahu, there will be loss of wealth through the king. The Moon aspecting (the said trio in the said house) will specifically cause more such losses.

पदारूढाद् व्यये सौम्ये शुभखेटयुतेक्षिते ।
ज्ञातिमध्ये व्ययो नित्यं पापदृक् कलहाद् व्ययः ॥१९॥

19. If Mercury is in the 12th from the Lagna Pada and be with or aspected by benefic similarly there will be expenses through paternal relatives. A malefic so related to the said Mercury will cause loss of wealth through disputes.

पदाद् व्यये सुराचार्ये वीक्षिते चान्यखेचरैः ।
करमूलाद् व्ययो वाच्यः स्वस्यैव द्विजसत्तम ! ॥२०॥

20. O Brahmin, if Jupiter is in the 12th from Lagna Pada, aspected by others, the expenses will be through taxes and on one's own.

आरूढाद् द्वादशे सौरे धरापुत्रेण संयुते ।
अन्यग्रहेक्षिते विप्र ! भ्रातृवर्गाद् धनव्ययः ॥२१॥

21. O Brahmin, if Saturn is in the 12th from the Lagna Pada along with Mars and is aspected by others, the expenses will be through one's co-born.

आरूढाद् द्वादशे स्थाने ये योगाः कथिता यथा ।
लाभभावे च ते योगा लाभयोगकरास्तथा ॥२२॥

22. *GAINFUL SOURCES :* Whatever sources of expenses are indicated above with reference to the 12th from Lagna Pada, gains through similar sources will occur if the 11th house so features with reference to Lagna Pada.

आरूढात् सप्तमे राहुरथवा संस्थितः शिखी ।
कुक्षिव्यथायुतो बालः शिखिना पीडितोऽथ वा ॥२३॥

23. *THE 7TH HOUSE FROM PADA (upto slaka 27)* : If Rahu or Ketu is placed in the 7th from Lagna Pada, the native will be troubled by stomachial disorders, or by fire.

आरूढात् सप्तमे केतुः पापखेटयुतेक्षितः।
साहसी श्वेतकेशी च वृद्धलिङ्गी भवेन्नरः॥२४॥

24. Should there be Ketu in the 7th from the Lagna Pada and be with aspect to or be conjunct another malefic, the native will be adventurous, will have (prematurely) grey hair and big male organ.

पदात्तु सप्तमे स्थाने गुरु-शुक्र-निशाकराः।
त्रयो द्वयमथैकोऽपि लक्ष्मीवान् जायते जनः॥२५॥

25. Should one, two or all the three of Jupiter, Venus and the Moon be in the 7th from Lagna Pada, the native will be very wealthy.

स्वतुङ्गे सप्तमे खेटः शुभो वाऽप्यशुभः पदात्।
श्रीमान् सोऽपि भवेन्नूनं सत्कीर्तिसहितो द्विज !॥२६॥

26. Whether a benefic or a malefic if be exalted in the 7th from Lagna Pada, the native will be affluent, and be famous.

ये योगाः सप्तमे स्थाने पदाश्च कथिता मया।
चिन्त्यास्तथैव ते योगा द्वितीयेऽपि सदा द्विज !॥२७॥

27. O Brahmin, these yogas as narrated by me with reference to the 7th from the Lagna Pada be also considered from the 2nd of Lagna Pada.

उच्चस्थो रौहिणेयो वा जीवो वा शुक्र एव वा।
एको बली धनगतः श्रियं दिशति देहिनः॥२८॥

28. Anyone of Mercury, Jupiter and Venus be exalted in the 2nd from Lagna Pada and be with strength, will make the subject rich.

ये योगाश्च पदे लग्ने यथावद् गदिता मया।
ते योगाः कारकांशेऽपि विज्ञेया बांधवर्जिताः॥२९॥

29. The yogas so far stated by me with reference to Lagna Pada be similarly evaluated from Karakamsa as well.

Notes : Karakamsa is the Navamsa occupied by Atmakaraka. For more information about Karakamsa, see ch. 39 *infra.* Atmakaraka etc. are discussed in ch. 32.

आरूढाद् वित्तभे सौम्ये सर्वदेशाधिपो भवेत् ।
सर्वज्ञो यदि वा स स्यात् कविर्वादी च भार्गवे ॥३०॥
आरूढात् केन्द्रकोणेषु स्थिते दारपदे द्विज ! ।
लग्नजायापदे वापि सबलग्रहसंयुते ॥३१॥
श्रीमांश्च जायते नूनं देशे विख्यातिमान् भवेत् ।
षष्ठेऽष्टमे व्ययस्थाने जातो दारपदेऽधनः ॥३२॥
पदे तत्सप्तमे वापि केन्द्रे वृद्धौ त्रिकोणके ।
सुवीर्यः संस्थितः खेटः भार्याभर्तृसुखप्रदः ॥३३॥
पदाद्दारपदे चैवं केन्द्रे कोणे च संस्थिते ।
द्वयोर्मैत्री भवेन्नूनं त्रिके वैरं न संशयः ॥३४॥
एवं लग्नपदाद् विप्र ! तनयादिपदे स्थिते ।
मित्रामित्रे विजानीयाल्लाभालाभौ विचक्षणः ॥३५॥
लग्नदारपदे विप्र ! मिथः केन्द्रगते यदि ।
त्रिलाभयोस्त्रिकोणे वा तथा राजा धराधिपः ॥३६॥
एवं लग्नपदादेव धनादिपदतो द्विज ! ।
स्थानद्वयं समालोक्य जातकस्य फलं वदेत् ॥३७॥

30-37. *GENERAL :* If Mercury is in the 2nd from Arudha Lagna, the native will lord over the whole country. Venus in the 2nd from Lagna Pada will make one a poet or a speaker. If the Dara Pada (i.e. the Pada of the 7th house) falls in an angle or in a trine counted from the Lagna Pada or if the Lagna Pada and Dara Pada both have strong planets, the native will be rich and be famous in his country. If the Dara Pada falls in the 6th/8th/12th from the Lagna Pada, then the native will be poor. If the Lagna Pada and the 7th therefrom or an angle/a trine/an upachaya therefrom be occupied by a strong planet, there will be happiness between the husbahd and wife. If the Lagna Pada and Dara Pada are mutually angular or trinal, there will be amity between the couple; if these be in mutually 6th/8th/12th, doubtlessly mutual enmity will crop up. O Brahmin, similarly mutual relationship or gain or loss through son etc. be known based on Lagna Pada and the relative Bhava Pada. If the Lagna Pada and Dara Pada are mutually angular or 3rd and 11th or trinal, the native will be a king ruling the earth. Similar deductions be made with reference to mutual positions of Lagna Pada and Dhana Pada.

अथोपपदाध्यायः ॥३०॥

Chapter 30
Upa Pada

अथोपपदमाश्रित्य कथयामि फलं द्विज ! ।
यच्छुभत्वे भवेन्नृणां पुत्रदारादिजं सुखम् ॥१॥
तनुभावपदं विप्र ! प्रधानं पदमुच्यते ।
तनोरनुचराद्यत् स्यादुपारूढं तदुच्यते ॥२॥
तदेवोपपदं नाम तथा गौणपदं स्मृतम् ।
शुभखेटगृहे तस्मिन् शुभग्रहयुतेक्षिते ॥३॥
पुत्रदारसुखं पूर्णं जायते द्विजसत्तम ! ।
पापग्रहयुते तत्र पापभे पापवीक्षिते ॥४॥
प्रव्राजको भवेज्जातो दारहीनोऽथ वा नरः ।
शुभदृग्योगतो नैव योगोऽयं दारनाशकः ॥५॥
रविर्नैवात्र पापः स्यात् स्वोच्चमित्रस्वभस्थितः ।
नीचशत्रुगृहस्थश्चेत्तदाऽसौ पाप एव हि ॥६॥

1-6. O Brahmin, now I tell you about Upa Pada, the auspiciousness of which will confer on then ative happiness from progeny, wife etc. The Pada of Lagna (i.e. Arudha Lagna) explained earlier is (of course) of prime importance. Upa pada is calculated for the bhava following the natal ascendant. This Upa Pada is also called Gauna Pada. O excellent of the Brahmins, if Upa Pada is conjunct or aspected by a benefic planet, one will obtain full happiness from progeny and spouse. Should the Upa pada be in a malefic's sign or is aspected by or is conjunct a malefic, one will become an ascetic and go without a wife. If (in the said circumstances) there be a benefic aspect (on upa pada or the related malefic), or conjunction, deprival of spouse will not come to pass. In this case, the Sun if exalted or in a friendly sign, is not a malefic. He is a malefic if in debilitation or in an enemy's sign.

Notes : Regarding Upa pada calculations, there are more than two views on the same sloka of Parasara or an identical Sutra from Jaimini. In our text, the word "अनुचर" *(Anuchara)* is used which denotes "the house following the ascendant at birth". Some interpret this as the 5th from ascendant while I feel it should be the house succeeding the natal ascendant, which is the 12th house in normal sense.

However, when we study other commentaries on Jaimini, (for example Chaukamba Hindi edition), we are taught that it is the 12th house from natal ascendant in the case of an odd sign ascending and it is the 2nd house from natal ascendant in the case of an even sign ascending. This argument, meseems, is more sound. Accordingly the Pada for the 12th or the 2nd from Lagna is called Upa pada. In calculating Upa pada, the rules mentioned in verses 4 and 5 of the previous chapter be kept in mind.

Now take the standard nativity. The ascendant is Scorpio, an even sign. Its 2nd house is Sagittarius whose lord Jupiter is 8 signs away from Sagittarius. Hence we count 8 signs from Jupiter (in Cancer). We so reach Aquarius which is the Upa pada in this case.

शुभग्रहाणां दृष्टिश्चेदुपारूढाद् द्वितीयके ।
शुभर्क्षे शुभयुक्ते च पूर्वोक्तं हि फलं स्मृतम् ॥७॥
उपारूढाद् द्वितीयं च नीचांशे नीचखेटयुक् ।
क्रूरग्रहसमायुक्तं जातको दारहा भवेत् ॥८॥
स्वोच्चांशे स्वोच्चसंस्थे वा तुङ्गदृष्टिवशात् तथा ।
भवन्ति बहवो दारा रूपलक्षणसंयुताः ॥९॥

उपारूढे द्वितीये वा मिथुने संस्थिते सति।
तत्र जातनरो विप्र ! बहुदारयुतो भवेत् ॥१०॥
उपारूढे द्वितीयेऽपि स्वस्वामिग्रहसंयुते।
स्वर्क्षगे तत्पतौ वापि यत्र कुत्रापि भूसुर ॥११॥
यस्य जन्मनि योगोऽयं स नरो द्विजसत्तम ! ।
उत्तरायुषि निर्दारो भवत्येव न संशयः ॥१२॥

7-12. *EFFECT OF 2ND FROM UPA PADA* : If the 2nd from Upa pada is a benefic sign or is aspected by or conjunct with a benefic, the same good results (as for wife and sons) will come to pass. If there be a planet in the 2nd from Upa pada in debilitation sign/Amsa or be conjunct with a debilitated/malefic planet, there will be destruction of wife. If the said occupant be in exaltation sign/Navamsa or be aspected by another planet, there will be many charming and virtuous wives. O Brahmin, if Gemini happens to be the 2nd from Upa pada, then also there will be many wives. O excellent of the Brahmins, if the Uparudha or the 2nd therefrom be occupied by its own lord or if the said lord is in his other own house, the death of wife will be at an advanced age.

Notes : In the example case, the Upa pada is in Aquarius, a malefic's sign and is powerfully aspected by malefic Mars and is without benefic's aspect. However, the 2nd from Upa pada is well fortified as its lord Jupiter is exalted and aspects the said 2nd house. Hence the native is happily married and endowed with progenic happiness.

Loss of wife is to be expected if the 2nd from Upa pada is occupied by a debilitated planet, or the occupant of the said 2nd is in debilitation Navamsa, or is conjunct a debilitated planet (i.e. a banefic debilitated joining a malefic in the 2nd from Upa pada) or a benefic joining a malefic in said 2nd house.

Taurus becoming the Upa pada is said to give many wives or plurality of marriage.

Although there may be combinations for early loss of spouse if the 2nd lord from Uparudha (or Upapada) is in the 2nd itself or is in his other sign, it will considerably protect the native from such a calamity. And the spouse as a result will live udto an advanced age.

स्वराशौ संस्थितेऽप्येवं नित्याख्ये दारकारके।
उत्तरायुषि निर्दारो भवत्येव न संशयः॥१३॥
उपारूढपतिः स्वोच्चे स्थिरस्त्रीकारकोऽथ वा।
सुकुलाद् दारलाभः स्यान्नीचस्थे तु विपर्ययात्॥१४॥
उपारूढे द्वितीये वा शुभसम्बधतो द्विज!।
जातस्य सुन्दरी भार्या भव्या रूपगुणान्विता॥१५॥

13-15. *WIFE FROM THE 2ND OF UPAPADA (upto sloka 22)* : If a planet being constant indicator of wife (i.e. 7th lord or Venus) is in own house, there will be loss of wife only at a later stage. If the lord of Upapada or the constant significator of wife is in exaltation, the wife will be from a noble family; reverse will be the case, if he is debilitated. O Brahmin, if the 2nd from Upapada is related to a benefic, the wife will be beautiful, fortunate and virtuous.

उपारूढाद् द्वितीये च शनिराहू स्थितौ यदि।
अपवादात् स्त्रियस्त्यागो नाशो वा जायते द्विज!॥१६॥

16 Should Saturn and Rahu be in the 2nd from Upa pada, the native will lose his wife on account of calumny or through death.

उपारूढे द्वितीये वा शिखिशुकौ यदा स्थितौ।
रक्तप्रदररोगार्ता जायते तस्य भामिनी॥१७॥

17. The native's wife will be troubled by disorder of blood, leucorrhoea (प्रदर) etc. if Venus and Ketu are in the 2nd from Upapada.

बुध-केतू स्थितौ तत्र तदाऽस्थिस्त्रावसंयुता।
तत्रस्थाः शनिराह्वर्कास्तदाऽस्थिज्वरसंयुता॥१८॥

18. Mercury with Ketu in the 2nd from Upapada will cause breakage of bones while Rahu, Saturn and the Sun will cause distress of bones.

स्थूलाङ्गी बुधराहूभ्यां तत्रस्थाभ्यां द्विजोत्तम!।
बुधक्षेत्रे कुजार्कौ चेन्नासिकारोगसंयुता॥१९॥

कुजक्षेत्रेऽप्येवमेव फलं ज्ञेयं द्विजोत्तम ! ।
बृहस्पतिशनी तत्र कर्णनेत्ररुजान्विता ॥२०॥
तत्रान्यगेहगौ विप्र ! बुद्धभौमौ स्थितौ यदा ।
यदा स्वर्भानु-देवेज्यौ भार्या दन्तरुजान्विता ॥२१॥
शनिराहू शनिक्षेत्रे पङ्गुर्वातरुजान्विता ।
शुभदृग्योगतो नेति फलं ज्ञेयं विपश्चिता ॥२२॥

19-22. Mercury and Rahu in the 2nd from Upapada will give a stout-bodied wife. If the 2nd from Upapada happens to be a sign of Mercury and is tenanted by Mars and Saturn, the wife of the native will suffer from nasal disorders. Similarly a sign of Mars becoming the 2nd from Upapada and occupied by Mars and Saturn will cause nasal disorders to one's wife. Jupiter and Saturn will, if be in the 2nd from Upapada, cause disorders of ears/eyes to the wife. If Mercury and Mars be in the 2nd from Upapada other than own signs or if Rahu is with Jupiter in the 2nd from Upapada, the native's wife will suffer from dental disorders. Saturn and Rahu together in a sign of Saturn which is the 2nd from Upapada will cause lamen-ess or windy disorders to the native's wife. These evils will not come to pass if there be conjunction or aspect from a benefic (or from another benefic in the case of affliction being caused by a benefic himself).

लग्नात् पदादुपारूढाद् यो राशिः सप्तमो द्विज ! ।
तस्मात् तत्स्वामिनः खेटात् तदंशाच्च द्विजोत्तम! ॥२३॥
एवमेव फलं ज्ञेयमित्याहुर्नारदादयः ।

23-23½. O Brahmin, all these effects be deduced from the natal ascendant, Lagna Pada, the 7th from Upapada and the lords thereof. So say Narada and others.

उक्तेभ्यो नवमे विप्र ! शनिचन्द्रबुधा यदि ॥२४॥
अपुत्रता तथाऽर्केज्यराहुभिर्बहुपुत्रता ।
चन्द्रेणैकसुतस्तत्र मिश्रैः पुत्रो विलम्बतः ॥२५॥
रवीज्यराहुयोगेन पुत्रो वीर्यप्रतापवान् ।
प्रचण्डविजयी विप्र ! रिपुनिग्रहकारकः ॥२६॥

उवतस्थाने कुजार्किभ्यां पुत्रहीनः प्रजायते।
दत्त पुत्रयुतो वापि सहोत्थसुतवान् भवेत् ॥२७॥
तत्रस्थे विषमे राशौ बहुपुत्रयुतो नरः।
स्वल्पापत्यः समे राशौ जायते द्विजसत्तम ! ॥२८॥

25-28. *ABOUT SONS :* If Saturn, the Moon and Mercury are together in the 9th from one of the said places (sloka 23), there will be no son at all while the Sun, Jupiter and Rahu so placed will give a number of sons. The Moon so placed will give a son while a mixture of planets will delay the obtainment of a son. The son caused by the conjunction of the Sun, Jupiter and Rahu above will be strong, valorous, greatly successful and will destroy enemies. If Mars and Saturn are in the said 9th, there will be no son, or a son will be obtained by adoption or brother's son will come in adoption. In all these cases, odd signs will yield many sons while even sign will cause only a few.

सिंहे चोपपदे विप्र ! निशानाथयुतेक्षिते।
अल्पप्रजोऽथ कन्यायां जातः कन्याप्रजो भवेत् ॥२९॥
सुतभावनवांशाच्च स्थिरसन्ततिकारकात्।
एवं त्रिशांशकुण्डल्यामपि योगं विचिन्तयेत् ॥३०॥

29-30. *MANY SONS AND MANY DAUGHTERS :* O Brahmin, if Leo happens to be Upapada and is aspected by the Moon, there will be a limited number of children. Similarly Virgo will cause many daughters.

शनिराहू त्रिलाभस्थौ पदाद् भ्रातुर्विनाशकौ।
ज्येष्ठस्यैकादशे तत्र कनिष्ठस्य तृतीयके ॥३१॥

31. *CO-BORN FROM LAGNA PADA (upto sloka 36) :* Rahu and Saturn in the 3rd/11th from Lagna Pada will destroy the co-born of the native—in the 11th elder brothers/sisters and in the 3rd younger ones.

दैतेज्ये तत्र गर्भस्य नाशो व्यवहितस्य च।
लग्ने वापि पदे रन्ध्रे दैत्याचार्ययुतेक्षिते ॥३२॥

32. If Venus is in the 3rd/11th from Lagna Pada, there would have been an abortion to the mother earlier. Same is the effect if Venus is in the 8th from natal ascendant, or from Lagnarudha.

तथैव फलमित्याहुर्निर्विशंकं मुनीश्चराः ! ।
तृतीयलाभयोर्विप्र ! चन्द्रेज्यबुधमङ्गलाः ॥३३॥
बह्वो भ्रातरस्तस्य बलवन्तः प्रतापिनः ।
शन्यारसंयुते दृष्टे तृतीयैकादशे द्विज ! ॥३४॥
कनिष्ठज्येष्ठयोर्नाशो दिवज्ञेयो द्विजसत्तम ! ।
शनिरेको यदा विप्र ! लाभगो वा तृतीयगः ॥३५॥
तदा स्वमात्रशेषः स्यादन्ये नश्यन्ति सोदराः ।
तृतीये लाभगे केतौ बहुलं भगिनीसुखम् ॥३६॥

33-36. These are the effects, O Brahmin, as stated by venerable sages for the 3rd and the 11th from Lagna Pada. Should the Moon, Jupiter, Mercury and Mars be in the 3rd/11th from the Lagna Pada, there will be many valorous co-born. Should Saturn and Mars be in the 3rd/11th from Lagna Pada or lend aspects thereto, younger and elder coborn will respectively be destroyed. If Saturn is alone in one of the said houses the native will be spared while the co-born will die. Ketu in the 3rd/11th will give abundant happiness from one's sisters.

आरूढात् षष्ठभावस्थे पापाख्ये शुभवर्जिते ।
शुभसम्बन्धरहिते चौरो भवति जातकः ॥३७॥

37. *OTHER MATTERS FROM LAGNA PADA (upto sloka 43)* : If the 6th from Lagna Pada is occupied by a malefic and is bereft of conjunction/aspect of a benefic, the native will be a thief.

सप्तमे द्वादशे स्थाने सैंहिकेययुतेक्षिते ।
ज्ञानवांश्च भवेद् बालो बहुभाग्ययुतो द्विज ! ॥३८॥

38. If Rahu is in the 7th/12th from Lagna Pada or aspect one of the said houses, the native will be endowed with spiritual knowledge and be very fortunate.

आरूढे संस्थिते सौम्ये सर्वदेशाधिपो भवेत्।
सर्वज्ञस्तत्र देवेज्ये, कविर्वादी च भार्गवे ॥३९॥

39. If Mercury is in Lagna Pada, the native will lord over whole country while Jupiter will make him a knower of all things Venus in this context denotes a poet/speaker.

Note : Also see verse 30, ch. 29.

उपारूढात् पदाद् वापि धनस्थे शुभखेचरे।
सर्वद्रव्याधिपो धीमाञ्जायते द्विजसत्तम ॥४०॥

40. O excellent of the B-ahmins, if benefics occupy the 2nd from the Upapada or from Lagna Pada, the native will be endowed with all kinds of wealth and be intelligent.

उपारूढाद्धनाधीशे द्वितीयभवनस्थिते।
पापखेचरसंयुक्ते चौरो भवति निश्चितम् ॥४१॥

41. One will surely become a thief if the lord of the 2nd from Upapada is in the 2nd house (from the natal ascendant), and be with a malefic planet.

तत्सप्तमगृहाधीशाद् राहौ धनगते द्विज!।
दंष्ट्रावान् जायते बालः स्तब्धवाक् केतुखेचरे ॥४२॥
शनैश्चरे कुरूपः स्यात्सप्तमेशाद् द्वितीयगे।
मिश्रग्रहसमायुक्ते फलं मिश्रं समादिशेत् ॥४३॥

42-43. O Brahmin, if Rahu is in the 2nd from the lord of 7th counted from Upapada, the native will have long and projected teeth. Ketu so placed will cause stammering, and Saturn so placed will make one look ugly. Mixed will be the effects if there are mixed planets.

अथाऽर्गलाध्यायः ॥३१॥

Chapter 31

Argala Or Planetary Intervention

भगवन् ! याऽर्गला प्रोक्ता शुभदा भवताऽधुना।
तामहं श्रोतुमिच्छामि सलक्षणफलां मुने ! ॥१॥

1. O illustrious sage, you have told of (some) auspicious effects related to Argala. Kindly narrate its conditions and effects.

मैत्रेय ! सार्गला नाम यया भावफलं दृढम्।
स्थिरं खेटफलं च स्यात् साऽधुना कथ्यते मया ॥२॥
चतुर्थे च धने लाभे ग्रहे ज्ञेया तदर्गला।
तद्बाधकाः क्रमात् खेटा व्योमरिष्फतृतीयगाः ॥३॥
निर्बला न्यूनसंख्या वा बाधका नैव सम्मताः।
तृतीये व्याधिकाः पापा यत्र मैत्रेय ! बाधकाः ॥४॥
तत्रापि चार्गला ज्ञेया विपरीता द्विजोत्तम ! ।
तथापि खेटभावानां फलमर्गलितं विदुः ॥५॥
पञ्चमं चार्गलास्थानं नवमं तद्विरोधकृत्।
तमोग्रहभवा सा च व्यत्ययाज् ज्ञायते द्विज ! ॥६॥
एकग्रहा कनिष्ठा सा द्विग्रहा मध्यमा स्मृता।
अर्गला द्वयधिकोत्पन्ना मुनिभिः कथितोत्तमा ॥७॥
राशितो ग्रहतश्चापि विज्ञेया द्विविधाऽर्गला।
निर्बाधका सुफलदा विफला च सबाधका ॥८॥
यत्र राशौ स्थितः खेटस्तस्य पाकान्तरं यदा।
तस्मिन् काले फलं ज्ञेयं निर्विशंकं द्विजोत्तम ! ॥९॥

2-9. *FORMATION OF ARGALA :* Maitreya, I explain below Argala to know definite effects of houses and planets. Planets in the 4th, 2nd and the 11th (from a house or a planet) cause Argala while obstructors of the Argala will be those in the 10th, 12th and 3rd. If the Argala causing planet is stronger than the obstructing one, the former will prevail. Or if the number of Argalas are more than the obstructing planets, then also the Argala will prevail. If there are 3 or more malefics in the 3rd, they will cause Vipareeta Argala (more effective intervention) which will also be harmless and be very favourable. The 5th is also an Argala place while the planet in the 9th will counteract such Argala. As the nodes have retrograde motions, the Argalas and obstructions be also counted accordingly in a reverse manner. Sages say that the Argala caused by one planet will yield limited effects, by two medium and more than two excellent effects. Argalas should be counted from a sign or a planet as the case may be. The Argala unobstructed will be fruitful while the one duly obstructed will go astray. The Argala effects will be derived in the Dasa periods of the Rasi or planet concerned.

Notes : 'Argala' in Sanskrit is figuratively used to denote an impediment or obstruction. Arga'a is calculated from a house or from a planet. The 4th, 2nd and 11th house occupants cause Argala for a bhava or a planet. A planet in the 10th (from where the Argala is calculated) will obstruct the Argala coming from the 4th. Similarly a planet in 12th will counteract Argala emanating from the 2nd while the one in 11th will impede the Argala from the 3rd. Some suggest that the Argala obstruction places are countable from the Argala places instead of from the origional place or planet. This is not logical and a glance into Gochara Vedha (or obstructions during transits) will confirm our findings.

Just as we mark the Gocnara Vedhas along with benefic places, let us have the Argala and their obstructions as under :

$$\frac{4}{10} \quad \frac{2}{12} \quad \frac{11}{3} \quad \frac{5}{9}$$

Now see a hypothetical geniture given on the next page for an easy grasp of the Argala scheme.

The ascendant in the hypothetical chart is Aries. Mars in the 4th, Sun and Mercury in the 2nd, and Jupiter in the 11th cause Argala for the ascendant. (An Argala by benefic goes under the name 'Subhargala' and is deemed favourable. But we will confine ourselves to the extent of Argala in simple sense).

Ven	Lagna	Sun Merc	Moon
Jup			Mars
Sat			
Ketu			

The Argala of 4th house Mars is countered by 10th house Saturn, that of Sun-Mercury in the 2nd by Venus in the 12th and that of Jupiter in the 11th by Moon-Rahu in the 3rd.

As far as the nodes are concerned these are calculated in a reverse manner. From Rahu, the 2nd house counted in reverse order contains Sun-Mercury causing Argala to Rahu which is, however, obstructed by Mars in the 12th from Rahu (counted in reverse manner), similarly in all cases these be properly understood.

By way of additional information, see Gochara Vedha and benefic places for example for the Sun which will prove that our interpretation of Argala obstructed is correct :

$$\frac{3}{9} \quad \frac{6}{12} \quad \frac{10}{4} \quad \frac{11}{5}$$

In the above figures, the upper ones denote the Sun's favourable transits from the Moon and the lower ones denote obstructive forces in such houses from the Moon. For example the Sun in the 3rd house from the Moon during transit will be favourable. But his favourable disposition will remain curbed if simultaneously the 9th from the Moon is transited by another planet (than of course Saturn, which is an exception). Again just as there is Vipareetargala (or Argala itself eliminated), there is also Vipareeta Vedha. Vipareeta Vedha will prove auspicious eliminating the Vedha or obstruction. Suppose the benefic effects of the Sun in the 3rd from the Moon are being obstructed by another in the 9th from the Moon. The moment another planet joins the Sun in the 3rd from the Moon, the Vedha in the 9th from the Moon is off and the Sun in the 3rd proves auspicious till he has a companion.

In the matter of Argala and its obstruction, also see the following verse.

अर्गलां प्रतिबन्धञ्च प्रथमांघ्रिचतुर्थयोः ।
द्वित्र्यङ्घ्रयोश्च मिथो विप्र! चिन्तयेदिति मे मतम् ॥१०॥

10. *SPECIAL :* The Argala caused by placement of a planet in the first one fourth part of the Rasi is countered by another placed in the 4th quarter of the respective obstructive Rasi. Similarly 2nd quarter's Argala is eliminated by the 3rd quarter placement.

Notes : We have learnt that an Argala, for example in the 4th from a bhava or a planet is eliminated by another placed in the 10th house from the original planet/house. Here, the rules for obstruction of Argala are still narrowed down. Accordingly, there are only two circumstances of Argala getting nullified. Make the sign in which the Argala occurs into four quarters (of 7° 30′ each). Similarly the sign where obstruction occurs is also made in four quarters. If the Argala causing planet is in the first quarter (or first 7° 30′ of the sign) while the obstructing planet is in the 4th quarter (i.e. 22° 30′—30°), the obstruction indeed will come to pass. Otherwise not. So to say Argala will operate and the obstruction will fail. Likewise while the Argala planet is in the 2nd quarter of the sign (i.e. 7° 30′—15°), the obstruction (planet in 15°—22° 30′ i.e. 3rd quarter) will combat the Argala.

पदे लग्ने मदे वापि निराभासार्गला यदा ।
तदा जातोऽतिविख्यातो बहुभाग्ययुतो भवेत् ॥११॥
यस्य पापः शुभो वापि ग्रहस्तिष्ठेत् शुभार्गले ।
तेन द्रष्ट्रेक्षितं लग्नं प्राबल्यायोपकल्प्यते ॥१२॥

सार्गले च धने विप्र! धनधान्यसमन्वितः।
तृतीये सोदरादीनां सुखमुक्तं मनीषिभिः ॥१३॥
चतुर्थे सार्गले गेहपशु-बन्धुकुलैर्युतः।
पञ्चमे पुत्रपौत्रादिसंयुतो बुद्धिमान्नरः ॥१४॥
षष्ठे रिपुभयं, कामे धनदारसुखं बहु।
अष्टमे जायते कष्टं धर्मे भाग्योदयो भवेत् ॥१५॥
दशमे राजसम्मानं लाभे लाभसमन्वितः।
सार्गले च व्यये विप्र! व्ययाधिक्यं प्रजायते ॥१६॥
शुभग्रहार्गलायां तु सौख्यं बहुविधं भवेत्।
मध्यं पापार्गलायां च मिश्रायामपि चोत्तमम् ॥१७॥

11-17. *ARGALA EFFECTS :* Should there be Argala for the Arudha Pada, for the natal ascendant, and for the 7th from both, the native will be famous and fortunate. A malefic or a benefic causing unobstructed Argala aspecting the ascendant will make one famous. Similarly aspect on the 2nd house denotes acquisition of wealth and grains, 3rd house—happiness from co-born; the 4th house—residences, quadrupeds and relatives; the 5th house—sons, grand sons and intelligence, the 6th house—fear from enemies; the 7th house—abundant wealth and marital happiness, the 8th house—difficulties, the 9th house—fortunes; the 10th house—royal honour; the 11th house—gains, and the 12th house—expenses. The Argala by benefics will give various kinds of happiness, while benefic effects will be meddling with malefic Argalas. Argala by both benefics and malefics will yield mixed results.

Notes : For our own benefit we should understand the word 'Argala' in a suitable manner apart from the manner the Argala functions vis-a-vis Argala elimination.

1. Argala can be caused by a benefic which is known as Subhargala. This Argala can be from a malefic also, so that the benefic causing Argala stalls the malefic role going against the native. If the benefic's Argala is obstructed by another, then the benefic will become ineffective in Argala and the first-mentioned malefic will operate freely.

2. Argala can be by a malefic with reference to a benefic so that the native does not enjoy good effects due to the benefic.

This is Papargala (or malefic Argala) If the Argala is eliminated by a benefic or a malefic, then again the first mentioned benefic will be at liberty to act according to his own disposition.

3. Argala is operable with reference to Bhavas (or houses) as well.

Other relative rules need be well understood before application of the Argala.

लग्नपञ्चमभाग्येषु सार्गलेषु द्विजोत्तम !।
जातश्च जायते राजा भाग्यवान् नात्र संशयः ॥१८॥

18. Should there be (unobstructed) Argala for the ascendant, the 5th and 9th the native will doubtlessly become a king and fortunate.

अथ कारकाध्यायः ॥३२॥

Chapter 32

Planetary Karakatwas (Indications)

अथाऽहं सम्प्रवक्ष्यामि ग्रहानात्मादिकारकान्।
सप्तरव्यादिशन्यन्तान् राह्वन्तान् वाऽष्टसंख्यकान् ॥१॥
अंशैः समौग्नहौ द्वौ चेद्राह्वन्तान् चिन्तयेत् तदा।
सप्तैव कारकानेवं केचिदष्टौ प्रचक्षते ॥२॥

1-2. I now detail below Atmakarka etc. obtainable from among the 7 planets *viz* the Sun to Saturn. Some say that Rahu will become a Karka when there is a state of similarity in terms of longitude between (two) planets. Yet some say that the 8 planets including Rahu will have to be considered irrespective of such a state.

आत्मा सूर्यादिखेटानां मध्ये ह्यंशाधिको ग्रहः।
अंशसाम्ये कलाधिक्यात् तत्साम्ये विकलाधिकः ॥३॥

बुधं राशिकलाधिवयाद् ग्राह्यो नैवात्मकारकः ।
अंशाधिकः कारकः स्यादल्पभागोऽन्त्यकारकः ॥४॥
मध्यांशो मध्यखेटः स्यादुपखेटः स एव हि ।
विलोमगमनाद्राहोरंशाः शोध्याः खवह्नितः ॥५॥
अंशक्रमादधोऽधःस्थाश्चराख्याः कारका इति ।
आत्माख्यकारकस्तेषु प्रधानं कथ्यते द्विज ! ॥६॥
स एव जातकाधीशो विज्ञेयो द्विजसत्तम ! ।
यथा भूमौ प्रसिद्धोऽस्ति नराणां क्षितिपालकः ॥७॥
सर्ववार्ताधिकारी च बन्धकृन्मोक्षकृत् तथा ॥८॥

3-8. *ATMA KARAKA DEFINED :* Among the planets from the Sun etc. whichever has traversed maximum number of degrees in a particular sign is called Atmakarka. If the degrees are identical, then the one with more minutes of arc and if the minutes are also identical then the one with higher seconds of arc will have to be considered. In that case, these three are called Anthyakaraka, Madhyakarka and Upakheta. In the case of Rahu, deduct his longitude in that particular sign from 30. The Karakas will have to be decided as above and as per further rules given below. Out of these Karakas, Atmakaraka is the most important and has a prime say on the native just as the king is the most famous among the men of his country and is the head of all affairs and is entitled to arrest and release men.

यथा राजाज्ञया विप्र ! पुत्रामात्यादयो जनाः ।
समर्था लोककार्येषु तथैवान्येपि कारकाः ॥९॥
आत्मानुकूलमेवात्र भवन्ति फलदायकः ।
प्रतिकूले यथा भूपे सर्वेऽमात्यादयो द्विज ! ॥१०॥
कार्यं कर्तुं मनुष्याणां न समर्था भवन्ति हि ।
तथाऽऽत्मकारके क्रूरे नाऽन्ये स्वशुभदायकः ॥११॥
अनुकूले नृपे यद्वत् सर्वेऽमात्यादयो द्विज ! ।
नाशुभं कुर्वते तद्वनान्ये स्वाशुभदायकाः ॥१२॥

9-12. *IMPORTANCE OF ATMAKARAKA :* O Brahmin, just as the minister cannot go against the king, the other karakas, *viz*, Putrakaraka, Amatyakarka etc. cannot predominate over Atmakaraka in the affairs of the native. If the Atmakarka is adverse, other karakas cannot give their benefic effects (fully). Similarly if Atmakaraka is favourable, other karakas cannot predominate with their malefic influences.

आत्माकारकभागेभ्यो न्यूनांशोऽमात्यकारकः ।
तस्मान्न्यूनांशको भ्राता तन्न्यूनोमातृसंज्ञकः ॥१३॥
तन्न्यूनांशः पितातस्मादल्पांशः पुत्रकारकः ।
पुत्रान्न्यूनांशको ज्ञातिर्ज्ञातेर्न्यूनांशको हि यः ॥१४॥
स दारकारको ज्ञेयो निर्विशंक द्विजोत्तम ! ।
चराख्यकारला एते ब्राह्मणा कथिताः पुरा ॥१५॥
मातृकारकमेवाऽन्ये वदन्ति सुतकारकम् ।
द्वौ ग्रहौ भागतुल्यौ चेज्जायेतां यस्य जन्मनि ॥१६॥
तदग्रकारकस्यैवं लोपो ज्ञेयो द्विजोत्तम ! ।
स्थिरकारकवशात्तस्य फलं ज्ञेयं शुभाऽशुभम् ॥१७॥

13-17. *OTHER KARAKAS :* The planet next to Atmakaraka in terms of longitude is called Amatyakaraka. Similarly follow one another in terms of longitude are Bhratru Karaka, Matru karaka, Pitru karaka, Putrakaraka, Gnati karaka and Streekaraka. These are chara karakas or inconstant significators. Some consider Matrukaraka and Putrakaraka as identical. If two planets have the same longitude, both become the same karaka in which case there will be a deficit of one karaka. In that circumstance, consider cons tant significator in the context of benefic/malefic influence for the concerned relative.

Notes : A total of eight Chara karakas (inconstant or variable significators) are suggested as under :

1. Atma Karaka (highest in longitude devoid of Rasis)
2. Amatya Karaka (next to Atma Karaka in longitude)
3. Bhratru Karaka (next to Amatya Karaka in longitude)
4. Matru Karaka (next to Bhratru Karaka in longitude)
5. Pitru Karaka (next to Matru Karaka in longitude)
6. Putra Karaka (next to Pitru Karaka in longitude)
7. Gnati Karaka (next to Pitru Karaka in longitude)
8. Stree Karaka (next to Gnati Karaka in longitude)

The sage also suggests a school of thought which considers only seven significators, treating Matru Karaka and Putra Karaka as identical. This section thus counts only 7 Karakas.

Since some advocate the use of 8 karakas, Rahu is also added to the seven planets from Sun to Saturn. The degrees traversed by Rahu should be counted from the end of the Rasi he is in. In the standard nativity (ch. 29) the following are the karaka planets. We take 8 Karkas into consideration.

Karaka	Planet	Longitude
Atmakaraka	The Moon	27° 35′ 46″
Amatyakaraka	Venus	27 17 50
Bhratru Karaka	Jupiter	26 7 13
Matru Karaka	Rahu	22 22 54
Pitru Karaka	Mercury	14 54 13
Putra Karaka	The Sun	7 12 18
Gnati Karaka	Mars	6 18 46
Dara Karaka	Saturn	3 9 41

If two planets have the same longitude identical to the second of arc, both of them will be qualified for that particular karakaatwa or significatorship. In that case, there will be shortage of planet for Dara Karakatwa. The constant indicator Venus should then be considered in the matter of marriage etc. as coming under Dara Karaka.

अधुना सम्प्रवक्ष्यामि स्थिराख्यान् कारकग्रहान् ।
स पितृकारको ज्ञेयो यो बली रवि-शुक्रयोः ॥१८॥
चन्द्रारयोर्बली खेटो मातृकारक उच्यते ।
भौमतो भगिनी श्यालः कनीयान् जननीत्यपि ॥१९॥
बुधान्मातृसजातीया मातुलाद्याश्च बान्धवाः ।
गुरोः पितामहः शुक्रात् पतिः, पुत्रः शनैश्चरात् ॥२०॥
विप्रान्तेवासिनः पत्नी पितरौ श्वशुरौ तथा ।
मातामहादयश्चिन्त्या एते च स्थिरकारका ॥२१॥

18-21. *CONSTANT SIGNIFICATORS :* I narrate below the constant significators as related to the planets. The stronger among the Sun and *Venus* indicates the father while the stronger among the Moon and *Mars* indicates the mother. Mars denotes sister, brother-in-law, younger brother and mother. Mercury rules maternal relative while Jupiter indicates paternal grand-father. Husband and sons are respectively denoted by Venus and Saturn. From Ketu note wife, father, mother, parents-in-law and maternal grand father. These are constant significators.

Notes : The above planetary significance can be tabulated as under :

Planet	Karakatwa
Sun/Venus	Stronger of the two indicates father,
Moon/Mars	Stronger of the two indicates mother.
Mars	Sister, brother-in-law, younger brother and mother.
Mercury	Maternal relatives
Jupiter	Paternal grand-father
Venus	Husband
Saturn	Sons
Ketu	Wife, father, mother, parents-in-law, maternal grand father.

The above may be linked with the views expressed in verses occurring in the rest of this chapter.

अथाऽहं कारकान् वक्ष्ये खेटभाववशाद्द्विज ! ।
रवितः पुण्यभे तातश्चन्द्रान्माता चतुर्थके ॥२२॥
कुजात् तृतीयतो भ्राता बुधात् षष्ठे च मातुलः ।
देवेज्यात् पञ्चमात् पुत्रो दाराः शुक्राच्च सप्तमे ॥२३॥
मन्दादष्टमतो मृत्युः पित्रादीनां विचिन्तयेत् ।
इति सर्वं विचार्यैव बुधस्तत्तत् फलं वदेत् ॥२४॥

22-24. *HOUSES RELATED :* These constant significances are derivable from the Bhavas counted from the said constant significators. The 9th from the Sun denotes father, the 4th from the Moon mother, the 3rd from Mars brothers, the 6th from Mercury maternal uncle, the 5th from Jupiter sons, the 7th from Venus wife and the 8th from Saturn death. The learned should consider all these and declare related effects accordingly.

Notes : From these three verses, the constant Karakas emerge as under as normally discussed in standard literature on astrology :

The Sun	—	father
The Moon	—	mother
Mars	—	brothers (and sisters)
Mercury	—	maternal relatives
Jupiter	—	Sons (and daughters)
Venus	—	wife (or husband)
Saturn	—	death (or longevity)

अथाऽहं सम्प्रवक्ष्यामि प्रसङ्गाद्योगकारकान् ।
खेटान् जन्मनि जातस्य मिश्रः स्थितिवशाद् द्विज ! ॥२५॥
स्वर्क्षे स्वोच्चे च मित्रर्क्षे मिथः केन्द्रगता ग्रहाः ।
ते सर्वे कारकास्तेषु कर्मगस्तु विशेषतः ॥२६॥
यथा लग्ने सुखे कामे स्वोर्क्षोच्चस्था ग्रहा द्विज ! ।
भवन्ति कारकाख्यास्ते विशेषेण च खे स्थिताः ॥२७॥
स्वमित्रोच्चर्क्षगो हेतुरन्योऽन्यं यदि केन्द्रगः ।
सुहृत् तद्गुणसम्पन्नः सोऽपि कारक उच्यते ॥२८॥
नीचान्वयेऽपि यो जातः विद्यमाने च कारके ।
सोऽपि राजसमो विप्र ! धनवान् सुखसंयुतः ॥२९॥
राजवंशसमुत्पन्नो राजा भवति निश्चयात् ।
एवं कुलानुसारेण कारकेभ्यः फलं वदेत् ॥३०॥

25-30. *YOGA KARAKAS (OR MUTUAL COWORKERS) :* O Brahmin, I make below a passing reference to Yogakarakas (or mutual co-workers). Planets become Yogakarakas if they are in mutual angles identical with own signs, exaltation, or friendly sign. In the 10th house, a planet will be significantly so. Planets simply (i e. not being in friendly & *C*) in the ascendant, the 4th and 7th do not become such yogakarakas. Even if they be placed in other houses but with such dignities as mentioned shall become yogakarakas. With such planets, even a person of mean birth will become a king and be affluent. One born of royal scion then will surely become a king. Thus the effects be declared considering the number of such planets and the order the native belongs to.

Notes : Rule 1 : If two planets are in mutual angles from the ascendant and be with dignities like exaltation, own sign or friendly sign, they act on behalf of each other and are known as Paraspara Karakas or co-workers. If one of the occupants is in the 10th house, the effects will still be pronounced. This is not to be considered from the Moon.

Rule 2 : Even though the condition of mutual angularity is fulfilled, if the two planets do not enjoy one of the three dignities required, then there is no correlationship between them.

Rule 3 : If two planets are mutually angular, both being endowed with dignities like exaltation, own sign or friendly sign, they will become coworkers although not placed in angles from the ascendant.

These rules are exemplified in the undernoted charts, with reference to the said three rules.

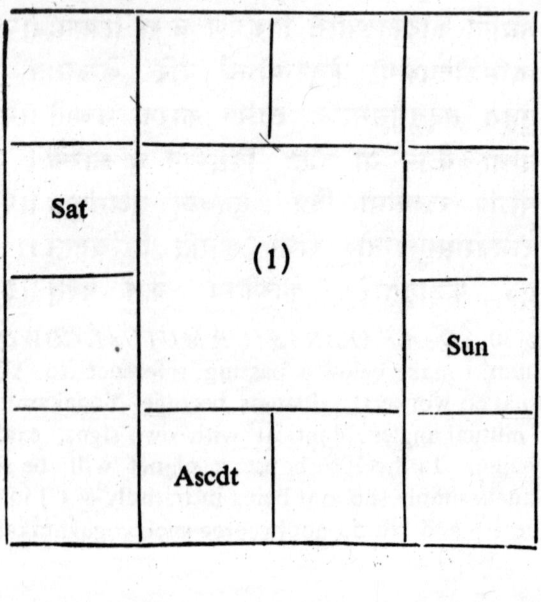

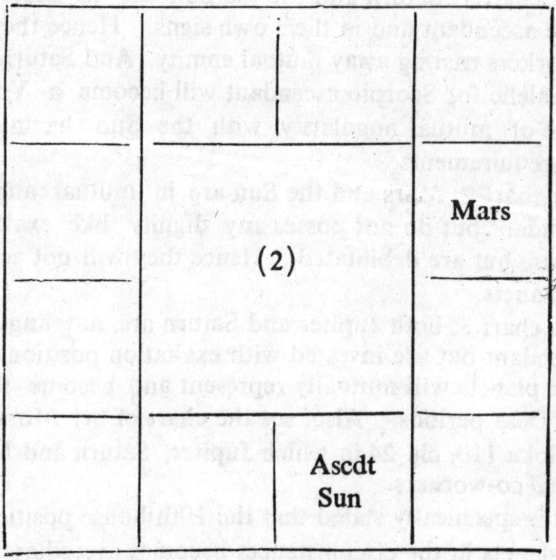
Mars
(2)
Ascdt
Sun

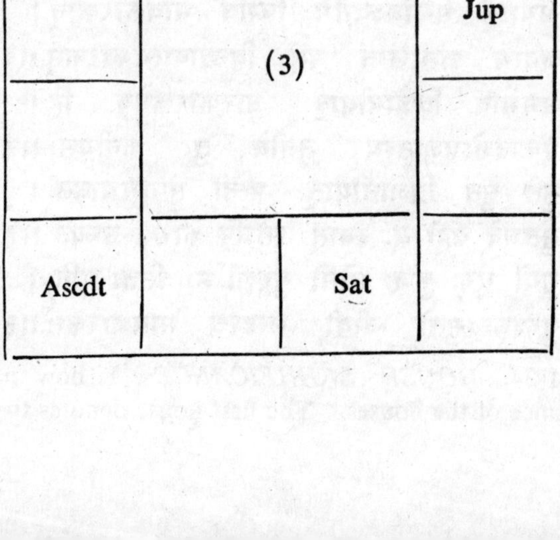
Jup
(3)
Ascdt
Sat

In chart 1, Saturn and the the Sun are in mutual angles from the ascendant and in their own signs. Hence they will act as co-workers casting away mutual enmity. And Saturn although a dire malefic for Scorpio ascendant will become a Yogakaraka by virtue of mutual angularity with the Sun having fulfilled dignity requirements.

In chart 2, Mars and the Sun are in mutual angles from the ascendant but do not posses any dignity like exaltation, or own house but are debilitated. Hence they will not act as Yoga giving planets.

In chart 3, both Jupiter and Saturn are not angular from the ascendant but are invested with exaltation positions. Hence both the planets will mutually represent and become favourable in their Dasa periods. Also, see the chart of Sri Morarji Desai under sloka 110, ch. 24 in which Jupiter, Saturn and Mars play as mutual co-workers.

It is specifically stated that the 10th house position for one of the planets in the circumstances becomes exceedingly favourable. In the example chart 1, the Sun is in the 10th with Paraspara Yogakaraka qualification in opposition to Saturn. Hence the Sun will exceedingly reveal beneficial results. Devoid of Saturn or any other co-worker, the Sun in the 10th will not be that powerful. In other words, by virtue of co-workership, the Sun's role gets immeasurably fortified.

There are some schools of thought which do not consider coworkership as given in rule 3 above.

अथाऽहं सम्प्रवक्ष्यामि विशेषं भावकारकान् ।
जनस्य जन्मलग्नं यत् विन्द्यादात्मकारकम् ।।३१।।
धनभावं विजानीयाद् दारकारकमेव हि ।
एकादशेऽग्रजातस्य तृतीये तु कनीयसः ।।३२।।
सुते सुतं विजानीयात् पत्नीं सप्तमभावतः ।
सुतभवे ग्रहो यः स्यात् सोऽपि कारक उच्यते ।।३३।।
सूर्यो गुरुः कुजः सोमो गुरुर्भौमः सितः शनिः ।
गुरुश्चन्द्रसुतो जीवो मन्दश्च भावकारकाः ।।३४।।

31-34. *HOUSE SIGNIFICANCE :* I now narrate the significance of the houses. The first house denotes the soul (and self), the 2nd house wife, the 11th preborn, the 3rd younger brothers/sisters, the 5th progeny and the 7th house wife. It is also said that a planet in the 5th becomes a karaka for wife. The significators of the house in order are : the Sun, Jupiter, Mars, the Moon, Jupiter, Mars, Venus, Saturn, Jupiter. Mercury, Jupiter and Saturn.

Notes : The karakatwas of each house are better signified in ch. 11 *supra*. The reader may consult the said chapter as well. Certain indications are additional in the present case.

The significator of each bhava is enunciated in sloka 34 above. For an easy grasp, these are :

1. The Sun : Ist house (self, soul, constitution etc.)
2. Jupiter : 2nd house (family, finance, wife etc.)
3. Mars : 3rd house (courage, later-born etc)
4. The Moon : 4th house (mother)
5. Jupiter : 5th house (progeny)
6. Mars : 6th house (enemies)
7. Venus : 7th house (wife, conjugal bliss etc)
8. Saturn : 8th house (longevity)
9. Jupiter : 9th house (fortunes, religion etc.)
10. Mercury : 10th house (honour)
11. Jupiter : 11th house (pre-born)
12. Saturn : 12th house (expenditure)

Although we have stated the significators of the bhavas to be certain planets, each bhava signifies more than what is stated above. In that case the significator can also be different. For example, Jupiter is karaka for the 9th house which means that he is holding the portfolio of the native's fortunes. When the question of father arises from the 9th house, the significator then is the Sun. Or take the case of 12th house. The significator is Saturn. The 12th house indicates final emancipation as well for which Saturn is not the indicator but Ketu. Thus a detailed approach to significance through bhavas is required.

पुनस्तन्वादयो भावाः स्थाप्यास्तेषां शुभाऽशुभम् ।
लाभस्तृतीयो रन्ध्रश्च शत्रुसंज्ञधनव्ययाः ॥३५॥
एते भावाः समाख्याताः क्रूराख्या द्विजसत्तम ! ।
एषां योगेन यो भावस्तस्य हानिः प्रजायते ॥३६॥

भावा भद्राश्च केन्द्राख्याः कोणाख्यौ द्विजसत्तम!।
एषां संयोगमात्रेण ह्यशुभोऽपि शुभो भवेत् ॥३७॥

35-37. O excellent of the Brahmins, after knowing the merits of the 1st house etc. the good and bad effects be declared. 11th, 3rd, 8th, 6th, 2nd and 12th are malefic bhavas. Association with these houses will inflict evils. Angles and trines are auspicious bhavas, the association with which turns even evils into auspiciousness.

Notes : The 6 bhavas *viz.* 11th, 3rd, 8th, 6th, 2nd and 12th are adverse. A planet owning or occupying one of the said houses will become a functional malefic and hence adversary.

The other 6 bhavas, viz. ascendant, 4th, 5th, 7th, 9th and 10th are good houses. Planets associated with these houses will prove favourable although by nature evil or adverse.

Also see ch. 34 for more information.

अथ कारकांशफलाध्यायः ॥३३॥

Chapter 33

Effects Of Karakamsa

अथाऽहं सम्प्रवक्ष्यामि कारकांशफलं द्विज!।
मेषादि-राशिगे स्वांशे यथावद् ब्रह्मभाषितम् ॥१॥

1. O Brahmin, as laid down by Lord Brahma, I now tell you about the effects of Karakamsa identical with Aries etc.

Notes : Karakamsa is the Navamsa occupied by the Atma Karaka planet. The Atmakaraka is the one who traversed the highest number of degrees etc. (devoid of Rasi), among the 8 planets, from Sun to Rahu. These have been explained in the previous chapters.

गृहे मूषकमार्जारा मेषांशे ह्यात्मकारके।
सदा भयप्रदा विप्र! पापयुक्ते विशेषतः ॥२॥

वृषांशकगते स्वस्मिन् सुखदाश्च चतुष्पदाः ।
मिथुनांशगते तस्मिन् कण्ड्वादिव्याधिसम्भवः ॥३॥
कर्कांशे च जलाद्भीतिः सिंहांशे श्वपदाद्भयम् ।
कण्डूः स्थौल्यञ्च कन्यांशे तथा वह्निकणाद्भयम् ॥४॥
तुलांशे च वणिग् जातो वस्त्रादिनिर्मितौ पटुः ।
अल्यंशे सर्पतो भीतिः पीडा मातुः पयोधरे ॥५॥
धनुरंशे क्रमादुच्चात् पतनं वाहनादपि ।
मकरांशे जलोद्भूतैर्जन्तुभिः खेचरस्तथा ॥६॥
शंख-मुक्ता-प्रवालाद्यैर्लाभो भवति निश्चितः ।
कुम्भांशे च तडागादि-कारको जायते जनः ॥७॥
मीनांशे कारके जातो मुक्तिभाग् द्विजसत्तम ! ।
नाऽशुभं शुभसंदृष्टे न शुभं पापवीक्षिते ॥८॥

2-8. *KARAKAMSA VARIOUS SIGNS :* If Atmakaraka be in Aries Navamsa, there will be nuisance from rats and cats at all times. A malefic joining will further increase the nuisance. Should Atmakaraka be in Taurus Navamsa, happiness from quadrupeds will result. Should he be in Gemini Navamsa, the native will be afflicted by itch etc. If he be in Cancer Navamsa, there will be fear from water etc. If he be in Leo Navamsa, fear will be from tiger etc. If he be in Virgo Navamsa, itch, corpulence, fire etc. will cause trouble while in Libra Navamsa, the Atmakaraka will make one a trader and skilful in making robes etc. Scorpio Navamsa holding the said planet will bring troubles from snakes etc. and also affliction to mother's breasts. There will be falls from height and conveyances etc. if it is Sagittarius Navamsa that is occupied by Atmakaraka. Capricorn Navamsa in this respect denotes gains from water-dwelling beings and conch, pearl, coral etc. If it is Aquarius Navamsa holding the said planet, the native will construct tanks etc. And in Pisces Navamsa the Atmakaraka will grant final emancipation. A beneflc's aspect will remove evils while that of a maleflc will cause no good.

कारकांशे शुभे विप्र ! लग्नांशे च शुभग्रहे ।
शुभसंवीक्षिते जातो राजा भवति निश्चितः ॥९॥

स्वांशाच्छुभग्रहाः केन्द्रे कोणे वा पापवर्जिताः।
धन-विद्यायुतो जातो मिश्रैर्मिश्रफलं वदेद् ॥१०॥
उपग्रहे च विप्रेन्द्र ! स्वोच्च-स्वर्क्ष-शुभर्क्षगे।
पापदृग्रहिते चाऽन्त्ये कैवल्यंतस्य निर्दिशेत् ॥११॥

9-11. O Brahmin, if there be only benefics in the Karakamsa and the Navamsa of Lagna and be aspected by benefics, the native will undoubtedly become a king. Should the angles/trines from the Karakamsa be occupied by benefics devoid of malefic association, the native will be endowed with wealth and learning. The combination of benefic and malefic will in this context yield mixed results. If the Upakheta (or upagraha, vide sloka 5 ch. 32) is in its exaltation sign, or own/frienly sign, and is devoid o f malefic aspect, the native will go to heavens after death.

चन्द्राऽऽरभृगुवर्गस्थे कारके पारदारिकः।
विपर्यस्थेऽन्यथा ज्ञेयं फलं सर्वं विचक्षणैः ॥१२॥

12. If the Atmakaraka is in the divisions of the Moon, Mars or Venus, the native will go to others' wives. Otherwise, the contrary will prevail.

कारकांशे रवौ जातो राजकार्यपरो द्विज ! ।
पूर्णेन्दौ भोगवान् विद्वान् शुक्रदृष्टे विशेषतः ॥१३॥
स्वांशे बलयुते भौमे जातः कुन्तायुधी भवेत्।
वह्निजीवी नरो वाऽपि रसवादी च जायते ॥१४॥
बुधे बलयुते स्वांशे कलाशिल्पविचक्षणः।
वाणिज्यकुशलश्चापि बुद्धि-विद्यासमन्वितः ॥१५॥
सुकर्मा ज्ञाननिष्ठश्च वेदवित् स्वांशगे गुरौ।
शुक्रे शतेन्द्रियः कामी राजकीयो भवेन्नरः ॥१६॥
शनौ स्वांशगत जातः स्वकुलोचितकर्मकृत्।
राहौ चौरश्च धानुष्को जातो वा लोहयन्त्रकृत् ॥१७॥
विषवैद्योऽथवा विप्र ! जायते नाऽत्र संशयः।
व्यवहारी गजादीनां केतौ चौरश्च जायते ॥१८॥

13-18. *EFFECTS OF PLANETS IN KARAKAMSA :* O Brahmin, if the Sun is in the Karakamsa, the native will be engaged in royal assignments. If the Full Moon is there, he will enjoy pleasures and be a scholar; more so if Venus aspects. If strong Mars is in Karakamsa, he will use the weapon spear, will live through fire and be an alchemist Should strong Mercury be in Karakamsa, he will be skilful in arts and trading, be intelligent and educated. Jupiter in Karakamsa denotes one doing good acts, endowed with spiritualism and Vedic learning. One will be endowed with a longevity of 100 years, be sensuous and will look after state affairs if Venus is in Karakamsa. Saturn in Karakamsa will give such livelihood as due to the native's family. Rahu in Karakamsa denotes a thief, a bowman, a machinery maker, and a doctor treating poisonous afflictions. If Ketu be in Karakamsa, one will deal in elephants and be a thief

रविराहू यदा स्वांशे सर्पाद् भीतिः प्रजायते।
शुभदृष्टौ भयं नैव पापदृष्टौ मृतिभवेत् ॥१६॥
शुभषड्वर्गसंयुक्तौ विषवैद्यो भवेत् तदा।
भौमेक्षिते कारकांशे भानुस्वर्भानुसंयते ॥२०॥
अन्यग्रहा न पश्यन्ति स्ववेश्मपरदाहकः।
तस्मिन् बुधेक्षि ते चापि वह्निदो नैव जायते ॥२१॥
पापर्क्षे गुरुणा दृष्टे समीपगृहदाहकः।
शुक्रदृष्टे तु विप्रेन्द्र ! गृहदाहो न जायते ॥२२॥

19-22. *RAHU-SUN IN KARAKAMSA :* Should Rahu and the Sun be in Karakamsa there will be fear from snakes; if a benefic aspects the said combination there will be no fear but a malefic aspects will bring death (through serpents). If Rahu and the Sun occupy benefic Shadvargas, being in Karakamsa, one will be a doctor treating poisonous afflictions while the aspect from Mars on the said combination denotes that the native will burn either his own house or that of others. Mercury's aspect, instead of that of Mars, will not cause the said effects. If Rahu and the Sun be in Karakamsa and be in a malefic's sign in aspect to Jupiter, one will burn neighbouring house while the aspect of Venus will not cause such an event.

गुलिकेन युते स्वांशे पूर्णचन्द्रेण वीक्षिते।
चौरैर्हृतधनो जातः स्वयं चौरोऽथवा भवेत् ॥२३॥
ग्रहादृष्टे सगुलिके विपदो वा विषैर्हतः।
बुधदृष्टे बृहद्बीजो जायते नाऽत्र संशयः ॥२४॥

23-24. *GULIKA IN KARAKAMSA :* Should the Full Moon aspect the Karakamsa-placed Gulika, the native will lose his wealth to thieves or will himself be a thief. If Gulika is in Karakamsa but is unaspected by others, one will administer poison to others or will himself die of poisoning. Mercury's aspect in this context will give large testicles.

सकेतौ कारकांशे च पापदृष्टे द्विजोत्तम!।
जातस्य कर्णरोगो वा कर्णच्छेदः प्रजायते ॥२५॥
भृगुपुत्रेक्षिते तस्मिन् दीक्षितो जायते जनः।
बुधार्किदृष्टे निर्वीर्यो जायते मानवो ध्रुवम् ॥२६॥
बुधशुक्रेक्षिते तस्मिन् दासीपुत्रः प्रजायते।
पुनर्भवासुतो वाऽपि जायते नाऽत्र संशयः ॥२७॥
तपस्वी शनिना दृष्टे जातः प्रेष्योऽथवा भवेत्।
शनिमात्रेक्षिते तस्मिन् जातः संन्यासिवेषवान् ॥२८॥
रविशुक्रेक्षिते तस्मिन् राजप्रेष्यो जनो भवेत्।
इति संक्षेपतः प्रोक्तं कारकांशफलं द्विज! ॥२९॥

25-29. *EFFECTS OF ASPECTS ON KETU IN KARAKAMSA :* If Ketu is in Karakamsa in aspect to a malefic, one's ears will be severed or he will suffer from diseases of ears. Venus aspecting denotes one initiated into religions order. One will be devoid of strength if Mercury and Saturn aspect. If Mercury and Venus aspect, he will be the son of a female slave or of a female remarried. With Saturn's aspect one will perform penance or be a servant or will be a pseudo-ascetic. Venus and the Sun together aspecting will make one serve the king. Thus, O Brahmin, are told briefly the effects of Karakamsa.

स्वांशाद्धने च शुक्रारवर्गे स्यात् पारदारिकः।
तयोर्दृग्योगतो ज्ञेयमिदमामरणं फलम् ॥३०॥

केतौ तत्प्रतिबन्धः स्याद् गुरौ तु स्त्रैण एव सः।
राहौ चाऽर्थनिवृत्तिः स्यात् कारकांशाद् द्वितीयगे ॥३१॥

30-31. *EFFECTS OF THE 2ND FROM KARAKAMSA :* If the 2nd from Karakamsa falls in the divisions of Venus/Mars, one will be addicted to others' wives and if Venus or Mars aspect the said 2nd, the tendency will last till death. If Ketu is the 2nd from Karakamsa in a division of Venus/Mars, such addiction will not prevail while the position of Jupiter will cause such an evil. Rahu in the said case will destroy wealth.

स्वांशात् तृतीयगे पापे जातः शूरः प्रतापवान्।
तस्मिन् शुभग्रहे जातः कातरो नात्र संशयः ॥३२॥

32. *EFFECTS OF THE 3RD FROM KARAKAMSA :* A malefic in the 3rd from Karakamsa will make onh valorous while a benfic will make one timid.

स्वांशाच्चतुर्थभावे तु चन्द्रशुक्रयुतेक्षिते।
तत्र वा स्वोच्चगे खेटे जातः प्रासादवान् भवेत् ॥३३॥
शनिराहुयुते तस्मिन् जातस्य च शिलागृहम्।
ऐष्टिकं कुज-केतुभ्यां गुरुणा दारवं गृहम् ॥३४॥
तार्णं तु रविणा प्रोक्तं जातस्य भवनं द्विज!।
चन्द्रे त्वनावृते देशे पत्नीयोगः प्रजायते ॥३५॥

33-35. *EFFECTS OF THE 4TH FROM KARAKAMSA :* If the 4th from Karakamsa be occupied by Venus and the Moon, one will own palacial (or large) buildings. Similar is the effect of an exalted planet in the said 4th. A house made of stones is denoted by the occupation of Rahu and Saturn. Mars and Ketu indicate a house made of bricks while Jupiter denotes one made of wood. The Sun so related will give a house of grass. If the Moon be in the 4th from Karakamsa, one will have union with his wife in an uncompounded house.

पञ्चमे कुजराहुभ्यां क्षयरोगस्य संभवः।
रात्रिनाथेन दृष्टाभ्यां निश्चयेन प्रजायते ॥३६॥
कुजदृष्टौ तु जातस्य पिटकादिगदो भवेत्।
केतुदृष्टौ तु ग्रहणी जलरोगोऽथवा द्विज! ॥३७॥

सराहुगुलिके तत्र भयं क्षुद्रविषोद्भवम् ।
बुधे परमहंसश्च लगुडी वा प्रजायते ।।३८।।
रवौ खड्गधरो जातः कुजे कुन्तायुधी भवेत् ।
शनौ धनुर्धरो ज्ञेयो राहौ च लोहयन्त्रवान् ।।३९।।
केतौ च घटिकायन्त्री मानवो जायते द्विज ! ।
भार्गवे तु कविर्वाग्मी काव्यज्ञो जायते जनः ।।४०।।

36-40. *EFFECTS OF THE 5TH FROM KARAKAMSA* : If Rahu and Mars are in the 5th from Karakamsa, one will suffer from a pulmonary consumption, more so if the Moon aspects them. The aspect of Mars on the said house will bring boils or ulcers. Ketu's aspect on the said house will cause dysentery and said diseases caused by (impure) water. If Rahu and Gulika be in the house there will be fear from mean people aud poison. Should Mercury be in the said house, the native will be an ascetic of the highest order or one holding staff. The Sun and Mars in the said house respectively denote one using a knife and spear. Saturn denotes a bowman in this context. Rahu and Ketu in the said house respectively denote a machinist and a watch maker. Venus in the said house will make one a poet and an eloquent speaker.

स्वांशे तत्पञ्चमे वाऽपि चन्द्रेज्याभ्यां च ग्रन्थकृत् ।
शुक्रेण किञ्चिदूनोऽसौ ततोऽप्यल्पो बुधेन च ।।४१।।
गुरुणा केवलेनैव सर्वविद् ग्रन्थकृत् तथा ।
वेदवेदान्तविच्चापि, न वाग्मी शाब्दिकोऽपि सन् ।।४२।।
नैयायिकः कुजेनासौ ज्ञेन मीमांसकस्तथा ।
सभाजडस्तु शनिना गीतज्ञो रविणा स्मृतः ।।४३।।
चन्द्रेण सांख्ययोगज्ञः साहित्यज्ञश्च गायकः ।
केतुना गणितज्ञोऽसौ राहुणाऽपि तथैव च ।।४४।।
सम्प्रदायस्य सिद्धिः स्यात् गुरुसम्बन्धतो द्विज ! ।
स्वांशाद् द्वितीयतः केचित् फलमेवं वदन्ति हि ।।४५।।

41-45. *EFFECTS OF KARAKAMSA AND THE 5TH THEREFROM* : If Jupiter and the Moon are in Karakamsa or the 5th thereof, the native will be an author. Venus in the said place will make one an ordinary writer while Mercury will give still lesser effects in this respect. Should Jupiter be alone in the said house, one will be a knower of everything, be a writer, and be versed in Vedas and Vedanta philosophy, but not an oratorian or a grammarian. Mars in this respect denotes a logician, Mercury a Mimamsaka (follower of Mimamsa philosophy, one of the six chief systems of Hindu philosophy), Saturn one dull-witted in the assembly, the Sun a musician, the Moon a follower of Sankhya Philosophy (of sage Kapila enumerating 25 true principles with emphasis on final bliss), and versed in rhetorics and singing, and Ketu or Rahu an astrologer. Should Jupiter be related to the said positions (caused by others than him), the effected stated will effectively come to pass. Some say that the 2nd from Karakamsa be also similarly considered.

स्वांशात् षष्ठगते पापे कर्षको जायते जनः ।
शुभग्रहेऽलसश्चेति तृतीयेऽपि फलं स्मृतम् ॥४६॥

46. *EFFECTS OF THE 6TH FROM KARAKAMSA :* If the 6th from Karakamsa is occupied by a malefic, the native will be an agriculturist while he will be indolent if a benefic is there. The 3rd from Karakamsa be also similarly considered.

द्यूने चन्द्रगुरू यस्य भार्या तस्यातिसुन्दरी ।
तत्र कामवती शुक्रे, बुधे चैव कलावती ॥४७॥
रवौ च स्वकुले गुप्ता, शनौ चापि वयोऽधिका ।
तपस्विनी रुजाढ्या वा राहौ च विधवा स्मृता ॥४८॥

47-48. *EFFECTS OF THE 7TH FROM KARAKAMSA :* If the Moon and Jupiter are in the 7th from Karakamsa, the native will beget a very beautiful wife. Venus in the said house denotes a sensuous wife while Mercury indicates a wife versed in arts. The Sun so related will give a wife confining domestic core while Saturn denotes a wife of a higher age bracket, or a pious/sick wife. Rahu in this context will bring a widow in marriage.

शुभस्वामियुते रन्ध्रे स्वांशाद् दीर्घायुरुच्यते ।
पापेक्षितयुतेऽल्पायुर्मध्यायुर्मिश्रदृग्युते ॥४९॥

49. *EFFECTS OF THE 8TH FROM KARAKAMSA* : If a benefic or the planet owning the 8th from Karakamsa be in the 8th from Karakamsa, the native will be long-lived while a malefic so placed will reduce the life span. Aspect/conjunction of both benefics and malefics will yield a medium span of life.

कारकांशाच्च नवमे शुभग्रहयुतेक्षित ।
सत्यवादी गुरौ भक्तः स्वधर्मनिरतो नरः ॥५०॥
स्वांशाच्च नवमे भावे पापग्रहयुतेक्षिते ।
स्वधर्मनिरतो बाल्ये मिथ्यावादी च वार्धके ॥५१॥
नवमे कारकांशाच्च शनि-राहुयुतेक्षिते ।
गुरुद्रोही भवेद् बालः शास्त्रेषु विमुखो नरः ॥५२॥
कारकांशाच्च नवमे गुरुभानुयुतेक्षिते ।
तदाऽपि गुरुद्रोही स्यात् गुरुवाक्यं न मन्यते ॥५३॥
कारकांशच्च नवमे शुक्रभौमयुतेक्षिते ।
षड्वर्गादिकयोगे तु मरणं पारदारिकम् ॥५४॥
कारकांशाच्च नवमे ज्ञेन्दुयुवतेक्षिते द्विज ! ।
परस्त्री सङ्गमाद् बालो बन्धको भवति ध्रुवम् ॥५५॥
नवमे केवलेनैवे गुरुणा च युतेक्षिते ॥
स्त्रीलोलुपो भवेज्जातो विषयी चैव जायते ॥५६॥

50-56. *EFFECTS OF THE 9TH FROM KARAKAMSA* : If the 9th from Karakasmsa is aspected or occupied by a benefic, the native will be truthful, devoted to elders and attached to his own religion. If a malefic is so related as above, one will be attached to his religion in boyhood but will take to falsehood in old age. If Saturn and Rahu are so related as above, one will betray his elders and be averse to ancient learning. If Jupiter and the Sun are so related as above, one will betray his elders and will be disobedient to them. Should Mars and Venus be so related as above, and joining in six identical vargas, a female ill-related to the native will die. Mercury and the Moon so related will cause imprisonment of the native due to association with a female not of his own. If Jupiter is alone related to the 9th from Karakamsa by aspect or by conjunction, the native will be addicted to females and be devoted to sensual enjoyments.

कारकांशाच्च दशमे शुभखेटयुतेक्षिते ।
स्थिरवित्तो भवेद् बालो गम्भीरो बलबुद्धिमान् ॥५७॥
दशमे कारकांशाच्च पापखेटयुतेक्षिते ।
व्यापारे जायते हानिः पितृसौख्येन वर्जितः ॥५८॥
दशमे कारकांशाच्च बुधशुक्रयुतेक्षिते ।
व्यापार बहुलाभश्च महत्कर्मकरो नरः ॥५९॥
कारकांशाच्च दशमे रविचन्द्रयुतेक्षिते ।
गुरुदृष्टयुते विप्र ! जातको राज्यभाग् भवेत् ॥६०॥

57-60. *EFFECTS OF THE 10TH FROM KARAKAMSA :* If the 10th from Karakamsa be aspected or conjoined by a benefic, the native will have firm riches, be sagacious, strong and intelligent. A malefic so related will cause harm to his profession and deprive him of paternal bliss. Mercury and Venus so related will confer many gains in business (or profession) and will make him do many great deeds. The luminaries so related to the 10th from Karakamsa and if be in aspect to or conjunction with Jupiter the native will acquire a kingdom.

स्वांशादेकादशे स्थाने शुभखेटयुतेक्षिते ।
भ्रातृसौख्ययुतो बालः सर्वकार्येषु लाभकृत् ॥६१॥
एकादशे सपापे तु कुमार्गाल्लाभकृन्नरः ।
विख्यातो विक्रमी चैव जायते नाऽत्र संशयः ॥६२॥

61-62. *EFFECTS OF THE 11TH FROM KARAKAMSA :* If the 11th from Karakamsa be aspected by or conjunct a benefic, the native will enjoy happiness from coborn apart from gaining in every undertaking of his. If a malefic is in the said 11th the native will gain by questionable means, be famous and valorous.

कारकांशाद् व्ययस्थाने सद्ग्रहे सद्व्ययो भवेत् ।
असद्व्ययोऽशुभे ज्ञेयो ग्रहाभावे च सत्फलम् ॥६३॥
कारकांशाद् व्ययस्थाने स्वभोच्चस्थे शुभग्रहे ।
सद्गतिर्जायते तस्य शुभलोकमवाप्नुयात् ॥६४॥
कारकांशाद् व्यये केतौ शुभखेटयुतेक्षिते ।
तदा तु जायते मुक्तिः सायुज्यपदमाप्नुयात् ॥६५॥

मेषे धनुषि वा केतौ कारकांशात् व्यये स्थिते।
शुभखेटेन सन्दृष्टे सायुज्यपदमाप्नुयात् ॥६६॥
व्यये च केवले केतौ पापयुक्तेक्षितेपि वा।
न तदा जायते मुक्तिः शुभलोकं न पश्यति ॥६७॥
रविणा संयुते केतौ कारकांशाद् व्ययस्थिते।
शिवभक्तिर्भवेस्यत्त निर्विशंकं द्विजोत्तम ! ॥६८॥
चन्द्रेण संयुते केतौ कारकांशाद् व्ययस्थिते।
गौर्यां भक्तिर्भवेत्तस्य शाक्तिको जायते नरः ॥६९॥
शुक्रेण संयुते केतौ कारकांशाद् व्ययस्थिते।
लक्ष्म्यां सञ्जायते भक्तिर्जातको सौ समृद्धिमान् ॥७०॥
कुजेन संयुते केतौ स्कन्दभक्तौ भवेन्नरः।
वैष्णवो बुधसौरिभ्यां गुरुणा शिवभक्तिमान् ॥७१॥
राहुणा तामसीं दुर्गां सेवते क्षुद्रदेवताम्।
भक्तिः स्कन्देऽथ हेरम्भे शिखिना केवलेन वा ॥७२॥
कारकांशाद् व्यये सौरिः पापराशौ यदा भवेत्।
तदाऽपि क्षुद्रदेवस्य भक्तिस्तस्य न संशयः ॥७३॥
पापर्क्षेऽपि शनौ शुक्रे तदाऽपि क्षुद्रसेवकः।
अमात्यकारकात् षष्ठेप्येवमेव फलं वदेत् ॥७४॥

63-74. *EFFECTS OF THE 12TH FROM KARAKAMSA :* If the 12th from Karakamsa has a benefic, the expensess will be on good account while a malefic will cause bad expenses. If the said 12th be vacant then also good effects (in respect of expenses) will follow. If there be a benefic planet in exaltation or in own house in the 12th from Karakamsa or if Ketu is so placed and aspected by or conjunct a benefic one will attain heavens after death. One will attain final emancipation if Ketu is in the 12th (from Karakamsa) identical with Aries/Sagittarius and is aspected by a benefic. If Ketu in the 12th from Karakamsa and be with aspect/conjunction of a malefic one will not attain final emancipation. If the Sun and Ketu are in the said 12th the native will worship Lord Siva. The Moon and Ketu in the said 12th denotes a worshipper of Gauri (a con-sort of Lord Siva) Venus and Ketu in the said 12th denotes a worshipper of Lakshmi (a consort of Lord Vishnu) and a wealthy person. Mars and Ketu in the said 12th denotes a worshipper of Lord Subramanya (an offspring of Lord Siva). Rahu in the 12th from Karakamsa will make one worship Durga or some mean deity. Ketu alone in the said 12th denotes Subramanya's or Ganesa's worshipper. If Saturn is in the said 12th in a malefic's sign one will worship mean deities. Venus and Saturn in the said 12th in a malefic's sign will also make one worship mean deities. Similar inferences can be drawn from the 6th Navamsa counted from Amatya Karaka's Navamsa.

कारकांशात् त्रिकोणस्थे पापखेटद्वये द्विज ! ।
मानवो मन्त्र-तन्त्रज्ञो जायते नाऽत्र संशयः ॥७५॥
पापेन वीक्षिते तत्र जातो निग्राहको भवेत् ।
शुभैर्निरीक्षिते तस्मिन् नरोऽनुग्राहको भवेत् ॥७६॥

75-76. *MISCELLANEOUS MATTERS (upto sloka 84)* : O Brahmin, if there are two malefics in a trine from Karakamsa, the native will have knowledge of **Mantras** (sacred spells) and **Tantras** (mystical formularies for the worship of deities for attainment of super-human powers). If a malefic simultaneously aspects the said yoga, the native will use these learnings for malevolent purposes while a benefic's aspect will make him use the same for public good

शुक्रदृष्टे विधौ स्वांशे रसवादी भवेन्नरः ।
बुधदृष्टे च सद्वैद्यः सर्वरोगहरो भवेत् ॥७७॥
शुक्रदृष्टे सुखे चन्द्रे पाण्डुश्वित्री भवेन्नरः
भौमदृष्टे महारोगी रक्तपित्तार्दितो भवेत् ॥७८॥
केतुदृष्टे सुखे चंद्रे नीलकुष्ठी प्रजायते ।
चतुर्थे पञ्चमेवाऽहि स्थितौ राहु-कुजौ यदि ॥७९॥
क्षयरोगो भवेत् तस्य चन्द्रदृष्टौ तु निश्चितः ।
स्वांशात् सुखे सुते वाऽपि केवलः संस्थितः कुजः ॥८०॥
पिटकादिर्भवेत् तस्य तदा रोगो न संशयः ।
ग्रहणी जलरोगो वा तत्र केतौ स्थिते सति ॥८१॥

स्वर्भानुगुलिकौ तत्र विषवैद्यो विषार्दितः।
स्वांशकात् पञ्चमे भावे केवले संस्थिते शनौ ॥८२॥
धनुर्विद्याविदा जाता भवन्त्यत्र न संशयः।
केतौ च केवले तत्र घटिकायन्त्रकारकः ॥८३॥
बुधे परमहंसो वा दण्डी भवति मानवः।
लोहयन्त्री तथा राहौ, रवौ खड्गधरो भवेत् ॥८४॥
केवले च कुजे तत्र जातः कुन्तास्त्रधारकः।

77-84½. If the Moon is in the Karakamsa in aspect to Venus, the native will be an alchemist and if be in aspect to Mercury he will be a doctor capable of curing all diseases. If the Moon is in the 4th from Karakamsa and be in aspect to Venus, the native be afflicted by white leprosy; if in aspect to Mars blood and bilious disorders, and if to Ketu black leprosy. Should Rahu and Mars be in the 4th or 5th from Karakamsa the native will suffer from pulmonary consumption and if there be Moon's aspect simultaneously this affliction will be certain. Mars alone in the 4th/5th from Karakamsa will cause/ulcers. If Ketu be in the 4th or 5th from Karakamsa one will suffer from dysentery and afflictions due to (impure) water. Rahu and Gulika in the 4th/5th from Karakamsa will make one a doctor curing poisonous afflictions or will cause troubles through poison. Should Saturn be alone in the 4th or 5th from Karakamsa, the native will be skilful in archery. Ketu lonely placed in the 4th/5th from Karakamsa will make one a maker of watches etc. Mercury so placed will make one an ascetic of the highest order or an ascetic holding staff. Rahu, Sun and Mars respectively in these places denote a machinist, a knife user and spear/arrow user.

स्वांशे वा पञ्चमे स्वांशाच्चन्द्रेज्यौ संस्थितौ तदा ॥८५॥
ग्रन्थकर्ता भवेज्जातः सर्वविद्याविशारदः।
तत्र दैत्यगुरौ किञ्चिदूनग्रन्थकरो भवेत् ॥८६॥

85-86. The Moon and Jupiter in the Karakamsa or the 5th therefrom denotes a writer well-versed in all branches of learning. The grade of writership will comparatively descend in the case of Venus and further in the case of Mercury if so placed as above.

बुधे तत्र ततोऽप्यूनग्रन्थकर्त्ता प्रजायते।
तत्र शुक्रे कविर्वाग्मी काव्यज्ञश्च प्रजायते ।।८७।।
सर्वविद्ग्रान्थिको जीवे न वाग्मी च सभादिषु।
शब्दज्ञश्च विशेषेण वेदवेदान्तवित् तथा ।।८८।।
सभाजडो भवेद् बाल उक्तस्थानगते शनौ।
मीमांसको भवेन्नूनमुक्तस्थानगते बुधे ।।८९।।
स्वांशे वा पञ्चमे भौमे जातो नैयायिको भवेत्।
चन्द्रे च सांख्ययोगज्ञः साहित्यज्ञश्च गायकः ।।९०।।
रवौ वेदान्तविच्चैव गीतज्ञश्च प्रजायते।
केतौ च गणितज्ञः स्याज्ज्योतिःशास्त्रविशारदः ।।९१।।
सम्प्रदायस्य संसिद्धिर्गुरुसम्बन्धतो भवेत्।
द्वितीये च तृतीये च स्वांशादेवं विचारयेत् ।।९२।।
भावे सूक्ष्मफलं ज्ञात्वा जातकस्य फलं वदेत्।

87-92½. *PLANETS IN 5TH FROM KARAKAMSA :* Should Venus be in the 5th from Karakamsa, the native will be a poet, be eloquent and be a poet. Jupiter replacing denotes that he will be an exponent and be all-knowing but be unable to speak in an assembly. He will be further a grammarian and a scholar in Vedas and Upanishads. Saturn in this context will make one ineffective in an assembly, while Mercury will make him a skilful in Meemamsa (one of the six chief Darsanas). Mars in Karakamsa or the 5th therefrom will make one Justice while the Moon denotes a Sankhya Yogi, a rhetor or a singer. The Sun in the said 5th will make one learned in Vedanta and music. Ketu in the said 5th will make one a nathematician and skilful in astrology. Should Jupiter be related to the said Ketu, these learnings will be by inheritance. All these as well apply to the 2nd/3rd from Karakamsa and to the Karakamsa itself apart from applying to the 5th from Karakamsa.

केतौ स्वांशाद्द्वितीये वा तृतीये स्तब्धवाग् भवेत् ।।९३।।
पापदृष्टे विशेषेण मानवो वक्तुमक्षमः।

93-93½. Should Ketu be in the 2nd/3rd from Karakamsa, the native will be defective in speech, more so if a malefic aspects Ketu as above.

स्वांशाल्लग्नात् पदाद्वाऽपि द्वितीयाऽटमभावयोः ।।९४।।
केमद्रुमः पापसाम्ये चन्द्रदृष्टौ विशेषतः ।
अत्राऽध्याये च ये योगाः सफलाः कथिता मया ।।९५।।
योगकर्तृदशायान्ते ज्ञेयाः सर्वे फलप्रदाः ।
एवं दशाप्रदाद्राशेर्द्वितीयाष्टमयोर्द्विज ! ।।९६।।
ग्रहसाम्ये च विज्ञेयो योगः केमद्रुमोऽशुभः ।
दशाप्रारम्भसमये सलग्नान् साधयेद् ग्रहान् ।।९७।।
ज्ञेयस्तत्रापि योगोऽयं पापसाम्येऽर्थरन्ध्रयोः ।
एवं तन्वादिभावानां सूर्यादीनां नभःसदाम् ।।९८।।
तत्तत्स्थित्यनुसारेण फलं वाच्यं विपश्चिता ।
इति संक्षेपतः प्रोक्तं कारकांशफलं मया ।।९९।।

94-99. If malefics be in the Karakamsa, Arudha Lagna and the 2nd and 8th from these places, there will be Kemadruma yoga; the effects of which will be still severer if the Moon's aspect be there. The effects due for these yogas will come to pass in the Dasa periods of the Rasis or planets eoncerned. Kemadruma Yoga will operate additionally if there are malefics in the 2nd and 8 from the Rasi whose Dasa will be in currency. The results of such yoga will also be inauspicious. If the 2nd and 8th in the chart cast for the beginning of a Dasa have malefics, then also Kemadruma prevails throughout the Dasa.

अथ योगकारकाध्यायः ।।३४।।

Chapter 34

Yoga Karakas

कारकांशवशादेवं फलं प्रोक्तं मया द्विज ! ।
अथ भावाधिपत्येन ग्रहयोगफलं शृणु ।।१।।

1. O Brahmin, thus I have told you about the effects derivable through Krakamsa. Now listen to the effects arising out of planetary house lord ships.

केन्द्राधिपतयः सौम्या न दिशन्ति शुभं फलम्।
क्रूरा नैवाऽशुभं कुर्युः शुभदाश्च त्रिकोणपाः ॥२॥
लग्नं केन्द्रत्रिकोणत्वाद् विशेषेण शुभप्रदम्।
पञ्चमं नवमं चैव विशेषधनमुच्यते ॥३॥
सप्तमं दशमं चैव विशेषसुखमुच्यते।
त्रिषडायाधिपाः सर्वे ग्रहाः पापफलाः स्मृताः ॥४॥
व्ययद्वितीयरन्ध्रेशाः साहचर्यात् फलप्रदाः।
स्थानान्तरानुरोधात्ते प्रबलाश्चोत्तरोत्तरम् ॥५॥
तत्र भाग्यव्ययेशत्वाद्रन्ध्रेशो न शुभप्रदः।
त्रिमदायाधिपत्वेऽथो कोणपत्वे तु सत्फलः ॥६॥
उक्तेष्वेषु बली योगो निर्बलस्य प्रबाधकः।
न रन्ध्रेशत्वदोषोऽत्र सूर्याचन्द्रमसोर्भवेत् ॥७॥

2-7. *NATURE DUE TO LORDSHIPS OF PLANETS :* Benefics owning angles will not give benefic effects while malefics owning angles *will not remain inauspicious,* The lord of a trine will give auspicious results. The lord of the ascendant is specially auspicious as the ascendant is an angle as well as trine. The 5th, and 9th houses are specially for wealth while the 7th and 10th are specially for happiness. Any planet owning the 3rd, 6th, or the 11th will give evil effects. The effects due to the lords of the 12th, and 8th will depend on their association. In each group, the significance will be in the ascending order. The 8th lord is not auspicious as he owns the 12th from the 9th. If the lord of the 8th simultaneously owns the 3rd, 7th or 11th, he will prove specifically harmful while his simultaneous ownership of a trine will bestow auspicious effects. The planet owning a predominant house will stall the effects due to another owning a less significant house and will give his own results. The 8th lordship of the Sun and the Moon is not evil.

Notes : The rules given in this part will help us to decide the good and bad planets for each ascendant based on lordships. A summary of these rules is given below to enable use of suitable application of lordships.

1. **Kendradhipatya Dosha :** This blemish goes to natural benefics by virtue of angular lordship. For example, for Gemini ascen-

dant the ownership of 4th and 7th goes to Jupiter and hence he is not a benefic for this ascendant. Lagna lord owning an angle i.e. 4th/7th/10th, shall not prove inauspicious. (Even if he owns an evil house, he is not classified as a malefic.) Natural benefics are increasing Moon, Mercury, Jupiter and Venus. Their angular lordship blemish will be in the ascending order. That is the Moon is the least malefic and Venus is the most malefic by such ownership.

2. **Malefic as owner of angle** : If a malefic owns an angle he will not be inauspicious. This does not mean that he will become auspicious. (The sage has cautiously worded his verse.) To be auspicious by virtue of angular lordship, the malefic should simultaneously own a trine. If he does not own a trine, he will be neutral by mere angular lordship; neither he will be disadvantageous. For Libra ascendant, Satrun is classified as unsullied yogakaraka because he owns the 4th (an angle) and the 5th (a trine). The Sun's beneficence to Taurus ascendant cannot be compared to Saturn's for Libra, because the Sun has only one house which is angular to the ascendant. For Leo ascendant Mars becomes a top rank benefic as he owns an angle (4th) and a trine (9th). Similarly for Cancer ascendant. The same Mars for Capricorn ascendant by virtue of angular lordship is not that superior because he does not simultaneously own a trine. Similarly his role for Aquarius ascendant. Weak Moon by virtue of angular lordship remains just neutral.

3. Primarily wealth-givers are the lords of 5th and 9th. The lords of 7th and 10th contribute to one's happiness. Each of them should be individually welldisposed. Trinal lordship to Jupiter will enable him give wealth abundantly and uninterruptedly. Venus becoming lord of 7th or 10th will give general happiness if the occupies an angle or a trine.

4. Lords of 3rd, 6th and 11th are classified as evil planets while the lords of 2nd, 12th and 8th will act according to association. If these lords simultaneously own such another house, they will be significantly harmful. If such a planet simultaneously owns a trine he will be favourable. For example, Jupiter is doubly evil for Libra ascendant as he owns the 3rd and 6th. Saturn, though owning the 8th, will be favourable for a Gemini nativity as he is the lord of the 9th as well. In considering two

lordships in any context, the Moolatrikona house has prime importance as against the other ordinary house. The Moolatrikona lordship will reveal itself effectively rather than the other own house.

5. When two planets are involved in a context, the one with good lordship will stall the evil effects of another planet owning a less powerful house. To wit, if the 9th lord and the 8th lord are both involved in a yoga, the 9th lord will give his good effects obstructing the evils due to the 8th lord.

6. We have the following two sets of good houses, (a) 1st, 4th, 7th and the 10th. (b) 5th and 9th. In each group the benefic disposition will ascend from house to house. That is, 7th lord is more powerful than the 4th. The 9th lord is so as against the 5th lord

7. Similarly two sets of evil houses are before us; (a) 3rd, 6th and 11th. (b) 12th, 2nd and 8th. Here again the maleficence will move in the ascending order. To wit, the 11th lord is the most evil in his group while the 8th lord is so in his group.

8. The summary of points 6 and 7 is : the 10th and 9th lords are the highest benefic planets while the 11th and 8th lords are the most adverse. Thus, the 10th lord's counterpart is the 11th lord and the 9th lord's counterpart is the 8th lord. (If we consider Saturn for Aries ascendant, he gets one best house and one worst house, i.e. the 10th and 11th houses. The 11th house being his Moolatrikona, he is predominantly the 11th lord rather than the 10th lord and hence very evil. Similarly his role for Gemini ascendant in which case the 9th lordship prevails over his 8th lordship and so he is not evil but favourable.)

9. The roles of various planets are generally based on these grounds and what we have had so far is a rough frame-work. However, no decision should be taken at one single point. For actual picture, the sage classifies the planets further in the succeeding verses.

10. As far as Rahu and Ketu are concerned, they act according to their position, association and dispositors, *vide* verse 16 *infra*.

गुरुशुक्रौ शुभौ प्रोक्तौ चन्द्रो मध्यम उच्यते ।
उदासीनो बुधः ख्यातः पापा रव्यार्किभूमिजाः ॥८॥

पूर्णेन्दुज्ञेज्यशुक्राश्च प्रबला उत्तरोत्तरम् ।
क्षीणेन्द्वर्कार्किभूपुत्राः प्रबलाश्च यथोत्तरम् ॥९॥
केन्द्राधिपत्यदोषो यः शुभानां कथितो हि सः ।
चन्द्रज्ञगुरुशुक्राणां प्रबलाश्चोत्तरोत्तरम् ॥१०॥

8-10. *NATURAL BENEFICS AND MALEFICS :* Jupiter and Venus are benefics while the Moon is mediocre in beneficence. Mercury is neutral (i.e. a benefic when associated with a benefic and a malefic when related to a malefic). Malefics are the Sun, Saturn and Mars. Full Moon, Mercury, Jupiter and Venus are stronger in the ascending order Weak Moon, the Sun, Saturn and Mars are stronger (in malefic disposition) in the ascending order. In revealing maleficence due to angular rulership, the Moon, Mercury, Jupiter and Venus are significant in the ascending order.

Notes : Jupiter and Venus are first rate benefics while the Moon is next to them. The Moon's variable dispositions have been given in the earlier pages. Mercury is neutral, i.e. a benefic in relation to a benefic and is a malefic in relation to a malefic. He has no disposition of his own. If he is alone, he will be favourable. Considering the Moon and Mercury in benefic classes, the four planets viz. Moon, Mercury, Jupiter and Venus are superior in the ascending order. That is Mercury is more beneficial than Moon, Jupiter is more beneficial than Mercury and Venus is the highest benefic. However, some exponents hold the view that Jupiter is the highest benefic, see **"Subhanampatih"**

As regards malefics, the Sun, Saturn and Mars come under this class when the nodes are excluded for they do not have their own disposition. Here again, the Sun is the least malefic, Saturn is more malefic than the Sun; and Mars is the highest malefic as against the Sun and Saturn.

केन्द्रकोणपती स्यातां परस्परगृहोपगौ ।
एकभे द्वौ स्थितौ वापि ह्येकभेऽन्यतरः स्थितः ॥११॥
पूर्णदृष्ट्येक्षितौ वापि मिथो योगकारौ तदा ।
योगेऽस्मिन् जायते भूपो विख्यातो वा जनो भवेत् ॥१२॥

11-12. *ANGULAR AND TRINAL LORDSHIPS* : If there be an exchange between an angular lord and a trinal lord, or if these two lords join in an angle or in a trine, or if a trinal lord is in angle or vice versa, or if there be full aspect between them, they cause a yoga. One born in such a yoga will become a king and be famous.

Notes : The following permutations will emerge from these two verses which yogas will make the native famous giving royal status. These are :

(1) exchange between an angular lord and a trinal lord. For example Gemini ascendant having Mercury in Aquarius and Saturn in Virgo.

(2) angular lord and trinal lord in a trine, whether they own or not.

(3) angular lord and trinal lord in an angle, whether they own or not.

(4) trinal lord in an angle, whether he owns or not.

(5) angular lord in a trine, whether he owns or not.

(6) angular lord and trinal lord in mutual opposition (as full aspect is required), particularly in good bhavas.

कोणेशत्वे यदैकस्य केन्द्रेशत्वं च जायते ।
केन्द्रे कोणे स्थितो वाऽसौ विशेषाद्योगकारकः ॥१३॥

13. If one and the same planet gets the lordships of a trine as well as an angle or if a planet is in an angle or in a trine, it will prove specially a yogakaraka.

केन्द्रेशत्वेन पापानां या प्रोक्ता शुभकारिता ।
सा त्रिकोणाधिपत्येऽपि न केन्द्रेशत्वमात्रतः ॥१४॥

14. *ANGULAR LORDSHIP* : **It has been said that a malefic owning an angle will become auspicious which is true only when it simultaneously lords over a trine and not by merely owning an angle.**

Note : This aspect has been clarified in the initial verses of the present chapter.

केन्द्रकोणाधिपावेव पापस्थानाधिपौ यदा ।
तयोः सम्बन्धमात्रेण न योगं लभते नरः ॥१५॥

15. If the lords of an angle or a trine owns simultaneously an evil house, he(i.e. the angular lord or the trinal lord)does not

cause a Rajayoga by mere relations stipulated (as per slokas 11 and 12 above).

Notes : In this context, if the evil house is Moolatrikona, that evil lordship will prevail. Alternatively if the angle or trine is Moolatrikona, the evil lordship is suppressed so that the good lordship shows up. Here such angular lord and such trinal lord by mere relations (as per verses 11 and 12) do not become Yogakaraka or status makers.

यद्भावेशयुतौ वापि यद्यद्भावसमागतौ ।
तत्तत्फलानि प्रबलौ प्रदिशेतां तमोग्रहौ ॥१३॥

16. *RAHU & KETU* : Rahu and Ketu give predominently the effects as due to their conjunction with a house lord or as due to the house they occupy.

Notes : As already stated, Rahu owns Aquarius and Ketu Scorpio. Still they do not have a disposition of their own in the matter of giving particular efferts. (In point of fact, these ownerships are for calculation of some of 'Jaimni' dasas etc. and not in a common context.) Inasmuch as they do not have a sign of their own, they have also not been specifically classified as malefic or benefic for the various ascendants as could be seen from the rules enunciated by sage Parasara in the current chapter. Hence it is suggested that the results to be given by Rahu and Ketu will depend on their association with other lords and occupation of houses. So to say, if they are related to good lords they will reveal effects favourable to the native, otherwise not. Alternatively they should be in favourable houses like angle, trine etc. so that good effects follow their position.

यदि केन्द्रे त्रिकोणे वा निवसेतां तमोग्रहौ ।
नाथेनान्यतरेणाढ्यौ दृष्टौ वा योगकारकौ ॥१७॥

17. If a node is in an angle in aspect to or association with a trinal lord or be in a trine in similar relation with an angular lord it will become Yogakaraka.

Notes : Two important positions are indicated for a node becoming Yogakaraka for a native. It should be in an angle in relation to a trinal lord or be in a trine in aspect to an angular lord. In such a situation Rahu or Ketu will become a Yogakaraka.

कस्मिल्लग्ने प्रजातस्य के ग्रहा योगकारकाः ।
के चाऽशुभप्रदाः खेटाः कृपया वद मे मुने ! ॥१८॥

18. O Sage, please narrate according to the signs rising as to which planet is a yogakaraka and which is inauspicious.

यथा पृष्टं त्वया विप्र ! तथोदाहरणं ब्रुवे ।
रन्ध्रेशत्वेऽपि भूपुत्रो भवेच्छुभसहायवान् ॥१९॥
मन्दसौम्यसिताः पापाः शुभौ गुरुदिवाकरौ ।
न शुभं योगमात्रेण प्रभवेच्छनि-जीवयोः ॥२०॥
पारतन्त्र्येण जीवस्य पापकर्मापि निश्चितम् ।
शुक्रः साक्षान्निहन्ता स्यान्मारकत्वेन लक्षितः ॥२१॥
मन्दादयोऽपि हन्तारो भवेयुः पापिनो ग्रहाः ।
मेषलग्नोद्भवस्यैवं फलं ज्ञेयं द्विजोत्तम ! ॥२२॥

19-22. *PLANETS & ARIES ASCENDANT :* O Brahmin, listen to these with examples. Even though Mars is the lord of the 8th, he will be helpful to (other) auspicious planets. Saturn, Mercury and Venus are malefics. Auspicious are Jupiter and the Sun. The mere conjunction of Saturn and Jupiter will not produce auspicious effects (although they own a trine and angle). If Jupiter is at the disposal of a malefic, he will surely give inauspicious results. Venus is a direct (or independent) killer. Saturn etc. will also inflict death if associated with an adverse planet (i.e. Venus). That is how the effects will be derived by an Aries native.

Notes : For Aries ascendant Mars is the ruler of the 1st and the 8th. The ascendant is his Moolatrikona sign while the 8th is his secondary sign. He will hence predominantly be favourable He cannot be independently auspicious but can help another favourable planet like the Sun or Jupiter or even the Moon through whom he will reveal his good qualities. It is also not illogical to conclude that if Mars is well related to Jupiter or the Sun or the Moon and is in good bhavas, favourable effects will come through him.

As regards other unsullied benefic planets for this ascendant we have only two. These are Jupiter and the Sun. Even if Jupiter is captured by another adversary, his good results will be stalled. Saturn, Mercury and Venus are malefics and will cause harm. Venus will prove a killer as he is the 2nd and 7th lord. Saturn and Mercury will also inflict death if related to Venus. The Moon's role is not discussed by the sage. The Moon will give mixed results according to association etc. as she is an angular ruler.

An association between Jupiter-Sun, Jupiter-Mars or Mars-Sun will be highly favourable for the ascendant in question. Jupiter-Saturn association will not prove to be helpful although they own the 9th and 10th. It is because, Saturn is 11th lord with prime emphasis on his Aquarius ownership.

जीवशुक्रेन्दवः पापाः शुभौ शनिदिवाकरौ।
राजयोगकरः सौरिर्बुधस्त्वल्पशुभप्रदः ॥२३॥
जीवादयो कुजश्चापि सन्ति मारकलक्षणाः।
वृषलग्नोद्भवस्यैवं फलान्यूह्यानि सूरिभिः ॥२४॥

23-24. *FOR TAURUS ASCENDANT :* Jupiter, Venus and the Moon are malefics. Saturn and the Sun are auspicious. Saturn will cause Rajayoga. Mercury is somewhat auspicious, Jupiter etc. and Mars will inflict death. These hints are for a Taurus native.

Notes : Jupiter is a malefic for Taurus ascendaut and will avail of the first opportunity to inflict harm as he owns the 8th and 11th houses both of which are evil. He is the first-rate adversary. The Moon being the 3rd lord is not auspicious. Venus is also classified here as an evil planet and a maraka planet. The words "जीवादयो" (Jeevadayo) indicate the Jupiter group, i.e. Jupiter, the Moon and Venus. According to the following words of **Susloka Sataka** —अलौ षष्टपदोषो न वृषभोपि न दोषभाक्—for Scorpio ascendant there is no blemish (to Mars) of the 6th lordship and also for Taurus ascendant (in the case of Venus). Sage Parasara apparently took into serious consideration the 6th lordship (Moolatrikona) of Venus and calssified him as an adversary. Though there are some more exponents to favour Susloka Sataka's line of thinking, Parasara being an undisputed authority should be given more weight. The Sun and Saturn are benefics. Saturn owns the best trine and best angle and hence he will bestow kingly status on the native. The Sun though a malefic by virtue of owning an angle proves auspicious. The rule that a malefic owning an angle should own a trine also, so that he becomes a Yogakaraka (vide sloka 14 supra) is naturally not applicable to the luminaries as they own only one sign each. As regards the role of Mercury, he is only of mixed nature for Taurus ascendant and he is not an excellent benefic by virtue of owning a Maraka house in addition to a trine. The 5th is his Moolatrikona and exaltation sign, If Mercury joins Saturn/Sun, he will act more effectively.

Mars is classified as a killer apart from Jupiter, Venus and the Moon. Mars is a killer for he owns the 7th and 12th. The role of Jupiter and Venus as killers is also understandable. Though the Moon is said to be a killer, she cannot independently do so for she is only the 3rd lord which is the least malefic among 3rd, 6th and 11th. The luminaries are considered not inauspicious even by ownership of the 8th house; as such the 3rd house lordshsp of the Moon in the case of Taurus be leniently viewed from the point of wiew of inflicting death. Her connections with Jupiter or Mars can empower her to inflict death on the Taurus native.

भौमजीवारुणाः पापाः एक एव कविः शुभः ।
शनैश्चरेण जीवस्य योगो मेषभवो यथा ॥२५॥
शशी मुख्यनिहन्ताऽसौ साहचर्याच्च पाकदः ।
द्वन्द्वलग्नोद्भवस्यैवं फलान्यूह्यानि पंडितैः ॥२६॥

25-26. *FOR GEMINI ASCENDANT* : Mars, Jupiter and the Sun are malefics while Venus is the only auspicious planet. The conjunction of Jupiter and Saturn is similar to that for Aries ascendant. The Moon is the prime killer, but it is dependant on her association. Thus have been explained by the scholars the effects for Gemini ascendant.

Notes : The three planets, viz. Jupiter, the Sun and Mars are adverse for Gemini ascendant. There is no hint on Saturn's role except that Saturn-Jupiter conjunction does not yield a yoga just as it does not do so for an Aries native. Saturn owns the

8th and the 9th while the 9th is his Moolatrikona. Jupiter owns the 7th and 10th. It is my personal feeling that an exchange between Saturn and Jupiter in the 9th and 10th or their placement in conjunction in the 9th/10th, or Saturn in the 9th as Jupiter is in the 10 will prove a very favourable point. (This line of thinking cannot be extended to Aries ascendant, i.e. exchange between 9th and 10th lords & *C* for Jupiter will be in fall in the 10th in a key house.)

For Gemini ascendant, Mars owns two evil houses, the 6th and 11th and hence he is a malefic. The Sun owning the 3rd will not be helpful.

Venus, the lord of the 5th and 12th, is declared to be highly favourable, as the 5th is his Moolatrikona. In view of the friendship between Venus and Mercury, the 12th lordship of Venus is not seriously considered adverse. On the same lines, Mercury for Libra ascendant is considered favourable although he owns the 12th, which is his Moolatrikona and exaltation—thus a predominant house.

भार्गवेन्दुसुतौ पापौ भूसुतेज्येन्दवः शुभाः ।
पूर्णयोगकरः साक्षान्मंगलो मंगलप्रदः ॥२७॥
निहन्ताऽर्कसुतोऽर्कस्तु साहचर्यात् फलप्रदः ।
कर्कलग्नोद्भवस्यैवं फलं प्रोक्तं मनीषिभिः ॥२८॥

27-28. *CANCER ASCENDANT :* Venus and Mercury are malefics, Mars, Jupiter and the Moon are auspicious. Mars is capable of conferring a full-fledged yoga and giving auspicious effects. Saturn and the Sun are killers and give effects according to association. These are Cancer ascendant's effects.

Notes : The role of the Sun is compared to that of Saturn as a killer. The Sun is the lord of the 2nd and Saturn rules the 7th and 8th for Cancer ascendant. Both the houses of Saturn are inauspicious and hence he is classified as a killer. However, they are not independently capable of doing bad or good but act as per their relationship with others.

Venus is inauspicious by virtue of angular lordship (4th house—Moolatrikona) and the 11th lordship. (The 11th lord for a movable sign is a malefic, i.e. Saturn for Aries, Venus for Cancer, the Sun for Libra and Mars for Capricorn ascendants.) Thus Venus gets a dual role to do evil for a Cancer native. The 3rd and 12th lordship of Mercury will inflict harm and hence he is inauspicious.

The best planet for this ascendant is Mars as he owns a trine as well as an angle. The 10th lordship will prevail much more favourably as the 10th is the best of the 4 angles and Aries is the Moolatrikona sign of Mars. The other two favourable planets are Jupiter and the Moon. Jupiter is the lord of the 6th and 9th. Though 6th is his Moolatrikona, the sage has given preference to the 9th lordship for obviously two reasons : firstly the 9th is best of the two trines and Jupiter is a close friend of the Moon, the ascendant lord. The 3rd favourable planet is the Moon who is the ascendant lord. The order of preference is Mars, Jupiter and the Moon, i.e. benefic tendency will descend from one to another and hence the Moon is the least benefic. If Mars is well related to Jupiter, the Moon or to the Sun, he can do wonders for a Cancer native, The best place as far as Saturn is concerned is Capricorn in the company of Mars or the Moon.

सौम्यशुक्रार्कजाः पापाः कुजेज्यार्काः शुभावहाः।
प्रभवेद्योगमात्रेण न शुभं गुरुशुक्रयोः ॥२९॥
मारकस्तु शनिश्चन्द्रः साहचर्यात् फलप्रदः।
सिंहलग्ने प्रजातस्य फलं ज्ञेयं विपश्चिता ॥३०॥

29-30. *LEO ASCENDANT :* Mercury, Venus and Saturn are malefics. Auspicious effects will be givin by Mars, Jupiter and the Sun. The conjunction of Jupiter and Venus (though Kendra Kona lords) will not produce auspicious results. Saturn and the Moon are killers who will give effects according to association. These are the effects applicable to Leo ascendant.

Notes : Just as the Sun is noted as a killer for Cancer ascendant, the Moon is similarly classified as a killer for Leo ascendant as she is the lord of the 12th house. This killer-role has not barred the Moon from becoming a Yogakaraka or an auspicious planet for Leo ascendant as per our experience. Saturn's adverse role is because of two prime reasons—firstly he is a sworn enemy of the ascendant lord and secondly he is the 7th lord apart from being the 6th lord. Mercury's role is equally ominous as the 2nd and 12th come under his regent. The 3rd and 10th lordship (a bad house and an angle respectively) makes Venus unreliable.

Mars is again the best planet for Leo ascendant followed by favourable roles to be enacted by Jupiter and the Sun. Mars rules the 4th and 9th; Jupiter the 5th and 8th and the Sun ascendant. Here again, the Sun is the 3rd in order.

कुजजीवेन्दवः पापाः बुध-शुक्रौ शुभावहौ ।
भार्गवेन्दुसुतावेव भवेतां योगकारकौ ॥३१॥
मारकोऽपि कविः, सूर्यः साहचर्यफलप्रदः ।
कन्यालग्नोद्भवस्यैवं फलान्यूह्यानि सूरिभिः ॥३२॥

31-32. *VIRGO ASCENDANT :* Mars, Jupiter and the Moon are malefics while Mercury and Venus are auspicious. The conjunction of Venus and Mercury will produce yoga. Venus is a killer as well. The Sun's role will depend on his association. These effects are for Virgo ascendant..

Notes : Mercury ruling the ascendant and the 10th house and Venus lording over the 2nd and 9th are classified as favourable planets. Venus by virtue of owning the 2nd will act as a killer also. (Mars ruling the 8th can also act as a killer.) Jupiter rules two angles—the 4th and the 7th—while the Moon is the 11th lord. For these reasons, these two are considered inauspicious. The Sun will be good if he joins good planets in good houses, for example in the 10th along with Mercury. There is no hint in the text about Saturn's role. By virtue of the 5th lordship and good relationship with the ascendant lord Mercury, he will prove auspicious. But the stain due to 6th lordship will cause a change in his disposition and he cannot be counted as an invariable dependent.

जीवार्कभूसुताः पापाः शनैश्चरबुधौ शुभौ ।
भवेतां राजयोगस्य कारकौ चन्द्रतत्सुतौ ॥३३॥
कुजो निहन्ति जीवाद्याः पापा मारकलक्षणाः ।
शुक्रः समः फलान्येवं विज्ञेयानि तुलोद्भवे ॥३४॥

33-34. *LIBRA ASCENDANT :* Jupiter, the Sun and Mars are malefics. Auspicious are Saturn and Mercury. The

Moon and Mercury will cause Rajayoga. Mars is a killer. Jupiter and other malefics will also acquire a disposition to inflict death. Venus is neutral. Thus should be known about Libra ascendant.

Notes : Although Venus is the ruler of the ascendant, he owns 8th as well, and hence the sage term him as neutral, Dire malefic is Jupiter, the lord of the 3rd and the 6th. The ruler of the 2nd and the 7th, Mars, is equally inauspicious while the Sun ruling the 11th will act as an obstructing force. These three planets, viz. Jupiter, Mars and the Sun are more malefic if mutually related but unrelated to Saturn, Mercury or the Moon. On the other hand, Mars or the Sun will act as primary benefics if they join Saturn, Mercury or Venus according to one school of thought.

सितज्ञशनयः पापाः शुभौ गुरुनिशाकरौ ।
सूर्यचन्द्रमसावेव भवेतां योगकारकौ ॥३५॥
कुजः समः सिताद्याश्च पापा मारकलक्षणाः ।
एवं फलं च विज्ञेयं वृश्चिकोदयजन्मनः ॥३६॥

35-36. *FOR SCORPIO ASCENDANT :* Venus, Mercury and Saturn are malefics. Jupiter and the Moon are auspicious. The Sun as well as the Moon are Yogakarakas. Mars is neutral. Venus and other malefics acquire the quality of causing death. These are for a Scorpio native.

Notes : Just as Venus is a neutral planet for Libra ascending, Mars is also neutral for Scorpio ascendant. Mars owns the ascendant and the 6th, the latter being his Moolatrikona. The Sun (lord of the 10th) and the Moon (lord of the 9th) are termed the best yogakarakas. Jupiter though ruling the 2nd (and the 5th), is auspicious just as Mercury for Taurus ascendant ruling the 2nd and the 5th. (of course Mercury's Moolatrikona is the 5th) Venus, Saturn and Mercury are malefics as well as death-dealing planets. Saturn can be practically auspicious if he is in the 5th/9th, being lord of an angle, from the point of view of status, finance etc.

एक एव कविः पापः शुभौ भौमदिवाकरौ ।
योगो भास्करसौम्याभ्यां निहन्ता भास्करात्मजः ॥३७॥

गुरुः समफलः ख्यातः शुक्रो मारकलक्षणः।
धनुर्लग्नोद्भवस्यैवं फलं ज्ञेयं विपश्चिता ॥३८॥

37-38. *SAGITTARIUS ASCENDANT :* Only Venus is inauspicious. Mars and the Sun are auspicious. The Sun and Mercury are capable of conferring a yoga Saturn is a killer. Jupiter is neutral. Venus acquires killing powers. These effects are for Sagittarius ascendant.

Notes : Venus is a first-rate malefic for Sagittarius ascendant as he owns the 6th and 11th. The sage hints that none is akin to Venus in giving malefic effects for this ascendant. Saturn is straightaway a killer, ruling the 2nd and the 3rd. Venus can also become a killer (if related to Saturn). Though Mercury rules two angles—the 7th and 10th—he is declared auspicious whereas for Virgo ascendant as well as Gemini ascendant, Jupiter is considered inauspicious. This supreme role of Mercury is possibly because of his ownership of the 10th house (moolatrikona and hence predominant against 7th house ownership) whereas Jupiter does not own Moolatrikona identical with the 10th house—best of the angles—for an ascendant ruled by Mercury. If the Sun (ruler of the 9th) joins Mercury, both of them will confer still superior Yoga for Sagittarius natives. Mars gives primarily his 5th house effects (moolatrikona) shedding his 12th lordship and hence is a favourable planet. Jupiter is neither a first-rate benefic nor an adversary for he owns the 4th (angular lordship's blemish). The Moon ruling the 8th cannot be a powerful Yogakaraka unless well-related to Mercury, the Sun or Mars. An association between the Moon and Jupiter can confer a yoga **par excellence.**

कुजजीवेन्दवः पापाः शुभौ भार्गवचन्द्रजौ।
मन्दः स्वयं न हन्ता स्याद् हन्ति पापाः कुजादयः ॥३९॥
सूर्यः समफलः प्रोक्तः कविरेकः सुयोगकृत्।
मृगलग्नोद्भवस्यैवं फलान्यूह्यानि सूरिभिः ॥४०॥

39-40. *CAPRICORN ASCENDANT :* Mars, Jupiter and the Moon are malefics, Venus and Mercury are auspicious. Saturn will not be a killer of his own. Mars and other malefics will inflict death. The Sun is neutral. Only Venus is capable of causing a superior yoga. These are the effects applicable to Capricorn ascendant.

Notes : The sage has listed Mars in the first place while mentioning adverse planets for Capricorn ascendant as Mars rules the 4th and 11th. Jupiter is lord of the 2nd and 12th, the latter being his important house. The 7th lord Moon is not quite a favourable planet.

Saturn and the Sun are neither very favourable nor very adverse. Saturn will reveal killing powers if he joins Jupiter, Mars or the Moon. While Venus and Mercury are both auspicious in their own way, the former is the best yogakaraka for this ascendant, for he is the lord of the 5th and 10th.

जीव-चन्द्र-कुजाः पापाः शुक्रसूर्यात्मजौ शुभौ ।
राजयोगकरो ज्ञेयः कविरेव, बृहस्पतिः ॥४१॥
सूर्यो भौमश्च हन्तारो बुधो मध्यफलः स्मृतः ।
कुम्भलग्नोद्भवस्यैवं फलान्यूह्यानि सूरिभिः ॥४२॥

41-42. *AQUARIUS ASCENDANT* : Jupiter, the Moon and Mars are malefics while Venus and Saturn are auspicious. Venus is the only Rajayoga causing planet. Jupiter, the Sun and Mars are killers. Mercury gives meddling effects. These effects are described by the learned for Aquarius ascendant.

Notes : The 2nd and 11th lord Jupiter is a dire malefic followed by the Moon (the 6th lord) and Mars (ruling the 3rd and 10th). While Venus and Saturn are both auspicious for Aquarius ascendant, Venus is the only planet that can be considered to have been vested with powers of Rajayoga. Saturn is not compared to Venus as he owns the 12th simultaneously. Venus is the lord of the 4th and the 9th. As the 9th is the best trine, he is relieved of blemish due to angular lordship. The Sun is termed as a killer as he rules the 7th, a maraka house. (Saturn plays a similar role for Leo ascendant owning the 7th in Moolatrikona). Jupiter ruling the 2nd and Mars owning the 3rd are also killers. Out of the 3 killers, Mars is the last in order. A strong relationship between two or all of these three killers will affect the longevity to decline severely. Mercury ruling the 5th and the 8th will give mixed results. If Mercury joins an adverse planet, he will be essentially adverse while in joining Venus or Saturn, he can considerably improve. Alone in bad houses, he will be evil and in good houses he will be favourable. This is how Mercury's role for this ascendant need be understood.

मन्दशुक्रांशुमत्सौम्याः पापा भौमविधू शुभौ ।
महीसुतगुरू योगकारकौ च महीसुतः ॥४३॥
मारकोऽपि न हन्ताऽसौ मन्दज्ञौ मारकौ स्मृतौ ।
मीनलग्नोद्भवस्यैवं फलानि परिचिन्तयेत् ॥४४॥

43-44. *PISCES ASCENDANT :* Saturn, Venus, the Sun and Mercury are malefics. Mars and the Moon are auspicious. Mars and Jupiter will cause a yoga. Though Mars is a killer, he will not kill the native (independently). Saturn and Mercury are killers. Thus should be judged the effects for a Pisces native.

Notes : Saturn owns two evil houses for Pisces ascendant. Hence he will reveal himself most awefully. Venus rules the 3rd and 8th—again two evil houses. And hence he is not a favourable planet. The Sun ruling the 6th will prove adverse though he has good terms with the lord of the ascendant, Jupiter Mars is the lord of the 2nd (Moolatrikona) and the 9th (the best of the trines). Inspite of owning a killer-house, he has been specifically exempt from acting as a killer independently and placed in the yogakaraka list. To be a killer, Mars must be instigated by another killer. viz. Saturn or Mercury. Jupiter is a very favourable planet (of course next to Mars) owning the ascendant and the 10th. Though there is no specific mention of Venus becoming a killer in such role can be seen in him as he owns the 8th house.

एवं भावाधिपत्येन जन्मलग्नवशादिह ।
शुभत्वमशुभत्व च ग्रहाणां प्रतिपादितम् ॥४५॥
अन्यानपि पुनर्योगान् नाभसादीन् विचिन्त्य वै ।
देहिना च फलं वाच्यं प्रवक्ष्यामि च तानहम् ॥४६॥

45-46. *GENERAL :* Thus the auspicious and inauspicious effects derivable through the planets due to their lordships according to the rising sign be estimated. Apart, the effects due to Nabhasa yogas etc. be also known which I narrate as under.

Notes : The good disposition, bad disposition and killing powers of the various planets are assigned by the sage on a particular understanding of lordships etc. for each of the 12 ascendants. From the current two verses, we take an important clue about the final role of a planet. To wit, if a planet is constituent of a favourable yoga, like, say, Daamini Yoga (one of the Nabhasa Yogas), his original malefic tendency of being an adverse planet for a particular ascendant, he will give the eftects of Daamini yoga and thus will become a Rajayogakaraka. Conversely, although a planet assumes good role by lordship, if he is involved in a bad yoga, like, say, Sarpa yoga (one of the Nabhasa yogas again) there will only be adverse results and not favourable results due to lordship. These causes should be properly estimated and effects denoted suitably. A killer is a killer irrespective of his having become a Rajayogakaraka or so. Killer and Yogakaraka should not be mixed together in respect of one and the same planet.

अथ नाभसयोगाध्यायः ॥३५॥

Chapter 35

Nabhasa Yogas

अधुना नाभसा योगाः कथ्यन्ते द्विजसत्तम !।
द्वात्रिंशत् तत्प्रभेदास्तु शतघ्नाष्टादशोन्मिताः ॥१॥
आश्रयाख्यास्त्रयो योगा दलसंज्ञं द्वयं ततः।
आकृतिर्विंशतिः संख्याः सप्त योगाः प्रकीर्तिताः ॥२॥

1-2. O excellent of the Brahmins, explained below are 32 Nabhasa yogas which have a total of 1800 different varieties. These consist of 3 Asraya yogas, 2 Dala yogas, 20 Akriti yogas, and 7 Sankhya yogas.

Notes : No additional notes and explanations are being given in the present volume on the following chapters :

Nabhasa yogas (ch, 35)

Lunar yogas (ch. 37)

Solar yogas (ch. 38)

These have been fully discussed and annotated in a clear manner in my English translations of **Saravali** and **Horasara.** The reader may refer to the said works.

रज्जुश्च मुसलश्चैव नलश्चेत्याश्रयास्त्रयः ।
मालाख्यः सर्पसंज्ञश्च दलयोगौ प्रकीर्तितौ ॥३॥
गदाख्यः शकटाख्यश्च शृङ्गाटक-विहंगमौ ।
हलवज्रयवाश्चैव कमलं वापियूपकौ ॥४॥
शर-शक्ति-दण्ड-नौका-कूट-च्छत्र-धनूंषि च ।
अर्धचन्द्रस्तु चक्रं च समुद्रश्चेति विंशतिः ॥५॥
संख्याख्या-वल्लकी-दाम-पाश-केदार-शूलकाः ।
युगो गोलश्च सप्तैते युक्ता दन्तमिता द्विज ! ॥६॥

3-6. *NAMES OF NABHASA YOGAS :* Asraya yogas are Rajju, Musala and Nala yogas. Dala yogas are Maala and Sarpa. The twenty Akriti yogas are : Geda, Sakata, Sringataka, Vihanga, Hala, Vajra, Yava, Kamala, Vaapi, Yupa, Sara, Sakthi, Danda, Nauka, Koota, Chatra, Dhanushi (or Chapa), Ardhachandra, Chakra and Samudra yogas. The seven Sankhya yogas are Vallaki, Daama, Paasa, Kedara, Soola, Yuga and Gola yogas. Thus these are 32 in total.

सर्वैश्चरे स्थितै रज्जुः स्थिरस्थैर्मुसलः स्मृतः ।
नलाख्यो द्विस्वभावस्थैराश्रयाख्या इमे स्मृताः ॥७॥

7. *RAJJU, MUSALA AND NALA YOGAS :* All the planets in movable signs cause Rajju yoga. All the planets in fixed signs cause Musala yoga. All the planets in dual signs cause Nala yoga.

केन्द्रत्रयगतैः सौम्यैः पापैर्वा दलसंज्ञकौ ।
क्रमान्मालाभुजंगाख्यौ शुभाशुभफलप्रदौ ॥८॥

8. *MAALA AND SARPA YOGAS :* If 3 angles are occupied by benefics Maala yoga is produced while malefics so placed will cause Bhujanga or Sarpa yoga. These yogas respectively produce benefic and malefic results.

आसन्नकेन्द्रद्वयगैः सर्वैर्योगो गदाह्वयः ।
शकटं लग्नजायास्थैः खाम्बुगैर्विहगः स्मृतः ॥९॥
योगः शृङ्गाटकं नाम लग्नात्मजतपःस्थितैः ।
अ यस्थानात् त्रिकोणस्थैः सर्वैर्योगो हलाभिधः ॥१०॥
लग्नजायास्थितैः सौम्यैः पापाख्यैः खाऽम्बुसंस्थितैः ।
योगो वज्राभिधः प्रोक्तः वीपरीतस्थितैर्यवः ॥११॥

9-11. *GADA, SAKATA, VIHAGA, SRINGATAKA, HALA, VAJRA AND YAVA YOGAS :* If all the planets occupy two successive angles, Gada yoga is formed. Sakata yoga occurs when all the planets are disposed in the ascendant and the 7th house. If all confine to the 4th and the 10th, then Vihaga yoga occurs. All planets in the ascendant, 5th and 9th cause Sringataka yoga while all planets are in the 2nd, 6th and the 10th or in the 3rd, 7th and 11th or in the 4th, 8th and 12th cause Halayoga. Vajra yoga is caused by all benefics in the ascendant and the 7th or all malefics in the 4th and 10th. In a contrary situation, i.e. all benefics in the 4th and the 10th or all malefics in the ascendant and the 7th, Yava yoga is generated.

सर्वकेन्द्रगतैः सर्वैर्मिश्रैः कमलसंज्ञकः ।
केन्द्रादन्यत्रगैः सर्वैर्योगो वापीसमाह्वयः ॥१२॥

12. *KAMALA AND VAPI YOGAS :* If all the planets are in the 4 angles, Kamala yoga is produced. If all of them be in all the cadent houses or in all the succedent houses Vapi yoga occurs.

यूपो लग्नाच्चतुर्भस्थैः शरस्तुर्याच्चतुर्भगैः ।
शक्तिर्मदाच्चतुर्भस्थैर्दण्डो मध्याच्चतुर्भगैः ॥१३॥

13. *YUPA, SARA, SAKTHI AND DANDA YOGAS :* If all the 7 planets are in the 4 houses commencing from the ascendant they cause Yupa yoga. If a similar occupation commences

from the 4th house Sara yoga, from the 7th house Sakthi yoga and from the 10th house Danda yoga are formed.

लग्नात् सप्तमगैर्नौका कूटस्तुर्याच्च सप्तमैः।
छत्राख्यः सप्तमादेवं चापं मध्याद् भसप्तगैः ॥१४॥

14. *NAUKA, KOOTA, CHATRA AND CHAPA YOGAS :* If all the planets occupy the seven houses from the ascendant, Nauka yoga occurs. Koota yoga, Chatra yoga and Chapa yoga occur respectively when the commencing houses are the 4th, 7th and 10th. Here again the planets should occupy seven continuous houses.

लग्नादेकान्तरस्थैश्च षड्भगैश्चक्रमुच्यते।
धनादेकान्तरस्थैस्तु समुद्रः षडगृहाश्रितै ॥१५॥

15. *CHAKRA AND SAMUDRA YOGAS :* If all the planets occupy six alternative signs commencing from the ascendant, Chakra yoga is formed. Samudra yoga is produced if these occupy similarly six alternative signs commencing from the 2nd from the ascendant.

एकराशिस्थितैर्गोलो युगाख्यो द्विभसंस्थितैः।
शूलस्तु त्रिभगैः प्रोक्तः केदारस्तु चतुर्भगैः ॥१६॥
पञ्चराशिस्थतैः पाशा दामाख्यः षड्गृहाश्रितैः।
वीणा सप्तभगैः सर्वैर्विहायान्यानुदीरितान् ॥१७॥

16-17 *SANKHYA YOGAS :* If all planets are in one sign Gola yoga is formed. Similarly if all are in 2 signs, Yuga yoga, 3 signs Soola yoga, 4 signs Kedara Yoga, 5 signs Paasa yoga, 6 signs Dama yoga and 7 signs Veena yoga is produced. None of these seven yogas will be operable, if another Nabhasa yoga explained earlier is derivable.

अटनप्रियाः सुरूपाः परदेशस्वास्थ्यभागिनो मनुजाः।
क्रूराः खलस्वभावा रज्जुप्रभवाः सदा कथिताः ॥१८॥

18. *EFFECTS OF NABHASA YOGAS (upto sloka 50) RAJJU YOGA :* One born in Rajju yoga will be fond of wandering, be charming, will earn in foreign countries, and be cruel and mischievous.

मानज्ञानधनाद्यैर्युक्ता भूपप्रियाः ख्याताः ।
बहुपुत्राः स्थिरचित्ता मुसलसमुत्था भवन्ति नराः ॥१६॥

19. *MUSALA YOGA :* One born in Musala yoga will be endowed with honour, wisdom, wealth etc., be dear to king, famous, will have many sons and be firm in disposition.

न्यूनातिरिक्तदेहा धनसञ्चयभागिनोऽतिनिपुणाश्च ।
बन्धुहिताश्च सुरूपा नलयोगे सम्प्रसूयन्ते ॥२०॥

20. *NALA YOGA :* One born in Nala yoga will have uneven physique, be interested in accumulating money, very skilful, helpful to relatives, and charming.

नित्यं सुखप्रधाना वाहनवस्त्रान्नभोगसम्पन्ना ।
कान्ता सुबहुस्त्रीका मालायां सम्प्रसूताः स्युः ॥२१॥

21. *MAALA YOGA :* One born in Maala yoga will be ever happy, endowed with conveyances. robes, food and pleasures, be splendorous and endowed with many females.

विषमाः क्रूरा निःस्वा नित्यं दुःखार्दिताः सुदीनाश्च ।
परभक्षपाननिरताः सर्पप्रभवा भवन्ति नराः ॥२२॥

22. *SARPA YOGA :* One born in Sarpa (Bhujanga) yoga will be crooked, cruel, poor, miserable and will depend on others for food and drinks.

सततोद्युक्तार्थवशा यज्वानः शास्त्रगेयकुशलाश्च ।
धनकनकरत्नसम्पत्संयुक्ता मानवा गदायां तु ॥२३॥

23 *GADA YOGA :* One born in Gada yoga will always make efforts to earn wealth, will perform sacrificial rites, be skilful in Sastras and songs and endowed with wealth, gold and precious stones

रोगार्ताः कुनखा मूर्खाः शकटानुजीविनो निःस्वा ।
मित्रस्वजनविहीनाः शकटे जाता भवन्ति नराः ॥२४॥

24. *SAKATA YOGA :* One born in Sakata yoga will be afflicted by diseases, will have diseased or ugly nails, be foolish,

will live by pulling carts, be poor and devoid of friends and relatives.

भ्रमणरुचयोविकृष्टा दूताः सुरतानुजीवनो धृष्टाः ।
कलहप्रियाश्च नित्यं विहगे योगे सदा जाताः ॥२५॥

25. *VIHAGA YOGA :* One born in V haga yoga will be fond of roaming, be a messenger, will live by sexual dealings, be shameless and interested in quarrels.

प्रियकलहाः समरसहाः सुखिनो नृपतेः प्रियाः शुभकलत्राः ।
आढ्या युवतिद्वेष्याः शृङ्गाटकसम्भवा मनुजाः ॥२६॥

26. *SRINGATAKA YOGA :* One born in Sringataka yoga will be fond of quarrels and battles, be happy, dear to king, endowed with an auspicious wife, be rich and will hate women.

बह्वाशिनो दरिद्राः कृषीवला दुःखिताश्च सोद्वेगा ।
बन्धुसुहृद्भिः त्यक्ताः प्रेष्याः हलसंज्ञके सदा पुरुषाः ॥२७॥

27. *HALA YOGA :* One born in Hala yoga will eat a lot, be very poor, be a farmer, be miserable, agitated, given up by friends and relatives and be a servant.

आद्यन्तवयःसुखिनः शूराः सुभगा निरीहाश्चः ।
भाग्यविहीना वज्रे जाताः खला विरुद्धाश्च ॥२८॥

28. *VAJRA YOGA :* One born in Vajra yoga will be happy in the beginning and at the end of life, be valorous, charming, devoid of desires and fortunes and be inimical.

व्रतनियममङ्गलपरा वयसो मध्ये सुखार्थपुत्रयुता ।
दातारः स्थिरचित्ता यवयोगभवाः सदा पुरुषाः ॥२९॥

29. *YAVA YOGA :* One born in Yava yoga will observe fasts and other religious rules, will do auspicious acts, will obtain happiness, wealth and sons in his mid-life, be charitable and firm.

विभवगुणाढ्याः पुरुषाः स्थिरायुषो विपुलकीर्तय शुद्धाः ।
शुभशतकाः पृथ्वीशाः कमलभवाः मानवा नित्यम् ॥३०॥

30. *KAMALA YOGA :* One born in Kamala yoga will be rich and virtuous, be long-lived, very famous, pure, will perform hundreds of auspicious acts and be a king.

निधिकरणे निपुणधियः स्थिरार्थसुखसंयुता सुतयुताश्च ।
नयनसुखसम्प्रहृष्टा वापीयोगेन राजानः ॥३१॥

31. *VAPI YOGA :* One born in Vapi yoga will be capable of accumulating wealth, be endowed with lasting wealth, and happiness and sons, be free from eye afflictions and be a king.

आत्मविदिज्यानिरतः स्त्रिया युतः सत्त्वसम्पन्नः ।
व्रतनियमरतमनुष्यो यूपे जातो विशिष्टश्च ॥३२॥

32. *YUPA YOGA :* One born in Yupa yoga will have spiritual knowledge, be interested in sacrificial rites, endowed with a wife, be strong, interested in fasts and other religious observations and be distinguished.

इषुकारा बन्धनपाः मृगयाधनसेविताश्च मांसादा ।
हिंस्राः कुशिल्पकाराः शरयोगे मानवाः प्रसूयन्ते ॥३३॥

33. *SARA YOGA :* One born in Sara yoga will make arrows, be head of prison, will earn through animals, will eat meat and indulge in torture and mean handiworks.

धनरहितविफलदुःखितनीचालसाश्चिरायुषः पुरुषाः ।
संग्रामबुद्धिनिपुणाः शक्त्यां जाताः स्थिराः शुभगाः ॥३४॥

34. *SAKTHI YOGA :* One born in Sakthi yoga will be bereft of wealth, be unsuccessful, miserable, mean, lazy, long-lived, interested and skilful in war, firm and auspicious.

हतपुत्रदारनिःस्वाः सर्वत्र च निर्घृणाः स्वजनबाह्याः ।
दुःखितनीचप्रेष्या दण्डप्रभवा भवन्ति नराः ॥३५॥

35. *DANDA YOGA :* One born in Danda yoga will lose his sons and wife, be indigent, unkind, away from his men, miserable and will serve mean people.

सलिलोपजीविविभवाः बह्वाशाः ख्यातकीर्तयो दुष्टाः ।
कृपणा मलिना लुब्धा नौसञ्जाताः खलाः पुरुषाः ॥३६॥

36. *NAUKA YOGA* : One born in Nauka yoga will derive his livelihood through water, be wealthy, famous. wicked, wretched, dirty and miserly.

अनृतकथनबन्धनपा निष्किञ्चनाः शठाः क्रूराः ।
कूटसमुत्था नित्यं भवन्ति गिरिदुर्गवासिनो मनुजाः ॥३७॥

37. *KOOTA YOGA* : One born in Koota yoga will be a liar, will head a jail, be poor, crafty, cruel and will live in hills and fortresses.

स्वजनाश्रयो दयावान्नानानृपवल्लभः प्रकृष्टमतिः ।
प्रथमेऽन्त्ये वयसि नराः सुखवान् दीर्घायुरातपत्री स्यात् ॥३८॥

38. *CHATRA YOGA* : One born in Chatra yoga will help his own men, be kind, dear to many kings, very intelligent, be happy at the beginning and end of his life and be long-lived.

आनृतिकगुप्तपालाश्चोराः कितवाश्च कानने निरताः ।
कार्मुकयोगे जाता भाग्यविहीनाः शुभा वयोमध्ये ॥३९॥

39. *CHAPA YOGA* : One born in Chapa yoga will be a liar, will protect secrets, be a thief, be fond of wandering in forests, be devoid of luck and be happy in the middle of his life.

सेनापतयः सर्वे कान्तशरीरा नृपप्रिया बलिनः ।
मणिकनकभूषणयुता भवन्ति योगेऽर्धचन्द्राख्ये ॥४०॥

40. *ARDHA CHANDRA YOGA* : One born in Ardha Chandra Yoga will lead an army, will possess a splendorous body, be dear to king, be strong and endowed with gems, gold and ornaments.

प्रणताऽऽशेषनराधिप-किरीटरत्नप्रभा-स्फुरितपादः ।
भवति नरेन्द्रो मनुजश्चक्रे यो जायते योगे ॥४१॥

41. *CHAKRA YOGA* : One born in Chakra yoga will be an emperor at whose feet will be the prostrating kings' heads, adoring gem-studded diadems.

बहुरत्नधनसमृद्धा भोगयुता धनजनप्रियाः ससुता ।
उदधिसमुत्थाः पुरुषाः स्थिरविभवाः साधुशीलाश्च ।।४२।।

42. *SAMUDRA YOGA :* One born in Samudra yoga will have many precious stones and abundant wealth, be endowed with pleasures, dear to people, will have firm wealth and be well-disposed.

प्रियगीतनृत्यवाद्या निपुणाः सुखिनश्च धनवन्तः ।
नेतारो बहुभृत्या वीणायां कीर्तिताः पुरुषाः ।।४३।।

4.3 *VEENA YOGA :* One born in Veena yoga will be fond of songs, dance and musical instruments, be skilful, happy, wealthy and be a leader of men.

दाम्नि सुजनोपकारी नयधनयुक्तो महेश्वरः ख्यातः ।
बहुसुतरत्नसमृद्धो धीरो जायेत विद्वांश्च ।।४४।।

44. *DAAMINI YOGA :* One born in Daamini yoga will be helpful to others, will have righteously earned wealth, be very affluent, famous, will have many sons and gems, be courageous and red-lettered.

पाशे बन्धनभाजः कार्ये दक्षाः प्रपञ्चकाराश्च ।
बहुभाषिणो विशीला बहुभृत्याः सम्प्रतानाश्च ।।४५।।

45. *PASA YOGA :* One born in Pasa yoga will be liable to be imprisoned, be skilful in work, be deceiving in disposition, will talk much, be bereft of good qualities and will have many servants.

सुबहूनामुपयोज्याः कृषीवलाः सत्यवादिनः सुखिनः ।
केदारे सम्भूताश्चलस्वभावा धनैर्युक्ताः ।।४६।।

46. *KEDARA YOGA :* One born in Kedara yoga will be useful to many, be an agriculturist, be truthful, happy, fickle-minded and wealthy.

तीक्ष्णालसधनहीना हिंस्राः सुबहिष्कृता महाशूराः ।
संग्रामे लब्धयशा शूले योगे भवन्ति नराः ।।४७।।

47. *SOOLA YOGA :* One born in Soola yoga will be sharp, indolent, bereft of wealth, be torturous, prohibited, valiant, and famous through war.

पाखण्डवादिनो वा धनरहिता वा बहिष्कृता लोके।
सुतमातृधर्मरहिता युगयोगे ये नरा जाताः ॥४८॥

48. *YUGA YOGA :* One born in Yuga yoga will be heretic, be devoid of wealth, be discarded by others, and be devoid of sons, mother and virtues.

बलसंयुक्ता विधना विद्याविज्ञानवर्जिता मलिना।
नित्यं दुःखितदीना गोले योगे भवन्ति नराः ॥४९॥

49. *GOLA YOGA :* One born in Gola yoga will be strong, be devoid of wealth, learning and intelligence, be dirty, sorrowful and miserable.

सर्वास्वपि दशास्वेते भवेयुः फलदायिनः।
प्राणिनामिति विज्ञेयाः प्रवदन्ति तवाग्रजाः ॥५०॥

50. Ancestors say that the results due to the said (Nabhasa) yogas will be felt throughout, in all the Dasa periods.

विविधयोगाध्यायः ॥३६॥

Chapter 36

Many Other Yogas

लग्ने शुभयुते योगः शुभः पापयुतेऽशुभः।
व्ययस्वगैः शुभैः पापैः क्रमाद्योगौ शुभाऽशुभौ ॥१॥
शुभयोगोद्भवो वाग्मी रूपशीलगुणान्वितः।
पापयोगोद्भवः कामी पापकर्मा परार्थयुक् ॥२॥

1-2. *BENEFIC & MALEFIC YOGAS :* If there be a benefic in the ascendant, Subha yoga is produced while a malefic therein causes Asubha yoga. Similarly benefics in both the 12th and the 2nd cause Subha yoga. Malefics in both the 12th and the 2nd also cause Asubha yoga. One born in Subha yoga will be eloquent, charming and virtuous while his counterpart will be sensuous, will do sinful acts and will enjoy (or swallow) others' wealth.

Notes : Subha yoga is of two kinds. It can be formed by a single benefic in the ascendant. It can also be formed by a benefic in the 2nd and by another simultaneously in the 12th. Obviously the latter Subha Yoga is still superior. (Needless to mention that if the ascendant, 2nd and 12th are simultaneously occupied by 3 benefics, even then Subha Yoga of a very great order is established.) This yoga gives physical beauty, excellent virtues and eloquent disposition. Though the text does not mention, additional effects are : a happy life, health, wealth, longevity, fame etc. These additional effects will not fully mature by a single ordinary benefic in the ascendant.

A malefic or malefics in these places will produce Asubha Yoga or inauspicious yoga. Each yoga is increasingly malefic. As a result, the subject will be libidinous, will indulge in unethical and sinful deeds and be capable of bracketing others' possessions. While a single malefic may not give so bad results, two or three in such positions will indeed produce most unfavourable results, apart from affecting health, longevity etc. adversely.

Needless to mention that in analysing the results due to good or bad combinations, one should take the planet's dignity, strength, relations with other planets and many such other factors into consideration. A malefic yoga can be nullified by other compensating factors while a good yoga may not be productive of expected good results when involved in adverse circumstances. For example, assume that for an Aquarius Mercury is in the 2nd house while Jupiter is in the 12th house. It will be detrimental to rush to the conclusion that the ascendant is surrounded by two benefics, and that Subha yoga results will improve the native. Conversely, this is worse than a typical Asubha Yoga.

Again take Asubha Yoga. Assume Virgo rises while Saturn is in exaltation in the 2nd and the Sun is in Leo in the

12th. This need not be dubbed as Asubha Yoga. These two malefics have their own merits and will prove favourable to the native.

This extension may wisely be made for every yoga—good or bad—and in every context throughout the analysis of the geniture. Only then will an agreeable picture emerge.

केन्द्रे देवगुरौ लग्नाच्चन्द्राद्वा शुभदृग्युते ।
नीचास्तारिगृहैर्हीने योगोऽयं गजकेसरी ।।३।।
गजकेसरिसञ्जातस्तेजस्वी धनवान् भवेत् ।
मेधावी गुणसम्पन्नो राजप्रियकरो नरः ।।४।।

3-4. *GAJAKESARI YOGA :* Should Jupiter be in an angle from the ascendant or from the Moon, and be conjunct or aspected by (another) benefic, avoiding at the same time debilitation, combustion and inimical sign, Gajakesari yoga is caused. One born in Gaja Kesari yoga will be splendorous, wealthy, intelligent endowed with many laudable virtues and will please the king.

Notes : The Parasari type of Gaja Kesari Yoga is constructed on a different footing. That Jupiter-Moon should be in mutual angles is a normally accepted yoga under this name. In my opinion this kind of angularity cannot yield supreme effects. The case of mere of Jupiter being in exaltation in a lunar angle can better be known as Pancha Maha Purusha Yoga, specifically Hamsa Yoga. In other cases the angularity between the two need not be given the name Gaja Kesari. In point of fact, the Moon-Jupiter mutual angular placement is called as simply Kesari Yoga, vide Phala Deepika, Ch. 6, sloka 14 etc. The effects given are : "The native will destroy the band of his enemies. He will be a lofty speaker in an assembly and will serve a king. He will be long lived and famous. He will be intelligent".

Referring to **Jataka Parijata**, there are two kinds of Gaja Kesari yogas mentioned therein. The first kind is formed by Jupiter being in an angle from the Moon. This is the common type of Yoga. Second alternative is : The Moon should be aspected by Mercury or Venus or Jupiter while the aspecting planet is free from debilitation and combustion.

Kumara Swameeyam a popular Tamil classic has this yoga stating that the Moon should be increasing (i.e. waxing) while Jupiter should be in the 4th or in the 10th from the said Moon. This comes to pass when a constituent is in Taurus, Pisces, Aquarius or Sagittarius. To wit, Gaja Kesari Yoga is applicable to only four placements That is, Jupiter should be in Aquarius while the Moon is in Taurus, or vice versa. Alternatively the Moon shoud be in Sagittarius while Jupiter is in Pisces, or vice versa. Please note that even Cancer is omitted which is exaltation sign for Jupiter and own sign for the Moon. In making such a specific statement, the author of **Kumara Swameeyam** must obviously have possessed an unparalleled authority.

Then we come to the Tamil translation of Parasara Hora by C.G. Rajan. His version states that the Moon and Jupiter should be in mutual angles, but the Moon should not have Mercury in the 5th from her, nor should she be in aspect to *Mercury* so that the Yoga obtained is not simultaneously given annulment. Further the *Moon* should be free from *combustion* and debilitation.

The Sanskrit edition of Parasara Hora of Sri Venkateswara Press, Bombay, has it in such a manner making it clear that Vaidyanatha of Jataka Parijata did take these verses from Parasara. (In fact many of the Raja Yogas given in our current chapter have been used by other works like *Phala Deepika, Kumara Swameeyam, Sata Yoga Manjari, Jataka Parijata etc).* Coming back to Gaja Kesari yoga given by the Bombay series, we find that the Jupiter-Moon mutual angularity finds place in the first kind of yoga as given by Vaidyanatha while the second version of Vaidyanatha occurs in the Bombay series in a different guise. It is stated there that Mercury aspecting or joining the Moon, not placed in debilitation nor being combust causes this yoga. In the second yoga, Venus and Jupiter are not given any place.

However, the two yogas given by Vaidyanatha are exactly identical with the ones given in Parasara Hora of Thakur Prasad Pustaka Bhandar edition from Varanasi.

The Chaukambha edition does not differ from our version.

Thus, I have placed all the different versions of Gaja Kesari Yoga before the reader. Though the name does not deserve any special consideration as for Gaja Kesari yoga, I would give less importance to the mere angular positions of Jupiter-Moon. From other formations, we may understand that Raja Yoga results will prevail in the following conditions in a descending order.

1. As given in **Kumara Swameeyam.**
2. As given in Chaukambha edition and our edition.
3. The second kind of yoga given by Jataka Parijata.
4. The second kind of yoga given by Bombay edition of Parasara Hora.

But, we do not understand the basis of C.G. Rajan why Mercury should not aspect the Moon or be in the 5th from her. Contrarily when Jupiter and the Moon are in mutual angles, Mercury in the 5th from the Moon will be an impetus to Gaja Kesari rather than becoming an impediment.

Gaja Kesari yoga formed in any of the four manners suggested above will give wealth, fame etc. in the Dasa periods of Jupiter, Moon and planets related to them. There is also a school of thought that one born in Kesari yoga will be rich in the dasa of Venus.

दशमेऽङ्गात्तथा चन्द्रात् केवलैश्च शुभैर्युते।
स योगोऽमलकीर्त्याख्यः कीर्तिराचन्द्रतारकी ।।५।।
राजपूज्यो महाभोगी दाता बन्धुजनप्रियः।
परोपकारी धर्मात्मा गुणढ्योऽमलकीर्तिजः ।।६।।

5-6. *AMALA YOGA* : If there be exclusively a benefic in the 10th from the ascendant or the Moon, Amala yoga exists. Amala yoga will confer fame lasting till the moon and stars exist and will make the native honoured by the king, enjoy abundant pleasures, be charitable, fond of relatives, helpful to others, pious and virtuous.

Notes : The 10th house from the Moon or from the ascendant should contain a benefic and be without a malefic occupation. If a malefic joins in the 10th simultaneously, the efficacy of the yoga will be void. A pure Amala Yoga gives name and fame lasting for decades and decades. Wealth is not indicated as a result of the yoga by the sage. Phala Deepika for example denotes wealth for this position.

It may be noted for what it is worth that the yogas mentioned by Bhava positions should be reckoned with reference to Bhava chart while dignity of the participant planets will depend on their sign position. An example chart for Amala Yoga is given below whose owner was born on 16th May, 1959 at 11gh 29vi at 26N29 80E21.

Ketu 17-36	Merc 12-18	Sun 1-17	Mars 27-17 Ven 12-57
	Rasi		Asc 6-09
			Moon 5-29
Sat 13-06	Jup 4-10		Rahu 17-36

This horoscope of a female was given by me in **Doctrines of Suka Nadi-Retold** on p. 37 in different context. There is a clear cut Amala Yoga caused by Mercury in the 10th from ascendant. Note that there is no planet accompanying Mercury, nor is there any adverse aspect on him. Further, there is an exchange between Mars and Mercury. This augurs the good effects of the yoga in the matter of wealth. As stated in Doctrines of Suka Nadi-Retold, the native started a business in the United States in sub period of Mercury during the major period of Venus. She has a well-settled show making steady progress.

सप्तमे चाऽष्टमे शुद्धे शुभग्रहयुतेऽथवा ।
केन्द्रेषु शुभयुक्तेषु योगः पर्वतसंज्ञकः ॥७॥

भाग्यवान् पर्वतोत्पन्नः वाग्मी दाता च शास्त्रवित् ।
हास्यप्रियो यशस्वी च तेजस्वी पुरनायकः ॥८॥

7-8. *PARVATA YOGA :* Benefics in angles will produce Parvatha yoga, as the 7th and 8th are vacant or are occupied by only benefics. One born in Parvatha yoga will be wealthy, eloquent, charitable, learned in Sastras, fond of mirth, famous, splendorous and be the leader of a city.

Notes : This yoga is formed at least in many ways according to different classical authors.

1. According to our version, there need be benefics in angles while the 7th and 8th are unoccupied or be in occupation by benefics alone. Then the yoga formed is known as Parvataa yoga.

2. The Tamil edition of Parasara Hora (translated by C.G. Rajan) has this yoga in two manners : That is, Benefics in angles and 6th and 8th. Alternatively benefics should be in angles and 9th.

3. The Sanskrit edition of Sri Venkateswara Press gives this yoga again in two forms thus ; (1) As per our version. (2) The lords of the ascendant and of the 12th in mutual angles and be aspected by friendly planets. These two are exactly followed by Sata Yoga Manjari (English translation by Prof. B. S. Rao).

4. Whereas the Sanskrit text of Sata Manjari Raja yoga (Hindi translation by Pt. G.K. Ojha) puts it thus : The dispositor of ascendant lord should be in his own sign or in his Moolatrikona sign which is identical with an angle or a trine reckoned from the ascendant. **Phala Deepika** exactly describes this yoga in this very manner.

5. Coming to **Jatakadesa Marga**, we find yet another version thus : If the ascendant, 4th, 7th and 10th are occupied by planets while the 8th and 12th are unoccupied, Parvata Yoga occurs. There is no mention of benefics or malefics in angles. That is these houses should remain occupied. **Horasara** (p. 233) has an identical version.

6. Chaukambha edition has it as given by C G. Rajan's first mentioned yoga.

7. The edition of Thakur Prasad Pustak Bhandar describes this yoga as per our version.

8, Now see Jataka Parijata. It has again two forms of this Yoga. The first one is formed in a manner identical with one mentioned in the Tamil version of Parasara Hora. The second type is formed as per the second yoga related to Bombay series of Parasara Hora. However, the Tamil version of **Jataka Parijata** (1926 edition by Sastra Sanjeevani Press) has it as our text has.

9. A version of Yavanas forms this yoga thus : The ascendant, 7th and 10th be occupied by benefics. So simple and no more pre-requisites. Note the 4th among angles is omitted by Yavanas. Thus there are so many varieties of Parvata Yoga.

When we consider the version given in our text, the maturity of this yoga will be during the Dasa periods of the benefics in the angles.

सुखेशेज्यौ मिथः केन्द्रगतौ बलिनि लग्नपे ।
काहलो वा स्वभोच्चस्थे सुखेशे कर्मपान्विते ॥९॥
ओजस्वी साहसी धूर्तश्चतुरङ्गबलान्वितः ।
यत्किञ्चिद् ग्रामनाथश्च काहले जायते नरः ॥१०॥

9-10. *KAHALA YOGA :* Should the 4th lord and Jupiter be in mutual angles while the ascendant lord is strong, Kahala yoga occurs. Alternatively the 4th lord being in his own or exaltation sign should be conjunct the 10th lord. In effect, the native will be energetic, adeventurous, cunning, endowed with a complete army consisting of chariots, elephants, horses and infantry and will lord over a few villages.

Notes : This yoga is given identically in the other three versions of Parasara Hora, viz. Venkateswara, Chaukamba and Thakur Prasad editions. Still others define this in different ways.

1. The first type of Kahala Yoga according to the Tamil version translated by C.G. Rajan is formed when the lords of the ninth and fourth are in mutual angles as the ascendant lord is endowed with strength. The second type of yoga mentioned by him is formed if the 4th lord is in his own sign or in exaltation in conjunction with or in aspect to the 10th lord. The aspect of the 10th lord is an addition in the Tamil version whereas in our version only a conjunction is noted. The native being foolish is

mentioned in the Tamil issue and Bombay issue, when giving effects of Kahala Yoga.

2. Mantreswara has it entirely differently thus : The dispositor of ascendant lord's dispositor should be in exaltation or own sign identical with a trine or angle reckoned from the ascendant. The effects mentioned are : prosperity, nobility, auspiciousness, benevolence and kindness.

3. **Jetakadsa Marga** mentions it in the same way as per C. G. Rajan's first type of yoga. **Jataka Parijata** follows **Jatakadesa Marga** while it adds the second version of Kahala Yoga given by our text.

लग्नेशे तुङ्गगे केन्द्रे गुरुदृष्टे तु चामरः।
शुभद्वये विलग्ने वा नवमे दशमे मदे ॥११॥
राजा वा राजपूज्यो वा चिरजीवी च पण्डितः।
वाग्मी सर्वकलाविद् वा चामरे जायते जनः ॥१२॥

11-12. *CHAMARA YOGA :* If the ascendant lord is exalted in an angle and be aspected by Jupiter, Chamara yoga is formed. This yoga also occurs if two benefics are in the ascendant, or 9th, or 10th or 7th. The effects of Chamara Yoga are : the native will be a king or honoured by the king, long-lived, scholarly, eloquent and versed in all arts.

Notes : While most texts are identical with our version, **Phala Deepika** puts it in a different way, viz. the ascendant be occupied by a benefic while the ascendant lord is in a good house or in exaltation. The effects attributed by Mantreswara are : long life, prospering like increasing Moon, fame, virtue and leadership. These are comparable [to what is generally stated for Chamara Yoga.

सबले लग्नपे पुत्र-षष्ठपौ केन्द्रगौ मिथः।
शंखो वा लग्नकर्मेशौ चरे बलिनि भाग्यपे ॥१३॥
धनस्त्रीपुत्रसंयुक्तो दयालुः पुण्यवान् सुधीः।
पुण्यकर्मा चिरञ्जीवी शंखयोगोद्भवो नरः ॥१४॥

13-14. *SANKHA YOGA :* If the ascendant lord is strong as the lords of the 5th and 6th are in mutual angles, then what is known as Sankha yoga is produced, Alternatively if the ascendant lord along with the 10th lord is in a movable sign as the 9th lord is strong, Sankha yoga is obtained. One born with Sankha yoga will be endowed with wealth, spouse and sons, be kindly disposed, propitious, intelligent, meritorious and long-lived.

सबले भाग्यपे भेरी खगैः स्वान्त्योदयास्तगैः ।
सबले भाग्यपे वाऽस्तौ केन्द्रे शुक्रेज्यलग्नपैः ॥१५॥
धनस्त्रीपुत्रसंयुक्तो भूपः कीर्तिगुणान्वितः ।
आचारवान् सुखी भोगी भेरीयोगे जनो भवेत् ॥१६॥

15-16. *BHERI YOGA :* If the 12th, ascendant, 2nd and 7th are occupied as the 9th lord is strong, the native obtains Bheri yoga. Again another kind of Bheri yoga is formed if Venus, Jupiter and the lord of thc ascendant are in an angle while the 9th lord is strong. The results of Bheri yoga are the native will be endowed with wealth, wife and sons, be a king, be famous, virtuous and endowed with good behaviour, happiness and pleasures.

सबले लग्नपे खेटाः केन्द्रे कोणे स्वभोच्चगाः ।
मृदङ्गयोगो जातोऽत्र भूपो वा तत्समः सुखी ॥१७॥

17. *MRIDANGA YOGA :* If the ascendant lord is strong as others occupy angles, trines, own houses or exaltation signs, Mridanga yoga is formed. The native concerned will be a king or equal to a king and be happy.

कामेशे कर्मगे तुङ्गे कर्मेशे भाग्यपान्विते ।
योगः श्रीनाथसंज्ञोऽत्र जातः शक्रसमो नृपः ॥१८॥

18. *SRINATHA YOGA :* If the 7th lord is in the 10th while the 10th lord is exalted and be in the company of the 9th lord, Srinatha yoga takes place. The native with this yoga will be equal to lord Devendra (the god of gods).

Notes : For Sagittarius ascendant, this yoga is simply formed if the Sun and Mercury are in the 10th in Virgo. But it is to be ensured that Mercury is in the first half of Virgo.

कर्मेशे सुतगे केन्द्रे बुधेऽर्के सबले स्वभे।
चन्द्रात् कोणे गुरौ ज्ञे वा कुजे लाभे च शारदः ॥१९॥
धनस्त्रीपुत्रसंयुक्तः सुखी विद्वान् नृपप्रियः।
तपस्वी धर्मसंयुक्तः शारदे जायते जनः ॥२०॥

19-20. *SARADA YOGA :* Should the 10th lord be in the 5th while Mercury is in an angle as the Sun with strength is in Leo, Sarda Yoga is formed. This will again obtain if Jupiter or Mercury is in a trine to the Moon, while Mars is in the 11th. One born in either kind of yoga will obtain wealth, spouse and sons, be happy, scholarly, dear to king, pious and virtuous.

धर्मलग्नगते सौम्ये पञ्चमे सदसद्युते।
पापे च चतुरस्रस्थे योगोऽयं मत्स्यसंज्ञकः ॥२१॥
कालज्ञः करुणामूर्तिर्गुणधीबलरूपवान्।
यशोविद्यातपस्वी च मत्स्ययोगे हि जायते ॥२२॥

21-22. *MATSYA YOGA :* Benefics in the 9th and the ascendant, mixed planets in the 5th and malefics in the 4th and 8th—this array of planets at birth will produce Matsya yoga. In effect, the native will be an astrologer, be a synonym of kindness, be virtuous, strong, beautiful, famous, learned and pious.

Notes : While our version and that of Chaukambha mention that the ascendant and the 9th be occupied by benefic planets, the versions of Sri Venkateswara Press, Thakur Prasad Pustaka Bhandar and C. G. Rajan stipulate that malefics and not benefics should be in the ascendant and the 9th. **Jakata Parijata** has the same view as given by the latter group requiring malefics in the 9th and in the ascendant.

That it is benefics that should be in the ascendant and the 9th is obviously correct as three groups are selected by Parasaa for this yoga, thus : Benefics in the first group, malefics in the second group and both (i.e. mixed) in the 3rd group.

पुत्रारिमदगाः सौम्याः स्वभोच्चसुहृदंशगाः।
त्रिलाभोदयगाः पापाः कूर्मयोगः स्वभोच्चगाः ॥२३॥

कूर्मयोगे जनो भूपो धीरो धर्मगुणान्वितः ।
कीर्तिमानुपकारी च सुखी मानवनायकः ॥२४॥

23-24. *KOORMA YOGA :* If the 5th, 6th and the 7th are occupied by benefic planets identical with own house or exaltation or friendly sign while malefics are in the 3rd 11th and the ascendant in own house or in exaltation, Koorma yoga is formed. The results of Koorma yoga are : the native will be a king, be courageous, virtuous, famous, helpful, happy and be leader of men.

भाग्येशे धनभावास्थे धनेशे भाग्यभावगे ।
लग्नेशे केन्द्रकोणस्थे खड्गयोगः स कथ्यते ॥२५॥
खड्गयोगे समुत्पन्नो धनभाग्यसुखान्वितः ।
शास्त्रज्ञो बुद्धिवीर्याढ्यः कृतज्ञः कुशलो नरः ॥२६॥

25-26. *KHADGA YOGA :* Should there be an exchange of signs between the lords of the 2nd and the 9th as the ascendant lord is in an angle or in a trine Khadga yoga is obtainable. One with Khadga yoga will be endowed with wealth, fortunes and happiness, be learned in sastras, be intelligent, mighty, grateful and skilful.

केन्द्रे मूलत्रिकोणस्थे भाग्येशे वा स्वभोच्चगे ।
लग्नाधिपे बलाढ्ये च लक्ष्मीयोगः प्रकीर्त्यते ॥२७॥
सुरूपो गुणवान् भूपो बहुपुत्र-धनान्वितः ।
यशस्वी धर्मसम्पन्नो लक्ष्मीयोगे जनो भवेत् ॥२८॥

27-28. *LAKSHMI YOGA :* If the 9th lord is in an angle identical with his Moolatrikona sign or own sign or exaltation sign while the ascendant lord is endowed with strength, Lakshmi yoga occurs. The native with this yoga will be charming, virtuous, kingly in status, endowed with many sons and abundant wealth, be famous and be of high moral merits.

लग्ने स्थिरे भृगौ केन्द्रे, चन्द्रकोणे शुभान्विते ।
मानस्थानगते सौरे योगोऽयं कुसुमाभिधः ॥२९॥
भूपो वा भूपतुल्यो वा दाता भोगी सुखी जनः ।
कुलमुख्यो गुणी विद्वान् जायते कुसुमाह्वये ॥३०॥

29-30 *KUSUMA YOGA :* Venus in an angle, the Moon in a trine along with a benefic and Saturn in the 10th—these planets thus cause Kusuma yoga for one born in a fixed sign ascending. Such a native will be a king or equal to him, be charitable, will enjoy pleasures, be happy, prime among his race men, virtuous and red-lettered

द्वितीये पञ्चमे जीवे बुधशुक्रयुतेक्षिते ।
क्षत्रे तयोर्वा सम्प्राप्ते योगः स च कलानिधिः ॥३१॥
कलानिधिसमुत्पन्नो गुणवान् भूपवन्दितः ।
रोगहीनः सुखी जातो धनविद्यासमन्वितः ॥३२॥

31-32. *KALANIDHI YOGA :* Should Jupiter be in the 2nd or the 5th and be aspected by Mercury and Venus, Kalanidhi yoga is caused. In effect, the native will be virtuous, honoured by the kings, bereft of diseases, be happy, wealthy and learned.

लग्नेश-तद्गतर्क्षेश-तद्गतर्क्षेश-तदंशपाः ।
केन्द्रे कोणे स्वतुङ्गे वा योगः कल्पद्रुमो मतः ॥३३॥
सर्वैश्वर्ययुतो भूपो धर्मात्मा बलसंयुतः ।
युद्धप्रियो दयालुश्च पारिजाते नरो भवेत् ॥३४॥

33-34. *KALPADRUMA YOGA :* Note the following four planets : (a) the ascendant lord, (b) the dispositor of the ascendant lord, (c) the dispositor of the planet at "b", (d) the Navamsa dispositor of the planet at "c". If all these are disposed in angles and trines from the ascendant, or be exalted, Kalpadruma yoga exists. One with this yoga will be endowed with all kinds of wealth, be a king, pious, strong, fond of war and merciful.

Notes : Kalpa Druma yoga is also known as Parijata Yoga. Kalpa Druma denotes the Celestial Tree while Parijata denotes the Celestial Flower. Both of these are known to grant any boon to the possessor who is said to be Devendra, the god of gods.

In the obtainment of yoga, there are four participants. This yoga can be noted in the following chart.

Born on July 23, 1856 at 0612 hrs at 18N32 73E57.

Jup Moon Rahu			Merc Sat
	RASI		Asc Sun Ven
		Mars	Ketu

Rahu	Merc		
Sat	Navamsa		
Asc Moon Jup	Mars		Ven Sun Ketu

Now see how Kalpa Druma yoga is formed in the chart. The constituents of the yoga are :

(a) The ascendant lord Moon.
(b) The ascendant lord's dispositor Jupiter.
(c) Jupiter is in own sign and hence no dispositor.
(d) Jupiter's Navamsa dispositor is Jupiter himself as he is in Sagittarius Navamsa.

All the above are in a trine from the natal ascendant who clearly form Kalpa-druma yoga. The effects mentioned by the sage were obtained by the owner of the chart, Bala Gangadhar Tilak, including fondness for war to get the country freed from foreign rule.

स्वान्त्याष्टस्थैर्द्वितीयेशाद् हरियोगः शुभग्रहैः ।
कामेशाद् बन्धुधर्माष्टस्थितैः सौम्यैर्हराभिधः ॥३५॥
लग्नेशाद् बन्धुकर्मायस्थितैर्ब्रह्माह्वयः स्मृतः ।
एषु जातः सुखी विद्वान् धनपुत्रादिसंयुतः ॥३६॥

35-36. *TRIMURTHI YOGAS :* Counted from the 2nd lord if benefics occupy the 2nd, 12th and 8th, Hari yoga is formed. If the 4th, 9th and 8th with reference to the sign occupied by the 7th lord are occupied by benefics, Hara yoga is obtainable. Brahma yoga is generated if, counted from the ascendant lord, benefics are in the 4th, 10th and 11th signs. One born in anyone of the said three yogas will be happy, learned and endowed with wealth and sons.

Notes : There are actually three different yogas given in the present two verses. These are Hari Yoga, Hara Yoga and Brahma Yoga. This represents the trinity of Hindu Gods and hence is known as Trimurthi yogas jointly. Some interpret this as one yoga knowing it as 'Hariharabrahma yoga' which is however incorrect.

For formation of Hari Yoga the 2nd lord's position is to be noted firstly. From the said position of the 2nd lord, each of the 2nd, 12th and 8th be occupied by benefics individually. See the chart on the next page.

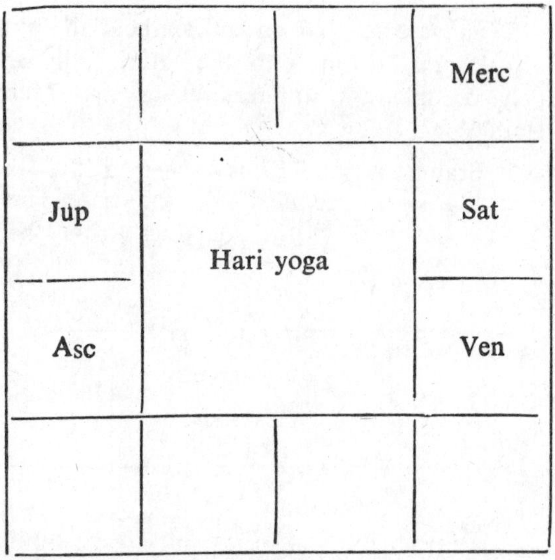

In the above case, the 2nd lord is Saturn. Note from Saturn, the 2nd is occupied by Venus, the 12th by Mercury and the 8th by Jupiter.

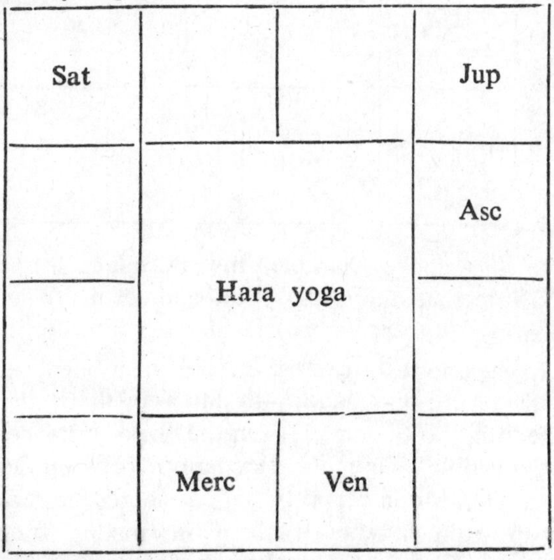

The second yoga is Hara Yoga (Hara denotes lord Siva.) See the chart given above for an easy grasp fulfilling the conditions laid down by Parasara.

In the above case, Saturn rules the 7th house and is placed in Pisces. From him the 4th, 8th and 9th are respectively occupied by Jupiter, Venus and Mercury. Thus forms Hara Yoga.

Lastly Brahma yoga. This is formed if the 4th, 10th and 11th from the sign occupied by the ascendant lord are tenented by benefics. Note this yoga from the following chart.

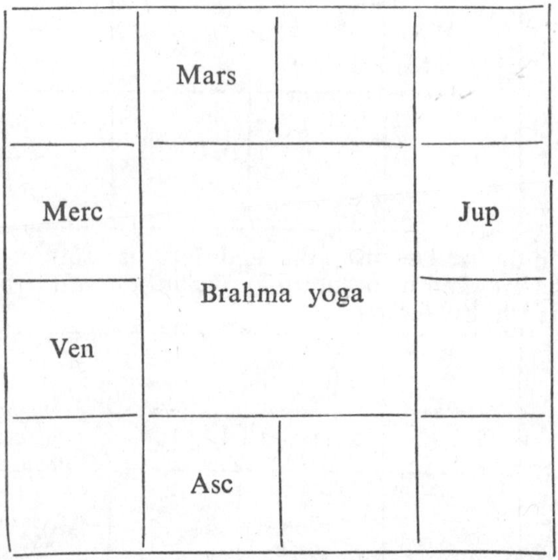

In the above example, the ascendant lord Mars is in Aries. Note that the 4th, 10th and 11th from Mars are occupied by Jupiter, Venus and Mercury in order.

In each yoga, three houses are mentioned, i.e. 2nd, 12th and 8th on the one hand; 4th, 8th and 9th on the other hand and the 4th, 10th and 11th in the third instance. This takes care of possible maximum elongation between Mercury and Venus. The Moon can also be considered in replacement of one of the said benefics if she is in waxing state. The Sun should not participate in these houses just like any malefic. If these Moon is herself a malefic her presence is also excluded in these yogas.

लग्नान्मदाष्टगैः सौम्यैः पापदृग्योगवर्जितैः ।
योगो लग्नाधियोगोऽस्मिन् महात्मा शास्त्रवित् सुखी ॥३७॥

37. *LAGNADHI YOGA :* Should benefics be in the 7th and the 8th counted from the ascendant and be devoid of conjunction/aspect of malefics, Lagnadhi yoga is produced making one a great person, learned in Sastras and happy.

Notes : Sage Parasara does not include the 6th house from the ascendant for Lagnadhi yoga. Only two houses are suggested, viz. the 7th and 8th from the ascendant. This is so given in the versions of Chaukamba, Sri Venkateswara Press, Thakur Prasad Pustaka Bhandara and C G. Rajan as well. The last three versions have an additional condition that the 4th house from the ascendant should at the same time be vacant. In Chandradhi yoga, the sage has included the 6th house, see ch.37 *infra*.

After a study of the various texts, we can conclude to the following effect : The 6th, 7th and 8th be occupied by benefics in any manner, i.e. the three benefics, viz. Jupiter, Mercury and Venus may be disposed in one, two or three houses in 6th, 7th and 8th. No other malefic should be in these houses nor aspect the occupants. The 4th from the ascendant or from the Moon. as the case may be, should remain unoccupied. Then Adhi yoga is obtained. The benefics mentonied should also be free from combustion and debilitation. If the yoga is formed in the above conditions, the native will be highly learned, wealthy and be among the most supreme men on the earth.

The best Adhi yoga is, however, with Mercury in the 6th, Jupiter in the 7th and Venus in the 8th house.

लग्नपे पारिजातस्थे सुखी, वर्गोत्तमे ह्यरुक् ।
गोपुरे धनधान्याढ्या, भूपः सिंहासने स्थिते ॥३८॥
विद्वान् पारावते श्रीमान् देवलोके स-वाहनः ।
ऐरावतस्थिते जातो विख्यातो भूपवन्दितः ॥३९॥

38-39. *EFFECTS OF ASCENDANT LORD'S DIVISIONADIGNITIES :* The ascendant lord in Parijathamsa will make one happy, in Vargothama immune to diseases, in Gopuramsa rich with wealth and grains, in Simhasanamsa a king, in Paravathamsa a scholar, in Devalokamsa opulent and endowed with conveyances, and in Iravatamsa famous and honoured by kings.

Notes : The dignities mentioned above could be found on p. 90 **supra**. Vargothama indicates a planet occupying the same Rasi and the same Navamsa.

अथ चन्द्रयोगाध्यायः ॥३७॥

Chapter 37

Lunar Yogas

सहस्ररश्मितश्चन्द्रे कण्टकादिगते क्रमात् ।
धनधीनैपुणादीनि न्यूनमध्योत्तमानि हि ॥१॥

1. If the Moon with reference to the Sun is in an angle, Panaphara or Apoklima, one's wealth, intelligence and skill will be respectively little, meddling and excellent.

स्वांशे वा स्वाधिमित्रांशे स्थितश्च दिवसे शशी ।
गुरुणा दृश्यते तत्र जातो धनसुखान्वितः ॥२॥
स्वांशे वा स्वाधिमित्रांशे स्थितश्च शशभृन्निशि ।
शुक्रेण दृश्यते तत्र जातो धनसुखान्वितः ॥३॥
एतद्विपर्ययस्थे च शुक्रेज्यानवलोकिते ।
जायतेऽल्पधनो बालो योगेऽस्मिन्निर्धनोऽथवा ॥४॥

2-4. In the case of a day birth if the Moon, placed in own Navamsa or in a friendly Navamsa, is aspected by Jupiter, one will be endowed with wealth and happiness. One born in night time will enjoy similar effects if the Moon is in own Navamsa or in friendly Navamsa in aspect to Venus. In a contrary situation, the aspect of Jupiter or of Venus on the Moon will make one go with little wealth or even without that.

चन्द्राद्रन्ध्रारिकामस्थैः सौम्यैः स्याधियोगकः ।
तत्र राजा च मन्त्री च सेनाधीशश्च बलक्रमात् ॥५॥

5. *ADHI YOGA FROM THE MOON :* If benefics occupy the 8th, 6th and 7th counted from the Moon, Adhi yoga obtains. According to the strength of the participating planets, the native concerned will be either a king or a minister or an army chief.

चन्द्राद् वृद्धिगतैः सर्वैः शुभैर्जातो महाधनी ।
द्वाभ्यां मध्यधनो जात एकेनाऽल्पधनो भवेत् ॥६॥

6. *DHANA YOGA :* Should all the (three) benefics be in Upachaya (i.e. 3rd, 6th, 10th and 11th) counted from the Moon, one will be very affluent; with two benefics so placed he will have medium effects in regard to wealth. If a single benefic is there, the wealth will be negligible.

चन्द्रात् स्वान्त्योभयस्थे हि ग्रहे सूर्यं बिना क्रमात् ।
सुनफाख्तोऽनफाख्यश्च योगो दुरधराह्वयः ॥७॥
राजा वा राजतुल्यो वा धीधनख्यातिमाञ्जनः ।
स्वभुजार्जितवित्तश्च सुनफायोगसम्भवः ॥८॥
भूपोऽगदशरीरश्च शीलवान् ख्यातकीर्तिमान् ।
सुरूपश्चाऽनफाजातो सुखैः सर्वैः समन्वितः ॥९॥
उत्पन्नसुखभुग् दाता धनवाहन-संयुतः ।
सद्भृत्यो जायते नूनं जनो दुरधराभवः ॥१०॥

7-10. *SUNAPHA, ANAPHA AND DURADHARA :* If there is a planet, other than the Sun, in the 2nd from the Moon Sunapha yoga, in the 12th Anapha yoga and planets in both places Duradhara yoga are caused. One with Sunapha yoga will be a king or equal to a king. endowed with intelligence, wealth, fame and self earned wealth. One born in Anapha yoga will be a king, be free from diseases, virtuous, famous charming and happy. One born in Duradhara yoga will enjoy pleasures, be charitable and endowed with wealth, conveyances and excellent serving force.

चन्द्रादाद्यधनाऽन्त्यस्थो विना भानुं न चेद्ग्रहः।
कश्चित् स्याद्वा विना चन्द्रं लग्नात् केन्द्रगतोऽथ वा ॥११॥
योगः केमद्रुमो नाम तत्र जातोऽतिगर्हितः।
बुद्धिविद्याविहीनश्च दरिद्रापत्तिसंयुतः ॥१२॥
अन्ययोगफलं हन्ति चन्द्रयोगो विशेषतः।
स्वफलं प्रददातीति बुधो यत्नाद् विचिन्तयेत् ॥१३॥

11-13. *KEMADRUMA YOGA :* Excluding the Sun, should there be no planet with the Moon or in the 2nd/12th from the Moon or in an angle from the ascendant, Kemadruma yoga is formed. One born in Kemadruma yoga will be very much reproached, be bereft of intelligence and learning and reduced to penury and perils.

अथ रवियोगाध्यायः ॥३८॥

Chapter 38

Solar Yogas

सूर्यात् स्वान्त्योभयस्थैश्च विना चन्द्रं कुजादिभिः।
वेशि-वोशिसमाख्यौ च तथोभयचरः क्रमात् ॥१॥

1. *VESI, VOSI AND UBHAYACHARI YOGAS :* Barring the Moon, if a planet among Mars etc. be in the 2nd from the Sun Vesi yoga, in the 12th Vosi yoga and planets in both the 2nd and the 12th Ubhayachari yoga are caused.

समदृक् सत्यवाङ् मर्त्यो दीर्घकायोऽलसस्तथा।
सुखभागल्पवित्तोऽपि वेशियोगसमुद्भवः ॥२॥
वोशी च निपुणो दाता यशोविद्याबलावन्तिः।
तथोभयचरे जातो भूपो वा तत्समः सुखी ॥३॥

2-3. *EFFECTS OF THESE YOGAS :* One born in Vesi yoga will be even sighted, truthful, long-bodied, indolent, happy and endowed with negligible wealth. One born with Vosi yoga will be skilful, charitable and endowed with fame, learning and strength. The Ubhayachari native will be a king or equal to a king and be happy.

शुभग्रहभवे योगे फलमेवं विचिन्तयेत् ।
पापग्रहसमुत्पन्ने योगे तु फलमन्यथा ॥४॥

4. Benefics causing these yogas will give the above mentioned effects while malefics will produce contrary effects.

अथ राजयोगाध्यायः ॥३९॥

Chapter 39
Raja Yogas

अथाऽतः सम्प्रवक्ष्यामि राजयोगान् द्विजोत्तम ! ।
येषां विज्ञानमात्रेण राजपूज्यो जनो भवेत् ॥१॥
ये योगाः शम्भुना प्रोक्ताः पुरा शैलसुताग्रतः ।
तेषां सारमहं वक्ष्ये तवाग्रे द्विजनन्दन ! ॥२॥

1-2. O excellent of the Brahmins, I now narrate below the Rajayogas making one entitled to royal honours. These were told to Parvati by Lord Siva once upon a time, the gist of which is as follows :

चिन्तयेत् कारकांशे वा जनुर्लग्नेऽथवा द्विज ! ।
राजयोगकरौ द्वौ द्वौ स्फुटौ खेटौ प्रयत्नतः ॥३॥
आत्मकारकपुत्राभ्यां योगमेकं प्रकल्पयेत् ।
तनुपञ्चमनाथाभ्यां तथैव द्विजसत्तम ! ॥४॥
लग्नपुत्रेशयोरात्मपुत्रकारकयोर्द्वयोः ।
सम्बन्धात् पूर्णमर्धं वा पादं वीर्यानुसारतः ॥५॥

3-5 These yogas are to be known from the Karakamsa ascendant and the natal ascendant. On the one hand the pair of Atmakaraka and Putrakaraka and on the other hand the natal ascendant lord and the 5th lord be considered. The effects due to such association will be full, or a half or a quarter according to their strengths.

Notes : Raja Yogas giving status can be formed with Karakamsa Lagna as the reckoning point. Similarly the natal ascendant is also another center wherefrom such yogas emanate. (Karakamsa Lagna is the Navamsa occupied by the Atma Karaka planet.)

If Karakamsa ascendant is oeing considered in evaluation of Raja yogas, the status of Putra Karaka is also to be taken into account. Here Putra Karaka is Chara Karaka. He is the 6th in status in the Atma Karaka scheme, as explained in slokas 13-17 of ch. 32 supra. On the other hand if natal ascendant is being considered the 5th lord from natal ascendant should also be scrutinized in terms of dignity, so that the real clues to the yoga are made out rightly. The 5th lord has been given a very important position in the analysis of Raja Yogas by the sage equating him with the 9th lord or even more, vide slokas 33 and 34 of the current chapter.

We shall now take an expanded clue of the two hints given in the present verses about the evaluation of Raja yogas.

There are certain Raja Yogas formed with reference to Karakamsa ascendant, Atma Karaka's position in the Rasi chart, Amatya Karaka, Upapada, Arudha pada etc.—so to say in the Jaimini style—as can be seen in our present text. For example take the rule given in sloka 22 of the current chapter where it is stated that Atma Karaka in benefic's Rasi or Navamsa will make one wealthy. In the chart given in ch. 29 (sloka 1-3), we have Atma Karaka Moon in Jupiter's Navamsa. So as per the rule the native should become rich. To strengthen this argument, we find Jupiter in exaltation. Putra Karaka (Chara scheme) for the said horoscope in the Sun. He aspects the ascendant. In the Navamsa chart, the Sun is placed in the 4th from Atma Karaka. All these indicate that the native should be wealthy. If Putra Karaka (Chara) and Karakamsa Lagna are not well related, the yogas related to that scheme will be futile.

Next take the natal ascendant lord and the 5th lord from the natal ascendant. In assessing the Raja yogas strength ralated to the natal ascendant, the strength and relationship between these two lords should be correctly understood. In the example chart cited above, the 5th lord is Jupiter who is exalted and is endowed with a Shadbala of 9.32 Rupas and Mars 7.32 Rupas. Their Vimsopaka strengths are respectively 16.45 and 16.80 points making them extremely well disposed to cause vigour to anyRaja yoga in the horoscope.

Hence it is apparent that the sage correlates the Chara Putra Karaka with the Karakamsa ascendant (or Atmakaraka) and the 5th lord from natal ascendant with the lord of the natal ascendant itself.

लग्नेशे पञ्चमे भावे पञ्चमेशे च लग्ने ।
पुत्रात्मकारकौ विप्र ! लग्ने च पञ्चमे स्थित ॥६॥
स्वोच्चे स्वांशे स्वभे वाऽपि शुभग्रहनिरीक्षितो ।
महाराजाख्ययोगोऽत्र जातः ख्यातः सुखान्वितः ॥७॥

6-7 *MAHA RAJA YOGA* : Should the ascendant lord and the 5th lord exchange their signs or if Atma karaka and Putra Karaka (Chara) are in the ascendant, the 5th, exaltation sign, own sign or own Navamsa in aspect to a benefic, Maha Raja yoga is produced. The native so born will be famous and happy.

Notes : An exchange between the ascendant lord and the 5th lord will bestow a supreme Raja yoga on the native. For example in the case of a Pisces-born, Jupiter in the 5th and the Moon in the ascendant.

In the second stage, the Atma Karaka and Putra Karaka (Chara) are brought in the picture. They can be jointly in the 5th or in the ascendant (or in Karakamsa Lagna and the 5th from there) or separately in these places. Alternatively, both of them should be in their respective exaltation signs, or in own signs, or in own Navamsas and be related to a benefic by aspect. In this respect, the horoscope of Mrs Gandhi will serve us with a perfect example. Her chart can be found with reference to sloka 50 in ch. 24 supra. The Atma Karaka is Saturn (21° 50') while Putra Karaka is Mercury

(13° 11′). It may be noted that Saturn is in the ascendant while Mercury is in the 5th lifting the native to Himalayan heights through the said Maha Raja yoga. Atma Karaka Saturn is in his own Navamsa and Merury is in the 10th from Karakamsa Lagna.

भाग्येशः कारको लग्ने पञ्चमे सप्तमेऽपि वा ।
राजयोगप्रदातारौ शुभखेटयुतेक्षितौ ॥८॥

8. If the ascendant lord and Atmakaraka are in the ascendant, 5th or 7th in conjunction with or in aspect to a benefic, there obtains a Raja yoga.

Notes : If the ascendant lord himself becomes the Atma Karaka his merc placement in the ascendant itself or in the 5th/7th from the ascendant in association with a benefic will cause a similar Raja yoga. In the case of Mrs Gandhi, the Atma Karaka is in the ascendant while the ascendant lord Moon is in exchange with him in the 7th. The Moon is favourably aspected by yoga karaka Jupiter from the 11th house speaking for the native's high and successful political career.

लग्नेशात् कारकाच्चापि धने तुर्ये च पञ्चमे ।
शुभखेटयुते भावे जातो राजा भवेद् ध्रुवम् ॥९॥
तृतीये षष्ठभे ताभ्यां पापग्रहयुतेक्षिते ।
जातो राजा भवेदेवं मिश्रे मिश्रफलं वदेत् ॥१०॥

9-10. Should there be benefics in the 2nd, 4th and 5th counted either from the ascendant lord or from Atmakaraka sign, one will become a king. Similarly malefics in the 3rd and 6th from the said places.

स्वांशे वा पञ्चमे शुक्रे जीवेन्दुयुतवीक्षिते ।
लग्ने लग्नपदे वाऽपि राजवर्गो भवेन्नरः ॥११॥

11. One will be related to royal circles if Venus is in the karakamsa, or in the 5th therefrom or in the ascendant or in Arudha ascendant in aspect to or in the company of Jupiter or the Moon.

Notes : The planet Venus should be in one of the four places, viz. Karakamsa ascedant, Arudha ascendant, natal ascendant and in the 5th from Karakamsa ascendant. (Arudha ascendant is also known as Arudha Pada, vide ch. 29 supra.) Being placed so, Venus must be related to the Moon or Jupiter by aspect/association.

Taking the example chart given in ch. 29, we find Venus is in the Karakamsa ascendant along with the Moon (the Atma Karaka). The native is thus related to people with high social status through his professional sphere.

जन्माङ्गे कालहोराङ्गे कलाङ्गे येन केनचित् ।
एकग्रहेण सन्दृष्टे त्रितये राजभाग् जनः ॥१२॥

12. Even if a single planet aspects the natal ascendant or Hora Lagna or Ghatika Lagna, the native will become a king.

Notes : Hora Lagna and Ghatika Lagna are narrated on page 63 **supra**. If a planet aspects one of the three ascendants, viz. natal ascendant, Hora Lagna and Ghatika Lagna, in becomes a Karaka planet or significator giving status etc. to the native.

लग्नषड्वर्गके चैवमेकखेटयुतेक्षिते ।
राजयोगो भवत्येव निर्विशंक द्विजोत्तम ! ॥१३॥
पूर्णदृष्टे पूर्णयोगमर्धदृष्टेऽर्धमेव च ।
पाददृष्टे पादयोगमिति ज्ञेयं क्रमात् फलम् ॥१४॥

13-14. If the six divisions (shadvargas) of the ascendanc is occupied or aspected by one and the same planet, a Raja"yoga is doubtlessly formed. Accordinz to the aspect is full, half or one fourth, results will be in order full, medium and negligible.

Notes : Rasi, Hora, Drekkana, Trimsamsa, Navamsa and Dvadasamsa constitute Shadvarga or six divisions. If a planet occupies the ascendant in all these 6 charts it causes a powerful Raja yaga. Aspects are referred to in the divisional charts here. I am unable to fully conceive the logic in aspects in divisional charts for the sage himself referred to longitudinal aspectual evaluations in an earlier chapter. Without commenting further on this controversial aspect I leave it at that, accepting my limitations to explain this fully.

लग्नत्रये स्वभोच्चस्थे खेटे राजा भवेद् ध्रुवम् ।
यद्वा लग्ने दृकाणेंऽशे स्वोच्चखेटयुते द्विज ! ॥१५॥

15. If the 3 ascendants (i.e. natal ascendant, Hora Lagna and Ghatika Lagna) are occupied by planets in exaltation/own sign or if the natal ascendant, Drekkana ascendant and Navamsa ascendant have exalted planets, Raja yoga is formed.

पदे शुभ स-चंद्रे च धने देवगुरौ तथा ।
स्वोच्चस्थखेटसन्दृष्टे राजयोगो न संशयः ॥१६॥

16. If the Moon and a benefic are in the Arudha Lagna, as Jupiter is in the 2nd from natal ascendant and both the places are aspected by planets in exaltation or in own sign, there will be a Raja yoga.

शुभे लग्ने शुभे त्वर्थे तृतीये पापखेचरे ।
चतुर्थे च शुभे प्राप्ते राजा वा तत्समोऽपि वा ॥१७॥

17. If the ascendant, 2nd and 4th are occupied by benefics while a malefic is in the 3rd, one will become a king or equal to a king.

स्वोच्चस्थो हरिणांको वा जीवो वा शुक्र एव वा ।
बुधो वा धनभावस्थः श्रियं दिशति देहिनः ॥१८॥

18. The native will be wealthy if one among the Moon, Jupiter, Venus and Mercury is exalted in the 2nd house.

षष्ठेऽष्टमे तृतीये वा स्व-स्वनीचगता ग्रहाः ।
लग्नं पश्येत् स्वभोच्चस्थो लग्नपो राज्ययोगदः ॥१९॥

19. If the 6th, 8th and the 3rd are occupied by debilitated planets as the ascendant lord is exalted or is in (his other) own house and aspects the ascendant, there is a Raja yoga.

षष्ठाऽष्टमव्ययाधीशा नीचस्था रिपुभेऽस्तगाः ।
स्वोच्चस्वभगलग्नेशो लग्नं पश्यंश्च राज्यदः ॥२०॥

20. Again a Raja yoga is formed if the 6th, 8th and 12th lords are in fall or in inimical signs or in combustion as the ascendant lord placed in his (other) own sign or in exaltation sign aspects the ascendant.

स्वोच्चस्वभस्थराज्येशो लग्नं पश्यंश्च राज्यदः।
शुभाः केन्द्रस्थिता वाऽपि राज्यदः नाऽत्र संशयः ॥२१॥

21. If the 10th lord, placed in his own house or in exaltation, aspects the ascendant, a Raja yoga is formed. Similar is the case if benefics are in angles.

शुभराशौ शुभांशे च कारको धनवान् भवेत्।
तदंशकेन्द्रेषु शुभे नूनं राजा प्रजायते ॥२२॥

22. If the Atmakaraka is in a benefic's Rasi/Navamsa, the native will be wealthy. If there are benefics in angels from Karakamsa Lagna, he will become a king.

लग्नारूढं दारपदं मिथः केन्द्र स्थितं यदि।
त्रिलाभे वा त्रिकोणे वा तदा राजा न संशयः ॥२३॥

23. If the Arudha Lagna and Darapada are in mutual angles or in mutual 3rd/11th or in mutual trines, the native will doubtlessly become a king.

Notes : Arudha Lagna is the Pada for the natal ascendant while Dara Pada is the Pada for the 7th house. (Chapter 29 may be referred in the context of such calculations.)

These two Padas should mutually be well placed, i.e. in mutual angles, mutual trines or mutually 3rd and 11th so that the native will enjoy a royal status.

Should these two Padas be in mutually 6th and 8th signs or 2nd and 12th signs, one will suffer from poverty not receiving the effects of the Raja yogas in the horoscope. The good relationship between Arudha Pada and Dara Pada is one of the essential pre-requisites for maturity of Raja Yogas.

भावहोराघटीसंज्ञलग्नानि च प्रपश्यति।
स्वोच्चग्रहो राजयोगो लग्नद्वयमथापि वा ॥२४॥

24. If two or all of Bhava Lagna, Hora Lagna, Ghatika Lagna are in aspect to exalted planets, a Raja yoga is formed.

राशेर्द्रेष्काणतोंऽशाच्च राशेरंशादथापि वा।
यद्वा राशिदृकाणाभ्यां लग्नद्रष्टा तु योगदः ॥२५॥

25. If the said 3 ascendants, their decanates and Navamas or the said ascendants and their Navamsas or the said ascendants and their decanates are aspected by a planet, a Raja yoga is formed.

पदे स्वोच्चखगाक्रान्ते चन्द्राक्रान्ते विशेषतः।
क्रान्ते च गुरु-शुक्राभ्यां केनाप्युच्चग्रहेण वा ॥२६॥
दुष्टार्गलग्रहाभावे राजयोगो न संशयः।
शुभारूढ़े तत्र चन्द्रे धने देवगुरौ तथा ॥२७॥

26-27. If Arudha Pada is occupied by an exalted planet particularly the Moon in exaltation or by Jupiter/Venus (with or without exaltation) while there is no Argala by a malefic, the native will become a king. If the Arudha Pada is a benefic sign containing the Moon while Jupiter is in the 2nd house, the same effect will prevail.

दुःस्थानेशोऽपि नीचस्थो यदि लग्नं प्रपश्यति।
तदाऽपि राजयोगः स्यादिति ज्ञेयं द्विजोत्तम! ॥२८॥

28. Even if one among the 6th, 8th and 12th lords being in debilitation aspects the ascendant there will be a Raja yoga.

चतुर्थदशमार्थाय-पतिदृष्टे विलग्नभे।
पदाल्लाभे तु शुक्रेण दृष्टेऽप्यारूढभे शुभे ॥२९॥
राजा वा तत्समो वापि जातको जायते ध्रुवम्।
षष्ठाष्टमगते नीचे लग्नं पश्यति वा तथा ॥३०॥
तृतीयलाभगे नीचे लग्नं पश्यति वा तथा।
लग्नांशकेन्द्रेषु शुभे निग्रहानुग्रहक्षमः ॥३१॥

29-31. The native will become a king if a planet ruling the 4th, 10th, 2nd or the 11th aspects the ascendant, while Venus aspects the 11th from Arudha Lagna as Arudha Lagna is occupied by a benefic. The same effect will be obtained if a debilitated planet aspects the ascendant and is placed in the 6th or the 8th.

Again similar result will prevail if a debilitated planet placed in the 3rd/11th lends aspect to the ascendant.

अथाऽहं सम्प्रवक्ष्यामि राजयोगादिकं परम् ।
ग्रहाणां स्थानभेदेन दृष्टियोगवशात् फलम् ॥३२॥

32. I now tell you of the Raja yogas based on the planets with different dignities and on the aspects and conjunctions of the planets.

तपःस्थानाधिपो मन्त्री मन्त्राधीशो विशेषतः ।
उभावन्योन्यसंदृष्टौ जातश्चेदिह राज्यभाक् ॥३३॥
यत्र कुत्रापि संयुक्तौ तौ वापि समसप्तमौ ।
राजवंशभवो बालो राजा भवति निश्चितम् ॥३४॥

33-34. The 9th lord is akin to a minister, and more especially the 5th lord. If these two planets mutually aspect, the native will obtain a kingdom. Even if these two are conjunct in any house or if be in mutually 7th places, one born of royal scion will become a king

वाहनेशस्तथा माने मानेशो वाहने स्थितः ।
बुद्धिधर्माधिपाभ्यां तु दृष्टश्चेदिह राज्यभाक् ॥३५॥

35. The native will attain kingdom if the 4th lord is in the 10th and the 10th lord is in the 4th and be in aspect to 5th and 9th lords.

सुतकर्म-सुहृल्लग्ननाथा धर्मपसंयुताः ।
यस्य जन्मनि भूपोऽसौ कीर्त्या ख्यातो दिगन्तरे ॥३६॥

36. If the lords of the 5th, 10th, 4th and the ascendant join in the 9th, one will become a ruler with fame spreading over the four directions

सुखकर्माधिपौ वापि मन्त्रिनाथेन संयुतौ ।
धर्मनाथेन वा युक्तौ जातश्चेदिह राज्यभाक् ॥३७॥

37. Should the lord of the 4th or of the 10th join either the 5th lord or the 9th lord, the native will obtain kingdom.

Notes : There are four Raja yogas mentioned in the above verse which can be understood as under :

(1) 4th lord joining the 5th lord.
(2) 4th lord joining the 9th lord.
(3) 10th lord joining the 9th lord.
(4) 10th lord joining the 5 lord.

It will be still superior if the 4th lord joins both the 5th lord and the 9th lord, or if the 10th lord joins the 5th and 9th lord. It may be noted that this is a yoga caused by an angular lord joinig a trinal lord.

सुतेशे धर्मनाथेन युते लग्नेश्वरेण वा ।
लग्ने सुखेऽथवा माने स्थिते जातो नृपो भवेत् ॥३८॥

38. If the 5th lord is in the ascendant, 4th or the 10th in the company of the 9th lord or of the ascendant lord, the native will become a king.

धर्मस्थाने स्थिते जीवे स्वगृहे भृगुसंयुते ।
पंचमाधिपयुक्ते वा जातश्चेदिह राजभाक् ॥३९॥

39. Should Jupiter be in his own sign identical with the 9th house and be in the company of either Venus or of the 5th lord, the native will obtain kinghood.

दिनार्धाच्च निशार्धाच्च परं सार्धद्विनाडिका ।
शुभा वेला तदुत्पन्नो राजा स्यात्तत्समोऽपि वा ॥४०॥

40. Two and half ghatis (i.e. 60 minutes of time) from mid-day or from mid-night is auspicious time. A birth during such an auspicious time will cause one to be a king or equal to him.

Notes : Though mid-day and mid-night are denoted in the translation for **Dinardha** and **Nisardha** a clarification is essential in regard to the implications of these. Mid-day simply denotes 12 Noon while mid-night zero hour as per common use. But what the sage implies is somewhat different. **Dinardha** means half of the day while Nisardha means half of the night, keeping in mind the Sun rise and Sun set at a given place. The verse has a yoga to indicate that if there is a birth within an hour of the said Dinardha or Nisardha, the native will be a king. I shall illustrate this with a practical case.

Take for instance a birth on 15th February 1947 at Jodhpur 73 E 2 and 26 N 18. The local sun rise is at 0638 hrs and sun set at 1749 hrs. Hence for this latitude and date, the day duration is 11h 11m and night duration 12h 49m. Divide the day duration by two to get Dinardha which indicates 5h 35m. Similarly dividing night duration by 2 we get Nisardha as 6h 24m. Add 5h 35m to Sun rise which will give half the day duration. Thus by adding 5h 35m to 6h 38m, we get 12h 13m. Similarly in the case of night, the night duration of 12h 49m be halved and the figure arrived at is to be added to sun set. Thus we get Oh 13m (i.e. 13 m later than the usual mid-night).

From the above we may understand that by simply taking 12 noon as mid-day and 0 hour as mid-night it will not serve our purpose in the context of the yoga suggested by the sage. Needless to mention that LMT is to be used for these calculations.

Uttara Kalamrita has two yogas in this respect, viz. Koteeswara yoga and Lakshadhikari yoga (vide ch 4, sloka 30). According to its author if there be a birth within 2 ghatikas (i.e. 48 minutes as against Parasara's mention of 60 minutes) of Dinardha and Nisardha, a king is born who will conquer his enemies and observe religious rules of conduct and be learned. He further adds that if in the said case an exalted planet is in the 2nd house, in aspect to another exalted planet, a Koteeswara is born. If the aspectig planet is in its own house (instead of being in exaltation) the native will then be only a Lakshadheewara. Suffice it to say that there will be relatively less riches in the second case.

चन्द्रः कविं कविश्चन्द्रमन्योऽन्यं त्रिभवस्थितः ।
मिथः पश्यति वा क्वापि राजयोग उदाहृतः ॥४१॥

41. Should the Moon and Venus be mutually in the 3rd and 11th and be in aspects, placed elsewhere, a Raja yoga is obtained.

Notes : As per the sloka in question, we find two conditions under which two Raja yogas form. In the first instance the Moon and Venus should be in mutually 3 and 11.

In the second instance, the Moon and Venus can be anywhere but should mutually aspect. This type of yoga is found in many standard texts.

चन्द्रे वर्गोत्तमांशस्थे सबले चतुरादिभिः।
ग्रहैर्दृष्टे च यो जातः स राजा भवति ध्रुवम् ॥४२॥

42. Should the Moon, endowed with strength, be in Vargothamsa and be aspected by four or more planets, the native will become a king.

उत्तमांशगते लग्ने चन्द्रान्यैश्चतुरादिभिः।
ग्रहैर्दृष्टेऽपि यो जातः सोऽपि भूमिपतिर्भवेत् ॥४३॥

43. One will become a king if the ascendant in Uttamamsa is aspected by four or more planets out of which the Moon should not be one.

त्र्यल्पैरुच्चस्थितैः खेटै राजा राजकुलोद्भवः।
अन्यवंशभवस्तत्र राजतुल्यो धनैर्युतः ॥४४॥

44. If one or two or three planets be in exaltation one of a royal scion will become a king while another will be equal to a king or be wealthy.

चतुर्भिः पञ्चभिर्वाऽपि खेटैः स्वोच्चत्रिकोणगैः।
हीनवंशभवश्चापि राजा भवति निश्चितः ॥४५॥

45. If 4 or 5 planets occupy their exaltation signs or Moolatrikona signs, even a person of base-birth will become a king.

षड्भिरुच्चगतैः खेटैश्चक्रवर्तित्वमाप्नुयात्।
एवं बहुविधा राज-योगा ज्ञेया द्विजोत्तम! ॥४६॥

46. If 6 planets are exalted, the native will become an emperor and will enjoy various kinds of royal paraphernalia.

एको गुरुर्भृगुर्वापि बुधो वा स्वोच्चसंस्थितः।
शुभग्रहयुते केन्द्रे राजा वा तत्समो भवेत् ॥४७॥

47. Even if one among Jupiter, Venus and Mercury is in

exaltation while a benefic is in an angle the native will become a king or be equal to him.

केन्द्रे स्थितैः शुभैः सर्वैः पापैश्च त्रिषडायगैः ।
हीनवंशोऽपि यो जातः स राजा भवति ध्रुवम् ॥४८॥

48. If all benefics are relegated to angles while malefics are in the 3rd, 6th and 11th, the native, though may be of mean descent will ascend, the throne.

अथ राजसम्बन्धयोगाध्यायः ॥४०॥

Chapter 40

Yogas For Royal Association

राज्यनाथे जनुर्लग्नादमात्येशयुतेक्षिते ।
अमात्यकारकेणापि प्रधानत्वं नृपालये ॥१॥

1. If the 10th lord from the ascendant is conjunct or aspected by the dispositor of Amatyakaraka or even conjunct or aspected by Amatya karaka himself, the native will be a chief in the king's court.

Notes : Amatya karaka is the immediate successor of Atma karaka as we have seen earlier. The lord of the sign occupied by Amatya Karaka should aspect or join the 10th lord counted from the ascendant; the native will then enjoy a high governmental position. The Amatya karaka taking the role of his dispositor in the above case will as well yield similar effects.

The yogas given in the chapter should be related to one's serving the government in various capacities depending on other combinations in his horosope.

लाभेशवीक्षिते लाभे पापदृग्योगवर्जिते ।
राज्यभावे तदा विप्र ! प्रधानत्वं नृपालये ॥२॥

2. If the 10th and 11th are devoid of malefic occupation/ aspect while the 11th is aspected by its own lord, the native will be a chief in the king's court.

Notes : This verse is open to another interpretation thus : the 11th be devoid of malefic aspect/occupation and be aspected by own lord while the 10th house should also be aspected by its lord and the 10th is also disposed in the same manner. That is, the 10th house should also be aspected by its lord and should be free from malefic aspect/occupation.

अमात्यकारकेणापि कारकेन्द्रेण संयुते।
तीव्रबुद्धियुतो बालो राजमन्त्री भवेद ध्रुवम् ॥३॥

3. Should Amatya karaka and the dispositor Atma karaka be together the native will be endowed with great intelligence and be a king's minister.

Notes : Karakendra is interpreted here as the dispositor of Atma karaka. Similarly Amatyesa means the dispositor of Amatya karaka.

अमात्यकारके विप्र ! सबले शुभसंयुते।
स्वक्षेत्रेस्वोच्चगे वापि राजमन्त्री भवेद् ध्रुवम् ॥४॥

4. If Amatya karaka is strong and be with a benefic or if Amatya karaka is in own house or in exaltation, one will surely becomea king's minister.

अमात्यकारके लग्ने पञ्चमे नवमेऽपि वा।
राजमन्त्री भवेद् बालो विख्यातो नाऽत्रसंशयः ॥५॥

5. There is no doubt in one's becoming a king's minister and famous if Amatya karaka is in the ascendant or the 5th or the 9th.

आत्मकारकतः केन्द्रे कोणे वाऽमात्यकारके।
तदा राजकृपायुवतो जातो राजाश्रितः सुखी ॥६॥

6. If Amatya karaka or Amatya karaka be in an angle or in a trine from the ascendant the native will beget royal mercy, royal patronage and happiness thereof.

कारकाच्च तथारूढात् लग्नाच्च द्विजसत्तम ! ।
तृतीये षष्ठभे पापैः सेनाधीशः प्रजायते ॥७॥

7. Should malefics be in the 3rd and 6th from Atma karaka or Arudha Lagna or the natal ascendant, one will become an army chief.

कारके केन्द्रे कोणेषु स्वतुङ्गे वा स्वभे स्थिते ।
भाग्यपेन युते दृष्टे राजमन्त्री भवेद् ध्रुवम् ॥८॥

8. If Atma karaka is in an angle or in a trine or in exaltation or in own house and be in aspect to the 9th lord, the native will be a king's minister.

कारके जन्मराशीशे लग्नगे शुभसंयुते ।
मन्त्रित्वे मुख्ययोगोऽयं वार्धकेनाऽत्र संशयः ॥९॥

9. Should the Moon sign lord become Atma karaka and be in the natal ascendant along with a benefic, the native will become a king's minister at his advanced age.

कारके शुभसंयुक्ते पञ्चमे सप्तमेऽपि वा ।
दशमे नवमे वाऽपि धनं राजाश्रयाद् भवेत् ॥१०॥

10. Should the Atmakaraka be in the 5th, 7th, 10th or the 9th and be with a benefic, one will earn wealth through royal patronage.

भाग्यभावपदे लग्ने कारके नवमेऽपि वा ।
राजसम्बन्धयोगोऽयं निर्विशंकं द्विजोत्तम ! ॥११॥

11. If the Arudha of the 9th house be itself the natal ascendant or if Atma karaka be in the 9th house the native will be associated with royal circles.

लाभेशे लाभभावस्थे पापदृष्टिविवर्जिते ।
कारके शुभसंयुक्ते लाभस्तस्य नृपालयात् ॥१२॥

12. One will gain through royal association if the 11th house is occupied by its own lord but be devoid of malefic aspect. The Atma karaka should at the same time be conjunct a benefic.

लग्नेशे राज्यभावस्थे राज्येशे लग्नसंस्थिते।
प्रबलो राजसम्बन्ध-योगोऽयं परिकीर्तितः ॥१३॥

13. An exchange of signs between the 10th lord and the ascendant lord will make the native associated with the king in a great manner.

कारकात् तुर्यभावस्थौ सितेन्दू द्विजसत्तम!।
यस्य जन्मनि जातोऽयं राजचिह्नेन संयुतः ॥१४॥

14. If Venus and the Moon are in the 4th from Karakamsa Lagna, the native will be endowed with royal insignia.

लग्नेशे कारके वाऽपि पञ्चमेशेन संयुते।
केन्द्रे कोणे स्थिते तस्मिन् राजमित्रं भवेन्नरः ॥१५॥

15. Should the ascendant lord or the Atma karaka be conjunct the 5th lord and be in an angle or in a trine, the native will be a king's minister.

अथ विशेषधनयोगाऽध्यायः ॥४१॥

Chapter 41

Combinations For Wealth

अथाऽतः संप्रवक्ष्यामि धनयोगं विशेषतः।
यस्मिन् योगे समुत्पन्नो निश्चितो धनवान् भवेत् ॥१॥

1. I now tell you of special combinations giving wealth. One born in these yogas will surely become wealthy.

पंचमे भृगुजक्षेत्रे तस्मिन् शुक्रेण संयुते।
लाभे भौमेन संयुवते बहुद्रव्यस्य नायकः ॥२॥

2. *YOGAS FOR GREAT AFFLUENCE (upto sloka 8)* : Should a sign of Venus be the 5th house and be occupied by Venus himself while Mars is in the 11th house, the native will obtain great riches.

Notes : This yoga applies to Capricorn and Gemini ascendants alone. For Capricorn ascendant, Venus will be in the 5th in own house while Mars will be in the 11th in own house. Similarly for Gemini ascendant. So to say for these two ascendants, the 5th and 11th lords in own houses will confer abundant riches.

पंचमे तु बुधक्षेत्रे तस्मिन् बुधयुते सति।
चन्द्रे भौमे गुरौ लाभे बहुद्रव्यस्य नायकः ॥३॥

3. Should a sign of Mercury be the 5th house and be occupied by Mercury himself as the 11th house is occupied by the Moon, Mars and Jupiter, the native will be very affluent.

Notes : This yoga applies to Aquarius ascendant and Taurus ascendant for which Mercury will be in the 5th in own house. It is quitc superior for Taurus ascendant keeping Aquarius native in the next place. In both cases, Jupiter ruling the 11th will be in own house along with his friends—the Moon and Mars.

पंचमे च रविक्षेत्रे तस्मिन् रवियुते सति।
लाभे शनीन्दुजीवाढ्ये बहुद्रव्यस्य नायकः ॥४॥

4. Should Leo be the 5th house and be occupied by the Sun himself as Saturn, the Moon and Jupiter are in the 11th, the native will be very affluent.

Notes *:* Here features Aries ascendant having the Sun in the 5th in Leo and Saturn, Jupiter and the Moon in the 11th in Aquarius. Please note Saturn occupies the 11th as its owner.

पंचमे तु शनिक्षेत्रे तस्मिन् शनियुते सति।
लाभे रवीन्दुसंयुक्ते बहुद्रव्यस्य नायकः ॥५॥

5. Should the Sun and Moon be in the 11th as Saturn is in the 5th identical with his own house, the native will be very affluent.

Notes : Saturn will be in the 5th in Capricorn for a Virgo native, and in Aquarius for a Libra native. The Sun and the Moon are required to be in the 11th. While being so, Cancer or Leo will be the 11th house as the case may be.

पंचमे तु गुरुक्षेत्रे तस्मिन् गुरुयुते सति।
लाभे चन्द्रसुते जातो बहुद्रव्यस्य नायकः ॥६॥

6. Should Jupiter be in the 5th identical with his own house as Mercury is in the 11th, the native will be very affluent.

Notes : Jupiter rules the 5th for Leo ascendant and for Scorpio ascendant while Mercury is the 11th lord for these two ascendants. Thus the 5th and 11th lords will be in own signs.

पंचमे तु कुजक्षेत्रे तस्मिन् कुजयुते सति।
लाभस्थे भृगुपुत्रे तु बहुद्रव्यस्य नायकः ॥७॥

7. If a sign of Mars be the 5th with Mars therein as Venus is in the 11th, the native will become very affluent.

Notes : Cancer and Sagittarius ascendant will attract this rule. Mars will be in own house in the 5th while Venus will be in the 11th in own house for these two ascendants.

पंचमे तु शशिक्षेत्रे तस्मिन् शशियुते सति।
शनौ लाभस्थिते जातो बहुद्रव्यस्य नायकः ॥८॥

8. If Cancer be the 5th house containing the Moon therein as Saturn is in the 11th, the native will become very affluent.

Notes : Here Pisces ascendant is considered with the Moon in the 5th and Saturn in the 11th.

Thus from slokas 2 to 8, the formula that stands for basic consideration is that the 5th lord should be in the 5th while the 11th lord is in the 11th itself. Only in case of the rule given in sloka 3 for Taurus and Aquarius ascendants, two more planets have been added for the 11th house position.

भानुक्षेत्रगते लग्ने तस्मिन् भानुयुते पुनः।
भौमेन गुरुणा युक्ते दृष्टे जातो युतो धनैः ॥९॥

9. *YOGAS FOR WEALTH* (*upto sloka 15*) : Should the Sun be in Leo identical with the ascendant and be conjunct or aspected by Mars and Jupiter, one will be wealthy.

चन्द्रक्षेत्रगते लग्ने तस्मिन् चन्द्रयुते सति।
बुधेन गुरुणा युक्त दृष्टे जातो धनी भवेत् ॥१०॥

10. Should the Moon be in Cancer identical with ascendant and be conjunct or aspected by Mercury and Jupiter one will be wealthy.

भौमक्षेत्रे गते लग्ने तस्मिन् भौमेन संयुते।
सौम्यशुक्रार्कजैर्युक्ते दृष्टे श्रीमान्नरो भवेत् ॥११॥

11. Should Mars be in the ascendant identical with his own sign and be conjunct or aspected by Mercury, Venus and Saturn, the native will be rich.

बुधक्षेत्रगते लग्ने तस्मिन् बुधयुते सति।
शनिजीवयुते दृष्टे जातो धनयुतो भवेत् ॥१२॥

12. Should Mercury's sign ascend with Mercury therein and be conjunct or aspected by Saturn aud Jupiter the native will be rich.

गुरुक्षेत्रगते लग्ने तस्मिन् गुरुयुते सति।
बुधभौमयुते दृष्टे जायते धनवान्नरः ॥१३॥

13. Should Jupiter be in the ascendant identical with his own sign and be conjunct or aspected by Mercury and Mars, the native will be rich.

भृगुक्षेत्रगते लग्ने तास्मन् भृगुयुते सति।
शनिसौम्ययुते दृष्टे यो जातः स धनी भवेत् ॥१४॥

14. If Venus be in the ascendant identical with his own sign and be conjunct or aspected by Saturn and Mercury, one will be wealthy.

शनिक्षेत्रगते लग्ने तस्मिन् शनियुते सति।
भौमेन गुरुणा युक्ते दृष्टे जातो धनैर्युतः ॥१५॥

15. If Saturn is in his own sign identical with ascendant be aspected by or conjunct Mars and Jupiter, the native will be wealthy.

धनदौ धर्मधीनाथौ ये वा ताभ्यां युता ग्रहाः ।
तेऽपि स्वस्वदशाकाले धनदा नाऽत्र संशयः ॥१६॥

16. *OTHER QUALIFIED PLANETS :* The 9th lord and th 5th lord are capable of bestowing wealth. Similarly planets conjunct such a lord. There is no doubt that these planets will give wealth during their Dasa periods.

Notes : The 5th lord and the 9th lord are primarily wealth-givers. If they are well placed in a horoscope, the native will become wealthy. If a favourable planet joins the 5th lord or the 9th lord, that planet will also become a significator of wealth.

ग्रहाणामुक्तयोगेषु क्रूरसौम्यविभागतः ।
बलाबलविवेकेन फलमूह्यं विचक्षणैः ॥१७॥

17. The yogas mentioned above (upto sloka 16) should be delineated after knowing favourable unfavourable dispositions of the participant planets and their strength and weakness.

केन्द्रेशः पारिजातस्थस्तदा दाता भवेन्नरः ।
उत्तमे ह्युत्तमो दाता गोपुरे पुरुषत्वयुक् ॥१८॥
सिंहासने भवेन्मान्यः शूरः पारावतांशके ।
सभाध्यक्षो देवलोके ब्रह्मलोके मुनिर्मतः ॥
ऐरावतांशके तुष्टो दिग्योगो नैव जायते ॥१९॥

18-19. *EFFECTS OF ANGULAR LORD'S DIVISIONAL DIGNITIES :* If the lord of an angle is in Parijatamsa, the native will be liberal, in Uttamamsa highly liberal, in Gopuramsa endowed with prowess, in Simhasanamsa honourable, in Paaravatamsa valorous, in Devalokamsa head of an assembly, in Brahmalokamsa a sage and in Iravatamsa delighted and be celebrated in all quarters.

Notes : From verse 18 to verse 34 of this chapter, the sage instructs us on the dignities of the 4 angular lords and two trinal lords.

The treatment is based on Dasa Varga divisions. For meanings of Parijata and other Amsas, sec ch. 6 supra. Shodasa

Varga scheme also can be applied to the rules given herein with suitable modification proportionately.

Lords of angles are those ruling the ascendant, the 4th, the 7th and the 10th. Their divisional dignities are discussed in the present group of verses. One of the said rulers having various dignities will yield following effects.

Parijatamsa	liberal
Uttamamsa	highly liberal
Gopuramsa	endowed with prowess and manliness
Simhasanamsa	honourable (prominent etc.)
Paravatmsa	valorous
Devalokamsa	head of men, leadership, high position etc.
Brahmalokamsa	sagely (spiritual achievements etc.)
Iravatmsa	delighted, ever happy etc. and be a celebrated personality from all viewpoints.

Here we must note the implied difference between the four lords ruling the various angles. The angular lords are powerful and more important in the ascending order. That is, the 4th lord is more powerful than the ascendant lord, the 7th lord is so against the 4th lord, and the 10th lord is the most powerful among the four lords. So the effects will also increase in the same order.

पारिजाते सुताधीशे विद्या चैव कुलोचिता।
उत्तमे चोत्तमा ज्ञेया गोपुरे भुवनांकिता ॥२०॥
सिंहासने तथा वाच्या साचिव्येन समन्विता।
पारावते च विज्ञेया ब्रह्मविद्या द्विजोत्तम ! ॥२१॥
सुतेशे देवलोकस्थे कर्मयोगश्च जायते।
उपासना ब्रह्मलोके भक्तिस्त्वरावतांशके ॥२२॥

20-22. *EFFECTS OF 5th LORD'S DIVISIONAL DIGNITIES :* If the 5th lord is in Parijatamsa, the native will take to the branch of learning befitting his race, if in Uttamamsa he will have excellent learning, if in Gopuramsa he will receive world-wide honours, in Simhasanamsa he will be endowed with ministership, in also paaravatamsa endowed with knowledge of Supreme Spirit; in Devalokamsa he will be a Karma Yogi (i.e. a performer of actions, worldly and religious rites), in Brahmalokamsa devoted to the Lord and in Iravatamsa pious.

Notes : While the four angular lords are treated in one and the same breath, the sage gives special importance to the 5th and 9th lords individually. The effects may suitably be understood based on the explanations given for angular lords above.

धर्मेशे पारिजातस्थे तीर्थकृत्त्वत्र जन्मनि ।
पूर्वजन्मन्यपि ज्ञेयस्तीर्थकृच्चोत्तमांशके ॥२३॥
गौपुरे मखकर्ता च परे चैवाऽत्र जन्मनि ।
सिंहासने भवेद्वीरः सत्यवादी जितेन्द्रियः ॥२४॥
सर्वधर्मान् परित्यज्य ब्रह्मैकपदमाश्रितः ।
पारावते च परमो हंसश्चैवात्र जन्मनि ॥२५॥
लगुडी वा त्रिदण्डी स्याद्देवलोके न संशयः ।
ब्रह्मलोके शक्रतदं याति कृत्वाऽश्वमेधकम् ॥२६॥
ऐरावते तु धर्मात्मा स्वयं धर्मो भविष्यति ।
श्रीरामः कुन्तिपुत्राद्यो यथा जातो द्विजोत्तम! ॥२७॥

23-27. *EFFECTS OF 9th LORD'S DIVISIONAL DIGNITIES :* If the 9th lord is in Parijatamsa, the native will visit holy places, if in Uttamamsa he had done so in the past births as well, if in Gopuramsa he will perform sacrificial rites, in Simhasanamsa he will be mighty, truthful, be a conquerer of his senses and will concentrate only on the Supreme Spirit giving up all religions, if in Paaravatamsa he will be the greates of ascetics, if in Devalokamsa he will be an ascetic holding a cudgel (लगुडी) or a religious mendicant that has renounced all mundane attachments and carrying three long staves tied together in his right hand (त्रिदंडिन्) and if in Brahmalokamsa he will perform Aswamedha yaga (**Horse Sacrifice**) and will attain the state of Lord Indra (god of gods). If the 9th lord is in Iravatamsa the person born will be a synonym of Dharma or virtues just as Lord Sri Rama and Yudhishtira (the eldest of Pandavas).

Notes : The 5th lord has been used in spiritual and material planes as well. Whereas the 9th lord is solely related to one's spiritual achievements as could be seen by the treatment given by Maharshi Parasara in the above 5 slokas.

The word Tridandi has been translated as above in the context of relating the native to a Sansyasi as these slokas exclusively concentrate on the spiritual achievements of the native. 'Tridandi' also means one who obtained command over mind, speech and deed. Without 'Trikarana Suddhi' or purity of these three it will not be possible for one to achieve divine bliss. One who thinks bad in his mind though good in the other two spheres, viz. speech and actions cannot be called a pure character. Or one who thinks of good and speaks similarly but acts in a contrary manner cannot be a successful spiritualist. Lastly one who speaks undesirable words though good in thinking and acting cannot also reach self realisation. Hence it is evident that one should be a 'Tridandi' or endowed with Trikarana Suddhi, so that he locates the Almighty at every point of space and time.

We have so far seen that 5th and 9th lords are primarily wealth givers. The sage also denotes the 5th and 9th lords as lords of 'Lakshmi sthanas'. Lakshmi though normally means wealth,further conveys a meaning splendour (our lustre). This relates to divine splendour acquired by a person through his spiritual merits. If a person is splendorous, we see in him what is called **Brahma Varchas** or the splendour making him look like God, free from any material attachment. In this context we cannot but recall great personages like Rama Krishna Parama Hamsa, Maharshi Ramana, Sankaracharyas of various orders and periods, Sivananda and so on and so forth. In all these cases, the 5th and 9th lords and 5th and 9th houses enabled them earn **that** splendour. The wealth they earned is such that it cannot be exhausted even after many centuries, i e. divine status.

विष्णुस्थानं च केन्द्रं स्याल्लक्ष्मीस्थानं त्रिकोणकम् ।
तदीशयोश्च सम्बन्धाद्राजयोगः पुरोदितः ॥२८॥

28. *ANGULAR AND TRINAL LORDS RELATED :* The angles are known as **Vishnusthaana** (i.e. houses of Lord Vishnu) while the trines are called **Lakshmi sthaanas** (i.e. houses of

Lakshmi). If the lord of an angle establishes relationship with a trinal lord, a Rajayoga will obtain.

Notes : The 4 houses, viz. the 1st, 4th, 7th and 10th are known as Vishnusthaanas while the 5th and and 9th are Lakshmisthaanas. In Hindu mythology, Lakshmi is a consort of Lord Vishnu, the supreme god. A relationship thus between an angular lord and a trinal lord is capable of causing a superior Rajayoga, just as one having the blessings of Sri Vishnu and His consort Lakshmi will be endowed with permanent wellbeing.

The kinds of relationship between planets that will be favourable are :

1. An exchange between these two lords.
2. Mutual aspects between these two lords.
3. Conjunction of these two lords.
4. Mutual angular placement existing between these two.
5. Mutual trinal placement between these two.

The first three kinds of relationships are more powerful while the last two cannot be equally powerful but in a lesser degree.

A sixth kind of relationship can also be extended in this context to Navamsa positions though I have no specific classic sanction for this. For example in a Capricornian's case, Mars in the Navamsa of Venus and Venus in that of Mars will confer a superior Raja yoga. This form of relationship will be eqally superior like the first 3 relationships mentioned by me in the earlier paragraph.

After seeing such a relationship between an angular lord and a trinal lord, their dignities like Parijata etc. will have to be seen to decide the extent of effects due as could be seen in the following six verses.

पारिजाते स्थितौ तौ चेन्नृपो लोकानुरक्षकः ।
उत्तमे चोत्तमो भूपो गजवाजिरथादिमान् ॥२९॥
गोपुरे नृपशार्दूलः पूजितांघ्रिर्नृपैर्भवेत् ।
सिंहासने चक्रवर्ती सर्वभूमिप्रपालकः ॥३०॥
अस्मिन् योगे हरिश्चन्द्रो मनुश्चैवोत्तमस्तथा ।
बलिर्वैश्वानरो जातस्तथान्ये चक्रवर्तिनः ॥३१॥

वर्तमानयुगे जातस्तथा राजा युधिष्ठिरः।
भविता शालिवाहाद्यस्तथैव द्विजसत्तम! ॥३२॥
पारावतांशकेऽप्येवं जाता मन्वादयस्तथा।
विष्णोः सर्वेऽवताराश्च जायन्ते देवलोकके ॥३३॥
ब्रह्मलोके तु ब्रह्माद्या जायन्ते विश्वपालकाः।
ऐरावतांशके जातः पूर्वं स्वायंभुवो मनुः ॥३४॥

29-34 *EFFECTS OF DIVISIONAL DIGNITIES OF THE TWO PLANETS SO RELATED :* Should an angular lord and a trinal lord having such a relationship (vide above slokas) be in Parijatamsa, the native will be king and will protect men, if Uttamamsa he will be an excellent king endowed with elephants, horses, chariots etc , if in Gopuramsa he will be a tiger of kings honoured by other kings, and if in Simhasanamsa he will be an emperor ruling over the entire earth; with the said Rajayoga relationship of the said planets in Simhasanamsa were born Harischandra, Manu, Bali, the Fire god (Agni Deva) and many other emperors. *In the present Yuga so born is Yudhishtira (or Dharma Raja of Maha Bharata). Salivahana's birth and that of others will also come with this yoga.* With these planets so related and in Paaravatamsa, Manu etc. were born. The Incarnations of Lord Vishnu took place when the said planets, being so related, were in Devalokamsa; and in Brahmalokamsa Lord Brahma and in Iravatamsa the Swayambhu Manu (the first of the 14 Manus identified as the second creator who produced the **Prajapatis** and to the said Manu the code of laws *viz.* **Manusmriti** is ascribed) were born.

Notes : The two planets, viz. an angular lord and a trinal lord with such a relationship, should be simultaneously in Parijatamsa. One in Parijatamsa and the other in a still higher Amsa will yield still better effects. The reader can intelligently manipulate the effects according to such Amsas.

When studying these slokas, we reach a crucial point as to the period of Parasara. There are baseless arguments that Parasara, author of **Brihat Parasara Hora,** could not be a sage that lived thousands of years ago; but a very recent author that should have lived after Varaha Mihira, Bhattotpala, Kalyana Varma and so on and so forth. This misconception does not deserve an answer at all and is worth being brushed aside as an idle gossip. The holders of such opinion may advance a million arguments in their own favour. Our query to them is: which exponent referred to the horoscopic positions of Lord Vishnu, Harischandra, Manu, Bali Chakravarthi, Agni Deva, Swayambhu Manu and last but not the least the Creater Brahma himself? Is it humanly possible, but for a sage, with divine contacts, to produce combinations existing in the sacred horoscopes of Vishnu, Brahma etc.? Also note with specific attention the statement of Parasara that "Dharma Raja (the eldest son of king Pandu, of Maha Bharata) of the **present age,** has this yoga". Does this not stand as an indisputable testimony of Parasara having lived in the Maha Bharata era ?

Yet, another clue about Parosara is served when in the above lines we find his prediction that Salivahana and others "will be born" with this yoga. The verb used is **bhavita** in future tense. That conveys that Parasara was a predecessor of Salivahana and not a successor of Bhattotpala etc.

Maharshi Jaimini, author of Poorva Mimamsa and propagator of Jaimini Astrology was a disciple of Parasara. If Parasara lived in the 17th century, what about Jaimini ?

Specific attention of the reader is drawn to the statement of Parasara in śloka 32 above, to the effect that "in the present Yuga" Dharma Raja is born with such a yoga. This is an ample proof that our sage was in Maha Bharata time and was the illustrious parent of illustrious Veda Vyasa.

Lastly, the following popular quotation enlists Parasara among the 18 exponents of **Jyotisha** :

सूर्यः पितामहो व्यासो वशिष्टोऽत्रि पराशर : ।
कश्यपो नारदो गर्गो मरीचिर्मनुरंगीरः ॥
लोमशः पौलशश्चैव च्यवनो यवनो मनुः 1
शौनकोऽष्टादशश्चैव ज्योतिःशास्त्र प्रवर्त्तकाः i।

This is again a proof that our sage was indeed a sage of Mahabharata era and is an authority with crown for Kali yuga astrology.

अथ दारिद्रय्योगाध्याय: ॥४२॥

Chapter 42

Combinations For Penury

बहवो धनदा योगा श्रुतास्त्वत्तो मया मुने! ।
दरिद्रजन्मदान् योगान् कृपया कथय प्रभो! ॥१॥

1. O Lord, you have stated many yogas rnlated to acquisition of wealth. Please tell me such yogas causing utter poverty.

लग्नेशे च व्ययस्थाने व्ययेशे लग्नमागते ।
मारकेशयुते दृष्टे निर्धनो जायते नर: ॥२॥

2. The native will be penniless if the ascendant lord is in the 12th as the 12th lord is in the ascendant along with a Maraka lord (death inflicting planet) or be in aspect to such a planet.

लग्नेशे षष्ठभावस्थे षष्ठेशे लग्नमागते ।
मारकेशेन युग्दृष्टे धनहीन: प्रजायते ॥३॥

3. The native will be penniless if the ascendant lord is in the 6th while the 6th lord is in the ascendant with conjuntion or aspect of a Maraka lord.

लग्नेन्दू केतुसंयुक्तौ लग्नपे निधनं गते ।
मारकेशयुते दृष्टे जातो वै निर्धनो भवेत् ॥४॥

4. Should the ascendant or the Moon be with Ketu while the ascendant lord is in the 8th, the person cencerned will be penniless.

षष्ठाष्टमव्ययगते लग्नपे पापसंयुते ।
धनेशे रिपुभे नीचे राजवंश्योऽपि निर्धन: ॥५॥

5. If the ascendant lord along with a malefic is in the 6th, 8th or 12th while the 2nd lord is in an enemy's sign or in debilitatton, even a native of royal scion will become penniless.

त्रिकेशेन समायुक्ते पापदृष्टे विलग्नपे।
शनियुक्तेऽथवा सौम्यैरदृष्टे निर्धनो नरः ॥६॥

6. If the ascendant lord is conjunct an evil house lord (one of the 6th, 8th and 12th lords) or Saturn and be devoid of benefic aspect the native will be penniless.

मन्त्रेशो धर्मनाथश्च क्रमात् षष्ठव्ययस्थितौ।
दृष्टौ चेन्मारकेशेन निर्धनो जयते नरः ॥७॥

7. Should the 5th and 9th lords be respectively found in the 6th and 12th and be in aspect to Maraka planets, the native will be penniless.

पापग्रहे लग्नगते राज्यधर्माधिपौ विना!।
मारकेशयुते दृष्टे जातः स्यन्निर्धनो भवेत् ॥८॥

8. If malefics, excepting the lords of the 10th and 9th, be in the ascendant in association with or aspect to Maraka planets, one will become penniless.

त्रिकेशा यत्र भावस्था तद्भावेशास्त्रिकस्थिताः।
पापदृष्टयुता बालो दुःखाक्रान्तश्च निर्धनः ॥९॥

9. Note the planets ruling the signs occupied by the lords of 6th, 8th and 12th. If the said dispositors are in such evil houses in turn and be associated with or aspected by malefics, the native will be miserable and indigent.

चन्द्राक्रान्तनवांशेशो मारकेशयुतो यदि।
मारकस्थानगो वाऽपि जातोऽत्र निर्धनो नरः ॥१०॥

10. The lord of the Navamsa occupied by the Moon joining a Maraka planet or occupying a Maraka house will make one penniless.

लग्नेशलग्नभागेशौ रिष्फरन्ध्रारिगौ यदि।
मारकेशयुतौ दृष्टौ जातोऽसौ निर्धनो नरः ॥११॥

11. Should the lord of natal ascendant and that of Navamsa ascendant be conjunct or be aspected by Maraka planets, one will be penniless.

शुभस्थानगताः पापाः पापस्थानगताः शुभाः।
निर्धनो जायते बालो भोजनेन प्रपीडितः॥१२॥

12. If inauspicious houses are occupied by benefics while auspicious houses are occupied by malefics, the native will be indigent and will be distressed even in the matter of food.

कोणेशदृष्टिहीना ये त्रिकेशैः संयुता ग्रहाः।
ते सर्वे स्वदशाकाले धनहानिकराः स्मृताः॥१३॥

13. A planet associated with one of the lords of the 6th, 8th and 12th, being bereft of a trinal lord's aspect, will in its Dasa periods cause harm to the native's financial aspects.

कारकाद् वा विलग्नाद् वा रन्ध्रेरिष्फे द्विजोत्तम!।
कारकाङ्गपयोदृष्टया धनहीनः प्रजायते॥१४॥

14. If the 8th/12th from Atmakaraka or from the natal ascendant be aspected by Atmakaraka Navamsa lord and the natal ascendant lord, the native will be bereft of wealth.

कारकेशो व्ययं स्वस्मात् लग्नेशो लग्नतो व्ययम्।
वीक्षते चेत् तदा बालो व्ययशीलो भवेद्ध्रुवम्॥१५॥

15. The native will be a spendthrift if the 12th from Atmakaraka is aspected by the dispositor of Atmakaraka or if the 12th from the natal ascendant is aspected by the ascendant lord.

अथ दारिद्र्ययोगांस्त् कथयामि सभङ्गकान्।
धनसंस्थौ तु भौमार्की कथितौ धननाशकौ॥१६॥
बुधेक्षितौ महावित्तं कुरुतो नात्र संशयः।
निःस्वतां कुरुते तत्र रविर्नित्यं यमेक्षितः॥१७॥
महाधनयुतं स्यातं शन्यदृष्टः करोत्यसौ।
शनिश्चापि रवेर्दृष्टया फलमेवं प्रयच्छति॥१८॥

16-18. Now I tell you some yogas for poverty along with conditions of their nullifications. Should Mars and Saturn be together in the 2nd house, the native's wealth will be destroyed.

Should Mercury aspet the said two planets in the 2nd, there will be great wealth. There is no doubt in it. The Sun in the 2nd in aspect to Saturn will cause penury while the Sun so placed if be not aspected by Saturn will give riches and fame. The same effects (i.e. poverty) be declared if Saturn is in the 2nd in aspect to the Sun.

अथायुर्दायाध्यायः ॥४३॥

Chapter 43
Longevity

धनाधनाख्ययोगौ च कथितौ भवता मुने !।
नराणामायुषो ज्ञानं कथयस्व महामते !॥१॥

1. O Sage, you have dealt with combinations for wealth and poverty. Kindly detail methods of ascertaining the life span of human beings.

साधु पृष्टं त्वया विप्र ! जनानां च हितेच्छया।
कथयाम्यायुषो ज्ञानं दुर्ज्ञेयं यत् सुरैरपि॥२॥
आयुर्ज्ञानविभेदास्तु बहुभिर्बहुधोदिताः।
तेषां सारांशमादाय प्रवदामि तवाऽग्रतः॥३॥

2-3. O Brahmin, for the benefit of mankind I narrate methods of ascertaining longevity, as knowing longevity is difficult even for gods. Many exponents have laid down various methods of longevity calculations. Following is the summary of such schools of thoughts.

Notes : Slokas 2-15 deal with Pindayu system of longevity calculations. After dealing with translation of these 14 slokas, the entire system of Pindayu is being fully explained by me with a practical example so that the reader follows the calculations involved thoroughly.

स्वोच्चनीचादि-संस्थित्या ग्रहा आयुःप्रदायकाः।
स्वस्ववीर्यवशैनैवं नक्षत्राणि च राशयः ॥४॥
पिण्डायुः प्रथमं तत्र ग्रहस्थितिवशादहम्।
कथयामि द्विजश्रेष्ठ ! श्रणुष्वेकाग्रमानसः ॥५॥
क्रमात् सूर्यादिखेटेषु स्वस्वोच्चस्थानगेष्विह।
नन्देन्दवस्तत्त्वमितास्तिथयोऽर्काः शरेन्दवः ॥६॥
प्रकृत्यो विंशतिश्चाब्दा आयुःपिण्डाः प्रकीर्तिताः।
नीचगेष्वेतदर्धञ्च ज्ञेयं मध्येऽनुपाततः ॥७॥
स्वच्चशुद्धो ग्रहः शोध्यः षड्भादूनो भमण्डलात्।
स्वपिण्डगुणितो भक्तो भादिमानेन वत्सराः ॥८॥

4-8. *PINDAYU* : The planets contribute longevity according to their being in exaltation or debilitation, and also based on their strengths and weaknesses and positions in Aswini etc. and in the various signs. First of all Pindayu, based on the planetary positions. O brahmin, listen to what I say, with singlemindedness. 19, 25, 15, 12, 15, 21 and 20 are the numper of years contributed by the planets from the Sun etc. when in (deep) exaltation. Thesr are half of the above in (deep) fall, and if the planets are in between exaltation and fall, rule of three process should be used, Deduct the actual position of the planet from its deep exaltation point. If the product is less than 6 signs, deduct it again from 12 signs. The product concerned be multiplied by the number of years allotted to the planet and divided by 12 to get the planet's actual contribution.

अस्तगस्तु हरेत्स्वार्धं विना शुक्रशनैश्चरौ।
वक्रचारं विना त्र्यंशं शत्रुराशौ हरेद् ग्रहः ॥९॥

9. *RECTIFICATIONS :* Excepting Venus and Saturn, the contributions made by others should be halved, if they are eclipsed, by the Sun. One third should be reduced if the planet is in its inimical sign. This does not apply to the one in retrogression (see **vakra charam**).

सर्वार्धत्रिचतुःपञ्चषष्ठभागं क्रमाद् ग्रहः।
व्ययाद्वामं स्थितः पापो हरेत् सौम्यश्च तद्दलम् ॥१०॥

एकभे तु बहुष्वेको हरेत्स्वांशं बली ग्रहः।
नाऽत्र क्षीणस्य चन्द्रस्य पापत्वं मुनिभिः स्मृतम् ॥११॥

10-11. *DEDUCTIONS FOR PLANETS IN VISIBLE HALF :* Full, half, one third, one fourth, one fifth and one sixth are the deductions of contributions made by malefics placed in the visible half of the zodiac. Benefics in such cases lose only half of what malefics lose. Should there be more than one planet in a house, the deduction due to the strongest will only prevail and not due to other planets in that particular house. Waning Moon is a benefic for this purpose.

लग्नांशलिप्तिका हत्वा प्रत्येकं विहगायुषा।
भाज्या मण्डललिप्ताभिर्लब्धं वर्षादि शोधयेत् ॥१२॥
स्वायुषो लग्नगे सूर्ये मङ्गले च शनैश्चरे।
तदर्धं शुभसंदृष्टे पातयेद् द्विजसत्तम ! ॥१३॥

12-13. *MALEFICS IN ASCENDANT :* In case the ascendant is occupied by malefics, adopt the following procedure: Convert the ascendant's sphuta into minutes of arc and multiply it by the years etc. contributed by the occupant and divide by 21600. The years etc. so arrived be deducted from the respective contribution which will be the net span donated by the planet. If there is benefic's aspect on the ascendant containing malefics, then the loss is only half (obtained through these calculations).

लग्नराशिसमाश्चाब्दा भागाद्यैरनुपाततः।
मासाद्यिका इतीच्छन्ति लग्नायुः केऽपि कोविदाः ॥१४॥
लग्नादायोंऽशतुल्यः स्यादन्तरे चाऽनुपाततः।
तत्पतौ बलसंयुक्ते राशितुल्यं च भाधिपे ॥१५॥

14-15. *ASCENDANT'S CONTRIBUTION :* The number of years contributed by the ascendant will correspond to the number of signs it gained (from Aries) while the degrees the ascendant gained in the particular sign will alsocorrespondingly donate (i.e. 30 degrees=1 year). If the Navamsa Ascendant lord is stronger than the ascendant lord, then the contribution be computed only based on the Navamsas gained (from

Aries), otherwise the computation will be for the Rasi ascendant only.

Notes : The seven planets from the Sun to Saturn respectively contribute 19, 25, 15, 12, 15, 21 and 20 years when on deep exaltation degree. The contributions are just halved when these are on deep debilitation degrees. The deep exaltation degrees for the 7 planets respectively from the Sun on are : Aries 10°, Taurus 3°, Capricorn 28°, Virgo 15°, Cancer 5°, Pisces 27° and Libra 20°. By adding 180°, to the said degrees, we get deep debilitation points for the concerned planets. After finding out the individual contributions of span of longevity, the same are to be rectified which method is being explained in appropriate place in the following paragraphs. To work out the longevitv through Pindayu method, we will take up the horoscope of a male born on 21.5.1944 at 19h 0lm 15s (WT) at 13N40 79E20. The Rasi and Bhava charts as reuqired for our purpose are :

	Merc Moon Ven	Sun	Sat
	Rasi		Mars Jup Rahu
Ketu			
	Asc		

	Merc	Moon Ven Sun	Sat
	Bhava		Mars Rahu
Ketu			Jup
	Asc		

The planetary longitudes in the respective signs as per Lahiri Ayanamsa (23-4-12) are : The Sun 7-12-18, the Moon 27-35-46, Mars 6-18-46, Mercury 14-54-13, Jupiter 26-7-13, Venus 27-17-50, Saturn 3-9-41 and ascendant 0-48-34. The bhava starting points are : lst—Libra 15-48-15, 2nd—Scorpio 15-48-15, 3rd—Sagittarius 15-47-39, 4th—Capricorn 15-47-2, 5th—Aquarius 15-47-1, 6th—Pisces 15-47-38, 7th—Aries 15-48-15, 8th—Taurus 15-48-15, 9th—Gemini 15-47-38, 10th—Cancer 15-47-1, 11th—Leo 15-47-1 and Virgo 15-47-38.

Based on the sage's instructions, we may device the following simple and common formula to know the number of years contributed by any of the 7 planets. (All concerned longitudes should be converted into decimals. The minutes and seconds be also considered. For example, 21° 32′ 49″ is converted into 21.547 degrees for easy calculation.) The formula to find out the basic planetary contribution is :

1. If "d" is less than 180°, then "c"
$$= f - (d \times f \div 360)$$

2. If "d" is above 180° 'c' $= \dfrac{d \times f}{360}$

Where "d" is distance between the planet's deep exaltation degree and its actual placement; "f" is the full number of years grantable by the planet and 'c' is the basic years actually granted by it due to its placement.

Take Saturn's case as an example. He can at best contribute 20 years. In the horoscope under evaluation, he is 223.1613 degrees away from his deep exaltation (Libra 20°). Hence to find out the basics ontribution of Saturn, we use rule 2 above, thus :

$$\frac{223.1613 \times 20}{360} = 12.3979 \text{ years}$$

On this basis, we have for the example nativity, the following basic donations of years by the 7 planets :

The Sun	:	17.5642 years
The Moon	:	24.6247 years
Mars	:	8.4036 years
Mercury	:	6.9968 years
Jupiter	:	14.1200 years
Venus	:	19.2327 years
Saturn	:	12.3979 years

These basic contributions will undergo the following reductions, as applicable.

1. Astangata Harana 2. Satru Kshetra Harana 3. Vyayadi Harana 4. Kroorodaya Harana. These may be understood from the following paragraphs.

1. **Astangata Harana** : If a planet is combust reduce the span by half. However, this does not affect Venus and Saturn in combustion.

2. **Satru Kshetra Harana** : If a planet is in its enemy's sign, reduce one third of the basic years and take only two third. An exception is that a retrograde planet, although placed in inimical sign, does not incur this liability. 'Vakrachara' is the expression made by Maharshi Parasara and hence it excepts a retrograde planet. Mars also does lose in an enemy's sign. Needless to mention, a planet in netural's sign (or in friend's sign) is not subjected to this reduction.

3. **Vyayadi Harana** : Planets entail reduction if placed anywhere between the 12th and 7th (reckoned in descending order).

This need not be mistaken to be Drisyardha Hani. Drisyardha means that half of the zodiac which is visible. Hence it is 180° behind the ascendental cusp, i.e. upto descendant via meridian. Vyayadi Harana figures are : full, half, 1/3, 1/4, 1/5 and 1/6h according to the planet being in 12th, 11th, 10th, 9th, 8th and 7th. These are for malefic planets while a benefic in this connection loses only half of what is noted for a malefie. The Moon is ever a benefic for longevity calculations, as per Maharshi Parasara. (Mercury although joining a malefic be treated as a benefic only, for all longevity calculations.) We find here that there is harmonic progression in these deductions and hence we ought to have a scientific and logical approach to the quantum of correction, rather than resorting to a flat check arbitrarily. There is no justification in straightaway eliminating the whole, for example, for a malefic in the 12th not giving heed to his actual degreewise placement. It should be full at the 12th bhava ending point, poroprtionately less on the 12th cusp and still lesser on the beginning point of 12th bhava or 11th bhava ending point. That is, starting with a 100% less on the 12th bhava ending we gradually arrive for a 50% reduction at the point where the 11th bhava ends. Thus it will be one sixth reduction at the end of 7th bhava while it will be 1/7th at the beginaing of the 7th bhava (or end of the 6th bhava). The reduction obtained by this method should be half in the case of a benefic (i.e. Jupiter, Venus, Mercury and the Moon). Without going through any difficult process, for each bhava, a common formula is given with which one can rectify the basic contributions of a planet in one of these houses.

The formula is :

$$\frac{\text{'c'}}{(14-\text{House}) - (\text{DP} \div \text{BL})} = \text{loss of years}$$

(DP=Distance of planet from bhava start; BL=Bhava length and 'House' is the bhava occupied by the planet under rectification.

To understand this formula, we will rectify Saturn's contribution He is in the 8th bhava and hence attracts this reduction. He is in Gemini 3-9-41 while the 8th house begins in Taurus at 15-48-15 and ends at 15-47-38 in Gemini. Thus the length of the 8th bhava is 29-59-33 or 29.9925 degrees, which is 'BL' for our purpose. The basic contribution of

Saturn is 12.3979 years. He is 17.3572 degreer ahead of the 8th bhava beginning. Therefore, his reduction is :

$$\frac{12\ 3979}{(14-8)-(17.3572 \div 29.9925)}=2.2869 \text{ years}$$

Thus, on account of Vyayadi Harana, Saturn entails a check of 2.2869 years. In the example horoscope, Mercury is not liable to this reduction as he is quite prior to the beginning of the 7th bhava. Others that attract this check are : The Sun, the Moon, Venus, Mars and Jupiter. The figures for these planets based on the present formula are :

Venus	(7th bhava)	:	1.4533 years
The Sun	(7th bhava)	:	2.7939 years
The Moon	(7th bhava)	:	1.8636 years
Saturn	(8th bhava)	:	2.2869 years
Mars	(9th bhava)	:	1.9472 years
Jupiter	(10th bhava)	:	1.9314 years

4. **Kroorodaya Harana** : Only malefics (i.e. Saturn, the Sun and Mars) entail this check if in the ascendant. Mercury, though joining a natural malefic will not be liable to this reduction. We do not require this reduction to any planet in the example horoscope, as there is none in the ascendant. Here the ascendant means the area between the starting and ending points of the sign rising. To find out this reduction, the ascendental cusp in degrees, minutes and seconds be multiplied by the number of basic years donated by the malefic concerned and divided by 21600. The divider is 21600 as these are the total minutes of arc in the zodiac. The figure so arrived should be reduced from the said malefic's basic contribution. However, if a benefic aspects the said malefic, reduce only half of the figure so suggested.

5. We have thus seen four types of reductions. At every stage the reduction should not be done instantaneously. After obtaining the reduction figures, wherever permitted, check up if there is more than one reduction for one and the same planet under various headings. The following may be remembered in this connection.

(a) If a planet attracts more than one reduction, the highest reduction is only to be done ignoring the others. For example, assume Mercury attracts a reduction of 7.5 years due to rule 1, followed by 2.3 years due to rule 2 and 4.35 years due to rule 3. The highest reduction is due to rule l and hence only 7.5 is to be deducted and the other two figures be ignored **in toto.**

(b) In case of Vyayadi Harana (rule 3), two or three planets may be in one bhava. In that case, the strongest loses and the other (or others) will not lose.

Not only the planets, but the ascendant also grants a certain number of years. This figure should also be found out before adding to the planetary contributions. To know the the number of years granted by the ascendant, firstly note the number of signs intervening between Aries and the sign before the ascendant. That is, if Sagittarius is the ascendant, count upto Scorpio beginning from Aries. This denotes 8 years. The degrees in the ascendant be also proportionately converted into years treating 30 degrees as one year, or 2.5 degrees as a month. The contribution of ascendant will be so calculated if the ascendant lord is stronger than the Navamsa Lagna lord.

In case the Navamsa Lagna lord is stronger than his counterpart, a different computation is to be resorted to, thus. Count from Aries till you reach a sign before Navamsa Lagna. In the case under study, the Navamsa Lagna lord, Moon, is stronger than the ascendant lord. Hence we compute Navamsa Lagna's contribution for our own use. The Navamsa Lagna is Cancer. Hence from Aries to Cancer we have three completed Navamsas which give 3 year. The ascending degree is 0-48-34 whereas one Navamsa is 3° 20′. Proportionately thus we get another 0.2428 years and have the total contribution of 3.2428 years as Ascendant's contribution. In case of Navamsa treat 3° 20′ as one full year. The ascendant's contribution undergoes no check.

Now we are ready for final reductions. There are 3 planets in the 7th house, viz. the Sun, the Moon and Venus. The Sun is the strongest and hence Vyayadi Harna (rule 3) applies to only the Sun while Venus and the Moon are rid of reduction on this score. The Sun is in enemy's camp and on this score he loses a third of 17 5642, which reduction is equal to 5.8547. This figure is higher than the one obtained for the

Sun as per rule 3 (i.e. Vyayadi Harana). Hence his final contribution turns to be 11.7095 years (i e. basic years minus Satru kshetra Harana). In the matter of Vyayadi Harana (rule 3) there is no other bhava where there is more than one planet.

Though the Moon has not lost on account of rule 3 (Vyayadi Harana), she is liable to reduction on account of her combustion (rule 1). Thus when her basic contribution (24.627) is halved, she is left with a net donation of 12.3124 years.

Except the Sun, no other planet is in enemy's sign. So, Satru Kshetra Harana (rule 2) does not apply to others. Now the final contributions may be noted as below :

Planet	Basic yrs.	Reduction	Reason	Net yrs.
Sun	17.5642	1/3rd	Rule 2	11.7095
Moon	24.6247	1/2	Rule 1	12.3124
Mars	08.4036	9th bhava	Rule 3	06.4564
Mercury	06.9968	Nil		06.9968
Jupiter	14.1200	10th bhava	Rule 3	12.1886
Venus	19.2327	7th bhava	exempted	19.2327
Saturn	12.3979	8th bhava	Rule 3	10.1110
Lagna				3 2428
			Total :	82 2502

These years are in Savanamana (360 days a year) as we have used 360° of the zodiac. To apply this to Gregorian calendar, we have to convert the same into Sauramana. By simply multiplying the said figure by 0.9856034, we can get Sauramana. Thus in the case of our example, we arrive at a net longevity in Sauramana as 81.06 years.

The dasa period so obtained are Pinda Dasa of the 7 planets and the Lagna. If the Sun is strongest in the horoscope, effects can be worked out on Pinda Dasa method.

अथ विप्र! निसर्गायुः खेटानां कथयाम्यहम्।
चन्द्रारज्ञसितेज्यार्कशनीनां क्रमशोब्दका ॥१६॥
एकद्वयंकनखा धृत्यः कृतिः पंचाशदेव हि।
जन्मकालात् क्रमाज् ज्ञेया दशाश्चैता निसर्गजाः ॥१७॥

16-17. *NISARGAYU :* O Brahmin, now I tell you about Nisargayu 1, 2, 9, 20, 18, 20 and 50 are the years allotted to the Moon, Mars, Mercury, Venus, Jupiter the Sun and Saturn from the period of birth.

Notes : Except giving the number of years applicable to Naisargayu, there is no other mention about rectification etc. in our version as well as in that of Chaukambha Sanskrit Sansthana. However, we have some more instructions in the version given by Thakur Prasad Pustak Bhandar. The relevant portion is as under :

वर्षमासदिनादिकं तद्धिपिंडायुः स्फुटं भवेत्।
एवं क्रिया निसर्गोपि हानिवृद्धिः पूर्ववत् ॥

This conveys to us that the years denoted for the planets are when they are in deep exaltation. These are halved at deep debilitation. Then the rectifications are the same as applicable to Pindayu. So to say, the four kinds of reductions suggested for Pindayu be performed for Nisargayu as well. Ascendant also contributes in Nisargayu. The method of its contribution in Nisargayu is also the same as seen in Pindayu scheme.

अथांऽशायु सलग्नानां खेटानां कथयाम्यहम्।
नवांशराशितुल्यानि खेटो वर्षाणि यच्छति ॥१८॥
भादि खगं खगैः सूर्यैर्हत्वा तद्भगणादिकम्।
कृत्वाऽर्कशेषितं ज्ञेयमब्दाद्यंशायुषः स्फुटम् ॥१९॥

18-19. *AMSAYU* : Now about Amsayu contributions by the ascendant and planets. The years correspond to the number of Navamsas counted from Aries. Multiply the longitude in question by 108. If the product exceeds 12, expunge multiples of 12 and consider the final product in Rasi, degrees etc. as years, months etc.

Notes : The 7 planets and the ascendant contribute to longevity as per Amsayurdhaya method based on the Navamsas covered. 3° 20′ longitude equals one year. Thus the basic contributions can be worked out as per the example given for the Lagna's longitude in the Pindayu scheme. Similar understanding can be extended to planetary longitudes. The basic contributions thus found out be rectified in the same manner as explained for Pindajayu. The sage puts forth a different suggestion as enunciated by another school of thought in regard to rectification of Amsayu, in the following slokas :

पिण्डायुरिव तत्रापि हार्निं कुर्याद् विचक्षणः ।
अत्राऽपरो विशेषोऽपि कैम्चिद् विज्ञैरुदाहृतः ॥२०॥
साधितायुः खगे स्वोच्चे स्वर्क्षे वा त्रिगुणं स्मृतम् ।
द्विगुणं स्वनवांशस्थे स्वद्रेष्काणे तथोत्तमे ॥२१॥
उभयत्र गते खेटे कार्यं त्रिगुणमेव हि ।
हानिद्वयेऽर्धहानिः स्यादित्यायुः प्रस्फुटं नृणाम् ॥२२॥

20-22. The same reductions as per Pindayu apply to Amsayu as well; i e. half for a combust planet, one third for inimical placement and the ones due for placements in the half of the zodiac counted from the 12th backwards. Some scholars suggest further corrections for Amsayu, viz. to increase threefold the contribution of a planet in exaltation or in own house and double the contribution if the contributor is in his own Navamsa or in own decanate. If doubling and trebling is warranted, only trebling be done. In case of reductions also, only halving is to be done if both halving and reducing a third are required. That is how the final life span of men be understood.

Notes : Rectification of Amsayu be done, taking the basic contributions as detailed below.

(a) Treble the basic years if the planet is exalted or in own sign.

(b) Double if in own Navamsa or own decanate.

(c) Among 'a' and 'b'. if both are needed only 'a' is to be effected.

(d) No clear instructions are found about halving the contribution or casting off a third. Halving, however, obviously applies to a debilitated planet while loss of a third part applies to a planet in inimical sign. In the matter of deduction also, only halving is to be effected if both reductions are required for one and the same planet.

एवं संसाध्य चान्येषां हन्यात् स्वस्वपरायुषा ।
नृणां परायुषा भक्त्वा तेषामायुः स्फुटं भवेत् ॥२३॥

23. *LONGEVITY FOR OTHER LIVING BEINGS :* For other living beings as well such computations be made. The said figure be multiplied by the figure corresponding to its full span of life and divided by the figure corresponding to full span of life for human beings.

अथायुः परमं वक्ष्ये नानाजातिसमुद्भवम् ।
अनन्तसंख्यं देवानामृषीणां च द्विजोत्तम ! ॥२४॥
गृध्रोलूक-शुकध्वांक्ष-सर्पाणां च सहस्रकम् ।
श्येन-वानर-भल्लूक-मण्डूकानां शतत्रयम् ॥२५॥
पंचाशदुत्तरशतं राक्षसानां प्रकीर्तितम् ।
नराणां कुञ्जराणां च विंशोत्तरशतं तथा ॥२६॥
द्वात्रिंशद् घोटकानाञ्च पंचविंशत् खरोष्ट्रयोः ।
वृषाणां महिषाणां च चतुर्विंशतिवत्सरम् ॥२७॥
विंशत्यायुर्मयूराणां छागादीनां च षोडश ।
हंसानां पंचनव च पिकानां द्वादशाब्दकाः ॥२८॥
शुनां पारावतानां च, कुक्कुटानां समाष्टकम् ।
बुद्बुदाद्यण्डजानां च परायुः सप्तवत्सराः ॥२९॥

24-29. *FULL LIFE SPAN OF VARIOUS LIVING BEINGS :* I now tell you the full life span figures for various living beings. Gods and sages enjoy endless life span (i.e. in astronomical proportions as against ordinary mortals). The full life span of eagles, owls, parrots, crows and snakes is one thousand years. Falcon, monkey, bear, and frog—tne full span of life in these cases is 300 years. Demon's life span in full is 150 years while it is 120 years for human beings. 32 years for horses, 25 years for donkeys and camels, 24 years for oxen and buffaloes, 20 years for peacocks, 16 years for goats and rams. 14 years for swans, 12 years for cuckoo, dog and dove, 8 years for hens etc. and 7 years for birds etc.—these are full life spans for various living beings.

यदेतदधुना प्रोक्तं त्रिधायुद्विजसत्तम ! ।
तेषु क्रिञ्च कदा ग्राह्यमिति ते कथयाम्यहम् ॥३०॥
विलग्नपे वलोपेते शुभदृष्टेंशसम्भवम् ।
रवौ पिंडोद्भवं ग्राह्यं चन्द्रे नैसर्गिकं तथा ॥३१॥

30-31. *CHOICE OF LONGEVITY* : I have narrated 3 different methods of longevity. Listen to me about the choice among the three systems. According to the ascendant, the Sun or the Moon being stronger than the other two, Amsayu, Pindayu or Nisargayu be respectively chosen.

बलसाम्ये द्वयोर्योगदलमायुः प्रकीर्तितम् ।
त्रयाणां त्रियुतेस्त्र्यंशसमं ज्ञेयं द्विजोत्तम ! ॥३२॥

32. *DOUBTFUL CASES* : If 2 among the ascendants the Sun and the Moon gain equal strength, then longevity be worked out as per both systems and the average of both (final) be considered. If all the 3 are equally strong, the average of the 3 be considered.

Notes : In slokas 30 and 31 above, we are asked to select one among the 3 systems, viz Pindayu, Naisargayu and Amsayu according to the Sun, the Moon and ascendant being the strongest. If two among the three have equal Shadbala, then the average of the respective systems will be the final longevity. If the three are of equal strength, the average of three systems be taken to be actual life duration of the native.

Take for example where the Sun and the Moon are equally strong and assume that Pindayu indicates a life span of 52.5 years while Nisargayu gives 40.7 years. The average of these two, i.e. 46.35 years will be the actual longevity.

Similarly assume that the luminaries and the ascendant are equally strong, and contribute 62.9 years Pindayu, 25.5 years

Nisargayu and 12.8 years of Amsayu. The average of these three, i.e. 33.73 years will be the actual longevity of the native.

अथाऽन्यदपि वक्ष्यामि शृणु त्वं द्विजसत्तम ! ।
कैश्चिल्लग्नाष्टमेशाभ्यां मन्देन्दुभ्यां तथैव च ॥३३॥
लग्नहोराविलग्नाभ्यां स्फुटमायुः प्रकीर्तितम् ।
आदौ लग्नाष्टमेशाभ्यां योगमेकं विचिन्तयेत् ॥३४॥
द्वितीयं मन्दचन्द्राभ्यां योगं पश्येद् द्विजोत्तम ! ।
लग्नहोराविलग्नाभ्यां तृतीयं परिचिन्तयेत् ॥३५॥
चरराशौ स्थितौ द्वौ चेत् तदा दीर्घमुदाहृतम् ।
एकः स्थिरेऽपरो द्वन्द्वे दीर्घमायुस्तथापि हि ॥३६॥
एकश्चरे स्थिरेऽन्यश्चेत् तदा मध्यमुदाहृतम् ।
द्वौ वा द्वन्द्वे स्थितौ विप्र ! मध्यमायुस्तथापि च ॥३७॥
एकश्चरेऽपरो द्वन्द्वे द्वौ वा स्थिरगतौ तदा ।
जातकस्य तदाऽल्पायुर्ज्ञेयमेवं द्विजोत्तम ! ॥३८॥
योगत्रयेण योगाभ्यां सिद्धं यद् ग्राह्यमेव तत् ।
योगत्रयविसंवादे लग्नहोराविलग्नतः ॥३९॥
लग्ने वा सप्तमे चन्द्रे ग्राह्यं मन्देन्दुतस्तदा ।
ह्रासो वृद्धिश्च कक्ष्याया विचिन्त्या सर्वदा बुधैः ॥४०॥

33-40. *OTHER CLUES TO LONGEVITY :* O excellent of the Brahmins, I give you details of other methods in the matter of longevity as under : This is based on the positions of the ascendant lord, 8th lord, Saturn, the Moon, natal ascendant and Hora ascendant (Hora Lagna). These six are grouped into three groups thus : the lords of the ascendant and of the 8th on the one hand, Saturn and the Moon on the other hand, and the natal ascendant and Hora ascendant on yet the other hand. Out of a group, if the two are in movable sign/signs long life is denoted. One in fixed sign and the other in a dual sign will also bestow long life. One in movable aign and the other in fixed sign will give medium life. If both are in dual sign then again medium life will be obtained. Short life is denoted if one is in a movable sign as the other is in a common sign, or if both are in fixed signs. The type of life denoted by three or two groups be only considered. If the three groups denote different scales, then the one indicated by the pair of natal ascendant and Hora ascendant be only considered. In case of three different indications if the Moon is in the ascendant or the 7th, then the one indicated by Saturn-Moon pair will only come to pass.

Notes: Three groups are considered here for this system of longevity calculations. Following are the three groups, each group consisting two of the six.

Ist group—natal ascendant lord and 8th lord from the ascendant.

2nd group—Saturn and the Moon.

3rd group—natal ascendant and Hora Langa. (For Hora Lagna, see p. 63).

Thus two planets in one group, two planets in another group and two ascendants in yet another group are selected. Now their positions will denote the basic longevity. Note the position of each of the constituent in each group thus :

1. Long life : If both the constituents are in movable signs (jointly or separately), long life will come to pass. One in fixed sign and another in a dual sign will also give same scale of longevity.

2. Medium life : One in movable sign and another fixed sign will give medium life. Both in dual signs will also give same effects.

3. Short life : One in movable sign and another in dual sign will indicate short life. Both of them in fixed signs will produce again short life.

Thus, all the six possible positions of a pair are covered. Which group is to be considered for arriving at life span and in what circumstances be understood thus.

4. Out of the three groups, the scale of span (viz. long, medium and short) indicated by two or three be considered. Suppose two groups indicate medium life while another short life, then take medium span as the basic one. Alternatively if three indicate identical scales, i e. long, short or medium, consider that as the case may be. It is also possible that one group denotes long life, another medium life and yet another short life. In that case follow point 5 given below.

5. If 3 groups denote variable spans, the group of natal ascendant and Hora ascendant will have a say on the indication. Whatever this pair denotes will be the basic span in case of three different indications.

6. Rule 5 has also an exception, thus. That is, in the case of three different indications (i.e. one long life, another medium life and yet another short life), see the position of the Moon in the natal horoscope. If she is in the ascendant or in the 7th, then the indication given by the pair of Hora-natal ascendants be ignored and the indication of Saturn-Moon be alone considered. If the Moon is neither in the ascendant nor in the 7th, then follow the indication of Hora-natal ascendants as given in rule 2 above.

दीर्घे योगत्रयेणैवं नखचन्द्रसमाब्दकाः ।
योगद्वयेन वस्वाशा योगैकेन रसांककाः ॥४१॥
मध्ये योगत्रयेणैवं खाष्टतुल्याब्दकाः स्मृताः ।
द्व्यगा योगद्वयेनाऽत्रयोगैकेनाब्धिषण्मिताः ॥४२॥
अल्पे योगत्रयेणाऽत्रद्वात्रिंशन्मितवत्सराः ।
योगद्वयेन षट्त्रिंशत् योगैकेन च खाब्धयः ॥४३॥
एवं दीर्घसमाल्पेषु खाब्धयो रसवह्नयः ।
खण्डा दन्तमितास्तेभ्यः स्फुटमायुः प्रसाधयेत् ॥४४॥

41-44. *FURTHER CLARIFICATIONS :* If long life is denoted by all the said three groups, the span is 120 years, if by two groups it is 108 years and if only by one group it is 96 years. If medium life is arrived at by three groups, it is 80 years, by 2 groups 72 years and by one group 64 years. If short life is denoted by the said three groups it is only 32 years, if by two groups 36 years and by one group 40 years. These are rectified as under.

Notes : Again, the sage fixes the quantum of years for long, short, and medium life spans, thus.

Long life : by 3 pairs—120 years (harmonic reduction of 12 years)

2 pairs—180 years

1 pair —96 years

Medium life : by 3 pairs—80 years (harmonic reduction of 8 years)
2 pairs—72 years
1 pair —64 years

Short life : by 3 pairs—32 years (progressive increase of 4 years)
2 pairs—36 years
1 pair —40 years

The indication has to be selected as per rules 4 to 6 given in the notes for slokas 33-40.

We will now work out the basic contribution of longevity for the same example as given for Pindayu calculations. The chart may be understood from Pindayu example, while Hora Lagna is Taurus 20° 32′ 12″.

The first group—ascendant lord is in a movable sign and the 8th lord is also in a movable sign. Hence long life.

The second group—Saturn and the Moon are respectively in dual sign and movable sign. Hence short life.

The third group—Hora Lagna and the natal ascendant are both in fixed signs. Again short life.

Two groups indicate short life. Hence we are left with no dilemma but to select the indications given by the two groups, i.e. short life. Two pairs indicate short life, hence 36 years will be the basic longevity.

This basic longevity will have to be rectified further as per the instructions given in the following verses.

पूर्ण राश्यादिगे चान्ते हानिर्मध्येऽनुपाततः ।
योगकारकखेटांशयोगस्तत्संख्यया हृतः ॥४५॥
लब्धांशास्तु यथाप्राप्तखण्डघ्नास्त्रिशतोद्धृताः ।
लब्धवर्षादिभिर्हीनं प्राप्तायुः अस्फुटं भवेत् ॥४६॥

45-46. *RECTIFICATIONS :* If the contributor is in the beginning of a sign, his donation will be full and it will be nil if he is at the end. For intermediary placements, rule of three process will apply. Add the longitudes of the contributors (devoid of signs) and the sum so arrived at be divided by the number of contributors. The latest product be multiplied by the number of basic years and divided by 30. This will yield the net longevity.

Notes : If the contributor is in the zero degree of the sign, his share will be full and if he is at the end, it will be zero. In between, his contribution is proportionately known. The longitudes of the contributors, according to being 2 or 4 or 6 as the case may be should be added together, devoid of signs. The resultant product be divided by 2 or 4 or 6 depending on the contributors. This figure should be multiplied by basic years and divided by 30 which will be net span of life. Basic years will also depend on whether one, two or three spans are being considered. When we are considering short life by 3 pairs, such figure will be 96 (i.e. 32×3) or when medium life by 2 pairs are being considered it will be 144, (i.e. 72×2) and so on and so forth.

In the example horoscope, we have short life contributed by 2 pairs and hence basic years for the time being be taken as 72 (i.e. 36 plus 36). The contributors are Moon, Saturn, Mars and Mercury. Their longitudes devoid of signs added denote 51° 58′ 26″. This is to be divided by 4, as there are 4 contributors. Thus we get 12° 59' 37". This is to be multiplied by 72 (basic years) and divided by 30. The net longevity in this process is 31.18 years.

Though Pindayu applies to the said horoscope, we have simply taken the same as an example in regard to the application of the current system.

योगहेतौ शनौ कक्ष्याह्रासोऽन्यैर्वृद्धिरुच्यते ।
न स्वर्क्षतुङ्गगे नो वा पापमात्रयुतेक्षिते ॥४७॥

47. *SPECIAL RULE FOR SATURN :* Should Saturn be a contributor, the class of longevity declines. Some advocate, contrarily, an increase of class in this context. If Saturn is in own sign or in exaltation, change in class will not occur. Even if he is aspected by or conjunct only a malefic, no change occurs.

लग्नसप्तमगे जीवे शुभमात्रयुतेक्षिते ।
कथितस्यायुषो विप्र ! कक्ष्यावृद्धिः प्रजायते ॥४८॥

48. *SPECIAL RULE FOR JUPITER :* If Jupiter is in the ascendant or in the 7th house, and be aspected by or conjunct only benefics, the class of longevity will increase.

अनायुश्चेद् भवेदल्पमल्पान्मध्यं प्रजायते ।
मध्यमाज्जायते दीर्घं दीर्घायुश्चेत्ततोऽधिकम् ॥४९॥
योगहेतौ गुरावेवं कक्ष्यावृद्धेश्च लक्षणम् ।
एतस्माद् वैपरीत्येन कक्ष्याह्रासः शनौ भवेत् ॥५०॥

49-50. *INCREASE AND FALL IN CLASS OF LONGEVITY :* From very short life to short life, from short life to medium life, from medium life to long life and from long life to extremely long life are the increases in the classification of longevity when Jupiter warrants an increase. The reverse is true if Saturn warrants a fall in the span of life.

आयुषो बहुधा भेदाः कथिता भवताऽधुना ।
कतिधा सा कदाऽनायुरमितायुः कदा भवेत् ॥५१॥

51. (Maitreya says) : You have narrated various kinds of longevlty computations. Please favour me by denoting subtle classes there of and poor and long life spans.

बालारिष्टं योगारिष्टमल्पं मध्यञ्च दीर्घकम् ।
दिव्यं चैवाऽमितं चैवं सप्तधायुः प्रकीर्तितम् ॥५२॥

52. (Parasara replies) : These are seven-fold, viz. Balarishta, yogarishta, short, medium, long, super-natural (Divya) and illimitable.

बालारिष्टे समा अष्टौ योगारिष्टे च विंशतिः ।
द्वात्रिंशद् वत्सरा अल्पे चतुष्षष्टिस्तु मध्यमे ॥५३॥
विंशाधिकशतं दीर्घे दिव्ये वर्षसहस्रकम् ।
तदूर्ध्वममितं पुण्यैरमितैराप्यते जनैः ॥५४॥

53-54. The life span in Balarishta is 8 years, in Yogarishta 20 years; in short, medium and long lives 32, 64 and 120 years in order are the spans. Super natural life span is for 1000 years. Above this supernatural life span of 1000 years it is Amitayu or illimitable longevity which can be acquired only by Merits.

चन्द्रेज्यौ च कुलीरांगे ज्ञसितौ केन्द्रसंस्थितौ।
अन्ये त्र्यायारिगाः खेटा अमितायुस्तदा भवेत् ॥५५॥

55. *LIMITLESS LONGEVITY :* Should Cancer ascend with Jupiter and the Moon there in while Venus and Mercury are in angles and others are in 3rd, 6th and 11th, the native will obtain limitless longevity.

सौम्याः केन्द्रत्रिकोणस्थाः पापास्त्र्यायारिगास्तथा।
शुभराशौ स्थिते रन्ध्रे दिव्यमायुस्तदा भवेत् ॥५६॥

56. *SUPER-NATURAL LONGEVITY :* One having benefics in angles/trines as malefics are in 3rd, 6th and 11th will obtain super-natural life span (one thousand years). The 8th house in this case should be one of benefic-owned signs.

गोपुरांशे गुरौ केन्द्रे शुक्रे पारावतांशके।
त्रिकोणे कर्कटे लग्ने युगान्तायुस्तदा द्विज ! ॥५७॥

57. *LIVING TILL THE END OF YUGA :* One born in Cancer ascendant will live till the end of the yuga if Jupiter is in an angle and be in Gopuramsa while Venus is in a trine and be in Paaravatamsa.

देवलोकांशके मन्दे कुजे पारावतांशके।
गुरौ सिंहासनांशेऽङ्गे जातो मुनिसमो भवेत् ॥५८॥

58. *LIVING THE LIFE SPAN OF A SAGE :* Jupiter in Simhasanamsa being in the ascendant, Saturn in Devalokamsa and Mars in Paaravatamsa—if these are so, one will enjoy the life span as due to a sage.

सुयोगैर्वर्धते ह्यायुः कुयोगैर्हीयते तथा।
अतो योगानहं वक्ष्ये पूर्णमध्याल्पकारकान् ॥५९॥

59. Good yogas increase the life span and bad yogas decrease the same (as arrived by mathematical means). Hence

I tell you such yogas as to know of full, medium and short span combinations.

केन्द्रे शुभग्रहैर्युक्ते लग्नेशे च शुभान्विते ।
सन्दृष्टे गुरुणा वाऽपि पूर्णमायुस्तदा भवेत् ॥६०॥

60. If an angle contains a benefic while the ascendant lord is conjunct or in aspect to a benefic or Jupiter in particular, the native will live a full span of life,

केन्द्रस्थिते विलग्नेशे गुरुशुक्रसमन्विते ।
ताभ्यां निरीक्षिते वाऽपि पूर्णमायुर्विनिर्दिशेत् ॥६१॥

61. Should the ascendant lord be in an angle in conjunction with or in aspect to Jupiter and Venus, full life span will result.

उच्चस्थितैस्त्रिभिः खेटैर्लग्नरन्ध्रेशसंयुतैः ।
अष्टमे पापहीने च पूर्णमायुर्विनिर्दिशेत् ॥६२॥

62. If at birth 3 planets are exalted, out of which the lords of ascendant and 8th are inclusive, as the 8th is devoid of a malefic in it, full life span will result.

अष्टमस्थैस्त्रिभि खेटैः स्वोच्चमित्रस्ववर्गगैः ।
लग्नेशे बलसंयुक्ते दीर्घमायुस्तदा भवेत् ॥६३॥

63. Long life is denoted if 3 planets are in the 8th, in exaltation, own/friendly divisions while the ascendant lord is strong.

स्वभोच्चस्थेन केनापि नभोगेन समन्वितः ।
अष्टमेशः शनिर्वापि दीर्घमायुर्विनिर्दिशेत् ॥६४॥

64. If Saturn or the ascendant lord is conjunct with any exalted planet, long life will result.

त्रिषडायगतैः पापैः शुभैः केन्द्रत्रिकोणगैः ।
लग्नेशे बलसंयुक्ते दीर्घमायुर्विनिर्दिशेत् ॥६५॥

65. Long life will be enjoyed if malefics are in 3rd, 6th and 11th while benefics are in angles.

षट्सप्तरन्ध्रभावेषु शुभखेटयुतेषु च ।
त्रिभवेषु च पापेषु पूर्णमायुर्विनिर्दिशेत् ॥६६॥

66. If the 6th, 7th and 8th are occupied by benefics while malefics are in 3rd and 11th, full life span will follow the birth.

शत्रुव्ययगताः पापा लग्नेशो यदि केन्द्रगः ।
रविमित्रं च रन्ध्रेशः पूर्णमायुस्तथापि हि ॥६७॥

67, If the 8th lord is friendly to the Sun while malefics are in the 6th and 12th as the ascendant lord is in an angle, the native will live the full span of life.

आयुः स्थानस्थिताः पापाः कर्मेशः स्वोच्चगो यदा ।
तथापि दीर्घमायु स्याद् विज्ञेयं द्विजसत्तम ! ॥६८॥

68. O excellent of the Brahmins, if a malefic is in the 8th while the 10 lord is exalted, one will be long-lived.

द्विस्वभावगृहे लग्ने लग्नेशे केन्द्रसंस्थिते ।
स्वोच्चराशित्रिकोणे वा दीर्घमायुर्विनिर्दिशेत् ॥६९॥

69. Long life will follow if a dual sign ascend at birth while its lord is in an angle oe in exaltation or in a trine.

द्विस्वभावगृहे लग्ने लग्नेशाद् बलसंयुतात् ।
द्वौ पापौ यदि केन्द्रस्थौ दीर्घमायुस्तदा भवेत् ॥७०॥

70. Should a common sign ascend while two malefics are in an angle with reference to strong ascendant lord, long life is indicated.

लग्नाष्टमेशयोर्मध्ये यः खेटः प्रबलो भवेत् ।
तस्मिन् केन्द्रगते दीर्घं मध्यं पणफरस्थिते ॥७१॥
आपोक्लिमे स्थिते स्वल्पमायुर्भवति निश्चितम् ।
लग्नेशे च रवेर्मित्रे दीर्घमायुः समे समम् ॥७२॥
शत्रौ स्वल्पं वदेदित्थमष्टमेशादपि स्मृतम् ।
मित्रमध्याऽरिभावस्थे तस्मिन्नेवं फलं वदेत् ॥७३॥

71-73. The stronger among the ascendant lord and the 8th lord if in an angle will confer long life and if in Panaphara

(2nd, 5th, 8th or 11th) medium life. If the said planet be in Apoklima (3rd, 6th, 9th or 12th) short life will come to pass. According to the ascendant lord being friendly, neutral or inimical to the Sun, long, medium or short life will result.

सहजाधीशभूपुत्रौ द्वौ रन्ध्रेशशनैश्चरौ ।
अस्तौ वा पापदृग्युक्तौ स्वल्पमायुः प्रयच्छतः ॥७४॥

74. Should Mars *and* the 3rd lord, *or* the 8th lord *and* Saturn be combust or (two of either pair) be conjunct malefics or aspected by malefics, there will be short life.

षष्ठेऽष्टमे व्यये वाऽपि लग्नेशे पापसंयुते ।
स्व पायुरनपत्यो वा शुभदृग्योगवर्जिते ॥७५॥

75. If the ascendant lord is in the 6th, 8th or 12th in the company of malefics and be devoid of conjunction/aspect of a benefic, short life will come to pass.

चतुष्टयगते पापे शुभदृष्टिविवर्जिते ।
बलहीने विग्लनेशे स्वल्पमायुर्विनिर्दिशेत् ॥७६॥

76. If malefics are in angles devoid of conjunction or aspect of benefics while the ascendant lord is not strong, only short life will result.

व्ययार्थौ पापसंयुक्तौ शुभदृग्योगवर्जितौ ।
स्वल्पमायुस्तदा ज्ञेयं निर्विशंकं द्विजोत्तम ! ॥७७॥

77. O excellent of Brahmins, if the 12th and 2nd are occupied by malefics and be devoid of benefic aspect or company, the native will be short-lived.

लग्नरन्ध्रेशयोरेवं दुःस्थयोर्बलहीनयोः ।
स्वल्पमायुर्बुधैर्ज्ञेयं मिश्रयोगाच्च मध्यमम् ॥७८॥

78. If the lords of the ascendant and the 8th are bereft of dignities and strength, short life will come to pass. If they are helped by others while being so, medium life will come to pass.

अथ मारकभेदाध्यायः ।।४४।।

Chapter 44

Maraka (Killer) Planets

बहुधाऽऽयुर्भवा योगाः कथिता भवताऽधुना ।
नृणां मारकभेदाश्च कथ्यन्तां कृपया मुने ! ।।१।।

1. O sage, you have mentioned a lot about longevity. Be kind enough to throw light on Marakas or killers.

तृतीयमष्टमस्थानमायुःस्थानं द्वयं द्विज ! ।
मारकं तद्व्ययस्थानं द्वितीयं सप्तमं तथा ।।२।।

2-5. O Brahmin, the 3rd and 8th are the two houses of longevity. The houses related to death are the 12th from each of these, i.e. the 2nd and 7th are Maraka houses.

Notes : The 3rd house is also a house of longevity as it is the 8th from the 8th. The 2nd house—12th from the 3rd—and the 7th house—12th from the 8th—are two principle Maraka houses. The lords of these houses will also acquire such qualities giving life or taking away life.

तत्रापि सप्तमस्थानाद् द्वितीयं बलवत्तरम् ।
तयोरीशौ तत्र गताः पापिनस्तेन संयुताः ।।३।।
ये खेटाः पापिनस्ते च सर्वे मारकसंज्ञकाः ।
तेषां दशाविपाकेषु सम्भवे निधनं नृणाम् ।।४।।
अल्प-मध्यम-पूर्णायुः प्रमाणमिह योगजम् ।
विज्ञाय प्रथमं पुंसां मारकं परिचिन्तयेत् ।।५।।

3. Out of the two (i.e 2nd and 7th) the 2nd is a powerful Maraka house (as against the 7th) The lords of the 2nd and the 7th, malefics in the 2nd and the 7th and malefics aceompanying the 2nd and the 7th lords are all known as Marakas. The major and sub periods of these planets will bring death on the native depending on whether he has a long life, medium life or short life.

Notes : The 2nd and 7th are denoted as Maraka houses. But the 2nd is given a more important place to kill than the 7th house. For the 2nd house acquires an additional qualification of being in the 7th from the 8th house. Thus, the 2nd is 12th from the 3rd, and 7th from the 8th.

If there is a malefic in the 2nd or in the 7th, he will be a prime killer while a benefic will not be so. The Dasa periods of such planets will inflict death.

अलाभे पुनरेतेषां सम्बन्धेन व्ययेशतुः ।
क्वचिच्छुभानां च दशास्वष्टमेशदशासु च ॥६॥
केवलानां च पापानां दशासु निधनं क्वचित् ।
कल्पनीयं बुधैर्नृणां मारकाणामदर्शने ॥७॥

6-7. The Dasa of a benefic planet related to the 12th lord may also inflict death. End may descend on the native in the 8th lord's Dasa. The Dasa of a planet which is an exclusive malefic (i.e. first-rate malefic) may also cause death.

Notes : The 12th house is also a house of death, for it is the terminal house. Malefics related to 2nd, 3rd, 7th and 8th will cause death while or not a benefic related to 12th will do so. The Dasa of a malefic, whether or not he is a lord of one of these houses, will also prove harmful for span of life. However, for Saturn, a different approach is recommended.

The rules given are just general and are hints to decide death givers. The life span should be ascertained through other Ayurdaya calculations, and the exact dasa periods be decided only later on. Simply saying that the 2nd lord's dasa will bring in death and so on and so forth will be a misnomer. The sage suggests that the occupants of the 3rd also will cause death. Thus the 8th and the 3rd, though known as houses of longevity, are simultaneously capable of causing death. For the information of the reader, the Maraka planets in the ascending are : occupants of or lords of 12th, 3rd, 8th, 7th and 2nd. The lords/occupants of 6th and 11th are second grade killers. The last group consists of occupants/lords of 5th, 9th, 10th, 4th and Ist. They are the least marakas. However, these can also become Marakas depending on the clues given in slokas 15-21 *infra*.

A difficult subject like longevity cannot be fully explained in a chapter like this. The reader may take basic guidelines from the present work and other standard works before forming an opinion on longevity.

सत्यपि स्वेन सम्बन्धे न हन्ति शुभभुक्तिषु ।
हन्ति सत्यप्यसम्बन्धे मारकः पापभुक्तिषु ॥८॥

8. The dasa of a malefic will not cause death in the Antardasa (sub period) of a benefic planet, although the former, is related to the latter, but in the sub period of a malefic planet though not related.

मारकग्रहसम्बन्धान्निहन्ता पापकृच्छनिः ।
अतिक्रम्येतरान् सर्वान् भवत्यत्र न संशयः ॥९॥

9. Shold Saturn be ill-disposed and be related to a maraka planet, he will be the first to kill in preference to other planets.

अथाऽन्यदपि वक्ष्यामि द्विज ! मारकलक्षणम् ।
त्रिविधाश्चायुषो योगाः स्वल्पायुर्मध्यमोत्तमाः ॥१०॥
द्वात्रिंशात् पूर्वमल्पायुर्मध्यमायुस्ततः परम् ।
चतुष्षष्ट्याः पुरस्तात् तु ततो दीर्घमुदाहृतम् ॥११॥
उत्तमायुः शतादूर्ध्वं ज्ञातव्यं द्विजसत्तम ! ।
जनैर्विंशतिवर्षान्तमायुर्ज्ञातुं न शक्यते ॥१२॥
जप-होम-चिकित्साद्यैर्बालरक्षां हि कारयेत् ।
म्रियन्ते पितृदोषैश्च केचिन्मातृग्रहैरपि ॥१३॥
केचित् स्वारिष्टयोगाच्च त्रिविधा बालमृत्यवः ।
ततः परं नृणामायुर्गणयेद् द्विजसत्तम ! ॥१४॥

10-14. O Brahmin, I tell you further about Marakas. Narrated earlier are three kinds of life spans, viz. short, medium and long. Short life is before 32 years, later on upto 64 it is medium life and from 64 to 100 it is long life. Beyond 100 the longevity is called supreme. O excellent of the Brahmins, it is impossible to decide upon longevity till the native is 20 year old. Till such year the child should be protected by sacred recitations, religious offerings (of ghee etc. to consecrated fire as prescribed by Vedas etc.) and medical treatments, for premature death may descend on the child due to sins of father or mother or of its own (in the previous birth).

अथाऽन्यदपि वक्ष्यामि नृणां मारकलक्षणम् ।
अल्पायुर्योगजातस्य विप भे च मृतिर्भवेत् ॥१५॥
मध्यायुर्योगजस्यैवं प्रत्यरौ च मृतिर्भवेत् ।
दीर्घायुर्योगजातस्य वधभे तु मृतिर्भवेत् ॥१६॥
द्वाविंशत्र्यंशपश्चैव तथा वैनाशिकाधिपः ।
विपत्तारा-प्रत्यरीशा वधभेशंस्तथैव च ॥१७॥
आद्यान्तपौ च विज्ञेयौ चन्द्राक्रान्तगृहाद् द्विज ! ।
मारकौ पापखेटौ तौ शुभौ चेद्रोगदौ स्मृतौ ॥१८॥
षष्ठाधिपदशायां च नृणां निधनसम्भवः ।
षष्ठाष्टरिष्फनाथानामपहारे मृतिर्भवेत् ॥१९॥
मारका बहवः खेटा यदि वीर्यसमन्विताः ।
तत्तद्दशान्तरे विप्र ! रोगकष्टादिसंभवः ॥२०॥
उक्ता ये मारकास्तेषु प्रबलो मुख्यमारकः ।
तदवस्थानुसारेण मृतिं वा कष्टमादिशेत् ॥२१॥

15-21. I further mention about the Maraka planets. One born with short life combinations may face death in the Dasa denoted by Vipat star (3rd from birth star); one of medium life may die in the dasa denoted by Pratyak star (5th from birth star). In the dasa denoted by Vadha star (7th from birth star), one with long life may obtain his end. The dasa of the lord of 22nd decanate or the one of 23rd, 3rd, 5th or 7th asterisms may also cause death. The lords of the 2nd and 12th counted from the Moon sign may bring death, this is true when the said ruler is a malefic and if he be a benefic there will be (only) diseases (but not death). Death may come to pass in the dasa of the 6th lord and in the sub periods of 6th/8th/12th lords. Should there be many Marakas (endowed with the power of killing) and be strong, there will be diseases, miseries etc. in the respective major and sub periods. Thus these are Marakas (as above) and are primarily related to descend death upon the native. According to their dispositions there may be death or difficulties.

Notes : The Maraka power of a planet may be correlated to the span of life arrived by other calculations. If both coincide there will be death. If there is a variation, there will not be death but difficulties equal to death like miseries, diseases, poverty etc.

राहुश्चेदथवा केतुर्लग्ने कामेऽष्टमे व्यये ।
मारकेशान्मदे वाऽपि मारकेशेन संयुतः ॥२२॥
मारकः स च विज्ञेयः स्वदशान्तर्दशास्वपि ।
मकरे वृश्चिके जन्म राहुस्तस्य मृतिप्रदः ॥२३॥
षष्ठाऽष्टरिष्फगो राहुस्तद्दाये कष्टदो भवेत् ।
शुभग्रहयुतो दृष्टो न तदा कष्टकृन्मतः ॥२४॥

22-24. *RAHU AND KETU AS MARAKAS* : If Rahu or Ketu be in the ascendant, 7th, 8th or 12th thereof, or be in the 7th from a Maraka lord or be with such a planet, they acquire powers of killing in their major or sub periods. For one born in Capricorn or in Scorpio, Rahu will be a Maraka. Should Rahu be in the 6th, 8th or 12th, he will give difficulties in his dasa periods. He will not, however, do so if aspected by or conjunct a benefic.

Notes : Important places for Rahu/Ketu to acquire power of killing are the ascendant, 7th, 8th or 12th. The 2nd house is naturally added as another node will be in the 2nd when one is in the specified 8th house. They will not be Marakas if they are in the 3rd, 9th, 5th and 11th houses. If a node joins a Maraka planet (or is in the house of a Maraka planet) it will act as a Maraka. Rahu is termed as a primary maraka for Capricorn and Scorpio ascendants. If he is in one of the adverse houses for these ascendants his dasa will bring death or intolerable difficulties.

लग्नात् तृतीयभावे तु बलिना रविणा युते ।
राजहेतोश्च मरणं तस्य ज्ञेयं द्विजोत्तम ! ॥२५॥
तृतीये चेन्दुना युक्ते दृष्टे वा यक्ष्मणा मृतिः ।
कुजेन व्रणशस्त्राग्नि-दाहाद्यैर्मरणं भवेत् ॥२६॥

तृतीये शनि-राहुभ्यां युक्ते दृष्टेऽपि वा द्विज ! ।
विषार्तितो मृतिर्वाच्या जलाद्वा वह्निपीडनात् ॥२७॥
गर्ताद्दुच्चात् प्रपतनाद् बन्धनाद् वा मृतिर्भवेत् ।
तृतीये चन्द्रमान्दिभ्यां युक्ते वा वीक्षिते द्विज ॥२८॥
कृमिकुष्ठादिना तस्य मरणं भवति ध्रुवम् ।
तृतीये बुधसंयुक्ते वीक्षिते वापि तेन च ॥२९॥
ज्वरेण मरणं तस्य विज्ञेयं द्विजसत्तम ! ।
तृतीये गुरुणा युक्ते दृष्टे शोफादिना मृतिः ॥३०॥
तृतीये भृगुयुग्दृष्टे मेहरोगेण तन्मृतिः ।
बहुखेटयुते तस्मिन् बहुरोगभवा मृतिः ॥३१॥

25-31. *THIRD HOUSE AND DEATH* : O excellent of Brahmins, if the Sun, being with strength, is in the 3rd house from the ascendant, one will obtain his death due to a king (or legal punishments). The Moon in the 3rd will cause death due to tuberculosis while wounds, weapons, fire and thirst will cause death through Mars in the 3rd. If the 3rd be aspected or occupied by Saturn and Rahu, death will be through poison, water or fire, or fall from heights or confinement. Death will surely come to descend through insects or leprosy if the Moon and Gulika occupy or aspect the 3rd house. Mercury aspecting or occupying the 3rd will bring death followed by fever. Jupiter in the 3rd or aspecting the 3rd will cause death by swelling or tumours. Urinary diseases will cause death if Venus is in the 3rd or aspects the 3rd. Many planets aspecting or occupying will bring death through many diseases.

Notes : The sage brings in the 3rd house in the context of death. According to the planets related to 3rd house by conjunction or aspect, death will descend on the native through the following causes.

The Sun	— legal punishments, death-awards etc. (also cardiac problem)
The Moon	— tuberculosis (lung disorders etc.)
Mars	— Wounds (accidents etc.), weapons (encounter), fire (also electricity) and thirst.
Saturn/Rahu	— poison, water, fire, confinement, falls etc.

Moon and Gulika — insects (scorpion, bees, snakes etc.) or leprosy.
Mercury — severe fever (typhoid etc.)
Jupiter — swelling, tumour, etc. (also jaundice, dropsy etc.)
Venus — urinary disorders (kidney troubles, venereal diseases etc.) (for females leucorrhea).
Mixed planets — various reasons

तृतीये च शुभैर्युक्ते शुभदेशे मृतिर्भवेत् ।
पापैश्च कीकटे देशे मिश्रैर्मिश्रस्थले मृतिः ॥३२॥

32, If the 3rd house is occupied by a benefic, death will be in an auspicious place (like a shrine) and if by a malefic in sinful places. Mixed occupation will yield mixed results in this regard.

तृतीये गुरु-शुक्राभ्यां युक्ते ज्ञानेन वै मृतिः ।
अज्ञानेनाऽन्यखेटैश्च मृतिर्ज्ञेया द्विजोत्तम ! ॥३३॥

33. Consciousness will prevail at the time of death if Jupiter or Venus be in the 3rd. With others therein, there will be unconsciousness before death.

चरराशौ तृतीयस्थे परदेशे मृतिर्भवेत् ।
स्थिरराशौ स्वगेहे च द्विस्वभावे पथि द्विज ! ॥३४॥

34. According to the 3rd house being a movable, fixed or dual sign, death will be in a foreign place (other than native place), in one's own house or on the way.

लग्नादष्टमभावाच्च निमित्तं कथितं बुधैः ।
सूर्येऽष्टमेऽग्नितो मृत्युश्चन्द्रे मृत्युर्जलेन च ॥३५॥
शास्त्राद् भौमे ज्वराज् ज्ञे च गुरौ रोगात् क्षुधा भृगौ ।
पिपासया शनौ मृत्युर्विज्ञेयो द्विजसत्तम ! ॥३६॥

35-36 : *OCCUPANTS OF THE 8TH HOUSE :* Note the occupant of the 8th house from the ascendant. If it is the Sun, death will be through fire, the Moon water, Mars weapons, Mercury fever, Jupiter diseases, Venus hunger and Saturn thirst.

अष्टमे शुभदृग्युक्ते धर्मपे च शुभैर्युते ।
तीर्थे मृतिस्तदा ज्ञेया पापाख्यैरन्यथा मृतिः ॥३७॥

37. Shou d the 8th house be occupied or aspected by a benefic while the 9th lord is conjunct a benefic the native will die in a shrine. If malefics take the role of benefics as above, death will be in a place other than a shrine.

अग्न्यम्बुमिश्रभत्र्यंशैर्ज्ञेयो मृत्युर्गृहाश्रितैः ।
परिणामः शवस्याऽत्र भस्मसंक्लेदशोषकैः ॥३८॥
व्यालवर्गदृकाणैस्तु विडम्बो भवति ध्रुवम् ।
शवस्य श्वशृगालाद्यैर्गृध्रकाकादिपक्षिभिः ॥३९॥

38-39. *FATE OF THE CORPSE :* Should there be a benefic's decanate in the 8th (i.e. the 22nd decanate being so), the corpse will be burnt in fire (as prescribed in Sastras); if a malefic's decanate be there, the body will be thrown away in water. If the decanate in question is owned by a mixed planet the dead body will only dry up. If it be a serpent decanate, the body will be eaten away by animals, crows etc.

कर्कटे मध्यमोऽन्त्यश्च वृश्चिकाद्यद्वितीयकौ ।
मीनेऽन्तिमस्त्रिभागश्च व्यालवर्गाः प्रकीर्तिताः ॥४०॥

40. *SERPENT DECANATES :* The 2nd and 3rd decanates in Cancer, the initial one in Scorpio and the last one in Pisces are designated as serpent decanates.

रविचन्द्रबलाक्रान्तत्र्यंशनाथे गुरौ जनः ।
देवलोकात् समायातो विज्ञेयो द्विजसत्तम ! ॥४१॥
शुक्रेन्द्वोः पितृलोकात्तु मर्त्याच्च रविभौमयोः ।
बुधाऽऽर्क्योर्नरकादेवं जन्मकालाद् वदेत् सुधीः ॥४२॥

41-42. *PRE-NATAL ABODE :* O excellent of **Brahmins** the stronger of the luminaries occupying a decanate of Jupiter denotes descent from the world of gods. If the said decanate be of Venus or the Moon the descent is from the world of the Manes, if be of the Sun or Mars it is from the world of the dead (of Yama) and if be of Mercury or Saturn it is from the hell.

गुरुश्चन्द्रसितौ सूर्यभौमौ ज्ञार्कौ यथाक्रमम् ।
देवेन्दुभूम्यधोलोकान् नयन्त्यस्तारिरन्ध्रगाः ॥४३॥
अथ तत्र ग्रहाभावे रन्ध्रारित्र्यंशनाथयोः ।
यो बली स निजं लोकं नयत्यन्ते द्विजोत्तम ! ॥४४॥
तस्य स्वोच्चादि-संस्थित्या वरमध्याऽधमाः क्रमात् ।
तत्तल्लोकेऽपि सञ्जाता विज्ञेया द्विजसत्तम ! ॥४५॥

43-45. *ASCENT AFTER DEATH :* According to the following planets in the 12th, 7th, 6th or the 8th, the native will attain such worlds after death: Juriter—heaven, the Mooo or Venus—the world of Manes, Mars/Sun—earth (i.e. rebirth), Mercury/Saturn—hell. Should the said houses be not occupied, the native will go to the world as indicated by stronger of the decanate lords related to the 6th and the 8th. The relative planet's exaltation etc. will denote the high, medium and low status the native will obtain in the said world.

अन्यान् मारकभेदांश्च राशिग्रहकृतान् द्विज ! ।
दशाध्यायप्रसंगेषु कथयिष्यामि सुव्रत ! ॥४६॥

46. Other planets and Rasis becoming Marakas are being discussed in the chapter related to Dasas.

अथ ग्रहावस्थाध्यायः ॥४५॥

Chapter 45

Avasthas Of Planets

अवस्थावशतः प्रोक्तं ग्रहाणां यत् फलं मुने ! ।
का साऽवस्था मुनिश्रेष्ठ! कतिधा चेति कथ्यताम्! ॥१॥

1. O sage, you have earlier stated that the Avasthas (states) of planets be considered in the context of planetary effects. Be kind to tell me about the same.

अवस्था विविधाः सन्ति ग्रहाणां द्विजसत्तम ! ।
सारभूताश्च यास्तासु बालाद्यास्ता वदाम्यहम् ।।२।।

2. O excellent of Brahmins, various kinds of planetary Avasthas have been expounded. Out of these, I tell you the summary of infant and other states (in the first instance).

क्रमाद् बालः कुमारोऽथ युवा वृद्धस्तथा मृतः ।
षडंशैरसमे खेटः समे ज्ञेयो विपर्ययात् ।।३।।

3. *INFANT STATE ETC :* Infant, youthful, adolescent, old and dead are the states of planets placed in the ascending order at the rate of six degrees in odd signs. This arrangement is reverse in the case of even signs.

Notes : These 5 Avasthas are known as Baaladi Avasthas. For odd signs, the placement concerned will denote the Avastha as under :

Infant state (Baalavastha)	— 0 to 6°
Youthful state (Kumaravastha)	— 6 to 12°
Adolescent state (Yuvavastha)	—12 to 18°
Advanced state (Vridhdhavastha)	—18 to 24°
In extremis (Mritavastha)	—24 to 30°

The above order is to be reversed for placement in an even sign.

फलं पादमितं बाले, फलार्धं च कुमारके ।
यूनि पूर्णं फलं ज्ञेयं वृद्धे किञ्चित् मृते च खम् ।।४।।

4. *RESULTS :* One fourth, half, full, negligible and nil are the grades of results due to a planet in infant, youthful, adolescent, old and dead states.

स्वभोच्चयोः समसुहृद्भयोः शत्रुभनीचयोः ।
जाग्रत्स्वप्नसुषुप्त्याख्या अवस्था नामदृक्फलाः ।।५।।

5. *AWAKENING, DREAMING AND SLEEPING STATES :* If a planet is in its own sign or in exaltation it is said to be in a state of awakening (or alertness). In the sign of a friend or of a neutral it is in dreaming state while in enemy's sign or in debilitation it is in a state of sleeping.

जागरे च फलं पूर्णं स्वप्ने मध्यफलं तथा ।
सुषुप्तौ तु फलं शून्यं विज्ञेयं द्विजसत्तम ! ॥६॥

6. According to a planet being in Awakening, Dreaming or Sleeping states, the results due to it will be full, medium or nil.

दीप्तः स्वस्थः प्रमुदितः शान्तो दीनोऽथ दुःखितः ।
विकलश्च खलः कोऽपीत्यवस्था नवधाऽपराः ॥७॥

7. *OTHER KINDS OF STATES :* There are nine kinds of other states, viz. Deepta, Swastha, Pramudita, Santa, Deena, Vikala, Khala, and Kopa.

स्वोच्चस्थः खेचरो दीप्तः स्वर्क्षे स्वस्थोऽधिमित्रभे ।
मुदितो मित्रभे शान्तः समभे दीन उच्यते ॥८॥
शत्रुभे दुःखितः प्रोक्तो विकलः पापसंयुतः ।
खलः खलगृहे ज्ञेयः कोपी स्यादर्कसंयुतः ॥९॥
यादृशो जन्मकाले यः खेटो यद्भावगो भवेत् ।
तादृशं तस्य भावस्य फलमुह्यं द्विजोत्तम ! ॥१०॥

8-10. If a planet is in its exaltation sign, it is in Deeptavastha, in own sign Swastha, in thick friend's sign Pramudita, in friendly sign Santa, in neutral's sign Deena, in the company of a malefic Vikala, in an enemy's sign Khala, and in being eclipsed by the Sun—Kopa. Depending on such a state of the planet, the house occupied by it will obtain corresponding effects.

लज्जितो गर्वितश्चैव क्षुधितस्तृषितस्तथा ।
मुदितः क्षोभितश्चैव ग्रहभावाः प्रकीर्तिताः ॥११॥
पुत्रगेहगतः खेटो राहुकेतुयुतोऽथवा ।
रविमन्दकुजैर्युक्तो लज्जितो ग्रह उच्यते ॥१२॥
तुङ्गस्थानगतो वाऽपि त्रिकोणेऽपि भवेत्पुनः ।
गर्वितः सोऽपि गदितो निर्विशंकं द्विजोत्तम ! ॥१३॥
शत्रुगेही शत्रुयुक्तो रिपुदृष्टो भवेद्यदि ।
क्षुधितः स च विज्ञेयः शनियुक्तो यथा तथा ॥१४॥

जलराशौ स्थितः खेटः शत्रुणा चाऽवलोकितः ।
शुभग्रहा न पश्यन्ति तृषितः स उदाहृतः ॥१५॥
मित्रगेही मित्रयुक्तो मित्रेण च विलोकितः ।
गुरुणा सहितो यश्च मुदितः स प्रकीर्तितः ॥१६॥
रविणा सहितो यश्च पापा पश्यन्ति सर्वथा ।
क्षोभितं तं विजानीयाच्छत्रुणा यदि वीक्षितः ॥१७॥
येषु येषु च भावेषु ग्रहास्तिष्ठन्ति सर्वथा ।
क्षुधितः क्षोभितो वापि तद्भावफलनाशनः ॥१८॥

11-18. *YET OTHER AVASTHAS :* Lajjita, Garvita, Kshudita, Trushita, Mudita and Kshobhita are the other kinds of (six) states due to the planets. Placed in the 5th house if a planet is associated with a node or with the Sun, Saturn or Mars, it is in **Lajjitavastha.** If a planet is in exaltation or in Moolatrikona, it is **Garvitavastha**. The avastha is **Kshudita** if the planet is in an enemy's sign, or conjunct an enemy or aspected by an enemy or even be in conjunction with Saturn. If a planet is in a watery sign and be in aspect to a malefic but not a benefic, the avastha is called **Trushita.** If a planet is in a friendly sign, or conjunct or aspected by a benefic or is conjunct Jupiter, it is said to be in **Muditavastha.** If a planet is conjunct the Sun and is aspected by or conjunct a malefic or is aspected by an enemy, it is said to be in **Kshobhitavashta.** The houses occupied by a planet in Kshuditavastha or Kshobhitavastha are destroyed.

एवं क्रमेण बोद्धव्यं सर्वभावेषु पण्डितैः ।
बलाऽबलविचारेण वक्तव्यः फलनिर्णयः ॥१९॥
अन्योन्यं च मुदा युक्तं फलं मिश्रं वदेत्पुनः ।
बलहीने तदा हानिः सबले च महाफलम् ॥२०॥
कर्मस्थाने स्थितो यस्य लज्जितस्तृषितस्तथा ।
क्षुधितः क्षोभितो वापि स नरो दुःखभाजनम् ॥२१॥
सुतस्थाने भवेद्यस्य लज्जितो ग्रह एव च ।
सुतनाशो भवेत्तस्य एकस्तिष्ठति सर्वदा ॥२२॥

क्षोभितस्तृषितश्चैव सप्तमे यस्य वा भवेत् !
म्रियते तस्य नारी च सत्यमाहुर्द्विजोत्तम ! ॥२३॥

19-23 The learned should estimate the effects due to a house in the manner cited above (i.e. with the help of various kinds of avasthas), after ascertaining the strength and weakness (of the various planets). Weak planets cause reduction in good effecs while stronger ones give greater effects. If a planet posited in the 10th house is in Lajjitavastha, Kshudhitavastha or Kshobhitavastha, the person w ll always be subjected to miseries. If a planet in the 5th house is in Lajjitavastha, there will be destruction of progeny, or there will be only or e surviving child. Surely the wife of the native will die if there is a planet in the 7th in Kshobhitavastha or in Trushitavastha.

नवालयारामसुखं नृपत्वं कलापटुत्वं विदधाति पुंसाम् ।
सदार्थलाभं व्यवहारवृद्धि फलं विशेषादिह गर्वितस्य ॥२४॥

भवति मुदितयोगे वासशालाविशाला
विमलवसनभूषाभूमियोषासु सौख्यम् ।
स्वजनजनविलासो भूमिपागारवासो
रिपुनिवहविनाशो बुद्धिविद्याविकाशः ॥२५॥

विशति लज्जितभाववशाद्रति विगतराममति विमतिक्षयम् ।
सुतगदागमनं गमनं वृथा कलिकथाभिरुचि न रुचि शुभे ॥२६॥

संक्षोभितस्यापि फलं विशेषाद्दरिद्रजातं कुमति च कष्टम् ।
करोति वित्तक्षयमंघ्रिबाधां धनाप्तिबाधामवनीशकोपात् ॥२७॥

क्षुधितखगवशाद्वै शोकमोहादिपातः
परिजनपरितापादाधिभीत्या कृशत्वम् ।
कलिरपि रिपुलोकैरर्थबाधा नराणा-
मखिलबलनिरोधो बुद्धिरोधो विषादात् ॥२८॥

तृषितखगभवे स्यादंगनासंगमध्ये
भवति गदविकारो दुष्टकार्याधिकारः ।
निजजनपरिवादादर्थहानिः कृशत्वं
खलकृतपरितापो मानहानिः सदैव ॥२९॥

24-29. *EFFECTS OF GARVITAVASTHA ETC.* : A planet in **Garvitavastha** will cause happiness through new houses and gardens, regalhood, skill in arts, financial gains at all times, and improvement in business. A planet in **Muditavastha** will give residences, clothes, ornaments, happiness from lands and wife, happiness from relatives, living in royal palaces, destruction of enemies and acquisition of wisdom and learning. A planet in **Lajjitavastha** will give aversion to God, loss of intelligence, loss of child, interest in evil speeches and listlessness in good things. A planet in **Kshobhitavastha** will give acute penury, evil disposition, miseries, financial debacles, distress to feet and obstruction to income due to royal wrath. A planet in **Kshudhitavastha** will cause downfal due to grief and passion, grief on account of relatives, physical decline, troubles from enemies, financial distress, loss of physical strength and an eclipsed mind due to miseries. A planet in **Trushitavastha** will cause diseases through association with females, leading over wicked (or evil) deeds, loss of wealth due to one's own men, physical weakness, miseries caused by evil people and decline of honour.

शयनं चोपवेशं च नेत्रपाणिप्रकाशनम् ।
गमनागमनं चाऽथ सभायां वसति तथा ॥३०॥
आगमं भोजनं चैव नृत्यं लिप्सां च कौतुकम् ।
निद्रां ग्रहाणां चेष्टां च कथयामि तवाग्रतः ॥३१॥
यस्मिन्नृक्षे भवेत्खेटस्तेन तं परिपूरयेत् ।
पुनरंशेन सम्पूर्य स्वनक्षत्रं नियोजयेत् ॥३२॥
यातदण्डं तथा लग्नमेकीकृत्य सदा बुधः ।
रविभिस्तु हरेद् भागं शेषं कार्ये नियोजयेत् ॥३३॥
नाक्षत्रिकदशारीत्या पुनः पूरणमाचरेत् ।
नामाद्यस्वरसंख्याढ्यं हर्तव्यं रविभिस्ततः ॥३४॥
रवौ पञ्च तथा देयाश्चन्द्रे दद्याद्द्वयं तथा ।
कुजे द्वयं च संयुक्तं बुधे त्रीत्रि नियोजयेत् ॥३५॥
गुरौ बाणाः प्रदेयाश्च त्रयं दद्याच्च भार्गवे ।
शनौ त्रयमथो देयं राहौ दद्याच्चतुष्टयम् ॥३६॥

त्रिभिर्भक्तं च शेषांकैः सा पुनस्त्रिविधा स्मृता ।
दृष्टिश्चेष्टा विचेष्टा च तत्फलं कथयाम्यहम् ॥३७॥

30-37. *CALCULATION OF SAYANA AND OTHER AVASTHAS :* I now tell you of the avasthas viz. Sayana, Upavesana, Netrapani, Prakasana, Gamana, Aagamana, Sabha, Agama, Bhojana, Nrityalipsa, Kautuka and Nidra, and the Chesthas of such avasthas. Note the number of the stars (from Aswini) occupied by the planet for which Avastha is to be calculated. Multiply that number by the number denoted by the planet (Sun 1, Moon 2 etc.). The figure so arrived at be again multiplied by the number of Navamsa the planet is in. Add to this the number of birth asterism, the number of ghatis of birth and the number of signs the ascendant gained from Aries. This figure be divided by 12 and the remainder will indicate the corresponding Avastha of the planet. The sub state in the said Avastha can be found out thus : Multiply the figure denoted by the Avastha concerned (i.e. Sayana 1, Upavesana 2 etc) by the same figure and increase it by the figure denoted by the Anka value for the first syllable of the native's personal name. Divide the product so obtained by 12. The remainder there of be further increased by constant planetary additaments, thus : Sun 5, Moon 2, Mars 2, Mercury 3, Jupiter 5, Venus 3, Saturn 3, Rahu 4 (and Ketu 4). (Here the planet means the one for whom the sub state is being known.) The product so arrived at be divided by 3. In th process if the remainder is 1, it is Drishti; if 2 Cheshta and if 0 Vicheshta.

Notes : So far narrated are three different groups of Avasthas. The present Avasthas are called Sayanadi Avasthas. These are of supreme importance as compared to the other kinds of Avasthas.

The following formula may be adopted to know about the planet's Avastha (Sayanadi) at birth.

$$\frac{(s \times p \times n) + (a+g+r)}{12} = \text{Avastha}$$

Where as 's' denotes the serial number of the star occupied by the planet, counted from Aswini at birth; 'p' denotes the status of the planet counted from the Sun (i.e. Sun 1, Mercury 4 etc; 'n' denotes the planet's Navamsa position (i.e. 1 to 9 Navamsas); 'a' denotes Janma Nakshatra (or ruling star, i.e. the one occupied by the Moon); 'g' denotes the ghati in which birth took place (i.e. 20gh 2 vigh is 21gh) and 'r' denotes the ascendant's order counted from Aries (i.e. Cancer 4, Leo 5, so on and so forth).

In place of 'n' given above, some translators interpret the word 'Amsa' as degree occupied by the planet which is obviously not correct. In this connection, the reader's attention is drawn to Balabhadra's **Hora Ratna**, ch 3 wherein the author Balabhadra himself gives an example for the Sun being in the 7th Navamsa of Leo and thus he considered only 7 as multiplier. He has not taken in to account the Sun's degree. He quotes **Adhbhuta Sagara** as his authority for calculation of Sayanadi Avasthas. It will thus be clear that 'Amsa' is Navamsa and not degree in this context.

Also please note that Aagamanavastha (the 6th one) is known as Gamanechchavastha by some exponents.

Take a case now as an example with the following data. The Sun in Krittika Nakshatra, 3rd Navamsa of Taurus (i.e in 7° 12′ Taurus), birth star Krittika, birth at 30gh 33vigh, and ascendant in Scorpio. With these we produce following information, keeping the formula given above.

$$s = 3 \qquad a = 3$$
$$p = 1 \qquad g = 31$$
$$n = 3 \qquad r = 8$$

Hence to find out the Avastha,

$$\frac{(3 \times 1 \times 3) + (3+31+8)}{12} = \frac{51}{12} = \text{remainder } 3$$

With the help of remainder 3, we count three Avastnas from Sayana. This indicates Netrapani Avastha for the Sun.

Similarly for 9 planets, such Avasthas be found out. In a given horoscope, the factors 's', 'g' and 'r' will be identical for all the 9 planets while factors 's', 'p' and 'n' will be variable.

After knowing the Avasthas of various planets, we have to find out the sub state of each Avastha. The formula for knowing sub-state is made in two stages, as under.

Stage 1 : $\frac{(A \times A) + fs}{12} = R$

Stage 2 : $(R + pa) \div 3 =$ sub state

Where 'A' is Avastha, 'fs' is first syllable's value with reference to the native's personal name, R is remainder in stage 1, and 'pa' is planetary additament denoted in the above slokas, such as Sun 5, Venus 3 etc. The remainder at stage 2 will denote sub state such as 1 is Drishti, 2 cheshta and 0 vicheshta.

We need information about Anka value or value for first syllable of the name of a person. These are :

1 for अ, क, छ, ड, ध भ and व

2 for इ, ख, ज, द, न, म and श

3 for उ, ग, झ, त, प, य and ष

4 for ए, घ, ट, थ; फ, र and म

5 for ओ, च, ठ, द, ब, ल and ह

Now with the above data, find the sub state for the Sun in Netrapani Avastha as per the example given supra. First syllable of the name is "Sa" (स). Hence,

Stage 1 : $\frac{(3 \times 3) + 4}{12} =$ Remainder 1

Stage 2 : $\frac{1+5}{3} = 0$

Remainder zero indicates sub state as Vicheshta, in Netrapani Avastha.

दृष्टौ मध्यफलं ज्ञेयं चेष्टायां विपुलं फलम् ।
विचेष्टायां फलं स्वल्पमेवं दृष्टिफलं विदुः ॥३८॥
शुभाऽशुभं ग्रहाणां च समीक्ष्याऽथ बलाऽबलम् ।
तुङ्गस्थाने विशेषेण बलं ज्ञेयं तथा बुधैः ॥३९॥

38-39. *EFFECTS OF CHESHTA ETC.* : If the sub state is Drishti in an Avastha, the results being stated for the Avastha will be medium, full in Cheshta and negligible in Vicheshta. The good and bad effects of planets be deciphered based on the strength and weakness of the planets. In exaltation, the planets reveal effects in a pronounded manner due to (good) avasthas.

Notes : If a planet is in good Avastha and is in Cheshta (sub state), the good effects will be full. If the sub state is Vicheshta, the good effects are neutralised. If the sub state is Drishti, good effects will be feebly felt. A planet in exaltation will give the good effects due to a particular Avastha in a fuller measure.

If a planet is in bad Avastha with Cheshta as sub state, the evil effects will be less. With Drishti, evil effects will be visibly felt. If Vicheshta is sub state, bad effects are neutralized. In debilitation, the evil effects due to an Avastha will be pronounced.

Each planet gives different effects—good or bad—according to the Avastha. No constant evaluation be made just with the name of an Avastha. This is what is conveyed in the following slokas.

मन्दाग्निरोगो बहुधा नराणां स्थूलत्वमङ्घ्रेरपिपित्तकोपः ।
व्रणं गुदे शूलमुरःप्रदेशे यदोष्णभानुः शयनं प्रयातः ॥४०॥
दरिद्रताभारविहारशाली विवादविद्याभिरतो नरः स्यात् ।
कठोरचित्तः खलु नष्टवित्तः सूर्यो यदा चेदुपवेशनस्थः ॥४१॥
नरः सदानन्दधरो विवेकी परोपकारी बलवित्तयुक्तः ।
महासुखी राजकृपाभिमानी दिवाधिनाथो यदि नेत्रपाणौ ॥४२॥
उदारचित्तः परिपूर्णवित्तः सभासु वक्ता बहुपुण्यकर्ता ।
महाबली सुन्दररूपशाली प्रकाशने जन्मनि पद्मिनीशे ॥४३॥
प्रवासशाली किल दुःखमाली सदालसी धीधनवर्जितश्च ।
भयातुरः कोपपरो विशेषाद्दिवाधिनाथे गमने मनुष्यः ॥४४॥
परदाररतो जनतारहितो बहुधागमने गमनाभिरुचिः ।
खलताकुशलो मलिनो दिवसाधिपतौ मनुजः कुमतिः कृपणः ॥४५॥
सभागते हिते नरः परोपकारतत्परः
सदार्थरत्नपूरितो दिवाकरे गुणाकरः ।
वसुन्धरानवांबरालयान्वितो महाबली
विचित्रमित्रवत्सलः कृपाकलाधरः परः ॥४६॥

क्षोभितो रिपुगणैः सदा नरश्चञ्चलः खलमतिः कृशस्तथा ।
धर्मकर्मरहितो मदोद्धतश्चागमे दिनपतौ तदा तदा ॥४७॥
सदाङ्गसन्धिवेदनापराङ्गनाधनक्षयो
बलक्षयः पदे पदे यदा यदा हि भोजने ।
असत्यता शिरोव्यथा तथा वृथान्नभोजनं
रवावसत्कथारतिः कुमार्गगामिनी मति ॥४८॥

विज्ञलोकैः सदा मण्डितः पण्डितः काव्यविद्यानवद्यप्रलापान्वितः ।
राजपूज्यो धरामण्डले सर्वदा नृत्यलिप्सागते पद्मिनीनायके ॥४९॥

सर्वदानन्दधर्ता जनो ज्ञानवान् यज्ञकर्ता धराधीशसद्मस्थितः ।
पद्मबन्धावरातेर्भयं स्वाननः काव्यविद्याप्रलापी मुदा कौतुके ॥५०॥

निद्राभरारक्तनिभे भवेतां निद्रागते लोचनपद्मयुग्मे ।
रवौ विदेशे वसतिर्जनस्य कलत्रहानिः कातिधार्थनाशः ॥५१॥

40-51. *EFFECTS OF THE SUN'S AVASTHAS AT BIRTH :* If the Sun is in **Sayanavastha**, the native will incur digestive deficiency, many diseases, stoutness of legs, bilious vitiation, ulcer in the anus, and heart strokes. If the Sun is in **Upavesanavastha**, the native will suffer poverty, will carry loads, will indulge in litigations, be hard-hearted, wicked, and will lose in his undertakings. If the Sun is in **Netrapani avastha,** the native will always be happy, wise, helpful to others, endowed with prowess and wealth, very happy, and will gain royal favours. If the Sun is in **Prakasanavastha,** the native will be liberal in disposition, will have plenty of wealth, be a significant speaker in the assembly, will perform many meritorious acts, be greatly strong and be endowed with charming beauty. If the Sun is in **Gamanavastha** the native will be disposed to live in foreign places, be miserable, indolent, bereft of intelligence and wealth, be distressed due to fear and be short-tempered. If the Sun is in **Agamanavastha,** the native will be interested in others' wives, be devoid of his own men, be interested in movements, skilful in doing evil deeds, be dirty, ill disposed and be tale-bearer. If the Sun is in **Sabhavastha,** the native will be disposed to help others, be always endowed with wealth and gems, be virtuous, endowed with lands, new houses and robes, be very strong, very affectionate to his friends and be very kindly disposed. If the Sun is in **Aagamavastha,** the native will be distressed due to enemies, fickle-minded, evil-minded, emaciated, devoid of virtuous acts and intoxicated with pride. If the Sun is in **Bhojanavastha,** the native will experience pains in joints, will lose money on account of others' females, will have strength declining off and on, be untruthful, will incur head-aches, will eat remnant food and will take to bad ways. If the Sun is in **Nrityalipsavastha,** the native will be honoured by the learned, be himself a scholar, will have knowledge of poetry etc., and be adored by kings on the earth. If the Sun is in **Kautukavastha,** the native will always be happy, be endowed with spiritual knowledge, will perform sacrificial rites, will move amidst kings, will have fear from enemies, be charming-faced and be endowed with knowledge of poetry. If the Sun is in **Nidravastha**, the native will possess eyes laden with sleepiness (i.e. be always drowsy), will live in foreign (or distant) places, will incur harm to wife and will face financial destruction.

Notes : Balabhadra gives some additional information in regard to planetary Avasthas based on 'Adbhuta Sagaram'. The same is correspondingly added for the benefit of the reader, along with my comments, avoiding repetition of the views of Parasara.

The Sun in Upavesanavastha will make one an artisan, black in complexion, devoid of learning, miserable and serve others. In Netrapani Avastha—all kinds of happiness, if the Sun is in the 5th, 9th and 10th or 7th house. In other houses, this Avastha of the Sun will give eye diseases and enmity with all. If in Prakasanavastha, the native will be meritorious, religious, liberal, will enjoy pleasures, be equal to a prince and enjoy the status of Kubera, the Hindu god of wealth. However, the said Prakasanavastha of the Sun placed in the 7th or the 5th house will cause loss of the first child and will produce many litigations. If the Sun is in Gamanavastha, the native will incur disease of the feet and be very mean. If in Agamanavastha, the Sun in 12th or in 7th will destroy progeny and will give very limited wealth. If in Aagamavastha, the Sun will give many miseries, ugly appearance, and foolishness. However, he will give wealth. The Sun in Bhojanavastha in the 9th house will cause many hindrances to spiritual and religious undertakings. In other houses, this position will cause head and ear diseases, apart from joint pains. Though Parasara states that the native with the Sun in Kautukavastha will have fear from enemies, Balabhadra exempts such evil effect før the 6th house position. The Sun in Kautukavastha in other houses will give a number of daughters, two wives, itch, excellence, liberality etc. If the Sun is in Nidravastha, the native will be predisposed to incur piles and elephantasis, be absolutely very peaceless and will be liable to lose his first child.

जानुःकाले क्षपानाथे शयनं चेदुपागते ।
मानी शीतप्रधानश्च कामी वित्तविनाशकः ॥५२॥
रोगार्दितो मन्दमतिर्विशेषाद्वित्तेन हीनो मनुजः कठोरः ।
अकार्यकारी परवित्तहारी क्षपाकरे चेदुपवेशनस्थे ॥५३॥
नेत्रपाणौ क्षपानाथे महारोगी नरो भवेत् ।
अनल्पजल्पको धूर्तः कुकर्मनिरतः सदा ॥५४॥
यदा राकानाथे गतवति विकाशं च जनने
विकाशः संसारे विमलगुणराशेरवनिपात् ।
नवाशामाला स्यात्करितुरगलक्ष्म्या परिवृता
विभूषा योषाभिः सुखमनुदिनं तीर्थगमनम् ॥५५॥
सितेतरे पापरतो निशाकरे विशेषतः क्रूरतरो नरो भवेत् ।
सदाक्षिरोगैः परिपीड्यमानो वलक्षपक्षे गमने भयातुरः ॥५६॥
विधावागमने मानी पादरोगी नरो भवेत् ।
गुप्तपापरतो दीनो मतितोषविवर्जितः ॥५७॥
सकलजनवदान्यो राजराजेन्द्रमान्यो
रतिपतिसमकान्तिः शान्तिकृत्कामिनीनाम् ।
सपदि सदसि याते चारुबिम्बे शशांके
भवति परमरीतिप्रीतिविज्ञो गुणज्ञः ॥५८॥
विधावागमके मर्त्यो वाचालो धर्मपूरितः ।
कृष्णपक्षे द्विभार्यः स्याद्रोगी दुष्टतरो हठी ॥५९॥

भोजने जनुषि पूर्णचन्द्रमा मानयानजनतासुखं नृणाम् ।
आतनोति वनितासुतासुखं सर्वमेव न सितेतरे शुभम् ॥६०॥

नृत्यलिप्सागते चन्द्रे सबले बलवान्नरः ।
गीतज्ञो हि रसज्ञश्च कृष्णे पापकरो भवेत् ॥६१॥

कौतुकभवनं गतवति चन्द्रे भवति नृपत्वं वा धनपत्वम् ।
कामकलासु सदा कुशलत्वं वारवधूरतिरमणपटुत्वम् ॥६२॥

निद्रागते जन्मनि मानवानां कलाधरे जीवयुते महत्त्वम् ।
हीनेऽङ्गनासञ्चितवित्तनाशः शिवालये रौति विचित्रमुच्चैः ॥६३॥

52-63. *EFFECTS OF THE MOON'S AVASTHAS AT BIRTH :* If the Moon is in **Sayanavastha**, the native will be honourable, sluggish, given to sexual lust, and will face financial destruction. If the Moon is in **Upavesanavastha**, the native will be troubled by diseases, be dull-witted, be not endowed with mentionable wealth (i.e. will have only negligible wealth), be hard-hearted, will do unworthy acts and will steal others' wealth. If the Moon is in **Netrapani avastha**, the native will be troubled by great diseases (long lasting in nature), be very garrulous, wicked and will indulge in bad deeds. Should the Moon be in **Prakasavastha**, the native will be famous in the world, will have his virtues exposed through royal patronage, be surrounded by horses, elephants, females and ornaments and will visit shrines. If the Moon is in **Gamanavastha**, with decreasing rays. the native will be sinful, cruel and always troubled by afflictions of sight; if with increasing rays, the native will be distressed due to fear. If the Moon is in **Agamanavastha**, the native will be honourable, will suffer diseases of feet, will secretly indulge in sinful acts, be poor and devoid of intelligence and happiness. If the Moon is in **Sabhavastha**, the native will be eminent among men, honoured by kings, and kings of kings, be very beautiful, wills ubdue the passion of women, be skilful in sexual acts and be virtuous. If the Moon is in **Agamavastha,** the native will be garrulous, and virtuous and if the said Moon is of dark fortnight the native will have two wives, be sick, highly wicked and be violent. If the Moon is in **Bhojanavastha,** the native will be endowed with honour, conveyances, attendants, social status, wife and daughters, provided she is Full (पूर्ण चन्द्र); if she is in dark fortnight these auspicious effects will fail to come. If the Moon is in **Nrityalipsavastha** and be endowed with (fortnightly) strength, the native will be strong, will have knowledge of songs and be a critic of beauty of things; if the said Moon is of dark fortnignt, the person will be sinful. If the Moon is in **Kautukavastha**, the native will attain kingship, lordship over wealth and skill in sexual acts and in sporting with harlots. Should increasing Moon conjunct Jupiter be in **Nidravastha**, the native will be quite eminent. Devoid of Jupiter's conjunction, if the Moon is in the said Avastha, the native will lose his wealth on account of females, and female jackals will be crying around his abode (as though if were a cemetery).

Notes : With the Moon in the ascendant in Sayanavastha, the native will incur diseases of rectum, be poor and highly irritable. In other houses, this condition will not give these defects so specifically. If weak Moon be in this Avastha (in any house), the right side of the native's body will incur damages caused by fire. There will be damage to teeth if the Moon is in Upavesanavastha. The Moon in Netrapani Avastha will bring eye diseases, elephantasis, etc. and will make the native garrulous. If the Moon is in Gamanavastha, it will cause diseases of the head and brain. There will be two wives and many daughters if the Moon is in Agamavastha. Bhojanavastha of the Moon will bring fear from snakes and water. The Moon in Nrityalipsavastha will give a very lean body and lasting sickness. Kautukavastha of the Moon will confer many sons. If the Moon is in Nidravastha in the 10th, the native will undergo miseries on account of his progeny. The Moon in the 5th or the 7th with the same Avastha will bring all kinds of auspicious effects. Should she join Rahu in the 5th or 7th, herself being in Nidravastha, everything of the native is destroyed and he will be laden with a thousand blemishes.

शयने वसुधापुत्रे व्रणयुक्तो जनो भवेत् ।
बहुना कण्डुना युक्तो दद्रुणा च विशेषतः ॥६४॥
बली सदा पापरतो नरः स्यादसत्यवादी नितरां प्रगल्भः ।
धनेन पूर्णो निजधर्महीनो धरासुतश्चेदुपवेशनस्थः ॥६५॥

यदा भूमिसुतो लग्ने नेत्रपाणिमुपागतः।
दरिद्रता तदा पुंसामन्यभे नगरेशता ॥६६॥

प्रकाशो गुणस्यापि वासः प्रकाशे धराधीशभर्तुः सदा मानवृद्धिः।
सुते भूसुते पुत्रकान्तावियोगो भवेद्राहुणा दारुणो वा निपातः ॥६७॥

गमने गमनं कुरुतेऽनुदिनं व्रणजालभयं वनिताकलहः।
बहुदद्रुककण्डुभयं बहुधा वसुधातनयो वसुहानिकरः ॥६८॥

आगमने गुणशाली मणिमालीवा करालकरवाली।
गजहन्ता रिपुहन्ता परिजनसन्तापहारको भौमे ॥६९॥

तुङ्गे युद्धकलाकलापकुशलो धर्मध्वजो वित्तपः
कोणे भूमिसुते सभामुपगते विद्याविहीनः पुमान्।
अन्तेऽपत्यकलत्रमित्ररहितः प्रोक्तेतरस्थानगे-
ऽवश्यं राजसभाबुधो बहुधनी मानी च दानी जनः ॥७०॥

आगमे भवति भूमिजे जनो धर्मकर्मरहितो गदातुरः।
कर्णमूलगुरुशूलरोगवानेव कातरमतिः कुसङ्गमी ॥७१॥

भोजने मिष्टभोजी च जनने सबले कुजे।
नीचकर्मंकरो नित्यं मनुजो मानवर्जितः ॥७२॥

नृत्यलिप्सागते भूसुते जन्मिनामिन्दिराराशिरायाति भूमीपतेः।
स्वर्णरत्नप्रवालैः सदा मण्डिता वासशाला नराणां भवेत्सर्वदा ॥७३॥

कौतुकी भवति कौतुके कुजे मित्रपुत्रपरिपूरितो जनः।
उच्चगे नृपतिगेहमण्डितः पूजितो गुणवरैर्गुणाकरैः ॥७४॥

निद्रावस्थां गते भौमे क्रोधी धीधनवर्जितः।
धूर्तो धर्मपरिभ्रष्टो मनुष्यो गदपीडितः ॥७५॥

64-75. *EFFECTS OF AVASTHAS OF MARS AT BIRTH :* If Mars is in **Sayanavastha,** the native will be troubled by wounds, itch and ulcer. If Mars be in **Upavesanavastha,** the native will be strong, sinful, untruthful, eminent, wealthy and bereft of virtues. If Mars be in the ascendant and be in **Netra-pani Avastha** there will be penury; in other houses this state will confer rulership of a city. Should Mars be in **Prakasavastha,** the native will shine with virtues and will be honoured by the king. Mars in **Prakasavastha** in the 5th house will, however, cause loss of children and of wife. If Mars is in the said state and be with Rahu, a severe (positional) fall will descend on the native. Should Mars be in **Gamanavastha** the native will be always roaming, will have fear of multiple ulcers, will incur misunderstandings with females, will be afflicted by boils, itches etc. and will incur financial decline. If Mars be in **Agamanavastha**, the native will be virtuous, endowed with precious gems, will adore a sharp sword, will walk with the (majestic) gait of an elephant (imparting surprise in the onlooker), will destroy his enemies and will remove the miseries of his people. If Mars be in **Sabhavastha** and be in exaltation the native will be skilful in conducting wars, will hold the flag of righteousness aloft and be wealthy; if Mars be in the said state in the 5th or 9th, the native will be bereft of learning, if in the 12th childlessness and no wife and no friends will result, and if Mars be in other houses than these in the said Avastha, the native will be a scholar in a king's court (i.e. be a poet laureate), be very wealthy, honourable and charitable. If Mars be in **Agamavastha**, the native will be devoid of virtues and good deeds, will be distressed by diseases, will acquire diseases of the root of the ears (कर्ण मूल रोग: & C पादमूलं ऊरूमूलं etc.), and severe gout pains, be timid and will befriend evil lot. If Mars be with strength while in Bhojanavastha, the native will eat sweet-food and if be devoid of strength, the native will indulge in base acts and be dishonourable. If Mars be **Nrityalipsavastha**, the native will earn wealth through king and will be endowed with fullness of gold, diamonds and corals in his house. If Mars be in **Kautukavastha** the native will be curious in disposition and be endowed with friends and sons, if Mars be simultaneously exalted, the native will be honoured by the king and the virtuous and be himself virtuous. If Mars be in **Nidravastha**, the native will be short-tempered. devoid of intelligence and wealth, be wicked, fallen from virtuous path and troubled by diseases.

Notes : If Mars is in Sayanavastha at birth, the native will be libidinous, learned, intelligent and irritable. Should this Avastha in particular occur in the 5th or in the 7th, the native will lose his first wife and first child as well. If Mars in 5th being in Sayanavastha is related to Saturn or Rahu, the native's head will be severed while with other malefics related to Mars in the said state ears/hand will be cut off.

Should Mars be in Upavesanavastha in the ascendant, the native will be extremely sinful, will incur several diseases, indigent and most unpeaceful. If the said Avastha occurs for Mars in the 9th house, the native will lose whole of his wealth apart from his wife and progeny. Mars in Netrapani Avastha in the ascendant will give poverty and will destroy the native's wife and progeny; in other houses this confers on the native all kinds of wealth and happiness from wife and children. However, the 2nd house position or the 7th house position of Mars in Netrapani Avastha will cause fear from lions and snakes apart from giving earnings from lands.Further the native's wife will predecease him. Should Mars bein Prakasanavastha in the 5th or in the 7th house, the native will lose his wife and all children. Placed in the 5th houie in Prakasanavastha if Mars is conjunct Saturn, the native will kill cows. Should Mars be in Gamanavastha, the native will be active in his assignments, will incur diseases of the joints, burning pains in eyes, dental afflictions and the like, will have fear from dogs and will adore the guise of a female. These effects are for the placement of Mars in the ascendant. In other houses, Mars in Gamanavastha will bring royal favours, leadership and luxuries of the life.

Shifting over to sloka 69 of our text, in the context of Mars being in Agamanavastha, the sage uses "गजहन्ता" which has been, however, interpreted as 'elephant killer' by some commentators. It is actually an indeclinable particle and conveys the meaning that the native will walk with the majestic gait of an elephant (imparting surprise in the onlookers.

Mars in Agamanavastha will cause piles and diseases of rectum.

If Mars is in Bhojanavastha or in Sayanavastha in the 5th house, or in the 8th house, there will be untimely death for the native. In other houses, Bhojanavsatha of Mars will confer wealth. Should Mars be in Nrityalipsavastha and be in the ascendant, 2nd, 7th or 10th, the native will receive all kinds of happiness; there will be miseries galore if Mars is in the 8th or 9th a part from incurring untimely death. In other houses, this state of Mars will make the native akin to Kubera. Mars in the

7th or in the 9th in Kautukavastha will give several diseases and death of first child and wife. In other houses, this state will confer scholarship, various kinds of wealth, two wives and more female children. In Nidravastha, Mars in the ascendant, 2nd, 3rd, 9th, 10th or 11th, will give scholarship, foolishness and poverty. The 5th house or 7th house placement of Mars in this Avastha will give many miseries and many male children. Should Rahu join Mars in Nidravastha in any house the native will have many wives, be miserable, and will suffer from some diseases on the surface of feet.

क्षुधातुरो भवेदंगे खञ्जो गुञ्जानिभेक्षणः ।
अन्यभे लम्पटो धूर्तो मनुजः शयने बुधे ॥७६॥

शशांकपुत्रे जनुरङ्गगेहे यदोपवेशे गुणराशिपूर्णः ।
पापेक्षिते पापयुते दरिद्रो हिते शुभे वित्तसुखी मनुष्यः ॥७७॥

विद्याविवेकरहितो हिततोषहीनो मानी
जनोभवति चन्द्रसुतेऽक्षि पाणौ ।
पुत्रालये सुतकलत्रसुखेन हीनः कन्या-
प्रजा नृपतिगेहबुधो वरार्थः ॥७८॥

दाता दयालुः खलु पुण्यकर्ता विकाशने चन्द्रसुते मनुष्यः ।
अनेकविद्यार्णवपारङ्गता विवेकपूर्णः खलवर्गहन्ता ॥७९॥

गमनागमने भवतो गमने बहुधा वसुधाधिपतेर्भवने ।
भवनं च विचित्रमलं रमया विदि नुश्च जनुःसमये नितराम् ॥८०॥

सपदि विदि जनानामुच्चगे जन्मकाले
सदसि धनसमृद्धिः सर्वदा पुण्यवृद्धिः ।
धनपतिसमता वा भूपता मंत्रिता वा
हरिहरपदभवितः सात्त्विकी मुक्तिलब्धिः ॥८१॥

आगमे जनुषि जन्मिनां यदा चन्द्रजे भवति हीनसेवया ।
अर्थसिद्धिरपि पुत्रयुग्मता बालिका भवति मानदायिका ॥८२॥

भोजने चन्द्रजे जन्मकाले यदा जन्मिनामर्थहानिः सदा वादतः ।
राजभीत्या कृशत्वंचलत्वं मतेरङ्गसङ्गो न जाया न जायासुखम् ॥८३॥

नृत्यलिप्सागते चन्द्रजे मानवो मानयानप्रवालव्रजैः संयुतः ।
मित्रपुत्रप्रतापैः सभापण्डितः पापभे वारवामारतो लम्पटः ॥८४॥
कौतुके चन्द्रजे जन्मकाले नृणामंगभे गीतविद्याऽनवद्या भवेत् ।
सप्तमे नैधने वारवध्वा रतिः पुण्यभे पुण्ययुक्ता मतिः सद्गतिः ॥८५॥
निद्राश्रिते चन्द्रसुते न निद्रासुखं सदा व्याधिसमाधियोगः ।
सहोत्थवैकल्यमनल्पतापो निजेन वादो धनमाननाशः ॥८६॥

76-86. : *EFFECTS OF MERCURY'S AVASTHAS AT BIRTH :* Should Mercury in **Sayanavastha** be in the ascendant, the native will be lame and will have reddish eyes (like the black bee); if Mercury be in the said Avastha in other houses, the native will be addicted to licentious pleasures and be wicked. If Mercury be in **Upavesanavastha** in the ascendant, the native will possess (the seven principle) virtues; if aspected by or conjunct malefics, penury will result and if by benefics financial happiness will follow. If Mercury be in **Netrapani Avastha,** the native will be devoid of learning, wisdom, wellwishers and satisfaction but be honourable; if Mercury be in the 5th house in the said Avastha, the subject will be bereft of happiness from wife and sons, be endowed with (more) female children and will gain abundant finance through royal patronage. If Mercury be in **Prakasavastha,** the native will be charitable, merciful, meritorious, will cross the boundaries of ocean in respect of many branches of learning, be endowed with great faculty of discrimination and will destroy evil people. If Mercury be in **Gamanavastha** the native will visit the court of kings on many occasions and Goddess **Lakshmi** (denoting wealth) will dwell in his abode. If Mercury be in **Agamanavastha,** the same effects due to his being in **Gamanavastha** will fructify. If Mercury be in **Sabhavastha**. and be in exaltation, the native will be affluent and meritorious at all times, be equal to Kubera (the lord of wealth in Hindu mythology) or be a king or a minister, be devoted to Lord Vishnu and Lord Siva, be virtuous and will attain final emancipation. Should Mercury be in **Agamavastha,** the native will serve base men and gain wealth thereby and will have two sons and one fame-bringing daughter. If Mercury be in **Bhojanavastha,** the native will face financial losses through litigations, will physically lose on account of fear from king (i.e. will become thin due to royal wrath), fickle-minded and will be bereft of physical and conjugal felicity. If Mercury be in **Nrityalipsavastha,** the native will be endowod with honour, cenveyances, corals (i.e. gems etc.), sons, friends, prowess and recognition in assembly due to his scholarship; if with the said state Marcury be in a malefic's sign the native will be addicted to prostitutes and will long for licentious pleasures. If Mercury be in **Kautukavastha,** and be in the ascendant, the native will be skilful in music; if be in the 7th/8th with the said Avastha one will be addicted to courtezans and if in the 9th, the native will be meritorious and attain heavens after death. If Mercury be in **Nidravastha,** the native will not enjoy comfortable sleep, be afflicted by neck or neck joint(समाधि) diseases, be devoid of coborn, afflicted by miseries galore, will enter into litigations with his own men will lose wealth and honour.

Notes : If Mercury is in the ascendant in Sayanavastha, the native will be a eunuch lacking productivity and will be devoid of a limb (whereas Parasara is specificly stating that the native will be lame), In other houses, this Avastha of Mercury will produce abstract penury. Should Mercury be in his own sign in Upavesanavastha, the native will be endowed with all kinds of happiness, be meritorious and liberal but will incur diseases of the sight. If Mercury is in Prakasavastha, the native will be interested in Vedic lore and will continue to be rich although he may be very charitable to give away anything. Gamanavastha of Mercury, will cause fear from snakes and water. Aagamanavastha of Mercury will bring many kinds of miseries and a wicked wife. Mercury in the 5th or in the 12th in Sabhavasha will give many female issues; in the 7th it will make the native black in complexion. Mercury in Agamavastha will cause urinary disorders. Bhojanavastha of Mercury gives poverty and many diseases at the time of one's end. If Mercury is in Nrityalipsavastha, the native will have five sons, 4 daughters and 2 wives. Mercury in Kautukavastha will cause piles and skin diseases. Mercury in Nidravastha will curtail longevity if the position is in ascendant or in the 10th house, whereas in other houses, this Avastha of Mercury will give abundant wealth.

वचसामधिपे तु जनुःसमये शयने बलवानपि हीनरवः ।
अतिगौरतनुः खलुदीर्घहनुः सुतरामरिभीतियुतो मनुजः ॥८७॥

उपवेशं गतवति यदि जीवे वाचालो बहुगर्वपरीतः ।
क्षोणीपतिरिपुजनपरितप्तः पदजंघास्यकरव्रणयुक्तः ॥८८॥

नेत्रपाणि गते देवराजार्चिते रोगयुक्तो वियुक्तो वरार्थश्रिया ।
गीतनृत्यप्रियः कामुकः सर्वदा गौरवर्णो विवर्णोद्भवप्रीतियुक् ॥८९॥

गुणानामानन्दं विमलसुखकन्दं वितनुते
सदा तेजःपुञ्जं व्रजपतिनिकुञ्जं प्रतिगमम् ।
प्रकाशं चेदुच्चे द्रुतमुपगतो वासवगुरु-
र्गुरुत्वं लोकानां धनपतिसमत्वं तनुभृताम् ॥९०॥

साहसी भवति मानवः सदा मित्रवर्गसुखपूरितो मुदा ।
पण्डितो विविधवित्तमण्डितो देवविद्यदि गुरौ गमं गते ॥९१॥

आगमने जनता वरजाया यस्य जनुःसमये हरिमाया ।
मुञ्चति नालमिहालयमद्धा देवगुरौ परितः परिबद्धा ॥९२॥

सुरगुरुसमवक्ता शुभ्रमुक्ताफलाढ्यः
सदसि सपदि पूर्णो वित्तमाणिक्यमानैः ।
गजतुरगरथाढ्यो देवताधीशपूज्यो
जनुषि विविधविद्यागर्विता मानवः स्यात् ॥९३॥

नानावाहनमानयानपटलीसौख्यं गुरावागमे
भृत्यापत्यकलत्रमित्रजसुखं विद्याऽनवद्या भवेत् ।
क्षोणीपालसमानतानवरतं चाऽतीव हृद्या मतिः
काव्यानन्दरतिः सदा हितगतिः सर्वत्र मानोन्नतिः ॥९४॥

भोजने भवति देवतागुरौ यस्य तस्य सततं सुभोजनम् ।
नैव मुञ्चति रमालयं तदा वाजिवारणरथैश्च मण्डितम् ॥९५॥

नृत्यलिप्सागते राजमानी धनी देवताधीशवन्द्यः सदा धर्मवित् ।
तन्त्रविज्ञो बुधैर्मण्डितः पंडितः शब्दविद्यानवद्यो हि सद्यो जनः ॥९६॥

कुतूहली सकौतुके महाधनी जनः सदा
निजान्वये च भास्करः कृपाकलाधरः सुखी ।

निलिम्पराजपूजिते सुतेन भूनयेन वा
युतो महाबली धराधिपेन्द्रसद्मपण्डितः ॥९७॥
गुरौ निद्रागते यस्य मूर्खता सर्वकर्मणि ।
दरिद्रतापरिक्रान्तं भवनं पुण्यवर्जितम् ॥९८॥

87-98. *EFFECTS OF JUPITER'S AVASTHAS AT BIRTH* : If Jupiter is in **Sayanavastha,** the native will be strong but will speak in whispers, be very tawny in complexion, will have prominent cheeks, and will have fear from enemies. If Jupiter be in **Upavesanavastha,** the native will be garrulous, very proud, be troubled by king and enemies and will have ulcers on feet, shanks, face and hands. If Jupitcr be in **Netrapani Avastha,** the native will be afflicted by diseases, devoid of wealth, be fond of music and dances, libidinous, tawny in complexion and be attached to other castemen. If Jupiter be in **Prakasavastha,** the native will enjoy virtues, be happy, splendorous and will visit placcs holy to Lord Krishna; if Jupiter in the said Avastha is exalted, the native will attain greatness among men, be equal to Kubera—the lord of wealth. If Jupiter is in **Gamanavastha** the native will be adventurous, be happy on account of friends. scholarly and endowed with various kinds of wealth and with Vedic learning, If Jupiter be in **Agamanavastha,** serving force, excellent women and the goddess of wealth will never leave the native's abode. If Jupiter be in **Sabhavastha,** the native will attain comparability with Jupiter (the God of speech) in the matter of speech. be endowed with superior corals, rubies and wealth, be rich with elephants, horses and chariots and will be supremely learned. If Jupiter be in **Agamavastha,** the native will be endowed with various conveyances, honours, retinue, children, wife, friends and learning, be equal to a king. extremely noble, fond of literature and will take to virtuous path. If Jupiter be in **Bhojanavastha** the native will always beget excellent food and horses, elephants and chariots while Lakshmi, the goddess of Lucre, will never leave his house. If Jupiter be in **Nrityalipsavastha,** the native will receive royal honours, be wealthy, endowed with knowledge of moral law (धर्म) and Tantra (a branch of learning dealing with magical or mystical formularies to attain superhuman powers), be supreme among the learned and be a great grammarian. If Jupiter bc in **Kautukavastha,** the native will be curious in disposition, very rich, will shine like the Sun in his circles, be exceedingly kind, be happy, honoured by the kings, endowed with sons, wealth and just disposition be very strong and be a scholar in the king's court. If Jupiter be in Nidravastha, the native will be foolish in all his undertakings, will suffer irredeemable penury and will be devoid of righteous acts.

Notes : If Jupiter is in Sayanavastha, the native will be fair in complexion but will suffer from colic pains. This Avastha of Jupiter placed in the ascendant, 7th or 10th will, however, give wealth and scholarship. Being in Upavesanavastha, if Jupiter occupies the 2nd, 3rd, 11th or 12th, the native will be virtuous and learned. In Netrapani Avastha, Jupiter will give head diseases and destroy the undertaking of the native. The native will be ever of doubtful disposition. If Jupiter is in Prakasana-vastha in a house other than the ascendant and the 10th, the native will incur diseases of privities and rectum. Jupiter in a house other than the 2nd, 5th, 7th and 10th, in Agamanavastha will bring fear from snakes. Sabhavastha of Jupiter will make the native rich through others' wealth. Should Sabhavastha occur to Jupiter in the 8th or in the 12th, the native will lose everything in his life. If Jupiter is in the asscendant in Bhojana-vastha, the native will be fond of flesh, be eloquent, libidinous and be happy in every manner. In other houses than the ascendant, 5th and the 9th, this state of Jupiter will produce many diseases. In Nrityalipsavastha, Jupiter placed in the ascendant, 5th, 9th or 10th will give abundant wealth while in other houses this cannot be expected of him. In Kautukavastha he will give wealth if in the ascendant, 10th or 7th only. Jupiter in Nidravastha will make one miserable, suffer eye diseases and wander all over. If he is in the 12th with this Avastha, there will be riches while this Avastha of Jupiter in the 5th, 7th or 10th wili destory the native's wife and children.

जनो बलीयानपिदन्तरोगी भृगौ महारोषसमन्वितः स्यात् ।
धनेन हीनः शयनं प्रयाते वारांगनासंगमलम्पटश्च ॥९९॥

यदि भवेदुशना उपवेशने नवमणिव्रजकाञ्चनभूषणैः ।
सुखमजस्रमरिक्षय आदरादवनिपादपि मानसमुन्नतिः ॥१००॥

नेत्रपाणिगते लग्नगेहे कवौ सप्तमे मानभे यस्य तस्य ध्रुवम् ।
नेत्रपाते निपातो धनानामलं चान्यभे वासशाला विशाला भवेत् ॥१०१॥
स्वालये तुंगभे मित्रभे भार्गवे तुंगमातंगलीलाकलापी जनः ।
भूपतेस्तुल्य एव प्रकाशं गते काव्यविद्याकलाकौतुकी गीतवित् ॥१०२॥
गमने जनने शुक्रे तस्य माता न जीवति ।
आधियोगो वियोगश्च जनानामरिभीतितः ॥१०३॥
आगमनं भृगुपुत्रे गतवति वित्तेश्वरो मनुजः ।
सत्तीर्थभ्रमशाली नित्योत्साही करांघ्रिरोगी च ॥१०४॥
अनायासेनालं सपदि महसा याति सहसा
प्रगल्भत्वंराज्ञः सदसि गुणविज्ञः किल कवौ ।
सभायामायाते रिपुनिवहहन्ता धनपतेः
समत्वं वा दाता बलतुरगगन्ता नरवरः ॥१०५॥
आगमे भार्गवे नागमो जन्मिनामर्थराशेररातेरतीव क्षतिः ।
पुत्रपातो निपातो जनानामपिव्याधिभीतिः प्रियाभोगहानिर्भवेत् ॥१०६॥
क्षुधातुरो व्याधिनिपीडितः स्यादनेकधारातिभयार्दितश्च ।
कवौ यदा भोजनगे युवत्या महाज्ञानी पण्डितमण्डितश्च ॥१०७॥
काव्यविद्यानवद्या च हृद्या मतिः सर्वदा नृत्यलिप्सागते भार्गवे ।
शंखवीणामृदंगादिगानध्वनिव्रातनैपुण्यमेतस्य वित्तोन्नतिः ॥१०८॥
कौतुकभवनं गतवति शुक्रे शक्रेशत्वं सदसि महत्त्वम् ।
हृद्या विद्या भविति च पुंसः पदमा निवसति सदमारतः ॥१०९॥
परसेवारतो नित्यं निद्रामुपगते कवौ ।
परनिन्दापरो वीरो वाचालो भ्रमते महीम् ॥११०॥

99-110. *EFFECTS OF AVASTHAS OF VENUS AT BIRTH :* If Venus be in Sayanavastha, the native although strong will incur dental diseases, be very short-tempered, bereft of wealth, will seek union with courtezans and be licentious. If Venus be in Upavesanavastha, the native will be endowed with multitude of nine gems (नवमणि वज) and golden ornaments, be ever happy, will destroy enemies be honoured by the king and will have highly increased honours. If Venus be in Netrapani

Avastha in the ascendant, the 7th or 10th, there will be loss of wealth on account of sight afflictions (i.e. heavy medical expenses due to severe eye diseases) and if the said Avastha occurs when Venus is in other houses, there will be large houses owned by the native. Should Venus be in **Prakasavastha** in own sign, exaltation sign of friendly sign, the native will sport like a lofty elephant, be equal to a king and be skilful in poetry and music. If Venus be in **Gamanavastha,** the native will not have a long living mother, will lament over separation from his own people and will have fear from enemies. If Venus be in **Agamanavastha**, the native will command abundant wealth, will undertake to visit superior shrines, be ever enthusiastic and will contract diseases of the hand and foot. If Venus be in **Sabhavastha** the native will earn eminence in the king's court, be very virtuous. will destroy enemies, be equal to Kubera in wealth, charitable, will ride on horses and will be excellent among men. If Venus is in **Agamavastha,** there will be no advent of wealth but troubles from enemies, separation from children and relatives, diseases and lack of pleasures from the wife. Should Venus be in **Bhojanavastha,** the native will be distressed due to hunger, diseases and many kinds of fear from enemies and if the said planet is in Virgo in Bhojanavastha, the native will be very rich and will be honoured by scholars. If Venus be in **Nrityalipsavastha**, the native will be skilful in literature, intelligent, will play musical instruments like lute, taber etc., be meritorious and very affluent. If Venus be in **Kautukavastha**, the native will be equal to Lord Indra, will attain greatness in the assembly, be learned and will have Lakshmi always dwelling in his abode. If Venus be in **Nidravastha,** the native will be interested in serving others, will blame others, be heroic, garrulous and wandering all over the earth.

Notes : Venus in Sayanavastha in the ascendant will confer riches; if in the 7th or in the 11th in the said Avastha, the native will be endowed with all kinds of happiness, will never face shortage of money and will have 7 sons and 5 daughters. In other houses than the ascendant, 7th and 11th, Venus in Sayanavastha will destroy the progeny of the native. If Venus is in Upavesanavastha, the native will have a defect or injury on the right side of the body. He will suffer from pains of joints as well. Should Upavesanavastha occur to Venus in exaltation or in own sign, the native will be endowed with all kinds of happiness. There will be sure loss of eye sight if Venus is in Netrapani Avastha. The 10th house placement of Venus in Netrapani Avastha is not praiseworthy for riches while in other houses than the ascendant, 7th and 10th this will bring abundant wealth apart from giving two wives. Prakasana Avastha of Venus placed in the 2nd, 7th, 9th or the ascendant will give wealth and sterling disposition. And if he be in the 10th or in exaltation or in friendly sign, the native will occupy a high position with the king. In other houses than these, Prakasavastha of Venus will give many diseases and miseries. If Venus is in Sabhavastha the native will receive royal favours and be akin to Kubera in wealth. Should Venus be in Sabhavastha in an enemy's sign or in aspect to an enemy, it will destroy everything. Nrityalipsavastha of Venus will confer a high degree of learning while Nidravastha will cause litigations, diseases, disputes and poverty. Kautukavastha of Venus will give abundant riches, wife and numerous children.

क्षुत्पिपासापरिक्रान्तो विश्रान्तः शयने शनौ ।
वयसि प्रथमे रोगी ततो भाग्यवतां वरः ॥१११॥

भानोः सुते चेदुपवेशनस्थे करालकारातिजनानुतप्ताः ।
अपायशाली खलु दद्रुमाली नरोभिमानी नृपदण्डयुक्तः ॥११२॥

नयनपाणिगते रविनन्दने परमया रमया रमयायुतः ।
नृपतितो हिततो मतितोषकृद्बहुकलाकलितो विमलोचितकृत् ॥११३॥

नानागुणग्रामधनाधिशाली सदा नरो बुद्धिविनोदमाली ।
प्रकाशने भानुसुते सुभानुः कृपानुरक्तो हरपादभक्तः ॥११४॥

महाधनी नन्दननन्दितः स्यादपायकारी रिपुभूमिहारी ।
गमे शनौ पण्डितराजभावं धरापतेरायतने प्रयाति ॥११५॥

आगमने गर्दभपदयुक्तः पुत्रकलत्रसुखेन विमुक्तः ।
भानुसुते भ्रमते भुवि नित्यं दीनमना विजनाश्रयभावम् ॥११६॥

रत्नावलीकाञ्चनमौक्तिकानां व्रातेन नित्यं व्रजति प्रमोदम् ।
सभागते भानुसुते नितान्तं नयेन पूर्णो मनुजो महौजाः ॥११७॥

आगमे गदसमागमो नृणामब्जबन्धुतनये यदा तदा।
मन्दमेव गमनं धरापतेर्याचनाविरहिता मतिः सदा ॥११८॥
संगते जनुषि भानुनन्दने भोजनं भवति भोजनं रसैः।
संयुतं नयनमन्दता तता मोहतापपरितापिता मतिः ॥११९॥
नृत्यलिप्सागते मन्दे धर्मात्मा वित्तपूरितः।
राजपूज्यो नरो धीरो महावीरो रणाङ्गणे ॥१२०॥
भवति कौतुकभावमुपागते रविसुते वसुधावसुपूरितः।
अतिसुखी सुमुखीसुखपूरितः कवितयामलया कलया नरः ॥१२१॥
निद्रागते वासरनाथपुत्रे धनी सदा चारुगुणैरुपेतः।
पराक्रमी चण्डविपक्षहन्ता सुवारकान्तारतिरीतिविज्ञः ॥१२२॥

111-122. *EFFECTS OF SATURN'S AVASTHAS AT BIRTH :* If Saturn is in **Sayanavastha,** the native will be troubled by hunger and thirst, will incur diseases in boyhood and later on will become wealthy. If Saturn be in **Upavesanavastha** the native will be troubled greatly by enemies, will contract dangers, will have ulcers allover the body, be self-respected and be punished by the king. If Saturn be in **Netrapani Avastha,** the native will be endowed with a charming female, wealth, royal favour and friends, will have knowledge of many arts and be an eloquent speaker. If Saturn be in **Prakasavastha,** the native will be very virtuous, very wealthy, intelligent, sportive, splendorous, merciful and devoted to Lord Siva. If Saturn be in **Gamanavastha,** the native will be very rich, endowed with sons; will grab enemie's lands and be a scholar at royal court. If Saturn be in **Agamanavastha,** the native will be akin to a donkey (i.e. foolish), bereft of happiness from wife and children, will always roam pitiably without anybody's patronage. If Saturn be in **Sabhavastha,** the native will have surprising (i.e. great) possessions of abundant precious stones and gold, be endowed with great judicial (or political) knowledge and be extremely brilliant. If Saturn be in **Agamavastha,** the native will incur diseases, and will not be skilful in earning royal patronage. If Saturn be in **Bhojanavastha,** the native will enjoy tastes of food, be weak-sighted and be fickle-minded due to mental delusion. If Saturn be in **Nrityalipsavastha,** the native will be righteous, extremely opulent, honoured by the king, brave and be heroic in warfield. If Saturn be **Kautukavastha** the native will be endowed with lands and wealth, be happy, endowed with pleasures through charming females and learned in poetry, arts etc. If Saturn be in **Nidravastha,** the native will be rich, endowed with charming virtues, valorous, will destroy even fierce enemies and be skilful in seeking pleasures through harlots.

Notes : If Saturn is in Sayanavastha in the 5th house, the native will be endowed with progeny and be happy in all manners; if in the ascendant, 6th or 8th, the native will live in alien places, be very poor and peaceless. This Avastha to Saturn will also cause diseases of the rectum (irrespective of the planet's placement). Saturn in Upavesanavastha will ever cause difficulties from the government and destruction of wealth. Saturn placed in the 10th or in the ascendant with Netrapani Avastha when unchecked will cause miseries in livelihood; in the 5th/7th there will be destruction of wealth, wife and progeny and in a house other than Ist, 5th and 7th, this Avastha of Saturn will give wealth and happiness from all sources. If Prakasanavastha occurs to Saturn while being in the 7th or the 9th, the native and his entire race will be "destroyed". Should Sabhavastha occur to Saturn in an enemy's sign or with an aspect from an enemy, there will be absolute destruction of the native's possession, Bhojanavastha of Saturn will cause digestive difficulties, piles and eye defects; if Saturn is in simultaneously exaltation or in own sign, the native will enjoy all kinds of happiness and be ever devoid of diseases. Kautukavastha of Saturn in the 5th/7th/9th will destroy everything and will leave the native with diseases alone. Should this Avastha occur to Saturn in another house than 5th/7th/9th, the native will be favoured by the king, will be very rich, meritorious, skilful, happy, learned and adorable. If Saturn is in Nidravastha, the native will be opulent, learned, will have two wives and many male issues and be very honourable for his sterlingness. Should Nidravastha occur to Saturn in the 10th house, there will be penury, diseases, living in alien places and obstruction to undertakings at every step. If he is in an angle or in a trine or in exaltation, these evil effects will not come to pass.

यदागमो जन्मनि यस्य राहौ क्लेशाधिकत्वं शयनं प्रयाते।
वृषेऽथ युग्मेऽपि च कन्यकायामजे समाजो धनधान्यराशेः ॥१२३॥
उपवेशनमिह गतवति राहौ दद्रुगदेन जनः परितप्तः।
राजसमाजयुतो बहुमानी वित्तसुखेन सदा रहितः स्यात् ॥१२४॥

नेत्रपाणावगौ नेत्रे भवतो रोगपोडिते।
दुष्टव्यालारिचौराणां भयं तस्य धनक्षयः ॥१२५॥
प्रकाशने शुभासने स्थितिः कृतिः शुभा नृणां।
धनोन्नतिर्गुणोन्नतिः सदा विदामगाविह।
धराधिपाधिकारिता यशोलता तता भवे-
न्नवीननीरदाकृतिर्विदेशतो महोन्नतिः ॥१२६॥
गमने च यदा राहौ बहुसन्तानवान्नरः।
पण्डितो धनवान् दाता राजपूज्यो नरो भवेत् ॥१२७॥
राहावागमने क्रोधी सदा धीधनवर्जितः।
कुटिलः कृपणः कामी नरो भवति सर्वथा ॥१२८॥
सभागतो यदा राहुः पण्डितः कृपणो नरः।
नानागुणपरिक्रान्तो वित्त सौख्यसमन्वितः ॥१२९॥

चेदगावागमं यस्य याते तदा व्याकुलत्वं सदारातिभीत्या भयम्।
महद्बन्धुवादो जनानां निपातो भवेद्वित्तहानिः शठत्वं कृशत्वम् ॥१३०॥

भोजने भोजनेनालं विकलो मनुजो भवेत्।
मन्दबुद्धिः क्रियाभीरुः स्त्रीपुत्रसुखवर्जितः ॥१३१॥
नृत्यलिप्सागते राहौ महाव्याधिविवर्द्धनम्।
नेत्ररोगी रिपोर्भीतिर्धनधर्मक्षयो नृणाम् ॥१३२॥
कौतुके च यदा राहौ स्थानहीनो नरो भवेत्।
परदाररतो नित्यं परवित्तापहारकः ॥१३३॥
निद्रावस्थां गते राहौ गुणग्रामयुतो नरः।
कान्तासन्तानवान् धीरो गर्वितो बहुवित्तवान् ॥१३४॥

123-134. *EFFECTS OF RAHU'S AVASTHAS AT BIRTH :* If Rahu be in Sayanavastha, the native will experience miseries galore; but if Rahu in the said Avastha be in Taurus, Gemini, Virgo or Aries the native will be endowed with wealth and grains. If Rahu be in **Upavesanavastha** the native will be distressed due to ulcers, be endowed with royl association, highly honourable and ever deviod of financial happiness. If Rahu be in **Netrapani Avastha,** the native will be troubled by eye diseases, will have fear from wicked people, snakes and thieves and will incur financial decline. If Rahu be in **Prakasavastha**, the native will acquire a high position, will perform auspicious acts, will obtain elevation of financial state, be highly virtuous. be a chief in the king's court, be charming like freshly formed clouds (that will cause soon rain) and be very prosperous in foreign places. If Rahu is in **Gamanavastha** the native will be endowed with numreous children, be scholarly, wealthy, charitable and honoured by the king. If Rahu is in **Agamanavastha,** the native will be very irritable, bereft of intelligence and wealth, crooked, miserly and libidinous. If Rahu is in **Sabhavastha** the native will be scholarly, miserly, and endowed with many virtues, wealth and happiness. If Rahu be in **Agamavastha**, the native will be always mentally distressed, will have fear from enemies and litigations with enemies, be bereft of his own men, will face financial destruction, and be crafty and emaciated. If Rahu be in **Bhojanavastha**, the native will be distressed without food, dull-witted, be not bold in his acts and be bereft of conjugal and progenic happiness. If Rahu be in **Nrityalipsavastha**, the native will contract a great and unsubduing disease. will have afflicted eyes and fear from enemies and will decline financially and righteously. If Rahu be in Kautukavastha, the native will be devoid of a position (or a place), be interested in others' famales and will steal others' wealth. If Rahu be in **Nidravastha**, the native will be a repository of virtues, be endowed with wife and children, bold, proud and very affluent.

Notes : If Rahu in Sayanavastha is in Leo, Virgo or Taurus, there will be all round happiness whereas in other signs he is adverse with this Avastha. Rahu's Upavesanavastha will destroy one's wealth and will cause difficulties in day-to-day affairs. His Netrapani Avastha in the ascendant or in the 7th will bring many evils and miseries while in other houses it will bring danger from animals. Rahu in Prakasanavastha in Leo or in Cancer will cause amputation of head; in other signs it gives wealth and royal service. Rahu's Sabhavastha in the 5th/10th/1st will destroy the native's progeny and spouse and will make him fickle-minded. This Avastha in other houses will give virtues, scholarship and wealth. With Rahu in the 10th or in the 7th Bhojanavastha the native will 'kill' his wife or he may abandon her or may not be happy in married life, and be irreligious. Nrityalipsavastha of Rahu in the ascendant will deprive the native of his progenic ability while in other houses this Avastha will give two wives and all kinds of happiness. Should Rahu be in Kautukavastha in a house other than 5th/7th/10th, the native will incur many kinds of miseries and be bereft of spouse and progeny. Nidravastha of Rahu will inflict utter poverty and make the native wander all over the earth aimlessly.

मेषे वृषेऽथ वा युग्मे कन्यायां शयनं गते।
केतौ धनसमृद्धिः स्यादन्यभे रोगवर्धनम् ॥१३५॥
उपवेशं गतौ केतौ दद्रुरोगविवर्द्धनम्।
अरिवातनृपव्यालचौरशंका समन्ततः ॥१३६॥
नेत्रपाणि गते केतौ नेत्ररोगः प्रजायते।
दुष्टसर्पादिभीतिश्च रिपुराजकुलादपि ॥१३७॥
केतौ प्रकाशने संज्ञे धनवान् धार्मिकः सदा।
नित्यं प्रवासी चोत्साही सात्त्विको राजसेवकः ॥१३८॥
गमेच्छायां भवेत्केतुर्बहुपुत्रो महाधनः।
पण्डितो गुणवान् दाता जायते च नरोत्तमः ॥१३९॥
आगमने च यदा केतुर्नानारोगो धनक्षयः।
दन्तघाती महारोगी पिशुनः परनिन्दकः ॥१४०॥
सभावस्थां गते केतौ वाचालो बहुगर्वितः।
कृपणो लम्पटश्चैव धूर्तविद्याविशारदः ॥१४१॥
यदागमे भवेत्केतुः केतुः स्यात्पापकर्मणाम्।
बन्धुवादरतो दुष्टो रिपुरोगनिपीडितः ॥१४२॥

भोजने तु जनो नित्यं क्षुधया परिपीडितः।
दरिद्रो रोगसंतप्तः केतौ भ्रमति मेदिनीम् ॥१४३॥
नृत्यलिप्साङ्गते केतौ व्याधिना विकलो भवेत्।
बुद्बुदाक्षो दुराघर्षो धूर्तोऽनर्थंकरो नरः ॥१४४॥
कौतुकी कौतुके केतौ नटवामारतिप्रियः।
स्थानभ्रष्टो दुराचारी दरिद्रो भ्रमते महीम् ॥१४५॥
निद्रावस्थां गते केतौ धनधान्यसुखं महत्।
नानागुणविनोदेन कालो गच्छति जन्मिनाम् ॥१४६॥

135-146. *EFFECTS OF KETU'S AVASTHAS AT BIRTH*: If Ketu is in **Sayanavastha** in Aries, Taurus, Gemini or Virgo, there will be plenty of wealth while in other signs increased diseases will follow. If Ketu be in **Upavesanavastha** the native will suffer from ulcers and will have fear from enemies. windy diseases snakes and thieves. Should Ketu be in **Netrapani Avastha**, the native will contract eye diseases, and will have fear from wicked people, snakes, enemies and people of royal family. If Ketu be in **Prakasanavastha**, the native will be wealthy, righteous will live in foreign places, be enthusiastic and genuine and will serve the king. If Ketu be in **Gamanavastha**, the native will be endowed with many sons, abundant wealth, be scholarly, virtuous, charitable and be excellent among men. If Ketu be in Agamanavastha, the native will incur many diseases, will face loss of wealth, will hurt (others) with his teeth (दन्तघातिन्), be a talebearer and will blame others. If Ketu be in **Sabhavastha,** the native will be garrulous, very proud, miserly, licentious and skilful in evil branches of learning. If Ketu be in **Agamavastha,** the native will be a notorious sinner, will enter into litigations with his relatives be wicked and troubled by diseases and enemies. If Ketu be in **Bhojanavastha**, the native will always be distressed with hunger, penury and diseases and will roam allover the earth. If Ketu be in **Nrityalipsavastha, the native** will be distressed due to diseases, will have a floral mark on the eye (i.e. white of the pupil), be impertinent, wicked and will plan evils. If Ketu be in **Kautukavastha**, the native will seek union with dancing females (i.e. prostitutes), will suffer positional displacement, will take to evil paths and will roam all over. If Ketu be in Nidravastha the native will be endowed with wealth and corns, be virtuous and will spend his time sportively.

शयने द्विज ! भावेषु यत्र तिष्ठन्ति सद्ग्रहाः।
नित्यं तस्य शुभज्ञानं निर्विशंकं वदेत् बुधः॥१४७॥

147. *GENERAL EFFECTS (upto sloka 155)* : O Brahmin, if a benefic planet is in Sayanavastha, there will be benefic effects at all times according to the learned.

भोजने येषु भावेषु पापास्तिष्ठन्ति सर्वथा।
तदा सर्वविनाशेऽपि नाऽत्र कार्या विचारणा॥१४८॥

148. If a malefic is in Bhojanavastha, everything (related to the house concerned) will be destroyed and there is no need of a second thought.

निद्रायां च यदा पापो जायास्थाने शुभं वदेत्।
यदि पापग्रहैर्दृष्टो न शुभं च कदाचन॥१४९॥

149. Should a malefic in the 7th be in Nidravastha auspicious effects will follow, provided there is no aspect from another malefic.

सुतस्थाने स्थितः पापो निद्रायां शयनेऽपि वा।
तदा शुभं भवेत्तस्य नाऽत्र कार्या विचारणा॥१५०॥

150. Declare without a second thought auspicious effects following the location of a malefic in the 5th but with Nidravastha or Sayanavastha.

मृत्युस्थानस्थितः पापो निद्रायां शयनेऽपि वा।
तदा तस्याऽपमृत्युः स्याद्राजतः परतस्तथा॥१५१॥

151. Untimely death due to royal wrath will come to pass if there is a malefic in the 8th in Nidravastha or Sayanavastha.

शुभग्रहैर्यदा युक्तः शुभैर्वा यदि वीक्षितः।
तदा तु मरणं तस्य गङ्गादौ च विशेषतः॥१५२॥

152. If in the above case there be a benefic aspect or conjunction, the said (untimely) death will be in the river Ganges, i e. Gangetic belt, shrines etc.

कर्मस्थाने यदा पापः शयने भोजनेऽपि वा।
तदा कर्मविपाकः स्यान्नानादुःखप्रदायकः ॥१५३॥

153. If there be a malefic in the 10th house in Sayana or Bhojanavastha, the native will face many miseries on account of his own deeds.

दशमस्थो निशानाथः कौतुके च प्रकाशने।
तदैव राजयोगः स्यान्निर्विशकं द्विजोत्तम ॥१५४॥

154. O excellent of the Brahmins, doubtlessly a Rajayoga will come to pass if the Moon is in the 10th in Kautukavastha or Prakasanavastha.

बलाऽबलविचारेण ज्ञातव्यञ्च शुभाऽशुभम्।
एवं क्रमेण बोद्धव्यं सर्वभावेषु बुद्धिमन्! ॥१५५॥

155. Thus the good and bad effects be guessed assessing the strength and weakness of the planets concerning all the Bhavas.

[To be concluded]

ERRATA

Page	Line	For	Read
18	26	AD 72	AD 78
57	23	257 59gh 47 5Vigh	257d 59gh 47.5 Vigh
60	20	4h 2m	4h 26m
79	22	11 2 3	11 2 5
121	23	tilour	valour
197	1	physicallp matiny	physically mating
218	14	downfull	downfall
221	7	blies	bliss
222	19	co-bron	coborn
236	14	progery	progeny
239	20	vives	vices
249	18	splenorous	splendorous
313			Rahu in Gemini (in the chart)
358	19	Geda	Gada
376	25	Jakata	Jataka
382	19	these	the
400	30	If Amatya	If Atma
431	23	another	another in
432	last but one	180	108
450	10	Vikala	Dukkhita, Vikala
454	7	stars	star
456	15	र and म	र and स
462	13	if	it

PROFESSION THROUGH ASTROLOGY

There are so many varieties of profession now-a-day. In olden times when classics on Astrology were written; there were selected professions only. Astrologers practising on traditional lines find them selves incompetent

in advising a profession. The author of this work is well versed in classic as well as modern Astrology; therefore has a firm grip on prescribing profession as per professional niceties of present times.

This work is a fine blend of classical professional predictaments and modern approach for choosing a profession. Sometimes the strongest planet in the chart has a say in the respect, while the other times Pancha Mahapurusha Yogas decide profession. This book is a must for a novice as well as a professional astrologer.

Rs. 80/-

LAL KITAB (Hindi)

LAL KITAB is yet a mystery to the lovers of Astrology. All believers of Astrology get fascinated by utility totkas of Lal Kitab to eradicate planetary evils. The totkas of Lal Kitab are too simple, do not require much need of mantras, tantras and Vedic rhymes and can be performed by articles of day to day domestic use. For example if Rahu is bad in the 8th house of the horoscope, drop some coins in the flowing water in a river, one would get relief from the evils of Rahu. If one's wife is ill and marital comforts are hampered, then give a chapati out of your food to a cow daily.

Thus, donating a chapati out of ones food to a cow, feeding the dogs, wearing a silver ring, dropping some coins in flowing water, donating something to teenage girls during Navratras are akin to Hindu social life and have descended to us through our forefathers social experiences for the cause of human well being. To us the author of Lai Kitab deserves and enjoys the same station as is ascribed to Mahatma Kabir in the world of practical devotion to God.

Rs. 80/-